Advanced Studies in Theoretical and Applied Econometrics

Volume 45

This book series aims at addressing the most important and relevant current issues in theoretical and applied econometrics. It focuses on how the current data revolution has affected econometric modeling, analysis and forecasting, and how applied work has benefited from this newly emerging data-rich environment. The series deals with all aspects of macro-, micro-, financial-, and econometric methods and related disciplines, like, for example, program evaluation or spatial analysis.

The volumes in the series are either monographs or edited volumes, mainly targeting researchers, policymakers, and graduate students.

This book series is listed in Scopus.

Chaohua Dong · Jiti Gao

Modern Series Methods in Econometrics and Statistics

Springer

Chaohua Dong
School of Statistics and Mathematics
Zhongnan University of Economics
and Law
Wuhan, China

Jiti Gao
Department of Econometrics and Business
Statistics
Monash University
Melbourne, VIC, Australia

ISSN 1570-5811 ISSN 2214-7977 (electronic)
Advanced Studies in Theoretical and Applied Econometrics
ISBN 978-981-96-2821-6 ISBN 978-981-96-2822-3 (eBook)
https://doi.org/10.1007/978-981-96-2822-3

This Springer imprint is published by the registered company Springer Nature Singapore Pte Ltd.
The registered company address is: 152 Beach Road, #21-01/04 Gateway East, Singapore 189721, Singapore

To our families

Preface

During the past four decades or so, a large number of textbooks and research monographs about nonparametric kernel-based estimation methods have been published, such as Härdle (1990), Fan and Gijbels (1996), Härdle et al. (2000), Fan and Yao (2003), Gao (2007), and Teräsvirta et al. (2010). While existing books on nonparametric estimation briefly mention and discuss series estimation, to the best of our knowledge, there is no such book that systematically introduces series methods for model estimation and specification testing problems that commonly occur in econometrics and statistics.

Answering the call for a systematic treatment of nonparametric series methods in econometrics and statistics, Modern Series Methods in Econometrics and Statistics focuses on orthogonal series-based estimation methods for model estimation and specification testing issues in a wide class of cross-sectional, nonlinear and nonstationary time series, and panel data settings.

This book focuses on several classes of regression models associated with series estimation. The structure of this book is organized as follows: (a) Chap. 1 gives some motivations for the writing of this book and also examples to show how series estimation works; (b) Chaps. 2 and 3 offer a summary of preliminary and preparatory results for mathematical expectations and simple series regressions, respectively; (c) Chap. 4 starts with standard density estimation and then show how to estimate density functions by an orthogonal series method; (d) Chap. 5 introduces a class of semiparametric models and then discusses some estimation results based on the orthogonal series method; (e) Chap. 6 considers a different class of nonparametric models with additive forms, for which the orthogonal series method has a natural advantage in terms of addressing the 'curse of dimensionality' and offering closed-form expressions for the resulting estimates; and (f) Chap. 7 offers a series based approach to estimating a class of semiparametric moment restriction models associated with some newly established results. The book also contains four appendices for function spaces, approximations in Space C and Hilbert space, and a comparison between kernel methods and series methods, respectively. The first three appendices summarize the main mathematical preparatory knowledge and tools for the reading and understanding of this book, including several crucial quantities for series methods some of which are overlooked by the relevant literature; and the fourth appendix shows the momentum behind the estimations of the kernel and series methods as well as their differences.

This book introduces and covers the main series-based estimation methods in econometrics and statistics and provides the necessary technical details. The empirical examples presented in the book enable researchers and graduate students to keep abreast of developments in the field. We hope that this book will serve as a useful tool for interested researchers.

While the authors of this book have tried their best to reflect the research work of many researchers in the field, some other closely related studies might still be inevitably omitted in this book. The authors, therefore, apologize for any omissions.

We would like to thank anyone who has encouraged and supported us to complete this book. Especially, we would like to thank the following coauthors and colleagues working in similar areas: Rong Chen, Xiaohong Chen, Tingting Cheng, Yongmiao Hong, Oliver Linton, Bin Peng, Peter Phillips, Liangjun Su, Dag Tjøstheim, Yundong Tu, Zhijie Xiao, Weilun Zhou, Yahong Zhou and Pingfang Zhu for their insightful discussions and comments during the years. Thanks also go to Miss Yueheng Hu for her assistance in the proofreading of this manuscript.

Our special thanks go to our family members. Chaohua Dong would like to thank his wife, Mrs. Jia Liu, and the lovely son, Yumo Dong, for their support. Jiti Gao offers his thanks to his wife, Mrs. Qun Jiang, and two sons, Robert and Thomas, for their continuing support.

Finally, Chaohua Dong would also like to acknowledge the financial support of the National Natural Science Foundation of China (NSFC 72073143 and 72473156). Thanks from Jiti Gao also go to the Australian Research Council Discovery Grants Program (DP130104229; DP150101012; DP170104421; DP200102769) for its financial support.

Without such support and cooperation, it would not be possible for us to complete the writing of this book.

Wuhan, China
Melbourne, Australia
August 2024

Chaohua Dong
Jiti Gao

References

Fan, J. & Gijbels, I. (1996). *Local polynomial modelling and its applications. Monographs on statistics and applied probability*. Chapman & Hall, New York.

Fan, J. & Yao, Q. (2003). *Nonlinear time series: Nonparametric and parametric methods*. Springer, New York.

Gao, J. (2007). *Nonlinear time series: Semiparametric and nonparametric methods. Monographs on statistics and applied probability*. Chapman & Hall, New York.

Härdle, W. (1990). *Applied nonparametric regression. Contributions to Economics and Statistics*. Cambridge University Press, UK.

Härdle, W., Liang, H., and Gao, J. (2000). *Partially linear models. Contributions to Economics and Statistics*. Springer-Verlag, Berlin.
Terasvirta, T., Tjostheim, D., and Granger, C. W. J. (2010). *Modelling nonlinear economic time series*. Oxford University Press, New York.

Contents

Chapter 1
Motivations

Series methods fall into the category of sieve methods in the context of nonparametric econometrics and statistics. Because of maximum flexibility, they are utilized in a variety of issues in econometrics and statistics accommodating, for example, not only traditional density estimation, regression, generalized method of moment (GMM) and maximum likelihood estimation (MLE), but also modern topics like nonstationary time series, high- and ultra-high-dimensional estimation and inference, and asymptotic theory related to big data, treatment effect, and machine learning.

1.1 How Do Series Methods Come into Play?

Studying conditional expectations, $\mathbb{E}(Y|X)$ say, has accounted for a large proportion of research in econometrics and statistics. Though $\mathbb{E}(Y|X)$ is known to be linear in X when (X, Y) is jointly normally distributed (Example 2.3.1 and Theorem 2.3.1 below), it remains an unknown function of X in almost all other circumstances in both theory and empirical studies; this is an example where one may encounter unknown functions. Thus, dealing with these unknown functions has been an ever-lasting theme in the fields.

On the other hand, in some function spaces a function can be expressed as an infinite series of functions, so that the partial sum of the series can approximate the function in some sense. Often, these functions in the infinite series constitute a basis in the function spaces; they can be orthogonal functions (e.g., trigonometric and Legendre polynomials), wavelet, and so on, and more importantly, they are associated with the function spaces, so they are known a priori. Moreover, there are other function spaces in which a function can be approximated by a combination of some known functions such as splines, deep neural networks, and Bernstein polynomials. *Sieve methods* use these approximations in the estimation of unknown functions in statistical and econometric models, and in particular, when the approximations of partial

C. Dong and J. Gao, *Modern Series Methods in Econometrics and Statistics*,
Advanced Studies in Theoretical and Applied Econometrics 45,
https://doi.org/10.1007/978-981-96-2822-3_1

sums of series are utilized the sieve methods reduce to *series methods*. Basically, whenever and wherever an unknown function exists in one's research issue (namely, semi/nonparametric issues, and the unknown function is called a nonparametric function), a series approximation may be used to replace the unknown function so that the nonparametric issue is parameterized but with diverging dimensions. Such a replacement is exactly the idea of series methods (also sieve methods) that is supported by sound and rigorous mathematical background. See Appendices A–C.

Specifically, suppose that there is an unknown function, $g(x)$ say, in one's research target that is about to estimate. One might have some idea about this function, for example, the domain where x belongs, whether it is continuous, whether it is smooth, and so on. Such characteristics and properties may be a piece of connotative information that one can grasp from the research issue, and also may be a requirement that the research conductor imposes on their research.

Bearing these basic properties in mind, one may find an appropriate function space that the unknown function $g(x)$ belongs to. All function spaces commonly used in econometrics and statistics will be introduced in the appendix chapters. In this function space, S say, that one finds out, the unknown function $g(x)$ can be approximated arbitrarily by a combination of a set of known functions; these functions normally form an (orthogonal) basis in S.

In a word, before estimating the unknown function, one needs to know which function space it resides in, or where one should consider to find it out. This is similar to the situation of estimating an Euclidean parameter. Normally, to estimate an unknown Euclidean parameter θ_0, statisticians and econometricians need to know which space it comes from, and which compact set it pertains to; these questions are so easy to answer that are often neglected, and often they suppose that $\theta_0 \in \Theta \subset \mathbb{R}^d$ and θ_0 is an interior point of the compact set Θ. Therefore, in this sense estimating $g(x) \in S$ is analogous to estimating $\theta_0 \in \Theta$.

Back to the unknown function estimation, the aforementioned combination of a set of known functions with unknown coefficients, along with the approximating residue, can be used in lieu of the unknown function ($g(x)$) in the relevant research. Thus, to solve the unknown function is equivalent to solving these unknown coefficients in the combination; this may be regarded as the parameterization of the nonparametric function and usually makes the thing much easier. This is the basic idea of series methods.

1.2 Why Do We Choose Series Methods?

As mentioned previously, series methods belong to sieve methods and there are quite a few such methods extensively studied in the literature. A natural question is why one prefers the series methods.

To answer this question, we show below the advantages and disadvantages of the series methods. Also, we make a rough comparison between series methods and its arch-rival kernel methods, in order to explain manifestly for the readers.

1.2.1 Advantages and Disadvantages

As stated above, the series methods change a nonparametric issue to a parametric question, but the number of parameters to estimate (namely, k in the following example) diverges with the sample size required by the convergence of infinite series; and on top of that, they are much more flexible so that they can be used, as far as we are aware, under any circumstances involving unknown function.

For example, under a high-dimensional setting, Dong et al. (2023) consider semiparametric moment restriction models

$$\mathbb{E}[m(W_i, X_i^\top \beta, g(Z_i))] = 0, \quad i = 1, \ldots, n, \tag{1.2.1}$$

where $\{(W_i, X_i, Z_i), i = 1, \ldots, n\}$ is an observed sample, $m(\cdots)$ is a known q-vector of functions, Euclidean parameter β and unknown function $g(\cdot)$ are about to estimate. Using an approximation to function $g(\cdot)$ suggested by series methods, say $g_k(\cdot)$ with k increasing to infinity, the β and $g(\cdot)$ can be simultaneously estimated.

More precisely, by the series method, $g_k(z)$ takes the form of $\sum_{j=0}^{k-1} c_j p_j(z)$, where k is a positive integer, and $\{p_j(z), j \geq 0\}$ is a sequence of basis functions in an appropriate function space that is known for econometricians and statisticians, while c_j $(j = 0, \ldots, k-1)$ are unknown. When $g(\cdot)$ is substituted by this kind of approximation function $g_k(z)$, the unknown function is translated into an unknown vector $(c_0, \ldots, c_{k-1})$. Though theoretically k has to increase with the sample size n, such translation changes a nonparametric issue to a parametric one. This is the merit of the series methods.

Dong et al. (2023) then obtain the estimates of β and $(c_0, \ldots, c_{k-1})$ by the generalized method of moments (GMM, discussed in the following chapter), denoted by $\widehat{\beta}$ and $(\widehat{c}_0, \ldots, \widehat{c}_{k-1})$; thereby the estimator of $g(x)$ is defined as

$$\widehat{g}(x) = \sum_{j=0}^{k-1} \widehat{c}_j \, p_j(x) \tag{1.2.2}$$

for any x in the domain of $g(\cdot)$.

Another example where series methods are used is for model specification testing. Hong and White (1995) propose two consistent one-sided specification tests for parametric regression models where testing statistics are constructed via the difference in sums of squared residuals between the parametric and nonparametric versions, while the nonparametric version is estimated by series regression. In a similar way in the case of nonstationary time series regression, a test statistic proposed for cointegrating model specification in Dong and Gao (2018) is driven by an orthogonal series.

With the further reading of the book, the readers may find more applications where possibly the unknown function is included in different and maybe much more complicated environments, such as

- Partial linear models, $\mathbb{E}(y|x, z) = x^\top \beta + g(z)$,

- Additive models, $\mathbb{E}(y|x, z) = g_1(x) + g_2(z)$,
- Single-index models, $\mathbb{E}(y|x) = g(x^\top \theta)$.

It is noteworthy that not only are used the series methods in mean regressions, but also in quantile regressions, least absolute deviation (LAD) and even M-estimation issues in the same fashion where the corresponding loss functions are used (such as the check function, absolute function, etc.) to replace the one used in the mean regression. See, e.g., Dong et al. (2024). Anyway, the flexibility of the series methods is one of the important reasons that are used in econometrics and statistics.

Moreover, since series methods estimate unknown function $g(x)$ by a combination of known functions, $\widehat{g}(x) = \sum_{j=0}^{k-1} \widehat{c}_j p_j(x)$, it is quite easy to implement any linear functional to $\widehat{g}(x)$, that is,

$$\mathcal{F}(\widehat{g}) = \sum_{j=0}^{k-1} \widehat{c}_j \mathcal{F}(p_j(x)), \tag{1.2.3}$$

where $\mathcal{F}$ is a linear functional in the function space. This is particularly convenient when one's target is to analyze $\mathcal{F}(g)$ for which $\mathcal{F}(\widehat{g})$ is a plug-in estimator. The most commonly used functionals include derivative and integral operators, and point functionals. More examples can be found in Sect. 3.1 of Das et al. (2003).

Furthermore, the series methods estimate functions globally, meaning that all observations are used to estimate unknown coefficients, and the estimated function is determined in its entire domain by these coefficients. This property might make series methods better for out-of-sample prediction.

However, before implementing the methods one needs to be familiar with some basic knowledge about related function spaces, whereas these function spaces are contained in several mathematical subjects such as mathematical analysis and functional analysis. Thus, this could be the first hurdle to use the series methods for some students and researchers. For example, what kind of function spaces are there available? And what are the bases of these spaces?

In addition, for theoretical researchers, they should make themselves have good grasp of infinite series in order to analyze their series estimators and residuals of series, so as to be able to establish their large sample theory. This could be the second hurdle.

Nonetheless, to help overcome these hurdles that is one of our main aims, we shall provide the readers with a detailed discussion on these function spaces in the appendix chapters. We also furnish with a comprehensive introduction to all approximating sequences of functions, including Bernstein polynomials, the best approximating polynomials in space C, and many orthogonal function sequences in Hilbert spaces. In particular, we show rigorously the mathematical properties of these function sequences and prove nearly all statements about them. We believe that these materials will be helpful in the use of the series methods.

1.2.2 Rough Comparison with Kernel Methods

One natural alternative to series methods is kernel methods. A rough comparison of the series methods with the kernel methods is given here, while a detailed discussion will be shown in Appendix D in the appendices of the book.

Consider a nonparametric regression,

$$Y = g(X) + e, \tag{1.2.4}$$

where $g(\cdot)$ is unknown, and the error term satisfies $\mathbb{E}[e|X] = 0$.

Based on a sample $\{(X_i, Y_i), i = 1, \ldots, n\}$, there are several ways to derive the so-called kernel estimator of the regression function $g(x) = \mathbb{E}[Y|X = x]$. Springing to our minds, one is calculating the conditional expectation through joint distribution of (X, Y) and marginal distribution of X, both of which can be estimated by the sample through the kernel methods; another one is a local constant estimation. Both of the two approaches yield

$$\widehat{g}(x) = \left[\frac{1}{n}\sum_{i=1}^{n}\frac{1}{h}K\left(\frac{X_i - x}{h}\right)\right]^{-1}\frac{1}{n}\sum_{i=1}^{n}\frac{1}{h}K\left(\frac{X_i - x}{h}\right)Y_i, \tag{1.2.5}$$

where $K(\cdot)$ is a kernel function (density function) and $h = h_n$ is a bandwidth in the jargon of kernel estimation that approaches zero with the increase of the sample size. With this formula and the help of computer, a researcher, even a beginner of nonparametric methods can calculate the value of $\widehat{g}(x)$ at every point x for which one assumes that there exists a neighborhood containing many observed points (X_i, Y_i). Although the precise choice of bandwidth h is difficult, the selection of $K(\cdot)$ does not make any significant difference.

It is clear that the kernel estimator $\widehat{g}(x)$ can be written as

$$\widehat{g}(x) = \sum_{i=1}^{n}\omega_{ni}(x)Y_i, \quad \omega_{ni}(x) = \left[\sum_{i=1}^{n}K\left(\frac{X_i - x}{h}\right)\right]^{-1}K\left(\frac{X_i - x}{h}\right), \tag{1.2.6}$$

which can be viewed as an average of Y_i's with weights $\omega_{ni}(x)$. The weights are large for those Y_i's when corresponding X_i's reside within some neighborhood of x while they are very small for Y_i's when corresponding X_i's are beyond some neighborhood of x. The mechanism governing the weights $\omega_{ni}(x)$ attributes to the kernel function $K(\cdot)$ and the bandwidth $h = h_n$; due to these, the estimator is regarded as a local average of Y_i's. In addition, the kernel estimator in (1.2.5) is essentially a statistic expression, instead of the usual mathematical formula of a function.

On the other hand, a series estimator of the regression function $g(x) = \mathbb{E}[Y|X = x]$, similar to the estimation in (1.2.1) and (1.2.2), will take the form of $\widehat{g}(x) = \sum_{j=0}^{k-1}\widehat{c}_j p_j(x)$, where $\{p_j(x)\}$ again is a sequence of basis functions in a suitable function space that contains $g(x)$, and $\widehat{c}_j$ are estimated from the regression equation

(1.2.4) along with the sample. In contrast to the kernel estimator, the series estimator is an explicit mathematical formula, valid on the entire domain of $g(x)$, though the observations $\{X_i, i = 1, \ldots, n\}$ might be in a subset of the domain. In addition, since x appears in the denominator, linear functional of the kernel estimator (1.2.5) is not as easily implemented as series estimator.

1.3 Examples: Applications of Series Methods

There are several interesting examples of series methods in Sect. 2 of Chen (2007). These examples include single spell duration models with unobserved heterogeneity, the shape-invariant system of Engel curves, and consumption-based asset pricing models. To motivate series methods, moreover, we shall provide several applications chosen from the literature on contemporary popular topics.

1.3.1 Density Estimation in Finance

Nonparametric estimation of density functions was the main momentum of nonparametric methods at the beginning of its history; one may find many earlier papers in the literature that dwelt on the questions using the series methods. See, for instance, Rosenblatt (1956), Watson and Leadbetter (1963), Schwartz (1967), Kronmal and Tarter (1968), Watson (1969), Wahba (1975), Walter (1977), Walter and Blum (1979), Anderson and Figueiredo (1980), Susarla and Walter (1981), Silverman (1982), Greblicki and Pawlak (1984, 1985), Hall (1980, 1981a, b, 1982, 1984, 1986). These researches mainly focus on the probabilistic and statistical insights of observable data.

In recent years, series estimation of density has been used in modeling economic and financial problems due to the flexibility of series methods. The densities of variables in finance are crucial as they give much valuable information on the movement of fortune; also in financial theory, density plays a key role in pricing.

For example, in the absence of arbitrage and market imperfection, there exists a state price density $f^*(x)$ for the payoff at maturity T such that the prices of European call and put options are formulated as

$$C(K) = e^{-r\tau}\mathbb{E}[(S_T - K)^+] = e^{-r\tau} \int_0^\infty (S_T - K)^+ f^*(S_T) dS_T, \quad (1.3.1)$$

$$P(K) = e^{-r\tau}\mathbb{E}[(K - S_T)^+] = e^{-r\tau} \int_0^\infty (K - S_T)^+ f^*(S_T) dS_T, \quad (1.3.2)$$

where K is the strick price, $\tau = T - t$, t is the current time, $x^+ = \max(x, 0)$, r is the risk-free interest rate, and S_T denotes the potential price of the underlying asset at time T. Thus, estimating $f^*(x)$ makes significant sense in finance.

To estimate $f^*(x)$ by the series method, Lu and Qu (2021) firstly adopt transformations

$$x = \frac{\log(S_T/S) - r\tau}{\sigma\sqrt{\tau}}, \quad \text{and } z = \frac{\log(K/S) - r\tau}{\sigma\sqrt{\tau}} \tag{1.3.3}$$

in $C(K)$ and $P(K)$, where S is the spot price of the underlying asset at t, σ is equal to the Black-Scholes implied volatility for the at-the-money call option of the same underlying asset and maturity. Thus,

$$C(z) = S\int \left(e^{\sigma\sqrt{\tau}x} - e^{\sigma\sqrt{\tau}z}\right)^+ f(x)dx, \tag{1.3.4}$$

$$P(z) = S\int \left(e^{\sigma\sqrt{\tau}z} - e^{\sigma\sqrt{\tau}x}\right)^+ f(x)dx, \tag{1.3.5}$$

where $f(x) = S_T\sigma\sqrt{\tau}f^*(Se^{r\tau+\sigma\sqrt{\tau}x})$.

Secondly, Lu and Qu (2021) use an orthogonal series expansion (introduced later) of $f(x)$ and available dataset of $\{C(z), P(z)\}$ that have the same maturity but different strike prices to estimate $f(x)$, so-called *option implied state price density*. Once $f(x)$ is estimated, $f^*(\cdot)$ is recovered accordingly. We shall go back to this question in the sequel chapter.

1.3.2 Average Treatment Effect

In the last two decades or so, there has been much interest in econometric methods for estimating the effects of active labor market programs such as job search assistance or classroom teaching programs. This interest has led to a surge in theoretical work focusing on estimating average treatment effects under various sets of assumptions.

Suppose there are N units, indexed by $i = 1, \ldots, N$, viewed as drawn randomly from a large population. Each unit is characterized by a pair of potential outcomes, $Y_i(0)$ for the outcome under the control treatment and $Y_i(1)$ for the outcome under the active treatment. In addition, each unit has a vector of characteristics, referred to as covariates, pre-treatment variables, or exogenous variables, denoted by X_i. It is important that these variables are not affected by the treatment. Finally, each unit is exposed to a single treatment, $W_i = 0$ if unit i receives the control treatment, and $W_i = 1$ if unit i receives the active treatment.

Suppose we observe for each unit the triple (Y_i, X_i, W_i), $i = 1, \ldots, N$, where Y_i is the realized outcome,

$$Y_i = \begin{cases} Y_i(0), & \text{if } W_i = 0, \\ Y_i(1), & \text{if } W_i = 1. \end{cases} \tag{1.3.6}$$

Hence, one may write $Y_i = Y_i(W_i) = (1 - W_i)Y_i(0) + W_iY_i(1)$. The average treatment effect is defined as $\mathbb{E}[Y(1) - Y(0)]$.

Also, define, for $w \in \{0, 1\}$, the two conditional expectation and variance functions

$$\mu_w(x) = \mathbb{E}[Y(w)|X = x], \quad \sigma_w^2(x) = \text{Var}[Y(w)|X = x]. \tag{1.3.7}$$

Note that a formal introduction on the conditional expectation will be given in the subsequent chapter. According to the series estimation procedure, one may have the estimates of $\mu_1(x)$ and $\mu_0(x)$ based on the observations of $\{(Y_i(w), X_i), i = 1, \ldots, n\}$, $w = 0, 1$.

To estimate $\mathbb{E}[Y_i|X_i = x]$, Hahn (1998, p. 323) uses the series method: Let $\{p_j(x)\}$ be the chosen orthogonal sequence, and define $y = (Y_1, \ldots, Y_n)^\top$, $Z_k(x) = (p_0(x), \ldots, p_{k-1}(x))^\top$, and $Z = (Z_k(X_1), \ldots, Z_k(X_n))^\top$. Then, we have

$$\widehat{\mathbb{E}}[Y_i|X_i = x] = Z_k(x)^\top \widehat{c}, \quad \widehat{c} = (Z^\top Z)^{-1} Z^\top y.$$

Theorem 6 of Hahn (1998, p. 323) establishes the efficiency of his estimator of average treatment effect $\mathbb{E}[Y(1) - Y(0)]$. In addition, Chen et al. (2008) use a series method to consider efficient estimation with an unknown propensity score under the GMM setting.

1.3.3 Machine Learning

Machine learning is an important component of the growing field of data science. Through the use of statistical methods, algorithms are trained to make classifications or predictions, uncovering key insights within data mining projects. These insights subsequently are applicable to decision-making within a variety of applications.

Machine learning, therefore, is a collection of modern, adaptive statistical learning methods for estimating regression functions and other statistical objects. These methods exploit structured parsimony restrictions (such as approximate sparsity) on regressions, together with various forms of regularization and model selection, to enable high-quality prediction in high-dimensional settings.

Machine learning classifiers fall into three primary categories: supervised learning, unsupervised learning, and semi-supervised learning. Density estimation can be viewed as unsupervised learning since it learns the density $f_X(x)$ from an observed sample $\{X_i, i = 1, \ldots, n\}$ where, as aforementioned, series methods are used extensively. By contrast, supervised learning is in spirit the same as a regression. From a machine learning point of view, supervised learning attempts to learn g in a model $Y = g(X) + \varepsilon$ by example through a teacher. One observes the system under study, both the inputs and outputs, and assembles a training set of observations $\{(X_i, Y_i), i = 1, \ldots, n\}$. The observed input values X_i to the system are also fed into an artificial system, known as a learning algorithm (usually a computer program), which also produces outputs $\widehat{g}(X_i)$ in response to the inputs. It is expected that the artificial and real outputs will be close enough to be useful for all sets of inputs likely to be encountered in practice. Hence, as a mainstream approach in nonparametric regressions, series methods are widely utilized in machine learning (Cucker & Zhou, 2007, p. 2; Hastie et al., 2008, p. 29).

Machine learning is different from other methods in ways that are useful in high-dimensional settings. For example, Lasso (Least absolute shrinkage and selection operator) has good properties with very many potential regressors (possibly many more than the sample size) when relatively few important regressors give a good approximation, but the identity of those few is not known (i.e., the regression is approximately sparse). In contrast, series regression is based on relatively few regressors, often many fewer than the sample size. Lasso and series regression are similar in that they both depend on a few regressors, giving a good approximation. They differ in that series regression requires that the identity of the important regressors is known, while with Lasso their identity need not be known.

Here are two examples. Chernozhukov et al. (2022) study automatic debiasing for linear and nonlinear functions of regressions. The structure of the identifying moment function is used to approximate an unknown function as a linear combination of a dictionary (i.e., basis). See Assumption 1 of Chernozhukov et al. (2022).

As another example, Qiu et al. (2021) estimate a finite-dimensional summary of one or more function-valued features of an underlying data-generating mechanism under a nonparametric model. The series estimator is proposed because it is convenient and its construction does not require efficiency theory; its tuning parameters can be selected data-adaptively, and they are universal in the sense that the same fits lead to efficient plug-in estimators for a rich class of estimands. Compared to traditional sieve estimators, these approaches are valid under more general conditions on the smoothness of the function-valued features by utilizing flexible estimates that can be obtained, for example, using machine learning methods.

References

Anderson, G. L., & Figueiredo, R. J. P. D. (1980). An adaptive orthogonal-series estimator for probability density functions. *The Annals of Statistics, 8*, 347–376.

Chen, X. (2007). *Handbook of econometrics*. Large sample sieve estimation of semi-parametric models (Vol. 6B, pp. 5550–5588). Amsterdam, North Holland: Elsevier.

Chen, X., Hong, H., & Tarozzi, A. (2008). Semiparametric efficiency in GMM models with auxiliary data. *Annals of Statistics, 36*, 808–843.

Chernozhukov, V., Newey, W. K., & Singh, R. (2022). Automatic debiased machine learning of causal and structural effects. *Econometrica, 90*, 967–1027.

Cucker, F., & Zhou, D.-X. (2007). *Learning theory: An approximation theory viewpoint.* Cambridge Monograph on Applied and Computational Mathematics. Cambridge: Cambridge University Press.

Das, M., Newey, W. K., & Vella, F. (2003). Nonparametric estimation of sample selection models. *The Review of Economic Studies, 70*, 33–58.

Dong, C., Chen, R., Xiao, Z., & Liu, W. (2024). Functional quantile autoregression. *Journal of Econometrics*, 244, 105765.

Dong, C., & Gao, J. (2018). Specification testing driven by orthogonal series for nonlinear cointegration with endogeneity. *Econometric Theory, 34*, 754–789.

Dong, C., Gao, J., & Linton, O. (2023). High dimensional semiparametric moment restriction models. *Journal of Econometrics, 232*, 320–345.

Greblicki, W., & Pawlak, M. (1984). Hermite series estimates of a probability density and its derivatives. *Journal of Multivariate Analysis, 15*, 174–182.

Greblicki, W., & Pawlak, M. (1985). Pointwise consistency of the Hermite series density estimate. *Statistics & Probability Letters, 3*, 65–69.

Hahn, J. (1998). On the role of the propensity score in efficient semiparametric estimation of average treatment effects. *Econometrica, 66*, 315–331.

Hall, P. (1980). Estimating a density on the positive half line by the method of orthogonal series. *Annals of the Institute of Statistical Mathematics, 32*, 351–362.

Hall, P. (1981a). On trigonometric series estimates of densities. *Annals of Statistics, 9*, 683–685.

Hall, P. (1981b). Laws of the iterated logarithm for nonparametric density estimators. *Zeitschrift für Wahrscheinlichkeitstheorie und Verwandte Gebiete, 56*, 47–61.

Hall, P. (1982). Comparison of two orthogonal series methods of estimating a density and its derivatives on an interval. *Journal of Multivariate Analysis, 12*, 432–449.

Hall, P. (1984). Central limit theorem for integrated square error of multivariate nonparametric density estimators. *Journal of Multivariate Analysis, 14*, 1–16.

Hall, P. (1986). On the rate of convergence of orthogonal series density estimators. *Journal of the Royal Statistical Society Series B, 48*, 115–122.

Hastie, T., Tibshirani, R., & Friedman, J. (2008). *The Elements of statistical learning- data mining, inference, and prediction.* Springer series in statistics. New York: Springer.

Hong, Y., & White, H. (1995). Consistent specification testing via nonparametric series regression. *Econometrica, 63*, 1133–1159.

Kronmal, R., & Tarter, M. (1968). The estimation of probability densities and cumulatives by fourier series methods. *Journal of the American Statistical Association, 63*, 925–952.

Lu, J., & Qu, Z. (2021). Sieve estimation of option-implied state price density. *Journal of Econometrics, 224*, 88–112.

Qiu, H., Luedtke, A., & Carone, M. (2021). Universal sieve-based strategies for efficient estimation using machine learning tools. *Bernoulli, 27*, 2300–2336.

Rosenblatt, M. (1956). Remarks on some nonparametric estimates of a density function. *Annals of Mathematical Statistics, 27*, 832–837.

Schwartz, S. (1967). Estimation of probability density by an orthogonal series. *The Annals of Mathematical Statistics, 38*, 1261–1265.

Silverman, B. W. (1982). On the estimation of a probability density function by the maximum penalized likelihood method. *Annals of Statistics, 10*, 795–810.

Susarla, V., & Walter, G. (1981). Estimation of a multivariate density function using delta sequences. *Annals of Statistics, 9*, 347–355.

Wahba, G. (1975). Optimal convergence properties of variable knot, kernel, and orthogonal series methods for density estimation. *Annals of Statistics, 3*, 15–29.

Walter, G. (1977). Properties of Hermite series estimation of probability density. *Annals of Statistics, 5*, 1258–1264.

Walter, G., & Blum, J. (1979). Probability density estimation using delta sequences. *Annals of Statistics, 7*, 328–340.

Watson, G. S. (1969). Density estimation by orthogonal series. *The Annals of Mathematical Statistics, 40*, 1496–1498.
Watson, G. S., & Leadbetter, M. R. (1963). On the estimation of the probability density, I. *The Annals of Mathematical Statistics, 34*, 480–491.

Part I
Series Methods

Conditional expectation is a basic concept on which many models in econometrics and statistics are built, and from which mean regression earns its name. Students and researchers need to be familiar with the definition and properties of conditional expectations. On top of that, we introduce this book's backbone concept, series methods, under the framework of mean regression. After understanding the working procedure of series methods in regression, readers may be able to use them in other circumstances.

Chapter 2
Conditional Expectations

2.1 Probability Spaces

Let Ω be an arbitrary set of points ω. In the probability theory context, we use Ω to collect all possible outcomes ω of a random experiment. *A random experiment* is a mechanism that produces a definite outcome that cannot be predicted with certainty. In this case, Ω is also called the *sample space* of the experiment.

For observing the number of heads in n tosses of a coin, the sample space $\Omega = \{0, 1, \ldots, n\}$; for describing the complete history of the n tosses, Ω is the space consisting of all 2^n n-long sequence of H's and T's; for the number of telephone calls arriving at an exchange, $\Omega = \{0, 1, 2, \ldots\}$; for the position of a particle, Ω is three-dimensional Euclidean space; for describing the motion of the particle, Ω is an appropriate space of functions.

Any subset of Ω is called an *event*. Empty set $\emptyset$ is always an event called an *impossible event*, while Ω itself as an event is called a *sure event*.

Definition 2.1.1 (*σ-field*) Let $\mathcal{F}$ be a class of subsets of Ω. We call $\mathcal{F}$ a σ-field (also σ-algebra) if

(1) $\Omega \in \mathcal{F}$.
(2) If $A \in \mathcal{F}$, then $A^c \in \mathcal{F}$.
(3) If $\{A_n, n \geq 1\}$ is a sequence of sets from $\mathcal{F}$, then $\bigcup_{n=1}^{\infty} A_n \in \mathcal{F}$. □

A σ-field is closed under the operations of complementation and countable union, and hence by the de Morgan laws, of countable intersection too.

The simplest σ-field is $\mathcal{F} = \{\emptyset, \Omega\}$ for any Ω, called the *trivial σ-field*; given an Ω, the largest σ-field is $\mathcal{F} = \{A, \ A \subset \Omega\}$ that is called the *power set* of Ω, denoted by 2^{Ω}. The power set of a set with n elements has 2^n elements, which accounts for its name and representation. When studying the subsets of a given set, particularly their measure-theoretic properties, the power set is often too big for anything very interesting or useful to be said about it.

C. Dong and J. Gao, *Modern Series Methods in Econometrics and Statistics*,
Advanced Studies in Theoretical and Applied Econometrics 45,
https://doi.org/10.1007/978-981-96-2822-3_2

Given a collection of sets, C, the intersection of all σ-fields containing C is called the *σ-field generated by C*, customarily denoted by $\sigma(C)$.

Example 2.1.1 Let $\Omega = \mathbb{R}, C = \{(-\infty, r], r \in \mathbb{Q}\}$ be the collection of closed half-line with rational endpoints. Then, $\sigma(C)$ is called Borel field of $\mathbb{R}$, generally denoted by $\mathcal{B}$.

A number of different base collections generate $\mathcal{B}$ as well. Since the countable union of open intervals can be a closed interval, and vice versa, the collection of open half-lines, $C = \{(-\infty, r), r \in \mathbb{Q}\}$, will also serve. Or, letting r_n be a decreasing sequence of rational numbers such that $r_n \downarrow x$,

$$(-\infty, x] = \bigcap_{n=1}^{\infty}(-\infty, r_n].$$

Such a sequence exists for any $x \in \mathbb{R}$, and hence $\mathcal{B}$ can be generated by the collection of half-lines with real endpoints, $C = \{(-\infty, x], x \in \mathbb{R}\}$. It follows easily that various other collections generate $\mathcal{B}$ as well, such as the open intervals of $\mathbb{R}$, the closed intervals, and the half-open intervals.

Example 2.1.2 Let $\Omega = \overline{\mathbb{R}}$, the extended real line. The Borel field of $\overline{\mathbb{R}}$ is easily given by

$$\overline{\mathcal{B}} = \{B, B \cup \{-\infty\}, B \cup \{+\infty\}, B \cup \{\pm\infty\} | \ B \in \mathcal{B}\}.$$

One may verify that $\overline{\mathcal{B}}$ is a σ-field.

Example 2.1.3 Let I be an interval on $\mathbb{R}$. Define $\mathcal{B}_I = \{B \cap I | B \in \mathcal{B}\}$. It is called the restriction of $\mathcal{B}$ to I, or the Borel field on I. In fact, $\mathcal{B}_I$ is generated by $C = \{(-\infty, r] \cap I, r \in \mathbb{Q}\}$.

The union of two σ-fields (in terms of the union of two sets) may not necessarily be a σ-field, because the unions of sets from one σ-field with those from another are not guaranteed in it. In view of this consideration, given two σ-fields, $\mathcal{F}$ and $\mathcal{G}$, the smallest σ-field containing all elements of $\mathcal{F}$ and all elements of $\mathcal{G}$ is denoted by $\mathcal{F} \vee \mathcal{G}$, called the *union of $\mathcal{F}$ and $\mathcal{G}$*. On the other hand, $\mathcal{F} \cap \mathcal{G} = \{A, \ A \in \mathcal{F}$ and $A \in \mathcal{G}\}$ is a σ-field, although for uniformity the notation $\mathcal{F} \wedge \mathcal{G}$ may be used for such an *intersection*. Formally, $\mathcal{F} \wedge \mathcal{G}$ denotes the largest of the σ-fields whose elements belong to both $\mathcal{F}$ and $\mathcal{G}$. Both of these operations can be generalized to countable cases, so that for a sequence of σ-fields $\mathcal{F}_n$, one may define $\bigvee_{n=1}^{\infty} \mathcal{F}_n$ and $\bigwedge_{n=1}^{\infty} \mathcal{F}_n$.

A *measurable space* is a pair $(\Omega, \mathcal{F})$ where Ω is any set and $\mathcal{F}$ is a σ-field of subsets of Ω.

Definition 2.1.2 (*Probability*) A probability measure $\mathbb{P}$ defined on a measurable space $(\Omega, \mathcal{F})$ is a mapping $\mathcal{F} \mapsto \mathbb{R}$ satisfying the axioms of probability:

(1) $\mathbb{P}(A) \geq 0, \forall A \in \mathcal{F}$,

(2) $\mathbb{P}(\Omega) = 1$,
(3) Countable additivity: for a disjoint collection $\{A_n, A_n \in \mathcal{F}\}$,

$$\mathbb{P}\left(\bigcup_{n=1}^{\infty} A_n\right) = \sum_{n=1}^{\infty} \mathbb{P}(A_n).$$

When $(\Omega, \mathcal{F})$ is a measurable space, the triple $(\Omega, \mathcal{F}, \mathbb{P})$ is called a *probability space*. More than one probability can be defined on the same measurable space, hence the distinction between measurable space and probability space is important.

Note that countable additivity implies finite additivity. Indeed, if $A_1, \ldots, A_n \in \mathcal{F}$ are disjoint, we may let $A_j = \emptyset$, $j \geq n+1$, and by the countable additivity,

$$\mathbb{P}\left(\bigcup_{j=1}^{n} A_j\right) = \mathbb{P}\left(\bigcup_{j=1}^{\infty} A_j\right) = \sum_{j=1}^{\infty} \mathbb{P}(A_j).$$

The convergence of the series implies $\mathbb{P}(\emptyset) = 0$, and then the finite additivity holds.

The axioms of the probability also imply that for any A, B and $\{A_j, j \geq 1\}$ in $\mathcal{F}$, (i) $0 \leq \mathbb{P}(A) \leq 1$; (ii) $\mathbb{P}(A^c) = 1 - \mathbb{P}(A)$; (iii) $\mathbb{P}(A) \leq \mathbb{P}(B)$ whenever $A \subset B$; (iv) $\mathbb{P}(A \cup B) = \mathbb{P}(A) + \mathbb{P}(B) - \mathbb{P}(A \cap B)$; (v) $\mathbb{P}(\cup_j A_j) \leq \sum_j \mathbb{P}(A_j)$; (vi) if $A_j \uparrow A$ or $A_j \downarrow A$, then $\mathbb{P}(A_j) \to \mathbb{P}(A)$ as $j \to \infty$.

In fact, due to finite additivity, $\mathbb{P}(A) + \mathbb{P}(A^c) = \mathbb{P}(A \cup A^c) = \mathbb{P}(\Omega) = 1$, so (i) and (ii) hold. Also when $A \subset B$, $B = A \cup (B \cap A^c)$, thus (iii) holds due to finite additivity again. For (iv), note that $A \cup B = A \cup (B \cap A^c)$, and therefore, $\mathbb{P}(A \cup B) = \mathbb{P}(A) + \mathbb{P}(B \cap A^c) = \mathbb{P}(A) + \mathbb{P}(B) - \mathbb{P}(A \cap B)$ where we used $B = (B \cap A) \cup (B \cap A^c)$. (v) follows from induction on j together with an implication of (iv) that $\mathbb{P}(A \cup B) \leq \mathbb{P}(A) + \mathbb{P}(B)$; note that (v) allows the right to be infinity. For (vi), notice that $\{\mathbb{P}(A_j)\}$ is a monotone sequence, so it must admit a limit. In addition, if $A_j \uparrow A$, then $A = \cup_j A_j$ and $\mathbb{P}(A)$ is the upper bound of $\{\mathbb{P}(A_j)\}$. Denote $B_0 = A_1$, $B_j = A_{j+1} - A_j$, $j \geq 1$. Then $A = \cup_{j=0}^{\infty} B_j$, $A_s = \cup_{j=0}^{s-1} B_j$ for $s \geq 1$, and $\{B_j, j \geq 0\}$ are disjoint mutually. As a result,

$$\mathbb{P}(A) = \sum_{j=0}^{\infty} \mathbb{P}(B_j),$$

and hence the partial sum $\mathbb{P}(A_s) \to \mathbb{P}(A)$ when $s \to \infty$, as desired.

If $A_j \downarrow A$, then $A = \cap_j A_j$, and the assertion holds if we consider $A_j^c \uparrow A^c$ and $A^c = \cup_j A_j^c$ that implies $\mathbb{P}(A_s^c) \to \mathbb{P}(A^c)$ when $s \to \infty$.

We now know that $\mathbb{P}(\emptyset) = 0$ and $\mathbb{P}(\Omega) = 1$. Nonetheless, $\emptyset$ might not be the only event that has probability zero, and it is also true that Ω might not be the only event that has probability one, as illustrated by the following example.

Example 2.1.4 In Example 2.1.3, let $I = [0, 1]$. Then we have $\mathcal{B}_I = \{B \cap I | B \in \mathcal{B}\}$ and measurable space $(I, \mathcal{B}_I)$, and further $(I, \mathcal{B}_I, m)$ is a probability space where m is Lebesgue measure. However, we know $m([0, 1]) = m((0, 1)) = 1$ and many other subsets of I that have probability one due to the definition of Lebesgue measure. Conversely, it is clear that there are many subsets of I (such as singletons) that have measure zero.

As implied by Example 2.1.4, to say an event cannot happen because it has probability zero is different from saying it cannot occur because the outcomes it possesses are not elements of Ω; similarly, to say an event has probability one is different from saying it is the sure event Ω. An event E is said to occur *almost surely* (a.s.), or equivalently, *with probability one* (w.p.1) if $E^c = \Omega \backslash E$ has probability zero. When there is ambiguity about probability measure being considered, the notation "a.s.[$\mathbb{P}$]" may be used.

More often than not, one encounters the completeness of a probability space, say $(\Omega, \mathcal{F}, \mathbb{P})$. Note that it enters probability theory in an essential way only in connection with the study of stochastic processes in continuous time. We say that a probability space $(\Omega, \mathcal{F}, \mathbb{P})$ is *complete* if $A \subset B$, $B \in \mathcal{F}$ and $\mathbb{P}(B) = 0$ together imply $A \in \mathcal{F}$ (and hence $\mathbb{P}(A) = 0$).

We shall generalize the idea in Examples 2.1.3 and 2.1.4. Suppose a random experiment represented by the space $(\Omega, \mathcal{F}, \mathbb{P})$ is modified to confine the possible outcomes to a subset of the sample space, say $A \subset \Omega$. Let $\mathcal{F}_A = \{A \cap B,\ B \in \mathcal{F}\}$. $\mathcal{F}_A$ is a σ-field and is called the *trace* of $\mathcal{F}$ on A. Define for $E \in \mathcal{F}_A$, $\mathbb{P}_A(E) = \mathbb{P}(E)/\mathbb{P}(A)$ when $\mathbb{P}(A) > 0$ that can be verified as a probability measure. Then, $(A, \mathcal{F}_A, \mathbb{P}_A)$ is called the *trace* of $(\Omega, \mathcal{F}, \mathbb{P})$ on A.

In probability theory, one interesting aspect is how the occurrence of a given event affects the possibility of other events occurring. For example, given the weather is cloudy tomorrow, how much possible would it rain? This is the so-called conditional probability in probability theory. The idea underlying conditional probability is that some but not all aspects of a random experiment have been observed. Precisely, if one observes that in $(\Omega, \mathcal{F}, \mathbb{P})$, $A \in \mathcal{F}$ has happened, how should we adjust the possibilities that other events possess?

Since A^c has been ruled out, clearly we should reduce Ω to A. Regarding of how possible an event $B \in \mathcal{F}$ would happen, we should focus on the event $B \cap A$. Thus, to normalize the probability of the "entire space" A has probability one (i.e., given that A has happened, the probability of A is one), we define

$$\mathbb{P}(B|A) = \frac{\mathbb{P}(B \cap A)}{\mathbb{P}(A)}, \text{ if } \mathbb{P}(A) > 0.$$

This is called the *conditional probability* of B given A. Note that $\mathbb{P}(A|A) = 1$. This consideration actually coincides with the trace of $(\Omega, \mathcal{F}, \mathbb{P})$ on A, $(A, \mathcal{F}_A, \mathbb{P}_A)$, as we know $B \cap A \in \mathcal{F}_A$ if $B \in \mathcal{F}$. As a set mapping on $\mathcal{F}$, $\mathbb{P}(\cdot|A)$ satisfies the axioms of probability.

A pair of events A and B in $\mathcal{F}$ is said to be *independent* if $\mathbb{P}(A \cap B) = \mathbb{P}(A)\mathbb{P}(B)$, or if $\mathbb{P}(B|A) = \mathbb{P}(B)$ whenever $\mathbb{P}(A) > 0$. For a class of events, C, if every pair of events of C is independent, we say that C is *pairwise independent*. In addition, C is said to be *totally independent* if

$$\mathbb{P}\left(\bigcap_{A \in \mathcal{L}} A\right) = \prod_{A \in \mathcal{L}} \mathbb{P}(A),$$

for every subset $\mathcal{L} \subset C$ that has at least two elements.

2.2 Random Variables and Expectations

Let $(\Omega, \mathcal{F}, \mathbb{P})$ be a probability space. A real *random variable* (r.v.) X is an $\mathcal{F}/\mathcal{B}$-measurable function on Ω, i.e., $\Omega \to \mathbb{R}$, where $\mathcal{B}$ is the Borel σ-field on $\mathbb{R}$. That is to say, $X(\omega)$ induces an inverse mapping from $\mathcal{B}$ to $\mathcal{F}$ such that $X^{-1}(B) = \{\omega,\ X(\omega) \in B\} \in \mathcal{F}$ for each $B \in \mathcal{B}$. The term "$\mathcal{F}$-measurable r.v. " may be applied when the role of $\mathcal{B}$ is understood. There are two important types of r.v.'s, discrete and continuous. A discrete random variable has distinct values that are countable and finite or countably infinite, whereas a continuous random variable has values that are uncountably infinite and form a continuous range of values.

Any r.v. X induces a probability measure on $\mathbb{R}$, say μ, such that $(\mathbb{R}, \mathcal{B}, \mu)$ becomes a probability space. Here, μ is given by $\mu(B) = \mathbb{P}(X^{-1}(B)) = \mathbb{P}(\{\omega, X(\omega) \in B\})$ for $B \in \mathcal{B}$. Because B can take interval $(-\infty, x]$, μ is synonymous with distribution. That is, $F_X(x) = \mathbb{P}(X \leq x) = \mathbb{P}(\{\omega, X(\omega) \leq x\})$ is the *cumulative distribution function* (c.d.f.) of X. Any c.d.f. is nonnegative, nondecreasing with $F_X(-\infty) = 0$ and $F_X(\infty) = 1$; it is right-continuous everywhere. According to discrete and continuous r.v., X possesses probability law or probability density function (p.d.f.). More detailed discussion about basic probability theory can be found in Davidson (1994).

To introduce the expectation of a r.v., we need the definition of integral of r.v. on sample space with respect to $\mathbb{P}$, though this definition is given with respect to a general measure μ in several books such as Billingsley (1995) (so that one has very general integral on abstract space with respect to a measure, for example, Lebesgue measure; however we do not pursue this generality in this book). First, let us consider nonnegative r.v. X on $(\Omega, \mathcal{F}, \mathbb{P})$ where $X(\omega) = \infty$ is allowed.

For each finite decomposition $\{A_i\}$ of Ω and $\{A_i\} \subset \mathcal{F}$, define the sum

$$\sum_i \left[\inf_{\omega \in A_i} X(\omega)\right] \mathbb{P}(A_i). \tag{2.2.1}$$

Here, some conventions on computing products involving infinity are: $0 \cdot \infty = \infty \cdot 0 = 0$, $x \cdot \infty = \infty \cdot x = \infty$ for $0 < x < \infty$, $\infty \cdot \infty = \infty$.

If $A_i = \emptyset$, the infimum in (2.2.1) is ∞ by the standard convention, while $\mathbb{P}(A_i) = 0$ so that this term has no contribution to the sum. The integral of X is defined as the supremum of (2.2.1),

$$\int_\Omega X(\omega)d\mathbb{P}(\omega) = \sup \sum_i \left[\inf_{\omega \in A_i} X(\omega) \right] \mathbb{P}(A_i), \tag{2.2.2}$$

where the supremum is taken over all finite partitions $\{A_i\}$ of Ω of $\mathcal{F}$-sets.

For a general r.v. X, let

$$X^+(\omega) = \begin{cases} X(\omega), & \text{if } 0 \le X(\omega) \le \infty; \\ 0, & \text{if } -\infty \le X(\omega) < 0 \end{cases} \tag{2.2.3}$$

be its positive part, and

$$X^-(\omega) = \begin{cases} -X(\omega), & \text{if } -\infty \le X(\omega) \le 0; \\ 0, & \text{if } 0 < X(\omega) \le \infty \end{cases} \tag{2.2.4}$$

be its negative part. These r.v.'s are nonnegative and $X = X^+ - X^-$. The definition of integral of X is given by

$$\int_\Omega X(\omega)d\mathbb{P}(\omega) = \int_\Omega X^+(\omega)d\mathbb{P}(\omega) - \int_\Omega X^-(\omega)d\mathbb{P}(\omega). \tag{2.2.5}$$

When it exists, the *expectation* or *mean* of a r.v. $X(\omega)$ in $(\Omega, \mathcal{F}, \mathbb{P})$ is the integral

$$\mathbb{E}(X) = \int_\Omega X(\omega)d\mathbb{P}(\omega). \tag{2.2.6}$$

For nonnegative r.v. X, $\mathbb{E}(X)$ is always defined (it may be infinite); for general r.v. X, $\mathbb{E}(X)$ is defined or X has an expected value, if at least one of $\mathbb{E}(X^+)$ and $\mathbb{E}(X^-)$ is finite, in which case $\mathbb{E}(X) = \mathbb{E}(X^+) - \mathbb{E}(X^-)$; and X is *integrable* if and only if $\mathbb{E}(|X|) < \infty$.

For $A \in \mathcal{F}$, define $I_A(\omega) = 1$ when $\omega \in A$ and $I_A(\omega) = 0$ when $\omega \notin A$, and we say that $I_A(\omega)$ is the *indicator function* of A. Though I_A is a r.v. for $A \in \mathcal{F}$, the indicator function can be defined beyond probability space. For instance, let $B \subset \mathbb{R}$, then define $I_B(x) = 1$ if $x \in B$ and $I_B(x) = 0$ if $x \notin B$. Such defined indicator function $I_B(\cdot)$ is a real function on $\mathbb{R}$.

$\mathbb{E}(X)$ has a dual characterization, as an abstract integral on the probability space and as Lebesgue-Stieljes integral on the line. It is equivalently written as

$$\mathbb{E}(X) = \int_\Omega X(\omega)d\mathbb{P}(\omega) = \int_{-\infty}^{\infty} x dF_X(x), \tag{2.2.7}$$

which of these representations is adopted is mainly a matter of convenience. The relationship (2.2.7) can be shown by virtue of induced measure of X on $\mathbb{R}$: $\mu(B) = \mathbb{P}(X^{-1}(B)) = \mathbb{P}(\{\omega, X(\omega) \in B\})$ for $B \in \mathcal{B}$. It follows that

$$\begin{aligned}\int_B x\mu(dx) &= \int_{-\infty}^{\infty} xI_B(x)\mu(dx) \\ &= \int_\Omega X(\omega)I_B(X(\omega))\mathbb{P}(d\omega) \\ &= \int_\Omega X(\omega)I_{X^{-1}(B)}(\omega)\mathbb{P}(d\omega) \\ &= \int_{X^{-1}(B)} X(\omega)\mathbb{P}(d\omega)\end{aligned}$$

for all $B \in \mathcal{B}$. In particular, noting $\mu(dx) = dF_X(x)$, $\mathbb{P}(d\omega) = d\mathbb{P}(\omega)$ and letting $B = \mathbb{R}$ we obtain (2.2.7).

The equivalence in (2.2.7) can be viewed as a special case of the change of variable for the transformation between two measurable spaces $(\Omega, \mathcal{F})$ and $(\Omega', \mathcal{F}')$. That is, in the above, $(\Omega', \mathcal{F}') = (\mathbb{R}, \mathcal{B})$ and $X(\omega)$ is regarded as the transformation. The general theorem about the change of variable can be founded in Billingsley (1995, p. 216).

We define the expectation of XI_A for any $A \in \mathcal{F}$,

$$\mathbb{E}(XI_A) = \int_A X(\omega)d\mathbb{P}(\omega) = \int_{X(A)} xdF_X(x), \tag{2.2.8}$$

where $X(A)$ is the set $\{X(\omega) : \omega \in A\}$. We say that X is a *simple r.v.* if it assumes only finitely many values and if $\{\omega : X(\omega) = x\} \in \mathcal{F}$ for each $x \in \mathbb{R}$. A finite sum

$$X(\omega) = \sum_i x_i I_{A_i}(\omega)$$

is a simple r.v. if and only if all $A_i \in \mathcal{F}$. It follows that

$$\begin{aligned}\mathbb{E}(X) &= \int_\Omega X(\omega)d\mathbb{P}(\omega) = \int_{\cup_i A_i} X(\omega)d\mathbb{P}(\omega) \\ &= \sum_i \int_{A_i} X(\omega)d\mathbb{P}(\omega) = \sum_i x_i \int_{A_i} d\mathbb{P}(\omega) \\ &= \sum_i x_i \mathbb{P}(A_i).\end{aligned}$$

Theorem 2.2.1 *If X is a nonnegative r.v. and $p > 0$, then*

$$\mathbb{E}(X^p) = p\int_0^\infty x^{p-1}\mathbb{P}(X > x)dx.$$

Proof For any $b > 0$, integration by parts gives

$$\begin{aligned}\int_0^b x^p dF_X(x) &= b^p F_X(b) - p\int_0^b x^{p-1} F_X(x)dx \\ &= p\int_0^b x^{p-1}dx F_X(b) - p\int_0^b x^{p-1}F_X(x)dx \\ &= p\int_0^b x^{p-1}[F_X(b) - F_X(x)]dx \\ &= p\int_0^b x^{p-1}\mathbb{P}(x < X \le b)dx.\end{aligned}$$

Letting $b \to +\infty$, the assertion holds. □

When the left has an limit infinite, so is the right. The theorem allows $\mathbb{E}(X^p) = \infty$. The assertion for $p = 1$ is often encountered in the literature, viz., $\mathbb{E}(X) = \int_0^\infty \mathbb{P}(X > x)dx$.

Theorem 2.2.2 (Markov's inequality) *For $\varepsilon > 0$ and $p > 0$,*

$$\mathbb{P}(|X| > \varepsilon) \le \frac{\mathbb{E}|X|^p}{\varepsilon^p}, \tag{2.2.9}$$

whenever the expectation exists, while a special inequality is called Chebyshev's inequality for $p = 2$. □

Proof Notice that

$$\begin{aligned}\varepsilon^p\mathbb{P}(|X| > \varepsilon) &= \varepsilon^p\int_{|x|>\varepsilon} dF_X(x) \le \int_{|x|>\varepsilon} |x|^p dF_X(x) \\ &\le \int |x|^p dF_X(x) = \mathbb{E}(|X|^p).\end{aligned}$$

The assertion holds. □

Let $I \subseteq \mathbb{R}$ be any interval. A function $\phi(\cdot) : I \mapsto \mathbb{R}$ is said to be *convex* on I if

$$\phi(\lambda x + (1-\lambda)y) \le \lambda\phi(x) + (1-\lambda)\phi(y) \tag{2.2.10}$$

for all $x, y \in I$ and $\lambda \in [0, 1]$.

Theorem 2.2.3 (Jensen's inequality) *Let a Borel function $\phi(\cdot)$ be convex on an interval I that contains the support of an integrable r.v. X. Moreover, suppose $\phi(X)$ is integrable. Then $\phi(\mathbb{E}(X)) \le \mathbb{E}\phi(X)$.* □

Proof Let $\ell(x) = ax + b$ be a supporting line of $\phi(x)$ through $(\mathbb{E}(X), \phi(\mathbb{E}(X)))$, i.e., a line lying entirely under the graph of $\phi(\cdot)$. Then $aX + b \le \phi(X)$, so that $a\mathbb{E}(X) + b \le \mathbb{E}\phi(X)$ but the left side equals $\phi(\mathbb{E}(X))$. □

A special case is $\phi(x) = |x|$. Then, the Jensen's inequality delivers $|\mathbb{E}(X)| \leq \mathbb{E}|X|$. Another example is $\phi(x) = x^2$, and the resultant Jensen's inequality reads $\mathbb{E}[X^2] \geq [\mathbb{E}(X)]^2$. We often derive it from $\mathbb{E}[X^2] - [\mathbb{E}(X)]^2 = \mathrm{Var}(X) \geq 0$.

Theorem 2.2.4 (Hölder's inequality) *For $p, q > 0$ and $p^{-1} + q^{-1} = 1$,*

$$\mathbb{E}|XY| \leq (\mathbb{E}|X|^p)^{1/p}(\mathbb{E}|Y|^q)^{1/q}, \tag{2.2.11}$$

whenever the expectations exist. A special case is called Cauchy-Schwarz inequality for $p = q = 2$.

When $0 < \alpha < \beta$, let $p = \beta/\alpha$, $q = \beta/(\beta - \alpha)$ and $Y = 1$ and X replaced by $|X|^\alpha$, Hölder's inequality gives Lyapounov's inequality

$$(\mathbb{E}|X|^\alpha)^{1/\alpha} \leq (\mathbb{E}|X|^\beta)^{1/\beta}. \tag{2.2.12}$$

Proof If $\mathbb{E}|X|^p = 0$, then $X = 0$ with probability one, hence $XY = 0$ with probability one, from which the assertion holds. If $a, b > 0$, let $s = p\ln(a)$ and $t = q\ln(b)$. Since e^x is convex, $\exp(p^{-1}s + q^{-1}t) \leq p^{-1}\exp(s) + q^{-1}\exp(t)$, or

$$ab \leq \frac{a^p}{p} + \frac{b^q}{q}.$$

This also holds for either $a = 0$ or $b = 0$. Now, let $u = (\mathbb{E}|X|^p)^{1/p}$ and $v = (\mathbb{E}|Y|^q)^{1/q}$, and we have

$$\left|\frac{XY}{uv}\right| \leq \frac{1}{p}\left|\frac{X}{u}\right|^p + \frac{1}{q}\left|\frac{Y}{v}\right|^q.$$

Taking expectation yields the inequality. □

2.3 Conditional Expectation Given Variable

Recall that the conditional density of continuous variable Y given X is

$$f_{Y|X}(y|x) = \frac{f_{X,Y}(x, y)}{f_X(x)}, \tag{2.3.1}$$

where $f_{X,Y}(x, y)$ is the joint density of X and Y, and $f_X(x)$ is the marginal density of X. Then, we may calculate

$$\mathbb{P}(a \leq Y \leq b|X = x) = \int_a^b f_{Y|X}(y|x)dy$$
$$= \frac{1}{f_X(x)} \int_a^b f_{X,Y}(x, y)dy.$$

Definition 2.3.1 Let X, Y be continuous variables. The conditional expectation of Y given $X = x$ is defined by

$$\mathbb{E}[Y|X = x] = \int y f_{Y|X}(y|x)dy.$$

Clearly, it is a function of x. But here x can be any point in the support of X; if we do not specify an x that X assumes, we obtain $\mathbb{E}[Y|X]$, a function of X. We also define *conditional variance* of Y given X as

$$\mathrm{Var}(Y|X) = \mathbb{E}[(Y - \mathbb{E}(Y|X))^2|X].$$

It is easy to show

$$\mathbb{E}[\mathbb{E}(Y|X)] = \int \mathbb{E}[Y|X = x] f_X(x)dx = \iint y f_{Y|X}(y|x)dy f_X(x)dx$$
$$= \int y \int f_{X,Y}(x, y)dxdy = \int y f_Y(y)dy = \mathbb{E}[Y].$$

Thus, $\mathbb{E}[\mathbb{E}(Y|X)] = \mathbb{E}(Y)$ for continuous variables.

Example 2.3.1 If $(\xi, \eta) \sim N((a_1, a_2), (\sigma_1^2, \sigma_2^2), \rho)$, then

$$\mathbb{E}(\eta|\xi) = a_2 + \rho\frac{\sigma_2}{\sigma_1}(\xi - a_1).$$

Proof The joint density of (ξ, η) is

$$f_{\xi,\eta}(x, y) = \frac{1}{2\pi|\Sigma|^{1/2}} \exp\left(-\frac{1}{2}u^\top \Sigma^{-1} u\right)$$

where we define $u = (x - a_1, y - a_2)^\top$, and Σ is the covariance matrix of (ξ, η),

$$\Sigma = \begin{pmatrix} \sigma_1^2 & \rho\sigma_1\sigma_2 \\ \rho\sigma_1\sigma_2 & \sigma_2^2 \end{pmatrix}, \quad \Sigma^{-1} = \frac{1}{|\Sigma|}\begin{pmatrix} \sigma_2^2 & -\rho\sigma_1\sigma_2 \\ -\rho\sigma_1\sigma_2 & \sigma_1^2 \end{pmatrix},$$

and $|\Sigma| = (1 - \rho^2)\sigma_1^2\sigma_2^2$, so that

$$u^\top \Sigma^{-1} u = \frac{1}{1 - \rho^2}\left[\frac{(x - a_1)^2}{\sigma_1^2} - 2\rho\frac{(x - a_1)(y - a_2)}{\sigma_1\sigma_2} + \frac{(y - a_2)^2}{\sigma_2^2}\right].$$

The marginal density of ξ is

$$f_\xi(x) = \frac{1}{\sqrt{2\pi}\sigma_1} \exp\left(-\frac{(x-a_1)^2}{2\sigma_1^2}\right).$$

Hence, the conditional density $f_{\eta|\xi}(y|x)$ is

$$\begin{aligned} f_{\eta|\xi}(y|x) &= \frac{f_{\xi,\eta}(x,y)}{f_\xi(x)} \\ &= \frac{1}{\sqrt{2\pi}\sqrt{1-\rho^2}\sigma_2} \exp\left[-\frac{1}{2(1-\rho^2)\sigma_1^2}\left(\rho(x-a_1) - \frac{\sigma_1}{\sigma_2}(y-a_2)\right)^2\right]. \end{aligned}$$

It follows that

$$\begin{aligned} \mathbb{E}(\eta|\xi) &= \int y f_{\eta|\xi}(y|\xi)dy = a_2 + \int (y-a_2) f_{\eta|\xi}(y|\xi)dy \\ &= a_2 + \int \frac{y}{\sqrt{2\pi(1-\rho^2)}\sigma_2} \exp\left[-\frac{1}{2(1-\rho^2)\sigma_1^2}\left(\rho(\xi-a_1) - \frac{\sigma_1}{\sigma_2}y\right)^2\right] dy \\ &= a_2 + \int \frac{y}{\sqrt{2\pi(1-\rho^2)}\sigma_2} \exp\left[-\frac{1}{2(1-\rho^2)\sigma_2^2}\left(y - \rho\frac{\sigma_2}{\sigma_1}(\xi-a_1)\right)^2\right] dy \\ &= a_2 + \rho\frac{\sigma_2}{\sigma_1}(\xi - a_1). \end{aligned}$$

This shows that the conditional expectation $\mathbb{E}(\eta|\xi)$ is linear in ξ when their joint distribution is normal. □

We do not know whether the linearity of $\mathbb{E}(\eta|\xi)$ is sufficient to the joint normal distribution of (ξ, η), but we do know in the representation of linearity, what are the intercept and slope.

Example 2.3.2 Suppose that r.v. ξ and η have means μ_ξ and μ_η, and variances σ_ξ^2 and σ_η^2, respectively; moreover, $\mathbb{E}(\eta|\xi) = a + b\xi$. Then,

$$a = \mu_\eta - b\mu_\xi, \qquad b = \rho\frac{\sigma_\eta}{\sigma_\xi},$$

where ρ is the correlation coefficient of ξ and η.

Proof We only illustrate the assertion for continuous variables, while the assertion can be shown in the same fashion for discrete variables after we give the relevant definition.

Let $f(x, y)$ be the joint density of (ξ, η), $f_\xi(x)$ the marginal density of ξ, $f_{\eta|\xi}(y|x)$ the conditional density of η given $\xi = x$. Then

$$\mathbb{E}(\eta|\xi = x) = \int y f_{\eta|\xi}(y|x)dy = \frac{1}{f_\xi(x)} \int y f(x, y)dy,$$

which in turn gives

$$\int y f(x, y)dy = (a + bx) f_\xi(x). \tag{2.3.2}$$

Integrating on the both sides of (2.3.2) w.r.t. x, we have

$$\mu_\eta = a + b\mu_\xi. \tag{2.3.3}$$

Further, multiplying on the both sides of (2.3.2) by x and integrating w.r.t. x, we have

$$\mathbb{E}(\xi\eta) = a\mu_\xi + b\mathbb{E}(\xi^2). \tag{2.3.4}$$

The system of Eqs. (2.3.3) and (2.3.4) leads to the result. □

After we show some properties on conditional expectation, the question in Example 2.3.2 can be solved in much more general situation. The following theorem is a more general result than Example 2.3.1.

Theorem 2.3.1 *Suppose $X \sim N_{p+q}(\mu, \Sigma)$, $\Sigma > 0$. Partition X, μ and Σ:*

$$X = \begin{pmatrix} X_1 \\ X_2 \end{pmatrix}, \quad \mu = \begin{pmatrix} \mu_1 \\ \mu_2 \end{pmatrix}, \quad \Sigma = \begin{pmatrix} \Sigma_{11} & \Sigma_{12} \\ \Sigma_{21} & \Sigma_{22} \end{pmatrix},$$

where X_1 and μ_1 are of p dimension, Σ_{11} is of $p \times p$. Given $X_1 = x_1$, the conditional distribution of X_2 is

$$X_2|X_1 = x_1 \sim N_q(\mu_2 + \Sigma_{21}\Sigma_{11}^{-1}(x_1 - \mu_1), \Sigma_{22\cdot1}),$$

where for simplicity we denote $\Sigma_{22\cdot1} = \Sigma_{22} - \Sigma_{21}\Sigma_{11}^{-1}\Sigma_{12}$. □

Proof Let

$$C = \begin{pmatrix} I_p & 0 \\ -\Sigma_{21}\Sigma_{11}^{-1} & I_q \end{pmatrix},$$

and define $Z = CX$ that follows normal distribution $N_{p+q}(C\mu, C\Sigma C^\top)$. Notice that

$$
\begin{aligned}
C\Sigma C^\top &= \begin{pmatrix} I_p & 0 \\ -\Sigma_{21}\Sigma_{11}^{-1} & I_q \end{pmatrix} \begin{pmatrix} \Sigma_{11} & \Sigma_{12} \\ \Sigma_{21} & \Sigma_{22} \end{pmatrix} \begin{pmatrix} I_p & -\Sigma_{11}^{-1}\Sigma_{12} \\ 0 & I_q \end{pmatrix} \\
&= \begin{pmatrix} \Sigma_{11} & \\ & \Sigma_{22\cdot 1} \end{pmatrix}.
\end{aligned}
$$

Hence,

$$
\begin{aligned}
Z = \begin{pmatrix} Z_1 \\ Z_2 \end{pmatrix} &= \begin{pmatrix} X_1 \\ X_2 - \Sigma_{21}\Sigma_{11}^{-1}X_1 \end{pmatrix} \\
&\sim N_{p+q}\left[\begin{pmatrix} \mu_1 \\ \mu_2 - \Sigma_{21}\Sigma_{11}^{-1}\mu_1 \end{pmatrix}, \begin{pmatrix} \Sigma_{11} & \\ & \Sigma_{22\cdot 1} \end{pmatrix}\right].
\end{aligned}
$$

Consequently, X_1 and $X_2 - \Sigma_{21}\Sigma_{11}^{-1}X_1$ are mutually independent, and $X_1 \sim N_p(\mu_1, \Sigma_{11})$, $X_2 - \Sigma_{21}\Sigma_{11}^{-1}X_1 \sim N_q(\mu_2 - \Sigma_{21}\Sigma_{11}^{-1}\mu_1, \Sigma_{22\cdot 1})$, from which the assertion follows. □

Corollary 2.3.1 *Under the condition in Theorem 2.3.1,* $\mathbb{E}[X_2|X_1 = x_1] = \mu_2 + \Sigma_{21}\Sigma_{11}^{-1}(x_1 - \mu_1)$. □

The assertion follows immediately from Theorem 2.3.1 but notice once again the conditional expectation is linear in the given variable.

Now we consider the discrete case. If Y is a discrete r.v. assuming $y_1, y_2, \ldots$, the conditional probability of Y given an event B is

$$
f(y_i|B) \equiv \mathbb{P}(Y = y_i|B) = \frac{\mathbb{P}(\{Y = y_i\} \cap B)}{\mathbb{P}(B)}, \quad \mathbb{P}(B) > 0.
$$

Definition 2.3.2 The conditional expectation of discrete Y given event B is

$$
\mathbb{E}[Y|B] = \sum_i y_i f(y_i|B).
$$

If $\{B_j, j = 1, \ldots, n\}$ is a partition of the sample space, Y assumes $y_1, y_2, \ldots$, then

$$
\begin{aligned}
&\sum_{j=1}^n \mathbb{E}[Y|B_j]\mathbb{P}(B_j) = \sum_{j=1}^n \sum_i y_i f(y_i|B_j)\mathbb{P}(B_j) \\
&= \sum_{j=1}^n \sum_i y_i \mathbb{P}(\{Y = y_i\} \cap B_j) = \sum_i y_i \sum_{j=1}^n \mathbb{P}(\{Y = y_i\} \cap B_j) \\
&= \sum_i y_i \mathbb{P}(\cup_{j=1}^n (\{Y = y_i\} \cap B_j)) = \sum_i y_i \mathbb{P}(\{Y = y_i\}) \\
&= \mathbb{E}[Y],
\end{aligned}
$$

which is the so-called Partition theorem, where we use $\mathbb{P}(E_1) + \mathbb{P}(E_2) = \mathbb{P}(E_1 \cup E_2)$ if $E_1 \cap E_2 = \emptyset$.

Let X and Y be two discrete random variables, assuming $x_1, x_2, \ldots$ and $y_1, y_2, \ldots$, respectively. For any j, $\mathbb{P}(X = x_j) \neq 0$, so $f(y_i|X = x_j) \equiv \mathbb{P}(Y = y_i|X = x_j)$ is well defined.

Definition 2.3.3 For two discrete variables X and Y, define

$$\mathbb{E}[Y|X = x_j] = \sum_i y_i f(y_i|X = x_j);$$

and conditional expectation $\mathbb{E}[Y|X]$ is a discrete variable that takes values $\mathbb{E}[Y|X = x_j]$, $j = 1, 2, \ldots$, with probability $\mathbb{P}(X = x_j)$. □

It follows from the definition that

$$\begin{aligned}\mathbb{E}[\mathbb{E}(Y|X)] &= \sum_j \mathbb{E}[Y|X = x_j]\mathbb{P}(X = x_j) = \sum_j \sum_i y_i f(y_i|X = x_j)\mathbb{P}(X = x_j) \\ &= \sum_j \sum_i y_i \mathbb{P}(Y = y_i, X = x_j) = \sum_i y_i \sum_j \mathbb{P}(Y = y_i, X = x_j) \\ &= \sum_i y_i \mathbb{P}(Y = y_i) = \mathbb{E}(Y).\end{aligned}$$

Again, for discrete variables, $\mathbb{E}[\mathbb{E}(Y|X)] = \mathbb{E}(Y)$.

Example 2.3.3 Roll a die until we get a 6. Let X be the total number of rolls and Y the number of 1's we get. Let us compute $\mathbb{E}[Y|X = x]$. The event $X = x$ means that there were $x - 1$ rolls that were not a 6 and then the xth roll was a 6. So, given this event, Y has a binomial distribution with $n = x - 1$ trials and probability of success $p = 1/5$. Thus,

$$\mathbb{E}[Y|X = x] = np = \frac{1}{5}(x - 1).$$

Now consider the following process. We do the experiment and get an outcome ω. In this example, ω is a string of $1, 2, 3, 4, 5$'s ending with 6. Then, $X(\omega) = x$ is the length of the string. Accordingly, we compute $\mathbb{E}[Y|X = x]$. This process gives a function

$$\omega \mapsto \mathbb{E}[Y|X(\omega) = x] = \frac{1}{5}(x - 1).$$

That is, $\omega \mapsto (x - 1)/5$ where $x = X(\omega)$, so we write $\omega \mapsto (X(\omega) - 1)/5$. It follows that $\mathbb{E}[Y|X] = (X - 1)/5$ is a function of X and hence a random variable. This will be true in general.

We calculate another conditional expectation in the same example, $\mathbb{E}[Y^2|X]$. Again, given $X = x$, Y has a binomial distribution with $n = x - 1$ and $p = 1/5$. Its variance is $np(1 - p) = 4(x - 1)/25$. So,

$$\begin{aligned}&\mathbb{E}[Y^2|X=x]-(\mathbb{E}(Y|X=x))^2\\=&\mathbb{E}((Y-\mathbb{E}(Y|X=x))^2|X=x)\\=&4(x-1)/25\end{aligned}$$

which gives

$$\mathbb{E}[Y^2|X=x]=\frac{1}{25}(x-1)^2+\frac{4}{25}(x-1).$$

Therefore,

$$E[Y^2|X]=\frac{1}{25}(X-1)^2+\frac{4}{25}(X-1)=\frac{1}{25}(X^2+2X-3),$$

a function of X too.

Theorem 2.3.2 *Let X, Y and Z be continuous. If $h(Y)$ is a function of Y that has finite expectation, then*

$$\mathbb{E}[h(Y)|X=x]=\int h(y)f_{Y|X}(y|x)dy. \tag{2.3.5}$$

If $h(Y,Z)$ is a function of Y and Z that has finite expectation, then

$$\mathbb{E}[h(Y,Z)|X=x]=\iint h(y,z)f_{Y,Z|X}(y,z|x)dydz, \tag{2.3.6}$$

where $f_{Y,Z|X}(y,z|x)$ is the conditional density of (Y,Z) given $X=x$, that is,

$$f_{Y,Z|X}(y,z|x)=\frac{f_{Y,Z,X}(y,z,x)}{f_X(x)}.$$

The theorem can be shown through the trace probability for $A=\{X=x\}$ if $\mathbb{P}(A)>0$ otherwise $A=\{|X-x|<\varepsilon\}$ with arbitrary $\varepsilon>0$, and in the final stage let $\varepsilon\to 0$. The proof is quite similar to the theorem for unconditional expectation and hence is omitted. See Billingsley (1995, pp. 274, 277). The theorem also has an analog for discrete variables that we do not show here due to clearness.

Regarding to conditional expectation, we have shown that $\mathbb{E}[\mathbb{E}(Y|X)]=\mathbb{E}(Y)$. In what follows, we give more properties about conditional expectation.

Theorem 2.3.3 *Conditional expectation has the following properties.*

(1) $\mathbb{E}(a|X)=a$ *where a is any constant.*
(2) $\mathbb{E}(aY+bZ|X)=a\mathbb{E}(Y|X)+b\mathbb{E}(Z|X)$ *for any $a,b\in\mathbb{R}$.*
(3) *Law of Iterated Expectation,* $\mathbb{E}[\mathbb{E}(Y|X)]=\mathbb{E}(Y)$.
(4) *If Y is integrable, for any r.v. X, Z, we have*

$$\mathbb{E}(Y|X)=\mathbb{E}[\mathbb{E}(Y|X,Z)|X].$$

(5) *If* $Y \geq 0$, *then* $\mathbb{E}[Y|X] \geq 0$.
(6) *If* X *and* Y *are independent, then* $\mathbb{E}[Y|X] = \mathbb{E}[Y]$.
(7) $|\mathbb{E}[Y|X]| \leq \mathbb{E}[|Y||X]$.
(8) *If* $\mathbb{E}(|g(X)Y|) < \infty$, *then*

$$\mathbb{E}(g(X)Y|X) = g(X)\mathbb{E}(Y|X).$$

In particular, $\mathbb{E}(g(X)|X) = g(X)\mathbb{E}(1|X) = g(X)$.
(9) *Let* $\phi(\cdot)$ *be a convex function on an interval containing the support of* X, $\mathbb{E}|\phi(X)| < \infty$. *Then, we have Jensen's inequality,* $\phi(\mathbb{E}[Y|X]) \leq \mathbb{E}[\phi(Y)|X]$.
(10) $Var(Y) = \mathbb{E}[Var(Y|X)] + Var[\mathbb{E}(Y|X)]$. □

Proof (1). Intuitively, this is true because a constant a averaging on any set remains unchanged. Firstly, we illustrate this for discrete X. Define $A = \{X = x\}$ and suppose $\mathbb{P}(A) > 0$. Let $Y = a$ with probability one. By Definition 2.3.2,

$$\mathbb{E}(a|X = x) = \mathbb{E}(Y|A) = a\frac{\mathbb{P}(\{Y = a\} \cap A)}{\mathbb{P}(A)} = a\frac{\mathbb{P}(A)}{\mathbb{P}(A)} = a.$$

Secondly, for continuous X, one may replace $A = \{X = x\}$ by $A = \{|X - x| \leq \varepsilon\}$ with arbitrary $\varepsilon > 0$. The proof is the same as the discrete case but the assertion holds due to the arbitrariness of ε.

(2). We only consider the case where all variables are continuous. Invoking (2.3.6), we have

$$\begin{aligned}
\mathbb{E}(aY + bZ|X = x) &= \iint (ay + bz) f_{Y,Z|X}(y, z|x)dydz \\
&= a \iint y f_{Y,Z|X}(y, z|x)dydz + b \iint z f_{Y,Z|X}(y, z|x)dydz \\
&= a \iint y f_{Y|X}(y|x)dy + b \iint z f_{Z|X}(z|x)dz \\
&= a\mathbb{E}(Y|X) + b\mathbb{E}(Z|X).
\end{aligned}$$

(4). For the continuous case, observe that

$$f_{Y|X,Z}(y|x, z) f_{Z|X}(z|x) = f_{Y,Z|X}(y, z|x),$$

and

$$\mathbb{E}(Y|X, Z) = \int y f_{Y|X,Z}(y|X, Z)dy.$$

Then,

$$
\begin{aligned}
\mathbb{E}[\mathbb{E}(Y|X, Z)|X] &= \int \mathbb{E}(Y|X, Z = z) f_{Z|X}(z|X) dz \\
&= \iint y f_{Y|X,Z}(y|X, z) dy f_{Z|X}(z|X) dz \\
&= \iint y f_{Y,Z|X}(y, z|X) dy dz \\
&= \int y f_{Y|X}(y|X) dy \\
&= \mathbb{E}(Y|X).
\end{aligned}
$$

For the discrete case, suppose that Y, X, Z assume $y_1, y_2, \ldots,\ x_1, x_2, \ldots,$ and $z_1, z_2, \ldots,$ respectively. Let us calculate $\mathbb{E}[\mathbb{E}[Y|Z, X]|X = x_j]$. Notice that $\mathbb{E}[Y|Z, X]$ is a random variable, denoted by ξ. Given $X = x_j$, ξ may assume $\mathbb{E}[Y|Z = z_k, X = x_j]$, $k = 1, 2, \ldots,$ and the probability $\xi = \mathbb{E}[Y|Z = z_k, X = x_j]$ is $\mathbb{P}(Z = z_k|X = x_j)$.

Hence,

$$
\begin{aligned}
&\mathbb{E}[\mathbb{E}[Y|Z, X]|X = x_j] \\
&= \sum_k \mathbb{E}[Y|Z = z_k, X = x_j]\mathbb{P}(Z = z_k|X = x_j) \\
&= \sum_k \sum_i y_i \mathbb{P}(Y = y_i|Z = z_k, X = x_j)\mathbb{P}(Z = z_k|X = x_j) \\
&= \sum_k \sum_i y_i \frac{\mathbb{P}(Y = y_i, Z = z_k, X = x_j)}{\mathbb{P}(Z = z_k, X = x_j)} \frac{\mathbb{P}(Z = z_k, X = x_j)}{\mathbb{P}(X = x_j)} \\
&= \sum_k \sum_i y_i \frac{\mathbb{P}(Y = y_i, Z = z_k, X = x_j)}{\mathbb{P}(X = x_j)} \\
&= \sum_i y_i \frac{\mathbb{P}(X = x_j, Y = y_i)}{\mathbb{P}(X = x_j)} = \sum_i y_i \mathbb{P}(Y = y_i|X = x_j) \\
&= \mathbb{E}[Y|X = x_j].
\end{aligned}
$$

The assertion holds since x_j is arbitrary that X can assume.

(5). It is obvious by the definition.

(6). We prove the continuous case only. If X and Y are independent, $f_{Y,X}(y, x) = f_Y(y) f_X(x)$. The assertion follows immediately.

(7). Define

$$
Y^+ = \max(0, Y), \quad \text{and} \quad Y^- = \max(0, -Y).
$$

Then, $|Y| = Y^+ + Y^-$ and $Y = Y^+ - Y^-$. Thus, by the linearity,

$$\begin{aligned}|\mathbb{E}[Y|X]| &= |\mathbb{E}[Y^+ - Y^-|X]| = |\mathbb{E}[Y^+|X] - \mathbb{E}[Y^-|X]| \\ &\le \mathbb{E}[Y^+|X] + \mathbb{E}[Y^-|X] = \mathbb{E}[Y^+ + Y^-|X] = \mathbb{E}[|Y||X].\end{aligned}$$

(8). Let us calculate $\mathbb{E}[Yg(X)|X]$ in discrete case. Suppose that X and Y assume $x_1, x_2, \ldots$ and $y_1, y_2, \ldots$, respectively. Given $X = x_j$, $Yg(X)$ assumes $y_i g(x_j), i = 1, 2, \ldots$, and the probability of taking $y_i g(x_j)$ given $X = x_j$ is $\mathbb{P}(Y = y_i|X = x_j)$. So,

$$\begin{aligned}\mathbb{E}[Yg(X)|X = x_j] &= \sum_i y_i g(x_j)\mathbb{P}(Y = y_i|X = x_j) \\ &= g(x_j)\sum_i y_i \mathbb{P}(Y = y_i|X = x_j) = g(x_j)\mathbb{E}[Y|X = x_j].\end{aligned}$$

The assertion holds due to the arbitrariness of x_j. Also, in the continuous case,

$$\begin{aligned}\mathbb{E}[Yg(X)|X = x] &= \int yg(x) f_{Y|X}(y|x)dy = g(x)\int y f_{Y|X}(y|x)dy \\ &= g(x)\mathbb{E}(Y|X = x).\end{aligned}$$

(9). Recall some facts about the convex function: If $\phi(\cdot)$ is convex then its left and right derivatives always exist and $\phi'_-(x) \le \phi'_+(x)$. Because $\phi(\cdot)$ is convex, we claim that there exists a function $h(\cdot)$ such that $h(x)(y - x) \le \phi(y) - \phi(x)$ for all x, y in the interval.

Indeed, recall the definition of convexity:

$$\phi((1 - \lambda)x + \lambda y) \le (1 - \lambda)\phi(x) + \lambda\phi(y),$$

for all $\lambda \in (0, 1)$ and x, y in the interval.

Rewrite

$$\frac{\phi(x + \lambda(y - x)) - \phi(x)}{\lambda} \le \phi(y) - \phi(x),$$

and furthermore,

$$\frac{\phi(x + \lambda(y - x)) - \phi(x)}{\lambda(y - x)}(y - x) \le \phi(y) - \phi(x).$$

For fixed $x < y$, letting $\lambda \to 0^+$ gives

$$\phi'_+(x)\,(y - x) \le \phi(y) - \phi(x);$$

while for fixed $x > y$, letting $\lambda \to 0^+$ gives

$$\phi'_-(x)\,(y - x) \le \phi(y) - \phi(x),$$

but $\phi'_-(x)(y - x) \ge \phi'_+(x)(y - x)$.

So, in either case $h(x) = \phi'_+(x)$ satisfies the inequality, and it always exists.

Letting $x = \mathbb{E}(Y|X)$, $y = Y$, we have

$$h(\mathbb{E}(Y|X))\,(Y - \mathbb{E}(Y|X)) \le \phi(Y) - \phi(\mathbb{E}(Y|X)).$$

Taking conditional expectation on X on both sides yields the conditional Jensen's inequality.

(10). Observe that

$$\begin{aligned}
\mathrm{Var}(Y) =& \mathbb{E}[Y - \mathbb{E}(Y)]^2 = \mathbb{E}[Y - \mathbb{E}(Y|X) + \mathbb{E}(Y|X) - \mathbb{E}(Y)]^2 \\
=& \mathbb{E}[Y - \mathbb{E}(Y|X)]^2 + \mathbb{E}[\mathbb{E}(Y|X) - \mathbb{E}(Y)]^2 \\
&+ 2\mathbb{E}\{[Y - \mathbb{E}(Y|X)][\mathbb{E}(Y|X) - \mathbb{E}(Y)]\} \\
=& \mathbb{E}[Y - \mathbb{E}(Y|X)]^2 + \mathbb{E}[\mathbb{E}(Y|X) - \mathbb{E}(Y)]^2 \\
=& \mathbb{E}[\mathrm{Var}(Y|X)] + \mathrm{Var}[\mathbb{E}(Y|X)],
\end{aligned}$$

where $\mathbb{E}\{[Y - \mathbb{E}(Y|X)][\mathbb{E}(Y|X) - \mathbb{E}(Y)]\} = 0$ by the Law of Iterated Expectations. □

One thing we should mention is that even if $\mathbb{E}(Y|X)$ exists, $\mathbb{E}(Y)$ may not exist. For example, let $X \sim$ Cauchy distribution, $\varepsilon \sim N(0, 1)$ independent of X, and $Y = X + \varepsilon$. Then, $\mathbb{E}(Y|X) = X$, but $\mathbb{E}(Y)$ does not exist. Conversely, if $\mathbb{E}(|Y|) < \infty$, $\mathbb{E}(Y|X)$ does exist by the definition of conditional expectation.

2.4 Conditional Expectation with Projection Viewpoint

It is known that $\mathbb{E}[Y]$ is the solution of $\min_a \mathbb{E}(Y - a)^2$, i.e., among all constants, $\mathbb{E}[Y]$ is the best predictor for Y in terms of mean square error. Now, given random variables X and Y, among all measurable functions $g(\cdot)$, we are about to find a $g_0(\cdot)$ such that

$$g_0 = \underset{\text{measurable } g}{\arg\min}\ \mathbb{E}[Y - g(X)]^2.$$

It follows from the property of conditional expectation that

$$\begin{aligned}
\mathbb{E}[Y - g(X)]^2 =& \mathbb{E}[Y - \mathbb{E}(Y|X)]^2 + \mathbb{E}[\mathbb{E}(Y|X) - g(X)]^2 \\
\ge& \mathbb{E}[Y - \mathbb{E}(Y|X)]^2
\end{aligned}$$

for any $g(X)$. Thus, $g_0(x) = \mathbb{E}[Y|X = x]$ is the solution, that is, $g_0(X) = \mathbb{E}[Y|X]$ is the best predictor of Y in terms of mean square error. Also, if we denote $e = Y - \mathbb{E}[Y|X]$, then $\mathbb{E}(e|X) = 0$, and hence $\mathbb{E}(e\, g(X)) = 0$ for any g. This actually is a depiction of conditional expectations from a projection viewpoint. We first introduce the notion of projection.

Definition 2.4.1 Let T be a r.v. with finite second moment, and $\mathcal{S} = \{S\}$ a collection of r.v.'s with finite second moment. All of these r.v. are defined on the same probability space. A r.v. S_0 is called a projection of T on $\mathcal{S}$ if $S_0 \in \mathcal{S}$ and S_0 minimizes

$$\min_{S \in \mathcal{S}} \mathbb{E}(T - S)^2.$$

From this definition and our derivation above, $g_0(X) = \mathbb{E}[Y|X]$ is the projection of Y onto the linear space of all measurable functions of X. Suppose that $\mathcal{S}$ is a linear space. Define inner product $\langle S_1, S_2\rangle = \mathbb{E}(S_1 S_2)$ in $\mathcal{S}$. If $\langle S_1, S_2\rangle = 0$, we say S_1 and S_2 are *orthogonal*. We then have the following theorem.

Theorem 2.4.1 *Let $\mathcal{S}$ be a linear space of r.v.'s with finite second moments. S_0 is the projection of T onto $\mathcal{S}$ if and only if*

$$\mathbb{E}[(T - S_0)S] = 0, \quad \forall\, S \in \mathcal{S}.$$

Every two projections of T onto $\mathcal{S}$ are equal almost surely. If $\mathcal{S}$ contains constant variables, then $\mathbb{E}T = \mathbb{E}S_0$ and $Cov(T - S_0, S) = 0$, for any $S \in \mathcal{S}$. □

Proof For $S, S_0 \in \mathcal{S}$, note that

$$\begin{aligned}\mathbb{E}(T - S)^2 &= \mathbb{E}(T - S_0 + S_0 - S)^2 \\ &= \mathbb{E}(T - S_0)^2 + \mathbb{E}(S_0 - S)^2 + 2\mathbb{E}[(T - S_0)(S_0 - S)].\end{aligned}$$

To see the sufficiency, note that if S_0 satisfies the orthogonality condition $\mathbb{E}[(T - S_0)S] = 0$, $\forall\, S \in \mathcal{S}$, the last term vanishes. Then, $\mathbb{E}(T - S)^2 \geq \mathbb{E}(T - S_0)^2$ and the equality holds if and only if $\mathbb{E}(S_0 - S)^2 = 0$. Thus, S_0 is a projection of T.

Conversely, for any α,

$$\begin{aligned}&\mathbb{E}(T - S_0 + \alpha S)^2 - \mathbb{E}(T - S_0)^2 \\ &\qquad = \alpha^2\mathbb{E}(S^2) + 2\alpha\mathbb{E}[(T - S_0)S] \geq 0.\end{aligned}$$

This implies $\mathbb{E}[(T - S_0)S] = 0$ due to the arbitrariness of α.

If there are two projections S_1 and S_2 of T, it follows from the first assertion that

$$\mathbb{E}[(T - S_1)(S_1 - S_2)] = 0, \tag{2.4.1}$$

$$\mathbb{E}[(T - S_2)(S_1 - S_2)] = 0. \tag{2.4.2}$$

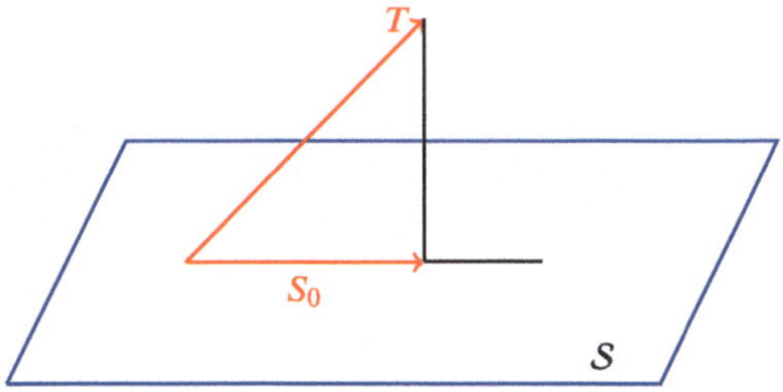

Fig. 2.1 Variable T is projected onto the space $\mathcal{S} = \{S\}$

Subtracting (2.4.1) from (2.4.2) yields $\mathbb{E}[(S_1 - S_2)^2] = 0$, implying that they are equal almost surely.

If there is a constant $c \neq 0$ in the space, then $\mathbb{E}[(T - S_0)c] = 0$ gives $\mathbb{E}T = \mathbb{E}S_0$; and hence $\mathbb{E}[(T - S_0)S] = 0$ implies $\text{Cov}(T - S_0, S) = 0$. □

From the theorem, the function $g_0(x) = \mathbb{E}[Y|X = x]$ is unique up to sets B of values x such that $\mathbb{P}(X \in B) = 0$. The theorem implies that the difference between T and its projection on $\mathcal{S}$ is orthogonal with all elements in $\mathcal{S}$. Here is a geometric explanation (Fig. 2.1):

Moreover, the theorem does not assert the existence of the projection, while the existence can be guaranteed by the closedness of the space.

Example 2.4.1 Most of the following properties of conditional expectation are shown in preceding sections, but here we prove them from a projection viewpoint.

(1) Due to Theorem 2.4.1, $\mathbb{E}[(Y - \mathbb{E}(Y|X))g(X)] = 0$ for any measurable g function. Then, letting $g(x) \equiv 1$ yields $\mathbb{E}[\mathbb{E}(Y|X)] = \mathbb{E}(Y)$. This is the Law of Iterated Expectation.

(2) If $Y = f(X)$, then $\mathbb{E}(Y|X) = Y$. This is because $\mathbb{E}[Y - g(X)]^2$ is minimized when $g = f$.

(3) If X and Y are independent, then $\mathbb{E}(Y|X) = \mathbb{E}(Y)$. This is because the orthogonality condition $\mathbb{E}[(Y - \mathbb{E}(Y))g(X)] = \mathbb{E}[Y - \mathbb{E}(Y)]\mathbb{E}[g(X)] = 0$ holds for any g, so that $\mathbb{E}(Y|X) = \mathbb{E}(Y)$ by Theorem 2.4.1.

(4) For any constant a and r.v. X, $\mathbb{E}(a|X) = a$. In fact, over all measurable functions $g(x)$, clearly $\mathbb{E}(a - g(X))^2$ is minimized when $g(x) = a$, which means $\mathbb{E}(a|X) = a$.

(5) $\mathbb{E}[f(X)Y|X] = f(X)\mathbb{E}(Y|X)$. Actually for any g,

$$\mathbb{E}\{[f(X)Y - f(X)\mathbb{E}(Y|X)]g(X)\} = \mathbb{E}\{[Y - \mathbb{E}(Y|X)]f(X)g(X)\} = 0,$$

by the Law of Iterated Expectation in Theorem 2.3.3. This verifies the assertion due to Theorem 2.4.1.

(6) $\mathbb{E}(Y + Z|X) = \mathbb{E}(Y|X) + \mathbb{E}(Z|X)$. Indeed, denoting $h(X) = \mathbb{E}(Y + Z|X)$, $h_1(X) = \mathbb{E}(Y|X)$ and $h_2(X) = \mathbb{E}(Z|X)$, invoking Theorem 2.4.1 for any measurable $g(x)$,

$$\mathbb{E}[(Y + Z - h(X))g(X)] = 0, \tag{2.4.3}$$
$$\mathbb{E}[(Y - h_1(X))g(X)] = 0, \tag{2.4.4}$$
$$\mathbb{E}[(Z - h_2(X))g(X)] = 0. \tag{2.4.5}$$

Adding Eqs. (2.4.4) and (2.4.5) and subtracting Eq. (2.4.3), we have

$$\mathbb{E}[(h(X) - h_1(X) - h_2(X))g(X)] = 0, \tag{2.4.6}$$

for any $g(X)$. In particular, Eq. (2.4.6) holds for $g(X) = h(X) - h_1(X) - h_2(X)$, that is,

$$\mathbb{E}[(h(X) - h_1(X) - h_2(X))^2] = 0,$$

which gives the assertion $h(X) = h_1(X) + h_2(X)$.

(7) For any X, Y, Z, $\mathbb{E}[\mathbb{E}(Y|X, Z)|X] = \mathbb{E}(Y|X)$. One may verify for any g,

$$\begin{aligned}&\mathbb{E}[(\mathbb{E}(Y|X, Z) - \mathbb{E}(Y|X))g(X)]\\ =&\mathbb{E}[\mathbb{E}(Yg(X)|X, Z)] - \mathbb{E}[\mathbb{E}(g(X)Y|X)] = 0.\end{aligned}$$

(8) Suppose that (X, Y) has joint density $f_{X,Y}(x, y)$, and $f_{Y|X}(y|x)$ is the conditional density of Y given $X = x$. Then

$$\mathbb{E}(Y|X) = \int y f_{Y|X}(y|X)dy.$$

In fact,

$$\begin{aligned}\mathbb{E}(Y - g(X))^2 =& \mathbb{E}(Y^2) - 2\mathbb{E}(g(X)Y) + \mathbb{E}(g^2(X))\\ =& \mathbb{E}(Y^2) - 2\int g(x)\left[\int y f_{Y|X}(y|x)dy\right] f_X(x)dx\\ &+ \int g^2(x) f_X(x)dx\\ =& \mathbb{E}(Y^2) + \int \left[g(x) - \int y f_{Y|X}(y|x)dy\right]^2 f_X(x)dx\\ &- \int\left[\int y f_{Y|X}(y|x)dy\right]^2 f_X(x)dx.\end{aligned}$$

To minimizes $\mathbb{E}(Y - g(X))^2$ over g, one should take $g(x) = \int y f_{Y|X}(y|x)dy$.

Other uses of projection in statistics can be found in van der Vaart (1998).

2.5 Conditional Expectation Given Sigma Field

A more general case of conditional expectation is conditioning on a σ-field, say $\mathbb{E}(Y|\mathcal{G})$. Recall that a r.v. X is said to be measurable w.r.t. $\mathcal{G}$ if for every $B \in \mathcal{B}$, Borel σ-field on $\mathbb{R}$,

$$X^{-1}(B) = \{\omega, X(\omega) \in B\} \in \mathcal{G}.$$

Definition 2.5.1 Let Y be an integrable r.v. on $(\Omega, \mathcal{F}, \mathbb{P})$, $\mathcal{G}$ be a σ-field and $\mathcal{G} \subset \mathcal{F}$. Conditional expectation $\mathbb{E}(Y|\mathcal{G})$ is an integrable r.v. measurable w.r.t. $\mathcal{G}$ such that

$$\int_G \mathbb{E}(Y|\mathcal{G})d\mathbb{P} = \int_G Y d\mathbb{P}, \quad \forall G \in \mathcal{G}. \tag{2.5.1}$$

The existence of $\mathbb{E}(Y|\mathcal{G})$ is considered firstly for nonnegative Y. Define a measure ν on $\mathcal{G}$ by $\nu(G) = \int_G Y d\mathbb{P}$ for any $G \in \mathcal{G}$. This measure is finite because Y is integrable, and it is absolutely continuous w.r.t. $\mathbb{P}$. By the Radon-Nikodym theorem there exists a function f, measurable w.r.t. $\mathcal{G}$, such that $\nu(G) = \int_G f d\mathbb{P}$. This f satisfies the definition above. If Y is not necessarily nonnegative, $\mathbb{E}(Y^+|\mathcal{G}) - \mathbb{E}(Y^-|\mathcal{G})$ satisfies the requirement.

There are possibly many r.v.'s that satisfy the definition of $\mathbb{E}(Y|\mathcal{G})$; any one of them is called a version of $\mathbb{E}(Y|\mathcal{G})$, and any two versions are equal with probability one.

Two extreme cases are $\mathbb{E}(Y|\mathcal{F}) = Y$ and $\mathbb{E}(Y|\mathcal{T}) = \mathbb{E}(Y)$ where $\mathcal{T} = \{\emptyset, \Omega\}$ the trivial sigma field. These are easy to check by the definition. A case in between is $\mathcal{G} = \{\emptyset, A, A^c, \Omega\}$, so that

$$\mathbb{E}(Y|\mathcal{G})(\omega) = \begin{cases} \mathbb{E}(Y|A), & \omega \in A, \\ \mathbb{E}(Y|A^c), & \omega \in A^c. \end{cases}$$

The value $\mathbb{E}(Y|\mathcal{G})(\omega)$ is to be interpreted as the expected value of Y for some one who knows for each $G \in \mathcal{G}$ whether or not it contains the point ω, which itself in general remains unknown.

Example 2.5.1 Let $\{B_i\}$ be a finite or countable partition of Ω generating σ-field $\mathcal{G}$ consisting of all possible unions of the B_i. Then $\mathbb{E}(Y|\mathcal{G})$ must be some constant value on B_i, say α_i, since it is measurable w.r.t. $\mathcal{G}$. It then follows from (2.5.1) that for $G = B_i$, $\alpha_i \mathbb{P}(B_i) = \int_{B_i} Y d\mathbb{P}$. Hence,

$$\mathbb{E}(Y|\mathcal{G})(\omega) = \frac{1}{\mathbb{P}(B_i)} \int_{B_i} Y d\mathbb{P}, \quad \omega \in B_i, \quad \mathbb{P}(B_i) > 0.$$

If $\mathbb{P}(B_i) = 0$, the value $\mathbb{E}(Y|\mathcal{G})$ over B_i is constant but arbitrary.

Example 2.5.2 For an indicator I_A r.v., $\mathbb{E}(I_A|\mathcal{G})$ is equal to $\mathbb{P}(A|\mathcal{G})$ where the conditional probability given σ-field is defined as follows. Let $\{B_i\}$ be a finite or countable partition of Ω generating σ-field $\mathcal{G}$. For $A \in \mathcal{F}$, define

$$g(\omega) = \mathbb{P}(A|B_i), \quad \omega \in B_i, \ i = 1, 2, \ldots \tag{2.5.2}$$

and we call this r.v. the conditional probability of A given $\mathcal{G}$, denoted by $\mathbb{P}(A|\mathcal{G})$. More generally, the conditional probability $\mathbb{P}(A|\mathcal{G})$ of A given $\mathcal{G}$ is a r.v. that is integrable and measurable w.r.t. $\mathcal{G}$ such that for any $G \in \mathcal{G}$ we have

$$\int_G \mathbb{P}(A|\mathcal{G})d\mathbb{P} = \mathbb{P}(A \cap G).$$

There are possibly many such r.v.'s but any two of them are equal with probability one. It is also clear that $\mathbb{P}(\cdot|\mathcal{G})$ satisfies the definition of probability, that is, $\mathbb{P}(\emptyset|\mathcal{G}) = 0$, $\mathbb{P}(\Omega|\mathcal{G}) = 1$, $\mathbb{P}(A|\mathcal{G}) \in [0, 1]$, and it satisfies additivity for disjoint sets.

Moreover, it is easy to check that for any simple variable $X = \sum_i \alpha_i I_{A_i}$, $\mathbb{E}(X|\mathcal{G}) = \sum_i \alpha_i \mathbb{P}(A_i|\mathcal{G})$.

If $\{X_t, t \in T\}$ is a collection of random variables, $\mathbb{E}(Y|X_t, t \in T) = \mathbb{E}(Y|\mathcal{G})$ where $\mathcal{G} = \sigma(X_t, t \in T)$ the σ-field generated by $\{X_t, t \in T\}$.

Theorem 2.5.1 *Properties of* $\mathbb{E}(Y|\mathcal{G})$.

(1) If Y is integrable and measurable w.r.t. $\mathcal{G}$, then $\mathbb{E}(Y|\mathcal{G}) = Y$; in particular, $Y = a$ implies $\mathbb{E}(a|\mathcal{G}) = a$ for constant a.
(2) Low of Iterated Expectations, $\mathbb{E}(\mathbb{E}(Y|\mathcal{G})) = \mathbb{E}(Y)$; if Sigma fields $\mathcal{D} \subset \mathcal{G} \subset \mathcal{F}$, then $\mathbb{E}(Y|\mathcal{D}) = \mathbb{E}(\mathbb{E}(Y|\mathcal{G})|\mathcal{D})$.
(3) Linearity, $\mathbb{E}(aX + bY|\mathcal{G}) = a\,\mathbb{E}(X|\mathcal{G}) + b\,\mathbb{E}(Y|\mathcal{G})$.
(4) $|\mathbb{E}(X|\mathcal{G})| \le \mathbb{E}(|X||\mathcal{G})$.
(5) If X is $\mathcal{G}$ measurable and $\mathbb{E}|XY| < \infty$, then $\mathbb{E}(XY|\mathcal{G}) = X\mathbb{E}(Y|\mathcal{G})$.
(6) If Y is integrable and $\mathbb{E}(Y|\mathcal{G}) = \mathbb{E}(Y)$ almost surely, then $Cov(X, Y) = 0$ for all integrable and $\mathcal{G}$ measurable X.
(7) If $X \le Y$ a.s., then $\mathbb{E}(X|\mathcal{G}) \le \mathbb{E}(Y|\mathcal{G})$ a.s. □

Proof (1). It is proven by the definition. Indeed, to make the equation $\int_A \xi d\mathbb{P} = \int_A Y d\mathbb{P}$ holds for any $A \in \mathcal{G}$, we simply let $\xi = Y$ that is measurable w.r.t. $\mathcal{G}$ and integrable. Thus, $\mathbb{E}(Y|\mathcal{G}) = Y$. Since $Y = a$ is measurable w.r.t. $\mathcal{G}$ and integrable, the assertion holds immediately.

(2). Taking $G = \Omega$ in the definition (2.5.1), the first assertion follows immediately. To show the second part, let $A \in \mathcal{D}$, then $A \in \mathcal{G}$. By definition,

$$\int_A \mathbb{E}(\mathbb{E}(Y|\mathcal{G})|\mathcal{D})d\mathbb{P} = \int_A \mathbb{E}(Y|\mathcal{G})d\mathbb{P} = \int_A Y d\mathbb{P}.$$

The most left equals the most right which implies $\mathbb{E}(Y|\mathcal{D}) = \mathbb{E}(\mathbb{E}(Y|\mathcal{G})|\mathcal{D})$.

(3). Using the definition repeatedly, for any $A \in \mathcal{G}$,

$$\begin{aligned}\int_A \mathbb{E}(aX + bY|\mathcal{G})d\mathbb{P} &= \int_A (aX + bY)d\mathbb{P}\\ &= a\int_A Xd\mathbb{P} + b\int_A Yd\mathbb{P} = a\int_A \mathbb{E}(X|\mathcal{G})d\mathbb{P} + b\int_A \mathbb{E}(Y|\mathcal{G})d\mathbb{P}\\ &= \int_A [a\mathbb{E}(X|\mathcal{G}) + b\mathbb{E}(Y|\mathcal{G})]d\mathbb{P},\end{aligned}$$

that is, $\mathbb{E}(aX + bY|\mathcal{G}) = a\mathbb{E}(X|\mathcal{G}) + b\mathbb{E}(Y|\mathcal{G})$ by the definition again.

(4). For nonnegative X, $\mathbb{E}(X|\mathcal{G})$ is nonnegative and thus the assertion holds.

For general X, define $X^+(\omega) = X(\omega)$ whenever $X(\omega) > 0$, otherwise zero, and $X^-(\omega) = -X(\omega)$ whenever $X(\omega) < 0$, otherwise zero. Both X^+ and X^- are nonnegative r.v.'s, and $X = X^+ - X^-$ and $|X| = X^+ + X^-$. Accordingly,

$$\begin{aligned}|\mathbb{E}(X|\mathcal{G})| &= |\mathbb{E}(X^+|\mathcal{G}) - \mathbb{E}(X^-|\mathcal{G})| \le \mathbb{E}(X^+|\mathcal{G}) + \mathbb{E}(X^-|\mathcal{G})\\ &= \mathbb{E}(X^+ + X^-|\mathcal{G}) = \mathbb{E}(|X||\mathcal{G}).\end{aligned}$$

(5). By definition, the assertion follows if for all $G \in \mathcal{G}$,

$$\int_G X\mathbb{E}(Y|\mathcal{G})d\mathbb{P} = \int_G XYd\mathbb{P}. \tag{2.5.3}$$

Let $X_{(n)} = \sum_{i=1}^n \alpha_i I_{E_i}$ be a $\mathcal{G}$-measurable simple r.v., where $E_1, \ldots, E_n \in \mathcal{G}$ form a partition of Ω. Then, Eq. (2.5.3) holds for $X = X_{(n)}$ since for all $G \in \mathcal{G}$,

$$\begin{aligned}\int_G X_{(n)}\mathbb{E}(Y|\mathcal{G})d\mathbb{P} &= \sum_{i=1}^n \alpha_i \int_{G\cap E_i} \mathbb{E}(Y|\mathcal{G})d\mathbb{P}\\ &= \sum_{i=1}^n \alpha_i \int_{G\cap E_i} Yd\mathbb{P} = \int_G X_{(n)}Yd\mathbb{P},\end{aligned}$$

in view of $G \cap E_i \in \mathcal{G}$.

Let $X \ge 0$ a.s. and let $\{X_{(n)}\}$ be a monotone sequence of simple $\mathcal{G}$-measurable r.v.'s converging to X for every $\omega \in \Omega$ (see Theorem 3.28 in Davidson, 1994). Then $X_{(n)}Y \to XY$ a.s. and $|X_{(n)}Y| \to |XY|$. Similarly, $X_{(n)}\mathbb{E}(Y|\mathcal{G}) \to X\mathbb{E}(Y|\mathcal{G})$ a.s. and

$$\begin{aligned}\mathbb{E}|X_{(n)}\mathbb{E}(Y|\mathcal{G})| &= \mathbb{E}|\mathbb{E}(X_{(n)}Y|\mathcal{G})| \le \mathbb{E}[\mathbb{E}(|X_{(n)}Y||\mathcal{G})]\\ &= \mathbb{E}|X_{(n)}Y| \le \mathbb{E}|XY| < \infty.\end{aligned}$$

It then follows from the Dominated Convergence Theorem that $\int_G X_{(n)}\mathbb{E}(Y|\mathcal{G})d\mathbb{P} \to \int_G X\mathbb{E}(Y|\mathcal{G})d\mathbb{P}$, and thus (2.5.3) holds for nonnegative X.

To extend to general X, note that $X = X^+ - X^-$ and

$$\begin{aligned}\mathbb{E}(XY|\mathcal{G}) &= \mathbb{E}(X^+Y - X^-Y|\mathcal{G}) = \mathbb{E}(X^+Y|\mathcal{G}) - \mathbb{E}(X^-Y|\mathcal{G})\\ &= (X^+ - X^-)\mathbb{E}(Y|\mathcal{G}) = X\mathbb{E}(Y|\mathcal{G}).\end{aligned}$$

(6). Observe that

$$\begin{aligned}\mathbb{E}(XY) &= \mathbb{E}(\mathbb{E}(XY|\mathcal{G})) = \mathbb{E}(X\mathbb{E}(Y|\mathcal{G}))\\ &= \mathbb{E}(X\mathbb{E}(Y)) = \mathbb{E}(X)\mathbb{E}(Y).\end{aligned}$$

Then, $\mathrm{Cov}(X, Y) = 0$.

(7). Notice by the definition that, for any $G \in \mathcal{G}$,

$$\begin{aligned}&\int_G [\mathbb{E}(X|\mathcal{G}) - \mathbb{E}(Y|\mathcal{G})]d\mathbb{P} = \int_G \mathbb{E}(X|\mathcal{G})d\mathbb{P} - \int_G \mathbb{E}(Y|\mathcal{G})d\mathbb{P}\\ &= \int_G Xd\mathbb{P} - \int_G Yd\mathbb{P} = \int_G [X - Y]d\mathbb{P} \le 0.\end{aligned}$$

Note also that $A = \{\omega : \mathbb{E}(X|\mathcal{G}) > \mathbb{E}(Y|\mathcal{G})\} \in \mathcal{G}$. It implies that $\mathbb{P}(A) = 0$. The assertion holds. □

Theorem 2.5.2 (Conditional Jensen's Inequality) *If $\phi(\cdot)$ is a convex function on the line, and X and $\phi(X)$ are both integrable, then*

$$\phi(\mathbb{E}(X|\mathcal{G})) \le \mathbb{E}(\phi(X)|\mathcal{G}), \quad a.s. \tag{2.5.4}$$

Proof For each $x_0 \in \mathbb{R}$ take a support line through $(x_0, \phi(x_0))$, $\phi(x_0) + A(x_0)(x - x_0) \le \phi(x)$. The slope $A(x_0)$ can be taken as the right-hand derivative of $\phi(\cdot)$, so that it is nondecreasing. Now, for $x_0 = \mathbb{E}(X|\mathcal{G})$ and $x = X$,

$$\phi(\mathbb{E}(X|\mathcal{G})) + A(\mathbb{E}(X|\mathcal{G}))(X - \mathbb{E}(X|\mathcal{G})) \le \phi(X).$$

Suppose that $\mathbb{E}(X|\mathcal{G})$ is bounded. Then, all the three terms above are integrable (since if $\phi(\cdot)$ is a convex function on the line, then $\phi(\cdot)$ and $A(\cdot)$ are bounded on bounded sets), and taking conditional expectation w.r.t. $\mathcal{G}$ gives (2.5.4).

In general, let $G_n = \{\omega, \ |\mathbb{E}(X|\mathcal{G})(\omega)| \le n\}$ for all positive integers. Hence, all G_n are $\mathcal{G}$ measurable. Then, $\mathbb{E}(I_{G_n}X|\mathcal{G}) = I_{G_n}\mathbb{E}(X|\mathcal{G})$ is bounded, and (2.5.4) holds for $I_{G_n}X$, that is, $\phi(I_{G_n}\mathbb{E}(X|\mathcal{G})) \le \mathbb{E}[\phi(I_{G_n}X)|\mathcal{G}]$. Now, $\mathbb{E}[\phi(I_{G_n}X)|\mathcal{G}] = \mathbb{E}[I_{G_n}\phi(X) + I_{G_n^c}\phi(0)|\mathcal{G}] = I_{G_n}\mathbb{E}[\phi(X)|\mathcal{G}] + I_{G_n^c}\phi(0) \to \mathbb{E}[\phi(X)|\mathcal{G}]$ as $n \to \infty$. On the other hand, $\phi(I_{G_n}\mathbb{E}(X|\mathcal{G})) \to \phi(\mathbb{E}(X|\mathcal{G}))$ by the continuity of ϕ. This finishes the proof. □

References

Billingsley, P. (1995). *Probability and Measure*. New York: Wiley.
Davidson, J. (1994). *Stochastic limit theory*. Advance texts in econometrics. New York: Oxford University Press.
van der Vaart, A. W. (1998). *Asymptotic Statistics*. Cambridge: Cambridge University Press.

Chapter 3
Regressions and Series Estimation

The regression problem has been studied for a long period of time. Already in 1632 Galileo Galilei used a procedure that can be interpreted as fitting a linear relationship to contaminated data. Such fitting of a line through chaotic points is a classical linear regression problem. A solution to this problem is provided by the famous principle of least squares, which was discovered independently by A. M. Legendre and C. F. Gauss, published in 1805 and 1809, respectively.

The term regression originated in an influential paper by Francis Galton (1886) where he examined the joint distribution of the stature (height) of parents and children. Effectively, he was estimating the conditional mean of children's height given their parent's height. Galton discovered that this conditional mean was approximately linear with a slope of 2/3. This implies that on average a child's height is more mediocre (average) than his or her parent's height. Galton called this phenomenon regression to the mean, and the label regression has stuck to this day to describe most conditional relationships.

Following these, linear regression analysis based on the concept of a regression function was introduced by F. Galton in 1889, whereas a probabilistic approach in the context of multivariate normal distributions was already given by A. Bravais in 1846.

This chapter is devoted to the principle of regression with a conditional expectation viewpoint. This viewpoint will reveal the rationale of regression, and in particular, show the mathematical expression of regression function from which several main nonparametric estimation methods have been developed. After understanding the procedure of using the series methods, one may use them in all kinds of nonparametric issues.

C. Dong and J. Gao, *Modern Series Methods in Econometrics and Statistics*,
Advanced Studies in Theoretical and Applied Econometrics 45,
https://doi.org/10.1007/978-981-96-2822-3_3

3.1 Regressions from Conditional Expectation Viewpoint

As it is well known, the conditional expectation $\mathbb{E}(Y|X)$ is a function of X, which is normally unknown to researchers and practitioners. Define $g(x) = \mathbb{E}(Y|X = x)$, the conditional expectation function (CEF). As pointed out in the preceding chapter, $g(X)$ is the projection of Y onto the space

$$\{m(X),\ m(\cdot) \text{ is measurable}\}. \tag{3.1.1}$$

Hence $g(X)$ satisfies the following definition.

Definition 3.1.1 Suppose that a statistic $T(\xi)$ in ξ is a predictor of η and it satisfies that for any statistic $\widetilde{T}(\xi)$,

$$\mathbb{E}(\eta - T(\xi))^2 \le \mathbb{E}(\eta - \widetilde{T}(\xi))^2. \tag{3.1.2}$$

Then we say that $T(\xi)$ has the least mean square error when predicting η. □

This is mainly a rephrasing of projection but from a mean square error point of view. It can be shown easily that $T(\xi) = \mathbb{E}(\eta|\xi)$. Indeed, for any function $\widetilde{T}(\xi)$,

$$\begin{aligned}\mathbb{E}(\eta - \widetilde{T}(\xi))^2 &= \mathbb{E}(\eta - T(\xi) + T(\xi) - \widetilde{T}(\xi))^2\\ &= \mathbb{E}(\eta - T(\xi))^2 + \mathbb{E}(T(\xi) - \widetilde{T}(\xi))^2\\ &\ge \mathbb{E}(\eta - T(\xi))^2\end{aligned}$$

by virtue of Theorem 2.4.1 and $\mathbb{E}[(\eta - T(\xi))(T(\xi) - \widetilde{T}(\xi))] = 0$ (or using the Law of Iterated Expectations). Therefore, projection, regression, and least mean square error predictor are synonym in statistics and econometrics.

Define $e = Y - \mathbb{E}(Y|X)$, and we then have

$$Y = g(X) + e, \tag{3.1.3}$$

which is called the *regression equation* for Y regressing on X, and e is the *error term*. We also call CEF $g(X) = \mathbb{E}(Y|X)$ *regression function*. Such defined error term has the following properties.

(1) $\mathbb{E}(e) = 0$, since $\mathbb{E}(e) = \mathbb{E}(Y) - \mathbb{E}(\mathbb{E}(Y|X)) = \mathbb{E}(Y) - \mathbb{E}(Y) = 0$;
(2) $\mathbb{E}(eX) = 0$, since $\mathbb{E}(eX) = \mathbb{E}(YX) - \mathbb{E}(X\mathbb{E}(Y|X)) = \mathbb{E}(YX) - \mathbb{E}(YX) = 0$;
(3) $\mathbb{E}(e|X) = 0$, because

$$\begin{aligned}\mathbb{E}(e|X) &= \mathbb{E}[Y - \mathbb{E}[Y|X]|X]\\ &= \mathbb{E}[Y|X] - \mathbb{E}[\mathbb{E}[Y|X]|X]\\ &= \mathbb{E}[Y|X] - \mathbb{E}[Y|X] = 0;\end{aligned}$$

(4) $\mathbb{E}[h(X)e] = 0$ for any $h(\cdot)$. This is due to $\mathbb{E}(e|X) = 0$.

It follows that $\mathbb{E}(e|X) = 0$ is weaker than the mutual independence between e and X, but stronger than the uncorrelation between them. More importantly, such defined regression (3.1.3) does not suffer from endogeneity because of property (2).

Therefore, we may conclude that a conditional expectation function $g(X) = \mathbb{E}(Y|X)$ implies a regression equation $Y = g(X) + e$; conversely, a regression equation $Y = g(X) + e$ coupled with $\mathbb{E}(e|X) = 0$ implies $g(X) = \mathbb{E}(Y|X)$ too. Hence, a regression is normally referred to as *conditional mean regression* or simply *mean regression*. By contrast, there are other kinds of regressions such as median regression and quantile regression, etc. Whereas we do not touch these regressions in this book, the reader may realize that series methods can be used in these regressions in the same way as in the mean regression.

Regression function $g(X) = \mathbb{E}(Y|X)$ can be viewed as the "explained portion of Y by X", while $e = Y - \mathbb{E}(Y|X)$ is the unexplained part of Y by X. Suppose now that X_1 and X_2 are two explanatory variables. Consider $e_1 = Y - \mathbb{E}(Y|X_1)$ and $e_2 = Y - \mathbb{E}(Y|X_1, X_2)$. If Var$(Y) < \infty$, then Var$(Y) \geq$Var$(e_1) \geq$Var$(e_2)$. In fact,

$$\begin{aligned}\mathrm{Var}(Y) =& \mathbb{E}[Y - \mathbb{E}(Y)]^2 = \mathbb{E}[e_1 + \mathbb{E}(Y|X_1) - \mathbb{E}(Y)]^2 \\ =& \mathbb{E}(e_1^2) + \mathbb{E}[\mathbb{E}(Y|X_1) - \mathbb{E}(Y)]^2 \\ \geq& \mathbb{E}(e_1^2) = \mathrm{Var}(e_1),\end{aligned}$$

since e_1 is uncorrelated with $\mathbb{E}(Y|X_1)$; and

$$\begin{aligned}\mathrm{Var}(e_1) =& \mathbb{E}(e_1^2) = \mathbb{E}[Y - \mathbb{E}(Y|X_1)]^2 \\ =& \mathbb{E}[e_2 + \mathbb{E}(Y|X_1, X_2) - \mathbb{E}(Y|X_1)]^2 \\ =& \mathbb{E}(e_2^2) + \mathbb{E}[\mathbb{E}(Y|X_1, X_2) - \mathbb{E}(Y|X_1)]^2 \\ \geq& \mathrm{Var}(e_2)\end{aligned}$$

since e_2 is uncorrelated with any function of X_1 and X_2. This means, regardless of whatever X_2 is, adding more explanatory variables might explain more for the dependent variable; and this is analog to the increase of R-squared in empirical applications when more explanatory variables are added in the regression equation.

Regression Eq. (3.1.3) is in population sense while in practice one observes a sample $\{(x_i, y_i), i = 1, \ldots, n\}$ from the population (X, Y) such that

$$y_i = g(x_i) + e_i, \tag{3.1.4}$$

where $g(\cdot)$ is either parametrically or nonparametrically unknown. For example, we have shown in Chap. 2 that when (X, Y) is normally distributed, $g(x) = \mathbb{E}(Y|X = x)$ is a linear function in x. In this case, the unknown function $g(x)$ is known up to a few constants (also called parameters in regression). This is an exemplar for linear regression. All these unknown parameters can be estimated using the ordinary least squares (OLS), maximum likelihood estimation (MLE), or method of moments (MM) as shown in existing econometric and statistical textbooks.

Definition 3.1.2 If among all linear function $T(\xi) = a + b\xi$, $T_0(\xi) = \alpha + \beta\xi$ satisfies

$$\mathbb{E}(\eta - T_0(\xi))^2 < \mathbb{E}(\eta - T(\xi))^2,$$

we say that $\mathbb{E}_L(\eta|\xi) = \alpha + \beta\xi$ is the linear least mean square error estimator for η given ξ. □

Logically, $\mathbb{E}(\eta - \mathbb{E}_L(\eta|\xi))^2 \geq \mathbb{E}(\eta - \mathbb{E}(\eta|\xi))^2$. Moreover, it is easy to verify that the intercept and slope of $\mathbb{E}_L(\eta|\xi) = \alpha + \beta\xi$ are

$$\alpha = \mathbb{E}(\eta) - \beta\mathbb{E}(\xi), \quad \text{and} \quad \beta = \rho\sigma_\eta/\sigma_\xi, \tag{3.1.5}$$

where ρ is the correlation coefficient between ξ and η. In effect, define

$$L(a, b) = \mathbb{E}(\eta - a - b\xi)^2,$$

and from the first-order condition,

$$\frac{\partial}{\partial a}L(a, b) = -2\mathbb{E}(\eta - a - b\xi) = 0,$$
$$\frac{\partial}{\partial b}L(a, b) = -2\mathbb{E}(\eta - a - b\xi)\xi = 0.$$

The assertion follows immediately by solving the system of the equations.

Interestingly, we have shown in Example 2.3.2 that if $\mathbb{E}(\eta|\xi) = \alpha + \beta\xi$, then α and β possess the expressions in (3.1.5). What is the relationship between $\mathbb{E}(\eta|\xi)$ and $\mathbb{E}_L(\eta|\xi)$? We illustrate this using the following example.

Example 3.1.1 Suppose that $Y = X + \varepsilon$ where $X \sim N(0, \sigma_X^2)$ and $\varepsilon \sim N(0, \sigma_\varepsilon^2)$ is independent of X. Then

$$\mathbb{E}_L(Y|X) = \frac{\text{Cov}(X, Y)}{\text{Var}(X)}X = X, \quad \text{and } \mathbb{E}(Y|X) = X.$$

Moreover,

$$\mathbb{E}_L(X|Y) = \frac{\text{Cov}(X, Y)}{\text{Var}(Y)}Y = \frac{\sigma_X^2}{\sigma_X^2 + \sigma_\varepsilon^2}Y, \quad \text{and } \mathbb{E}(X|Y) = \frac{\sigma_X^2}{\sigma_X^2 + \sigma_\varepsilon^2}Y,$$

where the assertion about $\mathbb{E}(X|Y)$ is derived from the joint normal distribution of (X, Y) with mean $(0, 0)$, variance $(\sigma_X^2, \sigma_X^2 + \sigma_\varepsilon^2)$, and covariance σ_X^2, and Example 2.3.1.

Suppose instead that $X \sim U[-\sqrt{3}\sigma_X, \sqrt{3}\sigma_X]$ and $\varepsilon \sim U[-\sqrt{3}\sigma_\varepsilon, \sqrt{3}\sigma_\varepsilon]$. They all have mean zero, and the variances σ_X^2 and σ_ε^2, respectively. It follows that

$$\mathbb{E}_L(X|Y) = \frac{\mathrm{Cov}(X, Y)}{\mathrm{Var}(Y)} Y = \frac{\sigma_X^2}{\sigma_X^2 + \sigma_\varepsilon^2} Y.$$

However, given $Y = \sqrt{3}(\sigma_X + \sigma_\varepsilon)$, the maximal value that Y might assume, $\mathbb{E}(X|Y) = \sqrt{3}\sigma_X$ because X has to be at its maximum. Evidently, $\mathbb{E}(X|Y) \neq \mathbb{E}_L(X|Y)$. Hence, $\mathbb{E}(X|Y)$ is a nonlinear function of Y.

Generally, the distribution of (X, Y) is unknown to econometricians, let alone the function $g(X) = \mathbb{E}(Y|X)$. Thus, $g(X) = \mathbb{E}(Y|X)$ is usually nonparametrically unknown; the topic of this book is the estimation of the unknown function $g(x) = \mathbb{E}(Y|X = x)$ in different situations. The main goal of regression analysis from (3.1.4) is to estimate $g(\cdot)$ and make statistical inferences. We shall discuss the classification of regressions in the next section.

3.2 Classification of Regressions

The regression of Y on X rests upon the regression function $g(x) = \mathbb{E}(Y|X = x)$ which is usually unknown to econometricians. To estimate $g(x)$ through a sample of (X, Y), it is necessary to make clear which class $g(x)$ belongs to.

A general regression model can be written as

$$Y = g(X; \theta_1, \ldots, \theta_p) + e, \tag{3.2.1}$$

which can be classified in terms of the relationship between g and its parameters:

(a) If $g(x; \theta_1, \ldots, \theta_p)$ is linear in $\theta_1, \ldots, \theta_p$ and known up to these parameters, model (3.2.1) is called *linear parametric regression*;
(b) If $g(x; \theta_1, \ldots, \theta_p)$ is nonlinear in some $\theta_1, \ldots, \theta_p$ and known up to these parameters, the model is called *nonlinear parametric regression*;
(c) If $g(x; \theta_1, \ldots, \theta_p) = g(x)$ and $g(\cdot)$ is unknown, the model is called *nonparametric regression*.

The first two classes constitute *parametric regression*, in contrast to the last one, *nonparametric regression*. For example, $g(x; \theta_1, \theta_2) = \theta_1 + \theta_2 x$ is a linear regression function, and $g(x; \theta_1, \theta_2) = \theta_1 e^{\theta_2 x}$ is a nonlinear regression function. Nonparametric regression models do not normally imply that there is no parameter to be estimated but rather that the parameter to be estimated is infinite dimensional. Indeed, the unknown regression function to be estimated can be regarded as an element of a function space that is infinite dimensional, as shown in the appendix chapters.

Parametric regression has some advantages if the model is specified correctly. For example, given the distribution of the error term, the maximum likelihood estimator of $\theta_0 = (\theta_1, \ldots, \theta_p)^\top$ converges to the true parameter vector at the rate of the inverse square root of the sample size (the so-called "root-n-consistent"), and can also be asymptotically normally distributed, with an asymptotic covariance matrix that is no larger than that of any other regular root-n-consistent estimator. Moreover, the parameter estimates may be used to help predict y for values of x, which fall outside the observed support of the regressors. On top of that, the estimates of these parameters are easily interpreted in the frame of economics and finance, etc. The drawback to parametric modeling is the requirement that the structural model and/or the error distribution are correctly specified. Correct specification may be particularly difficult for the error distribution, which represents the unpredictable component of the relation of Y to X.

Indeed, the usual assumption on parametric models is rather strong. As we have shown in Theorem 2.3.1 that when (X, Y) is jointly normal distributed, the regression function $\mathbb{E}(Y|X)$ is a linear function in X; and so far we have not found the second distribution that possesses this property. Thus, the assumed parametric model need not be the "actual" one if there is one, and the statistical and econometric methods developed for a particular parametric model could lead to erroneous conclusions when applied to the slightly perturbed model. These problems motivate the relevant literature to develop flexible non- and semiparametric methods for data analysis.

Nowadays, nonparametric modeling techniques have grown increasingly popular in both theoretical and applied econometrics, this is partially because economic theory seldom suggests any parametric functional relationships among economic variables, nor does it suggest particular parametric forms for error distributions. In addition, computing capacity boosts the use of flexible nonparametric models and methods.

The advantages and disadvantages of the nonparametric approach are the opposite of those for parametric modeling. Nonparametric modeling typically imposes few restrictions on the functional form of the joint distribution of the data (like smoothness or monotonicity), so there is little room for model misspecification, and consistency of an estimator of $g(x)$ is established under much more general conditions than those required for parametric modeling. On the other hand, when the estimating $g(x)$ requires smoothing of the empirical c.d.f. of the data, the rate of convergence of the estimator is usually slower than the parametric rate, due to the bias introduced by smoothing.

In particular, most nonparametric techniques suffer from the so-called "*curse of dimensionality*", because the rate of convergence of the resultant estimator depends on the dimension heavily. This may also be understood from a different perspective. Since the sparseness of the data becomes much more severe when the dimension of the data increases, nonparametric estimators converge more slowly to the true function as the dimension increases. For example, let x be uniformly distributed over the unit hypercube in $\mathbb{R}^{10}$ and consider local averaging in the hypercubical neighborhood; if the radii of the neighborhood are chosen to cover 10% of the range of each coordinate, then it will contain (on the average) only $(0.1)^{10}$ of the sample, and thus nearly always be empty. If, on the other hand, one adjusts the neighborhood to contain 10% of the sample, it will cover (on the average) $(0.1)^{1/10} \cong 80\%$ of the range of each coordinate.

Another example is as follows. For a kernel density estimator when the standard Gaussian is the target density, to achieve an accuracy comparable to $n = 50$ observations in one dimension, more than $n = 10^6$ observations are required in ten dimensions. See Nagler and Czado (2016) and the reference therein. This issue in general cannot be solved, as pointed out by Stone (1982, 1985). This phenomenon limits our ability to examine conditional mean functions or Lebesgue densities in a completely flexible way; this limitation of fully flexible models has motivated the development of *semiparametric modeling* methods discussed below, which offer a middle ground between fully parametric and fully nonparametric approaches.

Interestingly, not all nonparametric estimations face the curse of dimensionality. A leading example is the cumulative distribution function. As it can be expressed as the mean of a random variable defined using an indicator function, the finite-dimensional cumulative distribution can be estimated with root-n-consistency nonparametrically. See Appendix D.

Moreover, for the practical use of econometric modeling, there is a class of regressions that cannot be accommodated in either parametric or nonparametric regressions. This is *semiparametric regression.* As its name suggests, semiparametric regression is a hybrid of parametric and nonparametric regressions in order to tackle practical issues from economics and related disciplines. Typically, a semiparametric regression function contains both an unknown parameter but known to lie in a finite-dimensional Euclidean subspace and an unknown infinite-dimensional function parameter. Several leading semiparametric regression models are showcased as follows:

(a) Single-index models, $g(x) = h(\theta_0^\top x)$ where both the vector θ_0 and the function $h(\cdot)$ are unknown;
(b) Partially linear single-index models, $g(x) = x^\top \beta_0 + h(x^\top \theta_0)$ where the vectors β_0, θ_0 and function $h(\cdot)$ are unknown;
(c) Semilinear model, $g(x) = x_1^\top \beta_0 + h(x_2)$ where $x = (x_1^\top, x_2)$ and x_2 is a scalar, and β_0 and function $h(\cdot)$ are unknown;
(d) Additive nonparametric models, $g(x) = h_1(x_1) + \cdots + h_d(x_d)$ where $x = (x_1, \ldots, x_d)$, and all functions $h_i(\cdot)$, $i = 1, \ldots, d$, are unknown.

As a hybrid of the parametric and nonparametric regressions, semiparametric modeling shares the advantages and disadvantages of each. Because it allows a more general specification of the nuisance parameters, estimators of the parameters of interest for semiparametric models are consistent under a broader range of conditions than for parametric models, and these estimators are usually more precise (converging to the true values at the square root of the sample size) than their nonparametric counterparts. On the other hand, estimators for semiparametric models are generally less efficient than maximum likelihood estimators for a correctly specified parametric model and are still sensitive to misspecification of the structural function or other parametric components of the model.

While we introduce parametric, nonparametric, and semiparametric models in terms of regressions, these classifications are widely used in econometrics beyond regression. For instance, talking about parametric moment restriction models, we mean models such as

$$\mathbb{E}[m(W, \beta_0)] = 0, \tag{3.2.2}$$

where m is a q-vector of functions known up to a p-dimensional Euclidean parameter β_0, and variable W may consist of the response variable, explanatory variable, instrument variable, and so on. Given observations of W, the goal of studying (3.2.2) is to estimate β_0 that is fulfilled by *generalized method of moments* (GMM) for the case $q > p$. Moreover, talking about nonparametric moment restriction models we mean models like

$$\mathbb{E}[m(W, g(X))] = 0, \tag{3.2.3}$$

where m is a q-vector of known functions but the function g is unknown that is the target to estimate; furthermore, for semiparametric moment restriction models, we mean

$$\mathbb{E}[m(W, \beta_0, g)] = 0, \tag{3.2.4}$$

where again m is a q-vector of known functions but both Euclidean parameter β_0 and function g are about to estimate. We shall introduce a class of high-dimensional semiparametric moment restriction models in details in the subsequent chapter.

The reader is referred to Chapters in the Handbook of Econometrics such as Härdle and Linton (1994), Powell (1994), Chen (2007), and Ichimura (2007) for detailed discussions on nonparametric and semiparametric modelings.

3.3 Series Methods

Series methods are one class of the most popular nonparametric methods. Before introducing series methods, we show a big picture of nonparametric methods, and on which we know where the series methods are located. As is known, nonparametric methods include sieve methods, kernel methods, histograms, Fourier inversion, and so on; sieve methods include series methods, spline methods, wavelet methods, neural network methods, etc. See Fig. 3.1.

In any given semiparametric or nonparametric model where an unknown function $g(\cdot)$ is involved, *sieve methods* use an approximation $g_k(\cdot)$ to $g(\cdot)$ to replace it while $g_k(\cdot)$ depends only on a finite number of parameters. Moreover, $g_k(\cdot)$ belongs to a k-dimensional function space constructed maybe in terms of orthogonal series, spline, wavelet, neural network, etc., from which the corresponding terms (such as series methods, spline methods and so on) originated. These finite-dimensional function spaces are subspaces of infinite function spaces (e.g., space C, space L^2, and Sobolev space) that contain the target function $g(\cdot)$. As k increases, these subspaces approach their parent spaces, so that they are called *sieve spaces* and k their complexity. The term "method of sieve" was coined by Grenander (1981). The arch competitor to sieve methods is kernel methods, and we shall compare them in the appendix chapter of the book.

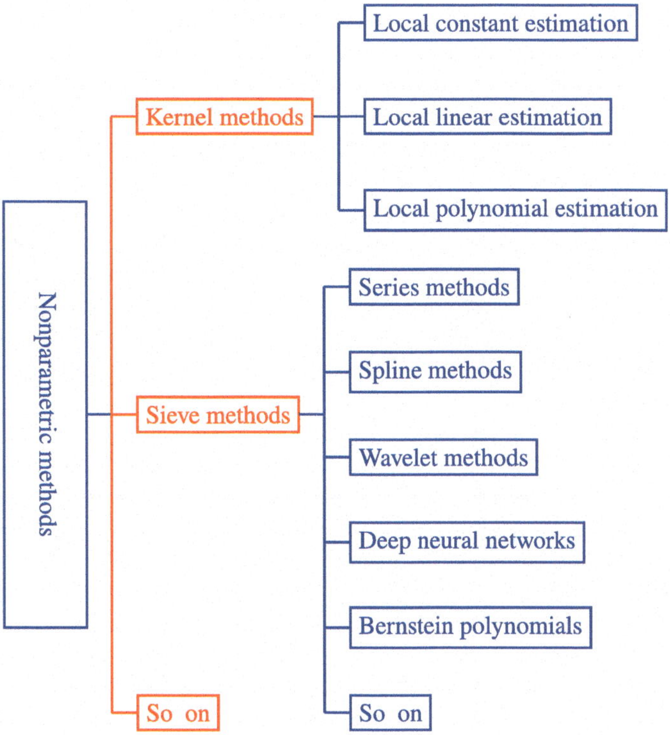

Fig. 3.1 The tree of inclusion relationship for nonparametric methods

3.3.1 Procedure of Series Estimation

As mentioned, *series methods* are a kind of sieve method that uses orthogonal function sequences such as orthogonal polynomials and trigonometric polynomials in the construction of sieve spaces. We shall use a regression model to explain the rudiment of series methods.

Suppose that we are interested in estimating a regression function $g(x) = \mathbb{E}(Y|X = x)$ given a sample of (Y, X), say $\{(y_i, x_i), i = 1, \ldots, n\}$. For convenience assume that X is a scalar. Thus,

$$y_i = g(x_i) + e_i, \qquad i = 1, \ldots, n. \tag{3.3.1}$$

Here, since we do not impose any restrictions on the function $g(\cdot)$, it is a nonparametric regression.

Before implementing a series estimation for the nonparametric regression (3.3.1), one needs to extract some useful information from the regression. That is, what kind of L^2 space $g(\cdot)$ belongs to. As may be well known, L^2 spaces are large enough to accommodate regression functions and, as Hilbert spaces, admit orthogonal basis. Therefore, L^2 space is the best candidate for series estimation.

To find the answer, the first step is to determine the *support* of $g(\cdot)$, namely, the closure of $\{x : g(x) \neq 0\}$. This in general is difficult but there might be some clues in the sample. For example, if x_i stands for a proportion, then $x_i \in [0, 1]$, so that $g(\cdot)$ has $[0, 1]$ as its support; if x_i stands for the return of a stock, usually $x_i \in [-1, 1]$, so that the support is $[-1, 1]$; if x_i signifies for a stock price, $x_i \geq 0$ and usually it is hardly to set an upper bound for it, so we may suppose $g(\cdot)$ has $[0, \infty)$ as its support; if x_i is a nonstationary time series process (a conventional symbol is x_t), we have to set the support to be the entire line $\mathbb{R} = (-\infty, \infty)$, due to the diverging nature of nonstationary time series. A rule of thumb for determining the support is when there is no clear information on the support a larger one is preferred and fortunately, the largest one is $\mathbb{R}$.

Having decided $[a, b]$, say, as the support of $g(\cdot)$, the second step is to determine whether the L^2 space is $L^2[a, b]$ or $L^2([a, b], \pi(x))$ with some density $\pi(x)$. Given that $[a, b]$ is a bounded interval, using any $\pi(x)$ is less relevant and people often prefer $\pi(x) \equiv 1$, viz., $L^2[a, b]$. While $[a, b]$ is an unbounded interval such as $\mathbb{R}$ or $[0, \infty)$, one normally has two options. For example, for the support of $\mathbb{R}$, one uses either $L^2(\mathbb{R})$ or $L^2(\mathbb{R}, \exp(-x^2))$. The main difference is that $L^2(\mathbb{R}) \subset L^2(\mathbb{R}, \exp(-x^2))$, and $L^2(\mathbb{R}, \exp(-x^2))$ is so large that contains all polynomials and power functions, whereas $L^2(\mathbb{R})$ does not. Consequently, once $L^2(\mathbb{R}, \exp(-x^2))$ is utilized, $g(x)$ could be a linear function that is a candidate model and will be determined by the sample with a nonparametric approach (estimation and inference). Therefore, one is able to make a comparison between linear regression and nonparametric regression. This is desirable in the most empirical analysis.

Now, we come to estimate the regression function $g(\cdot)$ in (3.3.1) that belongs to $L^2([a, b], \pi(x))$, say. This implies $\int_a^b g^2(x)\pi(x)dx < \infty$. Here, we suppose that $[a, b]$ is a bounded interval whereas the unbounded case will be discussed later. Suppose that $\{p_j(x)\}_{j=0}^{\infty}$ is an orthonormal basis in $L^2([a, b], \pi(x))$. The existence of the orthonormal basis is guaranteed by separable Hilbert space (Theorem C.2.6 in Appendix). While there may be more than one orthonormal basis in a Hilbert space, our experience suggests that the choice of $\{p_j(x)\}_{j=0}^{\infty}$ is unimportant, since different bases work similarly. Then, $g(\cdot)$ admits an orthogonal expansion

$$g(x) = \sum_{j=0}^{\infty} c_j \, p_j(x), \tag{3.3.2}$$

and by the theory of Hilbert space, the coefficients in the expansion are the inner product of $g(x)$ and $p_j(x)$ in the space, that is,

$$c_j = \int_a^b g(x)p_j(x)\pi(x)dx. \tag{3.3.3}$$

This is the mathematical expression of c_j, but we cannot calculate them using this integration because $g(x)$ is unknown. We use the regression (3.3.1) along with the sample to estimate these coefficients. Obviously, it is impossible to estimate all coefficients c_j in (3.3.3). What we can do is to estimate a few of c_j, while how many coefficients can be estimated in the end is a difficult and challengeable technique problem that we shall discuss later. Suppose $k \geq 1$ is a parameter by which we truncate the series (3.3.2), that is,

$$\begin{aligned} g(x) &= g_k(x) + \gamma_k(x), \\ g_k(x) &\equiv \sum_{j=0}^{k-1} c_j\, p_j(x), \quad \gamma_k(x) \equiv \sum_{j=k}^{\infty} c_j\, p_j(x). \end{aligned} \tag{3.3.4}$$

Hence, the regression equations can be rephrased as

$$y_i = g_k(x_i) + \gamma_k(x_i) + e_i, \quad i = 1, \ldots, n. \tag{3.3.5}$$

Since $g_k(x_i) = P_k(x_i)^\top c$ where $P_k(x) = (p_0(x), p_1(x), \ldots, p_{k-1}(x))^\top$ and $c = (c_0, c_1, \ldots, c_{k-1})^\top$, we write (3.3.5) in matrix form

$$y = Pc + \gamma + e, \tag{3.3.6}$$

in which $y = (y_1, \ldots, y_n)^\top$, $\gamma = (\gamma_k(x_1), \ldots, \gamma_k(x_n))^\top$, $e = (e_1, \ldots, e_n)^\top$ are n-vectors, and $P = (P_k(x_1), \ldots, P_k(x_n))^\top$ is a $n \times k$ matrix.

Thus far, the nonparametric regression (3.3.1) is completely parameterized as a linear model (3.3.6). By OLS, we then have the estimate of c,

$$\widehat{c} = (P^\top P)^{-1} P^\top y. \tag{3.3.7}$$

Naturally, the estimator of $g(\cdot)$ is defined as

$$\widehat{g}_k(x) = P_k(x)^\top \widehat{c}, \tag{3.3.8}$$

for any $x \in [a, b]$. All these constitute the implementation process of series methods in estimating $g(x)$ in regressions.

One criterion to measure the performance of the series estimator (3.3.8) is integrated mean squared error (IMSE), given by

$$\text{IMSE}_n(k) = \int_a^b (\widehat{g}_k(x) - g(x))^2 \pi(x) dx, \tag{3.3.9}$$

that is actually the squared norm of $\widehat{g}_k(x) - g(x)$ in the space $L^2([a, b], \pi(x))$.

Invoking the orthogonality of the basis and (3.3.7),

$$
\begin{aligned}
\mathrm{IMSE}_n(k) &= \int_a^b [P_k(x)^\top(\widehat{c}-c) - \gamma_k(x)]^2 \pi(x)dx \\
&= \|\widehat{c}-c\|^2 + \|\gamma_k(x)\|_{L^2}^2 \\
&= \|(P^\top P)^{-1}P^\top(\gamma+e)\|^2 + \|\gamma_k(x)\|_{L^2}^2
\end{aligned} \tag{3.3.10}
$$

that consists of the estimation error ($\|\widehat{c}-c\|^2$) and the truncation error ($\|\gamma_k(x)\|_{L^2}^2$).

In the following analysis, one will need to estimate $\|P^\top\gamma\|$ in which $\mathbb{E}\|P_k(x_i)\|^2$ is a key quantity. When $[a,b]=[-1,1]$, due to (C.5.2) in Appendix C and the monotone convergence theorem, as $k\to\infty$,

$$
\begin{aligned}
\frac{1}{k}\mathbb{E}\|P_k(x_i)\|^2 &= \int_{-1}^1 \frac{1}{k}\sum_{j=0}^{k-1} p_j^2(x) f_X(x)dx \\
&\to \frac{1}{\pi}\int_{-1}^1 \frac{1}{\pi(x)\sqrt{1-x^2}} f_X(x)dx.
\end{aligned}
$$

Thus, $\mathbb{E}\|P_k(x_i)\|^2 = O(k)$. This result may be true for general bounded interval $[a,b]$ since there is a one-one mapping between $[a,b]$ and $[-1,1]$.

Another quantity that we may be concerned in what follows is $\|P_k(x)\|$ the Euclidean norm of $P_k(x)$. When cosine sequence is used, Dong and Linton (2018) show that $\|P_k(x)\|^2 = k + O(1)$ for any $x\in[0,1]$ when $k\to\infty$; when $[a,b]=[-1,1]$, again due to (C.5.2), for orthonormal sequence $\|P_k(x)\|^2 = O(k)$. In the literature such as Newey (1997) and Chen (2007), one instead considers $\zeta_k \equiv \sup_{x\in[a,b]}\|P_k(x)\|^2$. It is clear that $\zeta_k = O(k)$ for Chebyshev polynomials of the first order and for cosine sequence. Some relevant quantities are discussed in Sect. C.5 in Appendix C.

In the sequel, we establish the asymptotic distribution of the proposed series estimator for the nonparametric regression.

Theorem 3.3.1 *Suppose that the regression function $g(x)$ in* (3.3.1) *has bounded support and is differentiable up to s order with $s\ge 2$, and that $\{(x_i,y_i), i=1,\ldots,n\}$ is an i.i.d. sequence, $\mathbb{E}(e_i|x_i)=0$, $\mathbb{E}(e_i^2|x_i)=\sigma^2$ a.s. Moreover, assume that $n^{-1}P^\top P = \Omega(1+o_P(1))$ and uniformly Ω has eigenvalues bounded below from zero and above from infinity. Then, $IMSE_n(k) = O_P(k/n + k^{-2s+2})$. Moreover, if $\sup_{1\le i\le n}\mathbb{E}(e_i^4|x_i)<\infty$ a.s. and $nk^{-2s+2}=o(1)$, we have, for any x in the support of $g(\cdot)$,*

$$
\frac{\sqrt{n}}{\sqrt{P_k(x)^\top\Omega^{-1}P_k(x)}}[\widehat{g}_k(x)-g(x)] \to_D N(0,\sigma^2), \tag{3.3.11}
$$

as $n\to\infty$. □

The normalizer is the same as what is commonly used in the literature that is of order $\sqrt{n/k}$; the condition $nk^{-2s+2}=o(1)$ is an undersmoothing condition that ensures the ignorance of the bias term $B_{nk}(x) \equiv P_k(x)^\top (P^\top P)^{-1} P^\top \gamma - \gamma_k(x)$. Alternatively, if taking into account the bias, one may have

$$\frac{\sqrt{n}}{\sqrt{P_k(x)^\top \Omega^{-1} P_k(x)}}[\widehat{g}_k(x) - g(x) - B_{nk}(x)] \to_D N(0, \sigma^2),$$

as $n \to \infty$, without the undersmoothing condition.

Proof (*Theorem* 3.3.1) Notice that

$$\begin{aligned}\|\widehat{c} - c\|^2 &= \|(P^\top P)^{-1} P^\top (\gamma + e)\|^2 \\ &\leq 2\|(P^\top P)^{-1} P^\top e\|^2 + 2\|(P^\top P)^{-1} P^\top \gamma\|^2.\end{aligned}$$

Moreover, given $X = (x_1, \ldots, x_n)$ we have

$$\begin{aligned}\mathbb{E}[\|(P^\top P)^{-1} P^\top e\|^2 | X] &= \mathrm{tr}\{(P^\top P)^{-1} P^\top \mathbb{E}[ee^\top | X] P (P^\top P)^{-1}\} \\ &= \sigma^2 \mathrm{tr}[(P^\top P)^{-1}] = \sigma^2 \frac{1}{n} \mathrm{tr}[\Omega^{-1}](1 + o_P(1)) \\ &= O_P(k/n);\end{aligned}$$

and

$$\begin{aligned}\|(P^\top P)^{-1} P^\top \gamma\| &= \frac{1}{n}\|\Omega^{-1} P^\top \gamma\|(1 + o_P(1)) \\ &\leq \lambda_{\min}^{-1}(\Omega)\frac{1}{n}\|P^\top \gamma\|\end{aligned}$$

while

$$\begin{aligned}\frac{1}{n}\mathbb{E}\|P^\top \gamma\| &\leq \frac{1}{n}\sum_{i=1}^n \mathbb{E}\|P_k(x_i)\||\gamma_k(x_i)| \\ &\leq \frac{1}{n}\sum_{i=1}^n (\mathbb{E}\|P_k(x_i)\|^2)^{1/2}(\mathbb{E}|\gamma_k(x_i)|^2)^{1/2} \\ &\leq C\sqrt{k}\left(\int_a^b |\gamma_k(x)|^2 f_X(x)dx\right)^{1/2}.\end{aligned}$$

Due to Theorems C.4.13 and B.2.7, we have

$$\max_{x \in [a,b]} |\gamma_k(x)| \leq (1 + \sqrt{k}) E_k(g) = o(k^{-s+1/2}),$$

where $E_k(g)$ is the best polynomial approximation error for $g(\cdot)$ with order no more than k. See Sect. B.2. Thus, $\|P^\top \gamma\|/n = o_P(k^{-s+1})$. It follows that

$$\|\widehat{c}-c\|^2 = O_P(k^{-2s+2}) + O_P(k/n). \tag{3.3.12}$$

Furthermore, due to Theorem C.4.7 and the sequential discussion, $\|\gamma_k(x)\|_{L^2}^2 = o(k^{-2s})$. Hence, $\mathrm{IMSE}_n(k) = O_P(k/n + k^{-2s+2})$.

To derive the asymptotic distribution of $\widehat{g}_k(x) - g(x)$, notice that

$$\begin{aligned}\widehat{g}_k(x) - g(x) &= P_k(x)^\top(\widehat{c}-c) - \gamma_k(x)\\ &= P_k(x)^\top(P^\top P)^{-1}P^\top(e+\gamma) - \gamma_k(x)\\ &= P_k(x)^\top(P^\top P)^{-1}\sum_{i=1}^n P_k(x_i)e_i + P_k(x)^\top(P^\top P)^{-1}P^\top\gamma - \gamma_k(x)\\ &\equiv I_1 + I_2 + I_3, \quad \text{say.}\end{aligned}$$

Here, I_1 is the leading term in deriving the asymptotic limit, whose conditional variance, given $X = (x_1, \dots, x_n)$, is

$$\begin{aligned}\mathbb{E}(I_1^2|X) &= \sigma^2 P_k(x)^\top(P^\top P)^{-1}\sum_{i=1}^n P_k(x_i)P_k(x_i)^\top(P^\top P)^{-1}P_k(x)\\ &= \sigma^2 P_k(x)^\top(P^\top P)^{-1}P_k(x)\\ &= \frac{1}{n}\sigma^2 P_k(x)^\top\Omega^{-1}P_k(x)(1+o_P(1)).\end{aligned}$$

Due to the i.i.d. data assumption, it is readily seen that after normalization, I_1 converges to a standard normal variable, that is,

$$\begin{aligned}\frac{\sqrt{n}}{\sqrt{P_k(x)^\top\Omega^{-1}P_k(x)}}I_1 &= \frac{\sqrt{n}}{\sqrt{P_k(x)^\top\Omega^{-1}P_k(x)}}P_k(x)^\top(P^\top P)^{-1}\sum_{i=1}^n P_k(x_i)e_i\\ &\to_D N(0,\sigma^2),\end{aligned}$$

as $n \to \infty$.

To fulfill the theorem, we need to show

$$\frac{\sqrt{n}}{\sqrt{P_k(x)^\top\Omega^{-1}P_k(x)}}I_2 = o_P(1), \qquad \frac{\sqrt{n}}{\sqrt{P_k(x)^\top\Omega^{-1}P_k(x)}}I_3 = o(1),$$

as $n \to \infty$. These are satisfied because $P_k(x)^\top\Omega^{-1}P_k(x) \asymp \|P_k(x)\|^2$, $I_2 = O_P(k^{-s+1}\|P_k(x)\|)$ and $I_3 = o(k^{-s+1/2})$. □

Another typical scenario of the regression one may encounter is that the support of regression function is unbounded since the regressor has unbounded support. This happens, for example, when the regressor is normally distributed or is integrated. Let us consider

$$y_i = m(x_i) + e_i, \quad i = 1, \dots, n, \tag{3.3.13}$$

where $\mathbb{E}(e_i|x_i) = 0$ and $m(\cdot)$ has support $\mathbb{R}$, $m(\cdot) \in L^2(\mathbb{R})$; other settings for $m(\cdot)$ with support $\mathbb{R}$ can be found in Dong et al. (2021b). Because Hermite function sequence $\{\mathscr{H}_j(x), j = 0, 1, \ldots\}$ forms an orthonormal basis in $L^2(\mathbb{R})$, we have

$$m(x) = \sum_{j=0}^{\infty} c_j \mathscr{H}_j(x), \tag{3.3.14}$$

and then rephrase (3.3.13) as

$$y = Hc + \gamma + e, \tag{3.3.15}$$

in which $y = (y_1, \ldots, y_n)^\top$, $\gamma = (\gamma_k(x_1), \ldots, \gamma_k(x_n))^\top$ with $\gamma_k(x) = \sum_{j=k}^{\infty} c_j \mathscr{H}_j(x)$, $e = (e_1, \ldots, e_n)^\top$ are n-vectors, $c = (c_0, c_1, \ldots, c_{k-1})^\top$, $H = (H_k(x_1), \ldots, H_k(x_n))^\top$ is a $n \times k$ matrix where $H_k(x) = (\mathscr{H}_0(x), \mathscr{H}_1(x), \ldots, \mathscr{H}_{k-1}(x))^\top$. As a result, $\widehat{c} = (H^\top H)^{-1} H^\top y$ by OLS, and one may define $\widehat{m}(x) = H_k(x)^\top \widehat{c}$ for any $x \in \mathbb{R}$ as the estimator of $m(x)$.

In this scenario $\mathrm{IMSE}_n(k)$ has the same form as (3.3.10). In fact,

$$\begin{aligned} \mathrm{IMSE}_n(k) &= \int [\widehat{m}(x) - m(x)]^2 dx \\ &= \|\widehat{c} - c\|^2 + \|\gamma_k(x)\|_{L^2}^2 \\ &= \|(H^\top H)^{-1} H^\top (e + \gamma)\|^2 + \|\gamma_k(x)\|_{L^2}^2. \end{aligned}$$

But remember that the basis in the expansion and the norm $\|\gamma_k(x)\|_{L^2}$ are different; the details can be found in Appendix C.

Theorem 3.3.2 *Let the support of $m(\cdot)$ be $\mathbb{R}$ and differentiable up to s order. Suppose that $\{(x_i, y_i), i = 1, \ldots, n\}$ is an i.i.d. sequence, $\mathbb{E}(e_i^2|x_i) = \sigma^2$ a.s. and $n^{-1} H^\top H = \Sigma(1 + o_P(1))$ where Σ has eigenvalues bounded below from zero and above from infinity uniformly in n. Then $\mathrm{IMSE}_n(k) = O_P(k/n + k^{-s+1})$. Moreover, if $\sup_{1 \le i \le n} \mathbb{E}(e_i^4|x_i) < \infty$ and $nk^{-s+1} = o(1)$, then*

$$\frac{\sqrt{n}}{\sqrt{H_k(x)^\top \Sigma^{-1} H_k(x)}} [\widehat{m}(x) - m(x)] \to_D N(0, \sigma^2)$$

as $n \to \infty$. □

The normalizer of $\widehat{m}(x) - m(x)$ is of order $\sqrt{n}/\|H_k(x)\|$ while according to (C.5.3) in Appendix C, $\|H_k(x)\| = O(k^{1/4})$. This implies that the estimator $\widehat{m}(x)$ of the regression function with unbounded support converges faster than its counterpart with bounded support if the series estimations involved use the same truncation parameter. In addition, the condition $nk^{-s+1} = o(1)$ is the undersmoothing condition that makes sure the bias term is negligible; however, it requires the smoothness order $s > 6$ in the setting $k = O(n^{1/5})$.

Proof (*Theorem* 3.3.2) Note that $\|(H^\top H)^{-1}H^\top(e+\gamma)\|^2 \le 2\|(H^\top H)^{-1}H^\top e\|^2 + 2\|(H^\top H)^{-1}H^\top \gamma\|^2$; calculating the conditional expectation given $X=(x_1,\dots,x_n)$ implies that the first term has order $O_P(k/n)$ while the second term has the same order as $\|n^{-1}H^\top\gamma\|^2$. Notice that

$$
\begin{aligned}
\frac{1}{n}\mathbb{E}\|H^\top\gamma\| &\le \frac{1}{n}\sum_{i=1}^{n}\int \|H_k(x)\||\gamma_k(x)|f_X(x)dx\\
&\le \left(\int \|H_k(x)\|^2 f_X(x)dx \int |\gamma_k(x)|^2 f_X(x)dx\right)^{1/2}\\
&\le C\left(\int \|H_k(x)\|^2dx \int |\gamma_k(x)|^2dx\right)^{1/2}\\
&\le C\sqrt{k}\|\gamma_k(x)\|_{L^2},
\end{aligned}
$$

where $f_X(x)$ is the density of x_i such that $f_X(x)\le C$, and $\|\gamma_k(x)\|_{L^2}$ is the norm of $\gamma_k(x)$ in $L^2(\mathbb{R})$. By Theorem C.4.8 in Appendix C, $\|\gamma_k(x)\|_{L^2}^2 = o(k^{-s})$. Hence, $\text{IMSE}_n(k) = O_P(k/n + k^{-s+1})$.

To derive the asymptotic distribution of $\widehat{m}(x) - m(x)$, observe that

$$
\begin{aligned}
\widehat{m}(x) - m(x) &= H_k(x)^\top(\widehat{c} - c) - \gamma_k(x)\\
&= H_k(x)^\top(H^\top H)^{-1}H^\top(e+\gamma) - \gamma_k(x)\\
&= H_k(x)^\top(H^\top H)^{-1}\sum_{i=1}^{n} H_k(x_i)e_i + H_k(x)^\top(H^\top H)^{-1}H^\top\gamma - \gamma_k(x)\\
&= I_1 + I_2 + I_3, \quad \text{say.}
\end{aligned}
$$

Again, the conditional variance of I_1 is equal to $\sigma^2 H_k(x)^\top(H^\top H)^{-1}H_k(x) = n^{-1}\sigma^2 H_k(x)^\top\Sigma^{-1}H_k(x)(1+o_P(1))$, given $X=(x_1,\dots,x_n)$. Due to i.i.d. data assumption, we have

$$
\frac{\sqrt{n}}{\sqrt{H_k(x)^\top\Sigma^{-1}H_k(x)}} I_1 \to_D N(0,\sigma^2)
$$

as $n\to\infty$. To fulfill the theorem, it suffices to show

$$
\frac{\sqrt{n}}{\sqrt{H_k(x)^\top\Sigma^{-1}H_k(x)}} I_2 = o_P(1), \qquad \frac{\sqrt{n}}{\sqrt{H_k(x)^\top\Sigma^{-1}H_k(x)}} I_3 = o_P(1).
$$

These are satisfied since $H_k(x)^\top\Sigma^{-1}H_k(x) \asymp \|H_k(x)\|^2$, $I_2 = o_P(k^{-(s-1)/2}\|H_k(x)\|)$ and $I_3 = o(k^{-s/2+5/12})$, because of $\sup_x|\gamma_k(x)| = o(k^{-s/2+5/12})$ by Theorem C.4.16. □

3.3.2 Selection Criteria of Truncation Parameter

This is the most difficult issue in empirical analyses when using series methods, although we have some theoretical requirements on k, such as $k \equiv k(n)$, $k \to \infty$ and $k/n \to 0$ as $n \to \infty$. This is because there are only a finite number of observations in empirical analysis, so this theoretical guidance might be useless. Thus, a data-driven approach to selecting the truncation parameter k is down-to-earth, and people normally use *cross-validation (CV) criterion* to fulfill the task. However, it is noteworthy that there are quite a few other selection criteria such as Mallows C_p, generalized cross-validation (GCV), Akaike information criterion (AIC), the corrected AIC, Bayesian information criterion (BIC), even least absolute shrinkage and selection operator (LASSO) and its variations. One may find these detailed discussion from Akaike (1973), Mallows (1973), Schwarz (1978), Li (1987), Andrews (1991), Gao et al. (2001, 2002), and Hansen and Racine (2012), among others. Here, we give a brief introduction to CV and GCV.

For each $i = 1, \ldots, n$, we calculate leave-one-out prediction error, that is, given k and for each i, we use $\{(y_j, x_j), j \neq i, 1 \leq j \leq n\}$ and the same procedure of series methods to have the estimate of coefficients in the orthogonal expansion from the regression (3.3.1), denoted by $\widetilde{c}_{k,-i}$,

$$\widetilde{c}_{k,-i} = \left(\sum_{j \neq i} P_k(x_j) P_k(x_j)^\top \right)^{-1} \sum_{j \neq i} P_k(x_j) y_j, \tag{3.3.16}$$

and then define prediction errors

$$\widetilde{e}_{k,i} = y_i - P_k(x_i)^\top \widetilde{c}_{k,-i}, \quad i = 1, \ldots, n. \tag{3.3.17}$$

Accordingly, the CV criterion is defined as

$$\mathrm{CV}_n(k) = \frac{1}{n} \sum_{i=1}^{n} \widetilde{e}_{k,i}^2. \tag{3.3.18}$$

Then, the estimator $\widehat{k}$ by CV criterion is the one from candidate set $\{1, 2, \ldots, K_n\}$ that has smallest value $\mathrm{CV}_n(k)$,

$$\widehat{k}_{\mathrm{CV}} = \underset{1 \leq k \leq K_n}{\arg\min}\, \mathrm{CV}_n(k). \tag{3.3.19}$$

Here, K_n is a predetermined integer that governs the complexity of the model we select, so K_n would not be too large since one normally prefers parsimonious models.

By contrast, for the same k, when obtaining the estimate of $\widehat{c}$ by the full data given by (3.3.7), we may compute the residual for each $i = 1, \ldots, n$ by

$$\widehat{e}_{k,i} = y_i - P_k(x_i)^\top \widehat{c} = y_i - P_k(x_i)^\top (P^\top P)^{-1} P^\top y.$$

The following theorem gives the relationship between $\widetilde{e}_{k,i}$ and $\widehat{e}_{k,i}$.

Theorem 3.3.3 *For the Leave-one-out prediction errors, we have*

$$\widetilde{e}_{k,i} = \frac{\widehat{e}_{k,i}}{1 - s_{ii}}, \tag{3.3.20}$$

where s_{ii} is the i-th diagonal element of matrix $P(P^\top P)^{-1}P^\top$, and precisely, $s_{ii} = P_k(x_i)^\top (P^\top P)^{-1} P_k(x_i)$. □

Proof We shall use the following identity for an invertible matrix A and a vector b,

$$(A - bb^\top)^{-1} = A^{-1} + (1 - b^\top A^{-1} b)^{-1} A^{-1} bb^\top A^{-1},$$

which is so-called the Sherman-Morrison formula, and easy to be verified.

It follows that

$$\begin{aligned}
\left(\sum_{j\neq i} P_k(x_j)P_k(x_j)^\top\right)^{-1} &= \left(P^\top P - P_k(x_i)P_k(x_i)^\top\right)^{-1} \\
&= (P^\top P)^{-1} + (1 - s_{ii})^{-1}(P^\top P)^{-1} P_k(x_i)P_k(x_i)^\top (P^\top P)^{-1}.
\end{aligned}$$

Accordingly,

$$\begin{aligned}
\widetilde{e}_{k,i} &= y_i - P_k(x_i)^\top \widehat{c}_{k,-i} \\
&= y_i - P_k(x_i)^\top \left(\sum_{j\neq i} P_k(x_j)P_k(x_j)^\top\right)^{-1} \sum_{j\neq i} P_k(x_j) y_j \\
&= y_i - P_k(x_i)^\top \left(\sum_{j\neq i} P_k(x_j)P_k(x_j)^\top\right)^{-1} (P^\top y - P_k(x_i)y_i) \\
&= y_i - P_k(x_i)^\top (P^\top P)^{-1} P^\top y + P_k(x_i)^\top (P^\top P)^{-1} P_k(x_i) y_i \\
&\quad - (1 - s_{ii})^{-1} P_k(x_i)^\top (P^\top P)^{-1} P_k(x_i) P_k(x_i)^\top (P^\top P)^{-1} (P^\top y - P_k(x_i) y_i) \\
&= \widehat{e}_{k,i} + s_{ii} y_i - (1 - s_{ii})^{-1} s_{ii} P_k(x_i)^\top (P^\top P)^{-1} P^\top y \\
&\quad + (1 - s_{ii})^{-1} s_{ii} P_k(x_i)^\top (P^\top P)^{-1} P_k(x_i) y_i \\
&= \widehat{e}_{k,i} + s_{ii} y_i - (1 - s_{ii})^{-1} s_{ii} P_k(x_i)^\top \widehat{c} + (1 - s_{ii})^{-1} s_{ii}^2 y_i \\
&= \widehat{e}_{k,i} + (1 - s_{ii})^{-1} s_{ii} [y_i - P_k(x_i)^\top \widehat{c}] \\
&= \widehat{e}_{k,i} + (1 - s_{ii})^{-1} s_{ii} \widehat{e}_{k,i} \\
&= (1 - s_{ii})^{-1} \widehat{e}_{k,i}.
\end{aligned}$$

This finishes the proof. □

The result of Theorem 3.3.3 shows that

$$\mathrm{CV}_n(k) = \frac{1}{n}\sum_{i=1}^{n}\frac{\widehat{e}_{k,i}^2}{(1-s_{ii})^2},$$

and we know that

$$\frac{1}{n}\sum_{i=1}^{n}(1-s_{ii}) = 1 - \frac{1}{n}\sum_{i=1}^{n}s_{ii}$$
$$= 1 - \frac{1}{n}\mathrm{tr}[P(P^\top P)^{-1}P^\top] = 1 - \frac{1}{n}k.$$

If roughly replacing all $1 - s_{ii}$ by their average, one has an excellent shortcut for computing $\mathrm{CV}_n(k)$ that delivers generalized cross-validation (GCV) criterion function

$$\mathrm{GCV}_n(k) = \left[1 - \frac{k}{n}\right]^{-2}\frac{1}{n}\sum_{i=1}^{n}\widehat{e}_{k,i}^2. \tag{3.3.21}$$

It can be seen that when k increases, $\mathrm{SSR}(k) \equiv \sum_{i=1}^{n}\widehat{e}_{k,i}^2$ decreases while $(1 - k/n)^{-2}$ becomes large. Thus, $\mathrm{GCV}_n(k)$ suggests a medium k that compromises between the accuracy and complexity of the model. Though approximately equal to $\mathrm{CV}_n(k)$, $\mathrm{GCV}_n(k)$ circumvents the heavy computation burden, so it is popular in choosing truncation parameters in sieve methods using $\mathrm{GCV}_n(k)$,

$$\widehat{k}_{\mathrm{GCV}} = \arg\min_{1\le k\le K_n} \mathrm{GCV}_n(k). \tag{3.3.22}$$

See Golub et al. (1979) for detailed discussion.

Example 3.3.1 We implement a simple example to compare the choices by CV and GCV criteria, respectively. Consider a nonparametric regression model, $y_t = g(x_t) + e_t$, $t = 1, \ldots, n$, where x_t is a scalar variable distributed uniformly over $[-1, 1]$, and $e_t \sim N(0, 1)$ is independent of x_t. For the regression function $g(x)$, two cases are investigated,

(1) $g(x) = 1 + p_2(x) - 2p_3(x)$ where $p_i(x)$, $i = 2, 3$, are orthonormal Legendre polynomials;
(2) $g(x) = x^2 + \sin(x)$.

In (1), we deliberately take $g(x)$ as a combination of a few Legendre polynomials in order to verify whether the CV and GCV criteria can find out the optimal truncation parameter $k_{\mathrm{opt}} = 4$.

Using $g(x) = 1 + p_2(x) - 2p_3(x)$, with $n = 200, 400, 600$, we generate data $\{x_t, y_t\}$ by the regression equation. Then we calculate $\mathrm{CV}(k)$ and $\mathrm{GCV}(k)$ for $k = 1, 2, \ldots, K_n$ with $K_n = 9$, and the results are reported in Table 3.1.

Table 3.1 CV(k) and GCV(k)

k	1	2	3	4	5	6	7	8	9
	$n = 200$								
CV(k)	1.7932	1.7945	1.6069	**1.0214**	1.0272	1.0275	1.0371	1.0484	1.0561
GCV(k)	1.7932	1.7901	1.5980	**1.0211**	1.0270	1.0270	1.0368	1.0458	1.0533
	$n = 400$								
CV(k)	1.7730	1.7819	1.5846	**1.0129**	1.0146	1.0134	1.0182	1.0187	1.0227
GCV(k)	1.7730	1.7797	1.5804	**1.0129**	1.0146	1.0132	1.0179	1.0182	1.0224
	$n = 600$								
CV(k)	1.7744	1.7805	1.5761	**1.0046**	1.0121	1.0113	1.0069	1.0099	1.0153
GCV(k)	1.7744	1.7791	1.5734	**1.0046**	1.0121	1.0111	1.0068	1.0098	1.0151

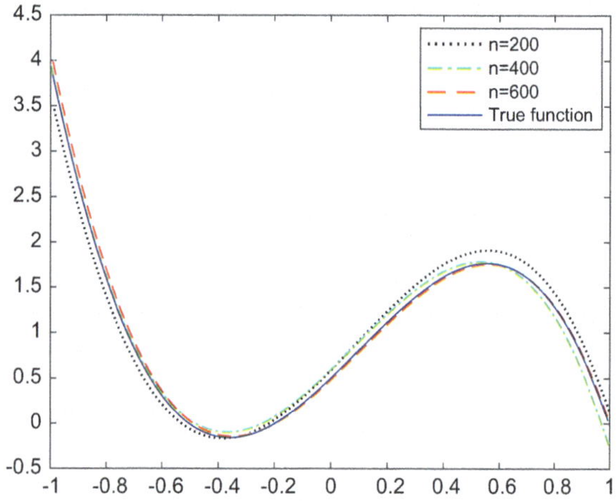

Fig. 3.2 Estimated $g(x) = 1 + p_2(x) - 2p_3(x)$

It is readily seen that both CV and GCV criteria determine $\widehat{k} = 4$ that coincides with the optimal truncation parameter $k_{\text{opt}} = 4$ for all sample size n. Also, all values of CV and GCV are quite close and many of them are equal. We plot the pictures for the estimates $\widehat{g}(x)$ with $\widehat{k} = 4$ in Fig. 3.2.

Similarly, using $g(x) = x^2 + \sin(x)$, with $n = 200, 400, 600$, we generate data $\{x_t, y_t\}$ by the regression equation. Then we calculate CV(k) and GCV(k) for $k = 1, 2, \ldots, K_n$ with $K_n = 9$, and the results are reported in Table 3.2.

As can be seen, the choices by the two criteria are consistent, i.e., for $n = 200$ and 400, they both choose $\widehat{k} = 3$, whereas for $n = 600$ they choose $\widehat{k} = 4$ simultaneously. This implication is crucial for series methods where the truncation parameter is required to increase by the theory of convergent series when n increases. We plot the pictures for the estimated $\widehat{g}(x)$ with $\widehat{k}$ corresponding to different sample sizes in Fig. 3.3.

Table 3.2 CV(k) and GCV(k)

k	1	2	3	4	5	6	7	8	9
	$n = 200$								
CV(k)	1.3654	1.1015	**1.0162**	1.0308	1.0211	1.0324	1.0402	1.0384	1.0491
GCV(k)	1.3654	1.1009	**1.0162**	1.0309	1.0204	1.0315	1.0389	1.0367	1.0464
	$n = 400$								
CV(k)	1.3721	1.0943	**1.0079**	1.0117	1.0092	1.0164	1.0174	1.0240	1.0226
GCV(k)	1.3721	1.0941	**1.0079**	1.0116	1.0091	1.0161	1.0171	1.0237	1.0222
	$n = 600$								
CV(k)	1.3611	1.0897	1.0085	**1.0047**	1.0088	1.0103	1.0115	1.0126	1.0187
GCV(k)	1.3611	1.0895	1.0085	**1.0047**	1.0087	1.0104	1.0114	1.0124	1.0184

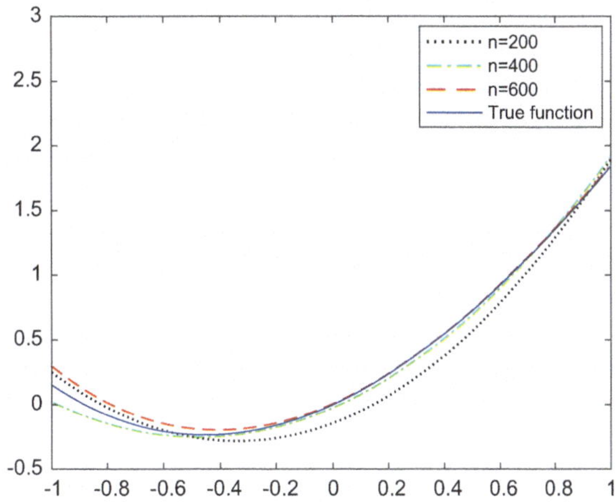

Fig. 3.3 Estimated $g(x) = x^2 + \sin(x)$

Example 3.3.2 We further consider the performance of CV and GCV criteria in selecting truncation parameter of series methods in nonparametric regression where the regressor has unbounded support. Precisely, let $\{y_t, x_t\}$ satisfy $y_t = g(x_t) + e_t$, $t = 1, \ldots, n$, where x_t is a scalar variable normally distributed $N(0, 1)$, $e_t \sim U(-1, 1)$ is independent of x_t.

Again, for the regression function $g(x)$, two cases are investigated,

(1) $g(x) = 1 + 0.5h_1(x) - 2h_2(x)$ where $h_i(x)$, $i = 1, 2, 3$, are orthonormal Hermite polynomials.
(2) $g(x) = x^2 + \sin(x)$.

Once more the design of $g(x) = 1 + 0.5h_1(x) - 2h_2(x)$ is deliberately to check whether CV and GCV criteria would find out the optimal truncation parameter $k_{\text{opt}} = 3$.

The $g(\cdot)$ is expanded using Hermite polynomials. Let $n = 150, 280, 500$ and $K_n = 9$.

Table 3.3 CV(k) and GCV(k)

k	1	2	3	4	5	6	7	8	9
	$n = 150$								
CV(k)	128.9658	134.4127	**0.3408**	0.3467	0.3579	0.4116	0.8107	6.5617	16.6838
GCV(k)	128.9658	127.6796	**0.3405**	0.3444	0.3453	0.3470	0.3486	0.3523	0.3559
	$n = 280$								
CV(k)	128.2596	132.8116	**0.3369**	0.3385	0.3429	0.3590	1.1723	1.0368	5.3229
GCV(k)	128.2596	129.0706	**0.3368**	0.3377	0.3393	0.3412	0.3410	0.3426	0.3440
	$n = 500$								
CV(k)	128.8952	132.2330	**0.3350**	0.3364	0.3385	0.3418	0.3620	0.4707	1.2455
GCV(k)	128.8952	130.1310	**0.3350**	0.3362	0.3375	0.3373	0.3393	0.3393	0.3394

Using $g(x) = 1 + 0.5h_1(x) - 2h_2(x)$, we generate data $\{x_t, y_t\}$ by the regression equation. Then we calculate CV(k) and GCV(k) for $k = 1, 2, \ldots, K_n$ and the results are reported in Table 3.3.

Though different values they might assume, both CV and GCV criteria make correct choice with $\widehat{k} = 3$ that is optimal by our design. We plot the pictures for the estimates $\widehat{g}(x)$ with $\widehat{k} = 3$ in Fig. 3.4.

Similarly, using $g(x) = x^2 + \sin(x)$, we generate data $\{x_t, y_t\}$ by the regression equation. Then we calculate CV(k) and GCV(k) for $k = 1, 2, \ldots, K_n$ and the results are reported in Table 3.4.

Once again, the two criteria have the same choice for different sample sizes, while their choice $\widehat{k}$ may be different according to the change in sample size. We plot the pictures for the estimates $\widehat{g}(x)$ with $\widehat{k}$ corresponding to different sample sizes in Fig. 3.5.

Fig. 3.4 Estimated $g(x) = 1 + 0.5h_1(x) - 2h_2(x)$

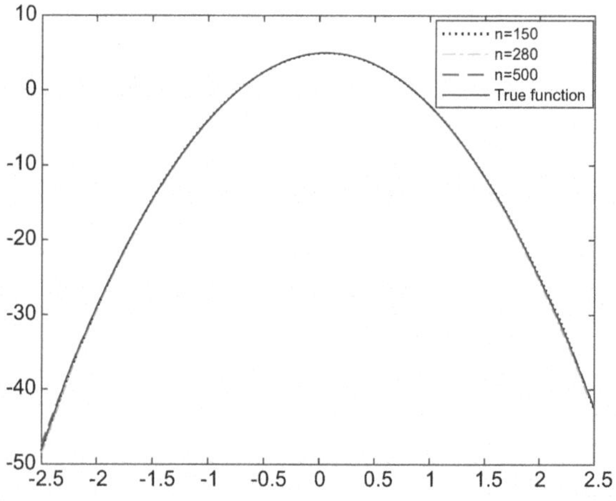

Table 3.4 CV(k) and GCV(k)

k	1	2	3	4	5	6	7	8	9
	$n = 150$								
CV(k)	2.7847	2.4674	0.4135	**0.3487**	0.3684	0.4481	0.8724	2.7680	53.0551
GCV(k)	2.7847	2.3620	0.3964	**0.3434**	0.3475	0.3504	0.3504	0.3523	0.3541
	$n = 280$								
CV(k)	2.7494	2.4237	0.4066	**0.3416**	0.3506	0.3630	0.4484	6.7748	7.0411
GCV(k)	2.7494	2.3659	0.3977	**0.3394**	0.3416	0.3412	0.3404	0.3427	0.3441
	$n = 500$								
CV(k)	2.7899	2.4224	0.4024	0.3426	0.3424	**0.3423**	0.3549	0.5079	2.6548
GCV(k)	2.7899	2.3893	0.3970	0.3393	0.3381	**0.3361**	0.3376	0.3394	0.3392

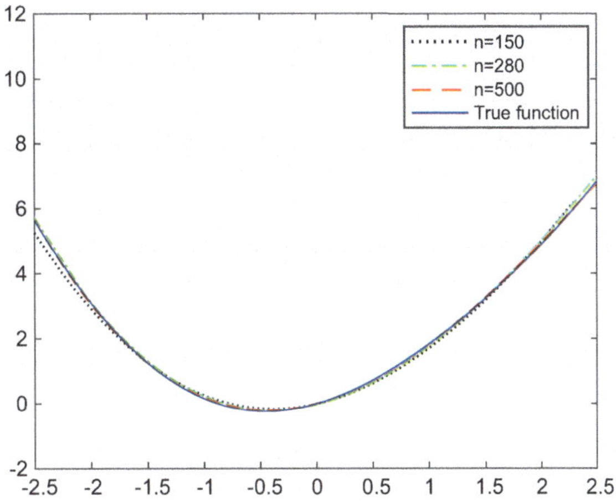

Fig. 3.5 Estimated $g(x) = x^2 + \sin(x)$

3.3.3 *Orthogonal Series Versus Power Functions*

When using series methods, one may be concerned about whether it is really necessary to use an orthogonal function sequence. The main reason for concern is from Taylor's theorem. For a function $g(x)$ defined on $[a, b]$, suppose it admits derivatives up to s order in (a, b), $s \geq 1$. Taylor's theorem says that, for different points $x, x_0 \in [a, b]$, there exists a point ξ between x and x_0 such that

$$g(x) = \sum_{j=0}^{s-1} \frac{g^{(j)}(x_0)}{j!}(x - x_0)^j + \frac{g^{(s)}(\xi)}{s!}(\xi - x_0)^s. \tag{3.3.23}$$

See Rudin (1976, p. 110). This gives an approximation of $g(x)$ by the combination of power functions $(x - x_0)^j$. Here, given the smoothness order s, the accuracy of the approximation depends on $|\xi - x_0|$ and $|g^{(s)}(\xi)|$ for which we usually do not have sufficient information where is ξ and how large is $|g^{(s)}(\xi)|$ since $g(x)$ is unknown. Roughly, $|\xi - x_0| \le |x - x_0|$, and hence the accuracy might be achieved in the neighborhood of x_0. Even if in the neighborhood of x_0, to improve the accuracy of Taylor expansion, one has to assume higher order derivatives. This price is not affordable in common nonparametric estimation.

Nonetheless, given smoothness order s of $g(x)$, as shown in Appendix C, the accuracy of the partial sum of its orthogonal series expansion approximating to $g(x)$ can be achieved by increasing the truncation parameter k. In a word, the accuracy of Taylor expansion is governed by the smoothness order that is also the number of the terms in its partial sum; by sharp contrast, the accuracy of orthogonal series expansion is governed by the truncation parameter given suitable smoothness order, that is, given the smoothness order of $g(\cdot)$, $g_k(x) - g(x) \to 0$ in some sense as $k \to \infty$ where $g_k(x)$ is the partial sum of the orthogonal series expansion of $g(x)$. This will be shown in the appendix chapters.

Actually, as early as 1980 White (1980) provided the answer to the concern. If Taylor's theorem is used in nonparametric regression (3.3.1), it is not clear which point x_0 should be used, and then some authors used the mean of explanatory variables as x_0. However, White (1980) showed that the first-order Taylor expansion has an evident difference from its estimation in both intercept and slope. White (1980, p. 152) concluded that OLS estimates do not necessarily provide reliable information about the local properties (derivatives, elasticities) of the unknown function.

This point is also supported by the following discussion on average marginal effect from Linton (2017). Let X and Y be scalar, and $\mathbb{E}(Y|X) = g(X)$ a smooth function. The effect of X on Y is measured by $g'(x)$ that varies over $X = x$. The average marginal effect is given by

$$\delta = \mathbb{E}[g'(X)] = \int g'(x) f_X(x) dx.$$

This quantity is widely used in nonlinear models to summarize the effect of the X on the Y. Clearly, if it is a linear regression, $g(x) = \alpha + \beta x$, $\delta = \beta$. For a general nonlinear model, many authors utilize the linear approximation of Taylor's theorem at the mean $\mu = \mathbb{E}(X)$,

$$g(X) = g(\mu) + g'(\mu)(X - \mu) + \frac{1}{2} g''(\xi)(X - \mu)^2,$$

where ξ is on the segment joining X and μ. They argue that $\beta = g'(\mu)$ and $\alpha = g(\mu) - \mu g'(\mu)$, i.e., the best linear fit provides an approximation to $g(X)$. This in general is not true. Though

$$\mathbb{E}\left|g(X) - g(\mu) - g'(\mu)(X - \mu)\right| \le \frac{1}{2} \sup_x |g''(x)| \operatorname{Var}(X),$$

both $\operatorname{Var}(X)$ and $\sup_x |g''(x)|$ are hardly close to zero.

Example 3.3.3 Let $Y = 1 + 2X + X^3 + \varepsilon, X \sim U[0, 2], \varepsilon \sim N(0, 1)$ independent of X. Thus, $\mu = \mathbb{E}(X) = 1$, $g(X) = \mathbb{E}(Y|X) = 1 + 2X + X^3$ and from (3.1.5),

$$\mathbb{E}_L(Y|X) = -\frac{3}{5} + \frac{28}{5}X,$$

while $\delta = \mathbb{E}[g'(X)] = 2 + 3\mathbb{E}(X^2) = 6$ and $g'(\mu) = g'(1) = 5$. These quantities we concern with are different. Accordingly, in some sense it denies the Taylor approximation to nonlinear regression.

It is noteworthy that there is a special case where $\delta = \mathbb{E}[g'(X)] = \beta$, the slope in $\mathbb{E}_L(Y|X)$. Let $Y = g(X) + \varepsilon, X \sim N(\mu, \sigma^2), \mathbb{E}(\varepsilon|X) = 0$. Then $\delta = \beta$. See Linton (2017, p. 79) for the proof.

Another concern is the construction of orthogonal polynomials. As is known, in an orthogonal polynomial sequence, $\{p_j(x)\}$, the s-th order polynomial $p_s(x)$ is merely a combination of $\{1, x, \ldots, x^s\}$. See Appendix C. Accordingly, the sieve space span$\{p_0(x), p_1(x), \ldots, p_k(x)\}$ =span$\{1, x, \ldots, x^k\}$. This concern is misleading in that one can use $\{1, x, \ldots, x^k\}$ to substitute $\{p_0(x), p_1(x), \ldots, p_k(x)\}$ in series estimation. What we can say is that though the span of the orthogonal polynomials is the same as power functions, their effects in series estimation are drastically different because the behaviors of x^j and $p_j(x)$ as regressors are totally different, as illustrated below.

Suppose that $\{h_j(x)\}$ is a sequence of polynomial functions, orthogonal or not, used to decompose $g(x)$ in nonparametric regression (3.3.1), say $g(x) = \sum_{j=0}^k c_j h_j(x)$. Here, to make the point crystal clear, we assume that the approximation error is zero (i.e., $c_j = 0$ for all $j > k$). Write $c = (c_0, c_1, \ldots, c_k)^\top$, $Y = (y_1, \ldots, y_n)^\top$, $H_k(x) = (h_0(x), \ldots, h_k(x))^\top$, and $H = (H_k(x_1), \ldots, H_k(x_n))^\top$. Thus, the least squares estimate of the coefficient vector c is

$$\widehat{c} = \frac{1}{n}(H^\top H/n)^{-1} H^\top Y.$$

The above estimate involves the inverse of the $(k + 1)$-dimensional square matrix $H^\top H/n$, that is,

$$\frac{1}{n}H^\top H = \frac{1}{n}\sum_{t=1}^{n} \begin{pmatrix} h_0^2(x_t) & h_0(x_t)h_1(x_t) & \cdots & h_0(x_t)h_1(x_t) \\ h_0(x_t)h_1(x_t) & h_1^2(x_t) & \cdots & h_1(x_t)h_k(x_t) \\ \vdots & \vdots & \ddots & \vdots \\ h_0(x_t)h_k(x_t) & h_1(x_t)h_k(x_t) & \cdots & h_k^2(x_t) \end{pmatrix}.$$

Let us compare the properties of this matrix under the setting of i.i.d. dataset for the two cases below. Case (I): $\{h_j(x)\}$ is an orthonormal sequence with respect to a density $\pi(x)$ that is also the density of x_t. That is, $\int h_i(x)h_j(x)\pi(x)dx = \delta_{ij}$ Kronecker delta. Again, to make things extremely clear we suppose here that the orthogonal density is exactly the density of the observed data. In this ideal case, by the strong

Law of Large Numbers (LLN), all the diagonal elements of $H^\top H/n$ converge almost surely to $\mathbb{E}[h_i^2(x_t)] = \int h_i^2(x)\pi(x)dx = 1$, while all other elements converge almost surely to $\mathbb{E}[h_i(x_t)h_j(x_t)] = \int h_i(x)h_j(x)\pi(x)dx = 0, i \neq j$. Thus, asymptotically $H^\top H/n$ is an identity matrix, which ensures its invertibility for sample size n large enough.

Case (II): $\{h_j(x) = x^j, j = 0, \ldots, k\}$. In this case, the elements of $H^\top H/n$ will converge almost surely to $\mathbb{E}(x_t^{i+j})$ by strong LLN again, for $i, j = 0, \ldots, k$. Hence, different from that in Case (I), $H^\top H/n$ no longer has the identity matrix as its limit. Note that the moments $\mathbb{E}(x_t^{i+j})$ can be highly heterogeneous across $i + j$, and the variables x_t^{i+j} can be highly correlated across $i + j$. Accordingly, $H^\top H/n$ can be ill-conditioned (the ratio of the largest to smallest eigenvalue can be quite large), thus inverting this matrix could lead to a computational error or poor approximation. Consequently, the least squares estimate of coefficient vector c could be inaccurate.

The above point is in line with what was made by Newey (1997). Newey (1997, p. 156) discussed approximation for multivariate function $g(x)$ with $x = (x_1, \ldots, x_d)$ by powers function $x^\lambda = \prod_{i=1}^d x_i^{\lambda_i}$ where $\lambda = (\lambda_1, \ldots, \lambda_d)$ multiple index, and wrote on page 156:

> *The theory to follow uses orthonormal polynomials, which may also have computational advantages. For the first step, replacing each power x^λ by the product of orthonormal polynomials of order corresponding to components of λ, with respect to some distribution may lead to reduced collinearity, particularly when the distribution closely matches that of the data.*

Newey's statement also implies that even if the densities for orthogonality and the variable x_t are not identical, the use of orthogonal polynomials would reduce collinearity. In addition, a fairly clear theoretical support to this point is Proposition 2.1 in Belloni et al. (2015) that gives a sufficient condition under which $H^\top H/n$ has eigenvalues bounded below from zero and above from infinity uniformly in n. So $H^\top H/n$ is not ill-conditioned uniformly in n when orthogonal series is used.

Due to the reasons discussed above, we highly recommend orthogonal function sequence including orthogonal polynomials and trigonometric functions when using series methods.

In the following chapters, we shall introduce the applications of series methods in dealing with semiparametric/nonparametric models. Although there are several alternatives in excellent monographs about nonparametric estimation, for example, Fan and Yao (2003), Gao (2007) and Li and Racine (2007), as mentioned, we advocate series estimation technique in appropriate situations for nonparametric and semiparametric issues, since this technique is much flexible for the use in many different circumstances than its arch-rival such as kernel methods, as illustrated by the subsequent chapters.

References

Akaike, H. (1973). Information theory and an extension of the maximum likelihood principle. In B. Petroc & F. Csake (Eds.), *Second International Symposium on Information Theory* (pp. 267–281). Budapest.

Andrews, D. W. (1991). Asymptotic optimality of generalized C_L, cross-validation and generalized cross-validation in regression with heteroskedastic errors. *Journal of Econometrics, 47*, 359–377.

Belloni, A., Chernozhukov, V., Chetverikov, D., & Kato, K. (2015). Some new asymptotic theory for least squares series: Pointwise and uniform results. *Journal of Econometrics, 186*, 345–366.

Chen, X. (2007). *Handbook of econometrics*. Large sample sieve estimation of semi-parametric models (Vol. 6B, pp. 5550–5588). Amsterdam, North Holland: Elsevier.

Dong, C., & Linton, O. (2018). Additive nonparametric models with time variable and both stationary and nonstationary regressors. *Journal of Econometrics, 207*, 212–236.

Dong, C., Linton, O., & Peng, B. (2021). A weighted sieve estimator for nonparametric time series models with nonstationary variables. *Journal of Econometrics, 222*, 909–932.

Fan, J., & Yao, Q. (2003). *Nonlinear time series: Nonparametric and parametric methods*. New York: Springer.

Galton, F. (1886). Regression towards mediocrity in hereditary stature. *The Journal of the Anthropological Institute of Great Britain and Ireland, 15*, 246–263.

Gao, J. (2007). *Nonlinear time series: Semiparametric and nonparametric methods*. Monographs on statistics and applied probability. New York: Chapman & Hall.

Gao, J., Tong, H., & Wolff, R. (2001). Adaptive orthogonal series estimation in additive stochastic regression models. *Statistic Sinica, 11*, 409–428.

Gao, J., Tong, H., & Wolff, R. (2002). Model specification tests in nonparametric stochastic regression models. *Journal of Multivariate Analysis, 83*, 324–359.

Golub, G., Heath, M., & Wahba, G. (1979). Generalized cross-validation as a method for choosing a good ridge parameter. *Technometrics, 21*, 215–224.

Grenander, U. (1981). *Abstract inference*. New York: Wiley.

Hansen, B. E., & Racine, J. S. (2012). Jackknife model averaging. *Journal of Econometrics, 167*, 38–46.

Härdle, W., & Linton, O. (1994). *Handbook of econometrics*. Applied nonparametric methods (Vol. IV, pp. 2295–2339). Amsterdam, North Holland: Elsevier.

Ichimura, H. (2007). *Handbook of Econometrics*. Implementing nonparametric and semiparametric estimators (Vol. 6B, pp. 5369–5468). Amsterdam, North Holland: Elsevier.

Li, K.-C. (1987). Asymptotic optimality for c_p, c_l, cross-validation and generalized cross-validation: Discrete index set. *Annals of Statistics, 15*, 958–975.

Linton, O. (2017). *Probability, statistics and econometrics*. Academic.

Li, Q., & Racine, J. (2007). *Nonparametric econometrics: Theory and practice*. Princeton: Princeton University Press.

Mallows, C. L. (1973). Some comments on c_p. *Technometrics, 15*, 661–675.

Nagler, T., & Czado, C. (2016). Evading the curse of dimensionality in nonparametric density estimation with simplified vine copulas. *Journal Multivariate Analysis, 151*, 69–89.

Newey, W. K. (1997). Convergence rates and asymptotic normality for series estimators. *Journal of Econometrics, 79*, 147–168.

Powell, J. (1994). *Handbook of econometrics*. Estimation of semiparametric models (Vol. IV, pp. 2443–2521). Amsterdam, North Holland: Elsevier.

Rudin, W. (1976). *Principles of mathematical analysis*. International series in pure and applied mathematics. New York: McGraw-Hill Inc.

Schwarz, G. (1978). Estimating the dimension of a model. *Annals of Statistics, 6*, 147–168.

Stone, C. (1982). Optimal global rates of convergence for nonparametric regression. *Annals of Statistics, 10*, 1040–1053.

Stone, C. (1985). Additive regression and other nonparametric models. *Annals of Statistics, 13*, 689–705.

White, H. (1980). Using least squares to approximate unknown regression functions. *International Economic Review, 21*, 149–170.

Part II
Applications of Series Methods

This part gives a variety of applications of series methods, such as density estimations, and estimations in additive nonparametric regressions, semiparametric single-index models and semiparametric moment restriction models. Since the data used in these models include different types, e.g., stationary and nonstationary time series and time trend, the circumstances where series methods are applied are diverse. Through these applications, one may be able to get familiar with series methods used in both theoretical and empirical analyses.

Chapter 4
Density Estimation and Its Applications

Density estimation has long been one of the research interests in the center of econometrics and statistics. It started with parametric estimation, assuming a family of densities with a few unknown parameters for a set of observations. Due to the natural defect, this methodology has gradually been replaced by nonparametric estimation in necessary situations. This means that estimating density needs nonparametric techniques. On the other hand, density estimation provides a vehicle with the development of nonparametric methods. For example, since a nonparametric regression function can be represented as a conditional expectation, once the joint and marginal densities are estimated, the estimator of the unknown function is obtained immediately.

Estimating density function and distribution function for a set of observations triggers nonparametric estimation methods because it has been a long history that researchers are interested in analyzing the distribution and its functionals of random variables to cater for the need of both theory and empirical analysis. Density estimation is a prominent part of nonparametric estimation, and nonparametric density estimators provide a straightforward way to look into densities of variable of interest through its sample. The first paper in the area of nonparametric functional estimation, in particular, nonparametric density estimation, is due to Rosenblatt (1956). Since the appearance of this paper, several methods have been developed for the nonparametric estimation of density functions, distribution functions, regression functions, failure rates, etc. From then on, there are extensive studies of density estimation in the literature by means of series methods in particular.

A surge of estimating density function began more than a half century ago when statisticians intended to find out information of population behind observations of a sample. In this period, people mainly focused on the estimation issue of densities and their functionals (e.g., derivatives) given an i.i.d. sample with different approaches. These studies include Rosenblatt (1956), Schwartz (1967), Kronmal and Tarter (1968), Watson (1969), Tarter and Kronmal (1970), Wahba (1975), Silverman (1982), Hall (1980, 1981a, b, 1982, 1984, 1986), Greblicki and Pawlak

C. Dong and J. Gao, *Modern Series Methods in Econometrics and Statistics*,
Advanced Studies in Theoretical and Applied Econometrics 45,
https://doi.org/10.1007/978-981-96-2822-3_4

(1984, 1985), Gallant and Nychka (1987), Gallant and Tauchen (1989), Fenton and Gallant (1996), and Laurent (1996).

Motivated by the estimate of density, economists and econometricians directly use such estimates in their studies about economic and financial issues. This is illustrated in the literature by van der Marel and Franx (1993), Aït-Sahalia (2002, 2008), Ángel León et al. (2009), Wu (2010), Xiu (2014), Necula et al. (2019), Lu and Qu (2021), and Aït-Sahalia et al. (2024). Thus, density estimation can help solve economic and related field issues.

4.1 Nonparametric Density Estimation

4.1.1 General Approach

Let $X_1, \ldots, X_n$ be an independent and identically distributed random variable sequence with common density $f(x)$. In what follows, we mainly consider the case that the support of $f(x)$ is $\mathbb{R}$, while in other cases, the estimation of $f(x)$ can be carried out similarly. Thus, to estimate $f(x)$ by the series methods, assume $f(x) \in L^2(\mathbb{R})$ (it is guaranteed particularly when $f(x)$ is bounded), wherein Hermite function sequence $\{\mathscr{H}_j(x)\}$ forms its basis. See Appendix C.

Accordingly, $f(x)$ admits an orthogonal series expansion

$$f(x) = \sum_{j=0}^{\infty} c_j \mathscr{H}_j(x), \quad c_j = \int f(x)\mathscr{H}_j(x)dx, \tag{4.1.1}$$

where the series converges in the norm sense. Note that Lemma 1 of Schwartz (1967) shows that if $f(x)$ is continuous, of bounded variation, belongs to $L^1(\mathbb{R}) \cap L^2(\mathbb{R})$, then series (4.1.1) converges uniformly in any interval interior to $\mathbb{R}$. Moreover, Dong et al. (2016) show a certain convergence rate the series (4.1.1) possesses when $f(x)$ is smooth. See Lemma C.1 in the supplement of Dong et al. (2016).

From (4.1.1), it is readily seen that $c_j = \mathbb{E}[\mathscr{H}_j(X)]$ where X is a variable having density $f(x)$. It is then reasonable to estimate c_j by the sample average,

$$\widehat{c}_j = \frac{1}{n}\sum_{i=1}^{n} \mathscr{H}_j(X_i), \tag{4.1.2}$$

and further propose an estimator of $f(x)$ as

$$\widehat{f}_n(x) = \sum_{j=0}^{k-1} \widehat{c}_j \mathscr{H}_j(x), \tag{4.1.3}$$

for any $x \in \mathbb{R}$, with positive integer $k = k(n)$ that is allowed to diverge with $n \to \infty$.

Clearly, $\mathbb{E}(\widehat{c}_j) = c_j$ implies the unbiasedness of $\widehat{c}_j$, and the variance

$$\begin{aligned}
\mathbb{E}(\widehat{c}_j - c_j)^2 &= \frac{1}{n^2}\mathbb{E}\left(\sum_{i=1}^{n}(\mathscr{H}_j(X_i) - c_j)\right)^2 \\
&= \frac{1}{n^2}\sum_{i=1}^{n}\mathbb{E}(\mathscr{H}_j(X_i) - c_j)^2 \\
&= \frac{1}{n}\mathrm{Var}(\mathscr{H}_j(X_i)) = O(n^{-1}),
\end{aligned}$$

where $\mathrm{Var}(\mathscr{H}_j(X_i)) = \mu_{j,2} - c_j^2$ and $\mu_{j,2} = \mathbb{E}(\mathscr{H}_j^2(X_i))$ which together with c_j is uniformly bounded in j, due to the uniform boundedness of Hermite functions and Parseval equality in Hilbert space.

Theorem 4.1.1 *Assume that $f(x) \in L^2(\mathbb{R})$, and the integer k is chosen such that $k/n \to 0$, $k \to \infty$, as $n \to \infty$. Then, MISE (mean integrated square error) $\mathbb{E}\int[\widehat{f}_n(x) - f(x)]^2 dx = o(1)$, as $n \to \infty$.*

Furthermore, assume that for some integer $r \geq 2$, $e^{x^2/2}[f(x)e^{-x^2/2}]^{(r)}$ exists and is square integrable over $\mathbb{R}$. Then,

$$\mathbb{E}\int[\widehat{f}_n(x) - f(x)]^2 dx = O(n^{-r/(r+1)}), \tag{4.1.4}$$

with $k = [n^{1/(r+1)}]$. □

Proof Note that

$$\begin{aligned}
\mathbb{E}\int[\widehat{f}_n(x) - f(x)]^2 dx =& \mathbb{E}\int\left[\sum_{j=0}^{k-1}(\widehat{c}_j - c_j)\mathscr{H}_j(x) + \sum_{j=k}^{\infty} c_j \mathscr{H}_j(x)\right]^2 dx \\
=& \sum_{j=0}^{k-1}\mathbb{E}(\widehat{c}_j - c_j)^2 + \sum_{j=k}^{\infty} c_j^2 \\
\leq& C\frac{k}{n} + \sum_{j=k}^{\infty} c_j^2 = o(1),
\end{aligned}$$

by the orthogonality of $\{\mathscr{H}_j(x)\}$.

Notice also that for Hermite polynomials, $[H_{j+1}(x)]' = 2(j+1)H_j(x)$, and Hermite functions $\mathscr{H}_j(x) = b_j^{-1}H_j(x)e^{-x^2/2}$ where $b_j = (\sqrt{\pi}2^j j!)^{1/2}$. For c_j, Integration by Parts gives

$$\begin{aligned}
c_j &= \frac{1}{b_j}\int f(x)H_j(x)e^{-x^2/2}dx \\
&= \frac{1}{2(j+1)b_j}\int f(x)H'_{j+1}(x)e^{-x^2/2}dx \\
&= -\frac{1}{2(j+1)b_j}\int [f(x)e^{-x^2/2}]'H_{j+1}(x)dx \\
&= \cdots \\
&= (-1)^r\frac{1}{2^r(j+1)\cdots(j+r)b_j}\int [f(x)e^{-x^2/2}]^{(r)}H_{j+r}(x)dx \\
&= \frac{(-1)^r b_{j+r}}{2^r(j+1)\cdots(j+r)b_j}\int e^{x^2/2}[f(x)e^{-x^2/2}]^{(r)}\mathscr{H}_{j+r}(x)dx \\
&= \frac{(-1)^r}{\sqrt{2^r(j+1)\cdots(j+r)}}\tilde{c}_{j+r},
\end{aligned}$$

where $\tilde{c}_{j+r}$ signifies the coefficient in the orthogonal expansion of $e^{x^2/2}[f(x)e^{-x^2/2}]^{(r)}$ in terms of Hermite functions.

It follows that

$$\begin{aligned}
\mathbb{E}\int [\widehat{f}_n(x) - f(x)]^2 dx &= \sum_{i=0}^{k-1}\mathbb{E}(\widehat{c}_j - c_j)^2 + \sum_{i=k}^{\infty} c_j^2 \\
&\leq C\frac{k}{n} + \sum_{i=k}^{\infty}\frac{1}{2^r(j+1)\cdots(j+r)}\tilde{c}_{j+r}^2 \\
&\leq C\frac{k}{n} + Ck^{-r}\sum_{i=k}^{\infty}\tilde{c}_{j+r}^2 \\
&= O(n^{-r/(r+1)}),
\end{aligned}$$

provided $k = [n^{1/(r+1)}]$. □

To investigate MSE (mean square error) at a given point x, define the partial sum of series (4.1.1),

$$f_k(x) = \sum_{i=0}^{k-1} c_j \mathscr{H}_j(x). \tag{4.1.5}$$

Theorem 4.1.2 *Assume that $f(x)$ is continuous, of bounded variation, and $f(x) \in L^1(\mathbb{R}) \cap L^2(\mathbb{R})$; the integer k is chosen such that $k^2/n \to 0$, $k \to \infty$, as $n \to \infty$. Then, the estimator $\widehat{f}_n(x)$ converges to $f(x)$ uniformly in MSE sense, viz., $\mathbb{E}[\widehat{f}_n(x) - f(x)]^2 = o(1)$ uniformly in x, as $n \to \infty$.*

Furthermore, assume for some integer $r \geq 3$, $e^{x^2/2}[f(x)e^{-x^2/2}]^{(r)}$ exists and is square integrable over $\mathbb{R}$. Then, MSE has rate

$$\mathbb{E}[\widehat{f}_n(x) - f(x)]^2 = O(n^{-(r-1)/(r+1)}), \tag{4.1.6}$$

in which $k = [n^{1/(r+1)}]$. □

Proof Because $\widehat{f}_n(x)$ is the unbiased estimate of $f_k(x)$,

$$\mathbb{E}[\widehat{f}_n(x) - f(x)]^2 = (f_k(x) - f(x))^2 + \mathbb{E}[\widehat{f}_n(x) - f_k(x)]^2.$$

According to Lemma 1 of Schwartz (1967), $\sup_x |f_k(x) - f(x)| = o(1)$ as $k \to \infty$. On the other hand,

$$\begin{aligned}
\mathbb{E}[\widehat{f}_n(x) - f_k(x)]^2 =& \mathbb{E}\left[\sum_{j=0}^{k-1} (\widehat{c}_j - c_j)\mathscr{H}_j(x)\right]^2 \\
=& \sum_{j=0}^{k-1}\sum_{s=0}^{k-1} \mathbb{E}(\widehat{c}_j - c_j)(\widehat{c}_s - c_s)\mathscr{H}_j(x)\mathscr{H}_s(x) \\
\leq& C\sum_{j=0}^{k-1}\sum_{s=0}^{k-1} [\mathbb{E}(\widehat{c}_j - c_j)^2\mathbb{E}(\widehat{c}_s - c_s)^2]^{1/2} \\
=& C\frac{k^2}{n} = o(1),
\end{aligned}$$

due to Cauchy-Schwarz inequality and the boundedness of Hermite functions. This finishes the first part.

To prove the second part, invoking

$$c_j = \frac{(-1)^r}{\sqrt{2^r(j+1)\cdots(j+r)}}\tilde{c}_{j+r}$$

derived in the previous theorem, we have

$$
\begin{aligned}
|f_k(x) - f(x)|^2 &= \left[\sum_{j=k}^{\infty} c_j \mathscr{H}_j(x)\right]^2 \\
&= \left[\sum_{j=k}^{\infty} \frac{(-1)^r}{\sqrt{2^r (j+1)\cdots(j+r)}} \tilde{c}_{j+r} \mathscr{H}_j(x)\right]^2 \\
&\le C \sum_{j=k}^{\infty} \frac{1}{(j+1)\cdots(j+r)} \sum_{j=k}^{\infty} \tilde{c}_{j+r}^2 \\
&= o(k^{-r+1}).
\end{aligned}
$$

Then, due to $k = [n^{1/(r+1)}]$ together with $\mathbb{E}[\widehat{f}_n(x) - f_k(x)]^2 = O(k^2/n)$, MSE has rate $O(n^{-(r-1)/(r+1)})$. □

Note that Walter (1977) makes use of particular properties of Hermite functions improving the convergence rate, Watson (1969) discusses weighted orthogonal series estimation, Tarter and Kronmal (1970) consider the estimation on multivariate densities, while Wahba (1975) compares series estimation of densities with other approaches and studies optimal convergence properties.

In particular, Anderson and Figueiredo (1980) propose an adaptive "two-pass" stratagem for density estimation. Let $w(x)$ be a density defined on (a, b) that is positive almost everywhere and satisfies $\int_a^b w(x)dx = 1$. Moreover, let $\{\varphi_j(x)\}$ be an orthonormal basis in $L^2((a, b), w(x))$.

Suppose that $f(x)$, the p.d.f. of random variable X, is such that $f/w \in L^2((a, b), w(x))$. Then, $f(x)$ may be expanded as

$$
f(x) = w(x) \sum_{j=0}^{\infty} c_j \varphi_j(x), \tag{4.1.7}
$$

where

$$
c_j = \int_a^b \frac{f(x)}{w(x)} \varphi_j(x) w(x) dx = \mathbb{E}[\varphi_j(X)],
$$

that implies an unbiased estimate

$$
\widehat{c}_j = \frac{1}{n} \sum_{i=1}^{n} \varphi_j(X_i), \tag{4.1.8}
$$

for c_j, given i.i.d. sample $X_1, \ldots, X_n$ drawn from X.

Consequently, we can construct an estimator of $f(x)$,

$$
\widehat{f}_n(x) = w(x) \sum_{j=0}^{k-1} \widehat{c}_j \varphi_j(x), \tag{4.1.9}
$$

with truncation parameter k diverging with n. A convenient error measure is

$$\int_a^b \frac{\mathbb{E}[\widehat{f}_n(x) - f(x)]^2}{w(x)} dx = \int_a^b \mathbb{E}\left[\frac{\widehat{f}_n(x) - f(x)}{w(x)}\right]^2 w(x)dx$$
$$= \int_a^b \mathbb{E}\left[\sum_{j=0}^{k-1}(\widehat{c}_j - c_j)\varphi_j(x) + \sum_{j=k}^{\infty} c_j\varphi_j(x)\right]^2 w(x)dx$$
$$= \sum_{j=0}^{k-1}\mathbb{E}(\widehat{c}_j - c_j)^2 + \sum_{j=k}^{\infty} c_j^2$$
$$= \frac{1}{n}\sum_{j=0}^{k-1}\mathrm{Var}(\varphi_j(X)) + \sum_{j=k}^{\infty} c_j^2.$$

Ideally, we would like to choose a family $\{\varphi_j(x)\}$ for which $f(x)$ can be approximated well by the first few terms. To select such an orthogonal sequence, let us consider the following strategy illustrated by Fourier series $\{\exp(2\pi ijx)\}$, $i = \sqrt{-1}$, $x \in [0, 1]$, instead of a general $\{\varphi_j(x)\}$.

Suppose that we have a transformation $G(x) : [0, 1] \mapsto [0, 1]$ that is one-to-one, increasing, and such that $g(x) = G'(x)$ is continuous. Define

$$u_j(x) = \exp(2\pi ijG(x)), \tag{4.1.10}$$

which is an orthonormal sequence w.r.t. $g(x)$. Indeed,

$$\int_0^1 u_j(x)u_\ell^*(x)g(x)dx = \int_0^1 \exp(2\pi i(j-\ell)x)dx = \delta_{j\ell},$$

where * signifies complex conjugate. This immediately yields a series-type estimator:

$$\widehat{f}_n(x) = \sum_{j=0}^{k-1}\widehat{c}_j u_j(x), \tag{4.1.11}$$

where

$$\widehat{c}_j = \frac{1}{n}\sum_{\ell=1}^{n} u_\ell^*(X_\ell). \tag{4.1.12}$$

By Anderson and Figueiredo (1980), if $G(x) = \int_0^x f(t)dt$, the new family $\{u_j(x)\}$ improves the estimate of $f(x)$. Moreover, in view of the dependence of $G(x)$ on the unknown $f(x)$, the paper proposes an adaptive (or two-pass) estimation procedure as follows.

Choose positive integers n_1 and n_2 such that $n_1 + n_2 = n$ and both of them are diverging with n. **Pass-one**: Let

$$\widehat{g}_n(x) = \sum_{j=-k}^{k} \widehat{a}_j \exp(2\pi i j x), \tag{4.1.13}$$

with

$$\widehat{a}_j = \frac{1}{n_1} \sum_{\ell=1}^{n_1} \exp(-2\pi i j X_\ell). \tag{4.1.14}$$

Pass-two: Define

$$\widehat{G}(x) = \int_0^x \widehat{g}_n(x) dx. \tag{4.1.15}$$

Then,

$$\widehat{f}_n(x) = \sum_{j=-k}^{k} \widehat{c}_j \exp(2\pi i j \widehat{G}(x)), \tag{4.1.16}$$

with

$$\widehat{c}_j = \frac{1}{n_2} \sum_{\ell=n_1+1}^{n} \exp(-2\pi i j \widehat{G}(X_\ell)). \tag{4.1.17}$$

The adaptive estimator (4.1.16) makes use of the preliminary estimation of the density in (4.1.13), so that the asymptotic property is enhanced, as shown in Anderson and Figueiredo (1980) where the readers are referred to find out more details.

4.1.2 Estimates of the Derivatives of Density

Another advantage of series estimation on densities is that one may obtain the estimates of derivatives directly from the density estimator. Hall (1982) and Greblicki and Pawlak (1984, 1985) are pioneer studies, as far as we are aware, that investigate the estimates of a density and its derivatives.

Observe that the normalized Legendre polynomials

$$p_j(x) = \sqrt{(2j+1)/2}\, P_j(x), \tag{4.1.18}$$

where $P_j(x)$ are Legendre polynomials of order j, form an orthonormal basis in $L^2[-1, 1]$. If density $f(x)$ has support confined to $(-1, 1)$, is continuous and of bounded variation on each interval $(-1+\varepsilon, 1-\varepsilon)$, $\varepsilon > 0$, and satisfies

$$\int_{-1}^{1} (1-x^2)^{-1/4} f(x) dx < \infty,$$

then the Legendre polynomial expansion of f, defined by

$$f(x) = \sum_{j=0}^{\infty} c_j p_j(x), \quad c_j = \int_{-1}^{1} p_j(x) f(x) dx, \tag{4.1.19}$$

converges uniformly to f on each interval $(-1+\varepsilon, 1-\varepsilon)$, $\varepsilon > 0$. See Sansone (1959, p. 236).

If $X_1, \ldots, X_n$ are independent random variables with common density f whose support is confined to $(-1, 1)$,

$$\widehat{c}_j = \frac{1}{n} \sum_{i=1}^{n} p_j(X_i) \tag{4.1.20}$$

are unbiased estimators of c_j. Further, we define

$$\widehat{f}_n(x) = \sum_{j=0}^{k-1} \widehat{c}_j p_j(x) \tag{4.1.21}$$

to be an estimate of $f(x)$ with truncation parameter k that may diverge with n. Conducting differentiation directly we obtain the estimate

$$\widehat{f_n^{(s)}}(x) = \sum_{j=0}^{k-1} \widehat{c}_j p_j^{(s)}(x) \tag{4.1.22}$$

of $f^{(s)}(x)$.

It follows from Lemma C.4.1 and Eq. (C.4.16) that $\{p_j^{(s)}(x), j \geq s\}$ is still orthogonal w.r.t. $(1-x^2)^s$.

Theorem 4.1.3 *Let $r \geq s \geq 0$ be integers. Suppose that f has r derivatives on $(-1, 1)$, $(1-x^2)^{1/4} f^{(r)}(x)$ is of bounded variation on $(-1, 1)$, and*

$$\int_{-1}^{1} (1-x^2)^{-3/4} |f^{(r)}(x)| dx < \infty.$$

Then,

$$\begin{aligned} &\int_{-1}^{1} \mathbb{E}[\widehat{f_n^{(s)}}(x) - f^{(s)}(x)]^2 (1-x^2)^s dx \\ &= \frac{k^{2s+1}}{n(2k+1)\pi} \int_{-1}^{1} (1-x^2)^{-1/2} f(x) dx + O(k^{2(s-r)-1}) + o(k^{2s+1} n^{-1}), \end{aligned} \tag{4.1.23}$$

as k and $n \to \infty$.

Moreover, for any $\varepsilon > 0$,

$$\sup_{|x|<1-\varepsilon} |\mathbb{E}[\widehat{f}_n^{(s)}(x) - f^{(s)}(x)]| = O(k^{(s-r)}). \tag{4.1.24}$$

If further $k^{2s+1}/n = o(1)$, then at each continuity point x of f in $(-1, 1)$, the random variable

$$Z_n(x) = \sqrt{\frac{n}{k^{2s+1}}}[\widehat{f}_n^{(s)}(x) - \mathbb{E}\widehat{f}_n^{(s)}(x)]$$

is asymptotically normal with zero mean and variance $\sigma_s^2(x) = f(x)/(2s+1)\pi(1-x^2)^{s+1/2}$. □

For the proof of the theorem, the readers are referred to Hall (1982). Next, consider the estimates of the derivatives of density on $\mathbb{R}$. Let X be a population random variable that possesses a density $f(x)$ with support $\mathbb{R}$, and $X_1, \ldots, X_n$ be i.i.d. sample drawn from X. Suppose $f^{(s)}(x) \in L^2(\mathbb{R})$, $s \geq 0$. Accordingly, $f^{(s)}(x)$ admits an orthogonal expansion in terms of Hermite function sequence $\{\mathscr{H}_j(x)\}$,

$$f^{(s)}(x) = \sum_{j=0}^{\infty} c_j \mathscr{H}_j(x), \tag{4.1.25}$$

and the coefficients

$$c_j = \int f^{(s)}(x)\mathscr{H}_j(x)dx = (-1)^s \int f(x)\mathscr{H}_j^{(s)}(x)dx. \tag{4.1.26}$$

This suggests the following estimate of $f^{(s)}(x)$,

$$\widehat{f}_n^{(s)}(x) = \sum_{j=0}^{k-1} \widehat{c}_j \mathscr{H}_j(x), \tag{4.1.27}$$

with

$$\widehat{c}_j = (-1)^s \frac{1}{n} \sum_{i=1}^{n} \mathscr{H}_j^{(s)}(X_i), \tag{4.1.28}$$

an unbiased estimator of c_j.

Theorem 4.1.4 *Let $f^{(s)}(x) \in L^2(\mathbb{R})$, $s \geq 0$. If $k \to \infty$, $k^{s+5/6}/n \to 0$ as $n \to \infty$, then*

$$\mathbb{E}\int (\widehat{f}_n^{(s)}(x) - f^{(s)}(x))^2 dx \to 0. \tag{4.1.29}$$

Suppose further for $r > s$, $t_r(x) \equiv (x - D)^r f(x) \in L^2(\mathbb{R})$ where D is differentiating operator, $\mathbb{E}|X|^{s/3} < \infty$. If $k \sim n^{2/(2r+1)}$, then

$$\mathbb{E} \int (\widehat{f}_n^{(s)}(x) - f^{(s)}(x))^2 dx = O(n^{-2(r-s)/(2r+1)}). \tag{4.1.30}$$

Proof Define $\mathscr{H}_{-j}(x) = \mathscr{H}_j(x)$. We have

$$\mathscr{H}_j'(x) = \sqrt{|j|/2}\mathscr{H}_{j-1}(x) - \sqrt{(|j|+1)/2}\mathscr{H}_{j+1}(x),$$

with $j = \pm 1, \pm 2, \ldots$ and

$$\mathscr{H}_0'(x) = \sqrt{1/2}\mathscr{H}_{-1}(x).$$

It then follows that

$$\mathscr{H}_j^{(s)}(x) = \sum_{\ell=-s}^{s} \alpha_{js\ell}\mathscr{H}_{j+\ell}(x), \tag{4.1.31}$$

where $|\alpha_{js\ell}| \leq K_s(|j| + s)^{s/2}$, and K_s is a constant depending on s only. Accordingly, one may rewrite

$$\widehat{c}_j = (-1)^s \frac{1}{n} \sum_{\ell=-s}^{s} \alpha_{js\ell} \sum_{i=1}^{n} \mathscr{H}_{j+\ell}(X_i), \tag{4.1.32}$$

from which we have

$$\mathrm{Var}(\widehat{c}_j) \leq (2s+1)K_s^2(j+s)^s \frac{1}{n}\mathbb{E} \sum_{\ell=-s}^{s} [\mathscr{H}_{j+\ell}(X)]^2. \tag{4.1.33}$$

Hence, by an inequality (Theorem 8.91.3 of Szego, 1975, p. 242),

$$\sup_x |\mathscr{H}_j(x)| \leq C(j+1)^{-1/12},$$

we have

$$\mathrm{Var}(\widehat{c}_j) \leq (2s+1)K_s^2 \frac{1}{n}(j+s)^s(j+1)^{-1/6}.$$

Moreover, observe that

$$\begin{aligned}
&\mathbb{E}\int(\widehat{f_n^{(s)}}(x)-f^{(s)}(x))^2dx\\
&=\sum_{j=0}^{k-1}\mathbb{E}(\widehat{c}_j-c_j)^2+\sum_{j=k}^{\infty}c_j^2\\
&\leq C\frac{1}{n}\sum_{j=0}^{k-1}(j+s)^s(j+1)^{-1/6}+\sum_{j=k}^{\infty}c_j^2\\
&=O(k^{s+5/6}/n)+o(1)=o(1).
\end{aligned}$$

Next, we prove (4.1.30). Notice by $\mathbb{E}|X|^{s/3}<\infty$ that

$$\mathbb{E}|\mathscr{H}_j(X)|^s\leq c(j+1)^{-s/4}. \tag{4.1.34}$$

This holds because

$$\max_{|x|\leq a}|\mathscr{H}_j(x)|\leq C_a(j+1)^{-1/4},\quad\text{and}\quad\max_{|x|>a}|x^{-1/3}\mathscr{H}_j(x)|\leq D_a(j+1)^{-1/4},$$

for any $a>0$.

Now, by (4.1.33) and (4.1.34) we have

$$\sum_{j=0}^{k-1}\mathbb{E}(\widehat{c}_j-c_j)^2=O(k^{s+1/2}/n).$$

On the other hand, by Walter (1977),

$$\sum_{j=k}^{\infty}c_j^2=O(k^{-(r-s)}).$$

The assertion follows immediately by combining the above two quantities. □

The uniform convergence of the estimate in this theorem is also discussed in Greblicki and Pawlak (1984). It is noteworthy that statistician Peter Hall made significant contributions to the density estimation, as illustrated by his consecutive papers Hall (1980, 1981a, b, 1982, 1984, 1986); in particular, he found the elegant law of the iterated logarithm for density estimators that are derived by kernel, trigonometric and orthogonal polynomial series, respectively. In this regard, about Hall's contribution, Cheng and Fan (2016) is an excellent review.

4.1.3 Guaranteed Positivity of Density Estimates

In estimating a density function by series methods, one may be concerned about whether the resultant estimate is assuredly positive. Indeed, this is not guaranteed, though we may have its consistency.

In a series of papers, Gallant and Nychka (1987), Gallant and Tauchen (1989), and Fenton and Gallant (1996), A. Ronald Gallant and his coauthors propose seminonparametric (SNP) estimation strategy, while, SNP, coined by Ibrahim et al. (1983), means a halfway between parametric and nonparametric inference procedures. The SNP estimator is a truncation (or sieve) estimator based upon a Hermite series expansion that possesses intriguing properties: its coefficients are determined by quasi maximum likelihood (QML) rather than by method of moments (MM), it is positive, and it is location and scale invariant.

To proceed, we need to introduce the following notation. For p with $p \geq 1$ the Sobolev norm of a real-valued function $f(u)$ with respect to a nonnegative weight function $\mu(u)$ defined on $\mathbb{R}^k$ is

$$\|f\|_{m,p,\mu} = \left(\sum_{|\lambda| \leq m} \int |D^\lambda f(u)|^p \mu(u) du \right)^{1/p}, \tag{4.1.35}$$

where $\lambda = (\lambda_1, \ldots, \lambda_k)$ is a k-vector with nonnegative integers as elements, $|\lambda| = \lambda_1 + \cdots + \lambda_k$, and

$$D^\lambda f(u) = \frac{\partial^{\lambda_1}}{\partial u_1^{\lambda_1}} \frac{\partial^{\lambda_2}}{\partial u_2^{\lambda_2}} \cdots \frac{\partial^{\lambda_k}}{\partial u_k^{\lambda_k}} f(u), \quad D^0 f(u) = f(u).$$

If the weight function is the identity, $\mu(u) = 1$, we write $\|f\|_{m,p,\mu} = \|f\|_{m,p}$; for $p = \infty$ and f with continuous partial derivatives to order m, define

$$\|f\|_{m,\infty,\mu} = \max_{|\lambda| \leq m} \sup_{u \in \mathbb{R}^k} |D^\lambda f(u)| \mu(u). \tag{4.1.36}$$

Again, if $\mu(u) = 1$, we write

$$\|f\|_{m,\infty} = \max_{|\lambda| \leq m} \sup_{u \in \mathbb{R}^k} |D^\lambda f(u)|.$$

Denote by $W_{m,p,\mu}$ the normed, linear space of real-valued functions f with finite $\|f\|_{m,p,\mu}$, and by $W_{m,p}$ the set of functions with finite $\|f\|_{m,p}$. For $p = 2$, $W_{m,2,\mu}$ is a Hilbert space with respect to the inner product

$$\langle f, g \rangle_{m,2,\mu} = \sum_{|\lambda| \leq m} \int D^\lambda f(u) D^\lambda g(u) \mu(u) du,$$

and similarly, $W_{m,2}$ is a Hilbert space with respect to

$$\langle f, g\rangle_{m,2} = \sum_{|\lambda|\le m} \int D^\lambda f(u) D^\lambda g(u) du.$$

In Gallant and Nychka (1987), the space of probability densities containing target density to estimate is

$$H = \left\{h(u) = f^2(u) + \varepsilon h_0(u)\right\}, \tag{4.1.37}$$

where $\|f\|_{m,2,\mu_0} < B_0$, $\|h_0\|_{m,2,\mu_0} < B_0$, $\varepsilon > \varepsilon_0$, $m_0 > k/2$, $\delta_0 > k/2$, some $B_0 > 0$, and small $\varepsilon_0 > 0$, $\mu_0(u) = (1 + \|u\|^2)^{\delta_0}$.

In the definition of H, B_0 is an a priori bound that not only imposes a smoothness restriction on the members of H but also bounds the tails of densities in H from above. The compactness of H effectively obtains from this bound. The density h_0 is a lower bound that is imposed both to be certain that densities in H are strictly positive and to bound the tails from below.

Then, sieve spaces H_K are defined as follows. Let m_0, B_0, ε_0, and μ_0 be as in the definition of H. Let $\phi(u)$ be a strictly positive probability density function on $\mathbb{R}^k$ that has a moment generating function and satisfies $\|P_K\phi\|_{m+m_0,2,\mu_0} < \infty$ for every polynomial of degree K for $K = 0, 1, \ldots$. Let H_K consist of those probability density functions with zero mean that are of the form

$$h(u) = [P_K(u)\phi(u)]^2 + \varepsilon h_0(u),$$

where $\|P_K(u)\phi(u)\|_{m+m_0,2,\mu_0} < B_0$ and $\varepsilon > \varepsilon_0$.

Let m and δ_0 be the same as in the definition of H, for some δ with $k/2 < \delta < \delta_0$ put $\|h\| = \|h\|_{m.\infty,\mu}$ where $\mu(u) = (1 + \|u\|^2)^\delta$. This norm is stronger than the one in the space defined before since for $|\lambda| < m$,

$$\int_{\mathbb{R}^k} |D^\lambda h_1(u) - D^\lambda h_2(u)| du \le \|h_1 - h_2\| \int_{\mathbb{R}^k} (1 + \|u\|^2)^{-\delta} du.$$

Gallant and Nychka (1987) show the following results:

(1) Let $\overline{H}$ denote the closure of H with respect to norm $\|h\|$. Then $\overline{H}$ is compact in the relative topology on $\overline{H}$ generated by the norm $\|h\|$.
(2) $\bigcup_{K=1}^{\infty} H_K$ is a dense subset of $\overline{H}$ with respect to norm $\|h\|$.

Given these properties available, the finite dimensional sieve space H_K can be used in series methods in density estimation.

The SNP estimator in Fenton and Gallant (1996) is defined as the quasi maximum likelihood estimator (QMLE),

$$\widehat{f}_{\text{SNP}} = \underset{f \in \mathscr{F}_n, \mu, \sigma > 0}{\arg\max} \frac{1}{n} \sum_{t=1}^{n} \ln\left[\frac{1}{\sigma} f\left(\frac{X_t - \mu}{\sigma}\right)\right], \tag{4.1.38}$$

where

$$\mathscr{F}_n = \left\{ f_n : f_n(x, \xi) = \left[\sum_{i=0}^{p_n} \xi_i x^i\right]^2 e^{-x^2/2} + \varepsilon_0 \phi(x), \ \xi \in \Xi_n \right\},$$

and $\Xi_n = \{\xi = (\xi_0, \ldots, \xi_{p_n}) : \int f_n(x, \xi) dx = 1\}$, p_n is an integer sequence increasing with sample size, ε_0 is a small positive number, and $\phi(x)$ stands for the density function of a standard normal variable.

Suppose that $\{X_t\}$ are observed data of random sample from the continuous density $f_0(x)$ that can be written as $f_0(x) = g_0^2(x)e^{-x^2/2} + \varepsilon_0\phi(x)$ where $g_0^{(j)}(x) \in L^2(\mathbb{R}, e^{-x^2/2})$ for $j = 0, 1, \ldots, k$. For every $B > 0$ and $a_0, a_1 \in \mathbb{R}$, there exist $k_0, k_1 > 0$ such that $\mathbb{P}(X^2 > a_0 + a_1 B) \leq k_0 e^{-k_1\sqrt{B}}$. Let $p_n = [n^\alpha]$ with $\alpha \in (0, 1)$. Fenton and Gallant (1996) show that

$$\int |f_0(x) - \widehat{f}_{\text{SNP}}(x)| dx = o_{a.s.}(n^{(\alpha-1)/2+\delta}) + o(n^{-k\alpha}) \tag{4.1.39}$$

for all sufficiently small $\delta > 0$.

The SNP technique in density estimation is used in Ángel León et al. (2009) and Necula et al. (2019) for option pricing and evaluation, to name a few.

4.2 Applications of Density Estimation

We notice that researchers and practitioners utilize density estimates by series methods in their studies, for example, Aït-Sahalia (2002, 2008), Wu (2010), Filipovic et al. (2013), Xiu (2014), Barletta et al. (2019), Lu and Qu (2021) and Aït-Sahalia et al. (2024), among others. While most of the papers are within a financial context, they witness series estimates to be a convenient approach.

4.2.1 Estimation of Parameters in Diffusion Process by MLE

Suppose X_t obeys a continuous time diffusion model

$$dX_t = \mu(X_t, \theta)dt + \sigma(X_t, \theta)dW_t, \tag{4.2.1}$$

where X_t is the state variable, W_t is a standard Brownian motion, μ and σ are known functions up to parameter θ, a Euclidean parameter with fixed dimension. Let the process $\{X_t\}$ be observed at discrete time points. To estimate θ by maximum likelihood estimation (MLE), the conditional density (also called transition function) of $X_{t+\Delta} = x$ given $X_t = x_0$, $p_X(\Delta, x|x_0, \theta)$, needs to be available explicitly or approximately; but for most diffusion models explicit transition function is impossible to obtain.

Under certain conditions on $\mu(x, \theta)$ and $\sigma(x, \theta)$, Aït-Sahalia (2002) proposes the following procedure to obtain an approximate of the transition function. First, let $Y \equiv \gamma(X, \theta) = \int^X du/\sigma(u, \theta)$. Thus, Y_t is a diffusion given by

$$dY_t = \mu_Y(Y_t, \theta)dt + dW_t. \tag{4.2.2}$$

It is shown in Aït-Sahalia (2002) that Y admits a smooth density $p_Y(\Delta, y|y_0, \theta)$ (the conditional density of $Y_{t+\Delta}|Y_t$) that is infinitely differentiable in Δ, y, y_0, while three times differentiable w.r.t. θ.

Second, for given $\Delta > 0$, $y_0 \in \mathbb{R}$ and $\theta \in \Theta$, define the "pseudo-normalized" increment of Y as $Z \equiv \Delta^{-1/2}(Y - y_0)$. By applying Jacobian formula for the change of density,

$$p_X(\Delta, x|x_0, \theta) = \sigma(x, \theta)^{-1} p_Y(\Delta, \gamma(x, \theta)|\gamma(x_0, \theta), \theta), \tag{4.2.3}$$

and

$$p_Y(\Delta, y|y_0, \theta) = \Delta^{-1/2} p_Z(\Delta, \Delta^{-1/2}(y - y_0)|y_0, \theta), \tag{4.2.4}$$

where $p_Z(\Delta, z|y_0, \theta)$ is the conditional density of Z.

Then, Aït-Sahalia (2002) uses orthogonal series expansion in terms of Hermite function sequence to approximate $p_Z(\Delta, z|y_0, \theta)$ by partial sum

$$p_Z^{(J)}(\Delta, z|y_0, \theta) = \phi(z) \sum_{j=0}^{J} \eta_Z^{(j)}(\Delta, y_0, \theta) H_j(z), \tag{4.2.5}$$

where $\phi(\cdot)$ is the density of standard normal variable, $H_j(z)$ are Hermite polynomials orthogonal w.r.t. $\exp(-x^2/2)$, $\eta_Z^{(j)}(\Delta, y_0, \theta)$ is the coefficients given by

$$\begin{aligned}
\eta_Z^{(j)}(\Delta, y_0, \theta) &= \frac{1}{j!} \int H_j(z) p_Z(\Delta, z|y_0, \theta) dz \\
&= \frac{1}{j!} \int H_j(\Delta^{-1/2}(y - y_0)) p_Y(\Delta, y|y_0, \theta) dy \\
&= \frac{1}{j!} \mathbb{E}[H_j(\Delta^{-1/2}(Y_{t+\Delta} - y_0))|Y_t = y_0, \theta].
\end{aligned}$$

Using (4.2.3) and (4.2.4) one can recover the estimates of the conditional densities by

$$p_Y^{(J)}(\Delta, y|y_0, \theta) = \Delta^{-1/2} p_Z^{(J)}(\Delta, \Delta^{-1/2}(y - y_0)|y_0, \theta),$$
$$p_X^{(J)}(\Delta, x|x_0, \theta) = \sigma^{-1}(x, \theta) p_Y^{(J)}(\Delta, \gamma(x, \theta)|\gamma(x_0, \theta), \theta).$$

With intriguing technology in dealing with these conditional expectations, Aït-Sahalia (2002) shows the asymptotic property of the MLE estimator $\widehat{\theta}$ by virtue of the approximated conditional density. We do not show the derivation of the asymptotic limit of $\widehat{\theta}$ in order not to deviate from our topic. In addition, a similar approach to the multivariate diffusion process is used for MLE estimation in Aït-Sahalia (2008).

4.2.2 *Exponential Series Estimator for Multivariate Densities*

Another application to cite is Wu (2010) where the author considers exponential series estimator (ESE) for multivariate densities which has an appealing information-theoretic interpretation. Precisely, for d-dimensional r.v. X with density $f_0(x)$, the ESE takes form

$$f_\theta(x) = \exp\left(\sum_{i_1=0}^{k_1-1} \cdots \sum_{i_d=0}^{k_d-1} \theta_{\mathbf{i}} \phi_{\mathbf{i}}(x)\right), \tag{4.2.6}$$

where $\mathbf{i} = (i_1, \ldots, i_d)$, $x = (x_1, \ldots, x_d)$, $\phi_{\mathbf{i}}(x) = \phi_{i_1}(x_1) \cdots \phi_{i_d}(x_d)$, and $\{\phi_i(\cdot)\}$ is an orthogonal function sequence, $(k_1, \ldots, k_d)$ is a set of truncation parameters. Such a form of density is estimated by maximum entropy subject to moment restrictions. To illustrate, consider a case of univariate ESE, that is

$$\max \; W(f_\theta) = \int f_\theta(x) \log(f_\theta(x)) dx, \tag{4.2.7}$$

subject to

$$\int f_\theta(x) dx = 1, \quad \int \phi_i(x) f_\theta(x) dx = \mu_i, \; i = 1, \ldots, m.$$

Since μ_i can be estimated by the sample average given observations drawn from the density to estimate, one may have the solution of (4.2.7) with estimated $\theta^* = (\theta_1^*, \ldots, \theta_m^*)$,

$$f_{\theta^*}(x) = \exp\left(\sum_{i=1}^{m} \theta_i^* \phi_i(x) - \psi(\theta^*)\right) \tag{4.2.8}$$

where the constant $\psi(\theta^*)$ is a normalizing factor such that $f_{\theta^*}(x)$ integrates to one,

$$\psi(\theta^*) = \log \int \exp\left(\sum_{i=1}^{m} \theta_i^* \phi_i(x)\right) dx.$$

For two densities p and q, define Kullback-Leibler information criterion (KLIC), also called cross or relative entropy,

$$D(p||q) = \int p(x) \log \frac{p(x)}{q(x)} dx \tag{4.2.9}$$

as a measure of discrepancy between p and q. It is well-known that $D(p||q) \geq 0$, and $D(p||q) = 0$ if and only if $p(x) = q(x)$ almost everywhere. Notice that $D(p||q)$ is not a metric since it is not symmetric and does not satisfy the triangle inequality.

It is shown in Wu (2010) that $D(f_0||f_{\theta^*}) \leq D(f_0||f_\theta)$. In addition, the maximum entropy problem is equivalent to the minimization of the relative entropy $D(f_\theta||f_0)$ with the same constraints. The resultant minimizing relative entropy takes the form

$$f_{\theta^*}(x) = f_0(x) \exp\left(\sum_{i=1}^{m} \theta_i^* \phi_i(x) - \psi(\theta^*)\right) \tag{4.2.10}$$

where

$$\psi(\theta^*) = \log \int f_0(x) \exp\left(\sum_{i=1}^{m} \theta_i^* \phi_i(x)\right) dx.$$

Given $\widehat{\mu}_i$ estimated by averaging $\phi_i(X)$ over a sample, one has $\widehat{\theta}$ by minimizing the relative entropy, so that $f_{\widehat{\theta}}(x)$ is obtained. Note that $D(f_0||f_{\widehat{\theta}}(x)) = D(f_0||f_{\theta^*}) + D(f_{\theta^*}||f_{\widehat{\theta}})$. This equation enables Wu (2010) to have the order of $D(f_0||f_{\widehat{\theta}}(x))$ by separably estimating $D(f_0||f_{\theta^*})$ and $D(f_{\theta^*}||f_{\widehat{\theta}})$.

For the following popular measures,

$$\begin{aligned} d_1(f_0, f_{\widehat{\theta}}) &= \int |f_0(x) - f_{\widehat{\theta}}(x)| dx \\ d_H(f_0, f_{\widehat{\theta}}) &= \left[\int \left(f_0^{1/2}(x) - f_{\widehat{\theta}}^{1/2}(x)\right)^2 dx\right]^{1/2} \\ d_{TV}(f_0, f_{\widehat{\theta}}) &= \sum_A \left| \int_A f_0(x) dx - \int_A f_{\widehat{\theta}}(x) dx \right|, \end{aligned}$$

it is shown that

$$\begin{aligned} d_1(f_0, f_{\widehat{\theta}}) &= O\left(\sqrt{D(f_0||f_{\widehat{\theta}}(x))}\right), \\ d_H(f_0, f_{\widehat{\theta}}) &= O\left(\sqrt{D(f_0||f_{\widehat{\theta}}(x))}\right), \\ d_{TV}(f_0, f_{\widehat{\theta}}) &= O\left(\sqrt{D(f_0||f_{\widehat{\theta}}(x))}\right). \end{aligned} \tag{4.2.11}$$

The paper then uses ESE to estimate joint density of monthly stock return indices of four markets: S & P 500 (U.S.), FTSE 100 (U.K.), Hangseng (H.K.) and Nikkei 225 (J.P.) using data from 1978 to 2006. For more details on ESE, the readers are referred to Wu (2010).

4.2.3 Thick-Tailed Density Estimation in Finance

Since thin-tailed, Gaussian density is not appropriate to depict extreme events in financial markets that happen not so rarely. For example, though the Black-Scholes model stipulates that the returns of underlying assets follow normal distribution, the features of actual returns often deviate from normal, e.g., they are asymmetric, thick-tailed, and skewed. The assumption of normality might be the major drawback of the celebrated Black-Scholes option pricing formula. Moreover, it is noteworthy that in the last three decades there have been several financial crises happened over the world, namely, 1997 Asian financial crisis, 2008 global financial crisis, and Feb 2020 the steep drop of financial market caused by COVID-19. Such black swan events happen with a higher probability than what normal distribution could depict; the financial industry realizes the use of heavy-tailed distribution such as student t to replace normal distribution or directly apply nonparametric estimation.

Given these observations, researchers employ heavier tail density in financial modeling. Let $g(x)$ be a probability density whose polynomial moments

$$\mu_r = \int_{\mathbb{R}} x^r g(x) dx \tag{4.2.12}$$

exist for all positive integers r. For example, $g(\cdot)$ may denote the pricing density in a financial market model. Typically, $g(\cdot)$ is not known in explicit form and needs to be approximated.

Let $w(x)$ be an auxiliary probability density function that has a finite exponential moment

$$\int_{\mathbb{R}} e^{-\lambda|x|} w(x) dx < \infty,$$

for some $\lambda > 0$. Then the set of polynomials is dense in the Hilbert space $L^2(\mathbb{R}, w(x))$ wherein $\{p_i(x), i \geq 0\}$ is an orthonormal polynomial sequence w.r.t. $w(x)$. Suppose further that $g(x)/w(x) \in L^2(\mathbb{R}, w(x))$. Thus,

$$\int_{\mathbb{R}} \frac{g^2(x)}{w(x)} dx < \infty,$$

and $g(x)/w(x)$ admits an infinite orthogonal series expansion in terms of $\{p_i(x), i \geq 0\}$, viz.

$$g(x) = w(x)\left[1 + \sum_{i=1}^{\infty} c_i p_i(x)\right], \quad c_i = \int_{\mathbb{R}} g(x) p_i(x) dx, \tag{4.2.13}$$

noting that $p_0(x) = 1$ and $c_0 = 1$.

Regarding the condition $g(x)/w(x) \in L^2(\mathbb{R}, w(x))$, it may be restrictive since it requires (4.2.12) to ensure the existence of all c_i in (4.2.13). By contrast, a series expansion for a generic density $f(x) \in L^2(\mathbb{R})$ is delivered by (4.1.1). Such $f(x)$ does not necessarily satisfy (4.2.12).

Accordingly, $g(x)$ can be approximated by

$$g_k(x) = w(x)\left[1 + \sum_{i=1}^{k} c_i p_i(x)\right]. \tag{4.2.14}$$

Though positiveness is not guaranteed, $g_k(x)$ always integrates to one, and clearly $g_k(x)/w(x) \to g(x)/w(x)$ in L^2 sense. A further result is given by Theorem 3.1 in Barletta et al. (2019) for the case where the support of $g(x)$ is included in $\mathbb{R}^+$.

In the literature, if $w(x)$ is a standard Gaussian density, (4.2.13) is the Gram-Charlier of $g(x)$, and $p_i(x)$ are Hermite polynomials (Necula et al., 2019), and then $g(x)$ can be approximated by the product of Gaussian density and a polynomial, illustrated by (4.2.14). This implies that $g(x)$ can possess a tail fatter than Gaussian density. On the other hand, (4.2.14) can be rephrased into a sum

$$g_k(x) = w(x) + w(x) \sum_{i=1}^{k} c_i p_i(x), \tag{4.2.15}$$

where the second summand plays a role of deviation from the standard Gaussian density of $g(x)$.

In (4.2.13), the choice of auxiliary density $w(x)$ is crucial. Ideally, we would like to choose $w(x)$ as close to $g(x)$ as possible, so that $g(x)/w(x)$ is close to one. This may be achieved if there are many $c_i = 0$, $i \geq 1$. Denote

$$\nu_r = \int_{\mathbb{R}} x^r w(x) dx,$$

the polynomial moments of $w(x)$. For any $n \geq 1$, if $\mu_r = \nu_r$ with $r \leq n$, then $c_r = 0$ for all $1 \leq r \leq n$. Indeed,

$$c_r = \int_{\mathbb{R}} p_r(x) g(x) dx = \int_{\mathbb{R}} p_r(x) w(x) dx = 0,$$

for $1 \leq r \leq n$, due to $p_0(x) = 1$ and the orthogonality of the sequence.

For particular applications of (4.2.13), see Filipovic et al. (2013) and Barletta et al. (2019).

4.2.4 Series Estimation of Option-Implied State Price Density

One more interesting application of the series estimation method on density is option pricing. A series estimator for the state price density (SPD) implied by a single cross-section of European options with different strikes and the same maturity is obtained that can help determine the distribution of the state price at the maturity.

The options market provides a natural laboratory for studying the dynamics of the SPD. Given a continuum of strikes over a sufficiently wide range, it is possible to recover this density from a cross-section of European option prices and the risk-free rate only.

Consider European options on a common underlying asset with the same maturity date denoted by T. In the absence of arbitrage and market imperfection, there exists a state price density $f_t^*(x)$ for the payoff at maturity T, such that the prices of the call and put options at time t satisfy

$$C_t(K) = e^{-r_t\tau}\int_0^\infty (S_T - K)^+ f_t^*(S_T)dS_T, \tag{4.2.16}$$

$$P_t(K) = e^{-r_t\tau}\int_0^\infty (K - S_T)^+ f_t^*(S_T)dS_T, \tag{4.2.17}$$

where K is the strike price, $\tau = T - t$, the function $u^+ = \max(u, 0)$, r_t is the risk-free rate at t, and S_T is the potential state price of the underlying asset at time T.

The proposed estimator of $f_t^*(\cdot)$ does not apply smoothing over t. As a result, we do not specify the state variables affecting $f_t^*(S_T)$. To reflect this feature, and to simplify the notation, we will suppress the subscript t in subsequent analysis. In particular, we will write $C_t(K)$, $P_t(K)$, r_t, and $f_t^*(S_T)$ as $C(K)$, $P(K)$, r, and $f^*(S_T)$, respectively.

Notice that the SPD is a dynamic object; its dispersion differs substantially between asset classes; and it varies significantly over time depending on, among other factors, market volatility, economic outlook, and time to maturity. To propose an estimator for general applications, we need a method to standardize the density or the data before approximating the SPD. In doing so, we adopt the following transformations,

$$x = \frac{\log(S_T/S) - r\tau}{\sigma\sqrt{\tau}}, \qquad z = \frac{\log(K/S) - r\tau}{\sigma\sqrt{\tau}}, \tag{4.2.18}$$

where S is the spot price of the state variable at t, σ is the Black-Scholes implied volatility for at-the-money call option of the same underlying asset and maturity.

Because the implied volatility is always reported as a summary statistic in options data, these two transformations are straightforward to compute. We denote the density after the change of variables by $f(x)$. With this density, (4.2.16) and (4.2.17) are rephrased as

$$C(z) = S \int \left(e^{x\sigma\sqrt{\tau}} - e^{z\sigma\sqrt{\tau}}\right)^+ f(x)dx, \tag{4.2.19}$$

$$P(z) = S \int \left(e^{z\sigma\sqrt{\tau}} - e^{x\sigma\sqrt{\tau}}\right)^+ f(x)dx. \tag{4.2.20}$$

The transformations in (4.2.18) are not new. For example, the second one is often used as a measure of moneyness to indicate how many standard deviations the option is in-the-money or out-of-the-money. However, their role in the current context is different, achieving the following two goals at once. First, the division by $\sqrt{\tau}\sigma$ serves as a variance-stabilizing transformation to ensure that the dispersion of $f(x)$ is insensitive to changes in market conditions and the time to maturity. In particular, if the dispersion of $f^*(x)$ increases abruptly due to a large negative shock, the Black-Scholes volatility will rise instantly, while the dispersion of $f(x)$ will remain relatively unchanged. Because σ is computed by inverting the Black-Scholes formula, it is not treated as an unknown parameter in the subsequent estimation. Consequently, the estimation problem remains linear in parameters after the transformation. Second, the logarithmic transformation $\log(S_T/S)$ shifts the density's support from the positive axis to the real line. If $f^*(x)$ is close to the log-normal density, $f(x)$ will be close to the normal density.

We shall use the series method to estimate $f(x)$. Once we have an ideal estimator for $f(x)$, $\widehat{f}(x)$ say, we may recover $f^*(\cdot)$ by reversing the monotonic transformation (4.2.18),

$$\widehat{f}^*(S_T) = \frac{1}{\sigma\sqrt{\tau}S_T}\widehat{f}\left(\frac{\log(S_T/S) - r\tau}{\sigma\sqrt{\tau}}\right). \tag{4.2.21}$$

To use the series methods, observe that the support of $f(x)$ is unbounded; this density is closely related to the normal density, especially when the stochastic process for the underlying asset is a geometric Brownian motion with drift r and volatility σ, this density is exactly of $N(0, 1)$; the density can have thicker tails than the normal distribution. These three features suggest that Hermite functions are suitable basis functions for the orthogonal series expansion of $f(x)$. Thus, suppose $f(x) \in L^2(\mathbb{R})$, and then

$$f(x) = \sum_{j=0}^{\infty} c_j \mathscr{H}_j(x), \quad c_j = \int f(x)\mathscr{H}_j(x)dx, \tag{4.2.22}$$

where $\mathscr{H}_j(x)$ are Hermite functions given by

$$\mathscr{H}_j(x) = (\sqrt{\pi}2^j j!)^{-1/2} H_j(x) e^{-x^2/2},$$

and $H_j(x)$ are Hermite polynomials orthogonal w.r.t. e^{-x^2}.

Let $\{(y_i, z_i), i = 1, \ldots, n\}$ denote the sample of observed option prices and transformed strike prices at time t. We assume that the data are ordered such that the first n_c observations are call options, and the remaining $n - n_c$ observations are put options. Then

$$y_i = S \int \left(e^{x\sigma\sqrt{\tau}} - e^{z_i\sigma\sqrt{\tau}}\right)^+ f(x)dx + e_i, \ \ i = 1, \ldots, n_c, \tag{4.2.23}$$

$$y_i = S \int \left(e^{z_i\sigma\sqrt{\tau}} - e^{x\sigma\sqrt{\tau}}\right)^+ f(x)dx + e_i, \ \ i = n_c + 1, \ldots, n, \tag{4.2.24}$$

where e_i represents the deviation of y_i from the theoretical prices due to market frictions and other factors.

Let k be a positive integer. It follows from (4.2.22) that $f(x) = f_k(x) + \gamma_k(x)$, where

$$f_k(x) = \sum_{j=0}^{k-1} c_j \mathscr{H}_j(x), \qquad \gamma_k(x) = \sum_{j=k}^{\infty} c_j \mathscr{H}_j(x).$$

Accordingly, regression equations (4.2.23) and (4.2.24) are rewritten as

$$y_i = x_i^\top \beta + e_i, \ \ i = 1, \ldots, n, \tag{4.2.25}$$

where $\beta = (c_0, \ldots, c_{k-1})^\top$, $x_i = (x_{i,0}, \ldots, x_{i,k-1})^\top$, in which

$$x_{i,j} = S \int \left(e^{x\sigma\sqrt{\tau}} - e^{z_i\sigma\sqrt{\tau}}\right)^+ \mathscr{H}_j(x)dx, \ \ i = 1, \ldots, n_c,$$

$$x_{i,j} = S \int \left(e^{z_i\sigma\sqrt{\tau}} - e^{x\sigma\sqrt{\tau}}\right)^+ \mathscr{H}_j(x)dx, \ \ i = n_c + 1, \ldots, n,$$

for $j = 0, \ldots, k-1$. Notice that Lu and Qu (2021) ignore $\gamma_k(x)$ in Eqs. (4.2.23) and (4.2.24), for this we do not advocate.

Define

$$\widehat{\beta} = \arg\min_{\beta \in \mathcal{H}_k} \sum_{i=1}^{n} (y_i - x_i^\top \beta)^2 + \beta^\top Q_\alpha \beta, \tag{4.2.26}$$

where Q_α is a regularization square matrix of order k,

$$\mathcal{H}_k = \left\{ \beta \in \mathbb{R}^k, \ \inf_{x \in \mathbb{R}} \sum_{j=0}^{k-1} \beta_j \mathscr{H}_j(x) \geq \eta \right\}$$

and η is a small negative number discussed later.

Moreover, define

$$\widehat{f}(x) = \sum_{j=0}^{k-1} \widehat{\beta}_j \mathscr{H}_j(x), \tag{4.2.27}$$

and optionally

$$\widetilde{f}(x) = \max(0, \widehat{f}(x))/c, \tag{4.2.28}$$

where $c > 0$ is such that $\widetilde{f}(x)$ integrates one.

We have the following comments on the estimator proposed. First, due to the truncation, $f_k(x) = f(x) - \gamma_k(x)$ might be negative at some point; the small negative number η in $\mathcal{H}_k$ is to account for this situation. In practice, η is suggested to be chosen between -10^{-4} and -10^{-3}. In the R code developed by Lu and Qu (2021), η is specified as an input parameter, so the user can apply different values, and compare the results.

Second, the term $\beta^\top Q_\alpha \beta$ is used to stabilize the estimate. Two specifications of Q_α are suggested. One is $Q_\alpha = \alpha I_k$; another one is $Q_\alpha = V D_\alpha V^\top$ where

$$D_\alpha = \text{diag}(\max\{\alpha - n\lambda_1, 0\}, \ldots, \max\{\alpha - n\lambda_k, 0\})$$

where $\lambda_1 \geq \cdots \geq \lambda_k$ are eigenvalues of $n^{-1}\sum_{i=1}^n x_i x_i^\top$, V contains all corresponding orthogonal eigenvectors.

Third, the parameter k controls the approximation error of $\gamma_k(x)$, while α controls the degree of regularization for a given k. Based on the theoretical and simulation results, Lu and Qu (2021) propose choosing k and α using the following procedure. Basically, this procedure specifies a sufficiently large k, and then uses α to regulate the estimates in case this k is larger than necessary. Step one, set $k = [2(n/\log(n))^{1/5}]$. Step two, for this k, determine α using the cross-validation (CV) method. See Lu and Qu (2021) for the details of the implementation of the CV method.

Fourth, the definition of (4.2.28) is actually the result of a L_2-projection approach that projects $\widehat{f}(x)$ on the class of nonnegative densities on the real line. That is, $\widetilde{f}(x)$ minimizes $\int[\widehat{f}(x) - g(x)]^2 dx$ over all nonnegative $g(x)$ such that $\int g(x)dx = 1$. In most simulations and empirical applications, the differences between $\widehat{f}(x)$ and $\widetilde{f}(x)$ are small.

We first show the assumptions that are necessary for the theoretical development in the sequel, and then establish the convergence rate of the estimator $\widehat{f}(x)$. Let $[\mathcal{K}_{c,L}, \mathcal{K}_{c,U}]$ and $[\mathcal{K}_{p,L}, \mathcal{K}_{p,U}]$ denote the spans of the call and put strikes, respectively. These two spans can be identical, or only partially overlap. Define $[\mathcal{K}_L, \mathcal{K}_U] = [\mathcal{K}_{c,L}, \mathcal{K}_{c,U}] \cup [\mathcal{K}_{p,L}, \mathcal{K}_{p,U}]$.

Assumption 4.2.1 There exists a Lipschitz continuous density over $x \in \mathbb{R}$ such that (4.2.16) and (4.2.17) hold for $K \in [\mathcal{K}_{c,L}, \mathcal{K}_{c,U}]$ and $K \in [\mathcal{K}_{p,L}, \mathcal{K}_{p,U}]$, respectively, where $[\mathcal{K}_{c,L}, \mathcal{K}_{c,U}] \cap [\mathcal{K}_{p,L}, \mathcal{K}_{p,U}] \neq \emptyset$.

Assumption 4.2.2 Let $z_{(1)}, \ldots, z_{(n)}$ be the order statistic of $z_1, \ldots, z_n$, and $F(x)$ be the CDF of $f^*(x)$. As $n \to \infty$, (i) $\max_{i \leq n-1} F(z_{(i+1)}) - F(z_{(i)}) \to_P 0$; (ii) $F(z_{(1)}) \to_P 0$ and $F(z_{(n)}) \to_P 1$.

Assumption 4.2.3 The density $f(x)$ and its Hermite coefficients satisfy: (i) there are $a > 0$ and $\kappa > 1$ such that $f(x) = O(\exp(-a|x|^\kappa))$ as $|x| \to \infty$; (ii) There exist $r > 0$ and $p > 0$ such that c_j in (4.2.22) satisfy $c_j = O(\exp(-pj^r))$ as $j \to \infty$.

Assumption 4.2.1 ensures the identifiability of the density in the pricing equations (4.2.16) and (4.2.17), see Lemma 1 in Lu and Qu (2021). Assumption 4.2.2 is in concert with the intuition that we need the option strikes to be dense asymptotically, and their range to cover all relevant positive out-of-the-money call and put option prices such that we can estimate the full SPD consistently.

To motivate Assumption 4.2.3, it is noted that the density $f(x)$ is defined by a Fredholm integral equation of the first kind with an unbounded support, where two kernel functions $S(\exp(\sqrt{\tau}\sigma x) - \exp(\sqrt{\tau}\sigma z))^+$ and $S(\exp(\sqrt{\tau}\sigma z) - \exp(\sqrt{\tau}\sigma x))^+$ are unbounded and are non-differentiable in x and z. For example, we may write $C(z) = \int H(z, x)f(x)dx$ with kernel function $H(z, x) = S(\exp(\sqrt{\tau}\sigma x) - \exp(\sqrt{\tau}\sigma z))^+$ that diverges for any fixed z as $x \to +\infty$. However, many asymptotic results for linear integral equations are obtained under settings where the kernel function is smooth and bounded, and the support is compact. Unfortunately, both conditions are violated with the current problem. There couldn't be any existing results that would imply our estimator's statistical properties, in particular, its rate of convergence. Fortunately, the option pricing problem has specific structures that can be exploited.

Assumption 4.2.3(i) requires imposing heavier tails than that of a normal distribution for $f(x)$ (other than $f^*(x)$). The density $f^*(x)$ does not satisfy this assumption even when the underlying asset price follows a geometric Brownian motion. As argued by Lu and Qu (2021), there are some sufficient conditions to guarantee Assumption 4.2.3(ii), but the entire conditions in Assumption 4.2.3 might be unnecessarily strong, and these could be replaced by certain differentiability at some order for $f(x)$. In particular, the decay rate of c_j should be an implication of some properties of $f(x)$.

Assumption 4.2.3(i) also rules out some heavy-tailed distributions. For example, if S_T has a Lévy distribution, i.e., $f^*(x) \sim x^{-3/2}$ as $x \to \infty$, then the SPD satisfies $f(x) \sim \exp(-\sigma\sqrt{\tau}x/2)$ as $x \to \infty$, violating the requirement $\kappa > 1$. However, because the mean of a Lévy distribution is infinite, the price of any call option with a finite strike is also infinite, casting doubt on whether such a distribution is directly useful for option pricing without any truncation.

Assumption 4.2.4 (i) (z_i, e_i) is independent of (z_j, e_j) for $i \neq j$; (ii) $\mathbb{E}(e_i) = 0$, $\mathbb{E}(e_i^2) = \sigma_i < \infty$, and e_i is independent of z_i for any i; (iii) $\max_{i>n_c} z_i = O_P(\log(n))$.

Assumption 4.2.5 As $n \to \infty$, (i) $\log(n)/k^r + k/n^{1/5} \to 0$; (ii) $\gamma = O_P(n^\nu), 0 < \nu < \infty$, where $\gamma = [\beta'(n^{-1}\sum_{i=1}^n x_i x_i')^{-1/2}\beta]^{1/2}$; (iii) $\alpha/n \to 0$; (iv) $\eta < 0$ and η is independent of n.

Assumption 4.2.4(i) is commonly encountered in the literature. Assumption 4.2.4(ii) allows for heteroskedasticity. Assumption 4.2.4(iii) ensures that the integral on $(-\infty, \infty)$ in $x_{i,j}$ right below (4.2.25) can be adequately approximated by $\int_{-\log(n)}^{\log(n)}$; it is for put options only. The detailed discussion on Assumption 4.2.4(iii) can be found in Lu and Qu (2021).

Assumption 4.2.5(i) requires the truncation order k to increase faster than $[\log(n)]^{1/r}$ to ensure that the bias from the Hermite series approximation is asymptotically negligible. Assumption 4.2.5(ii) imposes an upper bound on the decay

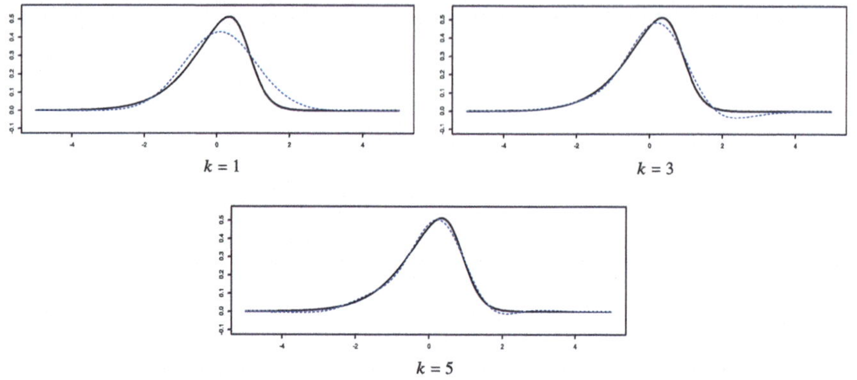

Fig. 4.1 Density is for the transformed variable x (crisis). Solid and dashed lines represent the true density and the approximation, respectively

rate of the Hermite coefficients relative to the eigenspace of $n^{-1}\sum_{i=1}^{n} x_i x_i^\top$. The parameter γ is related to, but different from, the sieve measure of ill-posedness τ_n defined in Blundell et al. (2007). To see this, let $\lambda_{\min}$ denote the smallest eigenvalue of $n^{-1}\sum_{i=1}^{n} x_i x_i^\top$, while let $u_{j\ell}$ be the (j, ℓ)th element of $(n^{-1}\sum_{i=1}^{n} x_i x_i^\top)^{-1/2}$. Then, $\gamma = (\sum_{j,\ell=1}^{k} u_{j\ell} c_{j-1} c_{\ell-1})^{1/2}$ and $\tau_n = \lambda_{\min}^{1/2}$. Under Assumption 4.2.3, $c_j \sim \exp(-pj^r)$, γ may diverge very much slower than $\lambda_{\min}^{-1/4}$ as $k \to \infty$. By imposing a restriction on γ, instead of on τ_n, this assumption allows the inverse problem to be severely ill-posed, as long as γ decays at the rate $O(k^\nu)$ for some $\nu > 0$.

The parameter α in Assumption 4.2.5(iii) appears in the regularization matrix Q_α that is given by either $Q_\alpha = \alpha I$ or $Q_\alpha = V D_\alpha V^\top$ discussed previously. These conditions in Assumption 4.2.5(ii) and (iii) determine the properties of Q_α, allowing us to derive the convergence rate. Finally, Assumption 4.2.5(iv) implies that the effect of η on the estimator $\widehat{f}(x)$ is negligible asymptotically.

Theorem 4.2.1 *Under Assumptions 4.2.1–4.2.5, for any $x \in \mathbb{R}$, we have*

$$\widehat{f}(x) - f(x) = O_P\left(\sqrt[4]{\frac{\alpha}{n}}\, k^{1/2+\nu} + \sqrt{\frac{k}{\alpha}}\right), \tag{4.2.29}$$

where the first term in the parentheses reflects the bias caused by the Tikhonov regularization

$$B(x) = -\mathbb{E}\left[h(x)^\top \left(\sum_{i=1}^{n} x_i x_i^\top + Q_\alpha\right)^{-1} Q_\alpha \beta\right],$$

where $h(x) = (\mathscr{H}_0(x), \ldots, \mathscr{H}_{k-1}(x))^\top$. □

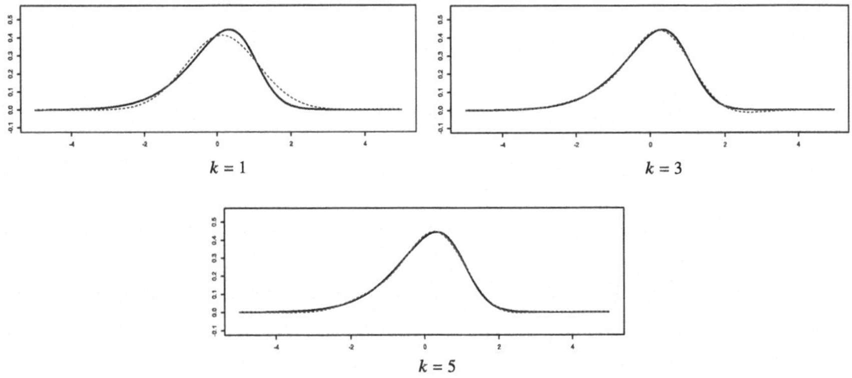

Fig. 4.2 Density is for the transformed variable x (expansion). Solid and dashed lines represent the true density and the approximation, respectively

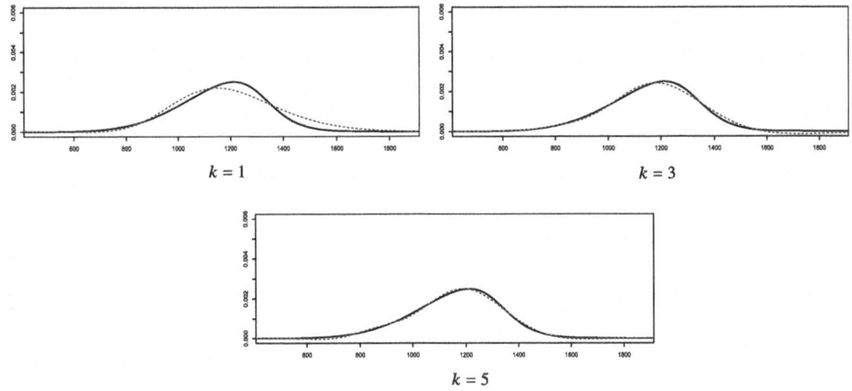

Fig. 4.3 Density is for original S (crisis). Solid and dashed lines represent the true density and the approximation, respectively

The proof can be found in Lu and Qu (2021). Notice that, by letting $k \sim (\log(n))^{1/r+c_1}$ for some finite c_1 and $\alpha = n^{c_2}$ with $2/7 < c_2 < 1/3$, we have $\widehat{f}(x) - f(x) = O_P(n^{-1/7})$. This rate corresponds to the optimal convergence rate when estimating the second-order derivative of a smooth function using a second-order polynomial and a second-order kernel.

To verify the effect of this estimation, the following stochastic volatility model with contemporaneous jumps in return and volatility (SVCJ) is used,

$$\frac{dS_t}{S_t} = r_t dt + \sqrt{V_t} dW_t + \left(e^{Z_t^s} - 1\right) dN_t - \lambda \bar{\mu} dt,$$
$$dV_t = \kappa(\theta - V_t)dt + \sigma_v \sqrt{V_t} dB_t + Z_t^v dN_t,$$

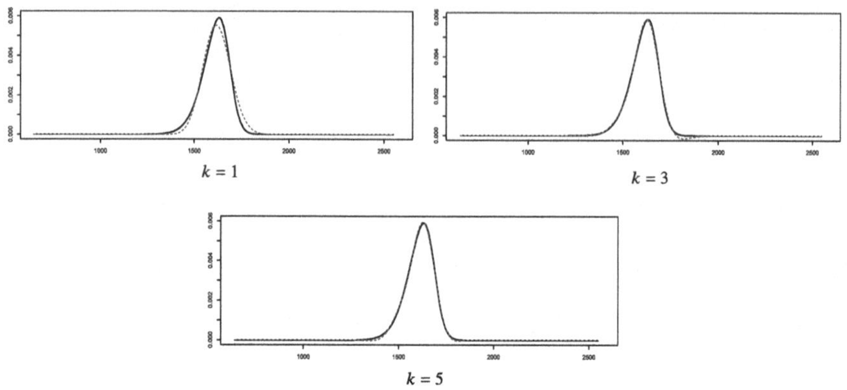

Fig. 4.4 Density is for original S (expansion). Solid and dashed lines represent the true density and the approximation, respectively

because Duffie et al. (2000) show that the SPDs implied by the SVCJ models have closed-form expressions (up to numerical integration).

The dataset used is drawn from the following two periods.

- Crisis period: 2008.10–2009.4
- Expansion period: 2013.6–2013.12.

The following are densities for original state price density and its estimates, and all pictures in Figs. 4.1, 4.2, 4.3 and 4.4 are taken from Lu and Qu (2021).

This chapter reviews the history of density estimation that actually is the start of nonparametric estimation. Though having been developed more than half century, the theory and applications are still active topics in contemporary economics and finance as well as related areas, while enormous challenges from big data have emerged.

References

Aït-Sahalia, Y. (2002). Maximum likelihood estimation of discretely sampled diffusions: A closed-form approximation approach. *Econometrica, 70*, 223–262.

Aït-Sahalia, Y. (2008). Closed-form likelihood expansions for multivariate diffusions. *Annals of Statistics, 36*, 906–937.

Aït-Sahalia, Y., Li, C., & Li, C. (2024). Maximum likelihood estimation of latent Markov models using closed-form approximations. *Journal of Econometrics, 240*, 105008.

Anderson, G. L., & Figueiredo, R. J. P. D. (1980). An adaptive orthogonal-series estimator for probability density functions. *The Annals of Statistics, 8*, 347–376.

Barletta, A., de Magistris, P. S., & Violante, F. (2019). A non-structural investigation of VIX risk neutral density. *Journal of Banking and Finance, 99*, 1–20.

Blundell, R., Chen, X., & Christensen, D. (2007). Semi-nonparametric IV esstimation of shape-invariant Engel curves. *Econometrica, 75*, 1613–1669.

Cheng, M., & Fan, J. (2016). Peter Hall's contributions to nonparametric function estimation and modeling. *The Annals of Statistics, 44*, 1837–1853.

Dong, C., Gao, J., & Tjøstheim, D. (2016). Estimation for single-index and partially linear single-index integrated models. *Annals of Statistics, 44*, 425–453.

Duffie, D., Pan, J., & Singleton, K. (2000). Transform analysis and asset pricing for affine jump-diffusions. *Econometrica, 68*, 1343–1376.

Fenton, V. M., & Gallant, A. R. (1996). Convergence rates of SNP density estimators. *Econometrica, 64*, 719–727.

Filipovic, D., Mayerhofer, E., & Schneider, P. (2013). Density approximations for multivariate affine jump-diffusion processes. *Journal of Econometrics, 176*, 93–111.

Gallant, A. R., & Nychka, D. W. (1987). Semi-nonparametric maximum likelihood estimation. *Econometrica, 55*, 363–390.

Gallant, A. R., & Tauchen, G. (1989). Seminonparametric estimation of conditionally constrained heterogeneous processes: Asset pricing applications. *Econometrica, 57*, 1091–1120.

Greblicki, W., & Pawlak, M. (1984). Hermite series estimates of a probability density and its derivatives. *Journal of Multivariate Analysis, 15*, 174–182.

Greblicki, W., & Pawlak, M. (1985). Pointwise consistency of the Hermite series density estimate. *Statistics & Probability Letters, 3*, 65–69.

Hall, P. (1981a). On trigonometric series estimates of densities. *Annals of Statistics,9*, 683–685.

Hall, P. (1981b). Laws of the iterated logarithm for nonparametric density estimators. *Zeitschrift für Wahrscheinlichkeitstheorie und verwandte Gebiete,56*, 47–61.

Hall, P. (1980). Estimating a density on the positive half line by the method of orthogonal series. *Annals of the Institute of Statistical Mathematics, 32*, 351–362.

Hall, P. (1982). Comparison of two orthogonal series methods of estimating a density and its derivatives on an interval. *Journal of Multivariate Analysis, 12*, 432–449.

Hall, P. (1984). Central limit theorem for integrated square error of multivariate nonparametric density estimators. *Journal of Multivariate Analysis, 14*, 1–16.

Hall, P. (1986). On the rate of convergence of orthogonal series density estimators. *Journal of the Royal Statistical Society Series B, 48*, 115–122.

Ibrahim, E., Gallant, A. R., & Souza, G. (1983). An elasticity can be estimated consistently without a priori knowledge of functional form. *Econometrica, 51*, 1731–1751.

Kronmal, R., & Tarter, M. (1968). The estimation of probability densities and cumulatives by fourier series methods. *Journal of the American Statistical Association, 63*, 925–952.

Laurent, B. (1996). Efficient estimation of integral functionals of a density. *Annals of Statistics, 24*, 659–681.

León, Ángel., Mencía, J., & Sentana, E. (2009). Parametric properties of semi-nonparametric distributions with applications to option valuation. *Journal of Business & Economic Statistics, 27*, 176–192.

Lu, J., & Qu, Z. (2021). Sieve estimation of option-implied state price density. *Journal of Econometrics, 224*, 88–112.

Necula, C., Drimus, G., & Farkas, W. (2019). A general closed form option pricing formula. *Review of Derivatives Research, 22*, 1–40.

Rosenblatt, M. (1956). Remarks on some nonparametric estimates of a density function. *Annals of Mathematical Statistics, 27*, 832–837.

Sansone, G. (1959). *Orthogonal functions*. Pure and applied mathematics. New York: Interscience Publishers Inc.

Schwartz, S. (1967). Estimation of probability density by an orthogonal series. *The Annals of Mathematical Statistics, 38*, 1261–1265.

Silverman, B. W. (1982). On the estimation of a probability density function by the maximum penalized likelihood method. *Annals of Statistics, 10*, 795–810.

Szego, G. (1975). *Orthogonal polynomials*. Providence, Rhode Island: Colloquium Publications XXIII, American Mathematical Association.

Tarter, M., & Kronmal, R. (1970). On multivariate density estimates based on orthogonal expansions. *The Annals of Mathematical Statistics, 41*, 718–722.

van der Marel, R. P., & Franx, M. (1993). A new method for the identification of non-Gaussian line profiles in elliptical galaxies. *The Astrophsical Journal, 407*, 525–539.

Wahba, G. (1975). Optimal convergence properties of variable knot, kernel, and orthogonal series methods for density estimation. *Annals of Statistics, 3*, 15–29.

Walter, G. (1977). Properties of Hermite series estimation of probability density. *Annals of Statistics, 5*, 1258–1264.

Watson, G. S. (1969). Density estimation by orthogonal series. *The Annals of Mathematical Statistics, 40*, 1496–1498.

Wu, X. (2010). Exponential series estimator of multivariate densities. *Journal of Econometrics, 156*, 354–366.

Xiu, D. (2014). Hermite polynomial based expansion of European option prices. *Journal of Econometrics, 179*, 158–177.

Chapter 5
Partially Linear Single-Index Regression Models

As a special case of partially linear single-index models, the semiparametric single-index model has been an important tool for practitioners to analyze data with both linear and nonlinear features. By virtue of a linear index and a nonparametric link function, the model circumvents the "curse of dimensionality" but maintains the flexibility to capture possible nonlinear relationships. The estimation of the index parameter and the nonparametric function has been intensively studied in the literature. This includes the semiparametric (profile) least square estimator (Härdle et al., 1993; Ichimura, 1993), the maximum quasi-likelihood estimator (Klein & Spady, 1993), the average derivative estimator (Härdle & Stocker, 1989; Power et al., 1989), the minimum average variance estimator (Xia et al., 2002), the penalized spline estimator (Yu & Ruppert, 2002; Ma et al., 2014), and the estimating function method (Cui et al., 2011), to cite a few.

With an extra linear part added into single-index models, partially linear single-index models draw considerable attentions from the researchers and practitioners and are studied extensively in the literature. See, for example, Carroll et al. (1997), Xia et al. (1999), Yu and Ruppert (2002), Zhu and Xue (2006), Liang et al. (2010), Lin and Kulasekera (2007), Ma and Zhu (2013), Chen et al. (2013), Ma et al. (2014), Huang et al. (2019), Lin et al. (2022), and Cai and Wang (2023). This is because a partially linear single-index model on the one hand can compensate the shortcomings of linear model such as misspecification, and on the other hand adds more element to single-index model. The partially linear single-index models can be viewed as a reasonable compromise between fully parametric and fully nonparametric modeling since they include parametric linear function and at the same time can achieve dimension reduction.

Moreover, in the last two decades or so, nonlinear (nonparametric or semiparametric) and nonstationary time series models have been studied extensively in the relevant literature, such as those based on nonparametric kernel methods by Karlsen and Tjøstheim (2001), Karlsen et al. (2007), Gao et al. (2009a, b), Phillips (2009),

C. Dong and J. Gao, *Modern Series Methods in Econometrics and Statistics*,
Advanced Studies in Theoretical and Applied Econometrics 45,
https://doi.org/10.1007/978-981-96-2822-3_5

Wang and Phillips (2009a, b, 2012), Gao (2012), Gao and Phillips (2013), Phillips et al. (2017), and series method-driven approaches by Dong et al. (2016), Dong and Linton (2018) and Zhou et al. (2024), among others. The main development in the field is the establishment of new estimation and specification testing procedures as well as the resulting asymptotic properties. Therefore, it is well worth studying single-index models and partially single-index models in the field of nonstationary time series.

5.1 Single-Index Models

As discussed in Ichimura (1993), a semiparametric single-index model takes the form

$$y_i = g(h(x_i, \theta_0)) + e_i, \quad i = 1, \ldots, n, \tag{5.1.1}$$

where $x_i \in \mathbb{R}^L$, $\theta_0 \in \mathbb{R}^M$, $h : \mathcal{X} \times \Theta \mapsto \mathbb{R}$, $\mathcal{X} \subset \mathbb{R}^L$, $\Theta \subset \mathbb{R}^M$, $h(\cdot, \cdot)$ is known up to θ_0, while $g(\cdot)$ is unknown. In the literature, θ_0 is called the index vector and $g(\cdot)$ is the link function to the single-index model.

Because $g(\cdot)$ is unknown, model (5.1.1) is semiparametric; otherwise, the model is a parametrically nonlinear model, and θ_0 can be estimated by nonlinear least squares under some regularity conditions. An example that leads to a single-index model is a latent dependent variable model where one does not observe y^* but y that is a transformation of y^*,

$$y^* = h(x, \theta_0) + v, \qquad y = \tau(y^*).$$

When τ is specified as

$$\tau(u) = \begin{cases} u, & \text{if } u > 0, \\ 0, & \text{if } u \leq 0, \end{cases}$$

the model becomes a censored Tobit model; when τ is specified as

$$\tau(u) = \begin{cases} 1, & \text{if } u > 0, \\ 0, & \text{if } u \leq 0, \end{cases}$$

the model reduces to a binary choice model. Anyway, if x and v are independent, and either the function $\tau(\cdot)$ or the distribution function of v is not specified, the mean regression $\mathbb{E}(y|x)$ is phrased as a semiparametric single-index model

$$\mathbb{E}(y|x) = \int \tau(h(x, \theta_0) + v) dF_v(v), \tag{5.1.2}$$

where $F_v(\cdot)$ is the distribution function of v.

Since the most popular choice for $h(\cdot, \cdot)$ is $h(x, \theta) = x^\top \theta$, more often than not, when talking about single-index models, it means

$$y_i = g(x_i^\top \theta_0) + e_i, \qquad i = 1, \ldots, n. \tag{5.1.3}$$

5.1.1 Identifiability

Before estimating model (5.1.3), one important issue is its identifiability. That is, under which conditions there are unique θ_0 and $g(\cdot)$ such that model (5.1.3) is identifiable and estimable. Intuitively, because $g(\cdot)$ is unknown, we should restrict θ_0, otherwise $g(x^\top \theta_0) = f(x^\top \tilde{\theta})$ for all x where $\tilde{\theta} = \theta_0 / \|\theta_0\|$ and $f(u) = g(\|\theta_0\| u)$ for all $u \in \mathbb{R}$. Thus, unknown pair (θ_0, g) takes the same role as unknown pair $(\tilde{\theta}, f)$ in the regression, and when $\|\theta_0\| \neq 1$, the two pairs are definitely different. In this case, we do not know which vector θ_0 and function $g(\cdot)$ we are about to estimate.

Lemma 5.1.1 *Let $m(x) = \mathbb{E}(y|x)$ be the mean function of y given x, and S be the support of $m(x)$ that is bounded and convex with at least one interior point. Suppose that for some unit vectors θ and β, of which the first nonzero elements are positive,*

$$m(x) = g(x^\top \theta) = f(x^\top \beta), \ \ \forall x \in S,$$

where $m(x)$ is continuous and non-constant. If $g(\cdot)$ and $f(\cdot)$ are continuous, then $\theta = \beta$ and $g = f$ on $\{x^\top \theta : x \in S\}$.

Proof It suffices to show $\theta = \beta$ since $f = g$ is a consequence.

Suppose $\theta \neq \beta$. Because $m(x)$ is continuous and non-constant, there exists a point $x_0 \in S$ and a neighborhood of x_0, $B = B(x_0, r) \subset S$, such that $m(x)$ is non-constant on B. Notice that $\|\theta\| = 1$, and hence for any $u \in (-r, r)$, $x_0 + u\theta \in B$. It follows that

$$g(x_0^\top \theta + u) = g(\theta^\top (x_0 + u\theta)) = f(\beta^\top (x_0 + u\theta)) = f(\beta^\top x_0 + u\beta^\top \theta),$$

and similarly,

$$f(x_0^\top \beta + u) = g(\theta^\top x_0 + u\beta^\top \theta).$$

Since the first nonzero elements of θ and β are positive, $\theta \neq -\beta$, and hence $|\theta^\top \beta| < 1$. Moreover, by recursion m times,

$$\begin{aligned} g(x_0^\top \theta + u) &= f(\beta^\top x_0 + u\beta^\top \theta) = g(\theta^\top x_0 + u(\beta^\top \theta)^2) = \cdots \\ &= g(\theta^\top x_0 + u(\beta^\top \theta)^m). \end{aligned}$$

Letting $m \to \infty$, we have $g(x_0^\top \theta + u) = g(x_0^\top \theta)$ for any $u \in (-r, r)$.

Now, for any $x \in B(x_0, r)$, $x = x_0 + u\gamma$ where $\|\gamma\| = 1$ and $u \in (-r, r)$. Thus, $m(x) = g(x^\top\theta) = g(x_0^\top\theta + u\gamma^\top\theta) = g(x_0^\top\theta)$, and this contradicts to the condition that $m(x)$ is non-constant on B. Therefore, $\theta = \beta$. □

The proof of the lemma is attributed to Lin and Kulasekera (2007). This lemma provides a theoretical verification of the most popular identification condition for single-index models in the literature, that is, $\|\theta_0\| = 1$ and the first nonzero element of θ_0 is positive. Notice also that another popular identification condition is that the first nonzero element of θ_0 is one. See Dong et al. (2015, 2016).

5.1.2 Estimation of Single-Index Models

Notice that the variation of y in model (5.1.3) normally comes from the variations of $x^\top\theta_0$ and e, while on the contour $x^\top\theta_0 = c$ it only results from e; however, on the contour line $x^\top\theta = c$ with $\theta \neq \theta_0$, the variation of y again comes from the variations of $x^\top\theta$ and e. Thus, the conditional variance

$$\mathrm{Var}(y|x^\top\theta) = \mathbb{E}\{[y - \mathbb{E}(y|x^\top\theta)]^2|x^\top\theta\}$$

measures the variation of y on each contour line $x^\top\theta = c$. Accordingly, Ichimura (1993) constructs an objective function from the sample analog of

$$\mathbb{E}\{w(x)[y - \mathbb{E}(y|x^\top\theta)]^2\},$$

where $w(x)$ is a weighting function and $\mathbb{E}(y|x^\top\theta)$ is replaced by its kernel estimator, and then define the estimator $\widehat{\theta}$ of θ_0 as the minimizer of the objective function. The consistency and the asymptotic normality of $\widehat{\theta}$ are both established, and the choice of $w(x)$ that achieves semiparametric efficiency bound is discussed as well in Ichimura (1993); nevertheless, the author does not show the estimator of the link function, let alone its asymptotics.

In model (5.1.3), moreover, let $\mathbb{E}(e|x) = 0$, and denote $G(x) = \mathbb{E}(y|x) = g(x^\top\theta_0)$. Here, we use x to signify both random regressor and its realization. Then

$$\nabla G(x) = \frac{\partial}{\partial x}G(x) = \frac{\partial}{\partial x}g(x^\top\theta_0) = g'(x^\top\theta_0)\theta_0.$$

Therefore, the derivative or gradient of the regression function at any point has the same direction as θ_0. Based on this observation, Härdle and Stocker (1989) and Power et al. (1989) propose to estimate θ_0 by $\mathbb{E}[\nabla G(x)]$, the so-called average derivative estimation (ADE) method. Let $f(x)$ be the density of x. Integration by parts gives

$$\mathbb{E}[\nabla G(x)] = -\mathbb{E}[y\nabla \log(f(x))].$$

Thus, instead of estimating $\nabla G(x)$, Härdle and Stocker (1989) and Power et al. (1989) propose to estimate $\ell(x) = \nabla \log(f(x))$ by high-order kernel smoothers. Because the nonparametric estimator of a high-dimensional density function is used, the ADE procedure still suffers from the "curse of dimensionality". Another disadvantage for the method is that when $\mathbb{E}[g'(x^\top\theta_0)] = 0$, the method gives a result in vain, since

$$\mathbb{E}[\nabla G(x)] = \mathbb{E}[g'(x^\top\theta_0)]\theta_0 = 0.$$

To circumvent this drawback, consider the outer product

$$\mathbb{E}[\nabla G(x)\nabla^\top G(x)] = \mathbb{E}[g'(x^\top\theta_0)]^2\theta_0\theta_0^\top,$$

that has one eigenvalue other than zero, whose corresponding eigenvector can be the estimator for θ_0. Xia (2006) uses this idea to estimate the gradients by local linear smoothing firstly, and then formulate the estimate of $\mathbb{E}[\nabla G(x)\nabla^\top G(x)]$ from which the estimator of θ_0 is defined to be its first eigenvector.

Recently, Dong et al. (2015) propose a single-index model for panel dataset of the form:

$$y_{it} = g(x_{it}^\top\theta_0) + \gamma_i + e_{it}, \quad t = 1, \ldots, T, \ i = 1, \ldots, N, \tag{5.1.4}$$

where $g \in L^2(\mathbb{R}, \exp(-x^2/2))$ is an unknown link function, x_{it} is of d dimension, γ_i is an individual effect that is allowed to be correlated with the regressors, and e_{it} is the error term. The aim therein is to estimate the index vector and link function.

As shown in Appendix C, Hilbert space $L^2(\mathbb{R}, \exp(-x^2/2))$ has Hermite polynomial system $\{H_j(x)\}$ as its orthogonal basis. Thus, the link function $g(\cdot)$ has orthogonal expansion

$$g(u) = \sum_{j=0}^{\infty} c_j h_j(u), \tag{5.1.5}$$

where $h_j(u) = H_j(u)/\sqrt{j!}$ that form an orthonormal sequence. Because θ_0 is a unit vector, by virtue of the property of Hermite polynomials it follows that, for a positive integer k,

$$\begin{aligned} g(x_{it}^\top\theta_0) &= \sum_{j=0}^{k-1} c_j h_j(x_{it}^\top\theta_0) + \sum_{j=k}^{\infty} c_j h_j(x_{it}^\top\theta_0) \\ &= \sum_{j=0}^{k-1}\sum_{|p|=j} a_{jp}(\theta_0)\mathcal{H}_p(x_{it}) + \delta_k(x_{it}^\top\theta_0) \end{aligned} \tag{5.1.6}$$

where $\delta_k(\cdot)$ is the truncation residue, $p = (p_1, \ldots, p_d)$ with components of nonnegative integers, and

$$a_{jp}(\theta_0) = c_j \sqrt{\binom{j}{p}} \theta_0^p, \qquad \theta_0 = (\theta_{01}, \ldots, \theta_{0d}), \ \ \theta_0^p = \theta_{01}^{p_1} \ldots \theta_{0d}^{p_d}$$

$$\mathcal{H}_p(x_{it}) = \prod_{\ell=1}^{d} h_{p_\ell}(x_{it,\ell}), \qquad \binom{j}{p} = \frac{j!}{p_1! \ldots p_d!}, \quad |p| = p_1 + \cdots + p_d.$$

The expansion of (5.1.6) separates x_{it} from θ_0 that allows to obtain a closed-form estimates, $\widehat{a}_{jp}$, of the coefficients $a_{jp}(\theta_0)$. However, since $a_{jp}(\theta_0)$ is the product of unknowns c_j and θ_0^p, one has to derive all estimates of $\widehat{c}_j$ and $\widehat{\theta}$ from $\widehat{a}_{jp}$, $j = 0, 1, \ldots, k-1$ and $|p| = j$ over all possible j. Fortunately, this is not very much difficult given the structure of $\widehat{a}_{jp}$. To see this, let $j = 1$. Then, all possible vectors p are $(1, 0, \ldots, 0)$, …, $(0, \ldots, 0, 1)$, and the corresponding terms in (5.1.6) are in the sum $c_1 x_{it}^\top \theta_0$. After algebra, one obtains all $\widehat{c}_j$ and $\widehat{\theta}$, and naturally define the estimator of the link function as

$$\widehat{g}(u) = \sum_{j=0}^{k-1} \widehat{c}_j h_j(u). \tag{5.1.7}$$

The convergence rate of $\widehat{\theta}$ is $1/\sqrt{NT}$, a parametric rate, while $\widehat{g}(u)$ has a conventional nonparametric rate; see Dong et al. (2015) for details.

Though appealing, the expansion of (5.1.6) as a partial sum of the orthogonal expansion has a drawback that increases the number of the terms drastically. In this case, the cardinality of the set $\{a_{jp}(\theta_0), \ |p| = j, j = 0, 1, \ldots, k-1\}$ is $O(k^d)$. It follows that when $d \geq 5$, it is impossible to use this strategy in the estimation since normally k is required to be $O(n^{1/5})$ in series estimation. This fact motivates Dong and Tu (2024) to study single-index regression under setting of increasing dimension of θ_0 and sparsity, and this study achieves variable selection in sparse single-index models using LASSO methodology.

5.2 Single-Index Models with Nonstationarity

As mentioned before, asymptotic theory for nonstationary time series has developed considerably in the last two decades or so. In the literature, however, most researchers only focus on the stationarity case so that their theoretical results are not applicable for such practitioners who use single-index models to deal with nonstationary time series data. For example, in macroeconomic context, practitioners may be concerned with inflation, unemployment rates, and other economic indicators. These variables exhibit nonstationary characteristics. Therefore, it is desirable in such circumstances to develop estimation theory for such single-index models associated with nonstationarity.

In earlier stages, two papers related to nonstationary single-index models are Chang and Park (2003) and Guerre and Moon (2006) in terms of the regressors being nonstationary. Chang and Park (2003) stipulate that

$$y_t = F(x_t, \theta_0) + e_t \tag{5.2.1}$$

with the regression function F further specified as

$$F(x, \theta) = \mu + p(x, \alpha) + q(x, \alpha)G(\nu + x^\top \beta), \tag{5.2.2}$$

where $\{x_t\}$ is a d-dimensional integrated process of order one, $\theta = (\mu, \alpha^\top, \nu, \beta^\top)^\top$ is a vector of parameters and $\theta_0 = (\mu_0, \alpha_0^\top, \nu_0, \beta_0^\top)^\top$ is the true but unknown vector in (5.2.1), both $p(x, \alpha)$ and $q(x, \alpha)$ are linear functionals on $\mathbb{R}^d$. The nonlinear part of the regression function F is specified as an index model with G, which is assumed to be a smooth distribution function-like transformation on $\mathbb{R}$. The model is purely parametrically nonlinear and is therefore not semiparametric.

Guerre and Moon (2006) study a binary choice model of the form:

$$y_t = \tau(y_t^*), \quad y_t^* = x_t^\top \beta_0 + u_t, \quad t = 1, \ldots, n, \tag{5.2.3}$$

where $\tau(x) = 1$ if $x \geq 0$ and 0 otherwise, x_t is d-dimensional I(1) process and u_t is an error term with unknown distribution. Let $\mathcal{F}_t$ be a sequence of Sigma fields and $F(\cdot)$ be the distribution of $-u_t$ given $\mathcal{F}_{t-1}$. Then,

$$\mathbb{E}(y_t|\mathcal{F}_{t-1}) = \mathbb{P}(y_t = 1|\mathcal{F}_{t-1}) = \mathbb{P}(-u_t \leq x_t^\top \beta_0|\mathcal{F}_{t-1}) = F(x_t^\top \beta_0).$$

Thus, we have $y_t = F(x_t^\top \beta_0) + \varepsilon_t$, a semiparametric single-index model. Guerre and Moon (2006) point out in the discussion section that their method developed for binary choice models may be applicable for the estimation of single-index models where the link function $g(x) \to \infty$ as $|x| \to \infty$.

More recently, when the regressor x_t is an I(1) process, Zhou et al. (2024) study a semiparametric single-index predictive regression of the form: $y_t = g_0(\theta_0^\top x_{t-1}) + e_t$, where θ_0 is the cointegrating coefficients of x_t, viz., $\theta_0^\top x_{t-1}$ is I(0). Under this setting and regularity conditions, the authors obtain the super-n convergence rate for the series estimator of θ_0.

We now consider a single-index model of the form:

$$y_t = g(\theta_0^\top x_t) + e_t, \quad t = 1, \ldots, n, \tag{5.2.4}$$

where y_t is a scalar process, the link function $g(\cdot)$ is an unknown nonlinear integrable function from $\mathbb{R}$ to $\mathbb{R}$, θ_0 is the true but unknown d-dimensional column vector of parameters, x_t is a d-dimensional integrated process, and e_t is an error process and n is sample size. Here, the link function is a generic function in $L^2(\mathbb{R})$ and model (5.2.4) is a cornerstone for the consequent study on partial linear single-index models.

Following the existing identifiability condition, we assume that $\|\theta_0\| = 1$ and the first component of θ_0 is positive. To facilitate the theoretical development in the following sections, we assume that θ_0 is an interior point located within a compact and convex parameter space Θ. To focus on the nonstationary case, we also assume throughout that the index component $x_t^\top \theta_0$ is still nonstationary. In other words, there exists a neighborhood of θ_0, $\mathcal{N}(\theta_0, \delta) \subset \Theta$, such that for any $\theta \in \mathcal{N}(\theta_0, \delta)$, $\theta^\top x_t$ is always an $I(1)$ process.

5.2.1 Estimation Procedure

Suppose that in model (5.2.4) the link function $g(\cdot) \in L^2(\mathbb{R})$, wherein the Hermite function sequence $\{\mathscr{H}_i(x)\}$ is an orthonormal basis. Thus, the function $g(\cdot)$ may be expanded into an orthogonal series,

$$g(x) = \sum_{i=0}^{\infty} c_i \mathscr{H}_i(x) \quad \text{and} \quad c_i = \int g(x)\mathscr{H}_i(x)dx. \tag{5.2.5}$$

Let k be a positive integer and define $g_k(x) = \sum_{i=0}^{k-1} c_i \mathscr{H}_i(x)$ as the truncation series and $\gamma_k(x) = \sum_{i=k}^{\infty} c_i \mathscr{H}_i(x)$ as the residue after truncation.

By virtue of (5.2.5) we write model (5.2.4) for $t = 1, \ldots, n$ as,

$$y_t = Z_k^\top(\theta_0^\top x_t)c + \gamma_k(\theta_0^\top x_t) + e_t,$$

where $Z_k^\top(\cdot) = (\mathscr{H}_0(\cdot), \ldots, \mathscr{H}_{k-1}(\cdot))$, $c^\top = (c_0, \ldots, c_{k-1})$ and k is the truncation parameter determined later.

Let $Y = (y_1, \ldots, y_n)^\top$, $Z = (Z_k(\theta_0^\top x_1), \ldots, Z_k(\theta_0^\top x_n))^\top$ an $n \times k$ matrix, $\gamma = (\gamma_k(\theta_0^\top x_1), \ldots, \gamma_k(\theta_0^\top x_n))^\top$ and $e = (e_1, \ldots, e_n)^\top$. Thereby, we have a matrix form equation

$$Y = Zc + \gamma + e$$

and hence by the OLS (ordinary least squares) method,

$$\widetilde{c} = \widetilde{c}(\theta_0) = (Z^\top Z)^{-1} Z^\top Y$$

is an estimator for c in terms of θ_0. Nonetheless, since θ_0 is unknown, $\widetilde{c}$ is infeasible and we only have a form of $\widetilde{c}$.

To estimate θ_0, define for $\theta \in \Theta$, $L_n(\theta) = \frac{1}{2}\sum_{t=1}^{n}[y_t - Z_k^\top(\theta^\top x_t)\widetilde{c}(\theta)]^2$. Then, we choose an optimum $\widehat{\theta}_n$ such that

$$\widehat{\theta}_n = \operatorname*{argmin}_{\theta \in \Theta} L_n(\theta), \tag{5.2.6}$$

as an estimator for θ_0. Once $\widehat{\theta}_n$ is available, we have a plug-in estimator

$$\widehat{g}_n(u) \equiv \widehat{g}_n(u; \widehat{\theta}_n) = Z_k(u)^\top \widehat{c}, \qquad \text{with } \widehat{c} = \widetilde{c}(\widehat{\theta}_n), \tag{5.2.7}$$

for any $u \in \mathbb{R}$, which is purely based on the sample and hence applicable. The estimation procedure proposed here is the so-called profile method (see, Severini & Wong, 1992; Liang et al., 2010).

Additionally, we define a normalized version of $\widehat{\theta}_n$ by $\widehat{\theta}_{n,\text{emp}} = \|\widehat{\theta}_n\|^{-1}\widehat{\theta}_n$ that satisfies the identification condition $\|\theta_0\| = 1$. Before we establish an asymptotic theory for $\widehat{\theta}_{n,\text{emp}}$ and $\widehat{\theta}_n$, we introduce the integrated processes that will be used frequently in the sequel in vector or scalar form.

Definition 5.2.1 (Integrated process) The regressor x_t used in what follows is an integrated process if $x_t = x_{t-1} + v_t$ for $t \geq 1$ and $x_0 = O_P(1)$, where $\{v_t\}$ is a linear process defined by $v_t = \sum_{j=0}^{\infty} \rho_j \varepsilon_{t-j}$, in which $\{\varepsilon_j, -\infty < j < \infty\}$ is a sequence of d-dimensional independent and identically distributed (i.i.d.) continuous random variables with $\mathbb{E}\varepsilon_1 = 0$, $\{\rho_j\}$ is a sequence of square matrices such that $\rho_0 = I_d$, $\sum_{j=0}^{\infty} j\|\rho_j\| < \infty$ and $\rho = \sum_{j=0}^{\infty}\rho_j$ is of full rank. Here, $\|\cdot\|$ is the norm of a matrix in element-wise sense. □

The integrated regressor x_t such defined is generated by a linear process v_t which has the i.i.d. sequence $\{\varepsilon_j, -\infty < j < \infty\}$ as building blocks. This is frequently used in the literature. See Park and Phillips (2000), Wang and Phillips (2009a, b, 2012), Gao et al. (2009a, b), Dong et al. (2016, 2021), Dong and Linton (2018), Dong and Gao (2018), Lin et al. (2020), among others. Because $\Delta x_t = v_t$ is stationary, usually we say that x_t is an I(1) process.

Meanwhile, asymptotic behaviors of x_t are important for the following theoretical development. Denote by L the lag operator, that is, $L\varepsilon_t = \varepsilon_{t-1}$, and also its powers are defined as $L^0 = I$ the identity operator and $L^j = L(L^{j-1})$ for $j \geq 2$. Hence, we may write

$$v_t = C(L)\varepsilon_t, \qquad C(L) \equiv \sum_{j=0}^{\infty}\rho_j L^j, \tag{5.2.8}$$

where $C(L)$ is an operator defined by the power series of the lag operator.

We then have the following symbolic calculation,

$$\begin{aligned}
C(L) = \sum_{j=0}^{\infty} \rho_j L^j &= \rho_0 I + \sum_{j=1}^{\infty} \rho_j L^j \\
&= \rho_0 I + \sum_{j=1}^{\infty} \rho_j [I + (L^j - I)] \\
&= \rho I + \sum_{j=1}^{\infty} \rho_j (L - I)(L^{j-1} + \cdots + I) \\
&= \rho I + (L - I) \sum_{j=1}^{\infty} \rho_j (L^{j-1} + \cdots + I) \\
&= \rho I + (L - I) \sum_{j=0}^{\infty} \left(\sum_{\ell=j+1}^{\infty} \rho_\ell \right) L^j \\
&\equiv \rho I + (L - I)\tilde{C}(L).
\end{aligned}$$

This for $C(L)$ is the so-called Beveridge-Nelson (BN) decomposition. See Phillips and Solo (1992, p. 972). Note that $I - L$ is the difference operator and $\tilde{C}(L)$ is the power series of the operator L. Hence,

$$v_t = C(L)\varepsilon_t = \rho\varepsilon_t + \tilde{\varepsilon}_{t-1} - \tilde{\varepsilon}_t \tag{5.2.9}$$

where $\tilde{\varepsilon}_t = \tilde{C}(L)\varepsilon_t$. Remarkably,

$$\begin{aligned}
x_t &= v_t + v_{t-1} + \cdots + v_1 + x_0 \\
&= \rho(\varepsilon_t + \cdots + \varepsilon_1) + \tilde{\varepsilon}_0 - \tilde{\varepsilon}_t + x_0.
\end{aligned} \tag{5.2.10}$$

One may show that, given $\sum_{j=0}^{\infty} j\|\rho_j\| < \infty$, we have $\sum_{j=0}^{\infty} \|\tilde{\rho}_j\| < \infty$ where $\tilde{\rho}_j = \sum_{\ell=j+1}^{\infty} \rho_\ell$. Thus, $\{\tilde{\varepsilon}_t\}$ is a stationary sequence and the nonsationarity of x_t is caused by $\rho(\varepsilon_t + \cdots + \varepsilon_1)$. It is readily seen that, letting $x_0 = 0$ a.s.,

$$\begin{aligned}
\mathbb{E}(x_t x_t^\top) &= \rho\mathbb{E}[(\varepsilon_t + \cdots + \varepsilon_1)(\varepsilon_t + \cdots + \varepsilon_1)^\top]\rho^\top \\
&\quad + \rho\mathbb{E}(\varepsilon_t + \cdots + \varepsilon_1)(\tilde{\varepsilon}_0 - \tilde{\varepsilon}_t)^\top \\
&\quad + \mathbb{E}(\tilde{\varepsilon}_0 - \tilde{\varepsilon}_t)(\varepsilon_t + \cdots + \varepsilon_1)^\top]\rho^\top \\
&\quad + \mathbb{E}(\tilde{\varepsilon}_0 - \tilde{\varepsilon}_t)(\tilde{\varepsilon}_0 - \tilde{\varepsilon}_t)^\top \\
&= t\rho\Omega\rho^\top - \Omega(\tilde{\rho}_t + \cdots + \tilde{\rho}_1)^\top \\
&\quad - (\tilde{\rho}_t + \cdots + \tilde{\rho}_1)\Omega + \mathbb{E}(\tilde{\varepsilon}_0 - \tilde{\varepsilon}_t)(\tilde{\varepsilon}_0 - \tilde{\varepsilon}_t)^\top \\
&= t\rho\Omega\rho^\top(1 + o(1)),
\end{aligned}$$

when t increases to infinity. Thus, the covariance matrix of x_t is proportional to t, and it is shown that, for $r \in [0, 1]$,

$$\frac{1}{\sqrt{n}} x_{[nr]} \to_D V(r) \tag{5.2.11}$$

in space $D[0, 1]^d$ as $n \to \infty$, where $[\cdot]$ is the biggest integer not exceeding the argument, and $V(r)$ is a Brownian motion with covariance matrix $\rho\Omega\rho^\top$. See Park and Phillips (2001). Here, $D[0, 1]^d$ is the Skorokhod space on $[0, 1]^d$, that is, the collection of functions defined on $[0, 1]^d$ that are everywhere right-continuous and have left limits everywhere. The convergence (5.2.11) is the origin of Assumption 5.7.1(e) in Sect. 5.7 for $V_n(r)$ and will be frequently used in the sequel to derive the limit theory for the estimators.

It is known that by Skorohod representation theorem (Pollard, 1984, p.71) there exists $(U_n^0(r), V_n^0(r))$ in a richer probability space such that $(U_n(r), V_n(r)) =_D (U_n^0(r), V_n^0(r))$ for which $(U_n^0(r), V_n^0(r)) \to_{a.s.} (U(r), V(r))$ uniformly on $[0, 1]^{d+1}$. To avoid the repetitious embedding procedure of $(U_n(r), V_n(r))$ to the richer probability space where $(U_n^0(r), V_n^0(r))$ is defined, we simply write $(U_n(r), V_n(r)) = (U_n^0(r), V_n^0(r))$ rather than $(U_n(r), V_n(r)) =_D (U_n^0(r), V_n^0(r))$. Notice that the theoretical results below are derived in this richer probability space, and we will not repeat this embeddedness again.

5.2.2 *Asymptotic Theory*

To derive an asymptotic theory for $\widehat{\theta}_n$ given by (5.2.6), let $S_n(\theta) = \frac{\partial}{\partial\theta} L_n(\theta)$ and $J_n(\theta) = \frac{\partial^2}{\partial\theta\partial\theta^\top} L_n(\theta)$ be the score and Hessian, respectively. As usual, we have the following expansion:

$$0 = S_n(\widehat{\theta}_n) = S_n(\theta_0) + J_n(\theta_n)(\widehat{\theta}_n - \theta_0), \tag{5.2.12}$$

where $J_n(\theta_n)$ is the Hessian matrix with the rows evaluated at a point θ_n between $\widehat{\theta}_n$ and θ_0.

To facilitate the development of an asymptotic theory, we consider coordinate rotation in $\mathbb{R}^d$. Let $Q = (\theta_0, Q_2)$ be an orthogonal matrix. Note that such Q does exist since $\theta_0 \neq 0$. We shall use the orthogonal matrix Q to rotate all vectors in $\mathbb{R}^d$. In particular,

$$\begin{aligned}
&\alpha_0 \equiv Q^\top\theta_0 = (\alpha_{10}, \alpha_{20}^\top)^\top, \text{ where } \alpha_{10} = \|\theta_0\|^2 = 1, \alpha_{20} = Q_2^\top\theta_0 = 0, \\
&z_t \equiv Q^\top x_t = (x_{1t}, x_{2t}^\top)^\top, \quad \text{where } x_{1t} \equiv \theta_0^\top x_t,\ x_{2t} \equiv Q_2^\top x_t, \\
&\alpha \equiv Q^\top\theta, \quad \text{for any generic } \theta.
\end{aligned} \tag{5.2.13}$$

Accordingly, we can rewrite the single-index model as $y_t = g(\theta_0^\top QQ^\top x_t) + e_t = g(\alpha_0^\top z_t) + e_t$. In addition, by Assumption 5.7.1 in Sect. 5.7, (5.2.11) and the continuous mapping theorem, we have, for $r \in [0, 1]$,

$$\frac{1}{\sqrt{n}} x_{1[nr]} \to_D V_1(r) = \theta_0^\top V(r), \text{ and } \frac{1}{\sqrt{n}} x_{2[nr]} \to_D V_2(r) = Q_2^\top V(r). \quad (5.2.14)$$

It is noteworthy that the rotation is not necessary in practice, as shown in the simulation section, and it is also logically impossible since θ_0 is unknown. The rotation is only used as a tool to derive an asymptotic theory for the proposed estimator.

If $\widehat{\alpha}_n$ is the nonlinear least squares estimator of α_0, then $\widehat{\alpha}_n = Q^\top \widehat{\theta}_n$. Moreover, the score function $S_n(\alpha)$ and the Hessian $J_n(\alpha)$ for the parameter α can be obtained from those for θ. More precisely, $S_n(\alpha) = Q^\top S_n(\theta)$ and $J_n(\alpha) = Q^\top J_n(\theta) Q$. Premultiplying equation (5.2.12) by $Q^\top$, we have

$$0 = S_n(\widehat{\alpha}_n) = S_n(\alpha_0) + J_n(\alpha_n)(\widehat{\alpha}_n - \alpha_0). \quad (5.2.15)$$

The following theorem, along with Assumptions 5.7.1 and 5.7.2 in Sect. 5.7, is given by Dong et al. (2016) that shows the asymptotic distributions for the score $S_n(\alpha_0)$, Hessian $J_n(\alpha_0)$ and $\widehat{\alpha}_n - \alpha_0$.

Theorem 5.2.1 *Denote $D_n = diag(n^{1/4}, n^{3/4} I_{d-1})$. Under Assumptions 5.7.1 and 5.7.2, as $n \to \infty$*

$$D_n^{-1} S_n(\alpha_0) \to_D R^{1/2} W(1) \quad \text{and} \quad D_n^{-1} J_n(\alpha_0) D_n^{-1} \to_P R, \quad (5.2.16)$$

where $W(1)$ is a d-dimensional vector of standard normal random variables independent of $V(r)$, and the symmetric block matrix $R = \begin{pmatrix} r_{11} & r_{12} \\ r_{21} & r_{22} \end{pmatrix}$ is given by

$$r_{11} = L_1(1, 0) \int s^2 \dot{g}^2(s) ds, \qquad r_{12} = \int_0^1 V_2^\top(r) dL_1(r, 0) \int s \dot{g}^2(s) ds,$$

$$r_{21} = r_{12}^\top, \qquad r_{22} = \int_0^1 V_2(r) V_2^\top(r) dL_1(r, 0) \int \dot{g}^2(s) ds,$$

in which V_1 and V_2 given by (5.2.14) are Brownian motions of dimension 1 and $d-1$, respectively, $L_1(r, 0)$ denotes the local time process of Brownian motion $V_1(\cdot)$, standing for the sojourning time of V_1 at zero over $[0, r]$.

As a result, under the same conditions, $\widehat{\alpha}_n$ is consistent and

$$D_n(\widehat{\alpha}_n - \alpha_0) \to_D R^{-1/2} W(1), \quad (5.2.17)$$

as $n \to \infty$. □

Here, the asymptotic limit depends on the local time of Brownian motion; we hereby briefly introduce it. If $W(r)$ is a standard Brownian motion, its *local time process* is defined by

$$L_W(r,a) = \lim_{\epsilon \to 0} \frac{1}{\epsilon} \int_0^r I(|W(u) - a| < \epsilon) du, \tag{5.2.18}$$

where $I(\cdot)$ is the indicator function. Note that $L_W(r, a)$ stands for the sojourn time of the process $W(\cdot)$ at the spatial point a over the time period $[0, r]$. A standard book introducing the local time process of Brownian motion is Revuz and Yor (2005).

In view of the structure of D_n, we have two limits from (5.2.17),

$$n^{1/4}(\widehat{\alpha}_{1n} - 1) \to_D \mathbf{MN}(0, \rho_{11}), \text{ and } n^{3/4}\widehat{\alpha}_{2n} \to_D \mathbf{MN}(0, \rho_{22}), \tag{5.2.19}$$

where $\widehat{\alpha}_n = (\widehat{\alpha}_{1n}, \widehat{\alpha}_{2n}^\top)^\top$, $\mathbf{MN}(0, \Xi)$ stands for mixture normal distribution for the case where the covariance matrix Ξ is stochastic, ρ_{11} and ρ_{22} are diagonal blocks on the matrix $R^{-1} = \begin{pmatrix} \rho_{11} & \rho_{12} \\ \rho_{21} & \rho_{22} \end{pmatrix}$,

$$\rho_{11} = (r_{11} - r_{12}r_{22}^{-1}r_{21})^{-1}, \quad \text{and} \quad \rho_{22} = (r_{22} - r_{21}r_{11}^{-1}r_{12})^{-1}. \tag{5.2.20}$$

Hence, $\widehat{\alpha}_n$ has two different convergence rates for its components.

Notice that $\alpha_0 = (1, 0, \ldots, 0)^\top$ is the coordinate of θ_0 under the coordinate system Q where θ_0 is an axis, and hence $\alpha_{10} = 1$ stands for the length of α_0 (also θ_0) while the vector $\alpha_{20} = (0, \ldots, 0)^\top$ represents the angles between θ_0 and each of the vectors orthogonal with θ_0. Thus, noting by (5.2.19), the estimator $\widehat{\alpha}_n$ of α_0 has dual convergence rates: the rate of the estimate for the length of α_0 (i.e. $\widehat{\alpha}_{1n}$) is $n^{-1/4}$ that is much slow, while the rate of adjustment of the angle (i.e. $\widehat{\alpha}_{2n}$) is as fast as $n^{-3/4}$. This difference in convergence rate can be explained in the following wa y. Due to the unit root behavior of $\{x_t\}$ its probability mass is spreading out in a Lebesgue type fashion. Since g is integrable, $g(\theta_0^\top x) \approx 0$ outside the effective range of g. This means that only moderate values of $\{x_t\}$ can contribute to g along θ_0, but in such directions that are orthogonal to θ_0, there is no restriction on $\{x_t\}$, so that even for far out values of $\{x_t\}$, they can contribute and hence increase the effective sample size. Certainly, no such effect can take place in univariate models.

Recall that $\widehat{\theta}_{n,\text{emp}} = \|\widehat{\theta}_n\|^{-1}\widehat{\theta}_n$. Intuitively, $\widehat{\theta}_{n,\text{emp}}$ might have a faster rate of convergence than that of $\widehat{\theta}_n$. This can be seen using the α-representation of the rotated system. Because of $\widehat{\theta}_n = Q\widehat{\alpha}_n$ and hence $\|\widehat{\theta}_n\| = \|\widehat{\alpha}_n\|$, $\widehat{\theta}_{n,\text{emp}} = Q\widehat{\alpha}_{n,\text{unit}}$, where $\widehat{\alpha}_{n,\text{unit}} = (\widehat{\alpha}_{n,\text{unit}}^1, (\widehat{\alpha}_{n,\text{unit}}^2)^\top)^\top = \|\widehat{\alpha}_n\|^{-1}\widehat{\alpha}_n$. The following results give the rates of convergence for $\widehat{\alpha}_{n,\text{unit}}$ and then for $\widehat{\theta}_n$ and $\widehat{\theta}_{n,\text{emp}}$, respectively.

Corollary 5.2.1 *Under Assumptions 5.7.1 and 5.7.2, we have as $n \to \infty$,*

$$n^{3/2}(\widehat{\alpha}_{n,unit}^1 - 1) \to_D -\frac{1}{2}\|\xi\|^2 \quad \textit{and} \quad n^{3/4}\widehat{\alpha}_{n,unit}^2 \to_D \xi,$$

where $\xi \sim \mathbf{MN}(0, \rho_{22})$ is the limit given by (5.2.19). □

See the proof in Dong et al. (2016). Note that, after the normalization, the slower rate in $\widehat{\alpha}_n$ becomes as fast as $n^{-3/2}$ whereas the faster rate remains the same. Note also that $\widehat{\alpha}_{n,\text{unit}}^1 = \|\widehat{\alpha}_n\|^{-1}\widehat{\alpha}_{1n} \leq 1$, so the limit of $\widehat{\alpha}_{n,\text{unit}}^1 - 1$ is negative. The intuitive reason for the faster rate of $\widehat{\alpha}^1_{n,\text{unit}}$ is that it takes advantage of the directions orthogonal to θ_0, where there is larger supply of information from far out x_t's as explained above. The rates are verified with Monte Carlo simulation. The resulting rates for $\widehat{\theta}_n$ are given in Theorem 5.2.2 below whose proof is shown in Dong et al. (2016) but we briefly present in Sect. 5.7.

Theorem 5.2.2 *Under Assumptions 5.7.1 and 5.7.2 in Sect. 5.7, we have as $n \to \infty$,*

$$n^{1/4}(\widehat{\theta}_n - \theta_0) \to_D \boldsymbol{MN}(0, \rho_{11}\theta_0\theta_0^\top), \tag{5.2.21}$$

$$n^{3/4}(\widehat{\theta}_{n,emp} - \theta_0) \to_D \boldsymbol{MN}(0, Q_2\rho_{22}Q_2^\top). \tag{5.2.22}$$

As can be seen, $\widehat{\theta}_n \to_P \theta_0$ at rate of $n^{-1/4}$ and $\widehat{\theta}_{n,\text{emp}} \to_P \theta_0$ at rate of $n^{-3/4}$. Again, roughly speaking, the normalization scales $\widehat{\theta}_n$ to the unit ball and hence accelerates the slower rate of $\widehat{\theta}_n$. Due to the fast convergence of $\widehat{\theta}_{n,\text{emp}}$, all the following assertions regarding estimates of quantities by plugging in $\widehat{\theta}_n$ remain true if $\widehat{\theta}_n$ is replaced by $\widehat{\theta}_{n,\text{emp}}$. We do not repeat this.

We would like to give some explanation for the faster and the slower rates about $\widehat{\theta}_n$ and $\widehat{\theta}_{n,\text{emp}}$ from a geometric point of view. As defined before, $\widehat{\theta}_n$ is the estimator of θ_0, and then $\widehat{\alpha}_n = Q^\top\widehat{\theta}_n = (\widehat{\alpha}_{1n}, \widehat{\alpha}_{2n}^\top)^\top$ is the coordinate of $\widehat{\theta}_n$ in the new system $Q = (\theta_0, Q_2)$. That is, $\widehat{\alpha}_{1n}$ is the coordinate of the estimator $\widehat{\theta}_n$ along the θ_0-axis, while $\widehat{\alpha}_{2n}$ is the coordinate of the estimator $\widehat{\theta}_n$ on Q_2, which by definition is consisting of all unit direction vectors orthogonal to θ_0.

Geometrically, $\widehat{\theta}_n$ is the composite of its coordinates $\widehat{\alpha}_{1n}$ and $\widehat{\alpha}_{2n}$. When $\widehat{\alpha}_{1n}$ and $\widehat{\alpha}_{2n}$ tend to their true values $\alpha_{10} = 1$ and $\alpha_{20} = 0$, $\widehat{\theta}_n$ approaches θ_0. Here is a picture in 2-dimensional case.

The convergence of $\widehat{\theta}_n$ to θ_0 can be viewed as a two-fold convergence: the length $\|\widehat{\theta}_n\|$ approaches $\|\theta_0\| = 1$ and the direction of $\widehat{\theta}_n$ approaches that of θ_0. It follows from the orthogonality of Q that

$$\begin{aligned}\|\widehat{\theta}_n\| = \|\widehat{\alpha}_n\| &= \left(\widehat{\alpha}_{1n}^2 + \|\widehat{\alpha}_{2n}\|^2\right)^{1/2} = \widehat{\alpha}_{1n}\left(1 + \widehat{\alpha}_{1n}^{-2}\|\widehat{\alpha}_{2n}\|^2\right)^{1/2}\\ &= \widehat{\alpha}_{1n}\left[1 + \frac{1}{2}O(\widehat{\alpha}_{1n}^{-2}\|\widehat{\alpha}_{2n}\|^2)\right]\end{aligned}$$

by Taylor expansion of $(1 + x)^{1/2}$ for small x, where due to consistency $\widehat{\alpha}_{1n}$ is positive in large probability. Thus, $\widehat{\alpha}_{1n}$ is the leading term of $\|\widehat{\theta}_n\|$.

On the other hand, the direction of $\widehat{\theta}_n$ approaching that of θ_0 is equivalent to that the angle τ_n between $\widehat{\theta}_n$ and Q_2 is tending to $\pi/2$. See Fig. 5.1. By the formula for the angle of two vectors,

$$\cos(\tau_n) = \frac{Q_2^\top\widehat{\theta}_n}{\|\widehat{\theta}_n\|} = \frac{\widehat{\alpha}_{2n}}{\|\widehat{\alpha}_n\|} = \widehat{\alpha}_{2n}[1 + O(\|\widehat{\alpha}_n\| - 1)],$$

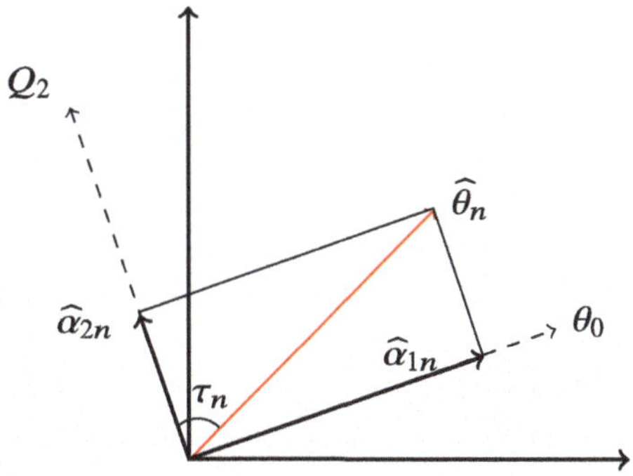

Fig. 5.1 The dual rates in single-index model

implying that $\widehat{\alpha}_{2n}$ is the leading term of $\cos(\tau_n)$. The faster rate of $\widehat{\alpha}_{2n}$ means that with the increase of sample size n, the estimator $\widehat{\theta}_n$ finds the correct direction quicker than matching the correct length.

Finally, let us now consider $\widehat{\theta}_{n,\text{emp}} = \|\widehat{\theta}_n\|^{-1}\widehat{\theta}_n$. Through the normalization $\widehat{\theta}_{n,\text{emp}}$ is always a unit vector, that is, artificially we make the norm of the estimator $\widehat{\theta}_n$ match that of θ_0. This compensates the slower rate of $\widehat{\alpha}_{1n}$ dramatically, as Corollary 5.2.1 indicates, $\widehat{\alpha}^1_{n,\text{unit}}$ converging to 1 possesses a rate of $n^{-3/2}$. By contrast, the normalization does not accelerate the rate of $\widehat{\alpha}_{2n}$, as shown in Corollary 5.2.1 where $\widehat{\alpha}^2_{n,\text{unit}}$ remains the same rate as that of $\widehat{\alpha}_{2n}$, namely $n^{-3/4}$.

Note further that the angle between $\widehat{\theta}_{n,\text{emp}}$ and Q_2 is still τ_n, the same angle between $\widehat{\theta}_n$ and Q_2. See Fig. 5.2. Because $\|\widehat{\theta}_{n,\text{emp}}\| = 1$, $\|Q_2\| = 1$ when $d = 2$ (for $d > 2$, all column vectors of Q_2 are unitary) and $\|\widehat{\theta}_n\| = \|\widehat{\alpha}_n\|$, we have

$$\cos(\tau_n) = Q_2^\top \widehat{\theta}_{n,\text{emp}} = \|\widehat{\theta}_n\|^{-1} Q_2^\top \widehat{\theta}_n = \|\widehat{\alpha}_n\|^{-1}\widehat{\alpha}_{2n} = \widehat{\alpha}^2_{n,\text{unit}},$$

and therefore,

$$\widehat{\theta}_{n,\text{emp}} \to_P \theta_0 \quad \Leftrightarrow \quad \tau_n \to_P \frac{\pi}{2} \quad \Leftrightarrow \quad \widehat{\alpha}^2_{n,\text{unit}} \to_P 0.$$

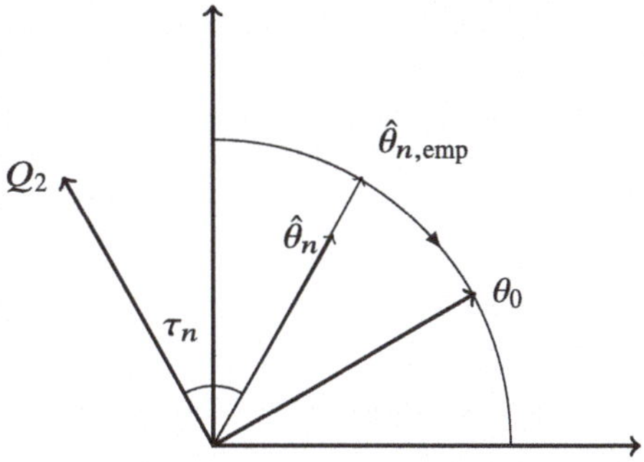

Fig. 5.2 The rate for normalized estimator in single-index model

As a result, $\widehat{\theta}_{n,\text{emp}}$ converges at a rate of $n^{-3/4}$ in Theorem 5.2.2, the same rate as that of $\widehat{\alpha}^2_{n,\text{unit}}$ (also as $\widehat{\alpha}_{2n}$).

In addition, we would like to have another look at the convergence rate of $\widehat{\theta}_{n,\text{emp}}$ directly from the results in Corollary 5.2.1, since Theorem 5.2.2 is proven by virtue of Corollary 5.2.1. Similarly to that $\widehat{\theta}_n$ is the composite of its coordinates $\widehat{\alpha}_{1n}$ and $\widehat{\alpha}_{2n}$, $\widehat{\theta}_{n,\text{emp}}$ is geometrically the composite of $\widehat{\alpha}^1_{n,\text{unit}}$ (with rate $n^{-3/2}$) and $\widehat{\alpha}^2_{n,\text{unit}}$ (with rate $n^{-3/4}$). Given the different rates for their components, intuitively $\widehat{\theta}_{n,\text{emp}}$ follows the rule of the slower one (i.e. $\widehat{\alpha}^2_{n,\text{unit}}$).

Furthermore, by Theorem 5.2.2, we have $\widehat{\theta}_n \sim \mathbf{MN}(\theta_0, n^{-1/4}\rho_{11}\theta_0\theta_0^\top)$. We next show that the estimator of the covariance matrix of $\widehat{\theta}_n$ is the inverse of the Hessian matrix of the form $[J_n(\widehat{\theta}_n)]^{-1}$ or even $[\widetilde{J}_n(\widehat{\theta}_n)]^{-1}$, where $\widetilde{J}_n(\theta) = \sum_{t=1}^n \dot{\widehat{g}}^2_n(\theta^\top x_t)x_t x_t^\top$ is the leading term of $J_n(\theta)$. Meanwhile, define the estimators of σ_e^2 and $L_1(1,0)$ by

$$\widehat{\sigma}_e^2 = \frac{1}{n}\sum_{t=1}^n [y_t - \widehat{g}_n(\widehat{\theta}_n^\top x_t)]^2 \text{ and } \widehat{L}_{n1}(1,0) = \frac{1}{\sqrt{n}}\sum_{t=1}^n \mathscr{H}_0^2(\widehat{\theta}_n^\top x_t), \qquad (5.2.23)$$

respectively, where $\mathscr{H}_0(\cdot)$ is the first function in the Hermite function sequence.

Corollary 5.2.2 *Under Assumptions 5.7.1 and 5.7.2 in Sect. 5.7, we have as* $n \to \infty$,

$$\widehat{\sigma}_e^2 \to_P \sigma_e^2, \quad \textit{and} \quad \widehat{L}_{n1}(1,0) - L_1(1,0) \to_P 0, \qquad (5.2.24)$$

and

$$\sqrt{n}[J_n(\widehat{\theta}_n)]^{-1} \to_P \rho_{11}\theta_0\theta_0^\top \ \textit{and} \ \sqrt{n}[\widetilde{J}_n(\widehat{\theta}_n)]^{-1} \to_P \rho_{11}\theta_0\theta_0^\top. \qquad (5.2.25)$$

The main result is the following central limit theorem for the estimator $\widehat{g}_n(u) = Z_k^\top(u)\widehat{c}$ for any $u \in \mathbb{R}$ that is shown in Dong et al. (2016) but we present in Sect. 5.7 for convenience.

Theorem 5.2.3 *Under Assumptions 5.7.1 and 5.7.2 in Sect. 5.7, as* $n \to \infty$, $\sup_{u\in\mathbb{R}} |\widehat{g}_n(u) - g(u)| \to_P 0$, *and*

$$\widehat{\sigma}_e^{-1}\widehat{L}_{n1}^{1/2}(1,0)n^{1/4}\|Z_k(u)\|^{-1}(\widehat{g}_n(u) - g(u)) \to_D N(0,1). \qquad (5.2.26)$$

The order involved in the normality is $O_P(1)n^{1/4}k^{-1/2}$ in view of $\|Z_k(u)\|^2 = O(k)$. This is comparable with the corresponding kernel estimation in the literature. Theorem 3.1 of Wang and Phillips (2009a, p.721) shows that, for univariate regression $y_t = f(x_t) + u_t$, the normalizer of $\hat{f}(x) - f(x)$ is $\left(h\sum_{t=1}^n K_h(x_t - x)\right)^{1/2}$ where h is a bandwidth, $K_h(\cdot) = K(\cdot/h)/h$ is a kernel function and $\hat{f}(x)$ is the kernel estimate of $f(x)$. Note that $\left(h\sum_{t=1}^n K_h(x_t - x)\right)^{1/2} = O_P(1)n^{1/4}h^{1/2}$. Thinking of k^{-1} as a counterpart to the bandwidth h, the normalizers in the two situations are quite comparable.

Moreover, noting that $\widehat{g}_n(u) - g(u) = Z_k^\top(u)(\widehat{c} - c) - \gamma_k(u)$ and by the orthogonality of the basis functions, $\int(\widehat{g}_n(u) - g(u))^2 du = \|\widehat{c} - c\|^2 + \|\gamma_k(u)\|^2$ where $\|\gamma_k(u)\|$ is the norm of $\gamma(u)$ in the function space. By Lemmas in Dong et al. (2016) and its supplementary document, $\|\widehat{c} - c\|^2 = O_P(kn^{-1/2})$ and $\|\gamma_k(u)\|^2 = O(k^{-m})$, one may find that $k^* = n^{1/2(m+1)}$ is an optimal truncation parameter since it makes $\|\widehat{c} - c\|^2$ and $\|\gamma_k(u)\|^2$ have the same order going to zero. Here, m is the smoothness order of $g(u)$.

5.3 Partially Linear Single-Index Models

Partially linear single-index models are popular because they are not as restrictive as parametric regression models. Meanwhile, they alleviate the problem of the "curse of dimensionality" associated with multivariate nonparametric models. Talking about partially linear single-index model, we mean

$$y = x^\top \beta_0 + g(x^\top \theta_0) + \varepsilon, \tag{5.3.1}$$

where β_0 and θ_0 are two unknown Euclidean vectors, and $g(\cdot)$ is an unknown link function.

Note that Li and Fan (1996) take a different form in nonparametric part in their partial linear model, and they consider the specification testings of partial linear models and single-index models based on kernel estimation; for regression function $h(x)$ with $x = (z^\top, w^\top)^\top$, their hypotheses for partial linear models are

$$H_0^a: \quad h(x) = z^\top \gamma + g(w), a.s. \text{ for some } \gamma \in \mathbb{R}^{q_2}, g: \mathbb{R}^{q_1} \mapsto \mathbb{R}$$

against

$$H_1^a: \quad h(x) \neq z^\top \gamma + g(w), \text{ for all } \gamma \in \mathbb{R}^{q_2}, g: \mathbb{R}^{q_1} \mapsto \mathbb{R}, \tag{5.3.2}$$

and their hypotheses for single-index models are

$$H_0^b: \quad h(x) = \phi(x^\top \gamma), a.s. \text{ for some } \gamma \in \mathbb{R}^q,$$

against

$$H_1^b: \quad h(x) \neq \phi(x^\top \gamma), \text{ for all } \gamma \in \mathbb{R}^q. \tag{5.3.3}$$

Carroll et al. (1997) use local linear estimation method to study partial linear single-index models; under identification condition, they estimate the two vectors of parameters and the unknown link function; Xia et al. (1999) explore partially single-index model (5.3.1), and, to ensure estimability, they assume that β_0 and θ_0 are perpendicular to each other with $\|\theta_0\| = 1$ and its first nonzero element positive. Otherwise, β_0 and $g(x^\top \theta_0)$ can be substituted by $\beta_0 - (\beta_0^\top \theta_0)\theta_0$ and $g(x^\top \theta_0) +$

$(\beta_0^\top \theta_0)\theta_0^\top x$, respectively. While Xia et al. (1999) show the identifiability of (5.3.1) under the assumptions of non-constant second derivative of $g(\cdot)$ and orthogonality between β_0 and θ_0, Lin and Kulasekera (2007) show the identifiability of partially linear single-index model under continuity, as given below.

Lemma 5.3.1 *Let $m(x) = \mathbb{E}(y|x)$ be the mean function of y given x, and S be the support of $m(x)$ that is bounded and convex with at least one interior point. Suppose that for two vectors $\beta_i \in \mathbb{R}^d$, and two unit vectors θ_i of which the first nonzero elements are positive, and $\beta_i \perp \theta_i$, $i = 1, 2$, such that*

$$m(x) = x^\top \beta_1 + g(x^\top \theta_1) = x^\top \beta_2 + h(x^\top \theta_2), \quad \forall x \in S, \tag{5.3.4}$$

where $m(x)$ is continuous and non-constant. If $g(\cdot)$ and $h(\cdot)$ are continuous, then $\theta_1 = \theta_2$, $\beta_1 = \beta_2$ and $g = h$ on $\{x^\top \theta_1 : x \in S\}$.

Proof Without loss of generality, we may assume that the origin is an interior point of S; otherwise, use the transformation $z = x - x_0$ where x_0 is an interior point of S and use z to replace x. In what follows, we only consider the case where $d = 2$ for simplicity.

Suppose $\theta_1 \neq \theta_2$. Then, (θ_1, θ_2) becomes a basis in $\mathbb{R}^2$; representing β_1 and β_2 in terms of (θ_1, θ_2). Accordingly, one can write $x^\top \beta_1 + g(x^\top \theta_1) = x^\top \beta_2 + h(x^\top \theta_2)$ as $\tilde{g}(x^\top \theta_1) = \tilde{h}(x^\top \theta_2)$ with $\tilde{g}(u) = au + g(u)$ and $\tilde{h}(u) = bu + h(u)$ for some scalars a and b. It then follows from Lemma 5.1.1 that $\theta_1 = \theta_2$, a contradiction. Thus, $\theta_1 = \theta_2 = \theta$. Moreover, $\beta \equiv \beta_1 - \beta_2 \perp \theta$. By (5.3.4), $f(x^\top \theta) = x^\top \beta$ where $f = h - g$. For any small t, let $x = t\beta \in S$. Hence, $f(0) = t\|\beta\|^2$ and by the arbitrariness of t, $\beta = 0$, yielding $\beta_1 = \beta_2$. Also, $g = h$ follows immediately. □

The lemma and its proof owes to Lin and Kulasekera (2007). In Liang et al. (2010), the authors propose a semiparametrically efficient profile least-squares estimators for the regression coefficients in a partially linear single-index model, and simultaneous variable selection and estimation of regression coefficients are achieved by using SCAD penalty function. In addition, a linear hypothesis test for the parametric coefficients and a goodness-of-fit test for the nonparametric component, respectively, are proposed.

Using a series expansion for the unknown link function $g(\cdot)$ in (5.3.1), similar to the profile method explained in the single-index model setting, one can estimate the two parameters β_0 and θ_0 as well as the link function. This estimation procedure is illustrated in the next section where the model is the same as (5.3.1) but the regressor is nonstationary.

5.4 Partially Linear Single-Index Models with Nonstationarity

In this section, we consider a nonstationary partially linear single-index model,

$$y_t = \beta_0^\top x_t + g(\theta_0^\top x_t) + e_t, \quad t = 1, \ldots, n, \tag{5.4.1}$$

where y_t is a scalar process, the link function $g(\cdot) : \mathbb{R} \mapsto \mathbb{R}$ is an unknown integrable function, β_0 and θ_0 are the true but unknown d-dimensional column vectors of parameters, x_t is a d-dimensional integrated process, e_t is an error process and n is sample size. The same as in the single-index model, we require $\|\theta_0\| = 1$ and the first element of θ_0 is positive for the sake of identifiability.

Model (5.4.1) can be viewed as an extension of linear parametric models since it would become a linear model under the particular choice of the link function. In addition, model (5.4.1) covers model (5.2.4) as a special case where $\beta_0 \equiv 0$. Taking these into account, models such as (5.4.1) are often used as a reasonable compromise between fully parametric and fully nonparametric modeling.

Standing on its own, model (5.2.4) has limited applicability since the regression function is integrable, and among other things, does not include the linear model. Coupled with the assumption that $\{x_t\}$ is a unit root process, this implies that only an order of $O(\sqrt{n})$ observations can be used in the estimations of θ_0 and g in (5.2.4). The function g is only capable of describing finite domain behavior in x_t, since when $\theta_0^\top x_t$ increases, $g(\theta_0^\top x_t)$ goes to zero.

When the g function is added as a component in model (5.4.1), one obtains a model whose behavior is governed by the linear component with g superimposed, whereas as x_t becomes large it reduces to the linear component. The resulting model (5.4.1) can be likened to a smooth transition regression model (STR model, Teräsvirta et al., 2010), whereas x_t increases, the model changes smoothly to a linear model. The model in this sense extends the STR model to a situation where there is an index involved and with a nonstationary input process. We believe that this is a situation which is of interest both theoretically and practically, as witnessed, for example, by our empirical study where quite different index behavior is obtained in the close domain as compared to the far-out region.

Theoretical results heavily depend on the level of nonstationarity of the integrated time series and the integrability of the link functions. These properties result in a slow rate of convergence for the link function involving an $I(1)$ process and fast rate of convergence for a linear regression with an $I(1)$ process. These are very different from the literature where regressors are stationary. In addition, Monte Carlo simulation generally needs relative larger sample size than cases where regressors are stationary if the regression function is integrable. This is because integrated process on one hand diverges at rate $\sqrt{n}$ and on the other hand, it possesses recurrent property making it possible to return to the effective domain of the integrable function g.

Existing studies, such as Xia et al. (1999), often impose an identification condition that β_0 is perpendicular to θ_0 on the partially linear single-index model setting. This is because when β_0 is not perpendicular to θ_0, a new vector $\beta_0 - (\beta_0^\top \theta_0)\theta_0$ can be used in the place of β_0 and the g function will be replaced by $g(u) + (\beta_0^\top \theta_0)u$. However, in model (5.4.1), the lack of orthogonality between β_0 and θ_0 does not affect the identifiability of the model at all due to integrability of the link function, as shown in Dong et al. (2016).

5.4.1 Estimation Procedure

Our estimation procedure for the partially linear single-index model setting in (5.4.1) is proposed as follows. By virtue of (5.2.5) again, for each t rewrite (5.4.1) as

$$y_t - \beta_0^\top x_t = Z_k(\theta_0^\top x_t)^\top c + \gamma_k(\theta_0^\top x_t) + e_t,$$

where $Z_k(\cdot)$, c and $\gamma_k(\cdot)$ are defined as before.

Denote $X = (x_1, x_2, \ldots, x_n)^\top$ an $n \times d$ matrix. Y, Z, γ, e remain the same as in the preceding section. We have a matrix form equation: $Y - X\beta = Zc + \gamma + e$. Then, the OLS gives that $\widetilde{c} = \widetilde{c}(\beta_0, \theta_0) = (Z^\top Z)^{-1} Z^\top (Y - X\beta_0)$. Due to the same reason as before, define for generic (β, θ), $L_n(\beta, \theta) = \frac{1}{2}\sum_{t=1}^n [y_t - \beta^\top x_t - Z_k^\top(\theta^\top x_t)\widetilde{c}(\beta, \theta)]^2$. Then, the estimator of (β_0, θ_0) is given by

$$(\widehat{\beta}_n, \widehat{\theta}_n) = \operatorname*{argmin}_{\theta\in\Theta,\beta} L_n(\beta, \theta). \tag{5.4.2}$$

Similarly, define $\widehat{g}_n(u) \equiv \widehat{g}_n(u; \widehat{\beta}_n, \widehat{\theta}_n) = Z_k^\top(u)\widehat{c}$ for any $u \in \mathbb{R}$ as an estimator for $g(u)$, where $\widehat{c} = \widetilde{c}(\widehat{\beta}_n, \widehat{\theta}_n)$ is a plug-in estimator, once the estimate of parameters is available; and the normalization $\widehat{\theta}_{n,\text{emp}} = \|\widehat{\theta}_n\|^{-1}\widehat{\theta}_n$ is defined to satisfy the identification condition.

5.4.2 Asymptotic Theory

Denote $\vartheta_0 = (\beta_0^\top, \theta_0^\top)^\top$ and $\vartheta = (\beta^\top, \theta^\top)^\top$ as a generic parameter for simplicity. Let $\mathfrak{S}_n(\vartheta)$ and $\mathfrak{J}_n(\vartheta)$ be the respective score and Hessian functions of $L_n(\vartheta)$ in the minimisation problem (5.4.2). Let $\widehat{\vartheta}_n$ be the estimator of ϑ_0. We then have the expansion:

$$0 = \mathfrak{S}_n(\widehat{\vartheta}_n) = \mathfrak{S}_n(\vartheta_0) + \mathfrak{J}_n(\vartheta_n)(\widehat{\vartheta}_n - \vartheta_0), \tag{5.4.3}$$

where $\mathfrak{J}_n(\vartheta_n)$ is the Hessian matrix with the rows evaluated at a point ϑ_n between $\widehat{\vartheta}_n$ and ϑ_0.

We also need to rotate our index vectors in model (5.4.1), namely, reparameterizing the model, in order to derive the asymptotics. Using the orthogonal matrix $Q = (\theta_0, Q_2)$ again, we can rewrite the model as

$$y_t = \beta_0^\top Q Q^\top x_t + g(\theta_0^\top Q Q^\top x_t) + e_t = \lambda_0^\top z_t + g(\alpha_0^\top z_t) + e_t, \tag{5.4.4}$$

where $\lambda_0 = Q^\top \beta_0 = (\lambda_{10}, \lambda_{20}^\top)^\top$ with $\lambda_{10} = \theta_0^\top \beta_0$ a scalar, $\lambda_{20} = Q_2^\top \beta_0$ a $(d-1)$-dimensional vector, $\alpha_0 = Q^\top \theta_0$, $z_t = Q^\top x_t$ are defined the same as before. Let $\lambda = Q^\top \beta$ and $\alpha = Q^\top \theta$ for the generic vector rotation. Also, group them by $\mu_0 = (\lambda_0^\top, \alpha_0^\top)^\top$ and $\mu = (\lambda^\top, \alpha^\top)^\top$.

Let $L_n(\mu)$ be the counterpart of $L_n(\beta, \theta)$ after reparameterization. If $\widehat{\mu}_n$, the minimizer of $L_n(\mu)$, is the estimator of μ_0, then $\widehat{\mu}_n = \text{diag}(Q^\top, Q^\top)\widehat{\vartheta}_n$. Moreover, the score function $\mathfrak{S}_n(\mu)$ and the Hessian $\mathfrak{J}_n(\mu)$ for the parameter μ can be obtained from those for ϑ. Namely, $\mathfrak{S}_n(\mu) = \text{diag}(Q^\top, Q^\top)\mathfrak{S}_n(\vartheta)$ and $\mathfrak{J}_n(\mu) = \text{diag}(Q^\top, Q^\top)\mathfrak{J}_n(\vartheta)\text{diag}(Q, Q)$. Premultiplying equation (5.4.3) by $\text{diag}(Q^\top, Q^\top)$, we have

$$0 = \mathfrak{S}_n(\widehat{\mu}_n) = \mathfrak{S}_n(\mu_0) + \mathfrak{J}_n(\mu_n)(\widehat{\mu}_n - \mu_0), \tag{5.4.5}$$

from which the following theorem is derived.

Theorem 5.4.1 *Under Assumptions 5.7.1 and 5.7.2 in Sect. 5.7, $\widehat{\mu}_n \to_P \mu_0$. Moreover, as $n \to \infty$,*

$$n(\widehat{\lambda}_n - \lambda_0) \to_D Q^\top \left(\int_0^1 V(r)V^\top(r)dr \right)^{-1} \int_0^1 V(r)dU(r), \tag{5.4.6}$$

$$D_n(\widehat{\alpha}_n - \alpha_0) \to_D R^{-1/2} W(1), \tag{5.4.7}$$

where $(U(r), V(r))$ is given in Assumption 5.7.1, D_n, R and W are the same as in Theorem 5.2.1. □

The proof is given by Dong et al. (2016) but we present it briefly in Sect. 5.7 for easy reference and convenience. Theorem 5.4.1 shows that for the partially linear single-index model, the estimators of the parameters in the linear part have the same rates of convergence as those in the linear model, while the estimator of the index vector retains the dual rates in the system of Q. Hence, there is a trio of rates of convergence accommodated in the partially linear single-index model setting. From Theorem 5.4.1, we may derive asymptotic distributions for both $\widehat{\beta}_n$ and $\widehat{\theta}_n$.

Theorem 5.4.2 *Under Assumptions 5.7.1 and 5.7.2, for $(\widehat{\beta}_n, \widehat{\theta}_n)$ given by* (5.4.2) *we have as $n \to \infty$*

$$n(\widehat{\beta}_n - \beta_0) \to_D \left(\int_0^1 V(r)V^\top(r)dr \right)^{-1} \int_0^1 V(r)dU(r), \tag{5.4.8}$$

$$n^{1/4}(\widehat{\theta}_n - \theta_0) \to_D \mathbf{MN}(0, \rho_{11}\theta_0\theta_0^\top). \tag{5.4.9}$$

Furthermore, using (5.4.7), for $\widehat{\theta}_n$, the results of Theorems 5.2.2–5.2.3 and Corollaries 5.2.1–5.2.2 with $\widehat{\theta}_{n,\text{emp}}$ and $\widehat{g}_n(u)$ defined in the same fashion remain true.

Theorem 5.4.3 *Under Assumptions 5.7.1 and 5.7.2, the results of Theorems 5.2.2–5.2.3 and Corollaries 5.2.1–5.2.2 also remain true for* $\widehat{\theta}_n$ *and* $\widehat{g}_n(u)$ *in model* (5.4.1) □

See the proofs of the above two theorems in Dong et al. (2016).

5.4.3 Extension to the General *H*-Regular Class

For integrated time series, the convergence rate of the estimates of the unknown parameters involved in a parametric regression function heavily depends on the functional form of the regression function under consideration. The relevant literature focuses on two classes of functions, i.e., the so-called I-regular class and H-regular class. Integrable functions belong to the I-regular class, while functions like power functions and polynomial functions are H-regular. For more details, we refer the readers to Park and Phillips (1999, 2001).

Observe that the partially linear single-index model is a combination of the two classes. As already stated, this can be seen as a smooth transition model whose behavior in the finite domain is a linear model perturbed by the g-function component, the influence of which is reduced for a large $\|x_t\|$. Such models have broad applications. Nonetheless, if the linear part is extended to a nonlinear form, the model will be more flexible and more applicable. To do so, we combine a general H-regular function with a general I-regular function to introduce a partially nonlinear single-index model of the form:

$$y_t = f(\beta_0^\top x_t) + g(\theta_0^\top x_t) + e_t, \quad t = 1, \ldots, n, \tag{5.4.10}$$

where $f(\cdot)$ is parametrically known and H-regular, $g(\cdot)$ is nonparametrically unknown and integrable, and β_0 and θ_0 are the unknown parameters.

In some circumstances, one may have some idea on the trend in y_t generated by an index variable $\beta^\top x_t$, e.g., linear or quadratic. Thus, model (5.4.10) should give an accurate description for such a relation. Certainly, the partially linear single-index model is a special case of model (5.4.10) with $f(u) = u$. Our goal is then to estimate (β_0, θ_0) and $g(\cdot)$ in model (5.4.10). Before we propose our estimation method, we give a definition for the H-regular class.

Definition 5.4.1 We say that a function $f(x)$ is asymptotically homogeneous, or H-regular, if for all $\eta > 0$

$$f(\eta x) = \upsilon(\eta)F(x) + \xi(\eta; x), \quad |\xi(\eta; x)| \le a(\eta)P(x) \tag{5.4.11}$$

where $F(x)$ and $P(x)$ are both locally integrable, and $\limsup_{\eta\to\infty} \frac{a(\eta)}{\upsilon(\eta)} = 0$. □

If f is H-regular, with υ and F satisfying (5.4.11), we call υ and F the *asymptotic order* and the *limit homogeneous function* of f, respectively. Note that any polynomial and power functions with positive power are H-regular. Note also that this definition is not the exact one in the reference above, since we modify the definition in Park and Phillips (1999, 2001) to adapt our situation in model (5.4.10).

The estimation procedure of model (5.4.10) is similar to that of model (5.4.1). Using the orthogonal expansion (5.2.5), for each t, rewrite (5.4.10) as $y_t - f(\beta_0^\top x_t) = Z_k(\theta_0^\top x_t)^\top c + \gamma_k(\theta_0^\top x_t) + e_t$, where $Z_k(\cdot)$, c and $\gamma_k(\cdot)$ are defined as before. Let $\widetilde{Y} = (y_1 - f(\beta_0^\top x_1), \ldots, y_n - f(\beta_0^\top x_n))^\top$, and Z, γ and e remain the same as before. We have the matrix form equation, $\widetilde{Y} = Zc + \gamma + e$. Then, the OLS gives $\widetilde{c} = \widetilde{c}(\beta_0, \theta_0) = (Z^\top Z)^{-1} Z^\top \widetilde{Y}$ but remember that it is infeasible.

Define $L_n(\beta, \theta) = \frac{1}{2} \sum_{t=1}^n [y_t - f(\beta^\top x_t) - Z_k^\top(\theta^\top x_t)\widetilde{c}(\beta, \theta)]^2$ for $\beta, \theta \in \mathbb{R}^d$. The estimator of (β_0, θ_0) is then given by

$$\begin{pmatrix} \widehat{\beta}_n \\ \widehat{\theta}_n \end{pmatrix} = \operatorname*{argmin}_{\theta \in \Theta, \beta} L_n(\beta, \theta). \tag{5.4.12}$$

Similarly, a plug-in estimator $\widehat{g}_n(u) \equiv Z_k(u)^\top \widehat{c}$ is defined for any real $u \in \mathbb{R}$, where $\widehat{c} = \widetilde{c}(\widehat{\beta}_n, \widehat{\theta}_n)$ is obtained once $(\widehat{\beta}_n, \widehat{\theta}_n)$ is available.

To derive asymptotic properties for $(\widehat{\beta}_n, \widehat{\theta}_n)$ in (5.4.12), using the orthogonal matrix $Q = (\theta_0, Q_2)$ again,

$$y_t = f(\beta_0^\top Q Q^\top x_t) + g(\theta_0^\top Q Q^\top x_t) + e_t = f(\lambda_0^\top z_t) + g(\alpha_0^\top z_t) + e_t,$$

where the notation used is the same as in (5.4.4), $\lambda = Q^\top \beta$ and $\alpha = Q^\top \theta$ for generic vector rotation. We also define $\mu_0 = (\lambda_0^\top, \alpha_0^\top)^\top$ and $\mu = (\lambda^\top, \alpha^\top)^\top$.

It is still true that if $\widehat{\mu}_n$ is the estimator of μ_0 given by the minimizer of $L_n(\mu)$, then $\widehat{\mu}_n = \text{diag}(Q^\top, Q^\top)\widehat{\vartheta}_n$. Moreover, $\mathfrak{S}_n(\mu) = \text{diag}(Q^\top, Q^\top)\mathfrak{S}_n(\vartheta)$ and $\mathfrak{J}_n(\mu) = \text{diag}(Q^\top, Q^\top)\mathfrak{J}_n(\vartheta)\text{diag}(Q, Q)$. The following two theorems and their proofs are given by Dong et al. (2016).

Theorem 5.4.4 *Suppose that (i) f is H-regular with asymptotic order υ and limit homogeneous function F; (ii) $\dot{f}$ and $\ddot{f}$ are H-regular with asymptotic order $\dot{\upsilon}$ and limit homogeneous function $\dot{F}$, asymptotic order $\ddot{\upsilon}$ and limit homogeneous function $\ddot{F}$, respectively; (iii) For $\beta \neq \beta_0$, $|F(\beta_0^\top x) - F(\beta^\top x)|$ is not a zero function on $\|x\| < \delta$ for some $\delta > 0$; (iv) $\upsilon(\sqrt{n})^{-1}\sqrt{k}^3 \to 0$, where k is the truncation parameter satisfying Assumption 5.7.2; (v) $|\dot{\upsilon}^{-2}(u)\ddot{\upsilon}(u)\upsilon(u)|$ is bounded in the region $u \geq M_0$ for some $M_0 > 0$.*

Under Assumptions 5.7.1 and 5.7.2 in Sect. 5.7, we have $\widehat{\mu}_n \to_P \mu_0$. Moreover, as $n \to \infty$,

$$n\dot{\upsilon}(\sqrt{n})(\widehat{\lambda}_n - \lambda_0) \to_D Q^\top \left(\int_0^1 [\dot{F}(\beta_0^\top V(r))]^2 V(r) V^\top(r) dr \right)^{-1} \times \int_0^1 \dot{F}(\beta_0^\top V(r)) V(r) dU(r), \tag{5.4.13}$$

$$D_n(\widehat{\alpha}_n - \alpha_0) \to_D R^{-1/2} W(1), \tag{5.4.14}$$

where $(U(r), V(r))$, D_n, R *and* W *are the same as in Theorem 5.2.1.* □

It is reasonable to require that the derivatives of f are H-regular if f is H-regular, as stated in Conditions (i) and (ii). Condition (iii) is simply an identification condition, while (iv) and (v) are technical requirements that can be fulfilled easily by many commonly used H-regular functions. Similar conditions for parameter estimation in regression models involving $I(1)$ processes can be found in Park and Phillips (2001). Particularly, $f(x) = x$ is a special case such that Conditions (i)–(v) are trivially satisfied.

Similar to Theorems 5.4.2 and 5.4.3, we derive some corresponding limit distributions for $\widehat{\beta}_n$ and $\widehat{\theta}_n$ as well as the plug-in estimate $\widehat{g}_n(u)$ below.

Theorem 5.4.5 *Under the same conditions as Theorem 5.4.4, we have as* $n \to \infty$,

$$n\dot{\upsilon}(\sqrt{n})(\widehat{\beta}_n - \beta_0) \to_D \left(\int_0^1 [\dot{F}(\beta_0^\top V(r))]^2 V(r) V^\top(r) dr \right)^{-1} \times \int_0^1 \dot{F}(\beta_0^\top V(r)) V(r) dU(r), \tag{5.4.15}$$

$$n^{1/4}(\widehat{\theta}_n - \theta_0) \to_D \mathbf{MN}(0, \rho_{11}\theta_0\theta_0^\top), \tag{5.4.16}$$

where the same notation is used as in Theorem 5.4.2.

Also, the plug-in estimator $\widehat{g}_n(u) = Z_k^\top(u)\widehat{c}$ *has the asymptotic normality as in Theorem 5.2.3. The results in Theorem 5.2.2 and Corollaries 5.2.1–5.2.2 remain valid.* □

5.5 Monte Carlo Simulations

This section investigates the finite-sample performance of the proposed estimators for both single index and partially linear single-index models. The generation of $\{x_t\}$ is the same as for the two types of models. Let $d = 2$, the dimension of x_t, and x_t is generated by

$$x_t = x_{t-1} + v_t \quad \text{with} \quad v_t = r_0 v_{t-1} + \varepsilon_t, \tag{5.5.1}$$

for $t = 1, \ldots, n$, where $r_0 = 0.1$, $\varepsilon_t \sim iiN(0, \sigma^2 I_2)$, and $x_0 = 0$. Let the sample size $n = 400$, 600, and 1000. The number of Monte Carlo replications is $M = 2000$. The truncation parameter is $k = [a \cdot n^\kappa]$ with $\kappa = \frac{5}{44}$ and $a = 3.65$, satisfying the conditions in Assumption 5.7.2 in Sect. 5.7.

5.5.1 Simulations for a Single-Index Model

Consider a single-index model $y_t = g(\theta_0^\top x_t) + e_t, e_t \sim N(0, 1), t = 1, \ldots, n$. There are two parts in the simulation, according as $\theta_0 = (0.6, -0.8)^\top$ and $\theta_0 = (1, 0)^\top$ that both satisfy $\|\theta_0\| = 1$.

We calculate the bias and standard deviation for $\widehat{\theta}_n = (\widehat{\theta}_{1n}, \widehat{\theta}_{2n})^\top$:

$$\text{Bias} = \bar{\widehat{\theta}}_n - \theta_0, \qquad \text{S.D.} = \left(\frac{1}{M} \sum_{\ell=1}^{M} (\widehat{\theta}_{n\ell} - \bar{\widehat{\theta}}_n)^{\otimes 2} \right)^{\otimes 1/2}, \tag{5.5.2}$$

where $\otimes$ denotes an element-wise operation, $\widehat{\theta}_{n\ell}$ stands for the ℓth replication of the estimate, and $\bar{\widehat{\theta}}_n = \frac{1}{M} \sum_{\ell=1}^{M} \widehat{\theta}_{n\ell}$.

In order to evaluate the asymptotic theory given in Theorem 5.2.2, we also calculate the bias and the standard deviation of $\widehat{\theta}_{n,\text{emp}} = \widehat{\theta}_n / \|\widehat{\theta}_n\|$ in the same way as in (5.5.2).

Part I. Set $\theta_0 = (0.6, 0.8)^\top$ that satisfies $\|\theta_0\| = 1$, $\sigma = 0.6$ and $g(u) = (1 + u^2)e^{-u^2}$. We use the proposed procedure to estimate θ_0.

As can be seen from Table 5.1, both the biases and the standard deviations for $\widehat{\theta}_n$ decrease as the sample size increases, and $\widehat{\theta}_{1n}$ and $\widehat{\theta}_{2n}$ have similar performance. Moreover, the biases and standard deviations of $\widehat{\theta}_{n,\text{emp}}$ indicate that $\widehat{\theta}_{n,\text{emp}}$ has a rate of convergence much faster than that of $\widehat{\theta}_n$, as shown in Theorem 5.2.2.

Part II. Put $\theta_0 = (1, 0)^\top$, while σ and $g(u)$ are the same as in Part I, i.e., $\sigma = 0.6$ and $g(u) = (1 + u^2)\exp(-u^2)$. As pointed out before, the rotation of the parameters is only for the derivation of the asymptotic theory. To evaluate the asymptotic theory given in Theorem 5.2.1, we directly take $\theta_0^\top = \alpha_0^\top = (1, 0)$ so that $\widehat{\alpha}_n = \widehat{\theta}_n$ in this experiment.

Table 5.1 Bias and standard deviation for single-index model

n	Bias			S.D.		
	400	600	1000	400	600	1000
$\widehat{\theta}_{1n}$	−0.0647	−0.0519	−0.0388	0.2678	0.2507	0.2042
$\widehat{\theta}_{2n}$	−0.0832	−0.0684	−0.0453	0.3461	0.3285	0.2586
$\widehat{\theta}^1_{n,\text{emp}}$	0.0043	0.0024	−0.0016	0.1005	0.0820	0.0679
$\widehat{\theta}^2_{n,\text{emp}}$	0.0063	0.0066	0.0050	0.0717	0.0659	0.0515

Table 5.2 Bias and standard deviation for single-index model

n	Bias			S.D.		
	400	600	1000	400	600	1000
$\widehat{\alpha}_{1n}$	0.0866	0.0768	0.0340	0.3803	0.3748	0.3338
$\widehat{\alpha}_{2n}$	0.0013	−0.0008	−0.0006	0.1388	0.1186	0.0898
$\widehat{\alpha}^1_{n,\text{unit}}$	−0.0073	−0.0061	−0.0031	0.0246	0.0237	0.0128
$\widehat{\alpha}^2_{n,\text{unit}}$	0.0011	−0.0018	−0.0003	0.1186	0.1080	0.0779

As can be seen from Table 5.2, both the biases and the standard deviations of $\widehat{\alpha}_{1n}$ and $\widehat{\alpha}_{2n}$ decrease as the sample size increases. Particularly, $\widehat{\alpha}_{2n}$ decreases much faster than $\widehat{\alpha}_{1n}$. This verifies the rates of convergence given in Theorem 5.2.1 that $\widehat{\alpha}_{2n} - \alpha_{20} = O_P(n^{-3/4})$, while $\widehat{\alpha}_{1n} - \alpha_{10} = O_P(n^{-1/4})$.

Nonetheless, shown by the standard deviations, $\widehat{\alpha}^1_{n,\text{unit}}$ converges significantly faster than $\widehat{\alpha}^2_{n,\text{unit}}$. This is also implied by Corollary 5.2.1 that $\widehat{\alpha}^1_{n,\text{unit}} - \alpha_{10} = O_P(n^{-3/2})$ and $\widehat{\alpha}^2_{n,\text{unit}} - \alpha_{20} = O_P(n^{-3/4})$. Note also that the biases of $\widehat{\alpha}^1_{n,\text{unit}}$ are always negative (by definition, $\widehat{\alpha}^1_{n,\text{unit}} \le \alpha_{10} = 1$) for each Monte Carlo experiment. As a result, the biases of $\widehat{\alpha}^1_{n,\text{unit}}$ approach zero relatively slower than those of $\widehat{\alpha}^2_{n,\text{unit}}$. In addition, $\widehat{\alpha}^2_{n,\text{unit}}$ and $\widehat{\alpha}_{2n}$ perform quite similarly since they have the same rate of convergence.

5.5.2 *Simulations for a Partially Linear Single-Index Model*

In this subsection, we examine the performance of proposed estimator for partially linear single-index model, $y_t = \beta_0^\top x_t + g(\theta_0^\top x_t) + e_t$, $t = 1, \ldots, n$, where $e_t \sim N(0, 1)$, $g(u) = (1 + u^2)\exp(-u^2)$, $\beta_0 = (0.3, 0.5)^\top$, $\theta_0 = (0.6, -0.8)^\top$ and $\sigma = 0.8$ involved in $\varepsilon_t \sim iiN(0, \sigma^2 I_2)$.

The formulae in (5.5.2) are used for $\widehat{\theta}_n$, $\widehat{\theta}_{n,\text{emp}}$ and $\widehat{\beta}_n$ in this experiment. All simulation results with sample size $n = 400, 600, 1000$ and $\sigma = 0.8$ are reported in Table 5.3. As can be seen, both the biases and the standard deviations decrease as the sample size increases. Moreover, the rate of $\widehat{\theta}_{n,\text{emp}}$ approaching the true value looks faster than that of $\widehat{\theta}_n$. This is supported by Theorems 5.4.2 and 5.4.3 that $\widehat{\theta}_n - \theta_0 = O_P(n^{-1/4})$ and $\widehat{\theta}_{n,\text{emp}} - \theta_0 = O_P(n^{-3/4})$.

Meanwhile, since $\widehat{\beta}_n = (\widehat{\beta}_{1n}, \widehat{\beta}_{2n})^\top$ possesses the fastest rate of convergence of n^{-1} by Theorem 5.4.2, both the biases and the standard deviations of $\widehat{\beta}_n$ support the large sample behavior. Therefore, the asymptotic theory established in the preceding section has been evaluated in these examples.

Table 5.3 Bias and standard deviation for partially linear single-index model

n	Bias			S.D.		
	400	600	1000	400	600	1000
$\widehat{\theta}_{1n}$	−0.0495	−0.0470	−0.0324	0.2652	0.2494	0.1991
$\widehat{\theta}_{2n}$	0.0676	0.0645	0.0435	0.3433	0.3340	0.2572
$\widehat{\theta}^1_{n,\text{emp}}$	0.0038	0.0031	0.0023	0.0934	0.0798	0.0597
$\widehat{\theta}^2_{n,\text{emp}}$	−0.0062	−0.0041	−0.0019	0.0761	0.0621	0.0475
$\widehat{\beta}_{1n}$	−0.0010	−0.0002	0.0001	0.0106	0.0068	0.0038
$\widehat{\beta}_{2n}$	−0.0007	0.0001	0.0001	0.0118	0.0067	0.0037

5.6 Empirical Study

In this section, we propose to use a partially linear single-index model to fit an empirical data set before we make comparisons with some candidate models.

The data. The aggregate US data on consumption, income, investment and interest rate are obtained from *Federal Reserve Economic Data (FRED)*. We consider a quarterly data set over 1960:1-2009:3 with 199 observations. Let r_t stand for the real interest rate, and $c_t = \log(C_t)$, $i_t = \log(I_t)$ and $v_t = \log(V_t)$, where C_t, I_t and V_t are the consumption expenditures, disposable incomes and investments, respectively, for $t = 1, \ldots, 199$. The data of c_t, i_t, v_t and r_t are plotted in (5.3a) of Fig. 5.3. It can be seen that all of them have trending components except r_t. To meet the theoretical assumptions, we de-trend the data for c_t, i_t and v_t. More precisely, suppose that $c_t = \mu_1 + c_{t-1} + u_{1t}$, $i_t = \mu_2 + i_{t-1} + u_{2t}$ and $v_t = \mu_3 + v_{t-1} + u_{3t}$ for $t = 2, \ldots, 199$, where u_{it}, $i = 1, 2, 3$, are error terms. Then, μ_i are estimated as: $\widehat{\mu}_1 = \frac{1}{198}\sum_{i=2}^{199}(c_t - c_{t-1}) = 0.1022$, $\widehat{\mu}_2 = \frac{1}{198}\sum_{i=2}^{199}(i_t - i_{t-1}) = 0.1302$, $\widehat{\mu}_3 = \frac{1}{198}\sum_{i=2}^{199}(v_t - v_{t-1}) = 0.0181$.

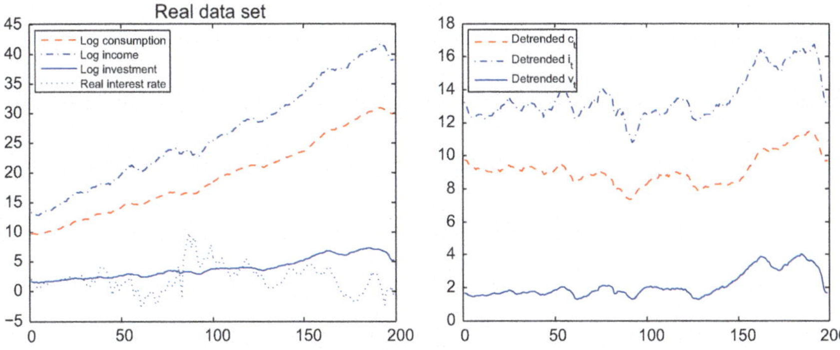

(a) The real data (b) The detrended data

Fig. 5.3 The real data and the de-trended data

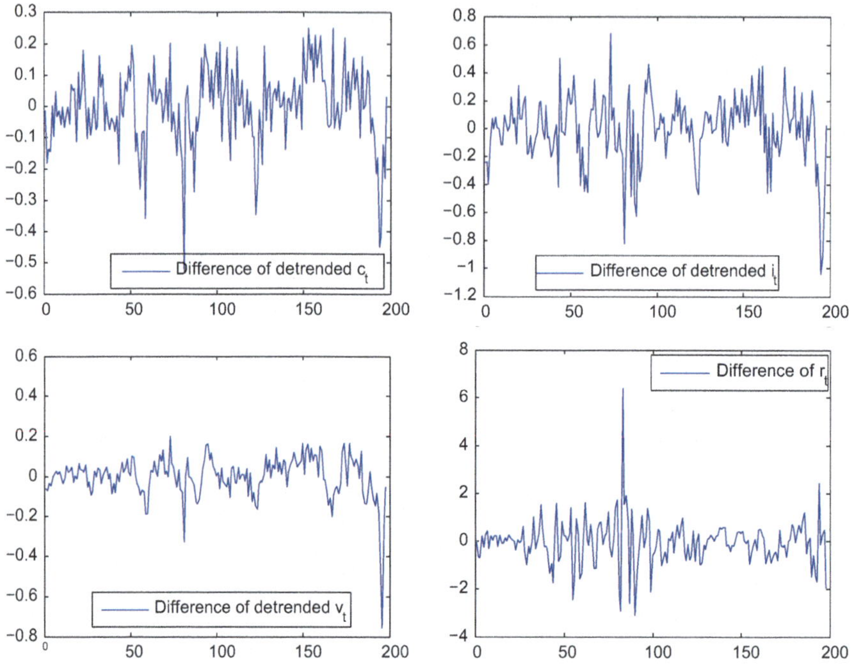

Fig. 5.4 Difference of dataset

Define for each t, $\tilde{c}_t = c_t - \widehat{\mu}_1 t$, $\tilde{i}_t = i_t - \widehat{\mu}_2 t$ and $\tilde{v}_t = v_t - \widehat{\mu}_3 t$. They are the de-trended versions being plotted in (5.3b) of Fig. 5.3, correspondingly.

An ADF test is applied to each of $\tilde{c}_t$, $\tilde{i}_t$, and $\tilde{v}_t$, respectively. The ADF test fails to reject the null of possessing a unit root with p-values 0.7595, 0.6293 and 0.7637, respectively. In addition, it is known from Gao et al. (2009b) that r_t is an $I(1)$ process. To visualize the I(1) processes, the plots of the differences are given in Fig. 5.4.

The model. A partially linear single-index model is proposed to fit the data $\tilde{c}_t$, $\tilde{i}_t$, $\tilde{v}_t$ as well as r_t in the following model,

$$y_t = \beta_0^\top x_t + g(\theta_0^\top x_t) + e_t, \tag{5.6.1}$$

where $t = 2, \ldots, 199$, $y_t = \tilde{c}_t$ and $x_t^\top = (x_{1t}, x_{2t}, x_{3t}, x_{4t}, x_{5t})$ in which $x_{1t} = \tilde{i}_{t-1}$, $x_{2t} = \tilde{i}_t$, $x_{3t} = \tilde{v}_t$, $x_{4t} = \tilde{v}_{t-1}$, $x_{5t} = r_t$, and $g(\cdot)$ is an unknown integrable function, e_t is the error term. Note that we only include the first lagged information in the discussion, as they are more relevant than the other lags.

Estimation. Before implementing our proposed procedures to estimate model (5.6.1), one issue is to determine a suitable truncation parameter k so that the function $g(\cdot)$ can be better approximated by the first k terms in $\{\mathscr{H}_i(x)\}$. Towards this end, we propose using the Generalized Cross-Validation (GCV) method (see Gao et al., 2002) as an initial step to select an optimal value k. Note that while there is no theory for such selection in the nonstationary time series case, the initial selection method works numerically in this example. Let $\widehat{k}$ denote an optimal value such that

$$\widehat{k} = \operatorname*{argmin}_{k \in K_n} \left(1 - \frac{k}{n}\right)^{-2} \widehat{\sigma}^2(k), \tag{5.6.2}$$

where $K_n = \{1, 2, \ldots, 12\}$ and $\widehat{\sigma}^2(k) = \frac{1}{n}\sum_{t=1}^{n}\left(y_t - \beta^\top x_t - Z_k(\theta^\top x_t)^\top \widetilde{c}(\beta, \theta)\right)^2$.

We have $\widehat{k} = 5$, and then $\widehat{\beta}_n = (-0.0479, 0.5701, -1.1689, 1.8685, -0.1223)^\top$ and $\widehat{\theta}_n = (0.2110, -0.3452, 0.0835, 2.6095, -0.2022)^\top$. Meanwhile, we have $\widehat{c} = \widetilde{c}(\widehat{\beta}_n, \widehat{\theta}_n) = (-89.64, 112.54, -74.65, 28.94, -3.33)^\top$. This suggests

$$\begin{aligned} \widehat{g}_5(u) =& [-89.64 b_0^{-1} H_0(u) + 112.54 b_1^{-1} H_1(u) - 74.65 b_2^{-1} H_2(u) \\ &+ 28.94 b_3^{-1} H_3(u) - 3.33 b_4^{-1} H_4(u)] e^{-u^2/2}, \end{aligned} \tag{5.6.3}$$

where $H_i(u)$ are the Hermite polynomials, and $b_i = (\sqrt{\pi} 2^i i!)^{1/2}$ are the norm of $H_i(u)$ in $L^2(\mathbb{R}, e^{-u^2})$ for $i = 0, 1, \ldots, 4$.

In comparison, the de-trended log consumption $y_t = \tilde{c}_t$ is plotted along with the fitted value by the partially linear single-index model $\widehat{y}_t = \widehat{\beta}_n^\top x_t + \widehat{g}_5(\widehat{\theta}_n^\top x_t)$ in (a) of Fig. 5.5.

Note also by (5.6.3) that the estimated link function $\widehat{g}_5(u)$ is integrable on $\mathbb{R}$. According to the normality in Theorem 5.2.3, we draw the confidence bands for $\widehat{g}_5(u)$ at the significance level of 80% in (b) of Fig. 5.5.

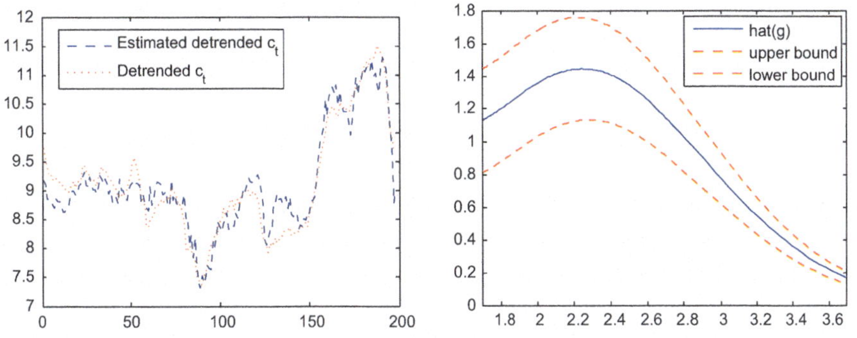

(a) Model (5.6.1) (b) Confidence interval curve

Fig. 5.5 Estimated data and estimated link function

Comparison. To check whether the estimated relationship by the partially linear model is a suitable one, we shall compare model (5.6.1) with two natural competitors of the form:

$$y_t = h(\theta_{10}^\top x_t) + e_{1t}, \tag{5.6.4}$$
$$y_t = \beta_{\text{linear}}^\top x_t + e_{2t}, \tag{5.6.5}$$

where $h(\cdot)$ is integrable and unknown, and $e_{\ell t}$ are the error terms for $\ell = 1, 2$.

To begin with, the linear model (5.6.5) is estimated by OLS with $\widehat{\beta}_{\text{linear}} = (-0.0628, 0.7952, -1.2315, 0.9414, -0.0644)^\top$. Moreover, GCV is applied for model (5.6.4) with $\widehat{\sigma}^2(k) = \frac{1}{n}\sum_{t=1}^{n}\left(y_t - Z_k(\theta^\top x_t)^\top \widetilde{c}(\theta)\right)^2$, and we have $\widehat{k} = 3$. Then, $\widehat{\theta}_{1n} = (-0.0014, 0.0152, -0.0229, 0.0176, -0.0016)^\top$. Meanwhile, the estimate of $\widehat{c} = \widetilde{c}(\widehat{\theta}_{1n}) = (237.05, -61.92, 315.32)^\top$ implies

$$\widehat{h}_3(u) = [237.05 b_0^{-1} H_0(u) - 61.92 b_1^{-1} H_1(u) + 315.32 b_2^{-1} H_2(u)] e^{-u^2/2}, \tag{5.6.6}$$

using the same notation as in (5.6.3).

To proceed further, we compare the so-called in-sample and out-of-sample mean square errors among the three models.

(i) In-sample mean square error (MSE_{in}): As above, all unknown parameters and functions in the three models (5.6.1), (5.6.4) and (5.6.5) are estimated based on the whole observations (x_t, y_t), $t = 2, \ldots, 199$. Once these have been done, we shall have estimated $\widehat{y}_t^\ell$ with $\ell = 1, 2, 3$ corresponding to models (5.6.1), (5.6.4), and (5.6.5) for $t = 2, \ldots, 199$,

$$\widehat{y}_t^1 = \widehat{\beta}_n^\top x_t + \widehat{g}_5(\widehat{\theta}_n^\top x_t), \quad \widehat{y}_t^2 = \widehat{h}_3(\widehat{\theta}_{1n}^\top x_t), \text{ and } \widehat{y}_t^3 = \widehat{\beta}_{\text{linear}}^\top x_t.$$

Then, the in-sample mean square errors are calculated, for $\ell = 1, 2, 3$, by

$$\text{MSE}_{in}(\ell) = \frac{1}{198}\sum_{t=2}^{199}(y_t - \widehat{y}_t^\ell)^2. \tag{5.6.7}$$

Meanwhile, to verify the choice of GCV, the MSE_{in} for model (5.6.1) with $k = 3, 4, 6, 7$ respectively and for model (5.6.4) with $k = 1, 2, 4, 5$, respectively are calculated as well.

(ii) Out-of-sample mean square error (MSE_{out}): Each time, one part of observations is used to estimate all unknown parameters and functions in the three models, then the next value of the dependent variable is forecasted using the estimated models. More precisely, letting $j = 1, 2, \ldots, 10$, we use the observations $\{(y_t, x_t) : 2 \le t \le 178 + 2j\}$ to estimate the unknown parameters and functions (with fixed $\widehat{k} = 5$ for model (5.6.1) and $\widehat{k} = 3$ for model (5.6.4)) in the three models, then the next y_{179+2j} is forecasted by the three models using the estimated parameters,

Table 5.4 The MSEs for models (5.6.1), (5.6.4), (5.6.5)

$k =$	Partially linear single-index model (5.6.1)					
	3	4	5	6	7	
MSE_{in}	0.0968	0.1018	0.0946	0.1460	0.1559	
MSE_{out}	0.2418	0.1761	0.1232	0.2146	0.1786	
$k =$	Single-index model (5.6.4)					Linear model (5.6.5)
	1	2	3	4	5	
MSE_{in}	0.3011	0.1641	0.1544	0.7709	1.4076	0.1666
MSE_{out}	0.6962	0.2733	0.2607	1.9060	3.0838	0.2598

$$\widehat{y}^1_{179+2j} = \widehat{\beta}_j^\top x_{179+2j} + \widehat{g}^j_5(\widehat{\theta}_j^\top x_{179+2j}),$$
$$\widehat{y}^2_{179+2j} = \widehat{h}^j_3(\widehat{\theta}_{1j}^\top x_{179+2j}), \text{ and } \widehat{y}^3_{179+2j} = \widehat{\beta}_{j,\text{linear}}^\top x_{179+2j}.$$

The MSE_{out} are evaluated, for $\ell = 1, 2, 3$, by

$$\text{MSE}_{out}(\ell) = \frac{1}{10}\sum_{j=1}^{10}(y_t - \widehat{y}^\ell_{179+2j})^2. \tag{5.6.8}$$

In addition, to assess the choice of GCV, the MSE_{out} for model (5.6.1) with $k = 3, 4, 6, 7$, respectively, and for model (5.6.4) with $k = 1, 2, 4, 5$, respectively, are computed as well. All MSE_{in} and MSE_{out} are given in Table 5.4.

In summary, among the three models, the partially linear single-index model (5.6.1) performs much better than the other two, in the sense that both its MSE_{in} and MSE_{out} are the smallest among the models. Particularly, model (5.6.1) outperforms models (5.6.4) and (5.6.5) over all choices of the truncation parameter regardless of whether or not it is chosen by the GCV method. This is possibly because model (5.6.1) is the combination of a linear trend and a local adjustment by the link function such that it is more flexible than the other two.

Note also that, with $\widehat{k} = 5$ model (5.6.1) has the best performance. Therefore, model (5.6.1) with $\widehat{k} = 5$ is the most favorable one to explain the empirical relationship between the consumption and the income, investment and real interest rate for the US data from the period of 1960 to 2009.

5.7 Mathematical Details

The assumptions and some theorems in this chapter are shown in this section, while the proofs of other theorems and related lemmas can be found in the supplementary material of Dong et al. (2016).

Assumption 5.7.1 (a) Let $\{\varepsilon_j, -\infty < j < \infty\}$ be a sequence of d-dimensional independent and identically distributed (i.i.d.) continuous random variables with $\mathbb{E}\varepsilon_1 = 0$, $\mathbb{E}[\varepsilon_1\varepsilon_1^\top] = \Omega > 0$ and $\mathbb{E}\|\varepsilon_1\|^p < \infty$ for some $p > 2$. The characteristic function of ε_1 is integrable, that is, $\int |\mathbb{E}\exp(iu^\top\varepsilon_1)|du < \infty$.

(b) Let $x_t = x_{t-1} + v_t$ for $t \geq 1$ and $x_0 = O_P(1)$, where $\{v_t\}$ is a linear process defined by $v_t = \sum_{j=0}^{\infty}\rho_j\varepsilon_{t-j}$, in which $\{\rho_j\}$ is a square matrix such that $\rho_0 = I_d$, $\sum_{j=0}^{\infty} j\|\rho_j\| < \infty$ and $\rho = \sum_{j=0}^{\infty}\rho_j$ is of full rank.

(c) There is a σ–field $\mathcal{F}_t$ such that $(e_t, \mathcal{F}_t)$ is a martingale difference sequence, that is, for all t, $\mathbb{E}(e_t|\mathcal{F}_{t-1}) = 0$ almost surely (a.s.). Also, $\mathbb{E}(e_t^2|\mathcal{F}_{t-1}) = \sigma_e^2$ a.s. and $\mu_4 := \sup_{1\leq t\leq n}\mathbb{E}(e_t^4|\mathcal{F}_{t-1}) < \infty$ a.s.

(d) x_t is adapted with $\mathcal{F}_{t-1}$.

(e) Let $V_n(r) = \frac{1}{\sqrt{n}}\sum_{t=1}^{[nr]} v_t$ and $U_n(r) = \frac{1}{\sqrt{n}}\sum_{t=1}^{[nr]} e_t$. Suppose that as $n \to \infty$

$$(U_n(r), V_n(r)) \to_D (U(r), V(r)),$$

where $(U(r), V(r))$ is a vector of $(d+1)$-dimensional Brownian motions.

Assumption 5.7.2 (a) $g(x)$ is differentiable on $\mathbb{R}$ and $g^{(m-\ell)}(x)x^\ell \in L^2(\mathbb{R})$ for $\ell = 0, 1, \ldots, m$ with some integer m.

(b) $k = [a \cdot n^\kappa]$ with some constant $a > 0$, $\kappa \in (0, 1/8)$ and $\kappa(m-3) \geq \frac{1}{2}$ with m as in (a) above.

Proof (*Theorem* 5.2.2) Noting that $\sqrt[4]{n}D_n^{-1} \to \text{diag}(1, \mathbf{0}_{d-1})$ as $n \to \infty$ where $\mathbf{0}_{d-1}$ is a zero matrix of $(d-1)\times(d-1)$, by the Continuous Mapping Theorem and Theorem 5.2.1 we have

$$\begin{aligned}\sqrt[4]{n}(\widehat{\theta}_n - \theta_0) &= \sqrt[4]{n}(D_nQ^\top)^{-1}D_nQ^\top(\widehat{\theta}_n - \theta_0)\\ &= Q\sqrt[4]{n}D_n^{-1}D_n(\widehat{\alpha}_n - \alpha_0)\\ &\to_D Q\,\text{diag}(1, \mathbf{0}_{d-1})R^{-1/2}W(1)\\ &= \mathbf{MN}(0, \rho_{11}\theta_0\theta_0^\top).\end{aligned} \tag{5.7.1}$$

In addition, it follows from $\widehat{\theta}_{n,\text{emp}} = Q\widehat{\alpha}_{n,\text{unit}}$, $\theta_0 = Q\alpha_0$ and Corollary 5.2.1 that

$$\begin{aligned}n^{3/4}\left(\widehat{\theta}_{n,\text{emp}} - \theta_0\right) &= Qn^{3/4}\begin{pmatrix}\widehat{\alpha}_{n,\text{unit}}^1 - 1\\ \widehat{\alpha}_{n,\text{unit}}^2\end{pmatrix}\\ &= (\theta_0\ Q_2)\begin{pmatrix}0\\ n^{3/4}\widehat{\alpha}_{n,\text{unit}}^2\end{pmatrix} + o_P(1)\\ &= Q_2n^{3/4}\widehat{\alpha}_{n,\text{unit}}^2 + o_P(1)\\ &\to_D \mathbf{MN}(0, Q_2\rho_{22}Q_2^\top).\end{aligned}$$

Proof (*Outline of Theorem* 5.2.3) The uniform consistency of $\widehat{g}_n(u)$ follows from Lemma A.3 of Dong et al. (2016) directly. Indeed, for large n and by the consistency of $\widehat{\theta}_n$ and the continuity of $\widetilde{c}(\theta)$ in θ, we have $\|\widehat{c} - c\|^2 = \|\widetilde{c}(\widehat{\theta}_n) - c\|^2 = O_P(1)\frac{k}{\sqrt{n}}$. Then,

$$\begin{aligned}\sup_{u\in\mathbb{R}}|\widehat{g}_n(u)-g(u)| &\le \sup_{u\in\mathbb{R}}|Z_k^\top(u)[\widehat{c}-c]|+\sup_{u\in\mathbb{R}}|\gamma_k(u)|\\ &\le \sup_{u\in\mathbb{R}}\|Z_k(u)\|\|\widehat{c}-c\|+\sup_{u\in\mathbb{R}}|\gamma_k(u)|\\ &= O_P(1)\sqrt{k}n^{-1/4+\kappa/2}+o(1)k^{-(m-1)/2-1/12}\\ &= o_P(1),\end{aligned}$$

where $\sup_{u\in\mathbb{R}}\|Z_k(u)\|\le C\sqrt{k}$ and $\sup_{u\in\mathbb{R}}|\gamma_k(u)|\le Ck^{-(m-1)/2-1/12}$ with some constant $C>0$ are given in Theorem C.4.16.

For the normality, in view of the consistency of $\widehat{\sigma}_e$ and $\widehat{L}_{n1}(1,0)$, we show the result with the replacement of σ_e and $L_1(1,0)$. Meanwhile, in order to correspond to the plug-in of $\widehat{\theta}_n$, denote by $\widehat{Z}$ the matrix Z that is defined before but replacing θ_0 by $\widehat{\theta}_n$. Noting that $\widetilde{c}=\widetilde{c}(\theta_0)=(Z^\top Z)^{-1}Z^\top Y$ and $Y=Zc+\gamma+e$,

$$\begin{aligned}\widehat{c}=\widetilde{c}(\widehat{\theta}_n) &= (\widehat{Z}^\top\widehat{Z})^{-1}\widehat{Z}^\top(Zc+\gamma+e)\\ &= c+(\widehat{Z}^\top\widehat{Z})^{-1}\widehat{Z}^\top(\gamma+e)+(\widehat{Z}^\top\widehat{Z})^{-1}\widehat{Z}^\top(Z-\widehat{Z})c.\end{aligned}$$

It follows from Lemma A.2 in Dong et al. (2016) that

$$\begin{aligned}\widehat{g}_n(u)-g(u) &= Z_k^\top(u)\widehat{c}-g(u)=Z_k^\top(u)(\widehat{c}-c)-\gamma_k(u)\\ &= Z_k^\top(u)(\widehat{Z}^\top\widehat{Z})^{-1}\widehat{Z}^\top(\gamma+e)+Z_k^\top(u)(\widehat{Z}^\top\widehat{Z})^{-1}\widehat{Z}^\top(Z-\widehat{Z})c-\gamma_k(u)\\ &= \frac{1}{\sqrt{n}}L_1^{-1}(1,0)Z_k^\top(u)\widehat{Z}^\top e(1+o_P(1))+\frac{1}{\sqrt{n}}L_1^{-1}(1,0)Z_k^\top(u)\widehat{Z}^\top\gamma\\ &\quad+\frac{1}{\sqrt{n}}L_1^{-1}(1,0)Z_k^\top(u)\widehat{Z}^\top(Z-\widehat{Z})c-\gamma_k(u)\\ &= \frac{1}{\sqrt{n}}L_1^{-1}(1,0)Z_k^\top(u)Z^\top e+\frac{1}{\sqrt{n}}L_1^{-1}(1,0)Z_k^\top(u)(\widehat{Z}-Z)^\top e\\ &\quad+\frac{1}{\sqrt{n}}L_1^{-1}(1,0)Z_k^\top(u)\widehat{Z}^\top\gamma+\frac{1}{\sqrt{n}}L_1^{-1}(1,0)Z_k^\top(u)\widehat{Z}^\top(Z-\widehat{Z})c\\ &\quad-\gamma_k(u).\end{aligned}$$

To fulfill the normality, we need to show

$$\begin{aligned}&(1).\ \sigma_e^{-1}L_1(1,0)^{-1/2}\frac{1}{\sqrt[4]{n}}\|Z_k(u)\|^{-1}Z_k^\top(u)Z^\top e\to_D N(0,1),\\ &(2).\ \frac{1}{\sqrt[4]{n}}\|Z_k(u)\|^{-1}Z_k^\top(u)\widehat{Z}^\top\gamma=o_P(1),\\ &(3).\ \frac{1}{\sqrt[4]{n}}\|Z_k(u)\|^{-1}Z_k^\top(u)\widehat{Z}^\top(Z-\widehat{Z})c=o_P(1),\\ &(4).\ \sqrt[4]{n}\|Z_k(u)\|^{-1}\gamma_k(u)=o(1),\\ &(5).\ \frac{1}{\sqrt[4]{n}}\|Z_k(u)\|^{-1}Z_k^\top(u)(\widehat{Z}-Z)^\top e=o_P(1).\end{aligned}$$

To begin with (1), observe that

$$\begin{aligned} &n^{-1/4}\sigma_e^{-1}L_1^{-1/2}(1,0)\|Z_k(u)\|^{-1}Z_k^\top(u)Z^\top e \\ =&n^{-1/4}\sigma_e^{-1}L_1^{-1/2}(1,0)\|Z_k(u)\|^{-1}\sum_{t=1}^{n} Z_k^\top(u)Z_k(\theta_0^\top x_t)e_t \end{aligned}$$

which is a martingale array in view of Assumption 5.7.1. We shall use Corollary 3.1 of Hall and Heyde (1980) to show the normality of (1).

The conditional variance process is, by Lemma A.2 in Dong et al. (2016),

$$\begin{aligned} &\frac{1}{\sqrt{n}}\sigma_e^{-2}L_1^{-1}(1,0)\|Z_k(u)\|^{-2}\sum_{t=1}^{n}(Z_k^\top(u)Z_k(\theta_0^\top x_t))^2\mathbb{E}(e_t^2|\mathcal{F}_{n,t-1}) \\ =&\frac{1}{\sqrt{n}}L_1^{-1}(1,0)\|Z_k(u)\|^{-2}\sum_{t=1}^{n}(Z_k^\top(u)Z_k(x_{1t}))^2 \\ =&\frac{1}{\sqrt{n}}L_1^{-1}(1,0)\|Z_k(u)\|^{-2}Z_k^\top(u)\left(\sum_{t=1}^{n} Z_k(x_{1t})^\top Z_k(x_{1t})\right)Z_k(u) \\ =&L_1^{-1}(1,0)\|Z_k(u)\|^{-2}Z_k^\top(u)\left(\frac{1}{\sqrt{n}}Z^\top Z\right)Z_k(u) \\ =&\|Z_k(u)\|^{-2}Z_k^\top(u)Z_k(u)(1+o_P(1)) = 1+o_P(1). \end{aligned}$$

Moreover, to fulfill the conditional Lindeberg's condition it suffices to show

$$\begin{aligned} &\|Z_k(u)\|^{-4}\frac{1}{n}\sum_{t=1}^{n}\mathbb{E}[(Z_k^\top(u)Z_k(x_{1t})e_t)^4|\mathcal{F}_{n,t-1}] \\ &\le C\|Z_k(u)\|^{-4}\frac{1}{n}\sum_{t=1}^{n}\|Z_k(u)\|^4\|Z_k(x_{1t})\|^4 \\ &=C\frac{1}{n}\sum_{t=1}^{n}\|Z_k(x_{1t})\|^4 = o_P(1) \end{aligned}$$

by a routine calculation using the density of $t^{-1/2}x_{1t}$ in Lemma A.1 in Dong et al. (2016). This finishes the normality for (1).

For the sake of brevity, we refer the reader to the supplementary material of Dong et al. (2016) for the proofs of (2)–(5). The outline then is completed. □

Proof (*Outline of Theorem* 5.4.1) For any $\vartheta = (\beta, \theta)$, denote

$$\mathfrak{S}_n(\vartheta) = \begin{pmatrix} \mathfrak{S}_{n,1}(\vartheta) \\ \mathfrak{S}_{n,2}(\vartheta) \end{pmatrix} = \begin{pmatrix} \frac{\partial L_n(\vartheta)}{\partial \beta} \\ \frac{\partial L_n(\vartheta)}{\partial \theta} \end{pmatrix},$$

$$\mathfrak{J}_n(\vartheta) = \begin{pmatrix} \mathfrak{J}_{n,11}(\vartheta) & \mathfrak{J}_{n,12}(\vartheta) \\ \mathfrak{J}_{n,21}(\vartheta) & \mathfrak{J}_{n,22}(\vartheta) \end{pmatrix} = \begin{pmatrix} \frac{\partial^2 L_n(\vartheta)}{\partial \beta \partial \beta^\top} & \frac{\partial^2 L_n(\vartheta)}{\partial \beta \partial \theta^\top} \\ \frac{\partial^2 L_n(\vartheta)}{\partial \theta \partial \beta^\top} & \frac{\partial^2 L_n(\vartheta)}{\partial \theta \partial \theta^\top} \end{pmatrix}.$$

Also, for any $\mu = (\lambda, \alpha)$, $\mathfrak{S}_n(\mu)$ and $\mathfrak{J}_n(\mu)$ are defined similarly but with the parameters rotated.

Denote $\widetilde{D}_n = \mathrm{diag}(nI_d, D_n)$. Thus, (5.4.5) may be equivalently written as

$$\widetilde{D}_n^{-1}\mathfrak{S}_n(\mu_0) + \widetilde{D}_n^{-1}\mathfrak{J}_n(\mu_n)\widetilde{D}_n^{-1}\widetilde{D}_n(\widehat{\mu}_n - \mu_0) = 0. \tag{5.7.2}$$

It follows from (5.7.2) that

$$\begin{aligned} & n^{-1}\mathfrak{S}_{n,1}(\mu_0) + n^{-2}\mathfrak{J}_{n,11}(\mu_n)n(\widehat{\lambda}_n - \lambda_0) \\ & \quad + n^{-1}\mathfrak{J}_{n,12}(\mu_n)D_n^{-1}D_n(\widehat{\alpha}_n - \alpha_0) = 0, \qquad (5.7.3) \\ & D_n^{-1}\mathfrak{S}_{n,2}(\mu_0) + D_n^{-1}\mathfrak{J}_{n,21}(\mu_n)n^{-1}n(\widehat{\lambda}_n - \lambda_0) \\ & \quad + D_n^{-1}\mathfrak{J}_{n,22}(\mu_n)D_n^{-1}D_n(\widehat{\alpha}_n - \alpha_0) = 0. \qquad (5.7.4) \end{aligned}$$

The results of (5.4.6) and (5.4.7) will be derived from (5.7.3) and (5.7.4), respectively. These are shown in the following two steps.

Step I: We first prove (5.4.7) from (5.7.4). First of all, note that $\mathfrak{S}_{n,2}(\mu_0)$ and $\mathfrak{J}_{n,22}(\mu_0)$ are exactly the $S_n(\alpha_0)$ and $J_n(\alpha_0)$ in Theorem 5.2.1, respectively, since $y_t - \beta_0^\top x_t$ in model (5.4.1) plays the same role as y_t in model (5.2.4). Therefore,

$$D_n^{-1}\mathfrak{S}_{n,2}(\mu_0) \to_D R^{1/2}W(1) \quad \text{and} \quad D_n^{-1}\mathfrak{J}_{n,22}(\mu_0)D_n^{-1} \to_P R, \tag{5.7.5}$$

where R and W are defined in Theorem 5.2.1.

To prove (5.4.7), it therefore suffices to show that

$$D_n(\widehat{\alpha}_n - \alpha_0) = [D_n^{-1}\mathfrak{J}_{n,22}(\mu_0)D_n^{-1}]^{-1}D_n^{-1}\mathfrak{S}_{n,2}(\mu_0) + o_P(1). \tag{5.7.6}$$

Theorem 10.1 of Wooldridge (1994) is used to prove (5.7.6). It is shown in detail in the supplemental material of Dong et al. (2016) that $n(\widehat{\lambda}_n - \lambda_0) = Q^\top n(\widehat{\beta}_n - \beta_0) = O_P(1)$ and $D_n^{-1}\mathfrak{J}_{n,21}(\mu_0)n^{-1} = o_P(1)$. Define for some $\delta > 0$, $\widetilde{C}_n = n^{-\delta}\widetilde{D}_n = \mathrm{diag}(n^{1-\delta}I_d, C_n)$ such that $\widetilde{C}_n\widetilde{D}_n^{-1} \to 0$ as $n \to \infty$, where $C_n = n^{-\delta}D_n$ is used in the proof of Theorem 5.2.1. It follows from (5.7.4) that

$$\begin{aligned}0 = D_n^{-1}\mathfrak{S}_{n,2}(\mu_0) + n^{-2\delta}C_n^{-1}[\mathfrak{J}_{n,21}(\mu_n) - \mathfrak{J}_{n,21}(\mu_0)]n^{-1+\delta}n(\widehat{\lambda}_n - \lambda_0) + o_P(1)\\ + D_n^{-1}\mathfrak{J}_{n,22}(\mu_0)D_n^{-1}D_n(\widehat{\alpha}_n - \alpha_0)\\ + n^{-2\delta}C_n^{-1}[\mathfrak{J}_{n,22}(\mu_n) - \mathfrak{J}_{n,22}(\mu_0)]C_n^{-1}D_n(\widehat{\alpha}_n - \alpha_0).\end{aligned}$$

The requirements (i)–(ii) in Theorem 10.1 of Wooldridge (1994) are trivially fulfilled and the requirement (iii) will be satisfied if we can show

$$\sup_{\{\mu:\|\widetilde{C}_n(\mu-\mu_0)\|<1\}} \|n^{-1+\delta}C_n^{-1}[\mathfrak{J}_{n,21}(\mu) - \mathfrak{J}_{n,21}(\mu_0)]\| = o_P(1) \tag{5.7.7}$$

$$\sup_{\{\mu:\|\widetilde{C}_n(\mu-\mu_0)\|<1\}} \|C_n^{-1}[\mathfrak{J}_{n,22}(\mu) - \mathfrak{J}_{n,22}(\mu_0)]C_n^{-1}\| = o_P(1). \tag{5.7.8}$$

With the choice of $\delta \in (0, 1/24)$, both (5.7.7) and (5.7.8) are proved in the supplemental material of Dong et al. (2016) and hence, the requirement (5.7.6) is verified if we choose $\delta \in (0, 1/24)$.

Furthermore, (5.7.5) shows that the condition (iv) in Wooldridge's theorem holds. Thus, the limit distribution (5.4.7) now follows directly.

Step II: We now turn to prove (5.4.6) from (5.7.3). Because $\mathfrak{J}_{n,12}(\mu_n) = \mathfrak{J}_{n,21}(\mu_n)^\top$, $D_n(\widehat{\alpha}_n - \alpha_0) = O_P(1)$ by Step I, $\mathfrak{J}_{n,11}(\mu_n)$ is independent of μ_n and $D_n^{-1}\mathfrak{J}_{n,21}(\mu_0)n^{-1} = o_P(1)$, we have $n(\widehat{\lambda}_n - \lambda_0) = (n^{-2}\mathfrak{J}_{n,11}(\mu_n))^{-1}n^{-1}\mathfrak{S}_{n,1}(\mu_0) + o_P(1)$ by (5.7.7). Note that

$$\begin{aligned}\frac{1}{n}\mathfrak{S}_{n,1}(\mu_0) &= \frac{1}{n}Q^\top\frac{\partial L_n(\vartheta_0)}{\partial\beta} = \frac{1}{n}Q^\top\sum_{t=1}^n(y_t - \beta_0^\top x_t - \widehat{g}_n(\theta_0^\top x_t))x_t\\ &= \frac{1}{n}\sum_{t=1}^n e_tQ^\top x_t + o_P(1) \to_D Q^\top\int_0^1 V(r)dU(r),\end{aligned}$$

when $n \to \infty$. Note also that

$$\frac{1}{n^2}\mathfrak{J}_{n,11}(\mu_n) = \frac{1}{n^2}Q^\top\sum_{t=1}^n x_tx_t^\top Q \to Q^\top\int V(r)V(r)^\top dr\,Q$$

almost surely using Theorem 3.1 of Park and Phillips (2001), from which equation (5.4.6) follows. The outline of the proof is completed. □

References

Cai, L., & Wang, S. (2023). Simultaneous confidence bands and global inferences for extended partially linear single-index models. *Applied Mathematical Modelling, 113*, 30–43.

Carroll, R. J., Fan, J., Gijbels, I., & Wand, M. P. (1997). Generalized partially linear single-index models. *Journal of the American Statistical Association, 92*, 477–489.

Chang, Y., & Park, J. Y. (2003). Index models with integrated time series. *Journal of Econometrics, 114*, 73–106.
Chen, J., Gao, J., & Li, D. (2013). Estimation in partially linear single-index panel data models with fixed effects. *Journal of Business and Economic Statistics, 31*, 315–330.
Cui, X., Hardle, W. K., & Zhu, L. (2011). The EFM approach for single-index models. *Annals of Statistics, 39*, 1658–1688.
Dong, C., & Tu, Y. (2024). Semiparametric estimation and variable selection for sparse single index models in increasing dimension. *Econometric Theory*, forthcoming, 1–46.
Dong, C., Linton, O., & Peng, B. (2021). A weighted sieve estimator for nonparametric time series models with nonstationary variables. *Journal of Econometrics,222*, 909–932.
Dong, C., & Gao, J. (2018). Specification testing driven by orthogonal series for nonlinear cointegration with endogeneity. *Econometric Theory, 34*, 754–789.
Dong, C., Gao, J., & Peng, B. (2015). Semiparametric single-index panel data models with cross-sectional dependence. *Journal of Econometrics, 188*, 301–312.
Dong, C., Gao, J., & Tjøstheim, D. (2016). Estimation for single-index and partially linear single-index integrated models. *Annals of Statistics, 44*, 425–453.
Dong, C., & Linton, O. (2018). Additive nonparametric models with time variable and both stationary and nonstationary regressors. *Journal of Econometrics, 207*, 212–236.
Gao, J. (2012). Identification, estimation and specification in a class of semi-linear time series models. http://mpra.ub.uni-muenchen.de/39256/.
Gao, J., King, M., Lu, Z., & Tjøstheim, D. (2009a). Nonparametric specification testing for nonlinear time series with nonstationarity. *Econometric Theory,25*, 1869–1892.
Gao, J., King, M., Lu, Z., & Tjøstheim, D. (2009b). Specification testing in nonlinear and nonstationary time series autoregression. *Annals of Statistics,37*(68), 3893–3928.
Gao, J., & Phillips, P. C. B. (2013). Semiparametric estimation in triangular system equations with nonstationarity. *Journal of Econometrics, 176*, 59–79.
Gao, J., Tong, H., & Wolff, R. (2002). Model specification tests in nonparametric stochastic regression models. *Journal of Multivariate Analysis, 83*, 324–359.
Guerre, E., & Moon, H. R. (2006). A study of a semiparametric binary choice model with integrated covariates. *Econometric Theory, 22*, 721–742.
Hall, P., & Heyde, C. C. (1980). *Martingale Limit Theory and Its Applications*. New York: Academic.
Härdle, W., Hall, P., & Ichimura, H. (1993). Optimal smoothing in single-index models. *Annals of Statistics, 21*, 157–178.
Härdle, W., & Stocker, T. W. (1989). Investigating smooth multiple regression by method of average derivatives. *Journal of the American Statistical Association, 84*, 986–995.
Huang, L., Jiang, H., & Wang, H. (2019). A novel partial-linear single-index model for time series data. *Computational Statistics and Data Analysis, 134*, 110–122.
Ichimura, H. (1993). Semiparametric least squares (SLS) and weighted SLS estimation of single-index models. *Journal of Econometrics, 58*, 71–120.
Karlsen, H. A., Mykelbust, T., & Tjøstheim, D. (2007). Nonparametric estimation in a nonlinear cointegration type model. *Annals of Statistics, 35*, 252–299.
Karlsen, H. A., & Tjøstheim, D. (2001). Nonparametric estimation in null recurrent time series. *Annals of Statistics, 29*, 372–416.
Klein, R. W., & Spady, R. H. (1993). An efficient semiparametric estimator for binary response models. *Econometrica, 61*, 387–421.
Liang, H., Liu, X., Li, R., & Tsai, C.-L. (2010). Estimation and Testing for partially linear single-index models. *Annals of Statistics, 38*(6), 3811–3836.
Li, Q., & Fan, Y. (1996). Consistent model specification tests: Omitted variables and semiparametric functional forms. *Econometrica, 64*, 865–890.
Lin, W., & Kulasekera, K. B. (2007). Identifiability of single-index models and additive-index models. *Biometrika, 94*, 496–501.
Lin, H., Shi, J., Tong, T., & Zhang, R. (2022). Partially linear single-index model in the presence of measurement error. *Journal of Systems Science and Complexity, 35*, 2361–2380.

Lin, Y., Tu, Y., & Yao, Q. (2020). Estimation for double-nonlinear cointegration. *Journal of Econometrics, 216*, 175–191.

Ma, S., Liang, H., & Tsai, C.-L. (2014). Partially linear single index models for repeated measurements. *Journal of Multivariate Analysis, 130*, 354–375.

Ma, Y., & Zhu, L. (2013). Doubly robust and efficient estimators for heteroscedastic partially single-index models allowing high dimension covariates. *Journal of the Royal Statistical Society: Series B (Statistical Methodology), 75*(2), 305–322.

Park, J. Y., & Phillips, P. C. B. (1999). Asymptotics for nonlinear transformations of integrated time series. *Econometric Theory, 15*, 269–298.

Park, J. Y., & Phillips, P. C. B. (2000). Nonstationary binary choice. *Econometrica, 68*, 1249–1280.

Park, J. Y., & Phillips, P. C. B. (2001). Nonlinear regression with integreted time series. *Econometrica, 69*(1), 117–161.

Phillips, P. C. B. (2009). Local time theory and spurious nonparametric regression. *Econometric Theory, 25*, 1466–1497.

Phillips, P. C. B., Li, D., & Gao, J. (2017). Estimating smooth structure change in cointegration models. *Journal of Econometrics, 196*, 180–195.

Phillips, P. C. B., & Solo, V. (1992). Asymptotics for linear processes. *Annals of Statistics, 20*(2), 971–1001.

Pollard, D. (1984). *Convergence of stochastic processes*. New York: Springer.

Power, J. L., Stock, J. H., & Stoker, T. M. (1989). Semiparametric estimation of index coefficients. *Econometrica, 57*, 1403–1430.

Revuz, D., & Yor, M. (2005). *Continuous martingales and brownian motion*. A Series of Comprehensive Studies in Mathematics 293. Springer.

Severini, T. A., & Wong, W. H. (1992). Profile likelihood and conditionally parametric models. *Annals of Statistics, 20*, 1768–1802.

Teräsvirta, T., Tjøstheim, D., & Granger, C. W. J. (2010). *Modelling nonlinear economic time series*. New York: Oxford University Press.

Wang, Q., & Phillips, P. C. B. (2009a). Asymptotic theory for local time density estimation and nonparametric cointegreting regression. *Econometric Theory,25*, 710–738.

Wang, Q., & Phillips, P. C. B. (2009b). Structure nonparametric cointegrating regression. *Econometrica,77*, 1901–1948.

Wang, Q., & Phillips, P. C. B. (2012). A specification test for nonlinear nonstationary models. *Annals of Statistics, 40*(2), 727–758.

Wooldridge, J. M. (1994). *Handbook of econometrics*, Estimation and inference for dependent processes (Vol. IV, pp. 2639–2738). Amsterdam: North Holland.

Xia, Y. (2006). Asymptotic distributions for two estimators of the single-index model. *Econometric Theory, 22*, 1112–1137.

Xia, Y., Tong, H., & Li, W. K. (1999). On extended partially linear single-index models. *Boimetrika, 86*, 831–842.

Xia, Y., Tong, H., Li, W. K., & Zhu, L.-X. (2002). An adaptive estimation of dimension reduction. *Journal of the Royal Statistical Society B, 64*, 363–410.

Yu, Y., & Ruppert, D. (2002). Penalized spline estimation for partially linear single-index models. *Journal of the American Statistical Association, 97*, 1042–1054.

Zhou, W., Gao, J., Harris, D., & Kew, H. (2024). Semi-parametric single-index predictive regression models with cointegrated regressors. *Journal of Econometrics, 238*, 105577.

Zhu, L., & Xue, L. (2006). Empirical likelihood confidence regions in a partially linear single-index model. *Journal of the Royal Statistical Society Series B, 68*, 549–570.

Chapter 6
Additive Nonparametric Models

In order to remove the constraint of linearity in generalized linear models, researchers propose a class of *generalized additive models* which replaces the linear form $g(x) = \beta_0 + x_1\beta_1 + \cdots + x_d\beta_d$ by a sum of unknown smooth functions $g(x) = \beta_0 + g_1(x_1) + \cdots + g_d(x_d)$. See, for example, Stone (1985, 1986), Hastie and Tibshirani (1986), Liu et al. (2013), and Wood (2017). Moreover, to relax the possible restriction of the generalized additive models, Stone (1985, 1986) also studies the approximation of additive form $\beta_0 + g_1(x_1) + \cdots + g_d(x_d)$ to a general regression function $g(x)$. In addition, the generalized additive models can be regarded as special models of projection pursuit regression (Friedman & Stuetzle, 1981), while some authors argue that generalized additive models are the extensions of additive models in the same way to the extension of linear models to generalized linear models in order to take into account of discrete response variables.

Our point of view, nonetheless, on the regression function $g(x) = \beta_0 + g_1(x_1) + \cdots + g_d(x_d)$ with unknown component functions is the simplification of fully nonparametric models where the regression function $g(x)$ is an unknown d-dimensional function in order to circumvent the curse of dimensionality. Thus, we refer to this kind of models as *additive nonparametric models*, given by

$$y = g_1(x_1) + \cdots + g_d(x_d) + e, \tag{6.0.1}$$

where $x = (x_1, \ldots, x_d)$ is covariate vector, $g_i(\cdot)$ $(j = 1, \ldots, d)$ are unknown univariate functions, and e is the error term. Note that whether an unknown constant β_0 is involved in model (6.0.1) depends on the identification of the model.

Introduced from the above two aspects, the additive models have a fine balance between model flexibility and interpretability stemming from the nonparametric setting and additivity, respectively, and consequently, there are some pros and cons in model (6.0.1) because of the same reasons:

C. Dong and J. Gao, *Modern Series Methods in Econometrics and Statistics*,
Advanced Studies in Theoretical and Applied Econometrics 45,
https://doi.org/10.1007/978-981-96-2822-3_6

(1) Because the regression function takes an additive form of univariate functions, model (6.0.1) no longer suffers from the so-called "curse of dimensionality" when d is greater than three.
(2) Model (6.0.1) is very much flexible in choosing nonlinear models and generalizable to different types of responses, whereas it remains possibility that model (6.0.1) reduces to a linear model.
(3) Because of the additivity, we can still interpret the contribution of each predictor while considering the other predictors fixed, similar to what we do in linear models.
(4) The series-based estimates of model (6.0.1) all have closed-form expression.
(5) While additivity is convenient, it is also one of its main limitations. This is mainly because model (6.0.1) might omit important nonlinear interactions among predictors.

6.1 Identification and Estimation

Stone (1985) considers in (6.0.1) that $g(x) = \mu + g_1(x_1) + \cdots + g_d(x_d)$ where $\mu = \mathbb{E}(y)$ and for the purpose of identifiability, assumes

$$\mathbb{E}[g_j(x_j)] = 0, \quad j = 1, \ldots, d. \tag{6.1.1}$$

These restrictions are generally adopted as identification conditions in additive nonparametric models while in some circumstances there might be a variation as discussed in Dong and Linton (2018).

Given an i.i.d. sample $\{(y_i, x_{1i}, \ldots, x_{di}), i = 1, \ldots, n\}$, Stone (1985) studies spline estimator $\widehat{g}(\cdot)$. Suppose $x \in [0, 1]^d$ and

(1) The distribution of x is absolutely continuous and its density $f(\cdot)$ is bounded away from zero and infinity on $[0, 1]^d$;
(2) $g(x)$ and $\text{Var}(y|x)$ are bounded on $[0, 1]^d$;
(3) Let $p = k + \beta > 0.5$ where k is a nonnegative integer, $\beta \in (0, 1]$, $M > 0$ a constant. Assume that Hölder condition is satisfied for all $g_j(\cdot)$, $j = 1, \ldots, d$, viz.

$$|g_j^{(k)}(u) - g_j^{(k)}(v)| \leq M|u - v|^{\beta}, \quad u, v \in [0, 1]. \tag{6.1.2}$$

Under conditions (1)–(3), Stone (1985) shows that the spline estimators $\widehat{g}_j(\cdot)$ have the following rates

$$\mathbb{E}\left[\|\widehat{g}_j^{(m)} - g_j^{(m)}\|_j^2 \Big| x_1, \ldots, x_n \right] = O_P(n^{-2(k-m)/(2p+1)}), \tag{6.1.3}$$

where $m \leq k$, $\|h\|_j^2 = \mathbb{E}[h^2(x_j)]$.

It is noteworthy that the rate $n^{-2(k-m)/(2p+1)}$, particularly $n^{-2p/(2p+1)}$ for $m = 0$ and p being the smoothness order, is universally acknowledged as the optimal rate in the relevant nonparametric estimation literature. Most nonparametric estimates except spline methods may attain this rate; see Dong and Linton (2018).

A commonly used method in estimating model (6.0.1) is the so-called backfitting technique. See Friedman and Stuetzle (1981), Linton and Nielsen (1995), Linton (1997), Mammen et al. (1999), Vogt (2012), and Vogt and Walsh (2019). Observe that for any $k : 1 \le k \le d$,

$$\mathbb{E}\left[y - \mu - \sum_{j=1,\neq k}^{d} g_j(x_j) \Big| x_k \right] = g_k(x_k). \tag{6.1.4}$$

This suggests an iterative algorithm for estimating all $g_j(\cdot)$:

(1) Let $\widehat{\mu} = \bar{y}$, $g_j^{(0)}(x_j) = 0$, $j = 1, \ldots, d$.
(2) For $k = 1, \ldots, d$, estimate $g_k(x_k)$ by

$$g_k^{(i+1)}(x_k) = \mathrm{Sm}\left(y - \widehat{\mu} - \sum_{j=1,\neq k}^{d} g_j^{(i)}(x_j) \Big| x_{j1}, \ldots, x_{jn} \right)$$

where "Sm" stands for some smoothing techniques such as kernel, series, and spline methods.
(3) Check whether $\|g_k^{(i+1)} - g_k^{(i)}\| < \delta$ for all $k = 1, \ldots, d$ and for the prespecified convergence tolerance $\delta > 0$. If so, let $g_k^{(i)}(x_k)$ be the estimate of $g_k(\cdot)$, otherwise, go back to step two.

Although such backfitting algorithm is popular in the estimation of additive models, it needs iteration incurring burden on computation. By contrast, if the series method is used, all unknown functions can be estimated simultaneously, as explained below.

To ease the notation, let $d = 3$ in model (6.0.1). Suppose $g_j(x_j) \in L^2(a_j, b_j)$, $j = 1, 2, 3$. Let $\{p_{ij}(\cdot), i = 0, 1, \ldots\}$ be the orthonormal basis in $L^2(a_j, b_j)$ with $p_{0j}(\cdot) \equiv 1$. Thus, we have orthogonal expansions, $j = 1, 2, 3$,

$$g_j(x_j) = \sum_{i=0}^{\infty} c_{ij} p_{ij}(x_j), \quad c_{ij} = \langle g_j, p_{ij} \rangle.$$

Let k be the truncation parameter. We write $g_j(x_j) = c_{0j} + Z_{jk}^\top(x_j)c_j + \gamma_{jk}(x_j)$, where

$$Z_{jk} = (p_{1j}(x_j), \ldots, p_{kj}(x_j))^\top, \quad \gamma_{jk}(x_j) = \sum_{i=k+1}^{\infty} c_{ij} p_{ij}(x_j),$$

and $c_j = (c_{1j}, \ldots, c_{kj})^\top$.

But notice that, due to $p_{0j}(\cdot) \equiv 1$, in each orthogonal expansion of the component function there is a constant, i.e., c_{0j}. If we keep all these constants in the regression equation, such constants may not be identifiable and estimable individually. This is the *identification issue* in additive model when series method is used, and this issue is also encountered when other estimation methods are utilized. For example, we have mentioned that Stone (1985) uses (6.1.1) as the identification condition that is also used in Ma et al. (2021).While nonparametric additive models have identifiability and estimability issues, different estimation methods address such issues individually. To address the issue in our situation, we retain one constant $c_0 = c_{01} + c_{02} + c_{03}$ in our regression. In other words, these functions $g_j(\cdot)$ are identified up to a constant. More often than not, whether we finally have the estimates of $g_j(\cdot)$ or $g_j(\cdot) - c_{0j}$ does not affect our understanding on the economic implication, since the difference between them is only a location in vertical direction.

Then, the regression Eq. (6.0.1) is rephrased as

$$\begin{aligned} y = c_0 + Z_{1k}^\top(x_1)c_1 + Z_{2k}^\top(x_2)c_2 + Z_{3k}^\top(x_3)c_2 \\ + \gamma_{1k}(x_1) + \gamma_{2k}(x_2) + \gamma_{3k}(x_3) + e. \end{aligned} \tag{6.1.5}$$

Given the observations of y and $x = (x_1, x_2, x_3)$ with sample size n, one may estimate $c = (c_0, c_1^\top, c_2^\top, c_3^\top)^\top$ from (6.1.5) by OLS,

$$\widehat{c} = (Z^\top Z)^{-1} Z^\top Y,$$

where Z is a $n \times (3k + 1)$ matrix with the values of $(1, Z_{1k}^\top(x_1), Z_{2k}^\top(x_2), Z_{3k}^\top(x_3))$ at the observed x at each row, $Y = (y_1, \ldots, y_n)^\top$. Note that $\gamma_{jk}(x_j)$ do not affect the OLS estimates since we have shown in the appendix they are negligible under smoothness conditions on $g_j(\cdot)$.

Once we have $\widehat{c}$, define the estimators

$$\widehat{g}_1(x_1) = \widehat{c}_0 + Z_{1k}^\top(x_1)\widehat{c}_1,\ \widehat{g}_2(x_2) = Z_{2k}^\top(x_2)\widehat{c}_2,\ \widehat{g}_3(x_3) = Z_{3k}^\top(x_3)\widehat{c}_3, \tag{6.1.6}$$

for any $x = (x_1, x_2, x_3)$ in the domain. Or in a more compact way,

$$\begin{pmatrix} \widehat{g}_1(x_1) \\ \widehat{g}_2(x_2) \\ \widehat{g}_3(x_3) \end{pmatrix} = \begin{pmatrix} 1 & Z_{1k}^\top(x_1) & \mathbf{0} & \mathbf{0} \\ 0 & \mathbf{0} & Z_{2k}^\top(x_2) & \mathbf{0} \\ 0 & \mathbf{0} & \mathbf{0} & Z_{3k}^\top(x_3) \end{pmatrix} \widehat{c}$$

where $\mathbf{0}$ is row vector of k zeros. These estimators are consistent for $g_j(\cdot)$, respectively, under identification condition $c_{02} = c_{03} = 0$ and regularity conditions, while their normality can also be established accordingly.

Therefore, using series methods can offer closed-form expressions, viz., (6.1.6), without involving recursive backfitting techniques.

6.2 Cointegrating Additive Nonparametric Models

In this section, we study a prototypical additive nonparametric model. The reason that we call this model "prototypical" is because it accommodates a stationary variable, a nonstationary variable and a deterministic time trend that are commonly encountered types of time series.

In practice, all these types of variables are important in economics, finance, and related fields. For example, aggregate consumption, disposable income and share prices are widely accepted as nonstationary variables, while interest rates and the volume of share trading are often taken as stationary variables. Some variables may also contain a deterministic time trend. Therefore, from a practical point of view, it is necessary to study regressions with these three kinds of regressors while the starting point is clearly this prototypical one.

Let us consider

$$y_t = \beta(\tau_t) + g(z_t) + m(x_t) + e_t, \tag{6.2.1}$$

where $t = 1, \ldots, n$, $\tau_t = t/n$, $\beta(\cdot)$, $g(\cdot)$ and $m(\cdot)$ are unknown smooth functions, z_t is a stationary process, x_t is an integrated process, and e_t is the error term.

Evidently, $\tau_t \in (0, 1)$ and then $\beta(\cdot)$ has compact support on $[0, 1]$; $g(\cdot)$ is defined on the support V_z of z_1 that could be a finite interval like $[a, b]$ or an infinite interval like $(-\infty, \infty)$ or $(0, \infty)$, while $m(\cdot)$ is defined on $\mathbb{R}$ since the second moment of the integrated process x_t is diverging (see, Definition 5.2.1 with $d = 1$).

Grenander and Rosenblatt (1957) provide a classic treatment of parametric deterministic trend models, while Phillips (2007, 2010) provides some updated discussions. There have been a number of papers that develop a theory for nonparametric regression with nonstationary variables alone. Karlsen et al. (2007) investigate the nonparametric regression situation where the single covariate is a recurrent Markov chain. Schienle (2008) investigates additive nonparametric regressions with Harris recurrent covariates and obtained a limit theory for kernel smooth backfitting estimators. Wang and Phillips (2009) consider an alternative treatment by making use of local time limit theory and, instead of recurrent Markov chains, working with partial sum representations. Phillips et al. (2017) consider a functional coefficient model where the covariates are unit root processes and the functional coefficient is driven by rescaled time τ_t. Wang (2015) gives a recent overview of the tools needed for the establishment of an asymptotic distribution theory in a variety of these settings.

The closest study to model (6.2.1) is Chang et al. (2001) where, although all the three regressors are contained, a parametrically nonlinear model is studied. In addition, there are a number of studies that contain regressors with two of these features and most of them are linear regression models with functional coefficients. Park and Hahn (1999) study linear regression with I(1) regressor and time-varying coefficients depending on the fixed design; Xiao (2009) studies functional-coefficient cointegration regression where the coefficients depend on a stationary variable and the regressor is an I(1) vector; Cai et al. (2009) study a similar model with more flexibility; more interestingly, Li et al. (2016) investigate asymptotic properties for sample covariance estimation for a trending time series model.

6.2.1 Estimation Procedure

We now discuss a series estimation method for model (6.2.1). By nature, these functions belong to different function spaces, and therefore we introduce these function spaces and their orthonormal bases used.

First, suppose that $\beta(\cdot) \in L^2[0,1] = \{u(r) : \int_0^1 u^2(r)dr < \infty\}$, in which an inner product is given by $\langle u_1, u_2\rangle = \int_0^1 u_1(r)u_2(r)dr$ and the induced norm $\|u\|^2 = \langle u, u\rangle$. Let $\varphi_0(r) \equiv 1$, and for $j \geq 1$, $\varphi_j(r) = \sqrt{2}\cos(\pi jr)$. Then, $\{\varphi_j(r), j \geq 0\}$ is an orthonormal basis in $L^2[0,1]$, $\langle\varphi_i(r), \varphi_j(r)\rangle = \delta_{ij}$ the Kronecker delta. Accordingly,

$$\beta(r) = \sum_{j=0}^{\infty} c_{1,j}\varphi_j(r), \quad \text{where } c_{1,j} = \langle\beta(r), \varphi_j(r)\rangle. \tag{6.2.2}$$

It is noteworthy that $\{\varphi_j(r), j \geq 0\}$ can be replaced by any other orthonormal basis in $L^2[0,1]$, as shown in Chen and Shen (1998), Gao et al. (2001) and Phillips (2005), among others. However, with this specific basis other than a general one we need not impose any additional assumption on it, and these quantities related to the basis can be easily and directly calculated.

Second, in order to expand $g(z)$, suppose that the function $g(\cdot)$ is in Hilbert space $L^2(V, dF(z)) = \{q(z) : \int_V q^2(z)dF(z) < \infty\}$ where $F(z)$ is a distribution on the support V of z_1. Moreover, let sequence $\{p_j(z), j \geq 0\}$ be an orthonormal basis in $L^2(V, dF(z))$ where an inner product is given by $\langle q_1, q_2\rangle = \int_V q_1(z)q_2(z)dF(z)$ and the induced norm $\|q\|^2 = \langle q, q\rangle$. Given the support $V \subset \mathbb{R}$, the choice of the density $dF(z)$ determines what function space we shall work with. It is well known that an orthogonal polynomial sequence can be constructed on a support with respect to a density by Gram-Schmidt orthonormalization theorem. See, for example, Dudley (2003, p. 168). If z_1 has support $V = \mathbb{R}$, the sequence is consisting of Hermite polynomials given $dF(z) = e^{-z^2/2}dz$; if z_1 has support $V = [0, \infty)$, the sequence is consisting of Laguerre polynomials given $dF(z) = e^{-z}dz$; if $V = [0,1]$, orthogonal trigonometric polynomials could be used; if $V = [-1, 1]$, the orthogonal polynomials are Chebyshev or Legendre polynomials.

Accordingly, the unknown function $g(z)$ has an orthogonal series expansion in terms of the basis of $\{p_j(z), j \geq 0\}$, viz.,

$$g(z) = \sum_{j=0}^{\infty} c_{2,j}p_j(z), \quad \text{where } c_{2,j} = \langle g(z), p_j(z)\rangle. \tag{6.2.3}$$

Third, because of Assumption 6.5.1 in Sect. 6.5, $x_t = O_P(\sqrt{t})$. Thus, the support of $m(\cdot)$ has to be $\mathbb{R}$. We therefore suppose $m(\cdot) \in L^2(\mathbb{R}) = \{f(x) : \int f^2(x)dx < \infty\}$ in which an inner product is given by $\langle f_1, f_2 \rangle = \int f_1(x) f_2(x)dx$ and the induced norm $\|f\|^2 = \langle f, f \rangle$. To expand $m(x)$, recall the sequence of the Hermite functions $\{\mathscr{H}_j(x)\}$ that is an orthonormal basis in $L^2(\mathbb{R})$. The unknown function $m(x)$ thence has an orthogonal series expansion in terms of $\{\mathscr{H}_j(x)\}$, viz.,

$$m(x) = \sum_{j=0}^{\infty} c_{3,j} \mathscr{H}_j(x), \quad \text{where } c_{3,j} = \langle m(x), \mathscr{H}_j(x) \rangle. \tag{6.2.4}$$

Let $k_i, i = 1, 2, 3$, be positive integers. Define the corresponding truncation series and residues with truncation parameter k_i for $\beta(r)$, $g(z)$ and $m(x)$ as follows,

$$\beta_{k_1}(r) = \sum_{j=1}^{k_1} c_{1,j}\varphi_j(r), \qquad \gamma_{1k_1}(r) = \sum_{j=k_1+1}^{\infty} c_{1,j}\varphi_j(r),$$

$$g_{k_2}(z) = \sum_{j=0}^{k_2-1} c_{2,j} p_j(z), \qquad \gamma_{2k_2}(z) = \sum_{j=k_2}^{\infty} c_{2,j} p_j(z),$$

$$m_{k_3}(x) = \sum_{j=0}^{k_3-1} c_{3,j}\mathscr{H}_j(x), \qquad \gamma_{3k_3}(x) = \sum_{j=k_3}^{\infty} c_{3,j}\mathscr{H}_j(x).$$

Note that we impose $c_{1,0} = 0$ in $\beta_{k_1}(r)$ for identification issue since normally $p_0(z) \equiv 1$ so that $c_{2,0}$ can remain as the intercept, whereas $\mathscr{H}_0(x)$ is a nonconstant function of x and hence $c_{3,0}$ can be identified by the variation of x and its observations. It follows that $\beta_{k_1}(r) \to \beta(r)$, $g_{k_2}(z) \to g(z)$ and $m_{k_3}(x) \to m(x)$ as $k_i \to \infty$ in some sense under certain conditions.

Denote $\phi_{k_1}(r) = (\varphi_1(r), \ldots, \varphi_{k_1}(r))^\top$, $a_{k_2}(x) = (p_0(x), \ldots, p_{k_2-1}(x))^\top$, and $b_{k_3}(x) = (\mathscr{H}_0(x), \ldots, \mathscr{H}_{k_3-1}(x))^\top$; $c_1 = (c_{1,1}, \ldots, c_{1,k_1})^\top$, $c_i = (c_{i,0}, \ldots, c_{i,k_i-1})^\top$, $i = 2, 3$. Accordingly, we have $\beta_{k_1}(r) = \phi_{k_1}(r)^\top c_1$, $g_{k_2}(x) = a_{k_2}(x)^\top c_2$ and $m_{k_3}(x) = b_{k_3}(x)^\top c_3$. Thus, model (6.2.1) is written as

$$\begin{aligned} y_t = {} & \phi_{k_1}(\tau_t)^\top c_1 + a_{k_2}(z_t)^\top c_2 + b_{k_3}(x_t)^\top c_3 \\ & + \gamma_{1k_1}(\tau_t) + \gamma_{2k_2}(z_t) + \gamma_{3k_3}(x_t) + e_t, \end{aligned} \tag{6.2.5}$$

where $t = 1, \ldots, n$.

To write all equations in (6.2.5) into a matrix form, let $Y = (y_1, \ldots, y_n)^\top$, $c = (c_1^\top, c_2^\top, c_3^\top)^\top$, $e = (e_1, \ldots, e_n)^\top$, and $\gamma = (\gamma(1), \ldots, \gamma(n))^\top$ where $\gamma(t) = \gamma_{1k_1}(\tau_t) + \gamma_{2k_2}(z_t) + \gamma_{3k_3}(x_t)$, $t = 1, \ldots, n$, and

$$B_{nk} = \begin{pmatrix} \phi_{k_1}(\tau_1)^\top & a_{k_2}(z_1)^\top & b_{k_3}(x_1)^\top \\ \vdots & \vdots & \vdots \\ \phi_{k_1}(\tau_n)^\top & a_{k_2}(z_n)^\top & b_{k_3}(x_n)^\top \end{pmatrix}$$

is a $n \times k$ matrix with $k = k_1 + k_2 + k_3$ for convenience. Consequently, we have

$$Y = B_{nk}c + \gamma + e, \tag{6.2.6}$$

which by the ordinary least squares (OLS) gives

$$\widehat{c} = (\widehat{c}_1^\top, \widehat{c}_2^\top, \widehat{c}_3^\top)^\top = (B_{nk}^\top B_{nk})^{-1} B_{nk}^\top Y,$$

provided that the matrix $B_{nk}^\top B_{nk}$ is nonsingular (which will be under our conditions with high probability).

Therefore, for any $r \in [0, 1]$, $z \in V$ and $x \in \mathbb{R}$, define naturally $\widehat{\beta}_n(r) = \phi_{k_1}(r)^\top \widehat{c}_1$, $\widehat{g}_n(z) = a_{k_2}(z)^\top \widehat{c}_2$ and $\widehat{m}_n(x) = b_{k_3}(x)^\top \widehat{c}_3$ as the estimators of the unknown functions β, g and m, which can be written into a vector version of the form:

$$(\widehat{\beta}_n(r), \widehat{g}_n(z), \widehat{m}_n(x))^\top = \Psi(r, z, x)^\top \widehat{c}, \tag{6.2.7}$$

where $\Psi(r, z, x)$ is a block matrix given by

$$\Psi(r, z, x) = \begin{pmatrix} \phi_{k_1}(r) & \mathbf{0} & \mathbf{0} \\ \mathbf{0} & a_{k_2}(z) & \mathbf{0} \\ \mathbf{0} & \mathbf{0} & b_{k_3}(x) \end{pmatrix},$$

in which $\mathbf{0}$'s are zero column vectors that may have different dimensions.

6.2.2 Asymptotic Theory

Note by Eq. (6.2.6) that $\widehat{c} - c = (B_{nk}^\top B_{nk})^{-1} B_{nk}^\top (\gamma + e)$. Thus, it is necessary to study the asymptotic behavior of $B_{nk}^\top B_{nk}$, which is done by Lemma 6.5.5 in Sect. 6.5.

Before we establish an asymptotic theory for the proposed estimators, we introduce some notation and preliminary results. Let $D_n = \mathrm{diag}(\sqrt{n} I_{k_1}, \sqrt{n} I_{k_2}, \sqrt{n/d_n} I_{k_3})$, a diagonal matrix of $k \times k$ ($k = k_1 + k_2 + k_3$), where $d_n = \sqrt{n}|\psi|(1 + o(1))$ and ψ is given by Assumption 6.5.1 in Sect. 6.5. Then, as shown in Lemma 6.5.5, $D_n^{-1} B_{nk}^\top B_{nk} D_n^{-1}$ is asymptotically approximated by a matrix in probability, viz., $\|D_n^{-1} B_{nk}^\top B_{nk} D_n^{-1} - U_k\| = o_P(1)$ as $n \to \infty$ on a richer probability space. Here, $U_k = \mathrm{diag}(I_{k_1}, U_{k_2}, L_W(1, 0) I_{k_3})$ where given in preceding chapter $L_W(1, 0)$ is the local time of $W(r)$ that is the weak limit of x_t/d_n, and $U_{k_2} = \mathbb{E}[a_{k_2}(z_1) a_{k_2}(z_1)^\top]$.

We allow for heteroskedasticity. In order to do so, suppose that $\mathbb{E}(e_t^2|\mathcal{F}_{n,t-1}) = \sigma^2(\tau_t)$, where $\sigma^2(\cdot)$ is a positive continuous function on $[0, 1]$ and $\mathcal{F}_{n,t}$ forms a filtration sequence that contains information up to time t. In order to tackle the heteroskedasticity, we also need to consider the limit of the conditional covariance matrix $B_{nk}^\top \Sigma_n B_{nk}$ where $\Sigma_n = \text{diag}(\sigma^2(\tau_1), \sigma^2(\tau_2), \dots, \sigma^2(\tau_n))$. Note that $\|D_n^{-1} B_{nk}^\top \Sigma_n B_{nk} D_n^{-1} - V_k\| = o_P(1)$ where $V_k = \text{diag}\left(V_*, \int_0^1 \sigma^2(r) dL_W(r, 0) I_{k_3}\right)$ in which $V_* = (V_{*ij})$ is a 2×2 symmetric block matrix with

$$
\begin{aligned}
V_{*11} &= \int_0^1 \phi_{k_1}(r)\phi_{k_1}(r)^\top \sigma^2(r)dr, \\
V_{*12} &= \int_0^1 \phi_{k_1}(r)\sigma^2(r)dr \mathbb{E}(a_{k_2}(z_1)^\top), \\
V_{*22} &= \int_0^1 \sigma^2(r)dr \mathbb{E}(a_{k_2}(z_1)a_{k_2}(z_1)^\top),
\end{aligned}
$$

which is given by Lemma 6.5.6.

In the homoskedasticity case, $V_k = \sigma^2 U_k$, where $\sigma^2(\cdot) \equiv \sigma^2$. To show the limit distribution of the estimators, define $L_\sigma = \text{diag}(1, 1, \int_0^1 \sigma^2(r) dL_W(r, 0))$, $L_3 = \text{diag}(1, 1, L_W(1, 0))$, $\bar{U}_k = \text{diag}(I_{k_1}, U_{k_2}, I_{k_3})$, $\bar{V}_k = \text{diag}(V_*, I_{k_3})$ and $\overline{\Psi}(r, z, x) = \Psi(r, z, x)\, \text{diag}(\|\phi_{k_1}(r)\|, \|a_{k_2}(z)\|, \|b_{k_3}(x)\|)^{-1}$ is the normalized $\Psi(r, z, x)$ defined in the preceding subsection.

The following theorem, along with the assumptions on which it is established, is given by Dong and Linton (2018), while for the sake of convenience and completeness, these assumptions are shown in Sect. 6.5.

Theorem 6.2.1 *Suppose that uniformly over all n, these eigenvalues of U_{k_2} and V_* are bounded below from zero and above from infinity. Let Assumptions 6.5.1–6.5.4 in Sect. 6.5 hold. Then, for any $r \in [0, 1]$, $z \in V$ and $x \in \mathbb{R}$,*

$$
\Omega_n^{-1/2} \begin{pmatrix} \frac{\sqrt{n}}{\|\phi_{k_1}(r)\|}[\widehat{\beta}_n(r) - \beta(r)] \\ \frac{\sqrt{n}}{\|a_{k_2}(z)\|}[\widehat{g}_n(z) - g(z)] \\ \sqrt{\frac{n}{d_n}} \frac{1}{\|b_{k_3}(x)\|}[\widehat{m}_n(x) - m(x)] \end{pmatrix} \to_D N(\mathbf{0}, L_3^{-1} L_\sigma L_3^{-1}) \tag{6.2.8}
$$

as $n \to \infty$, where $\Omega_n = \overline{\Psi}(r, z, x)^\top \bar{U}_k^{-1} \bar{V}_k \bar{U}_k^{-1} \overline{\Psi}(r, z, x)$, $\mathbf{0}$ is the 3-dimensional column vector of zeros. □

The boundedness of these eigenvalues of U_{k_2} and V_* is a commonly used assumption in the relevant literature, see, for example, Condition A.2 in Belloni et al. (2015, p. 347). Here, $U_{k_2} = \mathbb{E}[a_{k_2}(z_1)a_{k_2}(z_1)^\top]$, and V_* is formed in the same way but from deterministic basis functions and another basis functions of variable z_t. This condition, along with the block diagonal structure containing the local time $L_W(1, 0)$, is sufficient in the derivation of the normality in the theorem.

In the homoskedasticity case where $V_k = \sigma^2 U_k$, two requirements are reduced to that about U_{k_2} and researchers often normalize U_{k_2} to be the identity matrix. See, for example, Eq. (11) of Chen and Christensen (2015, p. 450) and the normalization of Belloni et al. (2015, p. 347).

Note that the matrix Δ_n has a diagonal block form

$$\Delta_n = \text{diag}\left([\Psi_1(r,z)^\top U_*^{-1} V_* U_*^{-1} \Psi_1(r,z)]^{1/2}, \left(\int_0^1 \sigma^2(r) dL_W(r,0)\right)^{1/2} \frac{\|b_{k_3}(x)\|}{L_W(1,0)}\right),$$

where we denote $\Psi_1(r,z)$ as the left-top 2×2 sub-matrix of $\Psi(r,z,x)$. This reveals some crucial asymptotic behaviors for the variables. Due to the divergence of the I(1) process x_t, all interactions between $m(x_t)$ and each one of $\beta(\tau_t)$ and $g(z_t)$ with proper normalization are asymptotically negligible and thence Δ_n has the above diagonal block form. The details can be found in Lemmas 6.5.5 and 6.5.6 below.

Therefore, we can separate the estimator $\widehat{m}_n(x)$ from the other estimators in (6.2.8) as follows:

$$[\Psi_1(r,z)^\top U_*^{-1} V_* U_*^{-1} \Psi_1(r,z)]^{-1/2} \begin{pmatrix} \sqrt{n}[\widehat{\beta}_n(r) - \beta(r)] \\ \sqrt{n}[\widehat{g}_n(z) - g(z)] \end{pmatrix} \to_D N(0, I_2), \quad (6.2.9)$$

$$\frac{L_W(1,0)}{\left(\int_0^1 \sigma^2(r) dL_W(r,0)\right)^{1/2}} \sqrt{\frac{n}{d_n \|b_{k_3}(x)\|^2}} (\widehat{m}_n(x) - m(x)) \to_D N(0,1). \quad (6.2.10)$$

All these results are comparable with the literature in the corresponding context. In fact, suppose without loss of generality, U_* is an identity matrix and $V_* = \sigma^2 U_*$. Then, the rates of (6.2.9) are $[\sqrt{n}/\|\phi_{k_1}(r)\|]^{-1}$ and $[\sqrt{n}/\|a_{k_2}(z)\|]^{-1}$ for $\widehat{\beta}_n(r) - \beta(r)$ and $[\widehat{g}_n(z) - g(z)]$, respectively, which are the same estimators as in Theorem 2 of Newey (1997) and Theorem 3.1 of Chen and Christensen (2015) in the case that the functional of the estimator in the papers is identical.

Meanwhile, the rate in (6.2.10) is about $n^{-1/4}\|b_{k_3}(x)\|$, very slow due to the divergence of x_t and the integrability of $m(x)$. This is the same as that in Theorem 3.3 of Dong et al. (2016) but note that $\|b_{k_3}(x)\| = Ck_3^{1/4}$ from Sect. C.5 of Appendix C. Overall, although the additive model has a mixture of deterministic trend, an unknown function of stationary variable, and an integrable function of the unit root variable, the estimators have their own rates of convergence.

The matrices U_* and V_* can be simplified in a special case where the function sequence $\{p_j(z)\}$ is orthogonal with respect to the density of z_1 (i.e., $dF(x)$ in the space $L^2(V, dF(x))$ is the density of z_1). Hence, $\mathbb{E}(a_{k_2}(z_1)) = 0$ and $\mathbb{E}(a_{k_2}(z_1)a_{k_2}(z_1)^\top) = I_{k_2}$. When $\sigma^2(\cdot) \equiv \sigma^2$, $V_* = \sigma^2 I_{k_1+k_2}$ and $U_* = I_{k_1+k_2}$, the limits of $\widehat{\beta}_n(r) - \beta(r)$ and $\widehat{g}_n(z) - g(z)$ in (6.2.9) can be further simplified.

More importantly, the conventional optimal rates of convergence of $\|\widehat{\beta}_n(r) - \beta(r)\|$ and $\|\widehat{g}_n(z) - g(z)\|$ can be jointly established where $\|\cdot\|$ stands for the norm of functions in the spaces defined previously. Here, the conventional rates are optimal according to what has been studied in Stone (1982, 1985). The following proposition and corollary are from Dong and Linton (2018).

Proposition 6.2.1 *Let Assumptions 6.5.1–6.5.4 in Sect. 6.5 hold. In model* (6.2.1) *we have jointly* $\|\widehat{\beta}_n(r) - \beta(r)\| = O_P(\sqrt{k_1/n} + k_1^{-s_1})$, $\|\widehat{g}_n(z) - g(z)\| = O_P(\sqrt{k_2/n} + k_2^{-s_2})$ *and* $\|\widehat{m}_n(x) - m(x)\| = O_P(\sqrt[4]{k_3/n} + k_3^{-s_3/2})$ *as* $n \to \infty$, *where the norms are of* L_2 *sense in the function spaces, respectively.* □

The proposition implies that the optimal rates of Stone (1982, 1985) are attainable jointly for the estimators $\widehat{\beta}_n(r)$ and $\widehat{g}_n(z)$. Indeed, if $k_i = O(n^{1/(2s_i+1)})$, the rates will be $O_P(n^{-s_i/(2s_i+1)})$, $i = 1, 2$, which are exactly the optimal rates in Stone (1982, 1985). Note also that in the literature as far as we know, there is no study dwelling on the optimal rates with respect to unit root regressors. While Newey (1997) and Chen and Christensen (2015, p. 451) obtain optimal rates for their sieve estimators in some specific situations, Proposition 6.2.1 establishes the optimal rates jointly for the estimators of two nonparametric functions of time trend and stationary variable, respectively, in an additive model, along with the convergence rate of nonparametric function of a unit root process.

In order to make statistical inference, the function $\sigma^2(\cdot)$ needs to be estimated. Though the estimation is possible by nonparametric method using the estimated residues, the main purpose would be deviated if we were about to do so. In what follows, we focus on the inference in the case of homoskedasticity. It can be seen from (6.2.9)–(6.2.10) that $V_* = \sigma^2 U_*$ and we need to estimate σ^2 and $nL_W(1,0)/d_n$ because $\int_0^1 \sigma^2(r) dL_W(r,0) = \sigma^2 L_W(1,0)$. Since the unknown parameter in d_n, viz., ψ, can be offset from the estimate of $L_W(1,0)$, we simply estimate the quantity $nL_W(1,0)/d_n$ directly. Define

$$\widehat{\sigma} = \left[\frac{1}{n}\sum_{t=1}^{n}(y_t - \widehat{\beta}_n(t/n) - \widehat{g}_n(z_t) - \widehat{m}_n(x_t))^2\right]^{1/2},$$

$$\Lambda_n = \sum_{t=1}^{n} f(x_t), \qquad \text{where } f(x) = \frac{1}{\sqrt{2\pi}} e^{-x^2/2}.$$

Corollary 6.2.1 *Suppose that Assumptions 6.5.1–6.5.4 in Sect. 6.5 hold. Then,* $\widehat{\sigma} \to_P \sigma$ *and* $\Lambda_n/(nL_W(1,0)/d_n) \to_P 1$ *as* $n \to \infty$. *As a result, with the replacement of* σ *by* $\widehat{\sigma}$ *and* $nL_W(1,0)/d_n$ *by* Λ_n, *we have, as* $n \to \infty$,

$$[\widehat{\sigma}^2 \overline{\Psi}_{12}(r,z)^\top U_*^{-1} \overline{\Psi}_1(r,z)]^{-1/2} \begin{pmatrix} \frac{\sqrt{n}}{\|\phi_{k_1}(r)\|}[\widehat{\beta}_n(r) - \beta(r)] \\ \frac{\sqrt{n}}{\|a_{k_2}(z)\|}[\widehat{g}_n(z) - g(z)] \end{pmatrix} \to_D N(0, I_2), \quad (6.2.11)$$

$$\sqrt{\Lambda_n}\frac{1}{\widehat{\sigma}\|b_{k_3}(x)\|}(\widehat{m}_n(x) - m(x)) \to_D N(0,1). \quad (6.2.12)$$

6.3 Monte Carlo Simulations

In this section, we conduct Monte Carlo simulations to investigate the performance of our estimators proposed in the last section in the finite sample situations. Let $M = 1000$ be the number of replications corresponding to each sample size specified below.

Example 6.3.1 In regression (6.2.1), let $\beta(r) = r - 1/2$ that satisfies $\int_0^1 \beta(r)dr = 0$, $g(z) = z^2 + \sin(z)$, and $m(x) = 1/(1 + x^4)$. Moreover, the cosine sequence given in (6.2.2) is utilized for the expansion of $\beta(r)$; the Chebyshev polynomials of the first kind, $p_j(z) = \cos(j \;\arccos(z))$, $j \geq 0$, are used to expand the function $g(\cdot)$; and the Hermite functions are used for the orthogonal expansion of $m(x)$.

Suppose that $\epsilon_i \sim N(0, 1)$, $w_t = \rho w_{t-1} + \epsilon_t$ with $\rho = 0.2$ and $w_0 \sim N(0, 1/(1 - \rho^2))$. This is the theoretical distribution of w_0 in the AR(1) process. Let $x_0 = 0$, $x_t = x_{t-1} + w_t$, $t \geq 1$. Moreover, let $z_t \sim i.i.U[-1, 1]$. Then, we generate $y_t = \beta(t/n) + g(z_t) + m(x_t) + e_t$, $t = 1, \ldots, n$, where $e_t \sim N(0, 1)$.

In the experiments below, the sample size is $n = 400, 600$, and 1200, respectively, and the truncation parameters $k_1 = k_2 = 3, 4, 5$ for $\beta(\cdot)$ and $g(\cdot)$, and $k_3 = 3, 4, 6$ for $m(\cdot)$, corresponding to each sample size. This indicates that the truncation parameters vary according to the sample sizes. It is noteworthy that, though in stationary case one may use the Generalized Cross Validation (GCV) (see, e.g., Gao, 2007) to determine the truncation parameter, there is no similar approach in nonstationary cases.

Having obtained all the estimators by our estimation procedure, we shall calculate their bias (denoted by $B_\beta(n)$, $B_g(n)$ and $B_m(n)$), standard deviation (denoted by $\pi_\beta(n)$, $\pi_g(n)$ and $\pi_m(n)$) and RMSE (denoted by $\Pi_\beta(n)$, $\Pi_g(n)$ and $\Pi_m(n)$). These quantities are defined as

$$B_\beta(n) \equiv \frac{1}{Mn}\sum_{t=1}^{n}\sum_{\ell=1}^{M}[\beta(t/n) - \bar{\widehat{\beta}}(t/n)],$$

$$\pi_\beta(n) \equiv \left(\frac{1}{Mn}\sum_{t=1}^{n}\sum_{\ell=1}^{M}[\widehat{\beta}^\ell(t/n) - \bar{\widehat{\beta}}(t/n)]^2\right)^{1/2},$$

$$B_g(n) \equiv \frac{1}{Mn}\sum_{t=1}^{n}\sum_{\ell=1}^{M}[g^\ell(z_t) - \bar{\widehat{g}}(z_t)],$$

$$\pi_g(n) \equiv \left(\frac{1}{Mn}\sum_{t=1}^{n}\sum_{\ell=1}^{M}[\widehat{g}^\ell(z_t) - \bar{\widehat{g}}(z_t)]^2\right)^{1/2},$$

$$B_m(n) \equiv \frac{1}{Mn}\sum_{t=1}^{n}\sum_{\ell=1}^{M}[m^\ell(x_t) - \bar{\widehat{m}}(x_t)],$$

$$\pi_m(n) \equiv \left(\frac{1}{Mn}\sum_{t=1}^{n}\sum_{\ell=1}^{M}[\widehat{m}^\ell(x_t) - \bar{\widehat{m}}(x_t)]^2\right)^{1/2},$$

where the superscript ℓ indicates the ℓ-th replication, $\overline{\widehat{\beta}}(\cdot) = \phi_{k_1}(\cdot)^\top \overline{\widehat{c_1}}$, $\overline{\widehat{g}}(\cdot) = a_{k_2}(\cdot)^\top \overline{\widehat{c_2}}$ and $\overline{\widehat{m}}(\cdot) = b_{k_3}(\cdot)^\top \overline{\widehat{c_3}}$ are the average of $\widehat{\beta}^\ell(\cdot)$, $\widehat{g}^\ell(\cdot)$ and $\widehat{m}^\ell(\cdot)$, respectively, over Monte Carlo replications $\ell = 1, \ldots, M$, $g^\ell(z_t)$ and $m^\ell(x_t)$ are the values of g and m evaluated for the z_t and x_t, respectively, in the ℓ-th replication; and

$$\Pi_\beta(n) \equiv \left(\frac{1}{Mn} \sum_{t=1}^{n} \sum_{\ell=1}^{M} [\beta(t/n) - \widehat{\beta}^\ell(t/n)]^2 \right)^{1/2},$$

$$\Pi_g(n) \equiv \left(\frac{1}{Mn} \sum_{t=1}^{n} \sum_{\ell=1}^{M} [g^\ell(z_t) - \widehat{g}^\ell(z_t)]^2 \right)^{1/2},$$

$$\Pi_m(n) \equiv \left(\frac{1}{Mn} \sum_{t=1}^{n} \sum_{\ell=1}^{M} [m^\ell(x_t) - \widehat{m}^\ell(x_t)]^2 \right)^{1/2}.$$

All results are reported in Table 6.1. It can be seen that all the statistics perform very well as these reported quantities decrease reasonably with the increase of the sample size. Nevertheless, there might be a visible slower rate for the estimator of m function than the other two. This is possible because the rate of convergence of the estimator $\widehat{m}_n(x)$ to $m(x)$ is the slowest among all estimators, in view of Theorem 6.2.1.

In addition, with the same estimators, we also calculate their values at particular points, i.e., $\widehat{\beta}^\ell(0.5)$, $\widehat{g}^\ell(-0.4)$ and $\widehat{m}^\ell(1.2)$ for all $\ell = 1, \ldots, M$. Then we may estimate the densities of $\widehat{\beta}^\ell(0.5) - \beta(0.5)$, $\widehat{g}^\ell(-0.4) - g(-0.4)$ and $\widehat{m}^\ell(1.2) - m(1.2)$ with normalization shown in Corollary 6.2.1. These are done in Matlab by the `ksdensity` function and are plotted in Figs. 6.1 and 6.2.

It can be seen from Figs. 6.1 and 6.2 that the curves of the estimated densities for $\widehat{\beta}_n(0.5) - \beta(0.5)$, $\widehat{g}(-0.4) - g(-0.4)$ and $\widehat{m}_n(1.2) - m(1.2)$ are gradually approaching the standard normal density. Particularly, the first two estimations seem visually to have a quicker convergence, which coincides again with our theoretical results in the preceding section.

Table 6.1 Bias, SD, and RMSE of the estimators

n	Bias			SD			RMSE		
	$B_\beta(n)$	$B_g(n)$	$B_m(n)$	$\pi_\beta(n)$	$\pi_g(n)$	$\pi_m(n)$	$\Pi_\beta(n)$	$\Pi_g(n)$	$\Pi_m(n)$
400	0.0012	−0.0605	0.0863	0.1040	0.1093	0.2117	0.0917	0.0831	0.1063
600	0.0004	−0.0496	0.0804	0.0992	0.0990	0.1429	0.0831	0.0775	0.0975
1200	0.0001	−0.0431	0.0497	0.0761	0.0725	0.1193	0.0707	0.0624	0.0774

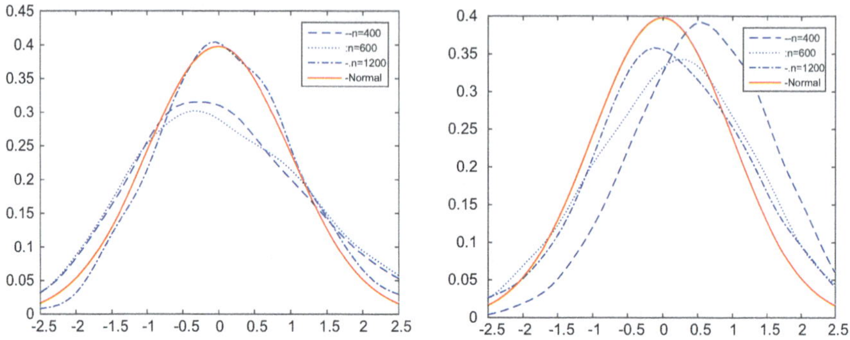

(a) Estimated density of $\widehat{\beta}_n(0.5) - \beta(0.5)$ (b) Estimated density of $\widehat{g}(-0.4) - g(-0.4)$

Fig. 6.1 The plot of estimated density functions

Fig. 6.2 Estimated density of $\widehat{m}_n(1.2) - m(1.2)$

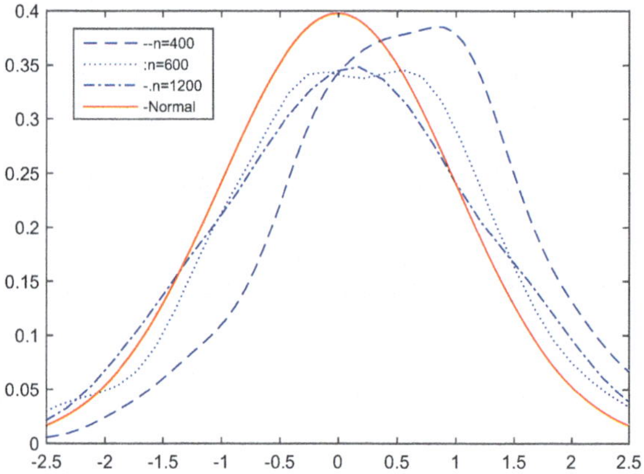

6.4 Empirical Study

In this section, we investigate the relationship between the stock prices of Coke and Pepsi using the proposed additive model. Let Y_t be the log adjusted close price of Coke, X_t be the log adjusted close price of Pepsi, and z_t be the ratio of the trading volume for Coke and that for Coke plus Pepsi such that we always have $0 \leq z_t \leq 1$. The time span is from the first of June, 1972 to the 31 August, 2016. We have $n = 11163$ observations excluding all weekends and public holidays; these data are plotted in Figs. 6.3 and 6.4.

The ADF test is employed to verify whether X_t is a unit root process. The test fails to reject the null hypothesis that X_t is a unit root process with the p-Value 0.9901. The same test is implemented on Y_t and results in the p-Value 0.9627, impling that Y_t is a unit root process too. In order to visualize the unit root processes, we also plot the daily returns of Coke and Pepsi in Fig. 6.5. The marginal price series appear to contain drifts and be nonrecurrent, viz., we may suppose that

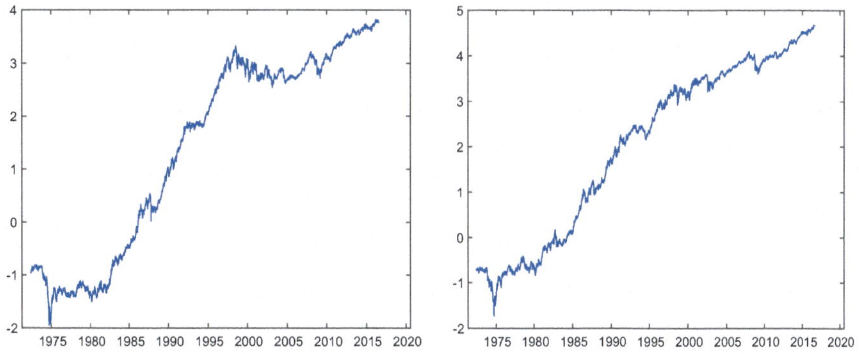

(a) Log price of Coke (b) Log price of Pepsi

Fig. 6.3 Plot data about Coke and Pepsi

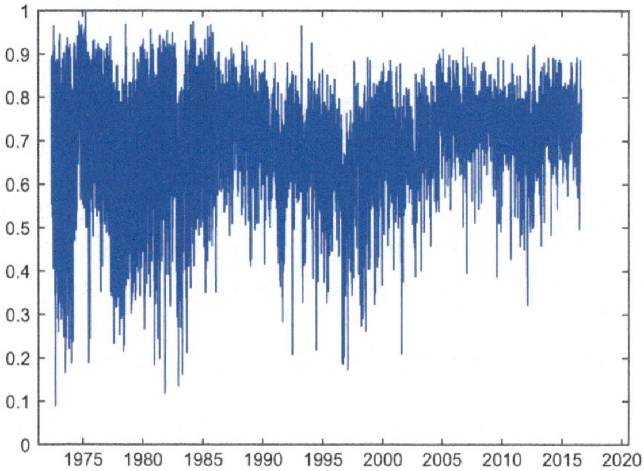

Fig. 6.4 Volume weight

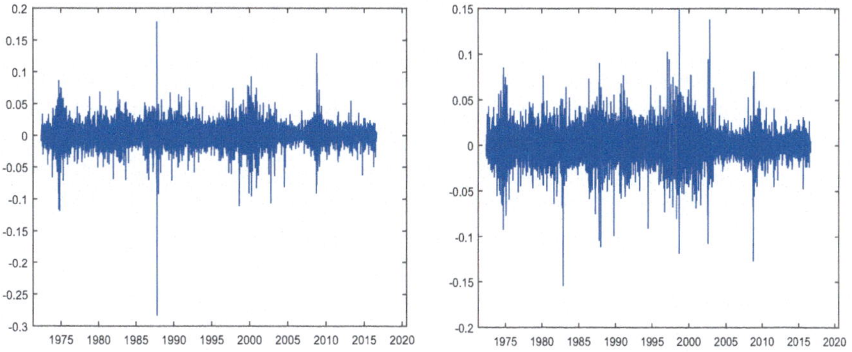

(a) Daily return of Coke (b) Daily return of Pepsi

Fig. 6.5 Daily returns of Coke and Pepsi

$X_t = \mu_1 + X_{t-1} + \xi_t$ and $Y_t = \mu_2 + Y_{t-1} + \zeta_t$, with $\mu_1, \mu_2 \neq 0$. This suggests that $X_t - \mu_1 t = X_0 + \sum_{j=1}^{t} \xi_j$ and $Y_t - \mu_2 t = Y_0 + \sum_{j=1}^{t} \zeta_j$ are recurrent processes that satisfy the theoretical requirement in the assumption in Sect. 6.5. We shall work with $x_t = X_t - \hat{\mu}_1 t$ and $y_t = Y_t - \hat{\mu}_2 t$, where $\hat{\mu}_1 = (X_n - X_0)/n$ and $\hat{\mu}_2 = (Y_n - Y_0)/n$ are consistent estimators of μ_1 and μ_2, respectively. More importantly, z_t and x_t might have certain correlation which our theory can deal with (see Assumption 6.5.2).

To investigate the relationship of the variables y_t, $\tau_t = t/n$, z_t and x_t, we use our model of the form:

$$y_t = \beta(\tau_t) + g(z_t) + m(x_t) + e_t, \tag{6.4.1}$$

for $t = 1, \ldots, n$, where all functions $\beta(\cdot)$, $g(\cdot)$ and $m(\cdot)$ are unknown and will be estimated using series methods. Since both $\beta(\cdot)$ and $g(\cdot)$ are defined on [0, 1], we use the cosine basis for their expansions, while for the expansion of $m(\cdot)$, Hermite function sequence is used.

One crucial issue in using series methods in practice is to determine the truncation parameter involved in the orthogonal series expansion in each case. Once the individual truncation parameter is chosen, the model can be implemented in practice. As mentioned in the preceding section, however, no theoretical guide exists for the choice of such parameters in such cases where the deterministic trend and both stationary and integrated processes are present. In view of this, we shall choose the truncation parameters for our model through evaluating the forecasting ability.

Precisely, the forecasting ability of a model is measured by the so-called out-of-sample mean square errors (MSE). We use data in the period $1 \leq t \leq n_1$ ($n_1 < n$), say, to estimate the model for given k_i ($i = 1, 2, 3$), then using the estimated model we forecast the dependent variable at $t = n_1 + 1$, obtaining $\widehat{y}_{n_1+1}$. Repeat this for other n_j's. The Out-of-Sample MSE with the given truncation parameters is defined by $J^{-1} \sum_{j=1}^{J} (\widehat{y}_{n_j+1} - y_{n_j+1})^2$ where $n_j < n_{j+1} < n$ for $j = 1, \ldots, J-1$. We say that a candidate model corresponding to a set of truncation parameters has the best forecasting ability if it has the smallest out-of-sample MSE among all possible candidates.

In what follows, let $J = 20$, and $n_j = 9162 + 100j$, $1 \leq j \leq J$. Because both are smooth functions on [0, 1], we shall use the same truncation parameter for $\beta(\cdot)$ and $g(\cdot)$, $k_1 = k_2$, while the parameter for $m(\cdot)$ is still denoted by k_3. All candidate models are these (k_1, k_2, k_3) that are not too large since from the complexity point of view this requirement is reasonable for a model. The Out-of-Sample MSEs are calculated for all feasible k_i, and the results are reported in Table 6.2.

From Table 6.2, we can see that the candidate model with $\widehat{k}_1 = \widehat{k}_2 = 2$ and $\widehat{k}_3 = 1$ has the smallest Out-of-Sample MSE 0.0146, viz., it has the best forecasting ability. Therefore, using $\widehat{k}_1 = \widehat{k}_2 = 2$, $\widehat{k}_3 = 1$ and our estimation procedure, we achieve

Table 6.2 Out-of-sample MSE for model (6.4.1)

k_3	$k_1(=k_2)$						
	2	3	4	5	6	7	8
1	0.0146	0.0515	0.0241	0.0364	0.0358	0.0251	0.0227
2	0.0752	0.0392	0.0190	0.0251	0.0454	0.0378	0.0342
3	0.0529	0.0316	0.0150	0.0191	0.0380	0.0332	0.0314
4	0.0329	0.0293	0.0197	0.0225	0.0367	0.0330	0.0318
5	0.0315	0.0290	0.0196	0.0224	0.0407	0.0383	0.0368
6	0.0260	0.0299	0.0226	0.0248	0.0388	0.0356	0.0338

$$
\begin{aligned}
\widehat{\beta}(r) &= -0.0223\varphi_1(r) - 0.0115\varphi_2(r), \quad r \in [0, 1], \\
\widehat{g}(z) &= -2.7906 + 0.1461\varphi_1(z), \quad z \in [0, 1], \qquad (6.4.2) \\
\widehat{m}(x) &= 3.4201e^{-x^2/2}, \quad x \in \mathbb{R},
\end{aligned}
$$

where $\varphi_j(r) = \sqrt{2}\cos(\pi jr)$ for $j \geq 1$. To visualize these functions, we plot their pictures and their confidence curves at 95% level in Fig. 6.6, respectively.

Notice from the estimated functions that the effect of relative trading volume is estimated as negative and close to linear, meaning that large amounts of trading in Coke relative to Pepsi are predictive of a decline in the price of Coke, ceteris paribus; the effect of Pepsi's price on Coke is symmetrical around zero, implying that Pepsi's price far away from its central range in either direction has a negative effect on the price of Coke, ceteris paribus. On the other hand, the estimated trend seems to be upward during the sample and bottoming out at the end, meaning that the price of Coke has increased over the sample period relative to the value predicted by a time-invariant relationship based on the chosen covariates.

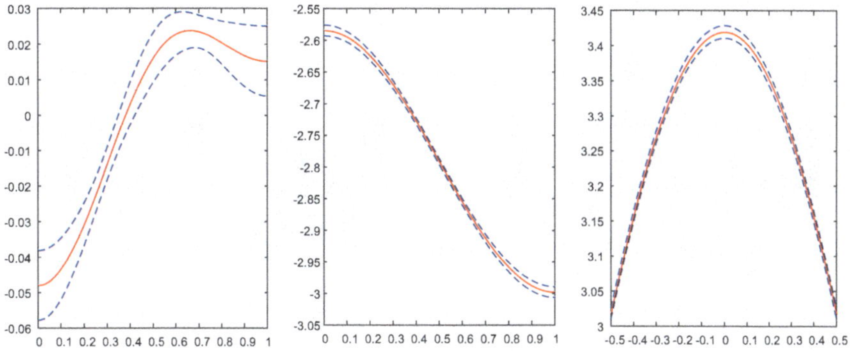

(a) Estimated $\boldsymbol{\beta}(r)$ (b) Estimated $\boldsymbol{g}(z)$ (c) Estimated $\boldsymbol{m}(x)$

Fig. 6.6 Estimated functions and their confidence curves at the 95% level

Table 6.3 Estimation and related statistics for model (6.4.3)

a_0	0.045	(0.0173, 0.0727)	a_1	0.1304	(0.1125, 0.1482)
a_2	0.3357	(−0.3735, −0.2980)	a_3	1.2609	(1.2506, 1.2711)
$R^2 = 0.8985$			$F = 32945$		
$f = 0$			$p = 0.0491$		

Comparison. In the sequel, the proposed model is compared with two competing models. One model is the linear parametric model, and the other is the model (6.4.1) plus a linear term in x_t,

$$y_t = a_0 + a_1 \tau_t + a_2 z_t + a_3 x_t + \varepsilon_{1t}, \quad (6.4.3)$$

$$y_t = \beta_1(\tau_t) + g_1(z_t) + \theta_0 x_t + m_1(x_t) + \varepsilon_{2t}. \quad (6.4.4)$$

We still evaluate the models in terms of their forecasting ability.

For model (6.4.3), we have the estimated coefficients, confidence intervals at the 95% significance level and related statistics using the full data reported in Table 6.3. The linear model is fitted well as the R^2 is close to one, $F \gg f$ and $p < 0.05$. However, its out-of-sample MSE is 0.0453 that is larger than that of the proposed model with functions in (6.4.2), though the residual plots in Fig. 6.7 are quite similar for the two models. So, we decline the linear model.

For model (6.4.4), we compute the Out-of-Sample MSEs with different combinations of feasible truncation parameters, shown in Table 6.4. The candidate model with $\widehat{k}_1 = \widehat{k}_2 = 4$ and $\widehat{k}_3 = 2$ has the smallest Out-of-Sample MSE, 0.0154. Though we seek the best model in a broad area of the truncation parameters, the resulting smallest Out-of-Sample MSE is larger than our proposed model.

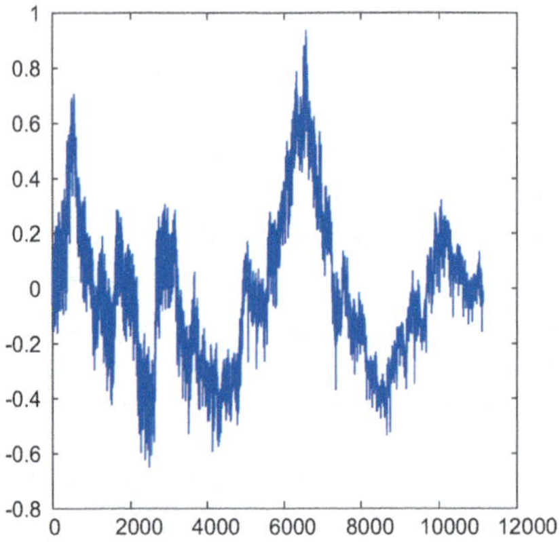

(a) Residuals of the proposed model

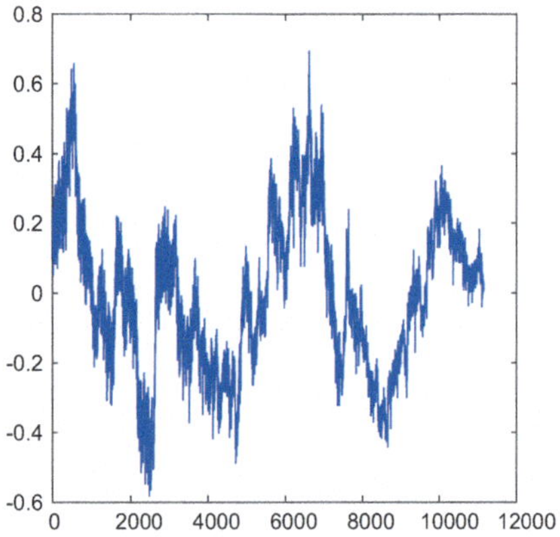

(b) Residuals of the linear model

Fig. 6.7 Plot of residuals for the proposed and linear models

Table 6.4 Out-of-sample MSE for model (6.4.4)

k_3	$k_1(= k_2)$						
	2	3	4	5	6	7	8
1	0.0462	0.0366	0.0167	0.0218	0.0319	0.0240	0.0227
2	0.0508	0.0313	0.0154	0.0195	0.0371	0.0322	0.0306
3	0.0457	0.0324	0.0181	0.0225	0.0356	0.0300	0.0286
4	0.0315	0.0289	0.0196	0.0223	0.0408	0.0386	0.0371
5	0.0313	0.0288	0.0195	0.0224	0.0408	0.0392	0.0376
6	0.0261	0.0293	0.0230	0.0259	0.0388	0.0370	0.0341

In conclusion, comparing with both models (6.4.3) and (6.4.4) in terms of out-of-sample MSE, we still recommend model (6.4.1) with functions in (6.4.2) for the given dataset.

Trading strategy. We examine the performance of our proposed model in a *pair trading strategy*. It is known that the strategy has more than 30 years history on Wall Street and is among the proprietary "statistical arbitrage" tools currently used by hedge funds as well as investment banks. The strategy uses the idea of cointegration between two related stocks: it opens short/long positions when they are apart from each other whereas closes the positions when they are converging. See Gatev et al. (2006) for details. Nonetheless, the conventional cointegration is described using a linear equation in the relevant literature. By contrast, we shall utilize the nonparametric nonlinear cointegration proposed in this section to define the pair strategy.

Take an integer $n_0 \in (1, n)$. With the proposed model (6.4.1) and (6.4.2), we calculate the estimated residuals $\widehat{e}_t = y_t - \widehat{\beta}(t/n_0) - \widehat{g}(z_t) - \widehat{m}(x_t)$, $1 \leq t \leq n_0$. Let α be a significance level specified below. Find out the empirical lower $(\alpha/2)$-quantile $\ell(\alpha/2)$ and upper $(\alpha/2)$-quantile $L(\alpha/2)$ from $\{\widehat{e}_t : 1 \leq t \leq n_0\}$.

The pair trading strategy is implemented as follows. Calculate for $t = n_0 + 1, \ldots, n$ all residuals $\widehat{e}_t = y_t - \widehat{\beta}(\tau_t) - \widehat{g}(z_t) - \widehat{m}(x_t)$. If $\widehat{e}_t > L(\alpha/2)$, we would short one dollar in Coke and long one dollar in Pepsi; if $\widehat{e}_t < \ell(\alpha/2)$, we would long one dollar in Coke and short one dollar in Pepsi; otherwise, we would close all positions held if any, and put positive gain into a risk-free bond account with rate r_0 and offset negative gain from the account. At the last trading day, we shall close all positions ignoring the location of the residual.

More precisely, at date $t \in [n_0 + 1, n]$, if $\widehat{e}_t > L(\alpha/2)$, we would owe $1/Y_t$ share of Coke and buy $1/X_t$ share of Pepsi; if $\widehat{e}_t < \ell(\alpha/2)$, we would owe $1/X_t$ share of Pepsi and buy $1/Y_t$ share of Coke; otherwise, we would clear all positions since last date of closing positions, say, date k. Hence, we obtain $\sum_{j=k}^{t-1} \Delta_j^t$, where

Table 6.5 Pair trading for Coke and Pepsi

	α	Nonlinear cointegration			Linear cointegration		
		$L(\alpha/2)$	$\ell(\alpha/2)$	Profit	$L(\alpha/2)$	$\ell(\alpha/2)$	Profit
$n_0 = 7000$	0.01	0.3511	−1.2710	0.0227	0.5678	−0.4937	0
	0.05	0.1130	−1.2025	0.6525	0.4631	−0.4324	0.0767
$n_0 = 7500$	0.01	0.3450	−1.2669	0.0227	0.5680	−0.4874	0
	0.05	0.1012	−1.1963	0.8162	0.4614	−0.4236	0.1389
$n_0 = 8000$	0.01	0.3401	−1.2647	0.0227	0.5681	−0.4828	0
	0.05	0.0806	−1.1913	0.9117	0.4580	−0.4167	0.1931
$n_0 = 8500$	0.01	0.3318	−1.2561	0.0145	0.5646	−0.4780	0
	0.05	0.0704	−1.1963	0.7515	0.4562	−0.4122	0.5708
$n_0 = 9000$	0.01	0.3234	−1.2622	0	0.5635	−0.4734	0
	0.05	0.0580	−1.2059	0	0.4547	−0.4153	0

$$\Delta_j^t = \begin{cases} (X_t/X_j - Y_t/Y_j)(1+r_0)^{n-t}, & \text{if } \widehat{e}_j > L(\alpha/2) \text{ and } X_t/X_j - Y_t/Y_j \geq 0, \\ X_t/X_j - Y_t/Y_j, & \text{if } \widehat{e}_j > L(\alpha/2) \text{ and } X_t/X_j - Y_t/Y_j < 0, \\ (Y_t/Y_j - X_t/X_j)(1+r_0)^{n-t}, & \text{if } \widehat{e}_j < \ell(\alpha/2) \text{ and } Y_t/Y_j - X_t/X_j \geq 0, \\ Y_t/Y_j - X_t/X_j, & \text{if } \widehat{e}_j < \ell(\alpha/2) \text{ and } Y_t/Y_j - X_t/X_j < 0. \end{cases}$$

Therefore, the total profit is $\sum_{t \in A} \sum_{j=k}^{t-1} \Delta_j^t$ where A is the set of all clearing dates.

We do not consider any cost in the trading such as transaction fee or price impact; we take $\alpha = 0.01$ and 0.05, and put $r_0 = 0.02/250$ per day. The trading results are presented in Table 6.5. We also show the trading results in the same table using model (6.4.3) in order to compare the model proposed with the linear model.

It can be seen that the results are sensitive to the length of the data history that determines the thresholds of taking action. More importantly, the proposed nonlinear cointegration model outperforms the linear model as it is more exquisite and can earn more money. Although it seems no action takes place for $t > 9000$ for both models, with $\alpha = 0.01$ the linear model in the experiment always has nothing to gain. We might conclude that nonparametric cointegration is a better alternative relationship to the linear cointegration in the literature on pair trading strategy.

6.5 Mathematical Details

This section presents all regularity assumptions, some technical lemmas and the proof of the main results that are from Dong and Linton (2018) for completeness.

Assumption 6.5.1 (a) Let $\{\epsilon_j, -\infty < j < \infty\}$ be a scalar sequence of independent and identically distributed random variables that have an absolutely continuous distribution with respect to the Lebesgue measure, and satisfy $\mathbb{E}[\epsilon_1] = 0, \mathbb{E}[\epsilon_1^2] = 1, \mathbb{E}|\epsilon_1|^{q_1} < \infty$ for some $q_1 \geq 4$. The characteristic function of ϵ_1 satisfies that $\int |\lambda||\mathbb{E}\exp(i\lambda\epsilon_1)|d\lambda < \infty$.

(b) Let $w_t = \sum_{j=0}^{\infty} \psi_j \epsilon_{t-j}$ where $\sum_{j=0}^{\infty} j|\psi_j| < \infty$ and $\psi \equiv \sum_{j=0}^{\infty} \psi_j \neq 0$.

(c) For $t \geq 1$, $x_t = x_{t-1} + w_t$, and $x_0 = O_P(1)$.

Though the integrated process x_t is defined the same as Assumption 5.7.1 with dimension $d = 1$, we restate it here because some notation has changed.

Assumption 6.5.2 (a) Suppose that (i) z_t is a strictly stationary and α-mixing process with mixing coefficients $\alpha(i)$ such that $\sum_{i=1}^{\infty} \alpha^{\delta/(2+\delta)}(i) < \infty$ for some $\delta > 0$. Or (ii) $z_t = \rho(\epsilon_t, \ldots, \epsilon_{t-d+1}; \eta_t)$ with fixed $d \geq 1$ and measurable function $\rho : \mathbb{R}^{d+1} \mapsto \mathbb{R}$, and z_t has finite second moment, where i.i.d.(0,1) sequence $\{\eta_j\}$ is independent of $\{\epsilon_j\}$.

(b) There exists an orthogonal function sequence $\{p_i(z), i \geq 0\}$ on the support V_z of z_1 and the orthogonality is with respect to $dF(z)$ where $F(z)$ is a distribution function on V_z. In addition, for $\delta > 0$ given by (a) above, we have either (i) $\mathbb{E}|p_j(z_1)|^{2(2+\delta)} = O(j)$ for large j or (ii) $\sup_{j\geq 0} \mathbb{E}|p_j(z_1)|^{2(2+\delta)} < \infty$.

(c) There is a filtration sequence $\mathcal{F}_{n,t}$ such that $(e_t, \mathcal{F}_{n,t})$ form a martingale difference sequence and (z_t, x_t) is adapted to $\mathcal{F}_{n,t-1}$. Moreover, almost surely $\mathbb{E}(e_t^2|\mathcal{F}_{n,t-1}) = \sigma^2(t/n)$, where $\sigma^2(\cdot)$ is a positive continuous function on $[0, 1]$ and $\max_{1\leq t\leq n} \mathbb{E}(|e_t|^{q_2}|\mathcal{F}_{n,t-1}) < \infty$ for some $q_2 \geq 4$.

Assumption 6.5.3 (a) The functions $\beta(\cdot)$, $g(\cdot)$ and $m(\cdot)$ are continuously differentiable up to orders s_1, s_2 and s_3, respectively. Moreover, $\beta^{(s_1)}(\cdot)$, $g^{(s_2)}(\cdot)$ and $m^{(s_3)}(\cdot)$ belong to the Hilbert spaces which contain the original functions, respectively.

(b) For $\beta(\cdot)$ function, let $\int_0^1 \beta(r)dr = 0$.

Assumption 6.5.4 All $k_i, i = 1, 2, 3$, diverge with n such that:

(a) If Assumption 6.5.2(b.i) holds, (1) $k_2^{2+2/(2+\delta)} = o(n)$, $k_3^5 = o(n)$, (2) $k_1 k_2^{1+1/(2+\delta)} = o(n)$, $k_1^2 k_3^3 = o(n)$, $k_2^2 k_3^{3/2} = o(n)$; if Assumption 6.5.2(b.ii) holds, (3) $k_2^2 = o(n)$, $k_3^5 = o(n)$, (4) $k_1 k_2 = o(n)$, $k_1^2 k_3^3 = o(n)$, $k_2^3 k_3^3 = o(n)$.

(b) Suppose that as $n \to \infty$, (5) $nk_1^{-(2s_1-1)} = o(1)$, $nk_2^{-(s_2-1)} = o(1)$ and $n^{1/2}k_3^{-(s_3-1)} = o(1)$ and (6) $nk_2k_1^{-2s_1} = o(1)$, $nk_3k_1^{-2s_1} = o(1)$, $nk_1k_2^{-s_2} = o(1)$, $nk_3k_2^{-s_2} = o(1)$, $n^{1/2}k_1k_3^{-s_3} = o(1)$, $n^{1/2}k_2k_3^{-s_3} = o(1)$.

Without loss of generality, let $x_0 = 0$ almost surely. It follows that

$$x_t = \sum_{\ell=1}^{t} w_\ell = \sum_{\ell=1}^{t} \sum_{i=-\infty}^{\ell} \psi_{\ell-i}\epsilon_i = \sum_{i=-\infty}^{t} \left(\sum_{\ell=\max(1,i)}^{t} \psi_{\ell-i} \right) \epsilon_i \equiv \sum_{i=-\infty}^{t} b_{t,i}\epsilon_i. \tag{6.5.1}$$

Taking into account that in Assumption 6.5.2, z_t may contain $\epsilon_t, \ldots, \epsilon_{t-d+1}$, we decompose, for $t > d$,

$$x_t = \sum_{i=t-d+1}^{t} b_{t,i}\epsilon_i + \sum_{i=-\infty}^{t-d} b_{t,i}\epsilon_i := x_t^{(d)} + x_t^{(t-d)}. \tag{6.5.2}$$

Thus, $x_t^{(d)}$ and $x_t^{(t-d)}$ are mutually independent, and $x_t^{(d)}$ is stationary since it is a combination of $\epsilon_t, \ldots, \epsilon_{t-d+1}$ with fixed coefficients $\psi_0, \ldots, \sum_{\ell=0}^{d-1}\psi_\ell$ (i.e., a MA(d) process), while $x_t^{(t-d)}$ is still nonstationary as we only take out fixed number of ϵ's from x_t.

Letting $1 \le s < t$, x_t also has the following decomposition:

$$x_t = x_s^* + x_{ts},$$

where $x_s^* = x_s + \bar{x}_s$ with $\bar{x}_s = \sum_{i=s+1}^{t}\sum_{a=-\infty}^{s}\psi_{i-a}\epsilon_a$ containing all information available up to s and $x_{ts} = \sum_{i=s+1}^{t} b_{t,i}\epsilon_i$ which captures all information containing in x_t on the time periods $(s, t]$. Let $d_{ts} := (Ex_{ts}^2)^{1/2} \sim \sqrt{t-s}$ for large $t-s$. Moreover, $\bar{x}_s = O_P(1)$ by virtue of Assumption 6.5.1.

Additionally, taking into account of that z_t and z_s may have $\epsilon_t, \ldots, \epsilon_{t-d}$ and $\epsilon_s, \ldots, \epsilon_{s-d}$ for $t - s \ge d$, we decompose

$$x_t = x_t^{(d)} + x_{ts}^{(d)} + x_s^{(d*)} + x_s^{(s-d*)}, \tag{6.5.3}$$

where

$$x_t^{(d)} = \sum_{i=t-d+1}^{t} b_{t,i}\epsilon_i, \quad x_{ts}^{(d)} = \sum_{i=s+1}^{t-d} b_{t,i}\epsilon_i$$

$$x_s^{(d*)} = x_s^{(d)} + \bar{x}_s^{(d)}, \quad x_s^{(s-d*)} = x_s^{(s-d)} + \bar{x}_s^{(s-d)},$$

recalling that $x_s^{(d)}$ and $\bar{x}_s^{(d)}$ are the sums of the first d terms of x_s and $\bar{x}_s$, respectively, whereas $x_s^{(s-d)}$ and $\bar{x}_s^{(s-d)}$ are the rest of them in x_s and $\bar{x}_s$, respectively. Obviously, all four components in (6.5.3) are mutually independent.

Lemma 6.5.1 *Suppose that Assumption 6.5.1 holds. For t or $t-s$ that is large,*

(1) $d_t^{-1}x_t$ have uniformly bounded densities $f_t(x)$ over all t and x satisfying a uniform Lipschitz condition $\sup_x |f_t(x+y) - f_t(x)| \le C|y|$ for any y and some constant $C > 0$. In addition, $\sup_x |f_t(x) - \phi(x)| \to 0$ as $t \to \infty$ where $\phi(x)$ is the standard normal density function.

(2) Let $1 \le s < t$. $d_{ts}^{-1}x_{ts}$ have uniformly bounded densities $f_{ts}(x)$ over all (t, s) and x satisfying the above uniform Lipschitz condition as well.

Lemma 6.5.2 *Let Assumption 6.5.1 hold. For t or $t-s$ that is large,*

(1) Let $\tilde{d}_t^2 = E[(x_t^{(t-d)})^2]$. $\tilde{d}_t^{-1}x_t^{(t-d)}$ have uniformly bounded densities $f_{t/d}(x)$ over all t and x satisfying a uniform Lipschitz condition $\sup_x |f_{t/d}(x+y) - f_{t/d}(x)| \le C|y|$ for any y and some constant $C > 0$. In addition, $\sup_x |f_{t/d}(x) - \phi(x)| \to 0$ as $t \to \infty$ where $\phi(x)$ is the standard normal density function.

(2) For $1 \le s < t$ and $t - s > d$, let $\tilde{d}_{ts}^2 = E[(x_{ts}^{(t-d)})^2]$. $\tilde{d}_{ts}^{-1}x_{ts}^{(t-d)}$ have uniformly bounded densities $f_{ts/d}(x)$ over all (t,s) and x satisfying the above uniform Lipschitz condition as well.

It is noteworthy that $\tilde{d}_t \sim \sqrt{t}$, the same order as d_t for large t, and $\tilde{d}_{ts} \sim \sqrt{t-s}$, the same order as d_{ts} for large $t-s$, noting that d is fixed.

Lemma 6.5.3 *Suppose that Assumptions 6.5.1 and 6.5.2(a.ii) hold.*

(1) Let $p(\cdot)$ be a function such that $\mathbb{E}|p(z_t)| < \infty$, $h(\cdot)$ be an integrable function on $\mathbb{R}$, i.e., $\int |h(x)|dx < \infty$. Then, for large t, $|\mathbb{E}p(z_t)h(x_t)| < C\tilde{d}_t^{-1}\mathbb{E}|p(z_t)| \int |h(x)|dx(1 + O(\tilde{d}_t^{-1}))$.

(2) Let $p_1(\cdot)$ and $p_2(\cdot)$ satisfy the above condition for $p(\cdot)$; $h_1(\cdot)$ is integrable and $h_2(\cdot)$ is such that $\int |xh_2(x)|dx < \infty$. For $1 \le s < t$ and $t-s > d$,

$$\begin{aligned}|\mathbb{E}[p_1(z_t)p_2(z_s)h_1(x_t)h_2(x_s)]| \le & C\tilde{d}_{ts}^{-1}\tilde{d}_s^{-1}\mathbb{E}|p_1(z_t)|\mathbb{E}|p_2(z_s)| \\ & \times \int |h_1(x)|dx \int |h_2(x)|dx(1 + O(\tilde{d}_{ts}^{-1})).\end{aligned}$$

This lemma is sufficient to deal with the correlation between z_t and x_t stipulated in Assumption 6.5.2.

Lemma 6.5.4 *(1) $\left\|\frac{1}{n}\sum_{t=1}^n \phi_{k_1}(\tau_t)\phi_{k_1}^\top(\tau_t) - I_{k_1}\right\|^2 = O(n^{-2}k_1^2)$ as $k_1/n \to 0$; (2) $\sup_{0\le r\le 1} \|\phi_{k_1}(r)\|^2 = k_1 + O(1)$ as $k_1 \to \infty$.*

Lemma 6.5.5 *Let $D_n = \mathrm{diag}(\sqrt{n}I_{k_1}, \sqrt{n}I_{k_2}, \sqrt{n/d_n}I_{k_3})$. Then, under Assumptions 6.5.1, 6.5.2, and 6.5.4, $\|D_n^{-1}B_{nk}^\top B_{nk}D_n^{-1} - U_k\| = o_P(1)$ as $n \to \infty$ on a richer probability space. Particularly,*

$$\left\|\frac{1}{n}\sum_{t=1}^n \phi_{k_1}(\tau_t)\phi_{k_1}(\tau_t)^\top - I_{k_1}\right\| = o(1),$$

$$\left\|\frac{1}{n}\sum_{t=1}^n a_{k_2}(z_t)a_{k_2}(z_t)^\top - U_{*22}\right\| = o_P(1), \text{ and}$$

$$\left\|\frac{d_n}{n}\sum_{t=1}^n b_{k_2}(x_t)b_{k_2}(x_t)^\top - L_W(1,0)I_{k_3}\right\| = o_P(1).$$

Lemma 6.5.6 *Under Assumptions 6.5.1, 6.5.2, and 6.5.4,* $\|D_n^{-1}B_{nk}^\top \Sigma_n B_{nk} D_n^{-1} - V_k\| = o_P(1)$ *as* $n \to \infty$ *on a richer probability space, where* $\Sigma_n = diag(\sigma^2(1/n), \ldots, \sigma^2(1))$ *and* D_n *is given in Lemma 6.5.5.*

The proofs of these lemmas can be found in Dong and Linton (2018).

Proof of Theorem 6.2.1 The theorem will be shown via the Cramér-Wold theorem. Notice that

$$\begin{aligned}\widehat{c} - c &= (B_{nk}^\top B_{nk})^{-1} B_{nk}^\top (\gamma + e)\\ &= D_n^{-1}[D_n^{-1}B_{nk}^\top B_{nk} D_n^{-1}]^{-1} D_n^{-1} B_{nk}^\top (\gamma + e),\end{aligned} \tag{6.5.4}$$

which implies

$$D_n(\widehat{c} - c) = [D_n^{-1}B_{nk}^\top B_{nk} D_n^{-1}]^{-1} D_n^{-1} B_{nk}^\top (\gamma + e).$$

Hence, for any $r \in [0, 1]$, $z \in V$ and $x \in \mathbb{R}$,

$$\begin{aligned}&\begin{pmatrix} \frac{\sqrt{n}}{\|\phi_{k_1}(r)\|}[\widehat{\beta}_n(r) - \beta(r)] \\ \frac{\sqrt{n}}{\|a_{k_2}(z)\|}[\widehat{g}_n(z) - g(z)] \\ \frac{\sqrt{n}}{\|b_{k_3}(x)\|\sqrt{d_n}}[\widehat{m}_n(x) - m(x)] \end{pmatrix}\\
&= \overline{\Psi}(r, z, x)^\top D_n(\widehat{c} - c) - \begin{pmatrix} \frac{\sqrt{n}}{\|\phi_{k_1}(r)\|}\gamma_{1k_1}(r) \\ \frac{\sqrt{n}}{\|a_{k_2}(z)\|}\gamma_{2k_2}(z) \\ \frac{\sqrt{n}}{\|b_{k_3}(x)\|\sqrt{d_n}}\gamma_{3k_3}(x) \end{pmatrix}\\
&= \overline{\Psi}(r, z, x)^\top [D_n^{-1}B_{nk}^\top B_{nk} D_n^{-1}]^{-1} D_n^{-1} B_{nk}^\top e \qquad (6.5.5)\\
&\quad + \overline{\Psi}(r, z, x)^\top [D_n^{-1}B_{nk}^\top B_{nk} D_n^{-1}]^{-1} D_n^{-1} B_{nk}^\top \gamma - \begin{pmatrix} \frac{\sqrt{n}}{\|\phi_{k_1}(r)\|}\gamma_{1k_1}(r) \\ \frac{\sqrt{n}}{\|a_{k_2}(z)\|}\gamma_{2k_2}(z) \\ \frac{\sqrt{n}}{\|b_{k_3}(x)\|\sqrt{d_n}}\gamma_{3k_3}(x) \end{pmatrix}, \qquad (6.5.6)\end{aligned}$$

Here, the leading term in the above is $\overline{\Psi}(r, z, x)^\top [D_n^{-1}B_{nk}^\top B_{nk} D_n^{-1}]^{-1} D_n^{-1} B_{nk}^\top e$ that will be dealt with first. To begin, by Lemma 6.5.5, $\|D_n^{-1}B_{nk}^\top B_{nk} D_n^{-1} - U_k\| = o_P(1)$ as $n \to \infty$, and making use of the block diagonal structure of U_k, it follows that

$$\begin{aligned}&\overline{\Psi}(r, z, x)^\top [D_n^{-1}B_{nk}^\top B_{nk} D_n^{-1}]^{-1} D_n^{-1} B_{nk}^\top e \qquad (6.5.7)\\
&= \overline{\Psi}(r, z, x)^\top U_k^{-1} D_n^{-1} B_{nk}^\top e(1 + o_P(1))\\
&= L_3^{-1}\overline{\Psi}(r, z, x)^\top \bar{U}_k^{-1} D_n^{-1} B_{nk}^\top e(1 + o_P(1)), \qquad (6.5.8)\end{aligned}$$

where $L_3 = \text{diag}(1, 1, L_W(1, 0))$ and $\bar{U}_k = \text{diag}(I_{k_1}, U_{k_2}, I_{k_3})$. As L_3 is independent of the sample size, we now focus on $\overline{\Psi}(r, z, x)^\top \bar{U}_k^{-1} D_n^{-1} B_{nk}^\top e$.

Write

$$\overline{\Psi}(r,z,x)^{\top}\bar{U}_k^{-1}D_n^{-1}B_{nk}^{\top}e=\sum_{t=1}^{n}\xi_{nt}e_t$$

where we denote

$$\xi_{nt}\equiv\overline{\Psi}(r,z,x)^{\top}\bar{U}_k^{-1}D_n^{-1}\begin{pmatrix}\phi_{k_1}(t/n)\\ a_{k_2}(z_t)\\ b_{k_3}(x_t)\end{pmatrix}.$$

Since $(e_t,\mathcal{F}_{nt})$ is a martingale difference sequence stipulated in Assumption 6.5.2, $\sum_{t=1}^{n}\xi_{nt}e_t$ is a martingale. We calculate the conditional variance as follows:

$$\begin{aligned}
&\sum_{t=1}^{n}\mathbb{E}[\xi_{nt}\xi_{nt}^{\top}e_t^2|\mathcal{F}_{n,t-1}]=\sum_{t=1}^{n}\xi_{nt}\xi_{nt}^{\top}\sigma^2(t/n)\\
&=\overline{\Psi}(r,z,x)^{\top}\bar{U}_k^{-1}D_n^{-1}B_{nk}^{\top}\Sigma_nB_{nk}D_n^{-1}\bar{U}_k^{-1}\overline{\Psi}(r,z,x)\\
&=\overline{\Psi}(r,z,x)^{\top}\bar{U}_k^{-1}V_k\bar{U}_k^{-1}\overline{\Psi}(r,z,x)(1+o_P(1))\\
&=\overline{\Psi}(r,z,x)^{\top}\bar{U}_k^{-1}\bar{V}_k\bar{U}_k^{-1}\overline{\Psi}(r,z,x)L_\sigma(1+o_P(1))\\
&\equiv\Omega_nL_\sigma(1+o_P(1))
\end{aligned}\tag{6.5.9}$$

by Lemma 6.5.6 and the structure of V_k, where $L_\sigma=\text{diag}(1,1,\int_0^1\sigma^2(r)dL(r,1))$, $\bar{V}_k=\text{diag}(V_*,I_{k_3})$ a deterministic matrix, and $\Omega_n=\overline{\Psi}(r,z,x)^{\top}\bar{U}_k^{-1}\bar{V}_k\bar{U}_k^{-1}\overline{\Psi}(r,z,x)$ is a 3×3 deterministic matrix as well. This means that the conditional variance of $\Omega_n^{-1/2}\sum_{t=1}^{n}\xi_{nt}e_t$ is approximated by L_σ in probability.

Here, we emphasize that $\Omega_n^{-1/2}$ is exchangeable with L_3, i.e., $\Omega_n^{-1/2}L_3=L_3\Omega_n^{-1/2}$. Indeed, notice that

$$\begin{aligned}
\Omega_n^{-1/2}&=\left[\overline{\Psi}(r,z,x)^{\top}\begin{pmatrix}U_*^{-1}V_*U_*^{-1}&0\\0&I_{k_3}\end{pmatrix}\overline{\Psi}(r,z,x)\right]^{-1/2}\\
&=\begin{pmatrix}[\overline{\Psi}_{12}(r,z)^{\top}U_*^{-1}V_*U_*^{-1}\overline{\Psi}_{12}(r,z)]^{-1/2}&0\\0&1\end{pmatrix},
\end{aligned}$$

where $\overline{\Psi}_{12}(r,z)=\text{diag}(\phi_{k_1}(r)/\|\phi_{k_1}(r)\|,a_{k_2}(z)/\|a_{k_2}(z)\|)$ is the left-top 2-by-2 sub-block matrix of $\overline{\Psi}(r,z,x)$, while the right-bottom block of $\overline{\Psi}(r,z,x)$ is $b_{k_3}(x)/\|b_{k_3}(x)\|$, and $U_*=\text{diag}(I_{k_1},U_{k_2})$. Then, it is obvious that $\Omega_n^{-1/2}$ is exchangeable with L_3. This point allows us to normalize the left-hand side of the Eq. (6.5.5) and the martingale $\sum_{t=1}^{n}\xi_{nt}e_t$ by $\Omega_n^{-1/2}$ simultaneously.

Hence, we shall show that the martingale $\Omega_n^{-1/2}\sum_{t=1}^{n}\xi_{nt}e_t$ converges to $N(0,L_\sigma)$ by the Cramér-Wold theorem and Corollary 3.1 of Hall and Heyde (1980, p. 58). To this end, let $\lambda=(\lambda_1,\lambda_2,\lambda_3)\neq0$ and we need to check for

$$\xi_n := \sum_{t=1}^{n} \lambda \Omega_n^{-1/2} \xi_{nt} e_t,$$

whether (1) Lindeberg condition and (2) the convergence of the conditional variance are fulfilled. We omit these, since readers who are interested in the details can find in Dong and Linton (2018). To finish the proof, one also needs to demonstrate that all reminder terms in (6.5.6) are negligible, that is, as $n \to \infty$,

$$\sum_{t=1}^{n} \xi_{nt} \gamma(t) = o_P(1), \quad \sqrt{n} \|\phi_{k_1}(r)\|^{-1} \gamma_{1k_1}(r) = o(1),$$
$$\sqrt{n} \|a_{k_2}(z)\|^{-1} \gamma_{2k_2}(z) = o(1), \quad \sqrt{n/d_n} \|b_{k_3}(x)\|^{-1} \gamma_{3k_3}(x)) = o(1),$$

which are also omitted due to the same reason. Hence, the sketch of the proof is finished.

6.6 Discussions

As it is well known, additive nonparametric models are commonly used and studied in econometrics and statistics. We are now in the place to provide some discussions. Eubank and Hart (1992) consider specification testing in the model

$$y_i = g(x_i) + e_i, \quad i = 1, \ldots, n, \tag{6.6.1}$$

with

$$H_0 : g(x) = \sum_{j=1}^{p} \beta_j g_j(x), \quad \forall\, x \in [0, 1],$$

against

$$H_1 : g(x) = \sum_{j=1}^{p} \beta_j g_j(x) + f(x), \quad \forall\, x \in [0, 1]$$

where all $g_j(\cdot)$ are known, β_j are unknown, $f(x)$ is not a linear combination of $g_j(\cdot)$'s. To construct testing statistic, Eubank and Hart (1992) propose a sequence of functions $\phi_{jn}(x)$, $j = 1, \ldots, n - p$, satisfying the orthogonality conditions

$$\sum_{i=1}^{n} \phi_{jn}(x_i)\phi_{ln}(x_i) = n\delta_{jl}, \quad j, l = 1, \ldots, n-p,$$

$$\sum_{i=1}^{n} \phi_{jn}(x_i)g_l(x_i) = 0, \quad j = 1, \ldots, n-p, l = 1, \ldots, p.$$

Suppose $\mathbb{E}(e_i) = 0$ and $\mathbb{E}(e_i^2) = \sigma^2$. To test H_0, consider fitting the alternative model

$$y_i = \sum_{j=1}^{p} \beta_j g_j(x_i) + \sum_{j=1}^{k} a_j \phi_{jn}(x_i) + e_i.$$

Let $Y = (y_1, \ldots, y_n)^\top$, $n \times p$ matrix $T = (g_j(x_i))$. Then $\beta = (\beta_1, \ldots, \beta_p)^\top$ is estimated by $\widehat{\beta} = (\widehat{\beta}_1, \ldots, \widehat{\beta}_p)^\top = (T^\top T)^{-1} T^\top Y$. Define the sample "Fourier" coefficients, $a_{jn} = \sum_{i=1}^{n} \phi_{jn}(x_i) y_i / n$. An estimate of the mean square error or risk is

$$\frac{1}{n}\sum_{i=1}^{n}\left(y_i - \sum_{j=1}^{p}\widehat{\beta}_j g_j(x_i) + \sum_{j=1}^{k} a_{jn}\phi_{jn}(x_i)\right)^2 + \frac{2\sigma^2(p+k)}{n}$$
$$= \frac{1}{n}\sum_{i=1}^{n}\left(y_i - \sum_{j=1}^{p}\widehat{\beta}_j g_j(x_i)\right)^2 - \sum_{j=1}^{k} a_{jn}^2 + \frac{2\sigma^2(p+k)}{n}. \tag{6.6.2}$$

An indication that H_0 is false is provided if (6.6.2) is minimized by some $k > 0$. Minimizing (6.6.2) is equivalent to maximizing

$$\sum_{j=1}^{k} a_{jn}^2 - \frac{2\sigma^2 k}{n}. \tag{6.6.3}$$

Eubank and Hart (1992) propose using as a test statistic the maximizer $\widehat{k}$ of

$$r(k) = \begin{cases} 0, & k = 0 \\ \sum_{j=1}^{k} a_{jn}^2 - \frac{\widehat{\sigma}^2 c_\alpha k}{n}, & k = 1, \ldots, n-p, \end{cases} \tag{6.6.4}$$

where $\widehat{\sigma}^2$ is any consistent estimator of σ^2, and c_α is such that $\mathbb{P}(\widehat{k} = 0) = 1 - \alpha$ under H_0.

The proposed test is formally given by: Reject H_0 if $\widehat{k} \geq 1$. The limit distribution of $\widehat{k}$ under H_0 is given and the power is shown approaching one in the paper.

In addition, Müller and Yao (2008) study functional additive models. To begin, let $X(s)$ be smooth, square integrable random function defined on domain $\mathcal{S}$, and the response $Y(t)$ a random function on $\mathcal{T}$. Their mean functions are $\mu_X(s) = \mathbb{E}(X(s))$ and $\mu_Y(t) = \mathbb{E}(Y(t))$. Denote $X^c(s) = X(s) - \mu_X(s)$ and $Y^c(t) = Y(t) - \mu_Y(t)$ the centered process. Consider the model

$$\mathbb{E}(Y(t)|X) = \mu_Y(t) + \int_S \beta(s,t)X^c(s)ds, \tag{6.6.5}$$

where $\beta(s,t)$ is assumed to be smooth and square-integrable.

Denote $G_X(s_1, s_2) = \mathrm{Cov}(X(s_1), X(s_2))$ and $G_Y(t_1, t_2) = \mathrm{Cov}(Y(t_1), Y(t_2))$. As defined in (C.4.35) of Appendix C, $G_X(s_1, s_2)$ and $G_Y(t_1, t_2)$ can generate integral operators on $L^2(\mathcal{S})$ and $L^2(\mathcal{T})$, respectively,

$$\mathcal{G}_X(\phi)(s) = \int_S G_X(s, s_2)\phi(s_2)ds_2, \quad \phi \in L^2(\mathcal{S}), \tag{6.6.6}$$

$$\mathcal{G}_Y(\psi)(t) = \int_{\mathcal{T}} G_Y(t, t_2)\psi(t_2)dt_2, \quad \psi \in L^2(\mathcal{T}). \tag{6.6.7}$$

Suppose that $\{\phi_k(s), \lambda_k\}_{k=1}^{\infty}$ and $\{\psi_m(t), \rho_m\}_{m=1}^{\infty}$ are eigenfunctions and eigenvalues associated with $\mathcal{G}_X$ and $\mathcal{G}_Y$, respectively. It is known that $\{\phi_k(s)\}_{k=1}^{\infty}$ and $\{\psi_m(t)\}_{m=1}^{\infty}$ are orthonormal sequences in $L^2(\mathcal{S})$ and $L^2(\mathcal{T})$, respectively; and two examples are given in Examples C.4.6 and C.4.7 of Appendix C.

The functional trajectories are not completely observed but rather are measured on a grid, and measurements are contaminated with measurement error. Denote by U_{ij} (resp. V_{il}) the noisy observations made of the random trajectories X_i (resp. Y_i) at times s_{ij} (resp. t_{il}), where (X_i, Y_i), $i = 1, \ldots, n$, correspond to an i.i.d. sample of processes (X, Y). The available observations are contaminated with measurement errors ϵ_{ij} (resp. ε_{il}), $1 \le j \le n_i$, $1 \le l \le m_i$, and $1 \le i \le n$, where n_i and m_i are the numbers of observations from X_i and Y_i. The errors are assumed to be i.i.d., with $\mathbb{E}(\epsilon_{ij}) = 0$, $\mathbb{E}(\epsilon_{ij}^2) = \sigma_X^2$, $\mathbb{E}(\varepsilon_{il}) = 0$, $\mathbb{E}(\varepsilon_{il}^2) = \sigma_Y^2$, and independent of functional principal component (FPC) scores

$$\xi_{ik} = \int_S (X_i(s) - \mu_X(s))\phi_k(s)ds, \quad k = 1, 2, \ldots \tag{6.6.8}$$

$$\zeta_{im} = \int_{\mathcal{T}} (Y_i(t) - \mu_Y(t))\psi_m(t)dt, \quad m = 1, 2, \ldots \tag{6.6.9}$$

Evidently, $\mathbb{E}(\xi_{ik}) = 0$, $\mathbb{E}(\xi_{ik}\xi_{ik'}) = 0$, $k \neq k'$ and $\mathbb{E}(\xi_{ik}^2) = \lambda_k$, and similarly, $\mathbb{E}(\zeta_{im}) = 0$, $\mathbb{E}(\zeta_{im}\zeta_{im'}) = 0$, $m \neq m'$ and $\mathbb{E}(\zeta_{im}^2) = \rho_m$.

Since $\beta(t,s)$ can be expanded by the tensor product of $\{\phi_k(s)\}_{k=1}^{\infty}$ and $\{\psi_m(t)\}_{m=1}^{\infty}$, from (6.6.5) and minimizing

$$\mathbb{E}\int_{\mathcal{T}} \left[Y^c(t) - \int_S \sum_{k=1}^{\infty}\sum_{m=1}^{\infty} b_{km}\phi_k(t)\psi_m(s)X^c(s)ds \right]^2 dt$$

over b_{km}, we obtain

$$\beta(t,s) = \sum_{k=1}^{\infty}\sum_{m=1}^{\infty} b_{km}\phi_k(s)\psi_m(t), \quad b_{km} = \frac{\mathbb{E}(\xi_k\zeta_m)}{\mathbb{E}(\xi_k^2)}, \tag{6.6.10}$$

$$\text{where } \xi_k = \int_{\mathcal{S}} \phi_k(s)X^c(s)ds, \quad \zeta_m = \int_{\mathcal{T}} \psi_m(t)Y^c(t)dt. \tag{6.6.11}$$

Moreover, the linear structure in the predictor scores and the uncorrelatedness of the FPC scores then imply that

$$\mathbb{E}(\zeta_m|X) = \int_{\mathcal{T}} \mathbb{E}[Y^c(t)|X]\psi_m(t)dt = \sum_{k=1}^{\infty} b_{km}\xi_k,$$

$$\text{and} \quad \mathbb{E}(\zeta_m|\xi_k) = b_{km}\xi_k.$$

Müller and Yao (2008) propose a nonparametric form to replace the linear function $\mathbb{E}(\zeta_m|\xi_k) = b_{km}\xi_k$, viz, $\mathbb{E}(\zeta_m|\xi_k) = f_{km}(\xi_k)$, resulting in a functional additive model (FAM)

$$\mathbb{E}(Y(t)|X) = \mu_Y(t) + \sum_{k=1}^{\infty}\sum_{m=1}^{\infty} f_{km}(\xi_k)\psi_m(t). \tag{6.6.12}$$

To ensure identifiability, Müller and Yao (2008) impose $\mathbb{E}(f_{km}(\xi_k)) = 0, \forall\, k, m$.

Given the observations U_{ij} for $X_i(s)$ at s_{ij}, $j = 1, \ldots, n_i$, one has

$$\begin{aligned} U_{ij} &= X(s_{ij}) + \epsilon_{ij} \\ &= \mu_X(s_{ij}) + \sum_{k=1}^{\infty} \xi_{ik}\phi_k(s_{ij}) + \epsilon_{ij}. \end{aligned}$$

Then $\widehat{\xi}_{ik}$ are obtained in which all unknown quantities μ_X, λ_k, ϕ_k and so on are substituted by their estimates from the entire data ensemble. Similarly, given the observations V_{il} for $Y_i(t)$ at t_{il}, $l = 1, \ldots, m_i$, one gets $\widehat{\zeta}_{im}$. Finally, Müller and Yao (2008) estimate f_{km} functions by the local linear method, and under regularity conditions establish their consistency, from which the estimate $\widehat{\mathbb{E}}(Y(t)|X)$ follows by (6.6.12).

Huang et al. (2010) study a variable selection issue for an additive nonparametric model of the form:

$$Y_i = \mu + \sum_{j=1}^{p} f_j(X_{ij}) + e_i, \tag{6.6.13}$$

where μ is an intercept, $X_i = (X_{i1}, \ldots, X_{ip})$ is explanatory variable and e_i is error term with mean zero and the same variance across i. f_j's are unknown functions but some may be zero. The problem addressed is to distinguishing the nonzero components from the zero components and estimating the nonzero components. Huang et al. (2010) allow $p > n$, and propose a penalized method for variable selection in (6.6.13) and show that the proposed method can correctly select the nonzero components with high probability.

It is noteworthy that additive components are approximated by truncated series expansions with B-spline bases. With this approximation, the problem of component selection becomes that of selecting the groups of coefficients in the expansion. The paper applies the adaptive group Lasso to select nonzero components, using the group Lasso to obtain an initial estimator and reduce the dimension of the problem; and it gives conditions under which the group Lasso selects a model whose number of components is comparable with the underlying model, and the adaptive group Lasso selects the nonzero components correctly with probability approaching one as the sample size increases and achieves the optimal rate of convergence.

Intriguingly, Xue (2009) also studies variable selection for additive nonparametric model. Towards this, Xue (2009) proposes a penalized polynomial spline method for simultaneous model estimation and variable selection in additive models. It approximates nonparametric functions by polynomial splines, and minimizes the sum of squared errors subject to an additive penalty on norms of spline functions. This approach sets estimators of certain function components to zero, thus performing variable selection.

Zhang et al. (2021) consider a functional additive quantile regression that models the conditional quantile of a scalar response based on the nonparametric effects of a functional predictor. Let y be a scalar response variable, $X(t)$, $t \in \mathcal{T}$, be a functional square-integrable predictor process on compact interval $\mathcal{T}$. They satisfy

$$Q_y(\tau|X) = \alpha(\tau) + \int_{\mathcal{T}} X(t)\beta(t,\tau)dt, \tag{6.6.14}$$

where $Q_y(\tau|X)$ is the conditional quantile of y given X at level $\tau \in (0,1)$, $\beta(t,\tau)$ is the square integrable coefficient function for a given τ.

Similar to Müller and Yao (2008), Zhang et al. (2021) use eigenvalues and eigenfunctions sequence $\{\phi_k(t), \lambda_k\}_{k=1}^{\infty}$ associated with the integral operator $\mathcal{G}_X$ generated by the covariance function $G(s,t)$ of $X(t)$. Then, $X(t)$ admits the Karhunen-Loeve expansion and $\beta(t,\tau)$ possesses an orthogonal expansion,

$$X(t) = \sum_{k=1}^{\infty} \xi_k \phi_k(t),$$

$$\beta(t,\tau) = \sum_{k=1}^{\infty} b_k(\tau)\phi_k(t).$$

Thus, (6.6.14) is reduced to

$$Q_y(\tau|X) = \alpha(\tau) + \sum_{k=1}^{\infty} b_k(\tau)\xi_k, \tag{6.6.15}$$

and then Zhang et al. (2021) extend it to a functional quantile regression

$$Q_y(\tau|X) = \alpha(\tau) + \sum_{k=1}^{\infty} f_{k\tau}(\zeta_k), \tag{6.6.16}$$

where all $f_{k\tau}$ are unknown functions satisfying $\mathbb{E}[f_{k\tau}(\xi_k)] = 0$ for identifiability, and $\zeta_k = \Phi(\lambda^{-1/2}\xi_k)$ in order to avoid possible scaling issue with $\Phi(\cdot)$ being continuously differentiable map $\mathbb{R} \mapsto [0, 1]$. Zhang et al. (2021) further suppose that there exists a sufficiently large s such that $f_{k\tau} \equiv 0$ for $k > s$.

Suppose $\{y_i, X_i(t)\}$ is an i.i.d. sample of $(y, X(t))$. The trajectories $\{X_i(t), t \in \mathcal{T}\}$ are observed intermittently on possible irregular grids $(t_{i1}, \ldots, t_{in_i})$. While all quantities $\mu(t)$, $G(s,t)$, ξ_{ik}, ζ_{ik}, and ϕ_k are estimated similar to Müller and Yao (2008), Zhang et al. (2021) estimate unknown functions $f_{k\tau}$ by the B-spline and the SCAD penalty method, and relevant statistical properties are established for the estimators.

Recently, Dong et al. (2024) propose a general functional quantile autoregression of the form:

$$q_t(\tau) = \int_0^1 H(\tau, u)q_{t-1}(u)du + g(\tau, x_t), \tag{6.6.17}$$

where $q_t(\tau)$ is the conditional quantile function of a stationary time series y_t, $H(\cdot,\cdot)$ is a smooth function on $[0, 1]^2$, x_t can be either the lagged y_t or other covariate, or both, $g(\cdot,\cdot)$ is smooth on $[0, 1] \times V$ where V is the support of x_t. The motivation of proposing the model (6.6.17) is that, as argued in the finance and economic literature, the information of various quantiles of the whole past distribution can have important influence on the future behavior of many economic variables; for example, the past income distributional information plays an important role on the future economic behavior. The model (6.6.17) thus answers the call in that it captures the systematic influences of the entire past distributional information on the future distribution of the response.

In (6.6.17) both $H(\cdot,\cdot)$ and $g(\cdot,\cdot)$ are unknown, and the authors utilize series methods to estimate them given the observations of $\{y_t, t = 1, \ldots, n\}$. The large sample properties of $\widehat{H}(\cdot,\cdot)$ and $\widehat{g}(\cdot,\cdot)$ as well as $\widehat{q}(\cdot)$ are established; Monte Carlo simulations are conducted to verify the performance of the estimators in finite sample situations, and an empirical study is used to show the usefulness of the model proposed.

References

Belloni, A., Chernozhukov, V., Chetverikov, D., & Kato, K. (2015). Some new asymptotic theory for least squares series: Pointwise and uniform results. *Journal of Econometrics, 186*, 345–366.

Cai, Z., Li, Q., & Park, J. (2009). Functional-coefficient cointegration models for nonstationary time series data. *Journal of Econometrics, 148*, 101–113.

Chang, Y., Park, J. Y., & Phillips, P. C. B. (2001). Nonlinear econometric models with cointegrated and deterministically trending regressors. *Econometrics Journal, 4*, 1–36.

Chen, X., & Christensen, T. (2015). Optimal uniform convergence rates and asymptotic normality for series estimators under weak dependence and weak conditions. *Journal of Econometrics, 188*, 447–465.

Chen, X., & Shen, X. (1998). Sieve extremum estimates for weakly dependent data. *Econometrica, 66*, 289–314.

Dong, C., Chen, R., Xiao, Z., & Liu, W. (2024). Functional quantile autoregression. *Journal of Econometrics*, 244, 105765.

Dong, C., Gao, J., & Tjøstheim, D. (2016). Estimation for single-index and partially linear single-index integrated models. *Annals of Statistics, 44*, 425–453.

Dong, C., & Linton, O. (2018). Additive nonparametric models with time variable and both stationary and nonstationary regressors. *Journal of Econometrics, 207*, 212–236.

Dudley, R. M. (2003). *Real Analysis and Probability*. Cambridge Studies in Advanced Mathematics 74. Cambridge University Press, Cambridge, U.K.

Eubank, R. L., & Hart, J. D. (1992). Testing goodness-of-fit in regression via order selection criteria. *Annals of Statistics, 20*, 1412–1425.

Friedman, J. H., & Stuetzle, W. (1981). Projection pursuit regression. *Journal of the American Statistical Association, 76*, 817–823.

Gao, J. (2007). *Nonlinear time series: Semiparametric and nonparametric methods*. Monographs on statistics and applied probability. New York: Chapman & Hall.

Gao, J., Tong, H., & Wolff, R. (2001). Adaptive orthogonal series estimation in additive stochastic regression models. *Statistic Sinica, 11*, 409–428.

Gatev, E., Goetzmann, W. N., & Rouwenhorst, K. G. (2006). Pairs trading: performance of a relative-value arbitrage rule. *The Review of Finance Studies, 19*, 797–827.

Grenander, U., & Rosenblatt, M. (1957). *Statistical analysis of stationary time series*. New York: Wiley.

Hall, P., & Heyde, C. C. (1980). *Martingale limit theory and its applications*. New York: Academic.

Hastie, T., & Tibshirani, R. (1986). Generalized additive models. *Statistical Science, 1*, 297–318.

Huang, J., Horowitz, J. L., & Wei, F. (2010). Variable selection in nonparametric additive models. *Annals of Statistics, 38*, 2282–2313.

Karlsen, H. A., Mykelbust, T., & Tjøstheim, D. (2007). Nonparametric estimation in a nonlinear cointegration type model. *Annals of Statistics, 35*, 252–299.

Linton, O. (1997). Efficient estimate of additive nonparametric models. *Biometrika, 84*, 469–474.

Linton, O., & Nielsen, J. P. (1995). A kernel method of estimating structured nonparametric regression based on marginal integration. *Biometrika, 82*, 93–100.

Li, D., Phillips, P., & Gao, J. (2016). Uniform consistency of nonstationary kernel-weighted sample covariance for nonparametric regressions. *Econometric Theory, 32*, 655–685.

Liu, R. L., Yang, L., & Hardle, W. K. (2013). Oracally efficient two-step estimation of generalized additive model. *Journal of the American Statistical Association, 108*, 619–631.

Ma, S., Linton, O., & Gao, J. (2021). Estimation and inference in semiparametric quantile factor models. *Journal of Econometrics, 222*, 295–323.

Mammen, E. O., Linton, O., & Nielsen, J. (1999). The existence and asymptotic properties of a backfitting projection algorithm under weak conditions. *Annals of Statistics, 27*, 1443–1490.

Müller, H.-G., & Yao, F. (2008). Functional additive models. *Journal of the American Statistical Association, 103*, 1534–1544.

Newey, W. K. (1997). Convergence rates and asymptotic normality for series estimators. *Journal of Econometrics, 79*, 147–168.

Park, J., & Hahn, S. (1999). Cointegrating regressions with time varying coefficients. *Econometric Theory, 15*, 664–703.

Phillips, P. C. B. (2010). The mysteries of trend. Discussion paper 1771, Cowles Foundation, Yale University.

Phillips, P. C. B. (2005). HAC estimation by automated regression. *Econometric Theory, 21*, 116–142.

Phillips, P. C. B. (2007). Regression with slowly varying regressors and nonlinear treads. *Econometric Theory, 23*, 557–614.

Phillips, P. C. B., Li, D., & Gao, J. (2017). Estimating smooth structure change in cointegration models. *Journal of Econometrics, 196*, 180–195.

Schienle, M. (2008). Nonparametric nonstationary regression. Doctoral thesis, Mannheim University, Mannheim, Germany.

Stone, C. (1982). Optimal global rates of convergence for nonparametric regression. *Annals of Statistics, 10*, 1040–1053.

Stone, C. (1985). Additive regression and other nonparametric models. *Annals of Statistics, 13*, 689–705.

Stone, C. (1986). The dimensionality reduction principle for generalized additive models. *Annals of Statistics, 14*, 590–606.

Vogt, M. (2012). Nonparametric regression for locally stationary time series. *Annals of Statistics, 46*, 2601–2633.

Vogt, M., & Walsh, C. (2019). Estimating nonlinear additive models with nonstationarities and correlated errors. *Scandinavian Journal of Statistics, 46*, 160–199.

Wang, Q. (2015). *Limit theorems for nonlinear cointegrating regression*. Singapore: World Scientific Press.

Wang, Q., & Phillips, P. C. B. (2009). Asymptotic theory for local time density estimation and nonparametric cointegreting regression. *Econometric Theory, 25*, 710–738.

Wood, S. N. (2017). *Generalized additive models: An introduction with R*. Chapman & Hall/CRC.

Xiao, Z. (2009). Functional-coefficient cointegration models. *Journal of Econometrics, 152*, 81–92.

Xue, L. (2009). Consistent variable selection in additive models. *Statistica Sinica, 19*, 1287–1296.

Zhang, Y., Lian, H., Li, G., & Zhu, Z. (2021). Functional additive quantile regression. *Statistica Sinica, 31*, 1331–1351.

Chapter 7
Semiparametric Moment Restriction Models

Moment restriction models (MRMs, hereafter) are very much popular in econometrics because many familiar models can be written in moment restriction forms. Due to this, MRMs have been studied extensively in the literature. Initially, researchers dwelled on parametric MRMs, that is, MRMs that only contain unknown Euclidean vector of parameters, and developed the generalized method of moments (GMM) to solve MRMs. See, Hansen (1982). Meanwhile, the efficiency of estimators is the highlight of these studies. Along with the development of nonparametric and semiparametric techniques as well as the advent of the big data era, people have started to investigate constrained MRMs (e.g., Chernozhukov et al., 2023), semiparametric MRMs, high-dimensional MRMs, and high-dimensional semiparametric MRMs.

7.1 Parametric MRMs

Parametric MRMs take the form

$$\mathbb{E}[m(v, \beta_0)] = 0, \tag{7.1.1}$$

where β_0 is an unknown vector in $\mathbb{R}^p$, and $m(\cdot)$ is a vector of known functions with dimension q, v is a vector of variables that are observable. Here, the aim is to find the estimate of β_0 based on an observation set $\{v_i, i = 1, \ldots, n\}$. The condition (7.1.1) is called orthogonality condition in the relevant literature.

A common genesis for MRMs (7.1.1) is a conditional moment restrictions model of the form:

$$\mathbb{E}[\rho(x, \beta_0)|z] = 0. \tag{7.1.2}$$

C. Dong and J. Gao, *Modern Series Methods in Econometrics and Statistics*,
Advanced Studies in Theoretical and Applied Econometrics 45,
https://doi.org/10.1007/978-981-96-2822-3_7

By virtue of Law of Iterated Expectation, orthogonality condition (7.1.1) holds with $m(v, \beta_0) = \rho(x, \beta_0) \otimes \varphi(z)$ where $\varphi(z)$ is any vector of functions in z, $v = (x, z)$.

Example 7.1.1 In a simple linear regression model, $y = x^\top \beta_0 + e$ where e is an error term with $\mathbb{E}(e) = 0$, often one imposes an exogeneity condition on it, $\mathbb{E}(e|x) = 0$. Apart from identifying possible intercept in the regression, the exogeneity condition implies the following orthogonality: $\mathbb{E}[(y - x^\top \beta_0)x] = 0$. This can be written into MRMs (7.1.1) with $p = q$, $m(v, \beta_0) = (y - x^\top \beta_0)x$ and $v = (x, y)$. Moreover, from the method of moments point of view, the orthogonality condition delivers $\beta_0 = (\mathbb{E}xx^\top)^{-1}\mathbb{E}(xy)$ from which one may derive the ordinary least squares estimator of β_0 based on observations $\{(x_i, y_i), i = 1, \ldots, n\}$.

Example 7.1.2 Again, consider $y = x^\top \beta_0 + e$ where $\mathbb{E}(e) = 0$ but this time $\mathbb{E}(e|x) \neq 0$. This is tantamount to saying that the model suffers from an endogeneity issue. Suppose we have a variable z of dimension q, so-called an instrumental variable, such that z is correlated with x and $\mathbb{E}(e|z) = 0$. Hence, we have MRMs (7.1.1) with $m(v, \beta_0) = (y - x^\top \beta_0)z$ and $v = (x, y, z)$.

Example 7.1.3 Suppose that vector y has expectation μ, then $\mathbb{E}(y - \mu) = 0$. This is the simplest version of MRMs. The solution of the sample version equation leads to the sample average of y_i to estimate μ.

To estimate β_0 in (7.1.1), it is necessary to ensure it is identifiable, that is, $\mathbb{E}[m(v, \beta)] = 0$ if and only if $\beta = \beta_0$. A necessary condition for identifiability is $q \geq p$, i.e., the number of moment restrictions is greater than or equal to the number of unknown parameters. If $q = p$, we say MRMs (7.1.1) is *exactly identified*; if $q > p$, we say MRMs (7.1.1) is *over-identified*. Both MRMs in Examples 7.1.1 and 7.1.3 are exactly identified, while MRMs in Example 7.1.2 could be over-identified if the dimension of z is greater than that of x.

Given the observation set $\{v_i, i = 1, \ldots, n\}$ from (7.1.1), one may form a function on β,

$$M_n(\beta) = \frac{1}{n}\sum_{i=1}^{n} m(v_i, \beta), \tag{7.1.3}$$

which is a vector of dimension q depending on the sample. We know that as n is large, $M_n(\beta_0)$ is close to $\mathbb{E}[m(v, \beta_0)] = 0$ if $\{v_i, i = 1, \ldots, n\}$ satisfies some conditions, for example, the sequence is identical and independent distributed (i.i.d.). Thus, intuitively under identification conditions the estimate of β_0, $\widehat{\beta}$, is such that $M_n(\beta)$ is as close to zero as possible over $\beta \in \Theta$ where Θ is a compact set in $\mathbb{R}^p$, and β_0 is an interior point of Θ. Mathematically, we define

$$\widehat{\beta} = \arg\min_{\beta \in \Theta} M_n(\beta)^\top W_n M_n(\beta), \tag{7.1.4}$$

where W_n is a $q \times q$ symmetric positive definite matrix that maybe depends on the sample $\{v_i, i = 1, \ldots, n\}$ and $W_n \to_P W$ as $n \to \infty$, W is positive definite as well.

If $q = p$, $\widehat{\beta}$ is the method of moments (MM) estimator, while if $q > p$, $\widehat{\beta}$ is the generalized method of moments (GMM) estimator.

Assumption 7.1.1 (a) Let $\{v_i, 1 \le i \le n\}$ be an i.i.d. sequence.
(b) Let $m(\cdot) = (m_1(\cdot), \ldots, m_q(\cdot))^\top$ and each component function be continuous in $\beta \in \Theta$.
(c) Suppose $q > p$.
(d) For any $\delta > 0$, there exists a small constant $\epsilon > 0$ such that

$$\inf_{\|\beta-\beta_0\|\ge\delta} \|\mathbb{E}(m(v, \beta))\| > \epsilon. \tag{7.1.5}$$

Condition 7.1.1 (a) makes our derivation below simple and readers easy to grasp the idea of consistency and normality shown in what follows. Condition 7.1.1 (b) is very mild while Condition 7.1.1 (c) indicates what we are studying is an over-identified MRM. Condition 7.1.1 (d) actually ensures the uniqueness of β_0 in MRM (7.1.1) but dictates in mathematical language, wherein the Eq. (7.1.5) says, as long as β deviates from β_0 at least with Euclidean metric δ, $\mathbb{E}[m(v, \beta)]$ will apart from zero at least with ϵ in Euclidean metric.

Theorem 7.1.1 *Let $W_n = I$, the identity matrix in* (7.1.4). *Under Assumption 7.1.1, we have $\widehat{\beta} \to_P \beta_0$ as $n \to \infty$.* □

Proof By the i.i.d. property, directly calculation yields $\|M_n(\beta_0)\| = O_P(n^{-1/2})$. Moreover, by definition,

$$\|M_n(\widehat{\beta})\|^2 = \inf_{\beta\in\Theta} \|M_n(\beta)\|^2 \le \|M_n(\beta_0)\|^2 = O_P(n^{-1})$$

which implies $n\|M_n(\widehat{\beta})\|^2 = O_P(1)$.

Moreover, for any $\beta \in \Theta$, we have

$$\begin{aligned}\|M_n(\beta)\|^2 =& \|M_n(\beta) - \mathbb{E}M_n(\beta) + \mathbb{E}M_n(\beta)\|^2 \\ =& \|M_n(\beta) - \mathbb{E}M_n(\beta)\|^2 + \|\mathbb{E}M_n(\beta)\|^2 \\ &+ 2[M_n(\beta) - \mathbb{E}M_n(\beta)]^\top \mathbb{E}M_n(\beta).\end{aligned}$$

Here,

$$\begin{aligned}&\mathbb{E}\|M_n(\beta) - \mathbb{E}M_n(\beta)\|^2 \\ =& \frac{1}{n}\mathbb{E}\left\|\frac{1}{\sqrt{n}}\sum_{i=1}^{n}[m(v_i, \beta) - \mathbb{E}m(v_i, \beta)]\right\|^2 \\ =& \frac{1}{n}\mathbb{E}\,\|m(v_i, \beta) - \mathbb{E}m(v_i, \beta)\|^2 \\ \le& \frac{1}{n}\sup_{\beta\in\Theta}\mathbb{E}\,\|m(v_i, \beta) - \mathbb{E}m(v_i, \beta)\|^2 = C\frac{1}{n},\end{aligned}$$

which implies $\|M_n(\beta) - \mathbb{E}M_n(\beta)\|^2 = O_P(n^{-1})$ uniformly in β, where the supremum is finite because of the continuity of $m(\cdot)$ in β and the compactness of Θ. Also, $\|\mathbb{E}M_n(\beta)\|^2 = \|\mathbb{E}m(v_i, \beta)\|^2 \leq \sup_{\beta\in\Theta} \|\mathbb{E}m(v_i, \beta)\|^2 < \infty$ again by the continuity and compactness.

Eventually, for any $\delta > 0$,

$$\begin{aligned}
\inf_{\|\beta-\beta_0\|>\delta} \|M_n(\beta)\|^2 &\geq \inf_{\|\beta-\beta_0\|>\delta} (\|M_n(\beta) - \mathbb{E}M_n(\beta)\|^2 + \|\mathbb{E}M_n(\beta)\|^2) \\
&\quad - 2 \sup_{\beta} \|M_n(\beta) - \mathbb{E}M_n(\beta)\| \|\mathbb{E}M_n(\beta)\| \\
&\geq \inf_{\|\beta-\beta_0\|>\delta} \|\mathbb{E}m(v_i, \beta)\|^2 - O_P(n^{-1/2}) \\
&\geq \epsilon, \qquad \text{in probability,}
\end{aligned}$$

where ϵ is given by Assumption 7.1.1 (d).

Now, for any $\delta > 0$, take a constant $M > 0$ to be determined at a later stage,

$$\begin{aligned}
&\mathbb{P}(\|\widehat{\beta} - \beta_0\| > \delta) \\
=&\mathbb{P}(\|\widehat{\beta} - \beta_0\| > \delta, n\|M_n(\widehat{\beta})\|^2 > M) \\
&+ \mathbb{P}(\|\widehat{\beta} - \beta_0\| > \delta, n\|M_n(\widehat{\beta})\|^2 \leq M) \\
\leq&\mathbb{P}(n\|M_n(\widehat{\beta})\|^2 > M) + \mathbb{P}\left(\inf_{\|\beta-\beta_0\|>\delta} n\|M_n(\beta)\|^2 \leq M\right) \\
=&\mathbb{P}(n\|M_n(\widehat{\beta})\|^2 > M) + \mathbb{P}\left(\inf_{\|\beta-\beta_0\|>\delta} \|M_n(\beta)\|^2 \leq M/n\right).
\end{aligned}$$

The first term can be arbitrarily small as n becomes large. Indeed, for any $\eta > 0$, since $n\|M_n(\widehat{\beta})\|^2 = O_P(1)$, we can take a sufficiently large M such that $\mathbb{P}(n\|M_n(\widehat{\beta})\|^2 > M) < \eta/2$. Fix this M, the second term is going to zero as $n \to \infty$ because $M/n \to 0$, but we have shown $\inf_{\|\beta-\beta_0\|>\delta} \|M_n(\beta)\|^2 > \epsilon$ in probability, so the event in the second term will shrink to the empty. This implies $\mathbb{P}\left(\inf_{\|\beta-\beta_0\|>\delta} \|M_n(\beta)\|^2 \leq M/n\right) < \eta/2$ when n is sufficiently large.

Finally, we show that for any $\delta > 0$ and $\eta > 0$, $\mathbb{P}(\|\widehat{\beta} - \beta_0\| > \delta) < \eta$ as $n \to \infty$. This completes the proof. □

Assumption 7.1.2 (a) Suppose $m(v, \beta)$ is continuously differentiable w.r.t. β up to the second-order. Moreover, $\partial^2 m(v, \beta)$ satisfies the Lipschitz condition.

(b) Let $B = \mathbb{E}[\frac{\partial}{\partial\beta} m(v, \beta_0)]$ that is of $p \times q$, and $A = BB^\top$. Suppose that A is of full rank.

Theorem 7.1.2 *Let* $W_n = I$, *the identity matrix in* (7.1.4). *Under Assumptions 7.1.1 and 7.1.2, as* $n \to \infty$ *we have*

$$\sqrt{n}(\widehat{\beta} - \beta_0) \to_D N(0, \Omega),$$

where $\Omega = A^{-1}B\Sigma B^\top A^{-1}$, $\Sigma = \mathbb{E}[m(v, \beta_0)m(v, \beta_0)^\top]$. □

Proof Observe that

$$\|M_n(\beta)\|^2 = \sum_{j=1}^{q}\left(\frac{1}{n}\sum_{i=1}^{n} m_j(v_i,\beta)\right)^2,$$

where we denote $m(\cdot) = (m_1(\cdot), \ldots, m_q(\cdot))^\top$. Denote

$$\begin{aligned} S_n(\beta) \equiv & \frac{\partial \|M_n(\beta)\|^2}{\partial \beta} \\ =& 2\sum_{j=1}^{q}\left(\frac{1}{n}\sum_{i=1}^{n} m_j(v_i,\beta)\right)\left(\frac{1}{n}\sum_{i=1}^{n}\frac{\partial}{\partial\beta} m_j(v_i,\beta)\right), \end{aligned}$$

and

$$\begin{aligned} H_n(\beta) \equiv & \frac{\partial^2 \|M_n(\beta)\|^2}{\partial\beta\partial\beta^\top} \\ =& 2\sum_{j=1}^{q}\left(\frac{1}{n}\sum_{i=1}^{n}\frac{\partial}{\partial\beta} m_j(v_i,\beta)\right)\left(\frac{1}{n}\sum_{i=1}^{n}\frac{\partial}{\partial\beta^\top} m_j(v_i,\beta)\right) \\ & + 2\sum_{j=1}^{q}\left(\frac{1}{n}\sum_{i=1}^{n} m_j(v_i,\beta)\right)\left(\frac{1}{n}\sum_{i=1}^{n}\frac{\partial^2}{\partial\beta\partial\beta^\top} m_j(V_i,\theta)\right). \end{aligned}$$

The estimator $\widehat{\beta}$ satisfies $S_n(\widehat{\beta}) = 0$ as the first-order condition. And by the consistency and the Mean Value Theorem,

$$0 = S_n(\widehat{\beta}) = S_n(\beta_0) + H_n(\beta^*)(\widehat{\beta} - \beta_0),$$

where β^* is on the line joining $\widehat{\beta}$ and β_0. Using Lipschitz condition, $\|H_n(\beta^*) - H_n(\beta_0)\| \le L\|\beta^* - \beta_0\|$ which gives

$$0 = S_n(\widehat{\beta}) = S_n(\beta_0) + H_n(\beta_0)(\widehat{\beta} - \beta_0) + \eta_n,$$

where $\|\eta_n\| \le L\|\widehat{\beta} - \beta_0\|^2$.

With high probability, $H_n(\beta_0)$ is positive definite. Write

$$\widehat{\beta} - \beta_0 = -H_n(\beta_0)^{-1}S_n(\beta_0) - H_n(\beta_0)^{-1}\eta_n$$

or

$$\sqrt{n}(\widehat{\beta} - \beta_0) = -H_n(\beta_0)^{-1}\sqrt{n}S_n(\beta_0) - H_n(\beta_0)^{-1}\sqrt{n}\eta_n.$$

The last term is negligible if we are able to show the convergence of the first term (that would be the leading term of $\sqrt{n}(\widehat{\beta} - \beta_0)$) since $\eta_n = O_P(\|\widehat{\beta} - \beta_0\|^2)$.

Using the following equations:

$$\begin{aligned}\sqrt{n}S_n(\beta_0) &= \sum_{j=1}^{q}\left(\frac{1}{\sqrt{n}}\sum_{i=1}^{n} m_j(v_i,\beta_0)\right)\left(\frac{1}{n}\sum_{i=1}^{n}\frac{\partial}{\partial\beta}m_j(v_i,\beta_0)\right)\\ &= \left[\frac{\partial}{\partial\beta}M_n(\beta_0)\right]\sqrt{n}M_n(\theta_0),\end{aligned}$$

and by the conventional CLT, we have

$$\sqrt{n}M_n(\theta_0) = \frac{1}{\sqrt{n}}\sum_{i=1}^{n} m(v_i,\beta_0) \to_D N(0,\Sigma),$$

where $\Sigma = \mathbb{E}[m(v,\beta_0)m(v,\beta_0)^\top]$.

Meanwhile, as $n \to \infty$,

$$\frac{\partial}{\partial\beta}M_n(\beta_0) = \frac{1}{n}\sum_{i=1}^{n}\frac{\partial}{\partial\beta}m(v_i,\beta_0) \to_P B.$$

Hence, by Slutsky theorem, $\sqrt{n}S_n(\beta_0) \to_D [\mathbb{E}\partial m(V,\beta_0)]\xi = B\xi$, as $n \to \infty$, where $\xi \sim N(0,\Sigma)$.

Moreover, by the WLLN again,

$$\begin{aligned}H_n(\beta_0) =& \sum_{j=1}^{q}\left(\frac{1}{n}\sum_{i=1}^{n}\frac{\partial}{\partial\beta}m_j(v_i,\beta_0)\right)\left(\frac{1}{n}\sum_{i=1}^{n}\frac{\partial}{\partial\beta^\top}m_j(v_i,\beta_0)\right)\\ &+\sum_{j=1}^{q}\left(\frac{1}{n}\sum_{i=1}^{n}m_j(v_i,\beta_0)\right)\left(\frac{1}{n}\sum_{i=1}^{n}\frac{\partial^2}{\partial\beta\partial\beta^\top}m_j(v_i,\beta_0)\right)\\ &\to_P[\mathbb{E}\partial m(v,\beta_0)][\mathbb{E}\partial m(v,\beta_0)]^\top = A.\end{aligned}$$

It finally follows from the Slutsky Theorem again and Continuous Mapping Theorem that

$$\sqrt{n}(\widehat{\beta}-\beta_0) \to_D A^{-1}B\xi \overset{d}{=} N(0,\Omega),$$

where $\Omega = A^{-1}B\Sigma B^\top A^{-1}$, and $\overset{d}{=}$ means equal in distribution. □

In Theorems 7.1.1 and 7.1.2, we take $W_n = I$ for simplicity. If remaining W_n in the estimator and recalling $W_n \to_P W$, we shall have

$$\sqrt{n}(\widehat{\beta}-\beta_0) \to_D N(0,\Omega(W)),$$

where $\Omega(W) = A^{-1}BW\Sigma WB^\top A^{-1}$, $A = BWB^\top$, $B = \mathbb{E}[\partial m(v, \beta_0)]$, and $\Sigma = \mathbb{E}[m(v, \beta_0)m(v, \beta_0)^\top]$.

Thus, W would affect the efficiency of $\widehat{\beta}$. Note that, if we take $W^* = \Sigma^{-1}$, then $\Omega(W^*) = [\mathbb{E}\partial m(V, \beta_0)\Sigma^{-1}\mathbb{E}\partial m(v, \beta_0)^\top]^{-1}$ and one can show that

$$\Omega(W) \geq \Omega(W^*)$$

for any positive definite W. That is, $W^* = \Sigma^{-1}$ (resp. W_n to be the sample version) makes the estimator efficient.

However, since W_n includes unknown β_0, W_n is infeasible in empirical study. To achieve efficiency, usually, a two-step method is applied:

(1) Let $W_n = I$ in (7.1.4), and obtain a consistent estimate $\widetilde{\beta}$;
(2) Define

$$\widehat{W}_n = \left[\frac{1}{n}\sum_{i=1}^{n} m(v_i, \widetilde{\beta})m(v_i, \widetilde{\beta})^\top\right]^{-1}.$$

Then, using $\widehat{W}_n$ as a weight matrix in (7.1.4), we can obtain $\widehat{\beta}$ that is asymptotically efficient.

When $q > p$, there may not be a solution in (7.1.1). One thus is interested in testing

$$H_0 : \mathbb{E}[m(v, \beta)] = 0, \quad \text{for some } \beta_0 \in \Theta, \tag{7.1.6}$$

against

$$H_1 : \mathbb{E}[m(v, \beta)] \neq 0, \quad \text{for any } \beta \in \Theta. \tag{7.1.7}$$

Hansen (1982) proposes the following testing statistic:

$$\tau_n = M_n(\widehat{\beta}^*)^\top \widehat{W}_n^{-1} M_n(\widehat{\beta}^*), \tag{7.1.8}$$

where $\widehat{\beta}^*$ is the estimator given by (7.1.4) with optimal $\widehat{W}_n$ and it is shown $n\tau_n \to_D \chi^2(q - p)$ under H_0 as $n \to \infty$. In the literature, the statistic τ_n is called J-test.

More interestingly, when H_0 is rejected for MRMs (7.1.1), it does not mean that all q moment conditions are not correct. Thus, Andrews (1999) considers a generalized method of moments estimation problem in which one has a vector of moment conditions, some of which are correct and others are incorrect. The paper introduces several procedures for consistently selecting the correct moment conditions. The procedures can also consistently determine whether there is a sufficient number of correct moment conditions to identify the unknown parameters of interest.

Despite its popularity and desirable large sample properties, it has been documented that the optimally weighted GMM estimator for MRMs has poor finite sample performance (see, e.g., Altonji & Segal, 1996). This drawback triggers a series of studies to propose an estimation method from the empirical likelihood estimation aspect that may have better performance in finite sample circumstances. Such studies include Owen (1990, 1991), Qin and Lawless (1994), Kitamura and Stutzer (1997), Imbens (1997), Imbens et al. (1998), and Newey and Smith (2004); and moreover, the last paper shows that for MRMs, the empirical likelihood estimator has better second-order properties than the optimally weighted GMM estimator.

7.2 Semiparametric MRMs

Along with the development of nonparametric techniques, semiparametric moment restriction models (SMRMs, hereafter) are proposed in econometrics. Apart from an unknown Euclidean vector of parameters, SMRMs include an infinite-dimensional parameter of unknown function, explicitly or implicitly; the simplest version of SMRMs is

$$\mathbb{E}[m(v, \beta_0, g(\cdot))] = 0, \tag{7.2.1}$$

where $m(\cdot)$ is a vector of q functions known up to $\beta_0 \in \mathbb{R}^p$ and $g(\cdot)$.

7.2.1 Conditional MRMs Estimated Through Conditional Density

It is noteworthy that conditional MRMs can be viewed as SMRMs because the conditional density therein is unknown, and it is involved in the study when the conditional expectation is specified. To deal with the unknown conditional density, a series of studies, Gallant and Nychka (1987), Gallant and Tauchen (1989), Fenton and Gallant (1996a, b), and Coppejans and Gallant (2002), discuss a seminonparametric (SNP) density estimation method. To elaborate, consider a conditional moment restriction model

$$\mathbb{E}[m(y, x, \beta_0)|x] = 0, \tag{7.2.2}$$

where $m(\cdot)$ is a vector of functions up to a finite-dimensional unknown parameter β_0. Let $f_0(y|x)$ be the true density function of y given x, and $f(y|x)$ denote any density function that satisfies the restriction for arbitrary β,

$$\int m(y, x, \beta) f(y|x) dy = 0, \quad f(y|x) > 0, \quad \int f(y|x) dy = 1.$$

Then, the true parameter (β_0, f_0) solves

$$\max_{f \in \mathcal{F}, \beta \in \Theta} \quad \mathbb{E}[\ln f(y|x)]$$

$$\text{subject to} \quad \int m(y, x, \beta) f(y|x) dy = 0,$$

where $\mathcal{F}$ stands for a density function space that contains the true density $f_0(y|x)$. Thus, the conditional MRMs (7.2.2) can be viewed as SMRMs.

Based on a sample $\{(x_i, y_i), i = 1, \ldots, n\}$, Gallant and Nychka (1987) and Gallant and Tauchen (1989) use SNP approximation $f_k(y|x, \beta, \theta_k)$ that always satisfies the constraints and tends to some function in $\mathcal{F}$ as $k \to \infty$, and propose the estimators that maximize the sample log likelihood function,

$$(\widehat{\beta}, \widehat{\theta}_k) = \arg\max_{\beta \in \Theta, \theta_k} \sum_{i=1}^{n} [\ln f(y_i|x_i, \beta, \theta_k)].$$

While most of the relevant literature only provide with the consistency of the estimators, Ai (2007) further investigates the so-called SNP maximum likelihood estimation method and establishes both asymptotic consistency and normality results.

7.2.2 Conditional MRMs Estimated Through SMD

There is a method called sieve minimum distance (SMD) to estimate conditional MRMs that eventually are converted to MRMs. Ai and Chen (2003) study a model of the form

$$\mathbb{E}[\rho(Z, \beta_0, h_0(\cdot))|X] = 0, \tag{7.2.3}$$

where $Z = (Y, X_z)$ and X_z is a subset of X, $\rho(\cdot)$ is a known vector of functions, $\alpha_0 \equiv (\beta_0, h_0)$ are parameters of interest that contain Euclidean parameter β_0 and a vector of infinite-dimensional functions $h_0 = (h_{01}, \ldots, h_{0d})$.

If the conditional distribution of Y given X, $F_{Y|X}(y|x)$, was known, $m(X, \alpha) = \mathbb{E}[\rho(Z, \beta, h(\cdot))|X]$ would be known. Thus, under the identification condition, the minimum distance estimation of α_0 is appropriate since model (7.2.3) implies that α_0 solves

$$\inf_{\alpha=(\beta,h)\in\Theta\times\mathcal{H}} \mathbb{E}\{m(X, \alpha)^\top [\Sigma(X)]^{-1} m(X, \alpha)\},$$

where $\Sigma(X)$ is a positive definite matrix for any given X.

Since the conditional distribution is actually unknown, $m(X, \alpha)$ is estimated by a sieve method. Let $\mathcal{H}$ be replaced by a sieve space $\mathcal{H}_n = \mathcal{H}_n^1 \times \cdots \times \mathcal{H}_n^d$ that has finite dimension and approaches $\mathcal{H}$ as $n \to \infty$. Let $\{p_{0j}(X), j = 1, 2, \ldots,\}$ denote a sequence of known basis functions (such as power series, splines, Fourier series, etc.), with the property that its linear combination can approximate any square integrable real-valued function of X. Denote $p^k(X) = (p_{01}(X), \ldots, p_{0k}(X))^\top$, and $m(X, \alpha) = (m_1(X, \alpha), \ldots, m_q(X, \alpha))^\top$. Then, for any fixed α, each $m_\ell(X, \alpha)$ can be approximated by $p^k(X)^\top \pi_\ell$ for some vector of coefficients π_ℓ as $k \to \infty$. It follows that, given i.i.d. sample $\{(X_i, Y_i), i = 1, \ldots, n\}$, the estimator of $m_\ell(X, \alpha)$ is obtained as $\widehat{m}_\ell(X, \alpha) = p^k(X)^\top \widehat{\pi}_\ell$ where $\widehat{\pi}_\ell$ is the coefficients of regressing

$\rho_\ell(Z_i, \alpha)$ on $p^k(X_i)$. To summarize, a consistent linear sieve estimator for $m(X, \alpha)$ is given by $\widehat{m}(X, \alpha) = (\widehat{m}_1(X, \alpha), \ldots, \widehat{m}_q(X, \alpha))^\top$ with

$$\widehat{m}_\ell(X, \alpha) = \sum_{i=1}^{n} \rho_\ell(Z_i, \alpha) p^k(X_i)^\top (P^\top P)^{-1} p^k(X),$$

where $P = (p^k(X_1), \ldots, p^k(X_n))^\top$. Finally, the SMD estimator is given by

$$\widehat{\alpha} = \underset{\alpha=(\beta,h)\in\Theta\times\mathcal{H}_n}{\arg\min} \frac{1}{n} \sum_{i=1}^{n} \widehat{m}(X_i, \alpha)^\top [\widehat{\Sigma}(X)]^{-1} \widehat{m}(X_i, \alpha)], \tag{7.2.4}$$

where $\widehat{\Sigma}(X)$ is a consistent estimate of $\Sigma(X)$ that is usually introduced to address potential heteroscedasticity.

It is interesting to point out that the estimator $\widehat{\alpha}$ in (7.2.4) is actually a GMM estimator as introduced in the preceding section. In order to see this, We choose $\widehat{\Sigma}(X) = I$. Then

$$\widehat{\alpha} = \underset{\alpha=(\beta,h)\in\Theta\times\mathcal{H}_n}{\arg\min} \left[\sum_{i=1}^{n} \rho(Z_i, \alpha) \otimes p^k(X_i)\right]^\top (I \otimes (P^\top P)^{-1}) \left[\sum_{i=1}^{n} \rho(Z_i, \alpha) \otimes p^k(X_i)\right],$$

where the objective function is the GMM criterion formulated with a weight matrix $I \otimes (P^\top P)^{-1}$ from moment conditions

$$\mathbb{E}[\rho(Z, \beta_0, h_0) p_{0j}(X)] = 0, \qquad j = 1, \ldots, k.$$

It then requires that $kq \geq p + dk$, i.e., the number of moment restrictions is greater than or equal to the number of parameters to estimate.

Under regularity conditions, Ai and Chen (2003) show the consistency and normality for $\widehat{\alpha}$. In addition, using the SMD method Ai and Chen (2007, 2012), Chen and Pouzo (2009, 2012, 2015) and Song (2015) study a series of problems in conditional MRMs including misspecified moments, nonsmooth residuals, efficiency bound, inference, measurement errors, etc.

7.2.3 *An Optimal Comparison of Misspecified MRMs*

Suppose that $\{v_i, i = 1, \ldots, n\}$ is an i.i.d. sequence of r-vectors drawn from the unknown probability measure μ_0 that satisfies

$$\mathbb{E}_{\mu_0}[g(v, \theta_0)] = 0, \tag{7.2.5}$$

where $g(\cdot)$ is a vector of functions known up to the unknown $\theta_0 \in \Theta \subset \mathbb{R}^{p_1}$. Here, we call the model by its moment function, for example, model g for (7.2.5). Let $\mathcal{M}$ be the set of all probability densities on $\mathbb{R}^r$, and define

$$\mathcal{P}_\theta^g = \{\mu \in \mathcal{M},\ \mathbb{E}_\mu[g(v,\theta)] = 0\}, \qquad \mathcal{P}^g = \bigcup_{\theta\in\Theta} \mathcal{P}_\theta^g. \tag{7.2.6}$$

that is, $\mathcal{P}_\theta^g$ is a set of measures satisfying the moment restrictions of model g at a given $\theta \in \Theta$, and $\mathcal{P}^g$ is a set of measures satisfying the moment restrictions at some $\theta \in \Theta$.

Then misspecification of model m is defined as follows: Model g is said to be misspecified if $\mu_0 \notin \mathcal{P}^g$.

An alternative moment restriction model is similarly defined as $\mathbb{E}_{\mu_0}[h(v,\beta_0)] = 0$, where h is a vector of functions known up to $\beta_0 \in B \subset \mathbb{R}^{p_2}$. The sets $\mathcal{P}_\beta^h$ and $\mathcal{P}^h$ are defined for model h as well.

Consider the situation where models g and h are both misspecified, and we wish to compare these models in terms of their goodness of fit. Let $D(g,\mu_0)$ and $D(h,\mu_0)$ be measures of fit of models g and h to the data generating measure μ_0, respectively. For example, Vuong (1989) adopted the KLIC:

$$D_{KL}(g,\mu_0) = \inf_{\mu\in\mathcal{P}^g} I(\mu_0||\mu),$$

where

$$I(\mu_0||\mu) = \begin{cases} \int \log\left(\frac{d\mu_0}{d\mu}\right) d\mu_0, & \text{if } \mu_0 \text{ is absolutely continuous w.r.t. } \mu, \\ +\infty & \text{otherwise.} \end{cases}$$

Another example, studied in depth by Hall and Pelletiel (2011), is the WE norm of (the violation of) the moment restrictions:

$$D_{WE}(g,\mu_0) = \inf_{\theta\in\Theta} \|\mathbb{E}_{\mu_0} g(v,\theta)\|_{W_g}^2,$$

where the weight matrix W_g may be unknown and needs to be estimated. The measures of fit $D_{KL}(h,\mu_0)$ and $D_{WE}(h,\mu_0)$ for model h are defined similarly.

Marmer and Otsu (2012) study the comparison between model g and h using any measure of fit D. This includes two kinds of testings:

(1) Two-sided comparison testing

$$H_0:\ \ D(g,\mu_0) = D(h,\mu_0),$$

against

$$H_1:\ \ D(g,\mu_0) \neq D(h,\mu_0).$$

(2) One-sided comparison testing

$$H_0: \ D(g, \mu_0) \leq D(h, \mu_0),$$

against

$$H_1: \ D(g, \mu_0) > D(h, \mu_0),$$

where the roles of models g and h are interchangeable. The following are two examples.

Example 7.2.1 (*Instrumental Variable Regression Models*) Let $v = (y, x, z_g, z_h)$ where y is a dependent variable, x is a vector of endogenous regressors, and z_g and z_h are different vectors of instruments for models g and h, respectively. Moment functions for models g and h are defined as $g(v, \theta) = z_g(y - x^\top\theta)$ and $h(v, \beta) = z_h(y - x^\top\beta)$, respectively. If one is interested in the WE measure of fit D_{WE}, the null hypothesis in two-sided testing for the model comparison is

$$H_0: \ \min_{\theta\in\Theta}\|\mathbb{E}_{\mu_0} z_g(y - x^\top\theta)\|^2_{W_g} = \min_{\beta\in B}\|\mathbb{E}_{\mu_0} z_h(y - x^\top\beta)\|^2_{W_h}.$$

Example 7.2.2 (*Linear Factor Asset Pricing Models*) Let f_g and f_h be two different vectors of factors (including a constant) used to define stochastic discount factors $f_g^\top\theta$ and $f_h^\top\beta$ based on linear factor asset pricing models g and h, respectively. Let R be an q-vector of asset returns and $v = (R, f_g, f_h)$. The moment functions for models g and h are defined as $g(v, \theta) = Rf_g^\top\theta - 1_q$ and $h(v, \beta) = Rf_h^\top\beta - 1_q$, respectively, where 1_q is the q-vector of ones, and the null hypothesis for the model comparison can be written as

$$H_0: \ \min_{\theta\in\Theta}\|\mathbb{E}_{\mu_0} Rf_g^\top\theta - 1_q\|^2_{W_g} = \min_{\beta\in B}\|\mathbb{E}_{\mu_0} Rf_h^\top\beta - 1_q\|^2_{W_h}.$$

Usually, in order to construct testing statistics, the generalized Neyman-Pearson (GNP) optimality criterion is used in related literature that compares the decay rate of the type II error probability under some restrictions on the decay rate of the type I error probability. To proceed, let $g_i(\theta) = g(v_i, \theta)$, $h_i(\beta) = h(v_i, \beta)$, $\bar{g}(\theta) = (1/n)\sum_{i=1}^n g_i(\theta)$, and $\bar{h}(\beta) = (1/n)\sum_{i=1}^n h_i(\beta)$; define

$$\widehat{\theta} = \arg\min_{\theta\in\Theta}\|\bar{g}(\theta)\|^2_{W_g}, \quad \text{and} \quad \widehat{\beta} = \arg\min_{\beta\in B}\|\bar{h}(\beta)\|^2_{W_h}.$$

Marmer and Otsu (2012) then propose the following testing statistic:

$$T_n = \min_{\eta_g\in\mathbb{R}^{q_1}, \eta_h\in\mathbb{R}^{q_2}, \|\eta_g\|^2_{W_g} = \|\eta_h\|^2_{W_h}} - 2n\ell(\eta_g, \eta_h),$$

where q_1 and q_2 are the number of restrictions for models g and h, respectively, and

$$\ell(\eta_g, \eta_h) = - \max_{\lambda_g \in \mathbb{R}^{q_1}, \lambda_h \in \mathbb{R}^{q_2}} \frac{1}{n} \sum_{i=1}^{n} \log \left[1 + \lambda_g^\top (g_i(\widehat{\theta}) - \eta_g) + \lambda_h^\top (h_i(\widehat{\beta}) - \eta_h) \right],$$

and under regular conditions they show that as $n \to \infty$, if H_0 holds, $T_n \to_D \chi_1^2$, while if H_1 holds, $\mathbb{P}(T_n > c) \to 1$ for any $c > 0$. Accordingly, picking the relevant critical value of χ_1^2, one may infer for the hypothesis H_0 against H_1.

7.3 High-Dimensional Semiparametric MRMs

Partially due to the recent advancements in data storage and computational power, high-dimensional data that have increasing dimensions have significantly occupied the mainstream in econometrics and statistical research. In gene expression datasets, for instance, it is not uncommon to encounter datasets with observations on at most a few hundred independent samples (subjects) and with information on tens or hundreds of thousands of genes per sample. Thus, high-dimensional data in the big data era are ubiquitous and are encountered on a regular basis by statisticians and econometricians in both academia and industry. Catering to the big data era, high-dimensional MRMs allow that both the number of parameters and the number of moment restrictions grow considerably along with the sample size.

We consider a class of semiparametric models that accommodate Euclidean parameters and unknown functions to estimate, where we allow the number of Euclidean parameters to increase to infinity. Two cases are considered sequentially: First, the dimensionality is moderate, and then the number of possible covariates is extremely large, i.e., sparse models. Large models are the focus of much current research; see Dong and Tu (2024), Athey et al. (2017), and Belloni et al. (2014b). We suppose that the model is defined through a set of unconditional moment conditions:

$$\mathbb{E}[m(V, \alpha_1^\top X_1, \ldots, \alpha_r^\top X_r, g_1(\theta_1^\top Z_1), \ldots, g_s(\theta_s^\top Z_s))] = 0, \tag{7.3.1}$$

where m is a known vector of functions whose dimension q is large, $\alpha_1, \ldots, \alpha_r$ are unknown Euclidean-valued parameters whose respective dimensions p_j may be large, while $g = (g_1, \ldots, g_s)$ is a vector of unknown smooth functions and the index vectors $\theta_1, \ldots, \theta_s$ are unit vectors with positive first elements satisfying the usual identification condition for the single-index model. Both r and s are fixed. The random variable V typically represents a dependent variable and possible instrumental variables, while the vectors $X_j (1 \le j \le r)$ and $Z_\ell (1 \le \ell \le s)$ are explanatory variables. We suppose that Z_j is of fixed finite dimension, but the dimension of X (and V) may be large, i.e., diverge. We suppose that a random sample $\{V_i, X_{ji}, Z_{\ell i}, 1 \le j \le r, 1 \le \ell \le s, i = 1, \ldots, n\}$ is observed and that $p = p(n) \to \infty$ and $q = q(n) \to \infty$ as $n \to \infty$ with $q > p \equiv p_1 + \cdots + p_r$ where p_j is the dimension of X_j.

For the case of moderate dimensionality, we consider the case where (at least) $p/n \to 0$, similar to Portnoy (1984, 1985), and Mammen (1989). The moment restriction model (7.3.1) features high-dimensionality in two ways: high-dimensional Euclidean parameters (α_j) and an unknown function vector $g(\cdot)$ with infinite-dimensional parameter elements (g_ℓ); the number of moment conditions necessarily increases to infinity. The setting includes as a special case the partial linear regression model with some weak instruments and endogeneity, Robinson (1988), except in our case the number of covariates in the linear part may increase to infinity with the sample size. There are sometimes many binary covariates whose effect can be restricted to be linear, perhaps after a transformation of response, but other continuous covariates whose effect is thought to be nonlinear. In panel data, one may wish to allow for many fixed effects in an essentially linear fashion, but capture the potential nonlinear effect of a critical covariate or a continuous treatment variable. If both the cross-sectional and time series dimensions are large then these quantities are all estimable. See, for example, Connor et al. (2012).

Chen et al. (2003) study a fixed-dimensional moment restriction model containing an unknown function. They consider two-step and profiled two-step methods. A similar approach is used in Chen and Liao (2015). Kernel estimation techniques, in particular, require an additional (albeit related) estimating equation for the unknown function, and either two-step or profile methods are common, see, for example, Powell (1994). By contrast, we use series methods to simultaneously estimate α_j, g_ℓ and θ_ℓ in the parameter spaces defined below. This approach also avoids high level assumptions, such as in Chen et al. (2003) and Han and Phillips (2006). The parameters of interest are particular functionals of α_j and g_ℓ for which we have plug-in estimators once we obtain the estimates of α_j and g_ℓ. We then establish the consistency and (self-normalized) asymptotic normality of the parameters of interest and provide a feasible CLT that allows a normal inference about the parameters of interest. We also propose some new test statistics to address the over-identification issue and establish their large sample properties.

Even though series methods can parameterize unknown functions, how to estimate θ_ℓ is still challenging. Note that the importance of the involvement of single-index structure in the conditional moment restriction model has been mentioned in Ai and Chen (2003, p. 1796), but there is no explicit treatment for the estimation of index vector, as far as we are aware, in the literature on moment or conditional moment restriction models. The reason might be, in our opinion, that the commonly used profile method dealing with single-index structure in regression models is not applicable because the moment function in general is no longer linear in its components. See, for example, Dong et al. (2016) and the reference therein for the use of the profile method in single-index regression. We offer a solution to deal with this situation.

Though a relatively simpler model

$$\mathbb{E}[m(V, \alpha_1^\top X_1, \ldots, \alpha_r^\top X_r, g_1(Z_1), \ldots, g_s(Z_s))] = 0. \tag{7.3.2}$$

is a special one of (7.3.1) where all vectors Z_ℓ are reduced to be scalar, this model also has wide applications because the number of unknown functions can be any fixed integer. For some discussions, we just consider the case of $r = 1$ and $s = 1$.

7.3.1 SMRMs Without Single-Index Structure

We start with model (7.3.2) in the special case of $r = s = 1$. The only price we pay for the case of $r > 1$ and/or $s > 1$ is the complexity of notation. Consider

$$\mathbb{E}[m(V, \alpha^\top X, g(Z))] = 0. \tag{7.3.3}$$

Here, we suppose that $g \in L^2(\mathbb{Z}, \pi) = \{f : \int_{\mathbb{Z}} f^2(z)\pi(z)dz < \infty\}$ a Hilbert function space, $\mathbb{Z} \subset \mathbb{R}^d$, where $\pi(\cdot)$ is a user-chosen density function on $\mathbb{Z}$. Roughly speaking, the choice of the density π relates to how large the Hilbert space is expected, since the thinner the tail of the density is, the larger the space is. For example, $L^2(\mathbb{R}, 1/(1+z^2)) \subset L^2(\mathbb{R}, \exp(-z^2))$. An inner product in the Hilbert space is given by $\langle f_1, f_2\rangle = \int_{\mathbb{Z}} f_1(z)f_2(z)\pi(z)dz$, and hence the induced norm $\|f\| = \sqrt{\langle f, f\rangle}$ for any $f_1(z), f_2(z), f(z) \in L^2(\mathbb{Z}, \pi)$.

Let $\{\varphi_j(\cdot)\}$ be a complete orthonormal function sequence in $L^2(\mathbb{Z}, \pi)$. Accordingly, for the function $g(z) \in L^2(\mathbb{Z}, \pi)$, we have an infinite orthogonal series expansion of the form:

$$g(z) = \sum_{j=0}^{\infty} \beta_j \varphi_j(z), \quad \text{where } \beta_j = \langle g, \varphi_j\rangle, \tag{7.3.4}$$

where the convergence is in the norm sense in the space. For positive integer K, define $g_K(z) = \sum_{j=0}^{K-1} \beta_j\varphi_j(z)$ as a truncated series and $\gamma_K(z) = \sum_{j=K}^{\infty} \beta_j\varphi_j(z)$ the residue. Then, $g_K(z) \to g(z)$ as $K \to \infty$. For better exposition, denote $\Phi_K(z) = (\varphi_0(z), \ldots, \varphi_{K-1}(z))^\top$ and $\beta = (\beta_0, \ldots, \beta_{K-1})^\top$ two K-vectors. Thus, $g_K(z) = \beta^\top \Phi_K(z)$.

Our primary goal is to estimate the unknown parameters (α, g) and their relevant functionals. Define $\Theta = \{(\mathbf{a}, f) : \mathbf{a} \in \mathbb{R}^p, f \in L^2(\mathbb{Z}, \pi)\}$, the parameter space for model (7.3.3), and

$$\|(\mathbf{a}, f)\| = \|\mathbf{a}\|_E + \|f\|_{L^2}, \tag{7.3.5}$$

where $\|\cdot\|_E$ denotes the Euclidean norm on $\mathbb{R}^p$ and $\|f\|_{L^2}$ signifies the norm on the Hilbert space, of which the subscript may be suppressed whenever no ambiguity is incurred.

To facilitate the implementation of nonlinear optimization, α should be confined to a compact subset of $\mathbb{R}^p$ and the truncated series $g_K(z)$ should be included in an expanding finite-dimensional bounded subset of $L^2(\mathbb{Z}, \pi)$. To this end, suppose that B_{1n} and B_{2n} are two positive real numbers diverging with n such that α in model (7.3.3) is included in $\Theta_{1n} := \{\mathbf{a} \in \mathbb{R}^p : \|\mathbf{a}\| \le B_{1n}\}$ and for sufficiently large n, $g_K(z)$ is included in $\Theta_{2n} := \{\mathbf{b}^\top \Phi_K(z) : \|\mathbf{b}\| \le B_{2n}\}$. Define $\Theta_n = \Theta_{1n} \otimes \Theta_{2n}$.

It is noteworthy that in an infinite-dimensional space, a bounded set may not necessarily be compact. See Ai and Chen (2012) for detailed discussion on compactness. However, our optimization is implemented over a compact set since it is of finite dimension and boundedness, so that our estimation procedure does not suffer from the *ill-posededness issue* that is encountered in the literature, such as Chen (2007) and Blundell et al. (2007).

Here, unlike in a standard single-index model, we do not require $\|\alpha\| = 1$ for identification. This is because the function $m(\cdot)$ is known, and hence we are able to identify any scaling for α. Assumption 7.3.2 in Sect. 7.3.6 allows for the bounds of α to diverge with the sample size that entertains the divergence of its dimensionality. Furthermore, since $\|g_K\| \le \|g\|$ it is clear that there exists an integer n_0 such that $g_K(z) \in \Theta_{2n}$ for all $n \ge n_0$. On the other hand, Θ_{2n}, the so-called linear sieve space in the literature, can approximate the entire function space with the increase of the sample size, because any $f(z) \in L^2(\mathbb{Z}, \pi)$ can be approximated by a combination of this type, $\mathbf{b}^\top \Phi_K(z)$, arbitrarily in the sense of norm. Thus, Θ can be approximated by Θ_n as $n \to \infty$. More importantly, our setting is similar to but broader than that discussed in Newey and Powell (2003).

We estimate α and β by

$$(\widehat{\alpha}, \widehat{\beta}) = \underset{\mathbf{a}\in\mathbb{R}^p, \mathbf{b}\in\mathbb{R}^K}{\operatorname{argmin}} \|M_n(\mathbf{a}, \mathbf{b})\|^2, \quad \text{subject to } \|\mathbf{a}\| \le B_{1n} \text{ and } \|\mathbf{b}\| \le B_{2n},$$
$$\text{where } M_n(\mathbf{a}, \mathbf{b}) = \frac{1}{\sqrt{q}}\frac{1}{n}\sum_{i=1}^{n} m(V_i, \mathbf{a}^\top X_i, \mathbf{b}^\top \Phi_K(Z_i)). \tag{7.3.6}$$

Here, the involvement of q in $M_n(\mathbf{a}, \mathbf{b})$ takes into account the divergent dimensions of the vector m in order to avoid the issue that $\|M_n(\mathbf{a}, \mathbf{b})\|$ could be large even if each element is small that would arise if we had not put q into $M_n(\mathbf{a}, \mathbf{b})$. This issue does not arise when the vector-valued m function has a fixed dimension. Define for any $z \in \mathbb{Z}$,

$$\widehat{g}(z) = \widehat{\beta}^\top \Phi_K(z), \tag{7.3.7}$$

as the estimator of $g(z)$.

Asymptotic properties of the estimators. The following theorem of the asymptotic consistency for all estimators is established by Dong et al. (2023), while the assumptions used are given in Sect. 7.3.6 for convenience and completeness.

Theorem 7.3.1 (Consistency) *Suppose that Assumptions 7.3.1–7.3.5 in Sect. 7.3.6 hold. Let* $B_{1n}^2 + B_{2n}^2 = o(n)$. *Then, we have* $\|(\widehat{\alpha} - \alpha, \widehat{g} - g)\| \to_P 0$ *as* $n \to \infty$ *for* $(\widehat{\alpha}, \widehat{g})$ *given by* (7.3.6) *and* (7.3.7). □

We then consider the limit distribution of the estimators. Nonetheless, we cannot establish a limit distribution for $\widehat{\alpha} - \alpha$ itself since the dimension of α diverges. Instead, we shall consider some finite-dimensional transformations of α, for which plug-in estimators are used. Likewise, we consider the functionals of $g(\cdot)$. In many applications, both types of quantities are of interest. For example, the weighted average marginal treatment effect (MTE) parameter in Carneiro et al. (2011) depends on both α and g. In financial econometrics, a leading example is the conditional value at risk, which depends on the parameters of the dynamic mean and variance model and the quantile of the error distribution.

Let $\mathscr{L}$ be a transformation from $\mathbb{R}^p \mapsto \mathbb{R}^\mu$ with $\mu \geq 1$ fixed, and let $\mathscr{F} = (\mathscr{F}_1, \ldots, \mathscr{F}_\nu)^\top$ with fixed ν be a vector of functionals on $L^2(\mathbb{Z}, \pi)$. Though in the literature, one usually takes linear $\mathscr{L}$ with $\mu = 1$ (see, e.g., Theorem 4.2 in Belloni et al., 2015, p. 352 and several results, such as Theorems 2 and 6 in Chang et al., 2015). We allow that $\mathscr{L}$ may have either linear or nonlinear components or both with $\mu \geq 1$. The elements of $\mathscr{F}$ can be, for example, as described in Newey (1997, p. 151), the integral of $\ln[g(z)]$ on some interval, which stands for consumer's surplus in microeconomics. Other examples include the partial derivative function, the average partial derivative, and the conditional partial derivative. Thus, we shall consider the limit distributions of $\mathscr{L}(\widehat{\alpha}) - \mathscr{L}(\alpha)$ and $\mathscr{F}(\widehat{g}) - \mathscr{F}(g)$.

Recall the Fréchet derivative operator for an operator from one Banach space to another. It is a bounded linear operator. The Fréchet derivative of $\mathscr{F}$ at $g(\cdot)$ is an s-vector of functionals, denoted by $\mathscr{F}'(g)$, such that

$$\mathscr{F}(\widehat{g}) - \mathscr{F}(g) = \mathscr{F}'(g) \circ (\widehat{g} - g) + \lambda(g, \widehat{g} - g),$$

where $\lambda(g, \widehat{g} - g) = o(\|\widehat{g} - g\|)$.

We are now ready to establish an asymptotic normality for our plug-in estimators. Define

$$\begin{aligned}
\Sigma_n^2 :=& \Gamma_n[\Psi_n\Psi_n^\top]^{-1}\Psi_n \Xi_n \Psi_n^\top [\Psi_n\Psi_n^\top]^{-1}\Gamma_n^\top, \quad \text{in which} \qquad (7.3.8)\\
\Gamma_n \equiv& \begin{pmatrix} \partial\mathscr{L}(\alpha)^\top & 0 \\ 0 & \mathscr{F}'(g)\circ\Phi_K{}^\top \end{pmatrix}_{(\mu+\nu)\times(p+K)},\\
\Xi_n :=& \mathbb{E}[m(V, \alpha^\top X, g(Z))m(V, \alpha^\top X, g(Z))^\top]_{q\times q},\\
\Psi_n \equiv& \mathbb{E}\begin{pmatrix} \frac{\partial}{\partial u} m(V, \alpha^\top X, g(Z))^\top \otimes X \\ \frac{\partial}{\partial w} m(V, \alpha^\top X, g(Z))^\top \otimes \Phi_K(Z) \end{pmatrix}_{(p+K)\times q},
\end{aligned}$$

provided that $\Psi_n\Psi_n^\top$ is invertible; here u and w stand for the second and the third arguments of the vector function $m(v, u, w)$, respectively.

Theorem 7.3.2 (Normality) *Let Assumptions 7.3.1–7.3.10 in Sect. 7.3.6 hold. Suppose also that $B_{1n}^2 + B_{2n}^2 = o(n)$. Then for $(\widehat{\alpha}, \widehat{g})$ given by (7.3.6) and (7.3.7), as $n \to \infty$*

$$\sqrt{n}\Sigma_n^{-1}\begin{pmatrix} \mathscr{L}(\widehat{\alpha}) - \mathscr{L}(\alpha) \\ \mathscr{F}(\widehat{g}) - \mathscr{F}(g) \end{pmatrix} \xrightarrow{d} N(0, I_{\mu+\nu}), \qquad (7.3.9)$$

provided that $\sqrt{n}\Sigma_n^{-1}(0_\mu^\top, (\mathscr{F}'(g)\circ\gamma_K)^\top)^\top = o(1)$, where Σ_n is given by the square root of Σ_n^2 defined in (7.3.8). □

Again, this normality is established by Dong et al. (2023). Given that the conditions in Theorem 7.3.1 hold in this theorem, the consistency of the estimator is valid before proving the normality. Apart from the diverging dimensions of Ψ_n and Ξ_n and the use of the transformation $\mathscr{L}$ and the functional $\mathscr{F}$, the form of the covariance matrices Σ_n^2 is the same as in the standard semiparametric literature, such as Hansen (1982), Pakes and Pollard (1989) and Chen et al. (2003).

In general, the convergence order of $\mathscr{F}(\widehat{g}) - \mathscr{F}(g)$ is proportional to $(\mathscr{F}'(g) \circ \Phi_K(z)^\top \mathscr{F}'^\top \circ \Phi_K(z))^{1/2} n^{-1/2}$, which is similar to the result in Theorem 2 of Newey (1997). Here, the matrix in the front of $n^{-1/2}$ is of dimension $\nu \times \nu$ and is associated with the derivative of the functional $\mathscr{F}$. To understand how it affects the rate, consider a special case that $\nu = 1$ and $\mathscr{F}(g) = g(z)$ for some particular z, implying $\mathscr{F}(\widehat{g}) - \mathscr{F}(g) = \widehat{g}(z) - g(z)$ and $\mathscr{F}'(g) \equiv 1$. Then, the matrix is a scalar and the rate becomes $\|\Phi_K(z)\| n^{-1/2}$, which coincides with the conventional nonparametric rate of convergence established in the literature. See, for example, Dong and Linton (2018).

The standard convergence order of $\mathscr{L}(\widehat{\alpha}) - \mathscr{L}(\alpha)$ is $n^{-1/2}$; however, Theorem 7.3.2 does not rule out the mildly *weak instrument case* where the matrix Σ_n is close to singular, i.e., $|\Sigma_n| \neq 0$ but $|\Sigma_n| \to 0$ with n at a certain rate; this would reduce the convergence rate of the estimators but the self-normalized distribution theory we have presented continues to hold under our conditions. However, we do rule out the more extreme cases considered in Han and Phillips (2006), which would change the limiting distribution.

The requirement that $\sqrt{n}\Sigma_n^{-1}(0_\mu^\top, (\mathscr{F}'(g) \circ \gamma_K)^\top)^\top = o(1)$ is an "undersmoothing" condition, playing a similar role to, for example, the condition $\sqrt{n} V_K^{-1} K^{-p/d} = o(1)$ in Corollary 3.1 of Chen and Christensen (2015, p. 454) and Comment 4.3 of Belloni et al. (2015). The precise form of the condition may vary according to the parameters of interest and the underlying model; it reflects the bias-variance trade-off that is relevant for the estimation of those quantities in the particular model.

In the large-dimensional α case, the bias-variance trade-off can be different from usual since the parametric part can contribute a large variance; the presence of weak instruments may also affect the bias-variance trade-off for certain parameters. For inference results about $g(z)$ it is a common practice to undersmooth/overfit to avoid the bias term. Some recent research advocates using extreme undersmoothing for better inference about finite-dimensional parameters in semiparametric models. See, for example, Cattaneo et al. (2018). Cattaneo et al. (2018) develop heteroskedasticity robust inference methods for the finite-dimensional parameters of a linear model in the presence of a large number of linearly estimated nuisance parameters in the case where essentially p is fixed but $K(n) \propto n$. In this case, the function $g(\cdot)$ is not consistently estimated. In our methodology, we pay equal attention to the function g, which itself can be of interest. Our methodology is also robust to conditional heteroskedasticity.

In Theorem 7.3.2, the limiting distribution involves unknown parameters in the matrix Σ_n. One would need a consistent estimator for this matrix in inference practice. It is easily seen that the estimator, $\widehat{\Sigma}_n$, in which we replace α and $g(\cdot)$ in Σ_n by $\widehat{\alpha}$ and

$\widehat{g}(\cdot)$, as well as the expectations in Ξ_n and Ψ_n by their sample versions, respectively, is consistent. More precisely, let

$$\widehat{\Sigma}_n^2 = \widehat{\Gamma}_n[\widehat{\Psi}_n\widehat{\Psi}_n^\top]^{-1}\widehat{\Psi}_n\widehat{\Xi}_n\widehat{\Psi}_n^\top[\widehat{\Psi}_n\widehat{\Psi}_n^\top]^{-1}\widehat{\Gamma}_n^\top,$$

where $\widehat{\Gamma}_n$ is Γ_n with replacement of $\partial\mathscr{L}(\alpha)$ by $\partial\mathscr{L}(\widehat{\alpha})$ and of $\mathscr{F}'(g)$ by $\mathscr{F}'(\widehat{g})$, and

$$\widehat{\Xi}_n \equiv \frac{1}{n}\sum_{i=1}^{n}[m(V_i,\widehat{\alpha}^\top X_i,\widehat{g}(Z_i))m(V_i,\widehat{\alpha}^\top X_i,\widehat{g}(Z_i))^\top], \tag{7.3.10}$$

$$\widehat{\Psi}_n \equiv \frac{1}{n}\sum_{i=1}^{n}\begin{pmatrix} \frac{\partial}{\partial u}m(V_i,\widehat{\alpha}^\top X_i,\widehat{g}(Z_i))^\top \otimes X_i \\ \frac{\partial}{\partial w}m(V_i,\widehat{\alpha}^\top X_i,\widehat{g}(Z_i))^\top \otimes \Phi_K(Z_i) \end{pmatrix}. \tag{7.3.11}$$

Then, the feasible version of the CLT (7.3.9), with $\widehat{\Sigma}_n$ replacing Σ_n, follows by similar arguments to those in the proof of Theorem 7.3.2. This allows the construction of simultaneous confidence intervals and consistent hypothesis tests about $\mathscr{L}(\alpha)$ and $\mathscr{F}(g)$.

Similar to the GMM literature, we may improve efficiency by using a weight matrix. Let W_n be a $q \times q$ positive definite matrix that may depend on the sample data. Then, $\|M_n(\mathbf{a},\mathbf{b})\|^2$, which measures the metric of $M_n(\mathbf{a},\mathbf{b})$ from zero, can be substituted by $M_n(\mathbf{a},\mathbf{b})^\top W_n M_n(\mathbf{a},\mathbf{b})$ in the minimization of (7.3.6), which is also a measure of the metric for the vector $M_n(\mathbf{a},\mathbf{b})$ from zero but in terms of the weight matrix W_n. Meanwhile, $\|M_n(\mathbf{a},\mathbf{b})\|^2$ can be viewed as a special case that W_n is the identity matrix. We require the matrix W_n to be not too close to being singular to prevent the possibility that $M_n(\mathbf{a},\mathbf{b})^\top W_n M_n(\mathbf{a},\mathbf{b})$ may be close to zero when $(\mathbf{a},\mathbf{b})$ is far from (α,β).

Proposition 7.3.1 *Suppose that the eigenvalues of W_n are bounded away from zero and above from infinity uniformly in n, and there exists a deterministic matrix W^* such that $\|W_n - W^*\| = o_P(1)$ as $n \to \infty$. Let $(\widetilde{\alpha},\widetilde{\beta})$ be the minimizer of $M_n(\mathbf{a},\mathbf{b})^\top W_n M_n(\mathbf{a},\mathbf{b})$ and define $\widetilde{g}(z) = \Phi_K(z)^\top\widetilde{\beta}$.*

Then, (1) Under the same conditions in Theorem 7.3.1, the consistency of the weighted estimator holds; (2) Under the same conditions in Theorem 7.3.2, the normality for the weighted estimator holds with Σ_n^2 replaced by

$$\Gamma_n[\Psi_n W^*\Psi_n^\top]^{-1}\Psi_n W^*\Xi_n W^*\Psi_n^\top[\Psi_n W^*\Psi_n^\top]^{-1}\Gamma_n^\top.$$

(3) If $W^* = \Xi_n^{-1}$, the optimal covariance matrices are obtained, $\Gamma_n[\Psi_n\Xi_n^{-1}\Psi_n^\top]^{-1}\Gamma_n^\top$. □

See Dong et al. (2023). Here, the optimal covariance is in the sense that

$$\Gamma_n[\Psi_n W\Psi_n^\top]^{-1}\Psi_n W\Xi_n W\Psi_n^\top[\Psi_n W\Psi_n^\top]^{-1}\Gamma_n^\top \geq \Gamma_n[\Psi_n\Xi_n^{-1}\Psi_n^\top]^{-1}\Gamma_n^\top,$$

for all W satisfying the conditions in the proposition. Though $W_n = \Xi_n^{-1}$ might make the estimator efficient, it is not feasible since Ξ_n involves the true parameters.

In practice, both Ξ_n and Ψ_n can be replaced by their sample versions of (7.3.10) and (7.3.11), so that the optimal covariance matrices are easily estimable. To do so, one will need to implement a two-step estimation method, as has normally been done in the literature, that is, at the first step, minimizing $\|M_n(\mathbf{a}, \mathbf{b})\|^2$ to have $\widehat{\alpha}$ and $\widehat{g}(\cdot)$ that are used to construct $\widehat{W}_n = \widehat{\Xi}_n^{-1}$; then at the second step one may minimize $M_n(\mathbf{a}, \mathbf{b})^\top \widehat{W}_n M_n(\mathbf{a}, \mathbf{b})$ to have a pair of optimal estimators, $(\widetilde{\alpha}, \widetilde{g}(\cdot))$.

Notice that there is an alternative way to achieve efficiency in one-step estimation, viz., the continuous updating estimator (CUE) and generalized empirical likelihood estimator; see Newey and Smith (2004) and Chang et al. (2015). Define $W_n(\mathbf{a}, \mathbf{b}) = [\Xi_n(\mathbf{a}, \mathbf{b})]^{-1}$, where

$$\Xi_n(\mathbf{a}, \mathbf{b}) := \frac{1}{n}\sum_{i=1}^{n}[m(V_i, \mathbf{a}^\top X_i, \mathbf{b}^\top \Phi_K(Z_i))m(V_i, \mathbf{a}^\top X_i, \mathbf{b}^\top \Phi_K(Z_i))^\top].$$

Then, $(\widetilde{\alpha}, \widetilde{g}(\cdot))$ can be estimated by minimizing $M_n(\mathbf{a}, \mathbf{b})^\top W_n(\mathbf{a}, \mathbf{b}) M_n(\mathbf{a}, \mathbf{b})$ over $(\mathbf{a}, \mathbf{b})$. For more details, we refer the reader to Hansen et al. (1996).

7.3.2 SMRMs with Single-Index Structure

Utilizing some particular property of Hermite polynomials, one approach introduced in this subsection is able to deal with the moment restriction models with a single-index structure. Similar to the preceding section, we only focus on the estimation procedure for model (7.3.1) in the case where $r = s = 1$,

$$\mathbb{E}[m(V, \alpha^\top X, g(\theta_0^\top Z))] = 0. \tag{7.3.12}$$

Our goal is to estimate α, θ_0 and $g(\cdot)$, where θ_0 satisfies the identification condition, viz., $\|\theta_0\| = 1$ and the first element is positive. Suppose that the function g has support $\mathbb{R}$ and $g \in L^2(\mathbb{R}, \exp(-w^2))$. Then, $g(w)$ admits an orthogonal expansion, $g(w) = \sum_{j=0}^{\infty} c_j h_j(w)$ where $h_j(w) = (\sqrt{\pi}2^j j!)^{-1/2} H_j(w)$ are normalized Hermite polynomials. Hence, by virtue of a property of Hermite polynomials given in Lemma B.1 in Dong et al. (2015) and $\|\theta_0\| = 1$ with $\theta_0 = (\theta_{01}, \ldots, \theta_{0d})^\top$, for any $k \geq 1$, we have

$$\begin{aligned} g(\theta_0^\top Z) &= \sum_{j=0}^{k-1} c_j h_j(\theta_0^\top Z) + \gamma_k(\theta_0^\top Z) \\ &= \sum_{j=0}^{k-1} \sum_{|u|=j} a_{ju}(\theta_0) \mathcal{H}_u(Z) + \gamma_k(\theta_0^\top Z), \end{aligned}$$

where $\gamma_k(\cdot)$ is the truncation residue, u is a multi-index, $u = (u_1, \ldots, u_d)$, $|u| = u_1 + \cdots + u_d$ and

$$a_{ju}(\theta_0) = \frac{\pi^{d/4} 2^{j/2} j!}{\sqrt{u_1! \cdots u_d!}} c_j \theta_0^u, \quad \theta_0^u = \prod_{j=1}^{d} \theta_{0j}^{u_j}, \quad \mathcal{H}_u(Z) = \prod_{j=1}^{d} h_{u_j}(Z_j).$$

Thus, $g(\theta_0^\top Z)$ can be approximated by a combination of $\beta^\top \Phi_K(Z)$ where $\Phi_K(Z)$ is a vector consisting of all $\mathcal{H}_u(Z)$ for $|u| = j$ and $0 \le j \le k-1$, and similarly β consists of all $a_{ju}(\theta_0)$ in the same order as $\Phi_K(Z)$, that is, $g(\theta^\top Z) = \beta^\top \Phi_K(Z) + \gamma_k(\theta_0^\top Z)$ and $\gamma_k(\cdot) = o(1)$ as $k \to \infty$ in some sense.

Therefore, similar to (7.3.6), we may estimate α and β by

$$\begin{aligned} (\widehat{\alpha}, \widehat{\beta}) = & \operatorname*{argmin}_{\mathbf{a} \in \mathbb{R}^p, \mathbf{b} \in \mathbb{R}^K} \|M_n(\mathbf{a}, \mathbf{b})\|^2, \\ & \text{subject to } \|\mathbf{a}\| \le B_{1n} \text{ and } \|\mathbf{b}\| \le B_{2n}, \end{aligned} \tag{7.3.13}$$

where

$$M_n(\mathbf{a}, \mathbf{b}) = \frac{1}{\sqrt{q}} \frac{1}{n} \sum_{i=1}^{n} m(V_i, \mathbf{a}^\top X_i, \mathbf{b}^\top \Phi_K(Z_i)) \phi(\|Z_i\|), \ \phi(v) = \exp(-v^2/2).$$

The involvement of $\phi(\cdot)$ in $M_n(\mathbf{a}, \mathbf{b})$ is to deal with the rapid divergence of the fourth moment of $h_j(\cdot)$. This technique is also used in Dong et al. (2021b) and Dong and Tu (2024).

Under similar conditions as in Theorem 7.3.1, $(\widehat{\alpha}, \widehat{\beta})$ given by (7.3.13) is consistent. We then detangle $\widehat{\beta}$ to have the estimates of c_j and θ_0, from which we can construct the estimator of $g(z)$. Specifically, if $c_1 \ne 0$, by the relationship $a_{1u}(\theta_0) = \sqrt{2}\pi^{d/4} c_1 \theta_0^u$ for all $|u| = 1$, along with the identification condition on θ_0, the estimate $\widehat{\beta}$ gives

$$\widehat{c}_1 = \operatorname{sgn}(\widehat{a}_{1u_0}) \frac{1}{\sqrt{2}\pi^{d/4}} \left(\sum_{|u|=1} \widehat{a}_{1u}^2 \right)^{1/2}, \quad \text{where } u_0 = (1, 0, \ldots, 0).$$

Because $\widehat{\beta}$ is consistent, $\widehat{c}_1 \ne 0$ with probability approaching one. Define

$$\widehat{\theta} = \frac{1}{\widehat{c}_1} Q \widehat{\beta},$$

as the estimator of θ_0, where $Q = (0_{d\times p}, I_d, 0_{d\times(K-d)})$ that chooses the corresponding estimates in $\widehat{\beta}$ of all a_{1u} with $|u| = 1$. As a result, $\widehat{\theta}$ is consistent by the consistency of $\widehat{\beta}$.

If $c_1 = 0$, without loss of generality, suppose that there exists some j_0, $2 \le j_0 \le k-1$, such that $c_{j_0} \ne 0$ (this can be almost surely guaranteed since k diverges).

Then, the estimate of θ_0 can be recovered by all estimates of $a_{j_0u}(\theta_0)$ in β, which is similar to but a bit complicated than the case of $c_1 \neq 0$. We omit this as it is the same as Dong et al. (2015, p. 304). It follows that we obtain the estimate $\widehat{\theta}$ of θ_0, along with that of c_j, from $\widehat{\beta}$. Therefore, $\widehat{g}(z)$ is defined through $\widehat{c}_j$ and the basis functions.

A straightforward algebra yields that the length of $\Phi_K(Z)$ is about $O(k^d)$, which limits the dimension of Z in a narrow range. If d is relatively large, this method would fail to work since k^d grows extremely fast. Thus, our method is only applicable to the case where d is small. When d is relatively large, we turn to consider another situation where the index vector θ_0 in model (7.3.12) satisfies one extra equation that helps estimate the vector. Indeed, as far as we are aware, in some economic theories, one may be able to estimate the unknown index vector by another equation.

With the estimate of θ_0 at hand, model (7.3.12) is reduced to model (7.3.3), so that α and g can be estimated by the procedure (7.3.6). The model of Carneiro et al. (2011) is in this situation. In their case, the marginal treatment effect (MTE) is $MTE(x, p) = x^\top\alpha + g'(p)$ and the parameter of interest is the weighted average MTE, $\Delta = \int_0^1 MTE(x, p)h(x, p)dp$ for some known weighting function h. The parameter θ_0 can be estimated from another moment equation, $\mathbb{E}\left[(\mathbb{I}(S = 1) - \Lambda(\theta_0^\top Z))\Psi_q(Z)\right] = 0$, with or without the specification of the function Λ, using the conventional technique for dealing with single-index models, such as Ai and Chen (2003) and Dong et al. (2016).

To facilitate the derivation of asymptotic distributions for the estimators of α and g where the estimate $\widehat{\theta}$ of θ_0 is obtained in the first step, one expects that $\widehat{\theta}$ is independent of the data used to estimate α and g. This is possible, and one way doing so is as follows. Let us split the observations $\{V_i, X_i, Z_i, i = 1, \ldots, n\}$ into two subsamples randomly, $\text{Sub}_1 := \{(V_i, X_i, Z_i), i = 1, \ldots, n'\}$ and $\text{Sub}_2 := \{V_i, X_i, Z_i, i = n' + 1, \ldots, n\}$, with $n' = [n/2]$. The ordering in both subsamples, in general, may not be the same as in the original sample, but we keep using subscript i after partition. The first subsample Sub_1 can be used to estimate θ_0 by an additional moment restriction (say), resulting in $\widehat{\theta}$, and the second Sub_2 is used to estimate the parameter α and function g. Here, due to the i.i.d. property of the sample, the independence property holds naturally. Additionally, $\sqrt{n}(\widehat{\theta} - \theta_0) = O_P(1)$ (e.g., Yu & Ruppert, 2002). The data-splitting technique can be found in the literature, for example, Bickel (1982) and Belloni et al. (2012).

7.3.3 Statistical Inference

In the GMM literature, the test of over-identification is crucial. Hansen (1982) proposes the J-test for over-identification in the situation where both p and q are fixed but $q > p$. This J-test has an asymptotic χ^2_{q-p} null distribution. In the case where an unknown infinite-dimensional parameter is involved, and both p and q are still fixed with $q > p$, Chen and Liao (2015) establish a statistic for over-identification testing that has an F distribution in large samples. By contrast, we propose a statistic for over-identification that has a normal limit distribution.

Consider the following hypotheses in model (7.3.3),

$$\begin{aligned} H_0 &: \ \mathbb{E}[m(V_i, \alpha^\top X_i, g(Z_i))] = 0 \ \text{ for some } (\alpha, g) \in \Theta, \\ H_1 &: \ \mathbb{E}[m(V_i, \mathbf{a}^\top X_i, h(Z_i))] \neq 0 \ \text{ for any } (\mathbf{a}, h) \in \Theta, \end{aligned} \tag{7.3.14}$$

where Θ is defined previously.

Define, for $\mathbf{a} \in \mathbb{R}^p$, $\mathbf{b} \in \mathbb{R}^K$ and any given $\kappa \in \mathbb{R}^q$ such that $\|\kappa\| = 1$,

$$L_n(\mathbf{a}, \mathbf{b}; \kappa) = \frac{1}{D_n(\mathbf{a}, \mathbf{b}; \kappa)} \sum_{i=1}^{n} \kappa^\top m(V_i, \mathbf{a}^\top X_i, \mathbf{b}^\top \Phi_K(Z_i)),$$

where $D_n(\mathbf{a}, \mathbf{b}; \kappa) = \left(\sum_{i=1}^n [\kappa^\top m(V_i, \mathbf{a}^\top X_i, \mathbf{b}^\top \Phi_K(Z_i))]^2\right)^{1/2}$.

Under the null hypothesis, the estimation procedure in the preceding section, and the conditions of Theorem 7.3.1, the estimator $(\widehat{\alpha}, \widehat{g})$ is consistent. As a result, the statistic $L_n(\widehat{\alpha}, \widehat{\beta}; \kappa)$ can be used to detect H_0 against H_1, as shown in Theorems 7.3.3 and 7.3.4 below. This test also works for the conventional moment restriction models with fixed p and q.

Theorem 7.3.3 *Suppose that there is no zero function in the vector m of functions. Let Assumptions 7.3.1 through 7.3.12 in Sect. 7.3.6 hold. For any $\kappa \in \mathbb{R}^q$ such that $\|\kappa\| = 1$, under H_0 we have,*

$$L_n(\widehat{\alpha}, \widehat{\beta}; \kappa) \to_D N(0, 1),$$

as $n \to \infty$, where $(\widehat{\alpha}, \widehat{\beta})$ is the estimator given by (7.3.6). □

Notice that if there is a zero function in m, the product $\kappa^\top m$ can be a zero function for some particular choice of κ. Thus, excluding the zero function is necessary. The theorem establishes the normality of the proposed statistic under the null that enables us to make statistical inferences.

Theorem 7.3.4 *Suppose that uniformly in n and $(\mathbf{a}, h) \in \Theta$, the eigenvalues of $\mathbb{E}[m(V, \mathbf{a}^\top X, h(Z))m(V, \mathbf{a}^\top X, h(Z))^\top]$ are bounded away from zero and infinity. Under H_1, suppose further that there exists a positive sequence δ_n such that $\inf_{(\mathbf{a},h)\in\Theta} \|E[m(V, \mathbf{a}^\top X, h(Z))]\| \geq \delta_n$ and $\liminf_{n\to\infty} \sqrt{n}\delta_n = \infty$. Then, for any vectors $\mathbf{a}$ and $\mathbf{b}$, there exists some $\kappa^* \in \mathbb{R}^q$ such that $\|\kappa^*\| = 1$ and $L_n(\mathbf{a}, \mathbf{b}; \kappa^*) \to_P \infty$, as $n \to \infty$.* □

See the proofs of the above theorems in Dong et al. (2023). The condition of the eigenvalues is commonly adopted in the literature, see, e.g., Chang et al. (2015) and Belloni et al. (2015). The κ^* that leads the divergence of the statistic is $\kappa^* = \mathbb{E}[m(V_i, \mathbf{a}^\top X_i, \mathbf{b}^\top \Phi_K(Z_i))]/\|\mathbb{E}[m(V_i, \mathbf{a}^\top X_i, \mathbf{b}^\top \Phi_K(Z_i))]\|$, where the denominator does not vanish guaranteed by H_1. Moreover, when $\delta_n = \delta$, the condition $\liminf_{n\to\infty} \sqrt{n}\delta_n = \infty$ is satisfied automatically, and this is the most commonly used assumption in the literature, see, Eq. (24) of Chang et al. (2015, p. 290). However, we allow the signal depending on the sample size, i.e., $\delta = \delta_n$, and $\delta_n \to 0$ with a rate slower than $n^{-1/2}$. Thus, our condition is much weaker than the one used in the literature.

We next propose another test for model (7.3.3) under H_0. Define $\widehat{m}(i) \equiv m(V_i, \widehat{\alpha}^\top X_i, \widehat{g}(Z_i))$ for simplicity and correspondingly, for later use define $m(i) \equiv m(V_i, \alpha^\top X_i, g(Z_i))$. Let $\widehat{e} = (\widehat{e}_1, \ldots, \widehat{e}_q)^\top$ and $\widehat{\sigma}^2 = (\widehat{\sigma}^2(i, j))_{q\times q}$, where

$$\widehat{e} \equiv \frac{1}{n}\sum_{i=1}^{n} \widehat{m}(i), \quad \text{and} \quad \widehat{\sigma}^2 \equiv \frac{1}{n}\sum_{i=1}^{n} \widehat{m}(i)\widehat{m}(i)^\top,$$

Here, $\widehat{e}$ and $\widehat{\sigma}^2$ may be understood as the estimated mean and covariance matrix of the error vector, respectively. Define

$$T_n \equiv \frac{1}{q}\sum_{j=1}^{q}\left(\frac{\sqrt{n}\,\widehat{e}_j}{\widehat{\sigma}(j, j)}\right)^2.$$

This statistic is constructed from $\sqrt{n}\widehat{e}_j/\widehat{\sigma}_n(j, j)$, which is somewhat like the traditional t-test. Evidently, the motivation of proposing T_n are the divergence of q and the asymptotic distribution of $\sqrt{n}\widehat{e}_j/\widehat{\sigma}_n(j, j)$ for each j.

Theorem 7.3.5 *Let Assumptions 7.3.1–7.3.12 listed in Sect. 7.3.6 hold. Suppose* $\mathbb{E}[m(i)m(i)^\top]$ *is a diagonal matrix with* $\min_{1\le j\le q}\mathbb{E}[m_j(i)^2] > c > 0$ *and* $\sup_{1\le j\le q}\mathbb{E}[m_j(i)^4] < C < \infty$ *for some constants* c *and* C. *Then, under* H_0, $\sqrt{q/2}(T_n - 1) \to_D N(0, 1)$ *as* $n \to \infty$. □

The requirement on the diagonal matrix of $\mathbb{E}[m(i)m(i)^\top]$ is not rigorous because, if not so, we may make a transformation $\tilde{m}(i) = (\mathbb{E}[m(i)m(i)^\top])^{-1/2}m(i)$ and then $\tilde{m}(i)$ would meet the requirement. These moment requirements are commonly used in the literature since $m_j(i)$ are generalized error terms, so we do not explain them in detail. The standard normal limit holds since qT_n behaves like a $\chi^2(q)$ but the degree of freedom q is diverging, and the statistic $\sqrt{q/2}(T_n - 1)$ is the normalized qT_n.

We then consider the consistency of T_n. For any vector $\mathbf{a} \in \mathbb{R}^p$ and function $h(\cdot)$, define $\widetilde{m}(i) \equiv \widetilde{m}(i; \mathbf{a}, h) = m(V_i, \mathbf{a}^\top X_i, h(Z_i))$, $\widetilde{e} = (\widetilde{e}_1, \ldots, \widetilde{e}_q)^\top$ and $\widetilde{\sigma} = (\widetilde{\sigma}_{ij})_{q\times q}$, where

$$\widetilde{e} = \frac{1}{n}\sum_{i=1}^{n} \widetilde{m}(i), \quad \text{and} \quad \widetilde{\sigma} = \frac{1}{n}\sum_{i=1}^{n} \widetilde{m}(i)\widetilde{m}(i)^\top.$$

Define also

$$\widetilde{T}_n := \frac{1}{q}\sum_{j=1}^{q}\left(\frac{\sqrt{n}\,\widetilde{e}_j}{\widetilde{\sigma}(j, j)}\right)^2.$$

Note that if H_0 is true, $\widetilde{T}_n$ would become T_n when $\mathbf{a}$ and $h(\cdot)$ are substituted by $\widehat{\alpha}$ and $\widehat{g}$, respectively; while if H_1 is true, $\widetilde{T}_n$ would diverge as shown in the following theorem.

Theorem 7.3.6 *Suppose that* $\max_{1\leq j\leq q}\sup_{\mathbf{a},h}\mathbb{E}[\widetilde{m}_j(i)^2]\leq C<\infty$ *for some constant* C. *Then, under the conditions in Theorem 7.3.4 and* H_1, *for any vector* $\mathbf{a}\in\mathbb{R}^p$ *and function* $h(\cdot)$, *as* $n\to\infty$, $\widetilde{T}_n\to_P\infty$ *provided that* $\sqrt{n/q}\,\delta_n\to\infty$ *where* δ_n *is given in Theorem 7.3.4.* □

Again, see the proofs of the above theorems in Dong et al. (2023). From statistical inference point of view, it is impossible to distinguish T_n from $\widetilde{T}_n$. In fact, one may use our estimation procedure to obtain the "estimates" of the parameters, then construct $\widetilde{T}_n$ and finally make an inference according to Theorem 7.3.5. The uniform boundedness of the second moment is reasonable in the i.i.d. setting. Compared with Theorem 7.3.4, the attenuation of δ_n is slowed down as we require $\sqrt{n/q}\,\delta_n\to\infty$. This is because of the difference in the constructions of T_n and $L_n(\mathbf{a},\mathbf{b};\kappa)$.

7.3.4 Ultra-High-Dimensional SMRMs

In this subsection, we consider the ultra-high-dimensional situation of model (7.3.3) where the potential number of covariates is much larger than the sample size (i.e., $p=e^{n^a}$ with $0<a<1$), but the parameter vector α has sparsity. That is, there are many zeros in α and only a number of elements are non-zero, but the identity of the non-zero elements is not known a priori. In addition, the coefficient vector β in the partial sum of the expansion of the nonparametric function may also possess sparsity in two potential scenarios: a) its elements may be zero if the unknown function is located in a subspace that has small dimensionality and b) the attenuation of its elements as the number of terms increases is guaranteed by Parseval equality in Hilbert space theory, so that many of them are negligible statistically. Hence, this section is devoted to estimating (α,g) under the sparsity condition. This "big-data" context is becoming increasingly relevant in applications.

There are some relevant existing papers on variable selection under sparsity. Belloni et al. (2014a) propose the combination of least squares and L_1 type lasso approach to select coefficients of the sieve in nonparametric regression. Also, Su et al. (2019) use L_1 type lasso approach to study continuous treatment in nonseparable models with high-dimensional data. In a high-dimensional conditional moment restriction model, Fan and Liao (2014) propose to use a folded concave penalty function combined with instrumental variables to select the important coefficients. Caner (2009) uses the same approach with a particular class of penalty functions to select variables. As Caner (2009, p. 271) argued, the Lasso-type GMM estimator selects the correct model much more often than GMM-BIC and the "downward testing" method proposed by Andrews and Lu (2001). We shall tackle the selection issue by the combination of a penalty function and our GMM approach.

Regarding of the GMM approach, to reduce the risk of misspecification, Andrews (1999) defines moment selection criterion (MSC) using J-test statistics and shows that the consistent moment selection can be achieved by choosing the vector minimizing the MSC. There are also other papers studying the selection issue using generalized empirical likelihood statistics. However, we mention that all of these methods are subject to pretest bias and in post-model selection inferential problems (Leeb & Pötscher, 2005).

We partition the parameter vectors as $\alpha = (\alpha_{0S}^\top, \alpha_{0N}^\top)^\top$ and $\beta = (\beta_{0S}^\top, \beta_{0N}^\top)^\top$, where the vectors α_{0S} and β_{0S} contain all "important coefficients" from α and β (i.e., non-zero coefficients), respectively, as referred in the literature such as Fan and Liao (2014), while α_{0N} and β_{0N} are zero.

For convenience, denote $v_0 = (\alpha^\top, \beta^\top)^\top \in \mathbb{R}^{p+K}$ the true parameter whose dimension varies with the sample size. In addition, $v_{0S} = (\alpha_{0S}^\top, \beta_{0S}^\top)^\top$ is referred to as an *oracle model*. Define $t_n = |v_{0S}|$ the dimension of v_{0S}, which may diverge with n.

Let $\widehat{v} \in \mathbb{R}^{p+K}$ be the estimated parameter of v_0 by the penalized GMM, which solves:

$$\widehat{v} = (\widehat{\alpha}^\top, \widehat{\beta}^\top)^\top = \underset{v=(\mathbf{a}^\top,\mathbf{b}^\top)^\top \in \mathbb{R}^{p+K}}{\operatorname{argmin}} \quad Q_n(v) \equiv \|M_n(v)\|^2 + \sum_{j=1}^{p+K} P_n(|v_j|), \quad (7.3.15)$$

where $M_n(v) = M_n(\mathbf{a}, \mathbf{b})$ is as defined in the preceding section, and $P_n(\cdot)$ is a penalty function discussed later. Our framework also accommodates the case where some components of α and β are entered without selection, as in Belloni et al. (2016), although we do not inscribe this in the notation for simplicity.

Let $T = \{j : 1 \le j \le p+K, v_{0j} \neq 0\}$ be the support of v_0, that is, the indexes of the non-zero components. We may equivalently say that T is the oracle model. Moreover, for a generic vector $v \in \mathbb{R}^{p+K}$, denote by v_T the vector in $\mathbb{R}^{p+K}$ whose jth element equals v_j if $j \in T$ and zero otherwise. Also, define v_S as the short version of v_T after eliminating all zeros in the position T^c (the complement set of T) from v_T. In the literature, the subspace $\mathcal{V} = \{v_T, v \in \mathbb{R}^{p+K}\}$ is called the *oracle space* of $\mathbb{R}^{p+K}$. Certainly, $v_0 \in \mathcal{V}$.

Define $S_n(\cdot)$ as the score vector that incorporates all partial derivatives of $\|M_n(\cdot)\|^2$. Also, denote $S_{nT}(v_S)$ as the vector of all partial derivatives of $\|M_n(v)\|^2$ with respect to v_j for $j \in T$, at v_T (bearing in mind that v_S is the short version of v_T). Hence, the vector $S_{nT}(v_S)$ has dimension $t_n = |T| = |v_S|$. Here and hereafter, for set T, $|T|$ stands for its cardinality, while for a vector v, $|v|$ stands for its dimension. Also, define in a similar fashion $H_{nT}(v_S)$ the $t_n \times t_n$ Hessian matrix for $\|M_n(v)\|^2$.

Let $P_n(\cdot)$ be a folded concave penalty functions (see Fan & Li, 2001). For any generic vector $v = (v_1, \ldots, v_{t_n})^\top \in \mathbb{R}^{t_n}$ with $v_j \neq 0$ for all j, define

$$\phi(v) = \limsup_{\epsilon \to 0+} \max_{j \le t_n} \sup_{u_1 < u_2, (u_1, u_2) \subset O(|v_j|, \epsilon)} -\frac{P_n'(u_2) - P_n'(u_1)}{u_2 - u_1},$$

where $O(\cdot, \cdot)$ is the neighborhood with specified center and radius, respectively, implying that $\phi(v) = \max_{j \le t_n} -P_n''(|v_j|)$ if P_n'' is continuous. Also, for the true parameter v_0, let

$$d_n = \frac{1}{2}\min\{|v_{0j}| : v_{0j} \neq 0, j = 0, \ldots, p + K\}$$

represent the strength of the signal.

Denoting the oracle model $T = T_1 \cup T_2$, where T_1 is the set of indices of non-zero elements in α and T_2 that of β, accordingly, we have $t_n = p_1 + K_1$ for the corresponding cardinalities. In what follows denote $\partial m/\partial u$ and $\partial m/\partial w$ the partial derivatives of m w.r.t the second and third arguments, respectively; and $F_{iS} = \mathrm{diag}(X_{iS}, \Phi_{KS}(Z_i))$ a $t_n \times 2$ matrix where X_{iS} is the sub-vector of X_i consisting of all X_{ij} for $j \in T_1$; $\Phi_{KS}(Z_i)$ is the sub-vector of $\Phi_K(Z_i)$ consisting of all $\varphi_j(Z_i)$ for $j \in T_2$.

To state the following theorem, define:

$$\begin{aligned}
\Sigma_{nT}^2 \equiv& \Gamma_n[\Psi_{nT}\Psi_{nT}^\top]^{-1}\Psi_{nT}\Xi_{nT}\Psi_{nT}^\top[\Psi_{nT}\Psi_{nT}^\top]^{-1}\Gamma_n^\top, \quad \text{in which} \qquad (7.3.16)\\
\Gamma_n \equiv& \begin{pmatrix} \partial\mathscr{L}(\alpha_{0S}) & 0 \\ 0 & \mathscr{F}'(g)\Phi_{KT}{}^\top \end{pmatrix}_{(\mu+\nu)\times(p_1+K_1)},\\
\Xi_{nT} \equiv& \mathbb{E}[m(V_1, \alpha_{0S}^\top X_{1S}, g(Z_1))m(V_1, \alpha_{0S}^\top X_{1S}, g(Z_1))^\top]_{q\times q},\\
\Psi_{nT} \equiv& \mathbb{E}\begin{pmatrix} \frac{\partial}{\partial u}m(V_1, \alpha_{0S}^\top X_{1S}, g(Z_1))^\top \otimes X_{1S} \\ \frac{\partial}{\partial w}m(V_1, \alpha_{0S}^\top X_{1S}, g(Z_1))^\top \otimes \Phi_{KT}(Z_1) \end{pmatrix}_{(p_1+K_1)\times q},
\end{aligned}$$

provided that $\Psi_{nT}\Psi_{nT}^\top$ is invertible; and the transformation $\mathscr{L}$ and vector functional $\mathscr{F}$ are defined in previous section.

Theorem 7.3.7 *Let Assumptions 7.3.1–7.3.3, 7.3.5, and 7.3.13–7.3.14 listed in Sect. 7.3.6 hold. Then, there exists a local minimizer $\widehat{v} = ((\widehat{\alpha}_S^\top, \widehat{\alpha}_N^\top)^\top, (\widehat{\beta}_S^\top, \widehat{\beta}_N^\top)^\top)$, for which we have (i)*

$$\lim_{n\to\infty} \mathbb{P}(\widehat{\alpha}_N = 0, \widehat{\beta}_N = 0) = 1.$$

In addition, the local minimizer $\widehat{v}$ is strict with probability arbitrarily close to one for all large n.

(ii) Let $\widehat{T} = \{j : 1 \le j \le p + K, \widehat{v}_j \neq 0\}$. Then,

$$\lim_{n\to\infty} \mathbb{P}(\widehat{T} = T) = 1.$$

(iii) Meanwhile, for the transformation $\mathscr{L}_{r\times p_1}$ and s-vector functional $\mathscr{F}$,

$$\sqrt{n}\Sigma_{nT}^{-1}\begin{pmatrix} \mathscr{L}(\widehat{\alpha}_S) - \mathscr{L}(\alpha_{0S}) \\ \mathscr{F}(\widehat{g}) - \mathscr{F}(g) \end{pmatrix} \xrightarrow{d} N(0, I_{\mu+\nu}),$$

as $n \to \infty$ *provided that* $\sqrt{n}\Sigma_{nT}^{-1}(0_{\mu}^{\top}, \mathscr{F}'(g)\gamma_K^{\top})^{\top} = o(1)$, *where* Σ_{nT} *is given by the square root of* Σ_{nT}^2 *defined in* (7.3.16). □

Note that the undersmoothing condition can be satisfied if Σ_{nT} with finite dimensionality has the smallest eigenvalue greater than a positive constant and γ_K decays to zero sufficiently fast. The estimators in this theorem are all local. This is why we exclude the identification condition in Assumption 7.3.4 currently, while in the next theorem, we shall discuss the global property of a local minimizer. The results (i) and (ii) indicate that under these conditions in the theorem, we are able to recover the sparsity in the model; meanwhile, the discussion on the result (iii) of the theorem is similar to Theorem 7.3.2.

Theorem 7.3.8 *In addition to the conditions of Theorem 7.3.7, suppose Assumption 7.3.4 holds. Then, the local minimizer* $\widehat{\upsilon}$ *satisfies that, for any* $\delta > 0$, *there exists* $\eta > 0$ *such that*

$$\lim_{n\to\infty} P\left(Q_n(\widehat{\upsilon}) + \eta < \inf_{\|\upsilon-\upsilon_0\|\ge\delta} Q_n(\upsilon)\right) = 1.$$

□

The theorem says that the local minimizer of the oracle space in Theorem 7.3.7 is also with high probability a global minimizer in $\mathbb{R}^{p+K}$. Note that by Theorems 7.3.7 and 7.3.8, the minimization in Eq. (7.3.15) enables one to recover the sparsity in the ultra-high-dimensional case since $q \ge p + K$, where q can be as large as $e^{n^{\epsilon}}$ for some $\epsilon > 0$. This is a bit different from Fan and Liao (2014) where there is no nonparametric function involved and $q = p$ (the number of IV is the same as that of regressors). Note that, given the consistency of the sparsity, the inference can be done in a similar way to Theorem 7.3.2.

The proofs of the above theorems are available in Dong et al. (2023).

7.3.5 *Simulation Experiments*

In this section, we investigate the performance of the proposed estimators in finite sample situations.

Example 7.3.1 Suppose $X_i = (X_{1i}, X_{2i}^{\top})^{\top}$, where X_{1i} assumes 1 and -1 with probability $1/2$, respectively, $X_{2i} \sim N(0, \Sigma_{p-1})$, where $\Sigma_{p-1} = (\sigma_{i,j})_{(p-1)\times(p-1)}$ with $\sigma_{i,i} = 1$, $\sigma_{i,j} = 0.3$ for $|i - j| = 1$ and $\sigma_{i,j} = 0$ for $|i - j| > 1$. Here, the first component of X_i is a discrete variable with which we intend to show that our theoretical results do not confine its applications to continuous variables only. Let Z_i be uniformly distributed on $(0, 1)$.

Our model considered is $\mathbb{E}[Y_i - \alpha^{\top} X_i - g(Z_i)|W_i] = 0$ with $W_i = Z_i$, and $g(\cdot) \in L^2[0, 1]$. Let $\varphi_0(r) \equiv 1$, and for $j \ge 1$, $\varphi_j(r) = \sqrt{2}\cos(\pi jr)$. It is known that $\{\varphi_j(r)\}$ is an orthonormal basis in $L^2[0,1]$. In this experiment, put $\alpha = (0.4, 0.1, 0, \ldots, 0)^\top \in \mathbb{R}^p$ and $g(z) = z^2 + \sin(z)$.

Define $m(V_i, \alpha^\top X_i, g(Z_i)) = (Y_i - \alpha^\top X_i - g(Z_i))\Phi_q(Z_i)$ where $V_i = (Y_i, W_i)$, $W_i = Z_i$ and $\Phi_q(\cdot) = (\varphi_0(\cdot), \ldots, \varphi_{q-1}(\cdot))^\top$. We have $\mathbb{E}[m(V_i, \alpha^\top X_i, g(Z_i))] = 0$ for $i = 1, \ldots, n$.

According to the estimation procedure in Sect. 7.3.1, define

$$(\widehat{\alpha}, \widehat{\beta}) = \operatorname*{argmin}_{\mathbf{a}\in\mathbb{R}^p, \mathbf{b}\in\mathbb{R}^K} \|M_n(\mathbf{a}, \mathbf{b})\|^2, \quad M_n(\mathbf{a}, \mathbf{b}) = \frac{1}{\sqrt{q}}\frac{1}{n}\sum_{i=1}^n m(V_i, \mathbf{a}^\top X_i, \mathbf{b}^\top \Phi_K(Z_i)).$$

Thus, $\widehat{\alpha}$ and $\widehat{g}(\cdot) \equiv \widehat{\beta}^\top \Phi_K(\cdot)$ are the estimates of $(\alpha, g(\cdot))$.

For $n = 200, 500$ and 1000, let $K = [n^{\tau_1}]$ with $\tau_1 = 1/4$, and $p = [n^{\tau_2}]$ with $\tau_2 = 1/5$. Also, let $q = p + K + \nu$ ($\nu \geq 0$ specified in the sequel) satisfy Assumption 7.3.3. The replication number of the experiment is $M = 1000$. We shall report the bias (denoted by $B_g(n)$), standard deviation (denoted by $\pi_g(n)$) and RMSE (denoted by $\Pi_g(n)$) of the estimate of the g function, that is,

$$B_g(n) \equiv \frac{1}{Mn}\sum_{\ell=1}^M\sum_{i=1}^n [\widehat{g}^\ell(Z_i) - g^\ell(Z_i)],$$

$$\pi_g(n) \equiv \left(\frac{1}{Mn}\sum_{\ell=1}^M\sum_{i=1}^n [\widehat{g}^\ell(Z_i) - \bar{\widehat{g}}(Z_i)]^2\right)^{1/2},$$

$$\Pi_g(n) \equiv \left(\frac{1}{Mn}\sum_{\ell=1}^M\sum_{i=1}^n [\widehat{g}^\ell(Z_i) - g^\ell(Z_i)]^2\right)^{1/2},$$

where the superscript ℓ indicates the ℓth replication, $\bar{\widehat{g}}(\cdot)$ is the average of $\widehat{g}^\ell(\cdot)$ over Monte Carlo replications $\ell = 1, \ldots, M$, $g^\ell(\cdot)$ means the value of g in the ℓth replication, and Z_i in functions such as $\widehat{g}^\ell(Z_i)$ correspond to the ℓth replication.

Regarding the parameter α, we report the following quantities, $B_\alpha(n) \equiv \|\alpha - \bar{\widehat{\alpha}}\|$ and $M_\alpha(n) \equiv \text{median}(\|\alpha - \widehat{\alpha}\|)$, where $\bar{\widehat{\alpha}}$ is the average of $\widehat{\alpha}^\ell$ and median$(\cdots)$ is the median of the sequence over Monte Carlo replications. Notice that, due to the divergence of the dimension, it might not make any sense to compare the estimated results for different sample sizes.

The results are reported in Table 7.1. It can be seen that all of the statistical quantities about the estimate of g are reasonably attenuated with the increase of both the sample size and ν that provides more information for the parameters being estimated. For the quantities about the estimate of α, we observe that they normally do not decrease with the sample size. This is because, as mentioned before, the dimension of α is increasing with the sample size; and hence, it does not make sense to compare them among different sample sizes. However, we find that, given the sample size, both quantities related to the estimate of α decrease with the increase of ν that gives more moment restrictions.

Table 7.1 Simulation results of Example 7.3.1, $q = p + K + \nu$

n	$\nu = 2$			n	$\nu = 4$		
	300	600	1000		300	600	1000
$B_g(n)$	0.0046	−0.0040	−0.0026	$B_g(n)$	−0.0023	−0.0019	0.0006
$\pi_g(n)$	0.3533	0.1965	0.1948	$\pi_g(n)$	0.1660	0.1530	0.1520
$\Pi_g(n)$	0.3401	0.1700	0.1682	$\Pi_g(n)$	0.1356	0.1217	0.1176
$B_\alpha(n)$	0.0700	0.0410	0.0684	$B_\alpha(n)$	0.0281	0.0271	0.0501
$M_\alpha(n)$	0.0355	0.0282	0.0665	$M_\alpha(n)$	0.0259	0.0244	0.0319
n	$\nu = 6$			n	$\nu = 8$		
	300	600	1000		300	600	1000
$B_g(n)$	0.0023	0.0019	−0.0000	$B_g(n)$	0.0009	0.0011	−0.0000
$\pi_g(n)$	0.1544	0.1445	0.1444	$\pi_g(n)$	0.1482	0.1370	0.1359
$\Pi_g(n)$	0.1218	0.1092	0.1031	$\Pi_g(n)$	0.1176	0.1015	0.0945
$B_\alpha(n)$	0.0124	0.0267	0.0265	$B_\alpha(n)$	0.0078	0.0048	0.0250
$M_\alpha(n)$	0.0254	0.0154	0.0464	$M_\alpha(n)$	0.0117	0.0098	0.0306

This can be explained as follows. Because the conditional moment $\mathbb{E}[Y_i - \alpha^\top X_i - g(Z_i)|Z_i]$ determines a function $U(z) \equiv \mathbb{E}[Y_i - \alpha^\top X_i - g(Z_i)|Z_i = z]$ and $\{\varphi_j(z)\}$ is an orthonormal sequence in the space that contains $U(z)$, the greater the ν is, the more axes in the space we use to explain the unknown function $U(z)$.

Additionally, the involvement of the discrete variable X_{1i} does not affect the performance of all measures. This might suggest for the practitioner that in this setting discrete variables are as tractable as continuous variables.

Example 7.3.2 We are about to verify the proposed schedule for variable selection and parameter estimation under sparsity studied in ultra-high SRMRs. The model is almost the same as that in Example 7.3.1 but the conditional variables are different. Suppose that

$$\mathbb{E}[Y_i - \alpha^\top X_i - g(Z_i)|W_i] = 0$$

where $(\alpha_1, \ldots, \alpha_4) = (2, -4, 3, 5)$, $\alpha_j = 0$ for $5 \le j \le p$. Here, $W_i = (X_{1i}, X_{2i})^\top$ and $g(\cdot) \in L^2[0, 1]$. The conditional moment gives the function $H(W) \equiv 0$, where $H(W) = \mathbb{E}[Y_i - \alpha^\top X_i - g(Z_i)|W_i = W]$. Thus, the instrument variable should be $\Psi_q(W_i)$, a basis vector of bivariate functions.

The same basis as in Example 7.3.1 is used for the orthogonal expansion of $g(z)$. Here, put $g(z) = 1 + \sqrt{2}\cos(\pi z)$. Thus, the expansion of $g(z)$ has coefficients $\beta_i = 1, i = 0, 1$, while $\beta_i = 0$ for all $i \ge 2$, implying the sparsity of the coefficient vector β (equivalently, the sparse nonparametric function $g(z)$).

Suppose that X_i are i.i.d. $N(0, I_p)$ and Z_i are i.i.d. $U(0, 1)$. Given the normal distribution of X_i, we use Hermite polynomial sequence to form $\Psi_q(W_i)$, that is, $\Psi_q(W_i) = (h_{j_1-1}(X_{1i})h_{j_2-1}(X_{2i}), j_1, j_2 = 1, \ldots, q_1)$, where $q_1 = [\sqrt{q+1}]$ and $\{h_j(\cdot)\}$ is the Hermite polynomial sequence. The rationale behind the formulation of

Table 7.2 Simulation results of Example 7.3.2 ($n = 100$)

λ	$p = 8, K = 6, q = 100$			λ	$p = 12, K = 6, q = 120$		
	0.4	0.2	0.08		0.4	0.2	0.08
$\text{MSE}_S(\alpha)$	0.2017	0.2811	0.1915	$\text{MSE}_S(\alpha)$	0.3065	0.2322	0.1970
$\text{MSE}_S(\beta)$	0.1288	0.1009	0.0789	$\text{MSE}_S(\beta)$	0.1900	0.0837	0.0624
$\text{MSE}_N(\alpha)$	0.0001	0.0026	0.0031	$\text{MSE}_N(\alpha)$	0.0015	0.0039	0.0016
$\text{MSE}_N(\beta)$	0.0000	0.0004	0.0001	$\text{MSE}_N(\beta)$	0.0000	0.0000	0.0008
$\text{TP}_S(\alpha)$	4	4	4	$\text{TP}_S(\alpha)$	4	4	4
$\text{TP}_S(\beta)$	2	2	2	$\text{TP}_S(\beta)$	2	2	2
$\text{TP}_N(\alpha)$	3.48	3.24	3.55	$\text{TP}_N(\alpha)$	6.88	6.72	5.90
$\text{TP}_N(\beta)$	3.28	3.40	2.96	$\text{TP}_N(\beta)$	3.46	3.36	2.92

$\Psi_q(w_1, w_2)$ is that the tensor product $\{h_{j_1}(w_1)h_{j_2}(w_2)\}$ is an orthogonal basis system to expand $H(w_1, w_2)$.

In the simulation, we use SCAD of Fan and Li (2001) with predetermined tuning parameters of λ as the penalty function. Therefore, the objective function is $\|M_n(v)\|^2 + \sum_{j=1}^{p+K} P_n(|v_j|)$, where $v = (\alpha^\top, \beta^\top)^\top$ a $(p+K)$-dimensional vector and $M_n(v) = \frac{1}{q_1 n}\sum_{i=1}^n (Y_i - \alpha^\top X_i - \beta^\top \Phi_K(Z_i))\Psi_q(W_i)$.

Four performance measures are reported. The first measure is the mean standard error (MSE_S) of the important regressors, that is, the average of $\|\widehat{\alpha}_S - \alpha_S\|$ and that of $\|\widehat{\beta}_S - \beta_S\|$ over Monte Carlo replications. The second measure is the mean standard error (MSE_N) of the unimportant regressors for α and β, respectively. The third measure, denoted by TP_S, is the number of correctly selected non-zero coefficients, and the fourth, TP_N, the number of correctly selected unimportant coefficients for α and β, respectively. The initial value for v in the simulation is taken as $(0, \ldots, 0)$. The results are reported in Table 7.2 with different parameters.

It can be seen from the table that all MSEs perform reasonably and particularly those for α_N and β_N are really well. They also seem to be smaller when both n and q become larger. Although the dimensions of α and β increase and $q \geq n$, the scheme can always correctly choose all the important coefficients. This is perhaps because all important coefficients in absolute are significantly greater than zero, as suggested by the literature that we do not pursue here. By contrast, some unimportant coefficients may be chosen as important ones, implying the scheme may not necessarily lead to parsimonious models.

7.3.6 Mathematical Details

This section gives the mathematical details involved Sect. 7.3, including all the regularity assumptions and the proofs of the main results.

Assumption 7.3.1 Suppose that $\{\varphi_j(\cdot)\}$ is a complete orthonormal function sequence in $L^2(\mathbb{Z}, \pi)$, that is, $\langle\varphi_i(\cdot), \varphi_j(\cdot)\rangle = \delta_{ij}$ the Kronecker delta.

Assumption 7.3.2 Suppose that B_{1n} and B_{2n} are positive real numbers diverging with n such that α in model (7.3.3) is included in $\Theta_{1n} := \{\mathbf{a} \in \mathbb{R}^p : \|\mathbf{a}\| \leq B_{1n}\}$ and for sufficiently large n, $g_K(z)$ is included in $\Theta_{2n} := \{\mathbf{b}^\top \Phi_K(z) : \|\mathbf{b}\| \leq B_{2n}\}$. Define $\Theta_n = \Theta_{1n} \otimes \Theta_{2n}$.

Assumption 7.3.3 Suppose that

(a) For each n, $\{(V_i, X_i^\top, Z_i^\top), i = 1, \ldots, n\}$ is an independent and identically distributed (i.i.d.) sequence (although the distribution depends on n, which we suppress notationally in the sequel) from (7.3.3);
(b) For the density f_Z of Z, there exist two constants, $0 < c < C < \infty$, such that $c\pi(z) \leq f_Z(z) \leq C\pi(z)$ on the support $\mathbb{Z}$ of Z, where $\pi(z)$ is given in the preceding section;
(c) Each moment function $m_j(\cdot, \cdot, \cdot)$, $j = 1, \ldots, q$, is continuous in the second and third arguments;
(d) $q(n) - p(n) \geq K$.

Assumption 7.3.4 Suppose that there is a unique function $g(\cdot) \in L^2(\mathbb{Z}, \pi)$ and for each n there is a unique vector $\alpha \in \mathbb{R}^p$ such that for any $\delta > 0$, there is a sufficiently small constant $\epsilon_n \equiv \epsilon_n(\delta) > 0$ such that

$$\inf_{\substack{(\mathbf{a}, f)\in\Theta \\ \|(\mathbf{a}-\alpha, f-g)\|\geq\delta}} q^{-1}\|\mathbb{E}m(V_i, \mathbf{a}^\top X_i, f(Z_i))\|^2 > \epsilon_n,$$

and possibly $\epsilon_n \to 0$ as $n \to \infty$ but with a rate slower than $\max(\|\gamma_K\|, n^{-1})$.

Assumption 7.3.5 Suppose that for each n, there is a measurable positive function $A(V, X, Z)$ such that

$$\begin{aligned} &q^{-1/2}\|m(V, \mathbf{a}_1^\top X, f_1(Z)) - m(V, \mathbf{a}_2^\top X, f_2(Z))\| \\ \leq &A(V, X, Z)[\|\mathbf{a}_1 - \mathbf{a}_2\| + |f_1(Z) - f_2(Z)|] \end{aligned}$$

for any $(a_1, f_1), (a_2, f_2) \in \Theta_n$, where (V, X, Z) is any realization of (V_i, X_i, Z_i) and $A(\cdot, \cdot, \cdot)$ satisfies that $\mathbb{E}[A^2(V_i, X_i, Z_i)] < \infty$.

Assumption 7.3.6 (a) Suppose that each element function m_j of the m function is differentiable with respect to its second and third arguments up to the second order; the second derivative functions satisfy a Lipschitz condition in a neighborhood of the (α, g):

$$\begin{aligned} &|\partial^{(u)}m_j(V, \alpha^\top X, g(Z)) - \partial^{(u)}m_j(V, \mathbf{a}^\top X, f(Z))| \\ \leq &B_j(V, \alpha^\top X, g(Z))(\|\alpha - \mathbf{a}\| + \|g - f\|)^\tau \end{aligned}$$

for some $\tau \in (0, 1]$, where u is a two-dimensional multiple index with $|u| = 2$, $\partial^{(u)}$ stands for the partial derivative of the function with respect to the second and third arguments, and B_j are positive functions such that $\max_{1\le j\le q} \mathbb{E}[B_j(V, \alpha^\top X, g(Z))^2] < \infty$.

(b) Let the g function be smooth with the smoothness order required being spelled out in Assumption 7.3.8.

Assumption 7.3.7 Suppose that

(a) $\mathbb{E}\left\|m(V, \alpha^\top X, g(Z))\right\|^2 = O(q)$, $\mathbb{E}\|X\|^2 = O(p)$ and $\mathbb{E}\|\Phi_K(Z)\|^2 = O(K)$;

(b) $\mathbb{E}\left\|\frac{\partial}{\partial u} m(V, \alpha^\top X, g(Z))\right\|^2 = O(q)$, and $\mathbb{E}\left\|\frac{\partial}{\partial w} m(V, \alpha^\top X, g(Z))\right\|^2 = O(q)$;

(c) $\mathbb{E}\left\|\frac{\partial}{\partial u} m(V, \alpha^\top X, g(Z)) \otimes X\right\|^2 = O(pq)$, and
$\mathbb{E}\left\|\frac{\partial}{\partial w} m(V, \alpha^\top X, g(Z)) \otimes \Phi_K(Z)\right\|^2 = O(Kq)$;

(d) $\mathbb{E}\left\|\frac{\partial^2}{\partial u^2} m(V, \alpha^\top X, g(Z)) \otimes XX^\top\right\|^2 = O(p^2 q)$, and
$\mathbb{E}\left\|\frac{\partial^2}{\partial w^2} m(V, \alpha^\top X, g(Z)) \otimes \Phi_K(Z)\Phi_K(Z)^\top\right\|^2 = O(K^2 q)$.

Assumption 7.3.8 Suppose that

(a) $\|\gamma_K\| p = o(1)$, $\quad n^{-1} p^2 = o(1)$;

(b) $\|\gamma_K\| K = o(1)$, $\quad n^{-1} K^2 = o(1)$.

Assumption 7.3.9 The partial derivatives of $m(v, u, w)$ satisfy

(a) $q^{-1/2}\left\|\frac{\partial}{\partial u} m(V, \mathbf{a}_1^\top X, f_1(Z)) - \frac{\partial}{\partial u} m(V, \mathbf{a}_2^\top X, f_2(Z))\right\| \le A_1(V, X, Z)[\|\mathbf{a}_1 - \mathbf{a}_2\| + |f_1(Z) - f_2(Z)|]$, where $\mathbb{E}[A_1(V, X, Z)^2] < \infty$ and $\mathbb{E}[A_1(V, X, Z)^2 \|X\|^2] = O(p)$.

(b) $q^{-1/2}\left\|\frac{\partial}{\partial w} m(V, \mathbf{a}_1^\top X, f_1(Z)) - \frac{\partial}{\partial w} m(V, \mathbf{a}_2^\top X, f_2(Z))\right\| \le A_2(V, X, Z)[\|\mathbf{a}_1 - \mathbf{a}_2\| + |f_1(Z) - f_2(Z)|]$, where $\mathbb{E}[A_2(V, X, Z)^2] < \infty$ and $\mathbb{E}[A_2(V, X, Z)^2 \|\Phi_K(Z)\|^2] = O(K)$.

Assumption 7.3.10 (a) The transformation $\mathscr{L}$ possesses continuous second partial derivatives and the Hessian matrix of each component $\mathscr{L}_j$ of $\mathscr{L}$ has uniformly bounded eigenvalues in a neighborhood of α, i.e., $\lambda_{\max}(\partial^2 \mathscr{L}_j) < \infty$ over n; moreover, the first partial derivative of $\mathscr{L}$ at α, $\partial\mathscr{L}(\alpha)$, has full rank. (b) The functional $\mathscr{F}$ possesses Fréchet derivative at $g(\cdot)$.

Assumption 7.3.11 Let $\overline{m}_n^*(\widehat{\alpha}, \widehat{g}; \kappa) = o_P(1)$ when $n \to \infty$, where we denote $\overline{m}_n^*(a, f; \kappa) = n^{-1/2}\sum_{i=1}^n \mathbb{E}[\kappa^\top m(V_i, a^\top X_i, f(Z_i))]$ for $(a, f) \in \Theta$ and κ such that $\|\kappa\| = 1$.

Assumption 7.3.12 Suppose that (i) $qp^2 = o(n)$ and $qK^2 = o(n)$; and (ii) $\sup_z \gamma_K^2(z) = o(q^{-1})$ as, along with $n \to \infty$, $K, p, q \to \infty$.

Assumption 7.3.13 The penalty function $P_n(u)$ satisfies (i) $P_n(0) = 0$; (ii) $P_n(u)$ is concave, nondecreasing on $[0, \infty)$, and has a continuous derivative $P_n'(u)$ for $u > 0$; $(iii) \sqrt{t_n}\, P_n'(d_n) = o(d_n)$; (iv) There exists $c > 0$ such that $\sup_{v \in O(v_{0S}, cd_n)} \phi(v) = o(1)$.

Assumption 7.3.14 (i) Let Assumptions 7.3.7–7.3.9 hold with p being replaced by p_1 and K by K_1. (ii) There exist $b_1, b_2 > 0$ such that for any $\ell \le q$ and $u > 0$,

$$\mathbb{P}(|m_\ell(V, \alpha^\top X, \beta^\top \Phi_K(Z))| > u) \le \exp(-(u/b_1)^{-b_2});$$

and $Var(m_\ell(V, \alpha^\top X, \beta^\top \Phi_K(Z)))$ are bounded away from zero and above from infinity uniformly for all ℓ. (iii) There are constants $C_1, C_2 > 0$ such that the minimum and maximum eigenvalues of $\mathbb{E}\partial m^\top(V_i, v_{0S}^\top F_{iS}) \otimes F_{iS})(\mathbb{E}\partial m^\top(V_i, v_{0S}^\top F_{iS}) \otimes F_{iS})^\top$, $C_1 \le \lambda_{\min} \le \lambda_{\max} \le C_2$. (iv) $P_n'(d_n) = o(n^{-1/2})$ and $\max_{\|v_S - v_{0S}\| < d_n/4} \phi(v_S) = o((t_n \log(q))^{-1/2})$; (v) $t_n^{3/2} P_n'(d_n)^2 = o(1)$, $t_n \max_{j \in T} P_n(|v_{0j}|) = o(1)$, and $t_n^{3/2} \log(q) = o(n)$.

Lemma 7.3.1 *Under Assumptions 7.3.1–7.3.5, we have*

1. $\|M_n(\alpha, \beta)\|^2 = O_P(\|\gamma_K\|^2) + O_P(n^{-1})$.
2. *Given* $B_{1n}^2 + B_{2n}^2 = o(n)$, $\sup_{\substack{\|\mathbf{a}\| \le B_{1n}, \|\mathbf{b}\| \le B_{2n} \\ \|(\mathbf{a}-\alpha, \mathbf{b}-\beta)\| > \delta}} \|M_n(\mathbf{a}, \mathbf{b})\|^{-2} = O_P(1/\epsilon_n)$ *for each* $\delta > 0$, *when n is large and where* $\epsilon_n \equiv \epsilon_n(\delta)$, *stipulated in Assumption 7.3.4.*

Denote $m(v, u, w) = (m_1(v, u, w), \ldots, m_q(v, u, w))^\top$, the Score and Hessian functions of $\|M_n(\mathbf{a}, \mathbf{b})\|^2$ as

$$S_n(\mathbf{a}, \mathbf{b}) = \begin{pmatrix} S_{1n}(\mathbf{a}, \mathbf{b}) \\ S_{2n}(\mathbf{a}, \mathbf{b}) \end{pmatrix} \equiv \begin{pmatrix} \frac{\partial}{\partial \mathbf{a}} \\ \frac{\partial}{\partial \mathbf{b}} \end{pmatrix} \|M_n(\mathbf{a}, \mathbf{b})\|^2,$$

$$H_n(\mathbf{a}, \mathbf{b}) = \begin{pmatrix} H_{11}(\mathbf{a}, \mathbf{b}) & H_{12}(\mathbf{a}, \mathbf{b}) \\ H_{21}(\mathbf{a}, \mathbf{b}) & H_{22}(\mathbf{a}, \mathbf{b}) \end{pmatrix} \equiv \begin{pmatrix} \frac{\partial^2}{\partial \mathbf{a} \partial \mathbf{a}^\top} & \frac{\partial^2}{\partial \mathbf{a} \partial \mathbf{b}^\top} \\ \frac{\partial^2}{\partial \mathbf{b} \partial \mathbf{a}^\top} & \frac{\partial^2}{\partial \mathbf{b} \partial \mathbf{b}^\top} \end{pmatrix} \|M_n(\mathbf{a}, \mathbf{b})\|^2.$$

Moreover, define

$$h_n(\alpha, g) = \frac{1}{q} \Psi_n \Psi_n^\top, \quad \text{and } s_n(\alpha, g) = \frac{1}{q} \Psi_n \frac{1}{n} \sum_{i=1}^{n} m(V_i, \alpha^\top X_i, g(Z_i)), \qquad (7.3.17)$$

where Ψ_n is given by (7.3.8).

Lemma 7.3.2 *Let Assumptions 7.3.1–7.3.2 and 7.3.5–7.3.9 hold. Then, as* $n \to \infty$, *(1)* $H_n(\alpha, \beta)$ *is asymptotically positive definite with probability one; (2)* $\|H_n(\alpha, \beta) - h_n(\alpha, g)\| = o_P(1)$*; (3)* $\|S_n(\alpha, \beta) - s_n(\alpha, g)\| = o_P(1)$.

The proofs of these two lemmas can be found in Dong et al. (2023).

Proof (*Theorem* 7.3.1) In Lemma 7.3.1, we have (i) $\|M_n(\alpha, \beta)\|^2 = O_P(u_n)$ with $u_n = \max(\|\gamma_K\|^2, n^{-1})$; and (ii) $\sup_{\substack{\|\mathbf{a}\| \le B_{1n}, \|\mathbf{b}\| \le B_{2n} \\ \|(\mathbf{a}-\alpha, \mathbf{b}-\beta)\| > \delta}} \|M_n(\mathbf{a}, \mathbf{b})\|^{-2} = O_P(1/\epsilon_n)$ for each $\delta > 0$.

Fix $\varepsilon > 0$ and $\delta > 0$. Assertion (ii) means that there exists a large but fixed M for which

$$\limsup \mathbb{P}\left(\epsilon_n \sup_{\substack{\|\mathbf{a}\| \le B_{1n}, \|\mathbf{b}\| \le B_{2n} \\ \|(\mathbf{a}-\alpha, \mathbf{b}-\beta)\| > \delta}} \|M_n(\mathbf{a}, \mathbf{b})\|^{-2} > M \right) < \varepsilon.$$

Meanwhile, by the definition of the estimator and (i), we have

$$\|M_n(\widehat{\alpha}, \widehat{\beta})\|^2 = \inf_{\|\mathbf{a}\| \le B_{1n}, \|\mathbf{b}\| \le B_{2n}} \|M_n(\mathbf{a}, \mathbf{b})\|^2 \le \|M_n(\alpha, \beta)\|^2 = O_P(u_n),$$

which gives $\epsilon_n \|M_n(\widehat{\alpha}, \widehat{\beta})\|^{-2} = O_P(\epsilon_n / u_n) \to_P \infty$ by Assumption 7.3.4 and hence

$$\mathbb{P}\left(\epsilon_n \|M_n(\widehat{\alpha}, \widehat{\beta})\|^{-2} > M\right) \to 1.$$

It follows that, with probability at least $1 - 2\varepsilon$, for all n large enough,

$$\epsilon_n \|M_n(\widehat{\alpha}, \widehat{\beta})\|^{-2} > M \ge \epsilon_n \sup_{\substack{\|\mathbf{a}\| \le B_{1n}, \|\mathbf{b}\| \le B_{2n} \\ \|(\mathbf{a}-\alpha, \mathbf{b}-\beta)\| > \delta}} \|M_n(\mathbf{a}, \mathbf{b})\|^{-2}.$$

Hence, the inclusion $(\widehat{\alpha}, \widehat{\beta}) \in \{(\mathbf{a}, \mathbf{b}) : \|\mathbf{a}\| \le B_{1n}, \|\mathbf{b}\| \le B_{2n}, \|(\mathbf{a} - \alpha, \mathbf{b} - \beta)\| > \delta\}$ holds with probability at most 2ε, $\mathbb{P}\left(\|(\widehat{\alpha} - \alpha, \widehat{\beta} - \beta)\| > \delta\right) \le 2\varepsilon$. As ε and δ are arbitrarily chosen, we then have $\|(\widehat{\alpha} - \alpha, \widehat{\beta} - \beta)\| \to_P 0$. Notice further that

$$\begin{aligned}
\|(\widehat{\alpha} - \alpha, \widehat{g}(z) - g(z))\|^2 =& \|\widehat{\alpha} - \alpha\|^2 + \int [\widehat{g}(z) - g(z)]^2 \pi(z) dz \\
=& \|\widehat{\alpha} - \alpha\|^2 + \int [(\widehat{\beta} - \beta)^\top \Phi_K(z) - \gamma_K(z)]^2 \pi(z) dz \\
=& \|\widehat{\alpha} - \alpha\|^2 + \|\widehat{\beta} - \beta\|^2 + \|\gamma_K(z)\|^2 \\
=& \|(\widehat{\alpha} - \alpha, \widehat{\beta} - \beta)\|^2 + \|\gamma_K(z)\|^2 \to_P 0,
\end{aligned}$$

as $n, K \to \infty$, by the orthogonality of the basis sequence, which then completes the proof. □

Proof (*Theorem* 7.3.2) Notice that the conditions of the theorem imply the consistency of the estimator that is used in the sequel. By the first-order condition $S_n(\widehat{\alpha}, \widehat{\beta}) = 0$, consistency and Taylor expansion, we have expansion

$$\begin{aligned}
0 = S_n(\widehat{\alpha}, \widehat{\beta}) =& S_n(\alpha, \beta) + H_n(\bar{\alpha}, \bar{\beta}) \begin{pmatrix} \widehat{\alpha} - \alpha \\ \widehat{\beta} - \beta \end{pmatrix} \\
=& S_n(\alpha, \beta) + H_n(\alpha, \beta) \begin{pmatrix} \widehat{\alpha} - \alpha \\ \widehat{\beta} - \beta \end{pmatrix} + [H_n(\bar{\alpha}, \bar{\beta}) - H_n(\alpha, \beta)] \begin{pmatrix} \widehat{\alpha} - \alpha \\ \widehat{\beta} - \beta \end{pmatrix},
\end{aligned}$$

where $(\bar{\alpha}, \bar{\beta})$ is some point on the joint line between $(\widehat{\alpha}, \widehat{\beta})$ and (α, β). Notice that the last term is of a smaller order in probability compared to the second term. Indeed, by the Lipschitz condition in Assumption 7.3.6, the last term in the norm is bounded by $O_P(p+K)[\|\widehat{\alpha}-\alpha\|+\|\widehat{\beta}-\beta\|]^{1+\tau}$, while the second term is $O_P(p+K)[\|\widehat{\alpha}-\alpha\|+\|\widehat{\beta}-\beta\|]$. Thus, we may write

$$0 = S_n(\widehat{\alpha}, \widehat{\beta}) = S_n(\alpha, \beta) + H_n(\alpha, \beta)\begin{pmatrix}\widehat{\alpha}-\alpha \\ \widehat{\beta}-\beta\end{pmatrix}(1+o_P(1)),$$

in view of the consistency and for simplicity we shall ignore the term $o_P(1)$ in the sequel. As shown in Lemma 7.3.2, under Assumptions 7.3.1–7.3.3, 7.3.5, 7.3.7–7.3.9, $H_n(\alpha, \beta)$ is asymptotically positive definite; meanwhile, $H_n(\alpha, \beta)$ and $S_n(\alpha, \beta)$ are approximated by $h_n(\alpha, g)$ and $s_n(\alpha, g)$ (defined in (7.3.17)), respectively, that is, $\|H_n(\alpha, \beta) - h_n(\alpha, g)\| = o_P(1)$ and $\|S_n(\alpha, \beta) - s_n(\alpha, g)\| = o_P(1)$. Hence, for large n,

$$\begin{pmatrix}\widehat{\alpha}-\alpha \\ \widehat{\beta}-\beta\end{pmatrix} = -H_n(\alpha, \beta)^{-1}S_n(\alpha, \beta) = -h_n(\alpha, g)^{-1}s_n(\alpha, g)(1+o_P(1)). \quad (7.3.18)$$

Note that $\mathscr{L}(\widehat{\alpha}) - \mathscr{L}(\alpha) = \partial\mathscr{L}(\alpha)^\top(\widehat{\alpha}-\alpha) + (\widehat{\alpha}-\alpha)^\top \otimes (\partial^2\mathscr{L}_1(\bar{\alpha}), \ldots, \partial^2\mathscr{L}_r(\bar{\alpha}))^\top \otimes (\widehat{\alpha}-\alpha)$ where $\mathscr{L}_j$ is the component of the transformation $\mathscr{L}$, and $\bar{\alpha}$ is on the segment joining α and $\widehat{\alpha}$. Due to Assumption 7.3.10, the second term above is negligible, and hence, $\widehat{g}(z) - g(z) = \Phi_K(z)^\top(\widehat{\beta}-\beta) - \gamma_K(z)$. By the linearity of Fréchet derivative and ignoring the higher-order term in the definition of Fréchet derivative, we have

$$\begin{aligned}
\begin{pmatrix}\mathscr{L}(\widehat{\alpha}) - \mathscr{L}(\alpha) \\ \mathscr{F}(\widehat{g}) - \mathscr{F}(g)\end{pmatrix} &= \begin{pmatrix}\partial\mathscr{L}(\alpha)^\top(\widehat{\alpha}-\alpha) \\ \mathscr{F}'(g)(\widehat{g}(z) - g(z))\end{pmatrix} \\
&= \begin{pmatrix}\partial\mathscr{L}(\alpha)^\top & 0 \\ 0 & \mathscr{F}'(g)\Phi_K(z)^\top\end{pmatrix}\begin{pmatrix}\widehat{\alpha}-\alpha \\ \widehat{\beta}-\beta\end{pmatrix} - \begin{pmatrix}0 \\ \mathscr{F}'(g)\gamma_K(z)\end{pmatrix} \\
&= \Gamma_n h_n(\alpha, g)^{-1}s_n(\alpha, g) - \begin{pmatrix}0 \\ \mathscr{F}'(g)\gamma_K(z)\end{pmatrix} \\
&= \Lambda_{1n} + \Lambda_{2n}, \quad \text{say.}
\end{aligned}$$

Recall $h_n(\alpha, g) = \frac{1}{q}\Psi_n\Psi_n^\top$ and $s_n(\alpha, g) = \frac{1}{q}\Psi_n\frac{1}{n}\sum_{i=1}^n m(V_i, \alpha^\top X_i, g(Z_i))$ by (7.3.17). Hence, $\Lambda_{1n} = \frac{1}{n}\Gamma_n(\Psi_n\Psi_n^\top)^{-1}\Psi_n\sum_{i=1}^n m(V_i, \alpha^\top X_i, g(Z_i))$. Then, the covariance matrix of $\sqrt{n}\Lambda_{1n}$ is

$$\Sigma_n^2 \equiv \Gamma_n(\Psi_n\Psi_n^\top)^{-1}\Psi_n\Xi_n\Psi_n^\top(\Psi_n\Psi_n^\top)^{-1}\Gamma_n^\top,$$

in which $\Xi_n \equiv \mathbb{E}[m(V_1, \alpha^\top X_1, g(Z_1))m(V_1, \alpha^\top X_1, g(Z_1))^\top]$. It follows from the standard Central Limit Theorem (i.i.d. innovations) that $\sqrt{n}\Sigma_n^{-1}\Lambda_{1n} \to_D N(0, I_{r+s})$ as $n \to \infty$. Then the assertion follows because of $\sqrt{n}\Sigma_n^{-1}(\mathbf{0}_r^\top, \mathscr{F}'(g)\gamma_K(z)^\top)^\top = o(1)$, yielding $\sqrt{n}\Lambda_{2n} = o(1)$. □

7.4 Panel Data SMRMs

There are many SMRMs proposed for penal data since they are very flexible and cover several classical models as special cases. Hahn (1997) considers asymptotically efficient estimation of the panel data models with sequential moment restrictions in an environment with i.i.d observations. It is shown that the GMM estimator with an increasing set of instruments attains the semiparametric efficiency bound of the model; the estimator considered therein allows for the heteroscedasticity of the unknown form.

Ullah et al. (2018) methodologically demonstrate how to detect and deal with endogeneity issues in panel data. For illustration purposes, they use a dataset consisting of observations over a 15-year period (i.e., 2002–2016) from 101 UK listed companies and examined the direct effect of R & D expenditures, corporate governance, and firms' characteristics on performance. Due to endogeneity bias, the result of their analyses indicates significant differences in findings reported under the ordinary least square (OLS) approach, fixed effects, and the GMM estimations.

Gørgens et al. (2019) investigate the relationship between moment restrictions and identification in simple linear AR(1) dynamic panel data models with fixed effects under standard minimal assumptions. The number of time periods is assumed to be small; the assumptions imply linear and quadratic moment restrictions, which can be used for GMM estimation.

Blundell and Bond (2023) consider the estimation of the dynamic error components model using two alternative linear estimators that are designed to improve the properties of the standard first differenced GMM estimator. Both estimators require restrictions on the initial conditions process; asymptotic efficiency comparisons and Monte Carlo simulations for the simple AR(1) model demonstrate the dramatic improvement in performance of the proposed estimators compared to the usual first-differenced GMM estimator, and compared to non-linear GMM.

Hong et al. (2023) study panel data models with interactive fixed effects where the regressors are allowed to be correlated with the idiosyncratic error terms. They propose a two-step profile GMM estimation procedure to estimate the parameters of interest; they also establish the asymptotic properties of the preliminary estimates and the iterative estimates, and propose an efficient profile GMM estimator; they additionally study the determination of the number of factors and propose Hausman tests for the exogeneity of the regressors.

The key difference between cross-sectional and penal data SMRMs is that penal data SMRMs have to take into account both individual and time-specific effects that cause the change of estimation procedure and inference. In this section, we mainly discuss high-dimensional panel data SMRMs.

7.4.1 High-Dimensional Panel Data SMRMs

Consider a class of high-dimensional moment restriction panel data models with interactive effects, where factors are unobserved and factor loadings are nonparametrically unknown smooth functions of individual characteristic variables. We allow the dimension of the parameter vector and the number of moment conditions to diverge with the sample size. Specifically, suppose that

$$\mathbb{E}[m(W_{it}, X_{it}^\top \beta, \lambda(V_i)^\top f_t)] = 0, \tag{7.4.1}$$

for $i = 1, \ldots, N$, $t = 1, \ldots, T$, where $m(\cdot)$ is a q-vector of known functions, W_{it} contains the dependent variable and possible instrumental variables, X_{it} is a p-vector of regressors, $\beta = (\beta_1, \ldots, \beta_p)^\top$ is a p-vector of unknown slope coefficients, f_t is a r-vector of unknown factors, and the factor loadings $\lambda(V_i) = (\lambda_1(V_{i1}), \ldots, \lambda_r(V_{ir}))^\top$ are unknown functions of individual characteristic variables $V_i = (V_{i1}, \ldots, V_{ir})^\top$, which are time invariant. The setting for the loading functions is also proposed by Connor et al. (2012), Ma et al. (2021), Dong et al. (2021a), etc. For example, Connor et al. (2012) allow that factor betas in the Fama-French model to depend on security characteristics, such as size, value, momentum, and own-volatility factors. We follow their work by considering unobservable factors due to popularity and wide applicability. Here we consider the case where the dimensions p and q are large, that is, $p = p(N, T) \to \infty$ and $q = q(N, T) \to \infty$, as $(N, T) \to (\infty, \infty)$, but not ultra-large since we require at least $qp^2/NT \to 0$ in the asymptotic distribution derived later. In addition, we also allow the number of factors r to be large. The dependence of the dimensionality (q, p and r) on the sample size is suppressed for the sake of simplicity. We are interested in estimating the unknown parameter β, unknown function $\lambda(\cdot)$ vector and f_t given $\{(W_{it}, X_{it}, V_i)\}$.

As is well known, a genesis of moment restrictions is conditional moment restrictions. Here are two examples.

Example 7.4.1 Let $\rho(W_{it}, X_{it}^\top \beta, \lambda(V_i)^\top f_t)$ be a known J-dimensional vector of generalized residual functions and Z_i be a sub-vector of V_i. Suppose that they satisfy a conditional moment restriction $\mathbb{E}[\rho(W_{it}, X_{it}^\top \beta, \lambda(V_i)^\top f_t)|Z_i] = 0$, almost surely. In fact, Arellano and Carrasco (2003), Breitung and Lechner (1995, 1998) are based on similar conditional moment conditions. Let $\Phi_k(z)$ be a sequence of functions that can approximate any square integrable function of Z in some sense arbitrarily as $k \to \infty$. Then the conditional restriction implies a set of unconditional moment restrictions $\mathbb{E}[\rho(W_{it}, X_{it}^\top \beta, \lambda(V_i)^\top f_t) \otimes \Phi_k(Z_i)] = 0$, where the symbol "$\otimes$" denotes the Kronecker product. Denote $m(W_{it}, Z_i, X_{it}^\top \beta, \lambda(V_i)^\top f_t) = \rho(W_{it}, X_{it}^\top \beta, \lambda(V_i)^\top f_t) \otimes \Phi_k(Z_i)$. Notice that the dimension of $m(\cdot)$ is Jk which increases with k. Therefore, (β, λ, f) can be solved from the above unconditional moment conditions by GMM.

Example 7.4.2 Let Y_{it} be a binary outcome assuming either 0 or 1. Suppose we have a binary panel data model of the form,

$$P(Y_{it} = 1|X_{it}, V_i, f_t) = F(\beta^\top X_{it} + \lambda(V_i)^\top f_t), \tag{7.4.2}$$

for $i = 1, \ldots, N,\ t = 1, \ldots, T$, where $\beta, X_{it} \in \mathbb{R}^p$, $V_i \in \mathbb{R}$ and $F(\cdot)$ is a known cumulative distribution function, e.g., the standard normal or standard logistic distribution. Model (7.4.2) has a similar form as Example 1 in Fernández-Val and Weidner (2016) and Example 2 in Chen et al. (2021) except that we allow factor loadings to be a vector of functions of random variable V_i while they assume λ_i is a parameter vector with fixed dimension. As mentioned in Fernández-Val and Weidner (2016), in a labor economics application, Y can be an indicator of female labor force participation and X can include fertility indicators and other socio-economic characteristics. Suppose that the function $\lambda(v)$ can be approximated arbitrarily in some sense by a linear combination of k known functions denoted as $\widetilde{\Phi}_k(v)$, that is, $\lambda(v) - \widetilde{\Phi}_k(v)^\top \alpha$ goes to zero in some sense as $k \to \infty$. Then under certain identification conditions given below, we can estimate β, α and f_t from the first-order conditions for maximum likelihood estimation.

Let $\lambda(v) = (\lambda_1(v_1), \ldots, \lambda_r(v_r))^\top$ be a vector of unknown functions, where $\lambda_\ell(v_\ell)$, $\ell = 1, 2, \ldots, r$, are univariate functions defined on $\mathbb{V}$, $\mathbb{V} \subset \mathbb{R}$. Let $\lambda_\ell(\cdot)$ belong to a Hilbert space $L^2(\mathbb{V}, \pi(v))$, where $\pi(v)$ is a user-chosen density function on $\mathbb{V}$. As usual, the inner product is defined as $\langle g_1, g_2 \rangle = \int_{\mathbb{V}} g_1(v) g_2(v) \pi(v) dv$ for functions in the space, and $\|g\|_{L^2} = \sqrt{\langle g, g \rangle}$ the induced norm. For the r-vector of functions $\lambda(\cdot)$, its norm is defined as $\|\lambda\|_{L^2} = \left(\sum_{\ell=1}^r \|\lambda_\ell\|_{L^2}^2\right)^{1/2}$.

Suppose that $\{\phi_j(\cdot), j \geq 0\}$ is an orthonormal basis in $L^2(\mathbb{V}, \pi(v))$. Thus, $\lambda_\ell(\cdot)$ admits an infinite orthogonal series expansion,

$$\lambda_\ell(v_\ell) = \sum_{j=0}^{\infty} \alpha_{\ell j} \phi_j(v_\ell), \text{ where } \alpha_{\ell j} = \langle \lambda_\ell, \phi_j \rangle,\ \ell = 1, \ldots, r. \tag{7.4.3}$$

For a positive integer k, define the partial sum $\lambda_\ell^{(k)}(v_\ell) = \sum_{j=0}^{k-1} \alpha_{\ell j} \phi_j(v_\ell) = \alpha_\ell^\top \Phi_k(v_\ell)$, where $\alpha_\ell = (\alpha_{\ell 0}, \ldots, \alpha_{\ell,k-1})^\top$ and $\Phi_k(v_\ell) = (\phi_0(v_\ell), \ldots, \phi_{k-1}(v_\ell))^\top$. Moreover, let $\lambda^{(k)}(v) = (\lambda_1^{(k)}(v_1), \ldots, \lambda_r^{(k)}(v_r))^\top = \widetilde{\Phi}_k(v)^\top \alpha$, where $\widetilde{\Phi}_k(v) = \mathrm{diag}(\Phi_k(v_1), \ldots, \Phi_k(v_r))$ and $\alpha = (\alpha_1^\top, \ldots, \alpha_r^\top)^\top$ is a (kr)-vector, containing all the coefficients in the truncation series. Define $\gamma_\ell^{(k)}(v_\ell) = \sum_{j=k}^{\infty} \alpha_{\ell j} \phi_j(v_\ell)$, the residue after truncation, and $\gamma^{(k)}(v) = (\gamma_1^{(k)}(v_1), \ldots, \gamma_r^{(k)}(v_r))^\top$. It is easy to see that $\lambda(v) = \lambda^{(k)}(v) + \gamma^{(k)}(v)$. It follows that $\lambda^{(k)}(v) \to \lambda(v)$ as $k \to \infty$, in some sense.

When factors are unobserved, the lack of identification of factors f_t and factor loadings λ_i is well known in the literature as they enter the model in a multiplicative way (see, for example, Bai 2009; Bai & Li, 2014). The following identification conditions fully make use of the interactive factor structure and the series expansions of the loading functions, and they are completely different from the existing conditions in the relevant literature.

Identification Conditions (IC)

(a) *If* $\phi_0(v) = 1$, $\alpha_{\ell 0} = \int_{\mathbb{V}} \lambda_\ell(v)\phi_0(v)\pi(v)dv = 0$ *for* $2 \le \ell \le r$;
(b) *The first coefficient in the orthogonal expansion of each* $\lambda_\ell(v)$ *not equal to zero is 1, that is,* $\alpha_{\ell j_{\ell,0}} = 1$, *while* $\alpha_{\ell j} = 0$ *for* $j < j_{\ell,0}$ *if any*;
(c) $P(f_{t\ell} \neq 0) = 1$, *for* $\ell = 1, 2, \ldots, r$, $t = 1, \ldots, T$.

The condition (a) is employed to normalize the additive terms such that the model can get rid of possible extra constants, which is standard in the additive model; see Assumption C.2 in Dong and Linton (2018) and the references therein. The condition (b) is similar to an identification in a single-index model. Although in the estimation of $y = g(\theta^\top x) + e$, a common IC is $\|\theta\| = 1$ and the first element $\theta_1 > 0$, another IC is also frequently seen, that is, $\theta_1 = 1$. Furthermore, the condition (c) stipulates $P(f_{t\ell} = 0) = 0$. This helps identify $\lambda_\ell(v)$ because eventually in our estimation procedure $\alpha_{\ell j} f_{t\ell}$ will be treated as coefficients to be estimated. If $P(f_{t\ell} = 0) > 0$, we have a positive failure probability of obtaining the estimates of $\alpha_{\ell j} f_{t\ell}$, and consequently fail to obtain the estimates of $\alpha_{\ell j}$. The total number of the identification conditions proposed are no more than $3k - 1$. In contrast to the identification condition in Bai (2009), this set of IC is simple and fully utilizes the proposed loading functions' orthogonal series expansion and factor structure to identify the factors and their loadings.

To illustrate how the IC works, let $r = 1$. The factor structure is $\lambda^{(k)}(V_i) f_t = \sum_{j=0}^{k-1} f_t \alpha_{\ell j} \phi_j(V_i)$. Due to the variation of $\phi_j(V_i)$, we are able to estimate $f_t \alpha_{\ell j}$, say b_j, for $j = 0, 1, \ldots, k-1$. Thus, $f_t = b_{j_{\ell,0}}$ due to IC(b) and then we know $\alpha_{\ell j} = b_j / b_{j_{\ell,0}}$ for $j = 0, 1, \ldots, k-1$. As said above, we are about to identify $(\alpha_{\ell 0}, \alpha_{\ell 1}, \ldots, \alpha_{\ell,k-1})$ and $f_{t\ell}$ from their product $(f_{t\ell}\alpha_{\ell 0}, f_{t\ell}\alpha_{\ell 1}, \ldots, f_{t\ell}\alpha_{\ell,k-1})$. Thus, $\alpha_{\ell j_{\ell,0}} = 1$ directly gives $f_{t\ell}\alpha_{\ell j_{\ell,0}} = f_{t\ell}$ and then we have all $\alpha_{\ell j}$ identified. On the other hand, the condition $\alpha_{\ell j_{\ell,0}}$ is equivalent to rescaling $\lambda_\ell(v)$ by $\alpha_{\ell j_{\ell,0}}$ if it is not one, $\lambda_\ell(v)/\alpha_{\ell j_{\ell,0}}$.

For each given (N, T), the parameter space for model (7.4.1) is defined as

$$\Theta_{NT} = \{(b, g_\ell, s_t) : b \in \mathbb{R}^p;\, g_\ell \in L^2(\mathbb{V}, \pi(v)), 1 \le \ell \le r;\, s_t \in \mathbb{R}^r, 1 \le t \le T\},$$

and for notational simplicity, we just use Θ hereafter. For $b \in \mathbb{R}^p$ and $g \in L^2(\mathbb{V}, \pi(v))$, we define

$$\|(b, g)\| = \left(\|b\|_E^2 + \|g\|_{L^2}^2\right)^{1/2},$$

where $\|\cdot\|_E$ denotes the Euclidean norm on $\mathbb{R}^p$ and $\|\cdot\|_{L^2}$ denotes the norm of function vector defined previously. The subscript will be suppressed hereafter whenever there is no ambiguity incurred.

Recall that $\lambda(v)=\lambda^{(k)}(v)+\gamma^{(k)}(v)$. Let $f_t^\top\lambda^{(k)}(v)=f_t^\top\widetilde{\Phi}_k(v)^\top\alpha=\Phi_k^r(v)^\top D_t$, where $D_t=(f_{t1}\alpha_1^\top,\ldots,f_{tr}\alpha_r^\top)^\top$. Then we rewrite the moment condition (7.4.1) as

$$\mathbb{E}\left[m\left(W_{it}, X_{it}^\top\beta, \Phi_k^r(V_i)^\top D_t+f_t^\top\gamma^{(k)}(V_i)\right)\right]=0. \tag{7.4.4}$$

Our estimation strategy is that we first estimate β and D_t simultaneously for each given t, and then we obtain the estimators of f_t and α by virtue of the identification conditions, and finally define the estimate of $\lambda(v)$ by $\widehat{\lambda}(v)=\widetilde{\Phi}_k(v)^\top\widehat{\alpha}$. Specifically, for each given t, we estimate β and D_t by

$$(\widehat{\beta}_t,\widehat{D}_t)=\underset{b\in\mathbb{R}^p,d_t\in\mathbb{R}^{kr}}{\arg\min}\ \|M_{Nt}(b,d_t)\|^2, \tag{7.4.5}$$
$$\text{subject to } \|b\|\le B_{1N} \text{ and } \|d_t\|\le B_{2N},$$

where $M_{Nt}(b,d_t)=\frac{1}{\sqrt{q}}\frac{1}{N}\sum_{i=1}^N m(W_{it},X_{it}^\top b,\Phi_k^r(V_i)^\top d_t)$, and B_{1N} and B_{2N} are two sequences of positive numbers diverging with N. In addition, the reason for including q in the function $M_{Nt}(b,d_t)$ is to take into account the divergence of the dimension of $m(\cdot)$.

Note that the subscript t in $\widehat{\beta}_t$ indicates that we only use the information at time t to estimate β. This strategy localizes a global parameter. To eschew this drawback, we define the final estimator for β by

$$\overline{\widehat{\beta}}=\frac{1}{T}\sum_{t=1}^T\widehat{\beta}_t. \tag{7.4.6}$$

The averaging converts the localized parameter back to global, and more importantly, this accelerates the convergence rate of $\widehat{\beta}_t$, as shown below, as if we estimate β using global information.

Write $\widehat{D}_t$ as $\widehat{D}_t=(\widehat{D}_{t1}^\top,\ldots,\widehat{D}_{tr}^\top)^\top$. Then it is easy to see that $\widehat{D}_{t\ell}$, for $1\le\ell\le r$, is the estimator of $f_{t\ell}\alpha_\ell=(f_{t\ell}\alpha_{\ell 0},f_{t\ell}\alpha_{\ell 1},\ldots,f_{t\ell}\alpha_{\ell,k-1})^\top$. By the IC(b) that the first non-zero coefficient $\alpha_{\ell j_{\ell,0}}=1$, we obtain the estimate of $f_{t\ell}$, and consequently, the estimate of α_ℓ, that is,

$$\widehat{f}_{t\ell}=\widehat{D}_{t\ell,j_{\ell,0}}=S_\ell^{(j_{\ell,0})}\widehat{D}_t,\quad \widehat{\alpha}_{t\ell}=\frac{\widehat{D}_{t\ell}}{\widehat{f}_{t\ell}}=\frac{S_\ell\widehat{D}_t}{S_\ell^{(j_{\ell,0})}\widehat{D}_t}, \tag{7.4.7}$$

where S_ℓ denotes a selection matrix drawing the corresponding sub-vectors from the parent vector and $S_\ell^{(j_{\ell,0})}$ denotes a selection vector drawing the $j_{\ell,0}$th element from $\widehat{D}_{t\ell}$. Notice that the subscript t in the notation $\widehat{\alpha}_{t\ell}$ implies the information at time t used for its estimation from which we define $\widehat{\lambda}_{t\ell}(v_\ell)=\Phi_k(v_\ell)^\top\widehat{\alpha}_{t\ell}$ as an estimator of $\lambda_\ell(v_\ell)$. To make use of the full information, we define the estimators of $\lambda_\ell(v_\ell)$, for $1\le\ell\le r$, as

$$\bar{\hat{\lambda}}_\ell(v_\ell) = \Phi_k(v_\ell)^\top \frac{1}{T}\sum_{t=1}^{T} \widehat{\alpha}_{t\ell}. \tag{7.4.8}$$

It is noteworthy that we can generalize the model by allowing the variable of characteristics V_i to vary with time, that is, each factor loading is a function of V_{it}. We may then use the series method to estimate $\lambda(V_{it})$ by $\widetilde{\Phi}_k(V_{it})^\top \alpha$ in a similar way, where α can be estimated using the same method as in (7.4.5). However, we focus on the case where the variable of characteristics is only indexed by i.

7.4.2 Asymptotic Theory

The following theorems, along with the regularity conditions, are given by Cheng et al. (2024), while for completeness, these assumptions are shown in Sect. 7.4.4.

Theorem 7.4.1 (Consistency) *Let Assumptions 7.4.1–7.4.9 in Sect. 7.4.4 and the IC hold. Suppose $B_{1N}^2 + B_{2N}^2 = o(N)$. Then, we have*

1. *As $(N, T) \to (\infty, \infty)$, $\|(\bar{\hat{\beta}} - \beta, \bar{\hat{\lambda}}_\ell(v) - \lambda_\ell(v))\| \to_P 0$.*
2. *As $N \to \infty$, for any given t, $\|\widehat{f}_{t\ell} - f_{t\ell}\| \to_P 0$.*

where $\ell = 1, 2, \ldots, r$. □

Given the consistency, one can further establish the convergence rates of estimators.

Theorem 7.4.2 (Convergence rate) *Let conditions in Theorem 7.4.1 hold. Then for $\ell = 1, 2, \ldots, r$, we have*

1. *As $(N, T) \to (\infty, \infty)$,*

$$\left\|\bar{\hat{\beta}} - \beta\right\| = O_P\left(\sqrt{\frac{p}{NT}}\right), \quad \bar{\hat{\lambda}}_\ell(v) - \lambda_\ell(v) = O_P\left(\sqrt{\frac{k}{NT}}\right) + O_P(\|\gamma_\ell^{(k)}\|).$$

2. *As $N \to \infty$, for any given t, $\widehat{f}_{t\ell} - f_{t\ell} = O_P\left(\sqrt{\frac{1}{N}}\right)$.* □

Note that p in the convergence rate of $\bar{\hat{\beta}}$ is due to the diverging dimensions of β. If the dimensions of β are fixed, then the rate of convergence of our estimators reduces to the traditional rate $(NT)^{-1/2}$. The convergence rates of $\bar{\hat{\lambda}}_\ell(V)$ and $\widehat{f}_{t\ell}$ are in line with the results from Dong et al. (2021a).

As the dimension of β diverges with the sample size (N, T), we may not be able to establish a limit distribution for $\bar{\hat{\beta}}$ directly. Instead, we consider some finite-dimensional transformations of β. See some examples for the functionals in Dong et al. (2023) and the reference therein. Let $\mathcal{L}$ be a transformation from $\mathbb{R}^p \mapsto \mathbb{R}^\eta$ with $\eta \geq 1$ fixed. Here we establish the limit distributions for $\mathcal{L}(\bar{\hat{\beta}}) - \mathcal{L}(\beta)$, $\bar{\hat{\lambda}}_\ell(v)$ and $\widehat{f}_{t\ell}$, $\ell = 1, 2, \ldots, r$.

Theorem 7.4.3 (Asymptotic normality) *Let Assumptions 7.4.1–7.4.9 and 7.4.10 (a)–(c) in Sect. 7.4.4 hold. Then,*

1. *As* $(N, T) \to (\infty, \infty)$, *we obtain* $\sqrt{NT}\left(\mathcal{L}(\widehat{\widehat{\beta}}) - \mathcal{L}(\beta)\right) \to_D N\left(0, \Sigma_{\mathcal{L}(\beta)}\right)$, *where*

$$\Sigma_{\mathcal{L}(\beta)} = \lim_{N,T\to\infty} \partial\mathcal{L}(\beta)^\top S_p(\Psi_N\Psi_N^\top)^{-1}\Psi_N\,\Xi_{q\times q}\Psi_N^\top(\Psi_N\Psi_N^\top)^{-1}S_p^\top\partial\mathcal{L}(\beta),$$

   where $S_p = (I_p, 0)_{p\times(p+kr)}$.

2. *As* $(N, T) \to (\infty, \infty)$ *and* $1 \le \ell \le r$, *we have* $\frac{\sqrt{NT}}{||\Phi_k(V)||}(\widehat{\widehat{\lambda}}_\ell(V) - \lambda_\ell(V)) \to_D N(0, \Sigma_{\lambda\ell})$, *where*

$$\Sigma_{\lambda\ell} = \lim_{N,T\to\infty} \frac{1}{||\Phi_k(V_\ell)||^2}\Phi_k(V_\ell)^\top S_\ell S_{kr}(\Psi_N\Psi_N^\top)^{-1}\Psi_N\widetilde{\Xi}_{q\times q} \times \Psi_N^\top(\Psi_N\Psi_N^\top)^{-1}S_{kr}^\top S_\ell^\top\Phi_k(V_\ell),$$

   and S_ℓ *is a selection matrix to select* $(\ell-1)k+1$ *to* ℓk *rows of a given matrix and* $S_{kr} = (0, I_{kr})_{(kr)\times(p+kr)}$.

3. *If, in addition, Assumption 7.4.10 (d) holds, as* $N \to \infty$, *for any given* t *and* $1 \le \ell \le r$, *we have* $\sqrt{N}\left(\widehat{f_{t\ell}} - f_{t\ell}\right) \to_D N\left(0, \Sigma_{f\ell}\right)$, *where*

$$\Sigma_{f\ell} = \lim_{N\to\infty} S_\ell^{(j_{\ell,0})}S_{kr}(\Psi_N\Psi_N^\top)^{-1}\Psi_N\Xi_m^*\Psi_N^\top(\Psi_N\Psi_N^\top)^{-1}S_{kr}^\top S_\ell^{(j_{\ell,0})\top}.$$

□

All these results are comparable with the parametric and nonparametric literature. For example, the covariance matrix $\Sigma_{\mathcal{L}(\beta)}$ has the same form as those in the standard GMM framework, except that here we have transformation $\mathcal{L}$, and Ψ_N and $\Xi_{q\times q}$ have diverging dimensions. From Theorem 7.4.3, we can see that the convergence rate of $\mathcal{L}(\widehat{\widehat{\beta}})$ is $(NT)^{-1/2}$, which is consistent with the existing studies that $\widehat{\beta} - \beta = O_P((NT)^{-1/2})$ (Bai, 2009). Under our setting, $\|\Phi_k(V)\|^2 = O(k)$, so the multiplier in (2) of Theorem 7.4.3 is in fact $\sqrt{NT/k}$.

7.4.3 Monte Carlo Experiments

In this section, we examine the performance of our proposed estimation procedure in finite sample settings using two experiments.

Example 7.4.3 (*Example* 7.4.1 *continued*) Suppose that we have the following linear regression model

$$Y_{it} = X_{it}^\top\beta + \lambda(V_i)^\top f_t + e_{it}, \tag{7.4.9}$$

where $X_{it} \sim N(0, I_p)$, p is the dimension of X_{it}, and $e_{it} \sim N(0, 1)$. Here we set $\beta = (0.4, 0.5, 0, \ldots, 0)^\top \in \mathbb{R}^p$; we have two common factors, $f_{t\ell} \sim \text{U}(-3, 3)$ for $\ell = 1, 2$. The corresponding factor loadings are $\lambda(V) = (\lambda_1(V_1), \lambda_2(V_2))^\top$ with $V_\ell \sim \text{U}(0, 1)$ and $\pi(v) = 1$. For simplicity, we let $\lambda_1(v) = \lambda_2(v) = \sqrt{2}\cos(\pi v)$. It is easy to check that the identification conditions (IC) is fulfilled. Our objective is to estimate β, $\lambda(\cdot)$ and f_t together with the series-based GMM proposed.

Suppose that $\mathbb{E}[e_{it}|V_i] = 0$. Let $\phi_0(v) = 1$, and for all $j \geq 0$, $\phi_j(v) = \sqrt{2}\cos(\pi j v)$. Then, $\{\phi_j(v)\}$ is an orthonormal basis in $L^2[0, 1]$. Let $m(W_{it}, X_{it}^\top\beta, \lambda(V_i)^\top f_t) = (Y_{it} - X_{it}^\top\beta - \lambda(V_i)^\top f_t)\Psi_q(V_i)$ where $W_{it} = (Y_{it}, V_i)$ and $\Psi_q(V_i)$ is a vector consisting of $\phi_{\ell_1}(V_{1i})\phi_{\ell_2}(V_{2i})$ with $\ell_1, \ell_2 \leq \sqrt{q}$. By Law of Iterated Expectations, we then have $\mathbb{E}[m(W_{it}, X_{it}^\top\beta, \lambda^\top(V_i)f_t)] = 0$. Note that the dimension of m function is q which is diverging. Thus, the parameters $(\beta, \lambda(\cdot), f_t)$ can be solved from the above unconditional moment restrictions using the estimation procedure outlined in the preceding section. Specifically, define $(\widehat{\beta}, \widehat{D}_t) = \arg\min \|M_{Nt}(b, d_t)\|^2$, where $M_{Nt}(b, d_t) = \frac{1}{\sqrt{q}}\frac{1}{N}\sum_{i=1}^N m(W_{it}, X_{it}^\top b, \Phi_k^r(V_i)^\top d_t)$. By virtue of the identification conditions (IC), we can get $\widehat{f}_t$ and $\widehat{\alpha}$ separately from $\widehat{D}_t$. Further, define $\widehat{\lambda}_1(v_1) = \Phi_k(v_1)^\top\widehat{\alpha}_1$ and $\widehat{\lambda}_2(v_2) = \Phi_k(v_2)^\top\widehat{\alpha}_2$, where $\widehat{\alpha}_1$ and $\widehat{\alpha}_2$ are the sub-vectors of $\widehat{\alpha}$ consisting of the first k elements and the remaining k elements in $\widehat{\alpha}$, respectively.

For each combination of (N, T) given below, $M = 100$ replications are executed. In this example, we assume $p = (NT)^{1/5}$, $k = (NT)^{1/5}$, and $q = p + kr + \nu$ with $\nu = 2$. Note that the choices of these parameters may not be the optimal ones, but they satisfy all the requirements in our assumptions.

To examine the performance of the estimator $\widehat{\beta}$, we compute bias and median which are defined as follows.

$$\text{Bias}(\beta) = \|\beta - \widehat{\beta}^*\|, \quad \text{Med}(\beta) = \text{median}(\|\beta - \widehat{\beta}^1\|, \ldots, \|\beta - \widehat{\beta}^M\|), \tag{7.4.10}$$

where the superscript s in $\widehat{\beta}^s$ indicates the estimate of the sth replication, $\widehat{\beta}^*$ is the average of $\widehat{\beta}^s$ for $s = 1, 2, \ldots, M$ over Monte Carlo replications.

To examine the performance of the estimators of loading functions $\widehat{\lambda}_\ell(v_\ell)$, we compute bias, standard deviation (Std), and root mean squared errors (RMSE) as follows.

$$\text{Bias}(\lambda_\ell) = \frac{1}{MN}\sum_{s=1}^M\sum_{i=1}^N \left(\widehat{\lambda}_\ell^s(V_i) - \lambda_\ell(V_i)\right), \tag{7.4.11}$$

$$\text{Std}(\lambda_\ell) = \left(\frac{1}{MN}\sum_{s=1}^M\sum_{i=1}^N \left(\widehat{\lambda}_\ell^s(V_i) - \widehat{\lambda}_\ell^*(V_i)\right)^2\right)^{1/2}, \tag{7.4.12}$$

$$\text{RMSE}(\lambda_\ell) = \left(\frac{1}{MN}\sum_{s=1}^M\sum_{i=1}^N \left(\widehat{\lambda}_\ell^s(V_i) - \lambda_\ell(V_i)\right)^2\right)^{1/2}, \tag{7.4.13}$$

where $\widehat{\lambda}_\ell^*(V_i)$ is the average of $\widehat{\lambda}_\ell^s(V_i)$ over Monte Carlo replications, $\ell = 1, 2$.

Similarly, to examine the performance of $\widehat{f_\ell}$, $\ell = 1, 2$, we compute

$$\text{Bias}(f_\ell) = \frac{1}{MT}\sum_{s=1}^{M}\sum_{t=1}^{T}\left(\widehat{f_{t\ell}^s} - f_{t\ell}\right), \tag{7.4.14}$$

$$\text{Std}(f_\ell) = \left(\frac{1}{MT}\sum_{s=1}^{M}\sum_{t=1}^{T}\left(\widehat{f_{t\ell}^s} - \overline{\widehat{f}}_{t\ell}\right)^2\right)^{1/2}, \tag{7.4.15}$$

$$\text{RMSE}(f_\ell) = \left(\frac{1}{MT}\sum_{s=1}^{M}\sum_{t=1}^{T}\left(\widehat{f_{t\ell}^s} - f_{t\ell}\right)^2\right)^{1/2}, \tag{7.4.16}$$

where $\overline{\widehat{f}}_{t\ell}$ is the average of $\widehat{f_{t\ell}^s}$ over Monte Carlo replications.

The results for $\overline{\widehat{\beta}}$ are reported in Table 7.3. It is readily seen that the bias and median of $\overline{\widehat{\beta}}$ are reasonably small for all sample sizes. Note that due to the divergence of the dimension, it might not make sense to compare the bias and median of $\overline{\widehat{\beta}}$ across different sample sizes.

Moreover, the results for $\overline{\widehat{\lambda}}$ and $\widehat{f}$ are given in Tables 7.4 and 7.5, respectively. As can be seen, with the increase of N, standard deviations, and root mean squared errors of $\widehat{f_\ell}$ decrease, but they do not change much with the increase of T. This is consistent with our theory that the convergence rate of $\widehat{f_\ell}$ is $O(N^{-1/2})$; with the increase of N and T, root mean squared errors of $\overline{\widehat{\lambda}}(v)$ decrease which verifies our theoretical results.

Table 7.3 Simulation results for $\overline{\widehat{\beta}}$ in Example 7.4.3

(N, T)	(50, 50)	(50, 100)	(50, 200)	(100, 50)	(100, 100)	(100, 200)	(200, 50)	(200, 100)	(200, 200)
Bias	0.0025	0.0031	0.0008	0.0013	0.0008	0.0008	0.0019	0.0002	0.0011
Med	0.0349	0.0217	0.0147	0.0231	0.0158	0.0112	0.0171	0.0111	0.0081

Table 7.4 Simulation results for $\overline{\widehat{\lambda}}_1$ and $\overline{\widehat{\lambda}}_2$ in Example 7.4.3

(N, T)	(50, 50)	(50, 100)	(50, 200)	(100, 50)	(100, 100)	(100, 200)	(200, 50)	(200, 100)	(200, 200)
$\overline{\widehat{\lambda}}_1$									
Bias	−0.0000	0.0000	−0.0001	−0.0000	0.0000	0.0000	0.0000	0.0000	−0.0001
Sd	0.0086	0.0053	0.0044	0.0064	0.0041	0.0030	0.0040	0.0034	0.0019
RMSE	0.0087	0.0053	0.0045	0.0064	0.0041	0.0030	0.0040	0.0034	0.0019
$\overline{\widehat{\lambda}}_2$									
Bias	−0.0000	−0.0001	−0.0000	−0.0001	−0.0001	0.0000	0.0001	−0.0001	0.0000
Sd	0.0101	0.0060	0.0041	0.0062	0.0047	0.0030	0.0043	0.0030	0.0024
RMSE	0.0101	0.0061	0.0041	0.0063	0.0048	0.0030	0.0044	0.0031	0.0024

Table 7.5 Simulation results for $\widehat{f_1}$ and $\widehat{f_2}$ in Example 7.4.3

(N, T)	(50, 50)	(50, 100)	(50, 200)	(100, 50)	(100, 100)	(100, 200)	(200, 50)	(200, 100)	(200, 200)
$\widehat{f_1}$									
Bias	−0.0007	−0.0011	−0.0021	−0.0009	0.0008	0.0006	−0.0003	−0.0002	−0.0001
Sd	0.1510	0.1041	0.0731	0.1508	0.1030	0.0739	0.1541	0.1033	0.0745
RMSE	0.1518	0.1046	0.0735	0.1517	0.1037	0.0742	0.1549	0.1038	0.0749
$\widehat{f_2}$									
Bias	−0.0022	0.0002	0.0015	0.0026	0.0013	0.0007	0.0010	0.0003	−0.0002
Sd	0.1425	0.1073	0.0730	0.1417	0.1064	0.0739	0.1429	0.1075	0.0734
RMSE	0.1430	0.1076	0.0734	0.1425	0.1071	0.0743	0.1437	0.1081	0.0738

Example 7.4.4 (*Example*7.4.17 *continued*) This example is about to verify the performance of series estimators for $Y_{it} = I\left[X_{it}^\top\beta + \lambda(V_i)^\top f_t - \varepsilon_{it} > 0\right]$ in finite sample situations. Note that

$$P(Y_{it} = 1|X_{it}, V_i, f_t) = F(X_{it}^\top\beta + \lambda(V_i)^\top f_t), \tag{7.4.17}$$

for $i = 1, \ldots, N$, $t = 1, \ldots, T$, where $\beta, X_{it} \in \mathbb{R}^p$, $f_t, V_i \in \mathbb{R}^2$, $\lambda(V) = (\lambda_1(V_1), \lambda_2(V_2))^\top$, $V = (V_1, V_2)$ and $F(u) = 1/(1 + \exp(-u))$ is the cumulative distribution function of ε_{it}. Assume $X_{it} \sim N(0, I_p)$. We set $\beta = (0.4, 0.5, 0, \ldots, 0)^\top \in \mathbb{R}^p$. For two common factors $f_{t\ell}$, $\ell = 1, 2$, let $f_{t\ell} \sim$ U$(-3, 3)$, while in loading functions $V_i \sim i.i.d.N(0_r, I_r)$ and $r = 2$. For simplicity, we set $\lambda_1(v) = \lambda_2(v) = \frac{\sqrt{2}}{\pi^{1/4}} v \exp(-v^2/2)$. We can see that the generation of loadings and factors satisfies the identification conditions (IC). The series-based GMM procedure can be used to estimate the unknown function $\lambda(V)$, unknown factor f_t and the parameter vector β.

From model (7.4.17), we have the log likelihood function

$$\ln\left[\prod_{i=1}^{N}\prod_{t=1}^{T} F^{Y_{it}}(\beta^\top X_{it} + \lambda(V_i)^\top f_t)\left(1 - F(\beta^\top X_{it} + \lambda(V_i)^\top f_t)\right)^{1-Y_{it}}\right].$$

Let $\Phi_k(v) = (p_0(v), \ldots, p_{k-1}(v))^\top$, where $\{p_j(x), j \geq 0\}$ is the sequence of Hermite functions that form an orthonormal basis in $L^2(\mathbb{R})$. Hence, we can approximate the log likelihood function by the following quantity Q^{NT} defined as

$$Q^{NT} = \ln \prod_{i=1}^{N} \prod_{t=1}^{T} F^{Y_{it}}(X_{it}^{\top}\beta + f_t^{\top}\widetilde{\Phi}_k(V_i)^{\top}\alpha)\left(1 - F(X_{it}^{\top}\beta + f_t^{\top}\widetilde{\Phi}_k(V_i)^{\top}\alpha)\right)^{1-Y_{it}}$$
$$= \ln \prod_{i=1}^{N} \prod_{t=1}^{T} F^{Y_{it}}(X_{it}^{\top}\beta + \Phi_k^r(V_i)^{\top}D_t)\left(1 - F(X_{it}^{\top}\beta + \Phi_k^r(V_i)^{\top}D_t)\right)^{1-Y_{it}}$$
$$= \sum_{t=1}^{T} Q_{Nt}, \tag{7.4.18}$$

where $Q_{Nt} = \sum_{i=1}^{N} \ln\left[F^{Y_{it}}(X_{it}^{\top}\beta + \Phi_k^r(V_i)^{\top}D_t)\left(1 - F(X_{it}^{\top}\beta + \Phi_k^r(V_i)^{\top}D_t)\right)^{1-Y_{it}}\right]$.

At each given t, to maximize Q_{Nt}, we derive the first-order conditions as follows.

$$\frac{\partial Q_{Nt}}{\partial \beta} = \sum_{i=1}^{N} \frac{(Y_{it} - F(X_{it}^{\top}\beta + \Phi_k^r(V_i)^{\top}D_t))F^{(1)}(X_{it}^{\top}\beta + \Phi_k^r(V_i)^{\top}D_t)}{F(X_{it}^{\top}\beta + \Phi_k^r(V_i)^{\top}D_t)(1 - F(X_{it}^{\top}\beta + \Phi_k^r(V_i)^{\top}D_t))} X_{it} = 0$$
$$\frac{\partial Q_{Nt}}{\partial D_t} = \sum_{i=1}^{N} \frac{(Y_{it} - F(X_{it}^{\top}\beta + \Phi_k^r(V_i)^{\top}D_t))F^{(1)}(X_{it}^{\top}\beta + \Phi_k^r(V_i)^{\top}D_t)}{F(X_{it}^{\top}\beta + \Phi_k^r(V_i)^{\top}D_t)(1 - F(X_{it}^{\top}\beta + \Phi_k^r(V_i)^{\top}D_t))} \Phi_k^r(V_i) = 0,$$

where $F^{(1)}(u) = \frac{dF(u)}{du}$. It is easy to see that the above first-order conditions are equivalent as $\frac{1}{N}\frac{\partial Q_{Nt}}{\partial \beta} = 0$ and $\frac{1}{N}\frac{\partial Q_{Nt}}{\partial D_t} = 0$, and this can be regarded as the sample version of the following moment conditions with $m(\cdot) = (m_1^{\top}(\cdot), m_2^{\top}(\cdot))^{\top}$:

$$\mathbb{E}[m_1(Y_{it}, X_{it}^{\top}\beta, \Phi_k^r(V_i)^{\top}D_t)]$$
$$= \mathbb{E}\left[\frac{(Y_{it} - F(X_{it}^{\top}\beta + \Phi_k^r(V_i)^{\top}D_t))F^{(1)}(X_{it}^{\top}\beta + \Phi_k^r(V_i)^{\top}D_t)}{F(X_{it}^{\top}\beta + \Phi_k^r(V_i)^{\top}D_t)(1 - F(X_{it}^{\top}\beta + \Phi_k^r(V_i)^{\top}D_t))} X_{it}\right] = 0,$$
$$\mathbb{E}[m_2(Y_{it}, X_{it}^{\top}\beta, \Phi_k^r(V_i)^{\top}D_t)]$$
$$= \mathbb{E}\left[\frac{(Y_{it} - F(X_{it}^{\top}\beta + \Phi_k^r(V_i)^{\top}D_t))F^{(1)}(X_{it}^{\top}\beta + \Phi_k^r(V_i)^{\top}D_t)}{F(X_{it}^{\top}\beta + \Phi_k^r(V_i)^{\top}D_t)(1 - F(X_{it}^{\top}\beta + \Phi_k^r(V_i)^{\top}D_t))} \Phi_k^r(V_i)\right] = 0.$$

Accordingly, define $(\widehat{\beta}, \widehat{D}_t) = \arg\min \|M_{Nt}(b, d_t)\|^2$, where

$$M_{Nt}(\beta, D_t) = \left(\frac{1}{N}\frac{\partial Q_{Nt}}{\partial \beta^{\top}}, \frac{1}{N}\frac{\partial Q_{Nt}}{\partial D_t^{\top}}\right)^{\top}.$$

Then, by the identification conditions (IC), we can get $\widehat{f}_t$ and $\widehat{\alpha}$. Further, $\widehat{\lambda}_1(V_1) = \Phi_k(V_1)^{\top}\widehat{\alpha}_1$ and $\widehat{\lambda}_2(V_2) = \Phi_k(V_2)^{\top}\widehat{\alpha}_2$, where $\widehat{\alpha}_1$ is the vector of the first k elements in $\widehat{\alpha}$ and $\widehat{\alpha}_2$ is the vector of the remaining k elements in $\widehat{\alpha}$.

We execute $M = 100$ replications for each sample size (N, T) given below. To do so, we take the truncation parameter $k = (NT)^{1/5}$, $p = (NT)^{1/5}$, $q = p + kr$

Table 7.6 Simulation results for $\overline{\widehat{\beta}}$ in Example 7.4.4

(N, T)	(50, 50)	(50, 100)	(50, 200)	(100, 50)	(100, 100)	(100, 200)	(200, 50)	(200, 100)	(200, 200)
Bias	0.1212	0.0816	0.0448	0.1316	0.0792	0.0464	0.1262	0.0786	0.0459
Med	0.1530	0.1018	0.0606	0.1443	0.0912	0.0558	0.1309	0.0837	0.0494

Table 7.7 Simulation results for $\overline{\widehat{\lambda}}_1$ and $\overline{\widehat{\lambda}}_2$ in Example 7.4.4

(N, T)	(50, 50)	(50, 100)	(50, 200)	(100, 50)	(100, 100)	(100, 200)	(200, 50)	(200, 100)	(200, 200)
$\overline{\widehat{\lambda}}_1$									
Bias	0.0153	−0.0002	0.0008	0.0075	0.0034	0.0019	−0.0085	0.0020	−0.0002
Sd	0.0410	0.0462	0.0134	0.0379	0.0142	0.0098	0.0238	0.0090	0.0068
RMSE	0.0442	0.0462	0.0134	0.0387	0.0146	0.0100	0.0253	0.0092	0.0069
$\overline{\widehat{\lambda}}_2$									
Bias	0.0096	−0.0008	0.0002	0.0045	0.0013	−0.0008	0.0024	0.0002	0.0001
Sd	0.0554	0.0201	0.0120	0.0237	0.0131	0.0083	0.0222	0.0089	0.0067
RMSE	0.0573	0.0201	0.0122	0.0242	0.0134	0.0085	0.0223	0.0092	0.0068

Table 7.8 Simulation results for $\widehat{f}_1$ and $\widehat{f}_2$ in Example 7.4.4

(N, T)	(50, 50)	(50, 100)	(50, 200)	(100, 50)	(100, 100)	(100, 200)	(200, 50)	(200, 100)	(200, 200)
$\widehat{f}_1$									
Bias	−0.0259	−0.1119	0.0032	−0.0545	−0.0589	−0.0206	−0.0476	−0.0788	−0.0208
Sd	0.9948	0.6756	0.4607	0.9861	0.6727	0.4597	0.9862	0.6790	0.4562
RMSE	1.0899	0.7426	0.4963	1.0725	0.7398	0.4952	1.0816	0.7533	0.4893
$\widehat{f}_2$									
Bias	−0.0702	0.0633	−0.0384	−0.0125	0.0063	−0.0179	0.0071	0.0045	−0.0220
Sd	0.9486	0.6962	0.4785	0.9529	0.7202	0.4874	0.9572	0.7158	0.4778
RMSE	1.0518	0.7641	0.5168	1.0411	0.7869	0.5217	1.0472	0.7878	0.5726

(exactly identified). To examine the performance of our estimators, we still use the measures defined in Example 7.4.3. The results are reported in Tables 7.6, 7.7 and 7.8.

Our findings are quite similar to that from Example 7.4.3. That is, (a) the bias and medians of $\overline{\widehat{\beta}}$ are reasonably small for all sample sizes. Note that due to the divergence of the dimension, it might not make sense to compare the bias and median of $\overline{\widehat{\beta}}$ across different sample sizes; (b) with the increase of N, standard deviations, and root mean squared errors of $\widehat{f}_\ell$ decrease, while they do not change much with the increase of T. This is consistent with our theory that the convergence rate of $\widehat{f}_\ell$ is $O(N^{-1/2})$ independent of T; (c) with the increase of N and T, root mean squared errors of $\overline{\widehat{\lambda}}(v)$ decrease.

7.4.4 Mathematical Details

The following are all the regularity assumptions used in Cheng et al. (2024) to derive the theoretical results in Sect. 7.4.

Assumption 7.4.1 Suppose that $\{\phi_j(\cdot), j \geq 0\}$ is an orthonormal basis in $L^2(\mathbb{V}, \pi(v))$, so that $\langle \phi_i, \phi_j \rangle = \delta_{ij}$ the Kronecker delta.

Assumption 7.4.2 Suppose that B_{1N} and B_{2N} are two sequences of positive numbers diverging with N, such that β in model (7.4.1) is in $\Theta_{1N} = \{b \in \mathbb{R}^p : \|b\| \leq B_{1N}\}$ and for sufficiently large N, $\lambda^{(k)}(v)^\top f_t$ is included in $\Theta_{2N} = \{\Phi_k^r(v)^\top d_t : \|d_t\| \leq B_{2N}\}$ where $\Phi_k^r(v) = (\Phi_k(v_1)^\top, \ldots, \Phi_k(v_r)^\top)^\top$.

Assumption 7.4.3 Suppose that

(a) Denote $W_t = (W_{1t}, \ldots, W_{Nt})^\top$ and $X_t = (X_{1t}, \ldots, X_{Nt})^\top$, and suppose that $\{(W_t, X_t, f_t), 1 \leq t \leq T\}$ is strictly stationary and α-mixing; denote $W_i = (W_{i1}, \ldots, W_{iT})^\top$ and $X_i = (X_{i1}, \ldots, X_{iT})^\top$, and suppose that $\{(W_i, X_i, V_i), 1 \leq i \leq N\}$ is identically distributed across i.
Moreover, denote $\alpha_{ij}(|t-s|)$ as the α-mixing coefficient between $(W_{it}, X_{it}, V_i, f_t)$ and $(W_{js}, X_{js}, V_j, f_s)$. Let

$$\sum_{i=1}^N \sum_{j=1}^N \sum_{k=1}^\infty \left(\alpha_{ij}(k)\right)^{\delta/(4+\delta)} = O(N),$$

and

$$\sum_{i=1}^N \sum_{j=1}^N \left(\alpha_{ij}(0)\right)^{\delta/(4+\delta)} = O(N),$$

where $\delta > 0$ is chosen such that

$$\mathbb{E}\left[|m_l(W_{it}, X_{it}^\top \beta, \lambda(V_i)^\top f_t)|^{2+\delta/2}\right] < \infty,$$
$$\mathbb{E}\left[\left|\frac{1}{f_{t\ell}} m_l(W_{it}, X_{it}^\top \beta, \lambda(V_i)^\top f_t)\right|^{2+\delta/2}\right] < \infty,$$

for $l = 1, \ldots, q$ and $\ell = 1, \ldots, r$.

(b) The density $f_V(v)$ of V_1 satisfies $c\pi(v) \leq f_V(v) \leq C\pi(v)$ on the support $\mathbb{V}$ of V_1 for some constants $C \geq c > 0$, where $\pi(v)$ is the density function used in the Hilbert space defined previously.
(c) The function $m(\cdot, \cdot, \cdot)$ is continuous in the second and third arguments.
(d) $q(N, T) - p(N, T) \geq kr$.

Assumption 7.4.4 Suppose that for each (N, t), there are unique $\lambda(\cdot)^\top f_t$ and $\beta \in \mathbb{R}^p$ such that model (7.4.1) is satisfied. In other words, for any $\delta > 0$, there is an $\epsilon > 0$ such that

$$\inf_{(b,d_t)\in\Theta,\|(b-\beta,\Phi_k^r(V_i)^\top d_t-\lambda(V_i)^\top f_t)\|\geq\delta} \frac{1}{q}\|\mathbb{E}m(W_{it}, X_{it}^\top b, \Phi_k^r(V_i)^\top d_t)\|^2 > \epsilon.$$

Assumption 7.4.5 (a) Suppose that for each (N, T), there is a measurable positive function $A(W, X, V)$ such that

$$\begin{aligned}&q^{-1/2}\|m(W, X^\top b_1, g_1(V)^\top s_1) - m(W, X^\top b_2, g_2(V)^\top s_2)\|\\ \leq& A(W, X, V)\left[\|b_1 - b_2\| + \|g_1(V)^\top s_1 - g_2(V)^\top s_2\|\right]\end{aligned}$$

for any $(b_1, g_1, s_1), (b_2, g_2, s_2) \in \Theta$, where (W, X, V) is any realization of (W_{it}, X_{it}, V_i) and the function A satisfies that $\mathbb{E}[A^2(W_{it}, X_{it}, V_i)] < \infty$.

(b) Assume that there exists $c > 0$ such that $0 < c \leq \lambda_{\min}(\frac{1}{q}\Psi_N\Psi_N^\top) \leq \lambda_{\max}(\frac{1}{q}\Psi_N\Psi_N^\top) \leq \frac{1}{c} < \infty$, where

$$\Psi_N = \mathbb{E}\begin{pmatrix} \frac{\partial}{\partial u}m(W_{it}, X_{it}^\top\beta, \lambda(V_i)^\top f_t)^\top \otimes X_{it} \\ \frac{\partial}{\partial w}m(W_{it}, X_{it}^\top\beta, \lambda(V_i)^\top f_t)^\top \otimes \Phi_k^r(V_i)\end{pmatrix}_{(p+kr)\times q}.$$

Assumption 7.4.6 Suppose that each element function m_j of the $m(\cdot, \cdot, \cdot)$ is differentiable with respect to its second and third arguments up to the second order. The second derivative functions satisfy a Lipschitz condition in a neighborhood of the $(\beta, \lambda^\top f)$,

$$\begin{aligned}&|\partial^{(u)}m_j(W, X^\top\beta, \lambda(V)^\top f) - \partial^{(u)}m_j(W, X^\top b, g(V)^\top s)|\\ &\leq B_j(W, X^\top\beta, \lambda(V)^\top f)(\|b - \beta\| + \|\lambda^\top f - g^\top s\|)^\tau\end{aligned}$$

for some $\tau \in (0, 1]$, where u is two-dimensional multiple index with $|u| = 2$, $\partial^{(u)}$ stands for the partial derivative of the function with respect to the second and third arguments, and B_j are positive such that $\max_{1\leq j\leq q}\mathbb{E}[B_j(W, X^\top\beta, \lambda(V)^\top f)^2] < \infty$.

Let $\frac{\partial}{\partial u}m(\cdots)$, $\frac{\partial}{\partial w}m(\cdots)$, $\frac{\partial^2}{\partial u^2}m(\cdots)$, $\frac{\partial^2}{\partial w^2}m(\cdots)$ and $\frac{\partial^2}{\partial u\partial w}m(\cdots)$ denote the partial derivatives of $m(v, u, w)$ with respect to its arguments u and w, respectively.

Assumption 7.4.7 Suppose that for any $i = 1, 2, \ldots, N$, $t = 1, 2, \ldots, T$,

(a) $\mathbb{E}\|m(W_{it}, X_{it}^\top\beta, \lambda(V_i)^\top f_t)\|^2 = O(q)$, $\mathbb{E}\|X_{it}\|^2 = O(p)$, $\mathbb{E}\|\Phi_k(V_i)\|^2 = O(k)$ and $\mathbb{E}\|f_t\|^2 = O(r)$;
(b) $\mathbb{E}\|\frac{\partial}{\partial u}m(W_{it}, X_{it}^\top\beta, \lambda(V_i)^\top f_t)\|^2 = O(q)$, and $\mathbb{E}\|\frac{\partial}{\partial w}m(W_{it}, X_{it}^\top\beta, \lambda(V_i)^\top f_t)\|^2 = O(q)$;

(c) $\mathbb{E}\|\frac{\partial}{\partial u}m(W_{it}, X_{it}^\top\beta, \lambda(V_i)^\top f_t) \otimes X_{it}\|^2 = O(pq)$, and
$\mathbb{E}\|\frac{\partial}{\partial w}m(W_{it}, X_{it}^\top\beta, \lambda(V_i)^\top f_t) \otimes \Phi_k^r(V_i)\|^2 = O(krq)$;
(d) $\mathbb{E}\|\frac{\partial^2}{\partial u^2}m(W_{it}, X_{it}^\top\beta, \lambda(V_i)^\top f_t) \otimes X_{it}X_{it}^\top\|^2 = O(p^2q)$, and
$\mathbb{E}\|\frac{\partial^2}{\partial w^2}m(W_{it}, X_{it}^\top\beta, \lambda(V_i)^\top f_t) \otimes \Phi_k^r(V_i)\Phi_k^r(V_i)^\top\|^2 = O(k^2r^2q)$;
(e) $\mathbb{E}\|\frac{\partial^2}{\partial u \partial w}m(W_{it}, X_{it}^\top\beta, \alpha^\top\widetilde{\Phi}_k(V_i)f_t) \otimes X_{it}\Phi_k^r(V_i)^\top\|^2 = O(pkrq)$.

Assumption 7.4.8 Suppose that

(a) $\|\gamma^{(k)}(V)\|^2p^2 = o(1), \quad N^{-1}p^2 = o(1)$;
(b) $\|\gamma^{(k)}(V)\|^2k^2r^2 = o(1), \quad N^{-1}k^2r^2 = o(1)$.

Assumption 7.4.9 The partial derivatives of $m(v, u, w)$ satisfy

(a)

$$q^{-\frac{1}{2}}\|\frac{\partial}{\partial u}m(W, X^\top b_1, g_1(V)^\top s_1) - \frac{\partial}{\partial u}m(W, X^\top b_2, g_2(V)^\top s_2)\|$$
$$\leq A_1(W, X, V)[\|b_1 - b_2\| + \|g_1(V)^\top s_1 - g_2(V)^\top s_2\|],$$

where $\mathbb{E}[A_1(W, X, V)^2] < \infty$ and $\mathbb{E}[A_1(W, X, V)^2\|X\|^2] = O(p)$.

(b)

$$q^{-\frac{1}{2}}\|\frac{\partial}{\partial w}m(W, X^\top b_1, g_1(V)^\top s_1) - \frac{\partial}{\partial w}m(W, X^\top b_2, g_2(V)^\top s_2)\|$$
$$\leq A_2(W, X, V)[\|b_1 - b_2\| + \|g_1(V)^\top s_1 - g_2(V)^\top s_2\|],$$

where $\mathbb{E}[A_2(W, X, V)^2] < \infty$ and $\mathbb{E}[A_2(W, X, V)^2\|\Phi_k^r(V)\|^2] = O(kr)$.

Assumption 7.4.10 (a) The transformation $\mathcal{L}$ possesses continuous second partial derivatives, and the Hessian matrix of each component $\mathcal{L}_j$ of $\mathcal{L}$ has uniformly bounded eigenvalues in a neighborhood of β; moreover, the first partial derivative of $\mathcal{L}$ at β, $\partial\mathcal{L}(\beta)$ has full rank.
(b) Suppose that

$$\frac{1}{NT}\sum_{i=1}^N\sum_{j=1}^N\sum_{t=1}^T\sum_{s=1}^T\mathbb{E}[m(W_{it}, X_{it}^\top\beta, \lambda(V_i)^\top f_t)m(W_{js}, X_{js}^\top\beta, \lambda(V_j)^\top f_s)^\top]$$
$$= \Xi_{q\times q} + o(1),$$

and $0 < c_1 \leq \lambda_{\min}(\frac{1}{q}\Xi_{q\times q}) \leq \lambda_{\max}(\frac{1}{q}\Xi_{q\times q}) \leq \frac{1}{c_1} < \infty$ for some constant $c_1 > 0$.

(c) Suppose that

$$\frac{1}{NT}\sum_{i=1}^{N}\sum_{j=1}^{N}\sum_{t=1}^{T}\sum_{s=1}^{T}\mathbb{E}\left[\frac{1}{f_{t\ell}f_{s\ell}}m(W_{it}, X_{it}^{\top}\beta, \lambda(V_i)^{\top}f_t)m(W_{js}, X_{js}^{\top}\beta, \lambda(V_j)^{\top}f_s)^{\top}\right]$$
$$= \widetilde{\Xi}_{q\times q} + o(1),$$

and $0 < c_2 \leq \lambda_{\min}(\frac{1}{q}\widetilde{\Xi}_{q\times q}) \leq \lambda_{\max}(\frac{1}{q}\widetilde{\Xi}_{q\times q}) \leq \frac{1}{c_2} < \infty$ for some constant $c_2 > 0$.

(d) Assume that for some selection matrix $\mathcal{S}$, we have

$$\mathcal{S}(\Psi_N\Psi_N^{\top})^{-1}\Psi_N\frac{1}{\sqrt{N}}\sum_{i=1}^{N}m(W_{it}, X_{it}^{\top}\beta, \lambda(V_i)^{\top}f_t) \to_D N(0, \mathcal{S}\Sigma_e\mathcal{S}^{\top}),$$

where $\Sigma_e = (\Psi_N\Psi_N^{\top})^{-1}\Psi_N\Xi_m^*\Psi_N^{\top}(\Psi_N\Psi_N^{\top})^{-1}$,

$$\Xi_m^* = \lim_{N\to\infty}\frac{1}{N}\sum_{i=1}^{N}\sum_{j=1}^{N}\mathbb{E}[m(W_{it}, X_{it}^{\top}\beta, \lambda(V_i)^{\top}f_t)m(W_{jt}, X_{jt}^{\top}\beta, \lambda(V_j)^{\top}f_t)^{\top}],$$

and $0 < c_3 \leq \lambda_{\min}(\frac{1}{q}\Xi_m^*) \leq \lambda_{\max}(\frac{1}{q}\Xi_m^*) \leq \frac{1}{c_3} < \infty$ for some constant $c_3 > 0$.

References

Ai, C. (2007). Seminonparametric maximum likelihood estimation of conditional moment restriction models. *International Economic Review, 48*, 1093–1118.

Ai, C., & Chen, X. (2003). Efficient estimation of models with conditional moment restrictions containing unknown functions. *Econometrica, 71*, 1795–1843.

Ai, C., & Chen, X. (2007). Estimation of possibly misspecified semiparametric conditional moment restriction models with different conditioning variables. *Journal of Econometrics, 141*, 5–43.

Ai, C., & Chen, X. (2012). The semiparametric efficiency bound for models of sequential moment restrictions containing unknown functions. *Journal of Econometrics, 170*, 442–457.

Altonji, J. G., & Segal, L. M. (1996). Small sample bias in GMM estimation of covariance structure. *Journal of Business and Economic Statistics, 14*, 353–366.

Andrews, D. W. (1999). Consistent moment selection procedures for generalized method of moments estimation. *Econometrica, 67*, 543–564.

Andrews, D. W., & Lu, B. (2001). Consistent model and moment selection procedures for GMM estimation with application to dynamic panel data models. *Journal of Econometrics, 101*, 123–165.

Arellano, M., & Carrasco, R. (2003). Binary choice panel data models with predetermined variables. *Journal of Econometrics, 115*(1), 125–157.

Athey, S., Imbens, G., Pham, T., & Wager, S. (2017). Estimating average treatment effects: Supplementary analysis and remaining challenges. *American Economic Review, 107*, 278–281.

Bai, J. (2009). Panel data models with interactive fixed effects. *Econometrica, 77*(4), 1229–1279.

Bai, J., & Li, K. (2014). Theory and methods of panel data models with interactive effects. *Annals of Statistics, 42*(1), 142–170.

Belloni, A., Chen, D., Chernozhukov, V., & Hansen, C. (2012). Sparse models and methods for optimal instruments with an application to eminent domain. *Econometrica, 80*, 2369–2429.

Belloni, A., Chernozhukov, V., & Hansen, C. (2014a). High-dimensional methods and inference on structural and treatment effects. *Journal of Economic Perspectives, 28*, 29–50.

Belloni, A., Chernozhukov, V., & Wang, L. (2014b). Pivitor estimation via square-root Lasso in nonparametric regression. *Annals of Statistics, 42*, 757–788.

Belloni, A., Chernozhukov, V., Chetverikov, D., & Kato, K. (2015). Some new asymptotic theory for least squares series: Pointwise and uniform results. *Journal of Econometrics, 186*, 345–366.

Belloni, A., Chernozhukov, V., Hansen, C., & Wei, Y. (2016). Post-selection inference for generalized linear models with many controls. *Journal of Business and Economic Statistics, 34*, 590–605.

Bickel, P. J. (1982). On adaptive estimation. *Annals of Statistics, 10*, 647–671.

Blundell, R., & Bond, S. (2023). Reprint of: Initial conditions and moment restrictions in dynamic panel data models. *Journal of Econometrics, 234*, 38–55.

Blundell, R., Chen, X., & Christensen, D. (2007). Semi-nonparametric IV esstimation of shape-invariant Engel curves. *Econometrica, 75*, 1613–1669.

Breitung, J., & Lechner, M. (1995). GMM-estimation of nonlinear models on panel data. Technical report.

Breitung, J., & Lechner, M. (1998). Alternative gmm methods for nonlinear panel data models. Technical report, SFB 373 Discussion Paper.

Caner, M. (2009). Lasso-type GMM estimator. *Econometric Theory, 25*, 270–290.

Carneiro, P., Heckman, J., & Vytlacil, E. (2011). Estimating marginal returns to education. *American Economic Review, 101*, 2754–2781.

Cattaneo, M. D., Jansson, M., & Newey, W. K. (2018). Inference in linear regression models with many covariates and heteroskedasticity. *Journal of the American Statistical Association, 113*, 1350–1361.

Chang, J., Chen, S., & Chen, X. (2015). High dimensional generalized empirical likelihood for moment restrictions with dependent data. *Journal of Econometrics, 185*, 283–304.

Chen, X. (2007). Large sample sieve estimation of semi-parametric models. *Handbook of Econometrics* (Vol. 6B, pp. 5550–5588). Elsevier: Amsterdam, North Holland.

Chen, X., & Christensen, T. (2015). Optimal uniform convergence rates and asymptotic normality for series estimators under weak dependence and weak conditions. *Journal of Econometrics, 188*, 447–465.

Chen, X., & Liao, Z. (2015). Sieve semiparametric two-step GMM under weak dependence. *Journal of Econometrics, 189*, 163–186.

Chen, X., & Pouzo, D. (2009). Efficient estimation of semiparametric conditional moment models with possibly nonsmooth residuals. *Journal of Econometrics, 152*, 46–60.

Chen, X., & Pouzo, D. (2012). Estimation of nonparametric conditional moment models with possibly nonsmooth generalized residuals. *Econometrica, 80*, 277–321.

Chen, X., & Pouzo, D. (2015). Sieve WALD and QLR inferences on semi/nonparametric conditional moment models. *Econometrica, 83*, 1013–1079.

Chen, X., Linton, O., & Keilegom, I. V. (2003). Estimation for semiparametric models when the criterion function is not smooth. *Econometrica, 71*, 1591–1608.

Chen, M., Fernández-Val, I., & Weidner, M. (2021). Nonlinear factor models for network and panel data. *Journal of Econometrics, 220*(2), 296–324.

Cheng, T., Dong, C., Gao, J., & Linton, O. (2024). GMM estimation for high-dimensional panel data models. *Journal of Econometrics, 244*, 105853.

Chernozhukov, V., Newey, W. K., & Santos, A. (2023). Constrained conditional moment restriction models. *Econometrica, 91*, 709–731.

Connor, G., Hagmann, M., & Linton, O. (2012). Efficient semiparametric estimation of the Fama-French model and extensions. *Econometrica, 80*, 713–754.

Coppejans, M., & Gallant, A. R. (2002). Cross-validated SNP density estimates. *Journal of Econometrics, 110*, 27–65.

Dong, C., & Tu, Y. (2024). Semiparametric estimation and variable selection for sparse single index models in increasing dimension. *Econometric Theory*, forthcoming:1–46.

Dong, C., & Linton, O. (2018). Additive nonparametric models with time variable and both stationary and nonstationary regressors. *Journal of Econometrics, 207*, 212–236.

Dong, C., Gao, J., & Peng, B. (2015). Semiparametric single-index panel data models with cross-sectional dependence. *Journal of Econometrics, 188*, 301–312.

Dong, C., Gao, J., & Tjøstheim, D. (2016). Estimation for single-index and partially linear single-index integrated models. *Annals of Statistics, 44*, 425–453.

Dong, C., Gao, J., & Peng, B. (2021a). Varying-coefficient panel data models with nonstationarity and partially observed factor structure. *Journal of Business & Economic Statistics, 39*(3), 700–711.

Dong, C., Linton, O., & Peng, B. (2021b). A weighted sieve estimator for nonparametric time series models with nonstationary variables. *Journal of Econometrics, 222*, 909–932.

Dong, C., Gao, J., & Linton, O. (2023). High dimensional semiparametric moment restriction models. *Journal of Econometrics, 232*, 320–345.

Fan, J., & Li, R. (2001). Variable selection via nonconcave penalized likelihood and its oracle properties. *Journal of the American Statistical Association, 96*, 1348–1360.

Fan, J., & Liao, Y. (2014). Endogeneity in high dimensions. *Annals of Statistics, 42*, 872–917.

Fenton, V. M., & Gallant, A. R. (1996a). Convergence rates of SNP density estimators. *Econometrica, 64*, 719–727.

Fenton, V. M., & Gallant, A. R. (1996b). Qualitative and asymptotic performance of SNP density estimators. *Journal of Econometrics, 74*, 77–118.

Fernández-Val, I., & Weidner, M. (2016). Individual and time effects in nonlinear panel models with large N, T. *Journal of Econometrics, 192*(1), 291–312.

Gallant, A. R., & Nychka, D. W. (1987). Semi-nonparametric maximum likelihood estimation. *Econometrica, 55*, 363–390.

Gallant, A. R., & Tauchen, G. (1989). Seminonparametric estimation of conditionally constrained heterogeneous processes: Asset pricing applications. *Econometrica, 57*, 1091–1120.

Gørgens, T., Han, C., & Xue, S. (2019). Moment restrictions and identification in linear dynamic panel data models. *Annals of Economics and Statistics, 134*, 149–176.

Hahn, J. (1997). Efficient estimation of panel data models with sequential moment restrictions. *Journal of Econometrics, 79*, 1–21.

Hall, A. R., & Pelletiel, D. (2011). Non-nested testing in models estimated via generalized method of moments. *Econometric Theory, 27*, 443–456.

Han, C., & Phillips, P. C. B. (2006). GMM with many moment conditions. *Econometrica, 74*, 147–192.

Hansen, L. P. (1982). Large sample properties of generalized method of moments estimators. *Econometrica, 50*, 1029–1054.

Hansen, L., Heaton, J., & Yaron, A. (1996). Finite-sample properties of some alternative GMM estimators. *Journal of Business and Economic Statistics, 14*, 262–280.

Hong, S., Su, L., & Jiang, T. (2023). Profile GMM estimation of panel data models with interactive fixed effects. *Journal of Econometrics, 235*, 927–948.

Imbens, G. W. (1997). One-step estimators for over-identified generalized method of moments models. *The Review of Economic Studies, 64*, 359–383.

Imbens, G. W., Spady, R. H., & Johnson, P. (1998). Information-theoretic approaches to inference in moment conditions models. *Econometrica, 66*, 333–357.

Kitamura, Y., & Stutzer, M. (1997). An information-theoretic alternative to generalized method of moments estimation. *Econometrica, 65*, 861–874.

Leeb, H., & Pötscher, B. M. (2005). Model selection and inference: Facts and fiction. *Econometric Theory, 21*, 21–59.

Ma, S., Linton, O., & Gao, J. (2021). Estimation and inference in semiparametric quantile factor models. *Journal of Econometrics, 222*, 295–323.

Mammen, E. (1989). Asymptotics with increasing dimension for robust regression with applications to the bootstrap. *Annals of Statistics, 17*, 382–400.
Marmer, V., & Otsu, T. (2012). Optimal comparison of misspecified moment restriction models under a chosen measure of fit. *Journal of Econometrics, 170*, 538–550.
Newey, W. K. (1997). Convergence rates and asymptotic normality for series estimators. *Journal of Econometrics, 79*, 147–168.
Newey, W. K., & Powell, J. L. (2003). Instrumental variable estimation of nonparametric models. *Econometrica, 71*, 1565–1578.
Newey, W. K., & Smith, R. (2004). Higher order properties of GMM and generalized empirical likelihood estimators. *Econometrica, 72*, 219–255.
Owen, A. (1990). Empirical likelihood ratio confidence regions. *Annals of Statistics, 18*, 90–120.
Owen, A. (1991). Empirical likelihood for linear models. *Annals of Statistics, 19*, 1725–1747.
Pakes, A., & Pollard, D. (1989). Simulation and the asymptotics of optimization estimators. *Econometrica, 57*, 1027–1057.
Portnoy, S. (1984). Asymptotic behaviour of M-estimators of p regression parameters when p^2/n is large. I: Consistency. *Annals of Statistics, 12*, 1298–1309.
Portnoy, S. (1985). Asymptotic behaviour of M-estimators of p regression parameters when p^2/n is large. II: Normal approximation. *Annals of Statistics, 13*, 1403–1417.
Powell, J. (1994). Estimation of semiparametric models. *Handbook of Econometrics* (Vol. IV, pp. 2443–2521). Elsevier: Amsterdam, North Holland.
Qin, J., & Lawless, J. (1994). Empirical likelihood and general estimating equations. *Annals of Statistics, 22*, 300–325.
Robinson, P. M. (1988). Root-N-consistent semiparametric regression. *Econometrica, 56*, 931–954.
Song, S. (2015). Semiparametric estimation of models with conditional moment restrictions in the presence of nonclassical measurement errors. *Journal of Econometrics, 185*, 95–109.
Su, L., Ura, T., & Zhang, Y. (2019). Non-separable models with high-dimensional data. *Journal of Econometrics, 212*, 646–677.
Ullah, S., Akhtar, P., & Zaefarian, G. (2018). Dealing with endogeneity bias: The generalized method of moments (gmm) for panel data. *Industrial Marketing Management, 71*, 69–78.
Vuong, Q. (1989). Likelihood ratio tests for model selection and non-nested hypotheses. *Econometrica, 57*(3), 307–333.
Yu, Y., & Ruppert, D. (2002). Penalized spline estimation for partially linear single-index models. *Journal of the American Statistical Association, 97*, 1042–1054.

Appendix A
Abstract Spaces

In this appendix, we introduce function spaces in particular space C and Hilbert spaces that are the cornerstone of series methods. To begin with, this chapter introduces vector, metric and normed vector spaces. Vector spaces are general abstract spaces while other spaces depicted later are their further restrictions. Metric in metric spaces is a basic tool to describe sequence convergence, and consequently there are completeness, closure, denseness and compactness of sets and equicontinuity of set of functions. Norm in normed spaces is defined for each element in contract with metric that is defined for each pair of elements in the spaces. Any norm can induce a metric, so the sequence in the normed space may converge in terms of norm. A space is called Banach space if it is complete normed space. All notions appear in this chapter are crucial to understand the function spaces in Appendixes B and C.

A.1 Vector Spaces

A *field* is, essentially, a set of numbers possessing addition, subtraction, multiplication, and division operations, and under which the set is closed. For example, rational numbers form a field.

A *vector space* over a field $\mathcal{F}$ is a set V together with two operations that satisfy the eight axioms listed below. Elements of V are commonly called *vectors*. Elements of $\mathcal{F}$ are commonly called *scalars*.

The first operation, called vector addition or simply addition, takes any two vectors $v \in V$ and $w \in V$ and assigns to them a third vector which is commonly written as $v + w \in V$, and called the sum of these two vectors.

The second operation, called scalar multiplication, takes any scalar $a \in \mathcal{F}$ and any vector $v \in V$ and gives another vector $a\,v \in V$.

C. Dong and J. Gao, *Modern Series Methods in Econometrics and Statistics*, Advanced Studies in Theoretical and Applied Econometrics 45,
https://doi.org/10.1007/978-981-96-2822-3

To qualify as a vector space, the set V and the operations of addition and multiplication must adhere to a number of requirements called axioms. In the list below, let u, v and w be arbitrary vectors in V, and a and b scalars in $\mathcal{F}$.

(1) Associativity of addition: $u + (v + w) = (u + v) + w$.
(2) Commutativity of addition: $u + v = v + u$.
(3) Identity element of addition: There exists an element $0 \in V$, called the zero vector, such that $u + 0 = u$ for all $u \in V$.
(4) Inverse elements of addition: For every $u \in V$, there exists an element $-u \in V$, called the additive inverse of u, such that $u + (-u) = 0$.
(5) Compatibility of scalar multiplication: $a(bu) = (ab)u$, for any $a, b \in \mathcal{F}$ and $u \in V$.
(6) Identity element of scalar multiplication: $1u = u$ for any $u \in V$, where 1 denotes the multiplicative identity in $\mathcal{F}$.
(7) Distributivity of scalar multiplication with respect to vector addition: $a(u + v) = au + av$ for any $a \in \mathcal{F}$ and $u, v \in V$.
(8) Distributivity of scalar multiplication with respect to field addition: $(a + b)u = au + bu$ for any $a, b \in \mathcal{F}$ and $u \in V$.

When the elements of the scalar field $\mathcal{F}$ are the real numbers in $\mathbb{R}$, the vector space is called a *real vector space*; when that are the complex numbers, it is called a *complex vector space*.

The notion of a vector space is defined even more generally in abstract algebra, by allowing the multiplier $\alpha, \beta, \ldots$ in $\mathcal{F}$ to be elements of an arbitrary commutative field. In this book, however, we confine ourselves to the two fields of real and complex numbers, respectively, and mostly to the former.

As can be seen, vector addition and scalar multiplication are operations, satisfying the closure property: $u + v$ and au are in V for all $a \in \mathcal{F}$, and all $u, v \in V$.

A finite set of vectors $v_1, \ldots, v_n \in V$ is *linearly dependent* if there exist scalars $\alpha_1, \ldots, \alpha_n \in \mathcal{F}$ not all zero, such that $\alpha_1 v_1 + \cdots + \alpha_n v_n = 0$. If the finite set $v_1, \ldots, v_n \in V$ is not linearly dependent, it is called *linearly independent*. In that case, a relation $\alpha_1 v_1 + \cdots + \alpha_n v_n = 0$ implies that $\alpha_1 = \cdots = \alpha_n = 0$. An infinite set S of vectors is called linearly independent if every finite subset of S is linearly independent; otherwise S is called linearly dependent.

Let V be a vector space. Suppose there is some positive integer n such that V contains a set of n vectors that are linearly independent, while every set of $n + 1$ vectors in V is linearly dependent. Then V is called *finite-dimensional* and n is called the *dimension* of V. If V is not finite-dimensional, it is called *infinite-dimensional*.

A nonempty subset W of a vector space V that is closed under addition and scalar multiplication (and therefore contains the 0-vector of V) is called a *linear subspace* of V, or simply a subspace of V. Subspaces of V are vector spaces (over the same field) in their own right. The intersection of all subspaces containing a given set S of vectors is called its *span* (the span of S), and it is the smallest subspace of V containing the set S. Expressed in terms of elements, the span is the subspace consisting of all the linear combinations of elements of S.

A subset S in a space V is called a *basis* of V if S is linearly independent and if the span of S is exactly V. It is readily seen that if V is n-dimensional, $n \geq 1$, then V has a basis consisting of n elements; conversely, if V has a basis of n elements, then V is n-dimensional.

A linear subspace of dimension 1 is a *vector line*. A linear subspace of dimension 2 is a *vector plane*. A linear subspace that contains all elements but one of a basis of the ambient space is a *vector hyperplane*. In a vector space of finite dimension n, a vector hyperplane is thus a subspace of dimension $n-1$.

Example A.1.1 Euclidean vector space $\mathbb{R}^k$ is of k dimension. In particular, $\mathbb{R}^1$ is interpreted as a line, $\mathbb{R}^2$ as a plane, and so on. In the geometrical interpretation of $\mathbb{R}^k$ we may regard an element x either as a point or as the vector from zero (the origin in $\mathbb{R}^k$) to that point.

Example A.1.2 Functions from any fixed set Ω to a field $\mathcal{F}$ form vector spaces, by performing addition and scalar multiplication pointwise. That is, the sum of two functions f and g is the function $(f+g)$ given by

$$(f+g)(w) = f(w) + g(w), \quad \forall\, w \in \Omega,$$

and similarly for multiplication $(af)(w) = a \cdot f(w),\ \forall\, w \in \Omega$.

Example A.1.3 Let $[a, b]$ (with $a < b$) be a finite closed interval of the real axis, and let $g(x)$ denote a continuous real-valued function on $[a, b]$. Let $C[a, b]$ be the set of all such functions, in which we define $g_1 + g_2$ and αg in the natural manner as given in the above example. It is clear that $C[a, b]$ is a real vector space. Moreover, it is infinite-dimensional, because for any $k \geq 1$, $\{1, x, \ldots, x^k\}$ is an independent set in $C[a, b]$.

Example A.1.4 As elements of a space consider infinite sequences $x = \{\xi_n, n = 1, 2, \ldots\}$ such that $\sum_{n=1}^{\infty} |\xi_n|^2 < \infty$. Define $\alpha x = \{\alpha \xi_n\}$ and $\{\xi_n\} + \{\eta_n\} = \{\xi_n + \eta_n\}$. It is readily seen (by Minkowski's inequality with $p = 2$) that this is an infinite-dimensional linear space. We denote it by ℓ^2. This space was first extensively studied by D. Hilbert in his work on quadratic forms in infinitely many variables, with applications to the theory of integrable equations. On this account, ℓ^2 is the classical prototype of what is known today as a Hilbert space. Hilbert spaces are linear spaces with a certain special kind of metrical structure that we introduce later on.

A.2 Metric Spaces

A metric space is a set in which every pair of elements is associated with a well-defined "distance". By utilizing the distance, we can define the convergence of sequences of elements by saying that a sequence $\{x_k\}$ of elements converges to an element x if the distance between x_k and x tends to zero when $k \to \infty$. Thus, by defining "distance" we are able to discuss the convergence of elements in terms of the usual convergence of the sequence of real numbers, namely the sequence of distances between x_k and x.

In the following definition, S is any set of elements, not necessarily a vector space.

Definition A.2.1 (*Metric and metric space*) A pseudometric for S is a function $\rho(\cdot, \cdot)$ from $S \times S$ into $[0, \infty)$ satisfying the following axioms:

(1) $\rho(x, y) \geq 0$; and $\rho(x, x) = 0$.
(2) $\rho(x, y) = \rho(y, x), \forall x, y \in S$.
(3) $\rho(x, y) \leq \rho(x, z) + \rho(z, y), \forall x, y, z \in S$.

If also

(4) $\rho(x, y) = 0$ implies $x = y$, then ρ is called a metric.

A metric space denoted by (S, ρ) consists of a set S and a metric on it. □

Axiom (1) is natural and reasonable for it is in concert with our common sense; due to this, we are able to identify any two elements x and y with $\rho(x, y) \neq 0$. Axiom (2), symmetric condition, states that the distance from x to y is identical to that from y to x, and is also a rather obvious requirement. Axiom (3) is called the "triangle inequality". This property guarantees, among others, the uniqueness of the limit of a sequence in metric space. Axiom (4) imposes an extra condition on the ρ to ensure a pseudometric to be a metric. It is important to keep in mind that different metrics ρ_1 and ρ_2 on a single space S define different metric spaces (S, ρ_1) and (S, ρ_2). By a *subspace* of a metric space we mean a metric space whose points form a subset of S and whose metric agrees with that on S.

Example A.2.1 Consider vector space $\mathbb{R}^2$. Let $x = (x_1, x_2)$ and $y = (y_1, y_2)$ be two generic points in $\mathbb{R}^2$. Define the following metrics on $\mathbb{R}^2$:

(1) $\rho_1(x, y) = |x_1 - y_1| + |x_2 - y_2|$;
(2) $\rho_2(x, y) = \sqrt{(x_1 - y_1)^2 + (x_2 - y_2)^2}$;
(3) $\rho_p(x, y) = [|x_1 - y_1|^p + |x_2 - y_2|^p]^{1/p}, 1 \leq p < \infty$;
(4) $\rho_\infty(x, y) = \max(|x_1 - y_1|, |x_2 - y_2|)$;
(5) $d(x, y) = \frac{\rho(x,y)}{1+\rho(x,y)}$ where ρ is any metric on $\mathbb{R}^2$.

The above metrics can be extended to the vector space $\mathbb{R}^n$, respectively, in a straightforward way.

Example A.2.2 Consider vector space of infinite sequences $x = \{\xi_n, n = 1, 2, \ldots\}$ (another element $y = \{\eta_n, n = 1, 2, \ldots\}$ used below).

(1) On the space of sequences for which $\sum_{n=1}^{\infty} |\xi_n| < \infty$ (the so-called ℓ^1 space),

$$\rho_1(x, y) = \sum_{n=1}^{\infty} |\xi_n - \eta_n|$$

is a metric;

(2) On the space of sequences for which $\sum_{n=1}^{\infty} |\xi_n|^p < \infty$, $1 \le p < \infty$ (the so-called ℓ^p space),

$$\rho_p(x, y) = \left(\sum_{n=1}^{\infty} |\xi_n - \eta_n|^p \right)^{1/p}$$

is a metric;

(3) On the space of bounded sequences,

$$\rho_\infty(x, y) = \sup_n |\xi_n - \eta_n|$$

is a metric;

(4) On the space of any infinite sequences,

$$\rho(x, y) = \sum_{n=1}^{\infty} \frac{1}{2^n} \frac{|\xi_n - \eta_n|}{1 + |\xi_n - \eta_n|}$$

is a metric.

Example A.2.3 Define the metric on an arbitrary set S,

$$\rho(x, y) = \begin{cases} 0, & \text{if } x = y; \\ 1, & \text{otherwise.} \end{cases}$$

This is called a discrete metric on S. While this is a rather uninteresting metric, it shows that we may make any arbitrary set into a metric space; in addition, it is often useful to employ this metric to produce counterexamples showing that "obvious properties of the metric may not hold in all metric spaces".

With an eligible metric defined on S, we are allowed to define convergence of sequence, open ball, bounded subset, etc., on metric space (S, ρ).

Definition A.2.2 A sequence $\{x_k\}$ of elements of (S, ρ) converges with respect to the metric to $x \in (S, \rho)$ if $\rho(x_k, x) \to 0$ as $k \to \infty$. The element x is called the limit of the sequence and we write $\lim_{k\to\infty} x_k = x$. □

If the limit exists, it is unique by virtue of the triangle inequality of the metric. In fact, if both x and y are the limit of $\{x_k\}$, then $\rho(x, y) \le \rho(x, x_k) + \rho(y, x_k) \to 0$ when $k \to \infty$, so $x = y$ since ρ is a metric. We can give an alternative characterization of convergence in a metric space by using the concept of a ball.

Definition A.2.3 The ball $B(x_0, r)$, $r > 0$, of all points $x \in (S, \rho)$ satisfying $\rho(x, x_0) < r$ is called an open ball with center x_0 and radius r. If the inequality is replaced by $\rho(x, x_0) \le r$, we speak of a closed ball. □

We then have that $\lim_{k\to\infty} x_k = x$ if and only if, for every ball $B(x, \varepsilon)$, there exists a $k_0 = k_0(\varepsilon)$ such that $x_k \in B(x, \varepsilon)$ for all $k > k_0$. This implies that every sphere centered at x must contain infinitely many elements of the sequence.

A subset of a metric space is called *bounded* if it is contained in some ball of finite radius.

Definition A.2.4 A sequence $\{x_k\}$ in a metric space (S, ρ) is said to be a Cauchy (or fundamental) sequence if $\rho(x_k, x_l) \to 0$ as $k, l \to \infty$. This means that for every $\varepsilon > 0$, there exists a positive integer N_ε such that $\rho(x_k, x_l) < \varepsilon$ for all $k, l > N_\varepsilon$.

Every convergence sequence is Cauchy, but a Cauchy sequence may not be convergent unless the metric space is complete, as defined below.

Definition A.2.5 A metric space (S, ρ) is said to be complete if every Cauchy sequence in (S, ρ) has a limit in (S, ρ). □

Here are two examples of metric space that are not complete.

Example A.2.4 Consider the set of all sequences $x = \{\xi_1, \xi_2, \ldots, \xi_k, \ldots\}$ in which only a few numbers of elements are not equal to zero, and we define metric

$$\rho_\infty(x, y) = \max_k |\xi_k - \eta_k|.$$

Let $x_k = \{1, 1/2, \ldots, 1/k, 0, 0, \ldots\}$. It is a Cauchy sequence since for $k \neq l$, $\rho_\infty(x_k, x_l) = \max_{k,l}\{1/(k+1), 1/(l+1)\}$ that tends to zero as $k, l \to \infty$. However, it can not have a limit that only has a finite number of nonzero terms. Thus, the metric space is not complete.

Example A.2.5 On $C[0, 1]$ define a metric

$$\rho_1(f, g) = \int_0^1 |f(x) - g(x)| dx.$$

Consider the sequence, $k \geq 2$,

$$f_k(x) = \begin{cases} 0, & \text{if } x \leq \frac{1}{2} - \frac{1}{k} \\ k(x - \frac{1}{2}) + 1, & \text{if } \frac{1}{2} - \frac{1}{k} < x \leq \frac{1}{2} \\ 1, & \text{if } \frac{1}{2} < x \leq 1. \end{cases}$$

See the plots of functions $f_k(x)$ with $= 2, 3, 4$ in Fig. A.1. Note that when $l > k \geq 2$,

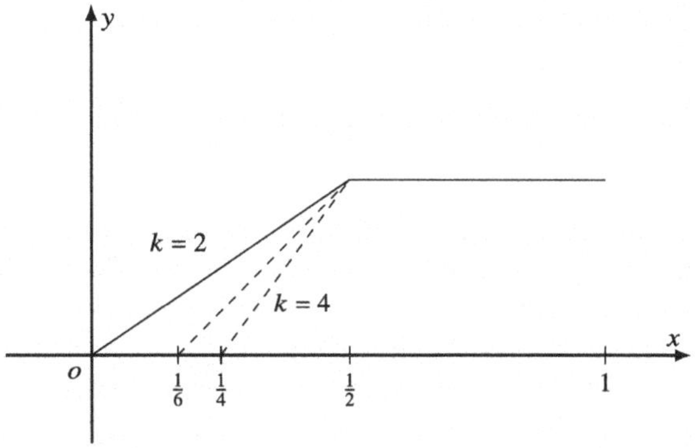

Fig. A.1 $f_k(x)$ with $k = 2, 3, 4$

$$\begin{aligned}\rho_1(f_k, f_l) &= \int_0^1 |f_k(x) - f_l(x)|dx \\ &= \int_{1/2-1/k}^{1/2-1/l} \left|k\left(x - \frac{1}{2}\right) + 1\right| dx + \int_{1/2-1/l}^{1/2} \left|(l-k)\left(\frac{1}{2} - x\right)\right| dx \\ &= \frac{1}{2}\left(\frac{1}{k} - \frac{1}{l}\right) \to 0,\end{aligned}$$

when $k, l \to \infty$. This is also true for $k > l$ obviously. Thus, $\{f_k(x)\}$ is Cauchy in $(C[0, 1], \rho_1)$.

Now suppose that $\{f_k(x)\}$ has a limit function $f(x)$ under ρ_1 that is continuous on $[0, 1]$. Observe that

$$\begin{aligned}\rho_1(f_k, f) = &\int_0^{1/2-1/k} |f(x)|dx + \int_{1/2-1/k}^{1/2} |f_k(x) - f(x)|dx + \int_{1/2}^1 |f(x) - 1|dx \\ &\to 0,\end{aligned}$$

as $k \to \infty$, implying that

$$f(x) = \begin{cases} 0, & \text{if } 0 < x < \frac{1}{2} \\ 1, & \text{if } \frac{1}{2} < x \leq 1. \end{cases}$$

But such $f(x)$ is impossible to be continuous, so the sequence has no limit in $C[0, 1]$ under metric ρ_1.

It seems that it is the continuity that hamstrings the completeness of the metric space. Let us abandon it and consider the set of all bounded functions on $[0, 1]$ with metric ρ_1. Unfortunately, this metric space is not complete too, as illustrated by the following example,

$$f_k(x) = \begin{cases} \sqrt{k}, & \text{if } 0 < x \leq \frac{1}{k} \\ 1/\sqrt{x}, & \text{if } \frac{1}{k} < x \leq 1. \end{cases}$$

This sequence is Cauchy, and it does not converge to any bounded function but to the function,

$$f(x) = \begin{cases} 0, & \text{if } x = 0 \\ 1/\sqrt{x}, & \text{if } 0 < x \leq 1. \end{cases}$$

In view of the unboundedness of the above limit function, let us further extend the set to include unbounded functions for which an improper integral exists, and interpret the integral under ρ_1 as an improper integral when necessary. The metric space so obtained again is not complete because the metric ρ_1 is defined in terms of the Riemann integral. One can construct sequences of functions which have, as limits, functions with an infinite number of finite discontinuities on [0, 1]. Such limit functions are not Riemann integral, and in order to proceed further, we have to invoke the more general Lebesgue integral.

Example A.2.6 (1) The space $\mathbb{R}$ with metric $\rho_1(x, y) = |x - y|$ is complete since the limits of rational sequences lead to the real numbers. This is a celebrated and fundamental result in analysis and will simply be assumed known. (2) Consequently, $\mathbb{R}^n$ with metric $\rho_1(x, y) = \sum_{i=1}^{n} |x_i - y_i|, x = (x_1, \ldots, x_n)^\top$ and $y = (y_1, \ldots, y_n)^\top$, is complete too.

Example A.2.7 Consider $C[0, 1]$ again but with metric

$$\rho_\infty(f, g) = \max_{x \in [0,1]} |f(x) - g(x)|.$$

This metric space is complete because the uniform limit of a sequence of continuous functions is continuous. To see this, let $\{f_k(x)\}$ be a Cauchy sequence in $C[0, 1]$, so that

$$\rho_\infty(f_k, f_l) = \max_{x \in [0,1]} |f_k(x) - f_l(x)| \to 0,$$

as $k, l \to \infty$. For every fixed $x \in [0, 1]$, the values of $\{f_k(x)\}$ will form a Cauchy sequence of real numbers. Thus, it has a limit, denoted by $f(x)$, and this determines a function on [0, 1].

We next show $f_k(x) \to f(x)$ uniformly on [0, 1]. For any given $\varepsilon > 0$, take N large such that, for all $k, l \geq N$, $|f_k(x) - f_l(x)| < \varepsilon$, for all $x \in [0, 1]$. Now let $l \to \infty$ for fixed x, giving

$$|f_k(x) - f(x)| < \varepsilon,$$

for all $k \geq N$ and all $x \in [0, 1]$. This means that $f_k(x) \to f(x)$ uniformly on [0, 1] as $k \to \infty$.

The final step is to show the continuity of $f(x)$. Let $x_0 \in [0, 1]$ be any point. It follows from the continuity of $f_k(x)$ at x_0 that, for any $\varepsilon > 0, \exists\, \delta > 0$, whenever $|x - x_0| < \delta$, $|f_k(x) - f_k(x_0)| < \varepsilon$. Also, due to uniform convergence, an N is chosen such that $|f_k(x) - f(x)| < \varepsilon$ for all $k \geq N$ and $x \in [0, 1]$. Thus,

$$|f(x) - f(x_0)| \leq |f(x) - f_k(x)| + |f_k(x) - f_k(x_0)| + |f_k(x_0) - f(x_0)|,$$

and each term on the right is less than ε when $|x - x_0| < \delta$ and $k \geq N$, so that $f(x)$ is continuous at x_0 and hence on $[0, 1]$.

A subset of a metric space is *closed* if the set contains the limit of every convergent sequence in the set. The *closure* of a set A, denoted by $\bar{A}$, is the set A together with the limits of all convergent sequences. If (S, ρ) is a complete metric space and (A, ρ) is a subspace of (S, ρ), then (A, ρ) is complete if and only if A is a closed set in (S, ρ).

Definition A.2.6 A subset A of the metric space (S, ρ) is said to be dense in (S, ρ) if, for every $x \in S$ and $\varepsilon > 0$, there exists a $y \in A$ such that $\rho(x, y) < \varepsilon$. □

In the real line $\mathbb{R}$ with the metric ρ_1, the rational numbers are a dense subset. Every real number can be approximated as close as we desire by a rational number. Similarly, in the vector space $\mathbb{R}^n$ with any metric, the set of vectors with rational coordinates is dense. More importantly, as will be seen in the next section in the Weierstrass theorem, the set of all polynomials is dense in $C[0, 1]$ with metric ρ_∞.

Theorem A.2.1 *Any incomplete metric space (S, ρ) can be embedded, as a dense subset, in a complete metric space. The latter is called a completion of (S, ρ). Any two completions are isometric and hence we may speak of the completion of (S, ρ).*

□

See Milne (1980) for the proof. Next, we introduce the concept of separable spaces that is motivated by the fact that all rational numbers on the axis are countable (that is, one may establish a one-one correspondence between all rational numbers and positive integers), whereas all real numbers are uncountable.

Definition A.2.7 A metric space is said to be separable if it contains a countable subset which is dense. A separable space may contain more than one set which is dense and countable. □

Example A.2.8 As mentioned before, the set of all polynomials is dense in $C[0, 1]$ with metric ρ_∞. Moreover, for each polynomial in $[0, 1]$ we can find a polynomial with rational coefficients that will approximate it as close as we desire. The set of polynomials with rational coefficients is countable, hence we conclude that $C[0, 1]$ with metric ρ_∞ is separable.

Example A.2.9 The space of infinite sequences

$$\left\{ x = (\xi_1, \ldots, \xi_n, \ldots), \sum_{n=1}^{\infty} \xi_n^2 < \infty \right\}$$

with metric ρ_2 is separable. To see this, let A be the subset of sequences of the form $(\alpha_1, \alpha_2, \ldots, \alpha_n, 0, 0, \ldots)$ having only a finite number of none-zero entries and in which the α_i are rational numbers. Let $x = (\xi_1, \ldots, \xi_n, \ldots)$ be an arbitrary element in the space. Since $\sum_{n=1}^{\infty} \xi_n^2 < \infty$, for any $\varepsilon > 0$, there exists an integer $N > 0$ such that

$$\sum_{i=N+1}^{\infty} \xi_i^2 < \frac{1}{2}\varepsilon^2.$$

Now choose an element $\tilde{x} = (\alpha_1, \alpha_2, \ldots, \alpha_N, 0, 0, \ldots)$ such that

$$\sum_{i=1}^{N} (\xi_i - \alpha_i)^2 < \frac{1}{2}\varepsilon^2.$$

We then have $\rho_2(x, \tilde{x}) < \varepsilon$. Because the set of finitely nonzero sequences with rational components is countable and we have shown that it is dense in $\{x, \rho_2(x, 0) < \infty\}$ where 0 is the sequence of zeros, the space is separable.

Example A.2.10 The space of bounded infinite sequences with the metric ρ_∞ is not separable. Consider the set $S = \{x = (\xi_1, \ldots, \xi_n, \ldots)\}$ in which ξ_i is either 1 or 0. This set is uncountable since we may consider the sequence as a binary representation of a number in $[0, 1]$. For any two different points $x, y \in S$, $\rho_\infty(x, y) = 1$. Now suppose there is a countable dense subset A in the space. Surround each of the elements of A with an open ball with a radius of $1/2$. Since S is uncountable, there are at least two elements of S that are included in one ball. This is impossible.

Most of the metric spaces that will be of value to us are separable, as we shall meet in the applications of series estimation, since such spaces deliver a countable basis.

One might think that the boundedness of a set is a strong property but in function space we need more stringent conditions. Consider a closed and bounded interval $[a, b]$ of the real line. For any $\varepsilon > 0$, one can find a finite number of points $x_n \in [a, b]$ such that for any $x \in [a, b]$, there exists x_n such that $|x - x_n| < \varepsilon$. For example, the point set $x_n = a + n(b - a)/N$, $n = 1, \ldots, N - 1$, will do if $(b - a)/N < \varepsilon$. This property illustrated right here is that of total boundedness.

Definition A.2.8 A subset A of a metric space (S, ρ) is said to be totally bounded if, for every $\varepsilon > 0$, A contains a finite set A_ε called an ε-net, such that for each $x \in S$, there is a $y \in A_\varepsilon$ such that $\rho(x, y) < \varepsilon$.

According to the definition we have several properties about totally bounded sets:

(a) Totally bounded set is bounded.
(b) Suppose A is totally bounded. For any given $\varepsilon > 0$, we may have a finite subset of A as an ε-net of A.
(c) Any totally bounded set A in a metric space (S, ρ) is separable.

In fact, (a) suppose that $A \subset S$ is totally bounded and (S, ρ) is a metric space and $\{x_1, \ldots, x_{n_0}\}$ is a 1-net of A. Then, for any $x \in A$, there is a x_k such that $\rho(x, x_k) < 1$. Thus,

$$\begin{aligned}\rho(x, x_1) &\le \rho(x, x_k) + \rho(x_k, x_1)\\ &\le 1 + \max_{1\le i,j\le n_0} \rho(x_i, x_j) \equiv d,\end{aligned}$$

which implies that all elements of A is covered by a ball $B(x_1, d)$. The assertion holds.

To show (b), note that for any given $\varepsilon > 0$, there is a finite $(\varepsilon/2)$-net of A, $\{x_1, \ldots, x_{n_0}\}$. Take any $\tilde{x}_k \in A \cap B(x_k, \varepsilon/2)$, $k = 1, 2, \ldots, x_{n_0}$. Then, $\{\tilde{x}_1, \ldots, \tilde{x}_{n_0}\}$ is a finite subset ε-net of A.

For (c), let A_n be a finite $(1/n)$-net of A and suppose $A_n \subset A$ due to (b). Note that $\cup_n A_n$ is a countable subset of A. For any $x \in A$, there exists $x_n \in A_n$ such that $\rho(x, x_n) < 1/n$. Thus, $x_n \to x$ and then the countable subset $\cup_n A_n$ is dense in A. The assertion holds.

The following is an example of a subset of a metric space which is bounded but not totally bounded.

Example A.2.11 Consider the space ℓ^2 of infinite sequences defined in Examples A.1.4 and A.2.2, $\{x = (\xi_1, \ldots, \xi_n, \ldots), \sum_{n=1}^{\infty} \xi_n^2 < \infty\}$ with metric ρ_2. The set of unit vectors e_k with unity in the kth place is bounded but not totally bounded. For $j \ne k$, we have $\rho_2(e_j, e_k) = \sqrt{2}$. Suppose an ε-net existed for $\varepsilon = 1/2$, then this would imply that $A_{1/2}$ contains points which are distant less than 1/2 from e_k, or equivalently, that $A_{1/2}$ must have points in each of the balls $B(e_k, 1/2)$. But the balls $B(e_k, 1/2)$ and $B(e_j, 1/2)$ are disjoint for $k \ne j$ and are at least countably infinite. Therefore a finite ε-net does not exist and the set is not totally bounded. Every totally bounded set is bounded, but as the example shows the converse is not true. Totally boundedness is a much stronger condition than boundedness.

Definition A.2.9 A metric space (S, ρ) is said to be compact (or sequentially compact) if it is complete and totally bounded. □

Compactness can be defined in several different ways, and it is a topological property. Sequential compactness for a metric space is coined because if a set A is compact in a metric space (S, ρ) every infinite sequence in A has a convergent subsequence with a limit in A.

Example A.2.12 (1) If A is a finite subset of a metric space then A is compact, for A is its own ε-net. (2) A set A on the real line $\mathbb{R}$ with the usual metric is compact if, and only if, it is closed and bounded. (This is a famous result in the analysis due to Heine and Borel. It can be extended to $(\mathbb{R}^n, \rho_2)$, that is, a bounded and closed subset of $(\mathbb{R}^n, \rho_2)$ is compact.) (3) In Example A.2.7 we have shown that $C[0, 1]$ with ρ_∞ is complete. Can we find a totally bounded subset? The closed ball $B(0, 1)$ will not do, since it is not totally bounded, and therefore, $B(0, 1)$ is not compact. Let us consider the set of functions that are Lipschitz, i.e., $|f(x) - f(y)| \le L|x - y|$ (the so-called Lipschitz condition). It can be shown that this set is totally bounded by exhibiting a finite set of piecewise linear functions that form a ε-net (see Exercise 3.2 9(d) in Milne, 1980). Thus, the set is compact. A more general result of this type exists called the Arzela-Ascoli theorem which states that compact subsets comprise those continuous functions which are (uniformly) bounded and equicontinuous.

Definition A.2.10 A collection of functions $f(x)$ defined on a closed interval is equicontinuous if, for any $\varepsilon > 0$, there exists a $\delta > 0$, such that $|x - y| < \delta$ implies $|f(x) - f(y)| < \varepsilon$ for all f in the collection. □

Theorem A.2.2 *A set* $A \subset C[a, b]$ *with metric* $\rho_\infty(f, g) = \max_{x\in[a,b]} |f(x) - g(x)|$ *is sequentially compact if and only if the following two conditions hold.*

(a) The set A *is uniformly bounded, that is, there exists a constant* K *such that for any* $f(x) \in A$, $|f(x)| \le K$, $\forall x \in [a, b]$.
(b) The set A *is equicontinuous.* □

Proof *Necessity*. Suppose $A \subset C[a, b]$ is sequentially compact. Then, A is bounded and Condition (a) holds. Now, let us consider Condition (b). For any $\varepsilon > 0$, there is a finite $(\varepsilon/3)$-net of A, $\{f_1(x), \ldots, f_{n_0}(x)\}$. Because $f_k(x)$ is continuous on $[a, b]$, it is uniformly continuous, and thus $\{f_1(x), \ldots, f_{n_0}(x)\}$ is equicontinuous. Then, for this $\varepsilon > 0$, there exists a $\delta > 0$, whenever $|x - y| < \delta$ we have

$$|f_k(x) - f_k(y)| < \frac{1}{3}\varepsilon,$$

for all $k = 1, \ldots, n_0$.

Taking any $f(x) \in A$, there is some $f_k(x)$ such that

$$|f(x) - f_k(x)| < \frac{1}{3}\varepsilon, \quad x \in [a, b].$$

Now, for any $x, y \in [a, b]$ and $|x - y| < \delta$, we have

$$\begin{aligned}|f(x) - f(y)| &\le |f(x) - f_k(x)| + |f_k(x) - f_k(y)| + |f_k(y) - f(y)| \\ &< \frac{1}{3}\varepsilon + \frac{1}{3}\varepsilon + \frac{1}{3}\varepsilon = \varepsilon.\end{aligned}$$

Since ε is arbitrary and δ depends on ε only, A is equicontinuous.

Sufficiency. Let A be uniformly bounded and equicontinuous. For any $\varepsilon > 0$, there exists a $\delta > 0$, whenever $|x - y| < \delta$,

$$|f(x) - f(y)| < \varepsilon \tag{A.2.1}$$

holds for all $f \in A$. Let n be a positive integer such that $(b - a)/n < \delta$. Partition $[a, b]$ into n equally spaced subintervals, $a = x_0 < x_1 < \cdots < x_n = b$. Thus, when both x and y are in the same subinterval, (A.2.1) holds.

For each $f(x) \in A$, construct a continuous function $f_n(x)$ and

$$f_n(x) = \begin{cases} f(x_k), \text{ if } x = x_k; \\ \text{linear}, \ x \in [x_k, x_{k+1}]. \end{cases}$$

If $f(x_k) \le f(x_{k+1})$, on $[x_k, x_{k+1}]$ we have

$$f(x_k) \le f_n(x) \le f(x_{k+1});$$

then for any $x \in [x_k, x_{k+1}]$,

$$f(x) - f(x_{k+1}) \le f(x) - f_n(x) \le f(x) - f(x_k).$$

In the converse case where $f(x_k) \ge f(x_{k+1})$, on $[x_k, x_{k+1}]$ we have

$$f(x_k) \ge f_n(x) \ge f(x_{k+1});$$

then for any $x \in [x_k, x_{k+1}]$,

$$f(x) - f(x_{k+1}) \ge f(x) - f_n(x) \ge f(x) - f(x_k).$$

Therefore, regardless of what happens we always have

$$|f(x) - f_n(x)| \le \max\{|f(x) - f(x_k)|, |f(x) - f(x_{k+1})|\} < \varepsilon.$$

And this holds actually for all $x \in [a, b]$, so that $\rho_\infty(f_n, f) < \varepsilon$, and the set $\{f_n(x)\}$ is a ε-net of A. Moreover, because of Condition (a),

$$|f_n(x)| \le |f(x)| + |f(x) - f_n(x)| < K + \varepsilon,$$

which says that the set $\{f_n(x)\}$ is uniformly bounded.

Notice that $f_n(x)$ is a broken-line that is determined by $n + 1$ vertical coordinates; the set $\{f_n(x)\}$ thus has a one-one correspondence with a bounded subset in $\mathbb{R}^{n+1}$ (that is sequentially compact by Example A.2.12). Accordingly, the set $\{f_n(x)\}$ is sequentially compact in $C[a, b]$, hence A is sequentially compact because the set $\{f_n(x)\}$ is a ε-net of A. □

A.3 Normed Vector Spaces

In this section, we introduce the concept of norm and then normed vector space that is a metric space with metric induced by the norm.

Definition A.3.1 A semi-norm on a vector space V is a real-valued function, $\|x\|$, defined for all $x \in V$ and which satisfies the following axioms:

(a) $\|x\| \geq 0$; $\|x\| = 0$ if $x = 0$;
(b) $\|x + y\| \leq \|x\| + \|y\|$;
(c) $\|\lambda x\| = |\lambda| \, \|x\|$, for any scalar λ.

A semi-norm $\| \cdot \|$ is called a norm if and only if $\|x\| = 0$ only for $x = 0$.

A normed vector space, denoted by $(V, \| \cdot \|)$, consists of a vector space V and a norm on V. □

Axiom (a) requires that the semi-norm of a vector is nonnegative and that the zero vector has zero semi-norm. Axiom (b) is a version of the triangle inequality for a vector space. Axiom (c) requires that the semi-norm of the vector λx should be $|\lambda|$ times the semi-norm of x, which is in accord with our intuition of multiplication by a scalar "stretching" a vector.

A normed vector space gives a natural metric by letting

$$\rho(x, y) = \|x - y\|.$$

It is not difficult to show that such defined $\rho(x, y)$ satisfies the axioms of a metric. Furthermore, $\rho(x, 0) = \|x - 0\| = \|x\|$, implying the norm of a vector is the distance from the origin to x.

Thus, a normed space is a particular type of metric space and we may apply all our previous concepts associated with metric spaces to normed vector spaces. It is important to note that there are metrics that are not generated by a norm in the above sense (one example is $d(x, y)$ in Example A.2.1(5)).

As for metric spaces, a single vector space V can generate several different normed vector spaces having different norm functions, $(V, \| \cdot \|_1)$ and $(V, \| \cdot \|_2)$, say. A *normed subspace* of a normed vector space V is always taken to mean an algebraic subspace of V having the same norm function as the parent space.

Since a normed vector space is a metric space, we can consider the questions of convergence of sequences, completeness, completion, separability, denseness and compactness to be settled. For example, in a normed vector space, a sequence of vectors $\{x_k\}$ converges to a vector x if $\|x_k - x\| \to 0$ as $k \to \infty$. This is called *convergence w.r.t. the norm* or *strong convergence*.

A complete normed vector space is called a *Banach space*. A subspace of a Banach space is itself a Banach space if and only if it is closed.

Example A.3.1 On $\mathbb{R}^n$ we define a family of norms by

$$\|x\|_p = \left(\sum_{i=1}^{n} |\xi_i|^p \right)^{1/p}, \quad 1 \leq p < \infty,$$

and

$$\|x\|_\infty = \max_{1 \leq i \leq n} (|\xi_i|).$$

The convergence w.r.t. these norms is equivalent componentwise convergence. The spaces $(\mathbb{R}^n, \|\cdot\|_p)$, $1 \leq p < \infty$, are Banach spaces. They are separable.

Example A.3.2 On the space of sequences for which $\sum_{i=1}^{\infty} |\xi_i|^p < \infty$ we define the norm

$$\|x\|_p = \left(\sum_{i=1}^{\infty} |\xi_i|^p\right)^{1/p}, \quad 1 \leq p < \infty.$$

This normed vector space is a Banach space usually denoted by ℓ_p. These spaces are separable.

Example A.3.3 On the space of bounded sequences we define the norm

$$\|x\|_\infty = \sup_{i \geq 1}(|\xi_i|).$$

This space is a Banach space usually denoted by ℓ_∞. It is not separable.

Example A.3.4 The space $C[0, 1]$ with ρ_∞ is a Banach space. Similarly, the Banach space of n-times continuously differentiable functions on $[0, 1]$ with

$$\|f\| = \sup_{x \in [0,1]} \sum_{k=0}^{n} |f^{(k)}(x)|$$

is usually denoted by $C^n[0, 1]$. These space are separable.

Example A.3.5 For the functions $f(x)$ defined on $[0, 1]$ for which

$$\int_0^1 |f(x)|^p dx < \infty, \qquad 1 \leq p < \infty,$$

we define the norm

$$\|f\|_p = \left(\int_0^1 |f(x)|^p dx\right)^{1/p}.$$

As we have already indicated in Example A.2.5, completion of this space involves the notion of Lebesgue integration. With this proviso we can say that the space of functions which are pth power integrable with the indicated norm is a Banach space. Clearly, functions can be identified by the norm up to a set of measure zero; these functions are called in an equivalent class. Let $L^p[0, 1]$ be the set of equivalent classes $f(x)$ such that $\|f\|_p$ defined above exists.

Appendix B
Approximation in Space C

This chapter gives approximation theorems in space C that include two well-known types of Weierstrass theorems and Jackson's theorems for polynomial approximations. While Bernstein polynomials are constructed to prove Weierstrass theorem, they may be used as a sieve method in nonparametric estimation particularly with shape restrictions. More importantly, we use the approximation order of the best approximation polynomials to a smooth function for the derivation of a convergence rate of the orthogonal polynomial series expansion of the smooth function in Appendix C. This is the main reason why we introduce the best approximation polynomials.

B.1 Weierstrass Theorem

Function space $C[a, b]$ defined in the preceding chapter is a collection of all functions continuous on $[a, b]$. One norm defined on $C[a, b]$ is the so-called *super norm*:

$$\|f\|_\infty = \sup_{x\in[a,b]} |f(x)|,$$

for any $f \in C[a, b]$, and therefore the distance of two functions in $C[a, b]$ is defined as

$$\|f - g\|_\infty = \sup_{x\in[a,b]} |f(x) - g(x)|,$$

which represents the maximum distance of the functions over $[a, b]$.

There are two forms of the Weierstrass theorem related with the space. One is stated in terms of algebraic polynomials, so-called the first Weierstrass theorem, and the other one is rephrased in terms of trigonometric polynomials, the second Weierstrass theorem.

Before showing the Weierstrass theorems, we introduce a crucial concept for continuous functions. The *modulus of continuity* of a continuous function measures

C. Dong and J. Gao, *Modern Series Methods in Econometrics and Statistics*, Advanced Studies in Theoretical and Applied Econometrics 45,
https://doi.org/10.1007/978-981-96-2822-3

its complexity of the intrinsic structure. Define the modulus of continuity for $f \in C[a, b]$ as,

$$\omega_f(\delta) = \sup_{\substack{|x-y|\leq\delta \\ x,y\in[a,b]}} |f(x) - f(y)|,$$

for $\delta > 0$.

Proposition B.1.1 (Properties of the modulus of continuity)

(a) $\omega_f(\delta)$ *is increasing in* δ*;*
(b) $f(x)$ *is uniformly continuous on* (a, b) *if and only if* $\lim_{\delta\to 0}\omega_f(\delta) = 0$*;*
(c) $\omega_f(\delta_1 + \delta_2) \leq \omega_f(\delta_1) + \omega_f(\delta_2)$*;*
(d) *For any positive integer* m*,* $\omega_f(m\delta) \leq m\,\omega_f(\delta)$*;*
(e) *For any* $\lambda > 0$*,* $\omega_f(\lambda\delta) \leq (\lambda + 1)\omega_f(\delta)$*;*
(f) $f(x) \in Lip_M(\alpha)$ *is equivalent to* $\omega_f(\delta) \leq M\delta^\alpha$*.* □

Proof These properties are easily to prove. Property (a) holds because for any $\delta > \delta' \geq 0$, we have $\{x, y \in [a, b] : |x - y| \leq \delta'\} \subset \{x, y \in [a, b] : |x - y| \leq \delta\}$, that implies, for any continuous function f, $\omega_f(\delta) \geq \omega_f(\delta')$ by the definition of modulus.

For (b), if f is uniformly continuous, for any $\varepsilon > 0$, there exists a $\delta > 0$ such that $|f(x) - f(y)| < \varepsilon$ whenever $|x - y| < \delta$. Thus, $\omega_f(\delta) < \varepsilon$ by the definition, and hence $\omega_f(\delta') < \varepsilon$ for all $\delta' < \delta$ by the monotonicity. This means $\lim_{\delta\to 0}\omega_f(\delta) = 0$. On the other hand, if $\lim_{\delta\to 0}\omega_f(\delta) = 0$, for any $\varepsilon > 0$, there exists a $\delta > 0$ such that $\omega_f(\delta') < \varepsilon$ whenever $\delta' < \delta$. We then have $|f(x) - f(y)| \leq \omega_f(|x - y|) < \varepsilon$ whenever $|x - y| < \delta$, implying the uniform continuity of f.

For (c), note that if $|x - y| \leq \delta_1 + \delta_2$, we can find at least a point z such that $|x - z| \leq \delta_1$ and $|y - z| \leq \delta_2$. Thus, $|f(x) - f(y)| \leq |f(x) - f(z)| + |f(y) - f(z)| \leq \omega_f(\delta_1) + \omega_f(\delta_2)$. The assertion then follows immediately.

Property (d) is a consequence of Property (c). For Property (e), notice that if $d - 1 < \lambda \leq d$ for some positive integer d, $\omega_f(\lambda\delta) \leq \omega_f(d\delta) \leq d\,\omega_f(\delta) \leq (\lambda + 1)\omega_f(\delta)$. Lastly, $f(x) \in \mathrm{Lip}_M(\alpha)$ means that $|f(x) - f(y)| \leq M|x - y|^\alpha$, so that $\omega_f(\delta) \leq M \sup_{|x-y|<\delta} |x - y|^\alpha = M\delta^\alpha$. Conversely, if $\omega_f(\delta) \leq M\delta^\alpha$, $|f(x) - f(y)| \leq \omega_f(|x - y|) \leq M|x - y|^\alpha$. □

Theorem B.1.1 (Weierstrass Theorem, the first, 1885) *Assume that* $g(x) \in C[a, b]$*. For any given* $\varepsilon > 0$*, there exists a polynomial* $P(x)$ *such that*

$$\|g(x) - P(x)\|_\infty < \varepsilon.$$

There are several versions of the proof for the theorem, among which Chebyshev's is the best known. To prove Theorem B.1.1, one only needs to consider $C[0, 1]$ since $x = (b - a)t + a$ maps $[0, 1]$ into $[a, b]$. The proof of the Weierstrass theorem we present here is due to the great Russian mathematician S. N. Bernstein in 1912. Bernstein's proof is of interest to us for a variety of reasons; perhaps most important is that Bernstein actually displays a sequence of polynomials that approximate a given $g(x) \in C[0, 1]$.

Define Bernstein polynomials for $g(x) \in C[0, 1]$, with $n = 1, 2, \ldots$,

$$B_n(x; g) = \sum_{k=0}^{n} g\left(\frac{k}{n}\right) C_n^k x^k (1 - x)^{n-k}. \tag{B.1.1}$$

It suffices to show that

$$\lim_{n\to\infty} \|g(x) - B_n(x; g)\|_\infty = 0.$$

Proof (*Method One*) Notice the binomial formula,

$$(x + y)^n = \sum_{k=0}^{n} C_n^k x^k y^{n-k}. \tag{B.1.2}$$

Differentiating w.r.t. x on both sides of (B.1.2) and multiplying x, we have

$$nx(x + y)^{n-1} = \sum_{k=0}^{n} k C_n^k x^k y^{n-k}. \tag{B.1.3}$$

Similarly, differentiating (B.1.2) twice w.r.t. x and multiplying x^2 yield

$$n(n-1)x^2(x + y)^{n-2} = \sum_{k=0}^{n} k(k-1) C_n^k x^k y^{n-k}. \tag{B.1.4}$$

Denote $r_{n,k}(x) = C_n^k x^k (1 - x)^{n-k}$, $0 \le k \le n$. Then from (B.1.2)–(B.1.4) we have

$$\begin{aligned}
&\sum_{k=0}^{n} r_{n,k}(x) = 1,\\
&\sum_{k=0}^{n} k r_{n,k}(x) = nx,\\
&\sum_{k=0}^{n} k(k-1) r_{n,k}(x) = n(n-1)x^2.
\end{aligned}$$

Hence,

$$\begin{aligned}
&\sum_{k=0}^{n} (k - nx)^2 r_{n,k}(x)\\
=& \sum_{k=0}^{n} k^2 r_{n,k}(x) - 2nx \sum_{k=0}^{n} k r_{n,k}(x) + n^2x^2 \sum_{k=0}^{n} r_{n,k}(x)\\
=& n^2x^2 - 2nx\, nx + n(n-1)x^2 + nx\\
=& nx(1 - x).
\end{aligned}$$

We may assume that $|g(x)| \le M$ on $[0, 1]$. By the uniform continuity, for $\forall\, \varepsilon > 0$, $\exists\, \delta > 0$,

$$|g(x) - g(x')| < \varepsilon, \quad \text{whenever } |x - x'| < \delta.$$

Then,

$$|g(x) - B_n(x; g)| = \left| \sum_{k=0}^{n} \left[g(x) - g\left(\frac{k}{n}\right) \right] r_{n,k}(x) \right|$$

$$\le \left| \sum_{|k-nx|<n\delta} \left[g(x) - g\left(\frac{k}{n}\right) \right] r_{n,k}(x) \right| + \left| \sum_{|k-nx|\ge n\delta} \left[g(x) - g\left(\frac{k}{n}\right) \right] r_{n,k}(x) \right|.$$

The first term is bounded above by $\varepsilon \sum_{|k-nx|<n\delta} r_{n,k}(x) \le \varepsilon$; the second term is bounded above by

$$2M \sum_{|k-nx|\ge n\delta} r_{n,k}(x) \le \frac{2M}{n^2\delta^2} \sum_{|k-nx|\ge n\delta} (k - nx)^2 r_{n,k}(x)$$

$$\le \frac{2M}{n^2\delta^2} \sum_{k=0}^{n} (k - nx)^2 r_{n,k}(x) = \frac{2M}{n^2\delta^2} nx(1 - x) \le \frac{M}{2n\delta^2},$$

which also can be arbitrarily small when δ is determined in the first term and then n is chosen sufficiently large. This finishes the proof. □

The second proof given below makes use of Bernoulli stochastic trials and Chebyshev inequality.

Proof (*Method Two*) Let $x \in [0, 1]$. Suppose there is a stochastic trial S and E is an associated event with $x = \mathbb{P}(E)$. Consider Bernoulli independent trials of S with n replicates. Let X_i be a random variable associated with the ith trial,

$$X_i = \begin{cases} 1, & \text{if } E \text{ happens}, \\ 0, & \text{otherwise}. \end{cases}$$

Then $S_n = X_1 + \cdots + X_n$ is the number that the E happens in the n trials, and S_n/n is the frequency, $\mathbb{E}[S_n/n] = x$. Moreover, $\mathbb{P}(S_n = k) = C_n^k x^k (1 - x)^{n-k} \equiv r_{n,k}(x)$, $k = 0, 1, \ldots, n$, and

$$\mathbb{E}[g(S_n/n)] = \sum_{k=0}^{n} g(k/n) r_{n,k}(x) = B_n(x; g).$$

It follows from Chebyshev inequality that

$$\mathbb{P}\left(\left|\frac{1}{n}S_n - x\right| \geq \delta\right) \leq \frac{1}{\delta^2}\mathrm{Var}\left(\frac{1}{n}S_n\right) = \frac{x(1-x)}{n\delta^2} \leq \frac{1}{4n\delta^2}, \quad \forall\, \delta > 0.$$

Then,

$$\begin{aligned}
|g(x) - B_n(x; g)| &= \left|g(x) - \mathbb{E}g\left(\frac{S_n}{n}\right)\right| \leq \mathbb{E}\left|g(x) - g\left(\frac{S_n}{n}\right)\right| \\
&= \mathbb{E}\left|g(x) - g\left(\frac{S_n}{n}\right)\right| I(|S_n/n - x| < \delta) \\
&\quad + \mathbb{E}\left|g(x) - g\left(\frac{S_n}{n}\right)\right| I(|S_n/n - x| \geq \delta) \\
&\leq \omega_g(\delta) + 2\|g\|_\infty \mathbb{E}[I(|S_n/n - x| \geq \delta)] \\
&= \omega_g(\delta) + 2\|g\|_\infty \mathbb{P}(|S_n/n - x| \geq \delta) \\
&\leq \omega_g(\delta) + \|g\|_\infty \frac{1}{2n\delta^2},
\end{aligned}$$

where $I(\cdot)$ is the indicator function.

For any $\forall\, \varepsilon > 0$, we choose $\delta > 0$ such that $\omega_g(\delta) < \varepsilon$; for this δ we may choose n large such that the second term is less than ε as well. □

There are other proofs, respectively, owe to Labesgue, Landau, Vallée-Poussin, Fejér, and Stone that we do not show here. Readers may find them in the literature, e.g., Landau's proof in Rudin (1976).

Generally, let us define polynomials associated with a sequence $\{b_{n,k}, k = 0, 1, \ldots, n\}$,

$$B_n(x) = \sum_{k=0}^{n} b_{n,k} r_{n,k}(x), \quad r_{n,k}(x) = C_n^k x^k (1-x)^{n-k}, \tag{B.1.5}$$

for $x \in [0, 1]$. Observe that

$$\begin{aligned}
r'_{n,0}(x) &= -n(1-x)^{n-1} = -n r_{n-1,0}(x), \\
r'_{n,k}(x) &= n r_{n-1,k-1}(x) - n r_{n-1,k}(x), \\
r'_{n,n}(x) &= n x^{n-1} = n r_{n-1,n-1}(x).
\end{aligned}$$

It follows that

$$B'_n(x) = n \sum_{k=0}^{n-1} (b_{n,k+1} - b_{n,k}) r_{n-1,k}(x). \tag{B.1.6}$$

Thus, (1) when $g(x) \in C[0, 1]$ is increasing (decreasing), so is $B_n(x; g)$; (2) when $\{b_{n,k}, k = 0, 1, \ldots, n\}$ is an increasing (decreasing) sequence, $B_n(x)$ in (B.1.5) is an increasing (decreasing) function on $[0, 1]$. It is noteworthy that the monotonicity of $\{b_{n,k}, k = 0, 1, \ldots, n\}$ is not a necessary condition for that of $B_n(x)$. For example, monotone increasing polynomial $B_3(x) = b_0(1-x)^3 + 3b_1 x(1-x)^2 + 3b_2 x^2(1 -$

$x) + b_3x^3$ does not imply $b_3 \geq b_2 \geq b_1 \geq b_0$ because it allows $b_2 < b_1$. Check for $b_0 = -1, b_1 = 0, b_2 = -2$ and $b_3 = 2$.

Similarly,

$$\begin{aligned}
r''_{n,0}(x) &= n(n-1)(1-x)^{n-2} = n(n-1)r_{n-2,0}(x),\\
r''_{n,1}(x) &= -2n(n-1)r_{n-2,0}(x) + n(n-1)r_{n-2,1}(x),\\
r''_{n,k}(x) &= n(n-1)[r_{n-2,k-2}(x) - 2r_{n-2,k-1}(x) + r_{n-2,k}(x)],\\
r''_{n,n-1}(x) &= n(n-1)[r_{n-2,n-3}(x) - 2r_{n-2,n-2}(x)],\\
r''_{n,n}(x) &= n(n-1)x^{n-2} = n(n-1)r_{n-2,n-2}(x).
\end{aligned}$$

Accordingly,

$$B''_n(x) = n(n-1)\sum_{k=0}^{n-2}(b_{n,k+2} - 2b_{n,k+1} + b_{n,k})r_{n-2,k}(x). \tag{B.1.7}$$

It then follows that (1) if $g(x) \in C[0, 1]$ is convex (concave), so is $B_n(x; g)$ for all n, and (2) if the sequence $\{b_{n,k}, k = 0, 1, \ldots, n\}$ satisfies $2b_{n,k+1} \leq (\geq) b_{n,k+2} + b_{n,k}$ for $0 \leq k \leq n-2$, then $B_n(x)$ in (B.1.5) is convex (concave). These merits of $B_n(x)$ can be used in nonparametric estimation with shape restriction. See, e.g., Ghosal et al. (2023).

We now give a more general result that is motivated by the observation from Bernstein polynomials. Most of the proofs of Weierstrass theorem can be unified in this general result. Recall that $B_n(x; g)$ defined before is associated with a function g in $C[0, 1]$. Accordingly, $B_n(x; g)$ can be viewed as an operator from $C[0, 1]$ to $C[0, 1]$, and we suppress x from $B_n(x; g)$ to emphasize g that generates the operator. $B_n(g)$ has the following properties:

(a) $B_n(f + g) = B_n(f) + B_n(g)$;
(b) $B_n(\alpha g) = \alpha B_n(g)$,
(c) $B_n(g)(x) \geq 0$, when $g(x)$ is positive, $\forall x$.

Properties (a) and (b) imply the linearity, while (c) means the positivity of $B_n(g)$. Operators satisfying these properties are called *linear and positive*.

Proposition B.1.2 *If operator T: $C[a, b] \mapsto C[a, b]$ is linear and positive, it is continuous.* □

Here, the continuity of T means when $\|g_n - g\|_\infty \to 0$, $\|T(g_n) - T(g)\|_\infty \to 0$ as $n \to \infty$, for any sequence $g_n(x)$ and function $g(x)$ in $C[a, b]$.

Proof Firstly, due to linearity and positivity, T is monotone. That is, if $f(x) \leq g(x)$, then $T(f) \leq T(g)$.

Secondly, for any $f \in C[a, b]$, since $-f, f \leq |f|$,

$$-T(f) \leq T(|f|), \text{ and } T(f) \leq T(|f|),$$

implying $|T(f)| \le T(|f|)$. Again, by monotonicity, $T(|f|) \le \|f\|_\infty T(1)$ where 1 is the constant function assuming 1 at any point. Thus,

$$\|T(f)\|_\infty \le \|f\|_\infty \|T(1)\|_\infty,$$

for any $f \in C[a, b]$. Finally, T is Lipschitz with constant $\|T(1)\|_\infty$,

$$\|T(f) - T(g)\|_\infty = \|T(f - g)\|_\infty \le \|f - g\|_\infty \|T(1)\|_\infty,$$

so that it is continuous. □

Bernstein's theorem is generalized very nicely when it is placed in this new setting. The following elegant theorem was proved independently by Bohman and Korovkin in, roughly, 1952.

Theorem B.1.2 (Bohman and Korovkin) *Let T_n: $C[0, 1] \mapsto C[0, 1]$ be a sequence of positive linear operators, and suppose that $T_n(f)$ converge uniformly to f in each of the three cases, $f_1(x) \equiv 1$, $f_2(x) = x$ and $f_3(x) = x^2$. Then $T_n(f) \to f$ uniformly for any $f(x) \in C[0, 1]$.* □

It is known that the operators such as $B_n(f)$ and the one used in Landau's proof fall into this category. In particular, $B_n(1) \equiv 1$, $B_n(x) \equiv x$ and $B_n(x^2) = x^2 + (x - x^2)/n \to x^2$ uniformly as $n \to \infty$.

Proof Let $x \in [0, 1]$ and let δ be a positive number. Let $t \in [0, 1]$. If $|t - x| > \delta$, then

$$\begin{aligned}|f(t) - f(x)| \le& \omega_f(|t - x|) \le (1 + \delta^{-1}|t - x|)\omega_f(\delta)\\ \le& (1 + \delta^{-2}|t - x|^2)\omega_f(\delta).\end{aligned}$$

Also, the inequality $|f(t) - f(x)| \le (1 + \delta^{-2}|t - x|^2)\omega_f(\delta)$ holds obviously for $|t - x| \le \delta$. It follows from the monotonicity of T_n that

$$\begin{aligned}|T_n(f)(x) - f(x)T_n(1)(x)| =& |(T_n(f - f(x))(x)| \le T_n(|f - f(x)|)(x)\\ \le& \omega_f(\delta)[T_n(1)(x) + \delta^{-2}T_n(|t - x|^2)(x)]\\ \le& \omega_f(\delta)[T_n(1)(x) + (\mu_n/\delta)^2],\end{aligned}$$

where $\mu_n^2 = \|T_n(|t - x|^2)(x)\|_\infty$.

If $\mu_n > 0$, take $\delta = \mu_n$. Then, $|T_n(f)(t) - f(x)T_n(1)(t)| \le \omega_f(\delta)\|T_n(1)(t) + 1\|_\infty$, and further

$$\begin{aligned}|T_n(f)(x) - f(x)| =& |T_n(f)(x) - f(x)T_n(1)(x) + f(x)T_n(1)(x) - f(x)|\\ \le& |T_n(f)(x) - f(x)T_n(1)(x)| + |f(x)T_n(1)(x) - f(x)|\\ \le& \omega_f(\delta)\|T_n(1)(x) + 1\|_\infty + \|f\|_\infty \|T_n(1)(x) - 1\|_\infty.\end{aligned}$$

If $\mu_n = 0$, then $|T_n(f)(x) - f(x)T_n(1)(x)| \leq \omega_f(\delta)T_n(1)(x)$ for any δ. Thus, $T_n(f)(x) = f(x)T_n(1)(x)$ by letting $\delta \to 0$. Consequently, $|T_n(f)(x) - f(x)| = |f(x)(T_n(1)(x) - 1)| \leq \|f\|_\infty \|T_n(1)(x) - 1\|_\infty \to 0$ as $n \to \infty$.

Note that

$$\begin{aligned}\mu_n^2 &= \|T_n(|t-x|^2)(x)\|_\infty = \|T_n(t^2)(x) - 2xT_n(t)(x) + x^2T_n(1)(x)\|_\infty \\ &\leq \|T_n(t^2)(x) - x^2\|_\infty + 2\|T_n(t)(x) - x\|_\infty + \|T_n(1)(x) - 1\|_\infty \\ &\to 0,\end{aligned}$$

as $n \to \infty$. Thus, for both cases that $\mu_n \to 0$ and $\mu_n = 0$, the assertion $\|T_n(f)(x) - f(x)\|_\infty \to 0$ holds. □

Next, to introduce the second Weierstrass theorem, we define and call

$$T(x) = a_0 + \sum_{j=1}^{k}(a_j \cos(jx) + b_j \sin(jx)) \tag{B.1.8}$$

a *trigonometric polynomial* of degree k if $a_k^2 + b_k^2 \neq 0$. Denote by $C_{2\pi}$ the collection of all continuous periodic functions on the real with period 2π. Clearly, $T(x) \in C_{2\pi}$.

Proposition B.1.3 *(a) The product of two trigonometric polynomials is a trigonometric polynomial with degree of the sum of the two; (b) If $T(x)$ is even, $T(x) = T(-x)$, then all $b_j = 0$. (c) If $T(x)$ is odd, $T(-x) = -T(x)$, then all $a_j = 0$.* □

The proposition can be shown straightforwardly and thus is omitted.

Theorem B.1.3 (Weierstrass Theorem, the second, 1885) *Suppose $f(x) \in C_{2\pi}$. For any $\varepsilon > 0$, there exists a trigonometric polynomial $T(x) \in C_{2\pi}$ such that*

$$\max_{x\in[-\pi,\pi]} |f(x) - T(x)| < \varepsilon.$$

Proof The proof can be implied from the first Weierstrass Theorem. Indeed, (1) if $f(x)$ is even, we consider the interval $[0, \pi]$. Let $x = \arccos(y)$, $y \in [-1, 1]$. Then $f(x) = f(\arccos(y))$ is continuous in y. By the first theorem, for any given $\varepsilon > 0$, there exists a polynomial $\sum_{k=0}^{n} c_k y^k$ such that

$$\max_{-1\leq y\leq 1} \left| f(\arccos(y)) - \sum_{k=0}^{n} c_k y^k \right| < \varepsilon,$$

or equivalently

$$\max_{0\leq x\leq \pi} \left| f(x) - \sum_{k=0}^{n} c_k \cos^k x \right| < \varepsilon.$$

Thus, $f(x)$ can be approximated well by an even trigonometric polynomial in view of the relationship among $\cos^k x$ and $\cos(jx)$.

(2) For any $f(x) \in C_{2\pi}$, both $[f(x) + f(-x)]\sin^2 x$ and $[f(x) - f(-x)]\sin x$ are even function. Thus, there are two even trigonometric polynomials $F_1(x)$ and $F_2(x)$ such that

$$|[f(x) + f(-x)]\sin^2 x - F_1(x)| < \varepsilon/2,$$
$$|[f(x) - f(-x)]\sin x - F_2(x)| < \varepsilon/2,$$

which is valid for any $x \in \mathbb{R}$. Or equivalently,

$$[f(x) + f(-x)]\sin^2 x = F_1(x) + \rho_1(x),$$
$$[f(x) - f(-x)]\sin x = F_2(x) + \rho_2(x),$$

which yield that $f(x)\sin^2 x = F_3(x) + \rho_3(x)$ where $F_3(x)$ is a trigonometric polynomial and $|\rho_3(x)| < \varepsilon/2$. Note that this holds for any $f(x)$, so $f(x - \pi/2)\sin^2 x = F_3(x) + \rho_3(x)$. Now we change $x \to x + \pi/2$, yielding

$$f(x)\cos^2 x = F_4(x) + \rho_4(x),$$

where $F_4(x) = F_3(x + \pi/2)$ and $\rho_4(x) = \rho_3(x + \pi/2)$. Combining the two expressions gives $f(x) = f(x)\sin^2 x + f(x)\cos^2 x = F_5(x) + \rho_5(x)$ where $F_5(x)$ is a trigonometric polynomial and $|\rho_5(x)| < \varepsilon$. □

The idea of the proof owes to Vallée-Poussin; it is also possible to derive the first given the second. In addition, there is a counterpart theorem to Bohman and Korovkin theorem in the case of continuous period functions, where $f_1(x) = 1$, $f_2(x) = \sin(x)$ and $f_3(x) = \cos(x)$.

B.2 Best Approximation Polynomials

Weierstrass theorem says that for any $g(x) \in C[a, b]$, we can choose a polynomial $p(x)$ such that $\|g(x) - P(x)\|_\infty$ is smaller than any given number. To achieve this target, however, the price we pay in general is that the order of the polynomial might have to be much high. It turns out that one may be interested in finding a polynomial with an order no more than a given number to have the best approximation in a sense that will be specified below. This is the so-called *best approximation polynomial* issue.

Let P_k be the set of all polynomials with order no higher than k and define for $g(x) \in C[a, b]$

$$E_k(g) = \inf_{p_k \in P_k} \|g(x) - p_k(x)\|_\infty.$$

Thus defined, $E_k(g)$ is the smallest uniform error approximating by polynomials with order no more than k. For each k, as shown in page 26 of Chap. 3 and proven in page 79 of Chap. 8 of Todd (1963), there exists a $p_k^* \in P_k$ such that $E_k(g) = \|g(x) - p_k^*(x)\|_\infty$ (known as Borel existence theorem (1905)). The $p_k^*(x)$ is called the best polynomial approximating to $g(x)$. We show here the existence of $p_k^*(x)$ as the consequence of a theorem below in the context of functional analysis.

Theorem B.2.1 *Let Y be a finite-dimensional subspace of a normed linear space V and $v \in V$. Then, there exists a (not necessarily unique) vector $y^* \in Y$ such that*

$$\|v - y^*\| = \min_{y \in Y} \|v - y\|.$$

Proof Since $0 \in Y$, if there exists such a y^* it must satisfy that $\|v - y^*\| \leq \|v\|$. Thus, it suffices to look for y^* in the compact set

$$K = \{y : \ \|y - v\| \leq \|v\|\}.$$

To do so, note that $f(y) = \|y - v\|$ is continuous because $|f(y_1) - f(y_2)| \leq \|y_1 - y_2\|$. Therefor, there exists a y^* at which $f(y)$ attains its minimum that finishes the proof. □

It follows immediately from Theorem B.2.1 that the best approximating polynomial $p_k^*(x)$ for any $g(x) \in C[a, b]$ exists since P_k is a finite-dimensional normed subspace of $C[a, b]$.

Corollary B.2.1 *For each $g(x) \in C[a, b]$ and fixed k, there exists a polynomial $p_k^*(x)$ of order no greater than k such that*

$$\|g - p_k^*\|_\infty = \min_{p_k \in P_k} \|g - p_k\|_\infty.$$

One may be concerned with the uniqueness of y^* in the above theorem. In fact, there is a sufficient condition under which the best approximation is unique. A norm $\|\cdot\|$ on a vector space V is said to be *strictly convex* if for any pair v and w, $v, w \in V$, and $v \neq w$ but $\|v\| = \|w\| = r$, we have $\|\lambda v + (1 - \lambda)w\| < r$ for any $\lambda \in (0, 1)$. If the norm in V in Theorem B.2.1 is strictly convex, then y^* is unique. Moreover, we have an equivalent condition for strictly convexity. A norm $\|\cdot\|$ in normed space V is strictly convex if and only if the triangle inequality is strict on nonparallel vectors; that is, if and only if

$$v \neq \alpha w, w \neq \alpha v, \forall \alpha, \Rightarrow \|v + w\| < \|v\| + \|w\|.$$

We firstly give a preliminary result about E_k by virtue of Bernstein polynomials.

Theorem B.2.2 *For any $g(x) \in C[0, 1]$,*

$$\|g(x) - B_k(x; g)\|_\infty \leq \frac{3}{2}\omega_g(k^{-1/2}),$$

where $B_k(x; g)$ *is the kth Bernstein polynomial constructed from g given by* (B.1.1). *Consequently,* $E_k(g) \le \frac{3}{2}\omega_g(k^{-1/2}) \to 0$ *as* $k \to \infty$. □

Proof Recall that $r_{k,\ell}(x) = C_k^\ell x^\ell (1-x)^{k-\ell}$. Notice that

$$
\begin{aligned}
|g(x) - B_k(x; g)| &= \left| \sum_{\ell=0}^{k} \left[g(x) - g\left(\frac{\ell}{k}\right) \right] r_{k,\ell}(x) \right| \\
&\le \sum_{\ell=0}^{k} \left| g(x) - g\left(\frac{\ell}{k}\right) \right| r_{k,\ell}(x) \\
&\le \sum_{\ell=0}^{k} \omega_g\left(\left| x - \frac{\ell}{k} \right| \right) r_{k,\ell}(x) \\
&\le \omega_g(k^{-1/2}) \sum_{\ell=0}^{k} \left(1 + k^{1/2} \left| x - \frac{\ell}{k} \right| \right) r_{k,\ell}(x) \\
&= \omega_g(k^{-1/2}) \left(1 + k^{1/2} \sum_{\ell=0}^{k} \left| x - \frac{\ell}{k} \right| r_{k,\ell}(x) \right)
\end{aligned}
$$

by virtue of the property of $\omega(\cdot)$ in preceding section, $\omega(\lambda\delta) \le (1+\lambda)\omega(\delta)$. Moreover, using the Cauchy-Schwarz inequality,

$$
\begin{aligned}
&\sum_{\ell=0}^{k} \left| x - \frac{\ell}{k} \right| r_{k,\ell}(x) \le \left(\sum_{\ell=0}^{k} \left| x - \frac{\ell}{k} \right|^2 r_{k,\ell}(x) \right)^{1/2} \left(\sum_{\ell=0}^{k} r_{k,\ell}(x) \right)^{1/2} \\
&= \left(\sum_{\ell=0}^{k} \left| x - \frac{\ell}{k} \right|^2 r_{k,\ell}(x) \right)^{1/2} = \left(\frac{1}{k^2} \sum_{\ell=0}^{k} |kx - \ell|^2 r_{k,\ell}(x) \right)^{1/2} \\
&= \left(\frac{1}{k^2} kx(1-x) \right)^{1/2} \le \frac{1}{2\sqrt{k}},
\end{aligned}
$$

due to the relationship derived in the proof of the first Weierstrass theorem. The first assertion follows while the second is its consequence. □

Analog to E_k, we may define the best approximation by trigonometric polynomials. Let H_k^* be the collection of all trigonometric polynomials with order no higher than k. For any $f(x) \in C_{2\pi}$, define

$$
E_k^*(f) = \inf_{T \in H_k^*} \| f(x) - T(x) \|_\infty .
$$

If $T^*(x) \in H_k^*$ is such that $\| f(x) - T^*(x) \|_\infty = E_k^*$, we say $T^*(x) \in H_k^*$ is the best approximation trigonometric polynomial to $f(x)$. The following results were reported in D. Jackson's doctoral dissertation thesis in 1911.

Theorem B.2.3 (Jackson's Basic Theorem) *If* $f(x) \in C_{2\pi}$, *then* $E_k^*(f) \leq C \omega_f(k^{-1})$ *where* C *is an absolute constant.* □

Theorem B.2.4 *If* $f(x) \in C_{2\pi}$ *and* $f(x) \in Lip_M(1)$, *then* $E_k^*(f) \leq Ck^{-1}$ *where* C *is an absolute constant.* □

Theorem B.2.5 *If* $f(x) \in C_{2\pi} \cap C^p(\mathbb{R})$, *i.e.,* f *is periodic and* $f^{(p)}$ *is continuous, then* $E_k^* \leq Ck^{-p}\omega_{f^{(p)}}(k^{-1})$. □

The last result is cited from Theorem 4.1 in Schultz (1969). It has a faster rate when the function is smooth and periodic. From a practical point of view, the periodicity assumption is restrictive whereas the following observation would release this anxiety.

Generally, we consider $f(x) \in C[a, b]$. Let

$$x = \frac{1}{2}[(b-a)t + b + a], \quad t \in [-1, 1]$$

which is a one-one mapping of $[-1, 1] \mapsto [a, b]$. We then have a function

$$\psi(t) = f\left(\frac{1}{2}[(b-a)t + b + a]\right)$$

defining on $[-1, 1]$. Let $t = \cos(\theta)$ and $g(\theta) = \psi(\cos(\theta))$ with $\theta \in [0, \pi]$.

Extend $g(\theta)$ to $[-\pi, 0]$ with $g(\theta) = g(-\theta)$, so that it becomes an even function on $[-\pi, \pi]$. Copy this $g(\theta)$ to every interval $[(2k+1)\pi, (2k+3)\pi]$ for all $k = 0, \pm 1, \pm 2, \ldots$, and then the resultant function, denoted by $h(\theta)$, is in $C_{2\pi}$, that is called *induced function* of $f(x)$. As a result, Jackson's basic theorem and Theorems B.2.4 and B.2.5 are applicable with the induced function of $f(x)$ if $h(\theta)$ satisfies their proviso conditions. The following are some relations between $f(x)$ and its reduced function in terms of the best approximation and modulus of continuity.

Proposition B.2.1 *Let* $E_k(f)$ *be the best approximation error for* $f(x) \in C[a, b]$, *and* $E_k^*(h)$ *be the best approximation error for the induced function* $h(\theta)$ *of* $f(x)$. *Then,* $E_k(f) = E_k^*(h)$. □

Proof There exists a polynomial p_k of degree at most k such that $|f(x) - p_k(x)| \leq E_k$. It is readily to see that the induced function $T(\theta)$ of $p_k(x)$ is a trigonometric polynomial of degree at most k. We have $|h(\theta) - T(\theta)| \leq E_k$, implying $E_k^*(h) \leq E_k(f)$.

On the other hand, for even function $h(\theta)$ we have an even trigonometric polynomial $T_k(\theta) = \sum_{j=0}^{k} a_j \cos(j\theta) = \sum_{j=0}^{k} c_j \cos^j(\theta)$ such that $|h(\theta) - T_k(\theta)| \leq E_k^*(h)$. This implies $|\psi(t) - \sum_{j=0}^{k} c_j t^j| \leq E_k^*(h)$ and then $|f(x) - p_k(x)| \leq E_k^*(h)$ for some polynomial p_k with order no higher than k. So, $E_k(f) \leq E_k^*(h)$. □

Proposition B.2.2 *Let $\omega_f(\delta)$ and $\omega_h(\delta)$ be the moduli of continuity for $f(x) \in C[a,b]$ and its induced function $h(\theta)$, respectively. Then,*

$$\omega_h(\delta) \leq \omega_f\left(\frac{1}{2}(b-a)\delta\right).$$

Proof By the definitions of the modulus of continuity and induced function,

$$\begin{aligned}
\omega_h(\delta) =& \sup_{|\theta_1-\theta_2|<\delta} |h(\theta_1) - h(\theta_2)| \\
=& \sup_{|\theta_1-\theta_2|<\delta} \left| f\left(\frac{1}{2}[(b-a)\cos\theta_1 + b + a]\right) - f\left(\frac{1}{2}[(b-a)\cos\theta_2 + b + a]\right)\right| \\
\leq& \sup_{|\cos\theta_1-\cos\theta_2|<\delta} \left| f\left(\frac{1}{2}[(b-a)\cos\theta_1 + b + a]\right) - f\left(\frac{1}{2}[(b-a)\cos\theta_2 + b + a]\right)\right| \\
=& \sup_{|x_1-x_2|<\delta} \left| f\left(\frac{1}{2}(b-a)x_1\right) - f\left(\frac{1}{2}(b-a)x_2\right)\right| \\
=& \sup_{|x_1-x_2|<(b-a)\delta/2} |f(x_1) - f(x_2)| \\
=& \omega_f\left(\frac{1}{2}(b-a)\delta\right).
\end{aligned}$$

Proposition B.2.3 *Let $[\alpha, \beta] \subset (a, b)$, and $\tilde{\omega}_f(\delta)$ be the modulus of continuity for f on $[\alpha, \beta]$. Then there exists a constant c depending on α, β, a, b only such that*

$$\tilde{\omega}_f(\delta) \leq \omega_h(c\delta).$$

Proof Using the mapping $t \mapsto x$, $[\alpha, \beta]$ is mapped to be $[\tau_1, \tau_2] \subset (-1, 1)$, where

$$\tau_1 = \frac{2\alpha - (b+a)}{b-a}, \quad \tau_2 = \frac{2\beta - (b+a)}{b-a}.$$

Let $\lambda = \min(\tau_1 + 1, 1 - \tau_2) > 0$. For any $x_i = \frac{1}{2}[(b-a)t_i + b + a] = \frac{1}{2}[(b-a)\cos(\theta_i) + b + a]$, $i = 1, 2$, if $|x_1 - x_2| < \delta$, $|t_1 - t_2| \leq 2\delta/(b-a)$. Thus, by the mean value theorem,

$$|\theta_1 - \theta_2| = |\arccos(t_1) - \arccos(t_2)| = \frac{1}{\sqrt{1-\xi^2}}|t_1 - t_2|$$

where t_1, t_2 are in between τ_1 and τ_2 while ξ is in between t_1 and t_2. Thus, $1 - \xi^2 = (1-\xi)(1+\xi) \geq \lambda^2$, which gives

$$|\theta_1 - \theta_2| \leq \frac{1}{\lambda}|t_1 - t_2| \leq \frac{2}{\lambda(b-a)}\delta.$$

Finally,

$$|f(x_1) - f(x_2)| = |h(\theta_1) - h(\theta_2)| \le \omega_h(\theta_1 - \theta_2)$$
$$\le \omega_h\left(\frac{2}{\lambda(b-u)}\delta\right),$$

from which $\tilde{\omega}_f(\delta) \le \omega_h(c\delta)$ with $c = \frac{2}{\lambda(b-a)}$. □

Theorem B.2.6 (Jackson's Theorem) *If $f(x) \in C[a,b]$, then $E_k(f) \le K\omega_f(k^{-1})$ where K is a constant depending on a and b only.* □

Proof Let $h(\theta)$ be the induced function of $f(x)$. We have

$$E_k(f) = E_k^*(h) \le A\omega_h(k^{-1}) \le A\omega_f\left(\frac{b-a}{2k}\right) \le K\omega_f\left(\frac{1}{k}\right).$$

Corollary B.2.2 *If $f(x) \in Lip_M(\alpha), 0 < \alpha \le 1$, $E_k(f) \le CMk^{-\alpha}$.* □

Corollary B.2.3 *If $f(x)$ is differentiable on $[a,b]$ and $|f'(x)| \le M$ for some $M > 0$, then $E_k(f) \le CMk^{-1}$.* □

Theorem B.2.7 *If $f(x) \in C^p[a,b]$, then for $k > p$,*

$$E_k(f) \le A_p \frac{1}{k^p}\omega_{f^{(p)}}\left(\frac{b-a}{2(k-p)}\right),$$

where A_p depends on p, a and b only. □

To prove the theorem, we introduce the following lemma first.

Lemma B.2.1 *If $f(x) \in C^1[a,b]$, we then have*

$$E_k(f) \le A\frac{1}{k}E_{k-1}(f').$$

Proof Let $p(x) \in P_{k-1}$ be the best approximation polynomial to $f'(x)$. Then $|f'(x) - p(x)| \le E_{k-1}(f')$. Denote $\varphi(x) = f(x) - \int_0^x p(u)du$, then $|\varphi'(x)| \le E_{k-1}(f')$ for $x \in [a,b]$ and $\varphi(x)$ is Lipschitz with order one. Then, by Corollary B.2.3, $E_k(\varphi) \le Ck^{-1}E_{k-1}(f')$. If $q(x)$ is the kth polynomial of the best approximation to $\varphi(x)$, then

$$|\varphi(x) - q(x)| = \left|f(x) - \int_0^x p(u)du - q(x)\right| \le A\frac{1}{k}E_{k-1}(f').$$

Then, the assertion holds since $\int_0^x p(u)du + q(x)$ is a polynomial of degree k. □

It is readily seen that Theorem B.2.7 holds by consecutively using Lemma B.2.1. Notice that the results on the best approximation polynomial will be used later in deriving the convergence rate of orthogonal polynomial series that is the backbone of the series methods. See Sect. C.4 in Appendix C.

Appendix C
Approximation in Hilbert Space

To introduce Hilbert spaces, this chapter introduces inner product spaces. With the inner product orthogonality of two elements being defined, Hilbert space is a complete inner product space. In terms of a closed subspace of Hilbert space, a direct sum decomposition of the space is defined and then associated projection operator is studied. Moreover, every Hilbert space is separable and has an orthogonal basis so that any element admits an orthogonal series expansion. This chapter then focuses on L^2 function spaces that involve almost all functions catered for nonparametric estimation issues in econometrics and statistics. In addition, mathematical properties of classical orthogonal sequences are discussed in detail.

Furthermore, the chapter summarizes convergence orders in both norm and pointwise sense of orthogonal expansions for functions in a variety of circumstances. In particular, several crucial quantities are shown that determine the rate of convergence in nonparametric series estimation. Such results are convenient for the reader when using series methods.

C.1 Inner Product Spaces

In metric space $\mathbb{R}^3$ with Euclidean norm $\|x\|_2 = (\xi_1^2 + \xi_2^2 + \xi_3^2)^{1/2}$, one may realize that the norm can be induced by the dot product $x \cdot y = \xi_1\eta_1 + \xi_2\eta_2 + \xi_3\eta_3$ that $\|x\|_2 = (x \cdot x)^{1/2}$. If we could make this connection in a class of metric spaces, there would be some profit. That is, we may define an inner operation between pairs of elements analogous to the dot product, and this operation yields the norm of an element as a special case. The operation we seek is called inner product; the resulting spaces are called inner product spaces.

Given the foregoing motivation for introducing an inner product, we now proceed on an axiomatic basis.

C. Dong and J. Gao, *Modern Series Methods in Econometrics and Statistics*, Advanced Studies in Theoretical and Applied Econometrics 45,
https://doi.org/10.1007/978-981-96-2822-3

Definition C.1.1 A *semi-inner product* on a real vector space V is a scalar-valued function $\langle x, y\rangle$ defined for all ordered pairs of vectors $x, y \in V$ which satisfies the following axioms:

(a) $\langle x, y\rangle = \langle y, x\rangle, \forall x, y \in V$;
(b) $\langle \alpha x + \beta y, z\rangle = \alpha\langle x, z\rangle + \beta\langle y, z\rangle, \forall x, y, z \in V$ and scalars α, β;
(c) $\langle\cdot,\cdot\rangle$ is nonnegative definite, i.e., $\langle x, x\rangle \geq 0$.

If further $\langle x, x\rangle = 0$ implies $x = 0$, the semi-inner product is called an *inner product*.

An *inner product space*, denoted by $(V, \langle\cdot,\cdot\rangle)$, consists of a vector space V and an inner product $\langle\cdot,\cdot\rangle$ on V. □

Axiom (a) imposes the property of symmetry on the semi-inner product. Axiom (b) indicates the linearity of the semi-inner product in the first argument and hence $\langle 0, 0\rangle = 0$. When the equivalent condition between $\langle x, x\rangle = 0$ and $x = 0$ is imposed, the semi-inner product enhances to be an inner product.

After we show the following inequality, the *Cauchy-Schwarz inequality*, we may conclude that in an inner product space, $\sqrt{\langle x, x\rangle}$ is a norm.

Theorem C.1.1 *In any inner product space V,*

$$|\langle x, y\rangle|^2 \leq \langle x, x\rangle\langle y, y\rangle, \qquad \forall x, y \in V.$$

Proof If $x = 0$ or $y = 0$ the inequality holds trivially. Otherwise, for all scalars α,

$$\begin{aligned} 0 &\leq \langle x - \alpha y, x - \alpha y\rangle \\ &= \langle x, x\rangle - 2\alpha\langle x, y\rangle + \alpha^2\langle y, y\rangle. \end{aligned}$$

In particular, letting $\alpha = \langle x, y\rangle/\langle y, y\rangle$ we have

$$0 \leq \langle x, x\rangle - \langle x, y\rangle^2/\langle y, y\rangle,$$

from which the assertion follows. □

Now, because $\langle x, x\rangle$ is nonnegative and $\langle \alpha x, \alpha x\rangle^{1/2} = |\alpha|\langle x, x\rangle^{1/2}$, if we show the triangle inequality for $\|x\| = \langle x, x\rangle^{1/2}$, it is a norm. In fact,

$$\begin{aligned} \|x + y\|^2 &= \langle x + y, x + y\rangle = \|x\|^2 + 2\langle x, y\rangle + \|y\|^2 \\ &\leq \|x\|^2 + 2\|x\|\|y\| + \|y\|^2 = (\|x\| + \|y\|)^2, \end{aligned}$$

and thus the triangle inequality holds immediately.

A familiar result of elementary geometry is that the sum of the squares of the sides of a parallelogram equals the sum of the squares of the diagonals. This so-called "parallelogram law" also holds in an inner product space, viz., $\|x + y\|^2 + \|x - y\|^2 = 2\|x\|^2 + 2\|y\|^2$. The readers may verify this using the property of the inner product.

Example C.1.1 (a) Euclidean space $\mathbb{R}^n$ with the inner product $\langle x, y\rangle = \xi_1\eta_1 + \cdots + \xi_n\eta_n$ is an inner product space. (b) The space ℓ_2 with the inner product $\langle x, y\rangle = \sum_{j=1}^{\infty} \xi_j\eta_j$ is an inner product space. (c) The space $L^2[0, 1]$ with the inner product $\langle f, g\rangle = \int_0^1 f(x)g(x)dx$ is an inner product space (see Example A.3.5 for the definition $L^2[0, 1]$). (d) Let Γ be a compact region in $\mathbb{R}^n$ and let $C(\Gamma)$ be the space of continuous functions on Γ. For any $f, g \in C(\Gamma)$, define the inner product $\langle f, g\rangle = \int_\Gamma f(x)g(x)dx$, then $C(\Gamma)$ becomes an inner product. (e) Let Γ be an open region in $\mathbb{R}^n$. Let $C^{(m)}(\Gamma)$ denote the space of functions which have continuous partial derivatives (in all variables) up to and including order m. Let $k = (k_1, \ldots, k_n)$ be a vector of integer entries, and let $|k| = k_1 + \cdots + k_n$. Define the differential operator D^k by

$$D^k f(x_1, \ldots, x_n) = \frac{\partial^{|k|} f(x_1, \ldots, x_n)}{\partial x_1^{k_1} \cdots \partial x_n^{k_n}}.$$

Take

$$\langle f, g\rangle^{(m)} = \int_\Gamma \sum_{|k|\le m} D^k f D^k g \, dx_1 \cdots dx_n.$$

Then, $C^{(m)}(\Gamma)$ becomes an inner product space.

Example C.1.2 Let V be a space of random variables defined on the same probability space that have a finite second-order moment. For any $X, Y \in V$, $\mathrm{Cov}(X, Y)$ is their covariance. It can be shown that $\langle X, Y\rangle = \mathrm{Cov}(X, Y)$ is an inner product. Hence, $(V, \langle\cdot, \cdot\rangle)$ is an inner product space. Accordingly, Theorem 2.2.4 is a particular form of the Cauchy-Schwarz inequality of Theorem C.1.1.

C.2 Hilbert Spaces

Since an inner product space is a particular normed space, we can ask whether the space is complete or not. An inner product space that is complete with respect to the norm induced by the inner product is called a *Hilbert space*. And we shall always refer the norm in Hilbert space as the induced norm.

We can give a rather significant geometric interpretation of the Cauchy-Schwarz inequality in a real inner product space. Note that, for any nonzero vectors $x, y \in V$, $\langle x, y\rangle/\|x\|\|y\|$ always has modulus less than 1. By analogy with $\mathbb{R}^3$, we could define the cosine of the "angle between x and y" by

$$\cos\widehat{xy} = \langle x, y\rangle/\|x\|\|y\|.$$

It then is reasonable to refer the vectors x and y as being orthogonal if $\cos\widehat{xy} = 0$, or equivalently, $\langle x, y\rangle = 0$. While the idea of angle is of very limited usefulness in real inner product space, the concept of orthogonality is of extreme importance.

Definition C.2.1 In an inner product space $(V, \langle\cdot,\cdot\rangle)$, two vectors x and y are said to be orthogonal, written as $x \perp y$, if $\langle x, y\rangle = 0$. The vector x is said to be orthogonal to a subset $S \subset V$, written as $x \perp S$, if x is orthogonal to every $y \in S$. The subsets S and W of V are orthogonal, $S \perp W$, if $\langle x, y\rangle = 0$ for all $x \in S$ and $y \in W$. The set of vectors $S^{\perp} = \{y \in V | y \perp x, x \in S\}$ is called the orthogonal complement of S.

The following assertions consequent upon Definition C.2.1 may be noted. (1) The zero vector is orthogonal to every element in the space. (2) $x \perp x$ if and only if $x = 0$. (3) If $x \perp y_k$ and $y_k \to y$ (in the sense of the induced norm), then $x \perp y$. (4) (The Pythagorean theorem) If $x \perp y$ then $\|x + y\|^2 = \|x\|^2 + \|y\|^2$. (5) If $x \perp \{y_1, y_2, \ldots, y_n\}$, then x is orthogonal to every element in the span of $\{y_k\}_1^n$.

For any subset $S \subset H$ and $x \in H$, define the distance from x to S as

$$\rho(x, S) = \inf_{y\in S} \|x - y\|.$$

Obviously, if $x \in S$, $\rho(x, S) = 0$.

If S is a closed subspace of a Hilbert space H, $S^{\perp}$ is clearly also a closed subspace and $S \cap S^{\perp} = \{0\}$. In addition, the direct sum decomposition holds:

$$H = S \oplus S^{\perp}.$$

This means that for any $x \in H$, we can uniquely write $x = y + y^{\perp}$ where $y \in S$, $y^{\perp} \in S^{\perp}$.

Theorem C.2.1 (The projection theorem) *Let S be a closed subspace of a Hilbert space H and let $x \in H$ be a vector. Then there exists a unique vector $y_0 \in S$ such that $\rho(x, S) = \|x - y_0\|$.*

A necessary and sufficient condition that y_0 is the unique minimizing vector is that $x - y_0 \perp S$. □

This theorem generalizes Theorem 2.4.1 where the orthogonality is defined in terms of covariance for r.v. with finite second moments (see Example C.1.2).

Proof Let $d = \rho(x, S) = \inf_{y\in S} \|x - y\|$ and choose a sequence of $y_k \in S$ such that $\lim_{k\to\infty} \|x - y_k\| = d$. By the parallelogram law,

$$\begin{aligned}\|y_k - y_j\|^2 &= \|(y_k - x) - (y_j - x)\|^2 \\ &= 2\|y_k - x\|^2 + 2\|y_j - x\|^2 - \|(y_k - x) + (y_j - x)\|^2 \\ &= 2\|y_k - x\|^2 + 2\|y_j - x\|^2 - 4\left\|\frac{1}{2}(y_k + y_j) - x\right\|^2.\end{aligned}$$

Since S is a linear space, $\frac{1}{2}(y_k + y_j) \in S$ for any k and j. Thus, by the definition of d, $\left\|\frac{1}{2}(y_k + y_j) - x\right\|^2 \geq d^2$. It follows that, as k and j go to infinity,

$$\|y_k - y_j\|^2 \leq 2\|y_k - x\|^2 + 2\|y_j - x\|^2 - 4d^2 \to 0,$$

which implies that $\{y_k\}$ is a Cauchy sequence in S. But S is a closed subspace in H, hence $\{y_k\}$ has a limit $y_0 \in S$. By the continuity of norm, $d = \|x - y_0\|$.

Suppose there is another vector $z_0 \in S$ such that $d = \|x - z_0\|$. Then,

$$\begin{aligned}\|y_0 - z_0\|^2 &= 2\|y_0 - x\|^2 + 2\|z_0 - x\|^2 \\ &\quad - 4\left\|\frac{1}{2}(y_0 + z_0) - x\right\|^2 \\ &= 4d^2 - 4\left\|\frac{1}{2}(y_0 + z_0) - x\right\|^2 \le 0,\end{aligned}$$

which gives that $y_0 = z_0$.

For the last part of the theorem we first show that if y_0 is the minimizing vector then $x - y_0 \perp S$. Let $y \in S$ and λ be any scalar, then $y_0 + \lambda y \in S$ and $\|x - (y_0 + \lambda y)\|^2 \ge \|x - y_0\|^2$. This implies

$$-2\lambda\langle x - y_0, y\rangle + \lambda^2\|y\|^2 \ge 0. \tag{C.2.1}$$

This is tantamount to saying $\langle x - y_0, y\rangle = 0$ by the arbitrariness of λ since if $\langle x - y_0, y\rangle \neq 0$, the inequality (C.2.1) could not hold for all λ.

On the other hand, if $x - y_0 \perp S$ for some $y_0 \in S$, then for any $y \in S$,

$$\begin{aligned}\|x - y\|^2 &= \|x - y_0 + y_0 - y\|^2 \\ &= \|x - y_0\|^2 + \|y_0 - y\|^2 \ge \|x - y_0\|^2\end{aligned}$$

so that $\|x - y\| \ge \|x - y_0\|$ for any $y \in S$. □

Theorem C.2.1 says that for any $x \in H$ and any closed subspace $S \subset H$, there exists a unique $y \in S$ such that $x - y \in S^\perp$. The direct sum decomposition follows, viz., $x = y + y^\perp$ where we denote $y^\perp = x - y$.

If $x = y + y^\perp$ where $y \in S$, $y^\perp \in S^\perp$, one may define a mapping $P_S : P_S(x) = y$ that is called the *orthogonal projection operator* generated by closed subspace S. P_S has the following properties:

(i) $P_S(\cdot)$ is linear, i.e., $P_S(a_1x_1 + a_2x_2) = a_1P_S(x_1) + a_2P_S(x_2)$.
(ii) $P_S(x) = x$ whenever $x \in S$.
(iii) $P_S(x) = 0$ whenever $x \in S^\perp$.
(iv) $\|P_S(x)\| \le \|x\|$ for all $x \in H$.

To see (i), let $x_1 = y_1 + y_1^\perp$ and $x_2 = y_2 + y_2^\perp$ where $y_1, y_2 \in S$ and $y_1^\perp, y_2^\perp \in S^\perp$. Then, $a_1x_1 + a_2x_2 = a_1y_1 + a_2y_2 + a_1y_1^\perp + a_2y_2^\perp$, $a_1y_1 + a_2y_2 \in S$ and $a_1y_1^\perp + a_2y_2^\perp \in S^\perp$. Thus, $P_S(a_1x_1 + a_2x_2) = a_1y_1 + a_2y_2 = a_1P_S(x_1) + a_2P_S(x_2)$. (ii) and (iii) are fairly clear; (iv) follows from $\|x\|^2 = \|y\|^2 + \|y^\perp\|^2$ if $x = y + y^\perp$. Accordingly, $\|P_S(x)\| = \|y\| \le \|x\|$.

Definition C.2.2 A subset $S = \{x_k\}$ of vectors in the inner product space V is said to be an orthogonal set of vectors if $x_k \perp x_j$ for each pair $k \neq j$. If in addition, for each k, $\|x_k\| = 1$, the set is said to be orthonormal. □

An orthogonal set of vectors $S = \{x_k\}$ is linearly independent. To see this, choose any finite collection of vectors $\{x_j\}$ and suppose that $\sum_j \alpha_j x_j = 0$. Taking any vector $x_p \in \{x_j\}$ and operating the inner product on both sides of the equation, one may find $|\alpha_p| \|x_p\|^2 = 0$ that yields $\alpha_p = 0$. Thus, the set is linearly independent.

Given a set of linearly independent vectors, there exists a systematic procedure for converting the set into an orthonormal set called the *Gram-Schmidt orthogonalization process*. Let H be any inner product space and $\{x_k\}$ any linearly independent sequence in H. Then there is an orthonormal sequence $\{e_k\}$ in H such that for each k, $\{x_1, \ldots, x_k\}$ and $\{e_1, \ldots, e_k\}$ have the same linear span.

In fact, let $e_1 = x_1/\|x_1\|$. This works for $k = 1$, i.e., the assertion holds when $k = 1$. Then recursively, given $e_1, \ldots, e_{k-1}$, let

$$g_k = x_k - \sum_{j=1}^{k-1} \langle x_k, e_j \rangle e_j.$$

Then $g_k \perp e_j$ for any $j \leq k - 1$, but $g_k \neq 0$ since x_k is not in the linearly span of $\{x_1, \ldots, x_{k-1}\}$, which is the same as the linear span of $\{e_1, \ldots, e_{k-1}\}$ by the induction hypothesis. Let $e_k = g_k/\|g_k\|$. Then the assertion holds for k.

Theorem C.2.2 (Bessel's inequality) *For any orthonormal set* $\{e_i, i \in I\}$ *and* $x \in H$ *where* H *is an inner product space,* $\|x\|^2 \geq \sum_{i \in I} |\langle x, e_i \rangle|^2$.

Proof Let $y = \sum_{i \in I} \langle x, e_i \rangle e_i$. Then by the linearity of the inner product, $\|y\|^2 = \sum_{i \in I} |\langle x, e_i \rangle|^2$ and

$$\langle x, y \rangle = \sum_{i \in I} |\langle x, e_i \rangle|^2 = \langle y, y \rangle,$$

implying $\langle x - y, y \rangle = 0$.

Hence, $\|x\|^2 = \|(x - y) + y\|^2 = \|x - y\|^2 + \|y\|^2 \geq \|y\|^2$. □

If S is a finite-dimensional closed subspace of Hilbert space H, and further suppose $S = \text{span}\{e_1, \ldots, e_n\}$ where $\{e_1, \ldots, e_n\}$ is an orthonormal set. For $x \in H$, finding the closest vector $y_0 = \sum_{i=1}^n a_i e_i \in S$ to x is, by Theorem C.2.1 (the projection theorem), equivalent to solving equations:

$$0 = \langle x - y_0, e_i \rangle = \langle x, e_i \rangle - a_i, \quad i = 1, \ldots, n$$

which gives $a_i = \langle x, e_i \rangle$ and thus $y_0 = \sum_{i=1}^n \langle x, e_i \rangle e_i$. This also means that $\|x - \sum_{i=1}^n a_i e_i\|$ is minimized when $a_i = \langle x, e_i \rangle$, $i = 1, \ldots, n$; and y_0 is the projection of x on S.

Theorem C.2.3 (Parseval-Bessel equality) *If* $\{e_i, i \in I\}$ *is an orthonormal set in* H, *and* $x, y \in H$ *with* $x = \sum_{i \in I} a_i e_i$ *and* $y = \sum_{i \in I} b_i e_i$ *where* H *is an inner product space, then* $a_i = \langle x, e_i \rangle$, $b_i = \langle y, e_i \rangle$ *and* $\langle x, y \rangle = \sum_{i \in I} a_i b_i$. □

Proof This is easily verified. □

Theorem C.2.4 (Riesz-Fischer Theorem) *For any Hilbert space H, any orthonormal set $\{e_i, i = 1, 2, \dots\}$ and any sequence $\{a_i, i = 1, 2, \dots\}$ such that $\sum_{i=1}^{\infty} a_i^2 < \infty$ if and only if the sum $\sum_{i=1}^{\infty} a_i e_i$ converges to some $x \in H$. If this is the case, $a_i = \langle x, e_i \rangle$.* □

Proof Suppose $\sum_{i=1}^{\infty} a_i^2 < \infty$ and define

$$x_k = \sum_{i=1}^{k} a_i e_i.$$

Then, for any $k > j$,

$$\|x_k - x_j\|^2 = \left\| \sum_{i=j+1}^{k} a_i e_i \right\|^2 = \sum_{i=j+1}^{k} a_i^2,$$

which tends to zero as $k, j \to \infty$. Whence, $\{x_k\}$ is a Cauchy sequence, and then $x_k \to x \in H$ for some x by the completeness of H.

For the sufficiency, if $\{x_k\}$ converges, it is a Cauchy sequence. Thus, $\|x_k - x_j\|^2 = \sum_{i=j+1}^{k} a_i^2 \to 0$ as $k, j \to \infty$, implying $\sum_{i=j+1}^{\infty} a_i^2 \to 0$ as $j \to \infty$. Consequently, $\sum_{i=1}^{\infty} a_i^2 < \infty$.

In the partial sum $x_k = \sum_{j=1}^{k} a_j e_j$, taking the inner product of both sides with e_i gives $\langle x_k, e_i \rangle = a_i$, $1 \le i \le k$. By the continuity of the inner product and $x_k \to x$, $\langle x_k, e_i \rangle \to \langle x, e_i \rangle$ as $k \to \infty$. □

Bessel's inequality implies $\sum_{i=1}^{\infty} |\langle x, e_i \rangle|^2 < \infty$, since $\sum_{i=1}^{k} |\langle x, e_i \rangle|^2 \le \|x\|^2$ for any k. It follows that $\sum_{i=1}^{\infty} \langle x, e_i \rangle e_i$ converges in H. Nonetheless, there is no reason to guarantee the series actually converges to x. Usually, the series $\sum_{i=1}^{\infty} \langle x, e_i \rangle e_i$ is called *Fourier expansion* of x, and the coefficients $\langle x, e_i \rangle$ are called *Fourier coefficients* of x. The next theorem sheds a light on the relationship of x and its Fourier expansion.

Theorem C.2.5 *Let $\{e_i, i = 1, 2, \dots\}$ be an orthonormal sequence in H. For any $x \in H$, the series*

$$\sum_{i=1}^{\infty} \langle x, e_i \rangle e_i$$

converges to an element $\tilde{x}$ in the closed subspace $S \subset H$ generated by the $\{e_i, i = 1, 2, \dots\}$. Furthermore, $x - \tilde{x} \perp S$. □

Proof As we have remarked, the Fourier series of x converges to $\tilde{x} \in S$. For any finite k and for every $j \le k$,

$$\langle x - x_k, e_j \rangle = \langle x, e_j \rangle - \sum_{i=1}^{k} \langle x, e_i \rangle \langle e_i, e_j \rangle = 0.$$

Since $x_k \to \tilde{x}, x - \tilde{x} \perp e_j$ by the continuity of the inner product, and hence $x - \tilde{x} \perp S$. □

Using the projection P_S generated by $S = \text{span}\{e_i, i = 1, 2, \dots\}$, $\tilde{x} = P_S(x) = \sum_{i=1}^{\infty} \langle x, e_i \rangle e_i$, and $H = S \oplus S^{\perp}$. Observe that if S is the whole space H, then $x - \tilde{x}$ must be the zero vector, namely, the Fourier expansion of x converges to x.

Definition C.2.3 An orthonormal set $\{e_i, i = 1, 2, \dots\}$ in a Hilbert space H is maximal if, and only if, the only vector orthogonal to each of the e_i is the zero vector. □

By this definition, if orthonormal set $\{e_i, i = 1, 2, \dots\}$ is maximal in H, and $x \in S^{\perp}$ with $S = \text{span}\{e_i, i = 1, 2, \dots\}$, then $x \perp e_i$ for all i, implying $x = 0$. Thus, $S^{\perp} = \{0\}$, so $H = S$, and $P_S(x) = x$. In this situation, every $x \in H$ can be represented as a Fourier series.

Definition C.2.4 A maximal orthonormal set $\{e_i, i = 1, 2, \dots\}$ in a Hilbert space H is called an orthonormal basis of H. □

When $\{e_i, i = 1, 2, \dots\}$ is an orthonormal basis, Bessel's inequality becomes an equality, viz.,

$$\|x\|^2 = \sum_{i=1}^{\infty} |\langle x, e_i \rangle|^2,$$

which usually is called Parseval's formula. Conversely, if Bessel's inequality holds as an equality, the orthonormal set $\{e_i, i = 1, 2, \dots\}$ is maximal, then a basis.

It is possible to show that every inner product space contains a maximal orthonormal set, and further, if the space is complete, this is tantamount to the existence of orthonormal basis in Hilbert space.

Theorem C.2.6 *Every Hilbert space has an orthonormal basis.* □

See Theorem 5.4.7 of Dudley (2003, p. 169).

For an orthonormal set $B := \{e_i, i = 1, 2, \dots\}$ the following conditions are equivalent.

(i) B is an orthonormal basis of H.
(ii) B is a "complete orthonormal set", that is, the only $x \in H$ such that $x \perp B$ is 0.
(iii) B spans H.
(iv) If $x \in H$ and $x_k = \sum_{i=1}^{k} a_i e_i$ where $a_i = \langle x, e_i \rangle$, then $x_k \to x$ as $k \to \infty$ in the norm.
(v) For all $x, y \in H$, $\langle x, y \rangle = \sum_{i=1}^{\infty} \langle x, e_i \rangle \langle y, e_i \rangle$.
(vi) For all $x \in H$, then $\|x\|^2 = \sum_{i=1}^{\infty} |\langle x, e_i \rangle|^2$.

Example C.2.1 In $L^2[-\pi, \pi]$ (complex space), the set of functions

$$f_k(t) = \frac{1}{\sqrt{2\pi}} e^{ikt}, \qquad k = 0, \pm 1, \pm 2, \dots$$

where $i = \sqrt{-1}$ is the imaginary unit, is maximal and hence an orthonormal basis. To demonstrate this, let $f(t) \in L^2[-\pi, \pi]$ and $f \perp f_k$ for all k, that is,

$$\int_{-\pi}^{\pi} f(t)e^{ikt}dt = 0, \qquad k = 0, \pm 1, \pm 2, \ldots.$$

We shall show that $f(t) \equiv 0$. Let

$$g(t) = \int_{-\pi}^{t} f(s)ds - \alpha,$$

where α will be determined later. Then $g(t)$ is continuous and $g'(t) = f(t)$.

Integrating by parts, we have, for $k \neq 0$,

$$\begin{aligned} 0 = \int_{-\pi}^{\pi} f(t)e^{ikt}dt &= g(t)e^{ikt}\Big|_{-\pi}^{\pi} - ik\int_{-\pi}^{\pi} g(t)e^{ikt}dt \\ &= (-1)^k(g(\pi) - g(-\pi)) - ik\int_{-\pi}^{\pi} g(t)e^{ikt}dt. \end{aligned}$$

Now, because of $f \perp f_0$, $g(\pi) - g(-\pi) = \int_{-\pi}^{\pi} f(t)dt = 0$. Hence, for $k \neq 0$,

$$\int_{-\pi}^{\pi} g(t)e^{ikt}dt = 0.$$

This relation can be extended to $k = 0$ by choosing α in such a way

$$\alpha = \frac{1}{2\pi}\int_{-\pi}^{\pi}\int_{-\pi}^{t} f(s)dsdt.$$

Thus,

$$\int_{-\pi}^{\pi} g(t)e^{ikt}dt = 0, \qquad k = 0, \pm 1, \pm 2, \ldots,$$

where $g(t)$ is continuous and periodic. It follows from the second Weierstrass theorem that there is a trigonometric polynomial

$$L_n(t) = \sum_{k=-n}^{n} \beta_k e^{ikt},$$

such that for any $\varepsilon > 0$,

$$|g(t) - L_n(t)| < \varepsilon, \qquad \forall t \in [-\pi, \pi].$$

Note that

$$\int_{-\pi}^{\pi} g(t)\overline{L_n}(t)dt = 0,$$

where $\overline{L_n}(t)$ is the complex conjugate of $L_n(t)$. Whence,

$$\begin{aligned}\int_{-\pi}^{\pi} |g(t)|^2 dt &= \int_{-\pi}^{\pi} \bar{g}(t)(g(t) - L_n(t))dt \\ &\leq \int_{-\pi}^{\pi} |g(t)||g(t) - L_n(t)|dt \leq \varepsilon \int_{-\pi}^{\pi} |g(t)|dt \\ &\leq (2\pi)^{1/2}\varepsilon \left(\int_{-\pi}^{\pi} |g(t)|^2 dt\right)^{1/2},\end{aligned}$$

by the Cauchy-Schwarz inequality, and then $\|g\|^2 \leq 2\pi\varepsilon^2$.

Accordingly, by the arbitrariness of ε, $g(t) = 0$ almost everywhere, i.e., $\int_{-\pi}^{t} f(s) ds = \alpha$ or $f(t) = 0$ almost everywhere.

In conclusion, in complex $L^2[-\pi, \pi]$, $\{f_k(t)\}$ is an orthonormal basis, while in real $L^2[-\pi, \pi]$, the set

$$\left\{\frac{1}{\sqrt{2\pi}}, \frac{1}{\sqrt{\pi}} \cos kt, \frac{1}{\sqrt{\pi}} \sin kt, k = \pm 1, \pm 2, \ldots\right\}$$

is an orthonormal basis.

C.3 L^p Spaces

We come down to the L^p spaces that are Banach spaces for $1 \leq p < \infty$ and in particular Hilbert spaces when $p = 2$.

Because a measure will be involved in the integrations discussed below, we first introduce some relevant concepts about the measure. Let X be an arbitrary set and $\mathcal{S}$ be a σ-field of subsets of X (see the definition of Sigma field in Chap. 2).

A *measure* on the σ-field $\mathcal{S}$ is a nonnegative, extended real-valued function μ on $\mathcal{S}$ such that whenever $\{A_i\}$ forms a finite or countable infinite collection of disjoint sets in $\mathcal{S}$, we have

$$\mu\left(\bigcup_i A_i\right) = \sum_i \mu(A_i).$$

A measure μ on a σ-field $\mathcal{S}$ is called *σ-finite*, if for any $S \in \mathcal{S}$ there exists a sequence $S_i \in \mathcal{S}$, $i = 1, 2, \ldots$, such that $S \subset \cup_{i=1}^{\infty} S_i$ and $\mu(S_i) < \infty$ for all i (or equivalently, the condition holds for X itself); it is *completion*, if $S \in \mathcal{S}$ and $\mu(S) = 0$, then whenever $S_1 \subset S$, $S_1 \in \mathcal{S}$ and $\mu(S_1) = 0$.

The triple $(X, \mathcal{S}, \mu)$ where X is an arbitrary set, $\mathcal{S}$ is a σ-algebra of some subsets of X and measure μ is σ-finite and completion, is called a *measure space*. In particular, when $\mu(X) = 1$, the measure space $(X, \mathcal{S}, \mu)$ reduces to a *probability space* that we normally denoted by $(\Omega, \mathcal{F}, \mathbb{P})$ and already introduced in Chap. 2.

By convention, a subset S of X with $\mu(S) = 0$ is called a *null set*. If a statement $p(x)$ about points $x \in X$ holds except a null set, we say that $p(x)$ holds almost everywhere (abbreviated a.e.), whereas in the case where $\mu(X) = 1$ (that is, the statement pertains to a probability space), we say that $p(x)$ holds almost surely (abbreviated a.s.).

For any measure space $(X, \mathcal{S}, \mu)$ and $0 < p < \infty$, $L^p(X, \mathcal{S}, \mu)$ denotes the set of all measurable functions f on X such that $\int_X |f|^p d\mu < \infty$, namely,

$$L^p(X, \mathcal{S}, \mu) = \left\{ f : \int_X |f|^p d\mu < \infty \right\},$$

and the values of f are real numbers except possibly on a null set, where f may be undefined or infinite. Here the integration is understood as in Doob (1994, p. 83), for example.

The notation $L^p(X, \mathcal{S}, \mu)$ will be abbreviated as L^p if there is no risk of confusion raised; also abbreviate L^1 to be L.

Example C.3.1 If $\mu(X) < \infty$, for $p > 1$, $L^p \subset L$. In effect, let $f \in L^p$ and define $A = \{x, |f(x)| > 1\}$ and $B = X \setminus A$. Then

$$\begin{aligned}
\int_X |f(x)| d\mu(x) &= \int_A |f(x)| d\mu(x) + \int_B |f(x)| d\mu(x) \\
&\le \int_A |f(x)|^p d\mu(x) + \int_B d\mu(x) \\
&\le \int_X |f(x)|^p d\mu(x) + \mu(X) < \infty.
\end{aligned}$$

Example C.3.2 If $\mu(X) = \infty$, the assertion of Example C.3.1 may not be correct. For instance, $X = [0, \infty)$, $f(x) = (1 + x)^{-1}$, then $f \in L^p$ for any $p > 1$ but $f \notin L$. Meanwhile, there exists some function $f \in L$ but $f \notin L^p$ for some $p > 1$. To see this, take

$$f(x) = \begin{cases} x^{-1/p}, & x \in (0, 1), \\ 0, & x \ge 1. \end{cases}$$

Then, $f \in L$ but $f \notin L^p$.

A measurable function f is called *essentially bounded* if and only if for some $M < \infty$, $|f| \le M$ almost everywhere (a.e.). The set of all essentially bounded real functions is called $L^\infty(X, \mathcal{S}, \mu)$.

Define respectively for $0 < p < \infty$ and $p = \infty$,

$$\|f\|_p = \left(\int |f|^p d\mu\right)^{1/p}, \quad \text{and} \quad \|f\|_\infty = \inf\{M : |f| \le M \text{ a.e.}\}.$$

Observe that when $\mu(X) < \infty$, if $f \in L^\infty$, then $f \in L^p$; in this case, moreover, $\lim_{p\to\infty} \|f\|_p = \|f\|_\infty$. In fact, for any $0 < \varepsilon < \|f\|_\infty$, denote $X_\varepsilon = \{x : |f(x)| > \|f\|_\infty - \varepsilon\}$, and we know $\mu(X_\varepsilon) > 0$. Then,

$$(\|f\|_\infty - \varepsilon)\mu(X_\varepsilon)^{1/p} \le \|f\|_p \le \|f\|_\infty \mu(X)^{1/p}.$$

The assertion follows if we firstly let $p \to \infty$ and then let $\varepsilon \to 0$.

Theorem C.3.1 *L^p is a linear space.* □

Proof For any scalar a and functions $f, g \in L^p$, note that

$$\int_X |af|^p d\mu = |a|^p \int_X |f|^p d\mu < \infty,$$

and according to the inequality $|f + g|^p \le 2^p(|f| \vee |g|)^p \le 2^p(|f|^p + |g|^p)$, we have

$$\int_X |f + g|^p d\mu \le 2^p \int_X |f|^p d\mu + 2^p \int_X |g|^p d\mu < \infty,$$

so that $af \in L^p$ and $f + g \in L^p$. □

To discuss further on L^p, we need two inequalities. Let p and q be positive number satisfying $1/p + 1/q = 1$, and call them *mutually adjoint numbers*.

Theorem C.3.2 (E. Hölder's inequality) *Let p and q be mutually adjoint numbers, $p > 1$ and $q > 1$. For any $f \in L^p$ and $g \in L^q$, we have $fg \in L$ and*

$$\left|\int_X fg d\mu\right| \le \|f\|_p \|g\|_q.$$

Proof Let $\alpha = 1/p$ and $\beta = 1 - \alpha = 1/q$. Consider function $y = x^\alpha$ on $x \ge 0$. It is concave because of $0 < \alpha < 1$, and thus its tangent line at $(1, 1)$, $y = \alpha x + \beta$, is on above the curve, viz.,

$$x^\alpha \le \alpha x + \beta, \qquad x \ge 0.$$

Letting $x = u/v$, we have $u^\alpha v^{-\alpha} \le \alpha u v^{-1} + \beta$, or

$$u^\alpha v^\beta \le \alpha u + \beta v, \qquad u, v > 0.$$

Now, let

$$u = \frac{1}{\|f\|_p^p}|f|^p, \quad v = \frac{1}{\|g\|_q^q}|g|^q,$$

and by the above inequality

$$\frac{1}{\|f\|_p\|g\|_q}|f(x)g(x)| \leq \frac{1}{p}\frac{1}{\|f\|_p^p}|f(x)|^p + \frac{1}{q}\frac{1}{\|g\|_q^q}|g(x)|^q.$$

Integrating on both sides yields

$$\frac{1}{\|f\|_p\|g\|_q}\int_X |f(x)g(x)|d\mu \leq \frac{1}{p}\frac{1}{\|f\|_p^p}\|f\|_p^p + \frac{1}{q}\frac{1}{\|g\|_q^q}\|g\|_q^q = 1.$$

The assertion follows immediately. □

Note that in the above proof we presume that $\|f\|_p \neq 0$ and $\|g\|_q \neq 0$, because otherwise the assertion is manifest. In addition, the inequality also holds for $p = 1$ (accordingly $q = \infty$) without needing the above derivation. Thus, we conclude the *Hölder inequality* holds for all adjoint numbers $p, q \geq 1$. In particular, when $p = q = 2$ the inequality reduces to the *Cauchy-Schwarz inequality*:

$$\left|\int_X fgd\mu\right| \leq \|f\|_2\|g\|_2, \qquad f, g \in L^2.$$

This is a particular form of the Cauchy-Schwarz inequality shown in Theorem C.1.1 when we regard the integration on the left as an inner product between f and g.

Theorem C.3.3 (H. Minkowski's inequality) *Assume that* $f, g \in L^p$, $p \geq 1$. *Then*

$$\|f + g\|_p \leq \|f\|_p + \|g\|_p.$$

Proof When $p = 1$, clearly

$$\int_X |f + g|d\mu \leq \int_X |f|d\mu + \int_X |g|d\mu,$$

so that the inequality holds for $p = 1$.

Now, consider $p > 1$. By the linearity of the space, $f + g \in L^p$, and consequently, $|f + g|^{p/q} \in L^q$ where q is the adjoint number of p. It thus follows from the Hölder's inequality for $|f|$ and $|f + g|^{p/q}$ that

$$\int_X |f||f + g|^{p/q}d\mu \leq \|f\|_p \left(\int_X |f + g|^p d\mu\right)^{1/q}.$$

By the same derivation we may have

$$\int_X |g||f + g|^{p/q}d\mu \leq \|g\|_p \left(\int_X |f + g|^p d\mu\right)^{1/q}.$$

Noting that $p - 1 = p/q$, we have

$$\begin{aligned}\|f+g\|_p^p &= \int_X |f+g|^p d\mu = \int_X |f+g||f+g|^{p-1} d\mu \\ &\le \int_X |f||f+g|^{p-1} d\mu + \int_X |g||f+g|^{p-1} d\mu \\ &\le (\|f\|_p + \|g\|_p)\left(\int_X |f+g|^p d\mu\right)^{1/q} \\ &= (\|f\|_p + \|g\|_p)\|f+g\|_p^{p/q},\end{aligned}$$

from which the Minkowski's inequality follows immediately. □

With Minkowski's inequality, we now safely conclude that the $\|\cdot\|_p$ defined above is a norm in L^p, $p \ge 1$. Thus, L^p are normed linear space, and further defining metric by $\rho(f, g) = \|f - g\|_p$ it becomes a metric space. Hence, the Cauchy sequence and the convergence in L_p-norm can be introduced into L^p spaces. The details are omitted since everything is clear from the abstract metric space in the preceding chapter, but we shall use it directly.

The reason that the case of $0 < p < 1$ is ignored is that the quantity $\|\cdot\|_p$ does not satisfy the triangle inequality. In fact, one can show that if $f \in L^p$ and $g \in L^q$, $0 < p < 1$, q is the adjoint number of p, then $\|fg\|_1 \ge \|f\|_p\|g\|_q$.

Theorem C.3.4 *Suppose $\{f_n\}$ is a Cauchy sequence in L^p, $p \ge 1$. Then there exists a function $f \in L^p$ such that $f_n \to f$ in L^p norm as $n \to \infty$.* □

Proof Since f_n is Cauchy, for every positive integer k, there exists a positive integer n_k such that

$$\|f_{n_k} - f_m\|_p < 2^{-k}, \quad \forall m > n_k.$$

Moreover, for every subset $S \subset X$ and $\mu(S) < \infty$ we have

$$\int_S |f_{n_k} - f_{n_{k+1}}| d\mu \le \|f_{n_k} - f_{n_{k+1}}\|_p \|1\|_q < [\mu(S)]^{1/q} 2^{-k},$$

due to Hölder's inequality.

Thus, the series $\sum_{k=1}^{\infty} \int_S |f_{n_k} - f_{n_{k+1}}| d\mu$ converges. It follows that the series

$$g(x) = |f_{n_1}(x)| + |f_{n_2}(x) - f_{n_1}(x)| + \cdots + |f_{n_{k+1}}(x) - f_{n_k}(x)| + \cdots$$

converges a.e. on every subset $S \subset X$ with $\mu(S) < \infty$, so does on X; also $\|g\|_p \le 1$. Consequently,

$$f(x) = f_{n_1}(x) + \sum_{k=1}^{\infty} (f_{n_{k+1}}(x) - f_{n_k}(x))$$

defines a function $f(x)$ in L^p and $f_{n_k}(x) \to f(x)$ a.e. as $k \to \infty$. In addition,

$$\|f(x) - f_{n_k}(x)\|_p \leq \sum_{\ell=k}^{\infty} \|f_{n_{\ell+1}}(x) - f_{n_\ell}(x)\|_p < 2^{-k+1},$$

that is, $f_{n_k}(x) \to f(x)$ in L^p norm and thus $\|f\|_p < \|f_{n_k}(x)\|_p + 2^{-k+1} < \infty$. □

By far, we know that L^p, $p \geq 1$, are Banach spaces. Next, we consider the separability of L^p, $p \geq 1$. Toward this end, we need several lemmas.

Lemma C.3.1 *If $f \in L^p$, $p \geq 1$, then for any $\varepsilon > 0$, there exists a bounded measurable function g such that $\|f - g\|_p < \varepsilon$.*

Proof For any $\varepsilon > 0$, by the absolute continuity of the integral, there exists a $\delta > 0$, such that whenever $S \subset X$ and $\mu(S) < \delta$,

$$\int_S |f|^p d\mu < \varepsilon^p.$$

Denote $A_k = \{x : |f(x)| > k\}, k = 1, 2, \ldots,$ and $A = \{x : |f(x)| = \infty\}$. Since $f \in L^p$, $p \geq 1$, for any subset S with $\mu(S) < \infty$, $f \in L(S)$. In addition, $\mu(A) = 0$ because of integrability. Noting that $\{A_k\}$ is decreasing, we have

$$0 = \mu(A) = \mu(\cap_{k=1}^{\infty} A_k) = \lim_{k\to\infty} \mu(A_k).$$

Thus, there exists k_0 such that $\mu(A_{k_0}) < \delta$. Let

$$g(x) = \begin{cases} f(x), & x \in X \setminus A_{k_0}, \\ 0, & x \in A_{k_0}. \end{cases}$$

Then $g(x)$ satisfies the requirement. Indeed, $g(x)$ is measurable and $|g(x)| \leq k_0$; and $\mu(f \neq g) = \mu(A_{k_0}) < \delta$. Thus,

$$\int_X |f - g|^p d\mu = \int_{f\neq g} |f - g|^p d\mu = \int_{f\neq g} |f|^p d\mu < \varepsilon^p.$$

The proof is complete. □

A class of simple functions is defined before we introduce the following lemma. If $f(x)$ takes a finite number of values for $x \in X$, we say $f(x)$ is a *simple function*. For any subset $S \subset X$, define the *characteristic function* or *indicator function* of S as

$$I_S(x) = \begin{cases} 1, & \text{if } x \in S, \\ 0, & \text{otherwise.} \end{cases}$$

Suppose $f(x)$ is simple and takes different values $c_1, \ldots, c_n$. Then, in terms of the characteristic function we can rephrase $f(x)$ as

$$f(x) = \sum_{j=1}^{n} c_j I_{A_i}(x),$$

where $A_i = \{x, f(x) = c_i\}$, $i = 1, 2, \ldots, n$, and they are disjoint.

Lemma C.3.2 *Suppose $g(x)$ is a measurable bounded function on X. Then for any $\varepsilon > 0$, there exists a simple function $\varphi(x)$ such that $\|g - \varphi\| < \varepsilon$.*

Proof First, consider the case where $X = [a, b]$. Assume $M = \sup_{x\in[a,b]} |g(x)|$ and $0 < M < \infty$. Note that g is integrable on X, so there exists a simple function $\varphi(x)$ on $[a, b]$ such that

$$\int_a^b |g(x) - \varphi(x)| d\mu < \varepsilon^p/(2M)^{p-1}.$$

Also, from the proof of Lemma C.3.1, we can require $\sup_{x\in[a,b]} |\varphi(x)| \le M$. Thus,

$$\int_a^b |g(x) - \varphi(x)|^p d\mu \le (2M)^{p-1} \int_a^b |g(x) - \varphi(x)| d\mu < \varepsilon^p,$$

which gives $\|g - \varphi\|_p < \varepsilon$.

Now consider the case where X is a general bounded measurable set. Suppose $X \subset [a, b]$ and let

$$g_1(x) = \begin{cases} g(x), & \text{if } x \in X, \\ 0, & \text{otherwise.} \end{cases}$$

Then, $g_1(x)$ is a measurable and bounded function on $[a, b]$, and hence there exists a simple function $\varphi_1(x)$ on $[a, b]$ such that $\|g_1 - \varphi_1\|_p < \varepsilon$. Let $\varphi(x)$ be the restriction of $\varphi_1(x)$ on X that still is a simple function. It follows that

$$\int_X |g(x) - \varphi(x)|^p d\mu \le \int_a^b |g_1(x) - \varphi_1(x)|^p d\mu < \varepsilon^p,$$

that completes the proof. □

Lemma C.3.3 *Suppose $\varphi(x)$ is a simple function on X. Then for any $\varepsilon > 0$, there exist a finite number of disjoint open sets $G_1, \ldots, G_n$ and each set G_i has all its component intervals possessing rational numbers as their endpoints; there also exists a simple function $\psi(x) = \sum_{j=1}^{n} r_j I_{G_i}(x)$, such that $\|\psi - \varphi\| < \varepsilon$.*

Proof Suppose $\varphi(x) = \sum_{j=1}^{n} c_j I_{X_i}(x)$, $X = \cup X_i$, where X_i are mutually disjoint. Then, there exists a closed set $F_i \subset X_i$ such that $\mu(X_i - F_i) < \varepsilon^p/2n(2M)^p$, $i = 1, 2, \ldots, n$. Clearly, F_i are mutually disjoint too. Hence, we can take open sets G_i, mutually disjoint, $G_i \supset F_i$, and G_i has all component intervals possessing rational numbers as their endpoints. Now, let $\psi(x)$ take r_i on G_i satisfying $|c_i - r_i| < \varepsilon(2\mu(X))^{-1/p}$ and $|r_i| \le |c_i|$, and $\psi(x) = 0$ for $x \notin \cup G_i$. Such $\psi(x)$ satisfies the requirement. In fact,

$$\begin{aligned}\int_X |\psi(x)-\varphi(x)|^p d\mu &= \int_{\cup X_i} |\psi(x)-\varphi(x)|^p d\mu \\ &= \int_{\cup F_i} |\psi(x)-\varphi(x)|^p d\mu + \int_{\cup(X_i - F_i)} |\psi(x)-\varphi(x)|^p d\mu \\ &< \frac{\varepsilon^p}{2\mu(X)}\mu(X) + (2M)^p \frac{\varepsilon^p}{2n(2M)^p} n = \varepsilon^p.\end{aligned}$$

Theorem C.3.5 *Suppose that X is a bounded measurable set, then $L^p(X)$ is separable.* □

Proof Let $f \in L^p(X)$, $p \geq 1$. Then, $f \in L(X)$. According to Lemma C.3.1, for any $\varepsilon > 0$, there exists a bounded measurable function $g(x)$, such that $\|f - g\| < \varepsilon/3$. By Lemma C.3.2, there exists a simple function $\varphi(x)$ such that $\|g - \varphi\| < \varepsilon/3$ and further by Lemma C.3.3, there exists a simple function $\psi(x)$ satisfying all conditions in the lemma such that $\|\varphi - \psi\| < \varepsilon/3$. Therefore,

$$\|f - \psi\| \leq \|f - g\| + \|g - \varphi\| + \|\varphi - \psi\| < \varepsilon.$$

Since all such $\psi(x)$ form a set S that has countable elements and we have shown the S is dense in $L(X)$, L^p is separable. □

Remark The theorem gives the separability of $L^p(X)$ when X is a bounded measurable set. When X is unbounded, the separability of $L^p(X)$ can be shown via the argument that for each bounded measurable $S \subset X$, $L^p(S)$ is separable.

Example C.3.3 $L^\infty[a,b]$ is not separable. Indeed, consider functions in the space,

$$f_s(x) = \begin{cases} 1, & a \leq x \leq s \\ 0, & s < x \leq b, \end{cases}$$

with all $s \in [a,b]$. For any $s \neq s'$, $\rho(f_s, f_{s'}) = 1$, but the potential of the set $\{f_s(x), s \in [a,b]\}$ is $\aleph$. If $L^\infty[a,b]$ is separable, there is a dense countable subset M_0, say. Make balls centered at each element of M_0 with radius $1/3$. Clearly, the set of all these balls is countable and is a cover of $L^\infty[a,b]$. Thus, there are at least two functions f_s, $f_{s'}$ in the same ball, so $\rho(f_s, f_{s'}) \leq 2/3$. Contradiction!

Next, let us consider when a subset A of $L^p[a,b]$ $(1 < p < \infty)$ is sequentially compact. Toward this end, define for $f(x) \in L^p[a,b]$,

$$f_h(x) = \frac{1}{2h}\int_{x-h}^{x+h} f(t)dt, \quad x \in [a,b], \quad h > 0.$$

In the integral if $t > b$ we let $f(t) = 0$. Clearly, $f_h(x) \in C[a,b]$, and thus $f_h(x) \in L^p[a,b]$. Now, we shall prove

$$\int_a^b |f_h(x)|^p dx \le \int_a^b |f(x)|^p dx.$$

Let q be the adjoint number of p, $1/p + 1/q = 1$. We have

$$\begin{aligned}
\int_a^b |f_h(x)|^p dx &\le \int_a^b \left(\frac{1}{2h}\int_{x-h}^{x+h} |f(t)|dt\right)^p dx \\
&\le \int_a^b \frac{1}{(2h)^p}\left(\int_{x-h}^{x+h} dt\right)^{p/q} \int_{x-h}^{x+h} |f(t)|^p dt dx \\
&= \frac{1}{2h}\int_a^b \int_{x-h}^{x+h} |f(t)|^p dt dx \\
&= \frac{1}{2h}\int_a^b \int_{-h}^{h} |f(t+x)|^p dt dx \\
&= \frac{1}{2h}\int_{-h}^{h} \int_a^b |f(t+x)|^p dx dt \\
&\le \frac{1}{2h}\int_{-h}^{h} \int_a^b |f(x)|^p dx dt \\
&= \int_a^b |f(x)|^p dx.
\end{aligned}$$

It follows that for two functions $f, g \in L^p[a, b]$,

$$\int_a^b |f_h(x) - g_h(x)|^p dx \le \int_a^b |f(x) - g(x)|^p dx,$$

or $\rho(f_h, g_h) \le \rho(f, g)$ with $\rho(f, g) = \left(\int_a^b |f(x) - g(x)|^p dx\right)^{1/p}$.

Theorem C.3.6 *A subset A of $L^p[a, b]$ $(1 < p < \infty)$ is sequentially compact if and only if the following two conditions hold.*

(a) There exists a constant $K > 0$ such that for any $f \in A$, we have

$$\int_a^b |f(x)|^p dx \le K^p$$

(b) For any $\varepsilon > 0$, there exists a $\delta = \delta(\varepsilon) > 0$, whenever $0 < h < \delta$, $\rho(f_h, f) < \varepsilon$ holds for all $f \in A$. □

Proof (1) *Necessity*. A is bounded because of sequentially compactness that implies (a). Moreover, for any $\varepsilon > 0$, there is a finite $(\varepsilon/3)$-net B, say. In addition, for any $f \in L^p[a, b]$ there is a continuous function $\varphi(x)$ such that $\varphi(a) = \varphi(b) = 0$, and $\rho(f, \varphi)$ can be arbitrarily small. Here, the boundary condition $\varphi(a) = \varphi(b) = 0$ makes it possible to continuously extend the function beyond $[a, b]$ such that it is everywhere zero out of $[a, b]$. Therefore, without loss of generality, we may assume the set B admits such continuous functions:

$$f_1(x), \ldots, f_{n_0}(x).$$

Invoking the continuity and the Mean Value Theorem, when $h \to 0$,

$$f_{k,h}(x) = \frac{1}{2h}\int_{x-h}^{x+h} f_k(t)dt = f_k(x+\theta h) \to f_k(x),$$

uniformly in x and $k = 1, \ldots, n_0$, where $0 \le \theta < 1$. Thus, when $h \to 0$,

$$\rho(f_{k,h}, f_k) \to 0$$

uniformly in $k = 1, \ldots, n_0$. Thus, for ε given above, there exists $\delta > 0$ such that whenever $0 < h < \delta$,

$$\rho(f_{k,h}, f_k) < \frac{1}{3}\varepsilon$$

holds for all k.

Now, taking any $f \in A$, there is a $f_k \in B$ such that

$$\rho(f, f_k) < \frac{1}{3}\varepsilon.$$

Thus, when $0 < h < \delta$,

$$\begin{aligned}\rho(f, f_h) &\le \rho(f, f_k) + \rho(f_k, f_{k,h}) + \rho(f_{k,h}, f_h)\\ &\le 2\rho(f, f_k) + \rho(f_k, f_{k,h}) < \frac{2}{3}\varepsilon + \frac{1}{3}\varepsilon\\ &= \varepsilon.\end{aligned}$$

(2) *Sufficiency*. By (a), we are about to show that the set $\{f_h(x), f(x) \in A\}$ is equicontinuous. In fact, for any $x, t \in [a, b]$, $x > t$,

$$\begin{aligned}|f_h(x) - f_h(t)| &= \frac{1}{2h}\left|\int_{x-h}^{x+h} f(s)ds - \int_{t-h}^{t+h} f(s)ds\right|\\ &= \frac{1}{2h}\left|\int_{t+h}^{x+h} f(s)ds - \int_{t-h}^{x-h} f(s)ds\right|\\ &\le \frac{1}{2h}\left(\int_{t+h}^{x+h} |f(s)|ds + \int_{t-h}^{x-h} |f(s)|ds\right)\end{aligned}$$

$$\leq \frac{1}{2h} 2(x-t)^{1/q} \left(\int_a^b |f(s)|^p ds \right)^{1/p}$$
$$\leq \frac{K}{h}(x-t)^{1/q}.$$

It follows that, for each fixed h, the set is equicontinuous.

Moreover, we shall show, for each fixed h, the set is bounded in $C[a,b]$. Actually,

$$|f_h(x)| \leq \frac{1}{2h} \left(\int_{x-h}^{x+h} dt \right)^{1/q} \left(\int_{x-h}^{x+h} |f(t)|^p dt \right)^{1/p}$$
$$= \left(\frac{1}{2h} \right)^{1/p} \left(\int_{x-h}^{x+h} |f(t)|^p dt \right)^{1/p}$$
$$\leq \left(\frac{1}{2h} \right)^{1/p} \left(\int_a^b |f(t)|^p dt \right)^{1/p}.$$

Thus, the set $\{f_h(x), f(x) \in A\}$ satisfies the two conditions in Theorem A.2.2, and hence it is sequentially compact in $C[a,b]$ for each fixed h.

Invoking (b) which says $\{f_h(x), f(x) \in A\}$ is a ε-net of A as long as h is sufficiently small, it follows that A is sequentially compact. □

C.4 L^2 Spaces and Orthogonal Sequences

Among all L^p spaces, L^2 space has some special properties. Apart from being a Banach space, it is a Hilbert too. For any $f, g \in L^2$, Cauchy-Schwarz inequality yields $\|fg\| \leq \|f\|_2\|g\|_2$ that guarantees $fg \in L$.

For convenience, from now on we specify $L^2(X, \mathcal{S}, \mu)$ as $L^2([a,b], w(x))$. Here $[a,b]$ is an interval on $\mathbb{R}$ that can be bounded or unbounded (in this case we also say it is an infinite interval); $w(x)$ is a *density* on $[a,b]$. By convention, $w(x)$ is nonnegative and the set $\{x : w(x) = 0, x \in [a,b]\}$ has Lebesgue measure zero. Without loss of generality we assume $\int_a^b w(x)dx = 1$ but not compulsively. $w(x)$ is called the *weight function* for $L^2([a,b], w(x))$.

Often $L^2([a,b], w(x))$ is abbreviated as $L^2[a,b]$ if $w(x) \equiv 1$, even L^2 if there is no ambiguity raised.

In $L^2([a,b], w(x))$ an inner product and its induced norm are

$$\langle f, g\rangle = \int_a^b f(x)g(x)w(x)dx, \qquad \|f\|_2 = \left(\int_a^b f^2(x)w(x)dx \right)^{1/2}.$$

Also, according to the inner product space, if $\langle f, g\rangle = 0$ we say f and g are orthogonal w.r.t. $w(x)$; equipped with the norm $\|\cdot\|_2$ and inner product $\langle f, g\rangle$, L^2 is a

Banach space and further separable Hilbert space; and thus L^2 admits an orthonormal sequence as its basis.

Example C.4.1 Trigonometric function sequence $\{\varphi_j(x), j \geq 0\}$:

$$\varphi_0(x) \equiv 1, \quad \varphi_{2j-1}(x) = \cos(jx), \quad \varphi_{2j}(x) = \sin(jx),$$

is orthogonal in $L^2[-\pi, \pi]$. The sequence is also a basis in $L^2[-\pi, \pi]$, known as *Fourier trigonometric polynomial system*, shown in Example C.2.1.

Example C.4.2 Trigonometric function sequence $\{\varphi_j(x), j \geq 0\}$ with $\varphi_0(x) \equiv 1$, $\varphi_j(x) = \sqrt{2}\cos(\pi jx)$, $j \geq 1$, is an orthonormal basis in $L^2[0, 1]$.

This is a consequence of the induced function approach introduced in Sect. B.2. Indeed, let $f(x) \in L^2[0, 1]$, and then define

$$g(x) = \begin{cases} f(x/\pi), & x \in [0, \pi], \\ f(-x/\pi), & x \in [-\pi, 0). \end{cases}$$

Notice that $g(x)$ can be viewed as a periodic even function in $L^2[-\pi, \pi]$. Thus, the class of all these functions restricted on $[0, \pi]$ forms a subspace of $L^2[0, \pi]$ in which, implied from Example C.4.1, $\{1, \cos(x), \cos(2x), \ldots\}$ is an orthogonal basis. Noting that $f(x) = g(\pi x)$, $x \in [0, 1]$, and the $\{\varphi_j(x), j \geq 0\}$ now becomes an orthonormal basis in $L^2[0, 1]$.

Example C.4.3 Consider differential equations of Sturm-Liouville type: $y'' + \lambda w(x)y = 0$, $y(a) = y(b) = 0$. Except the trivial solution $y \equiv 0$, the equation has a sequence of solution y_j according to eigenvalue λ_j and the y_j is unique up to a constant. If $\lambda_i \neq \lambda_j$, then y_i and y_j are orthogonal w.r.t. $w(x)$ on (a, b).

Indeed, since $y_i'' + \lambda_i w(x)y_i = 0$ and $y_j'' + \lambda_j w(x)y_j = 0$, multiplying them by y_j and y_i, respectively, and then taking difference give $(y_j y_i' - y_i y_j')' + (\lambda_i - \lambda_j)w(x)y_i y_j = 0$.

It follows that

$$\int_a^b (y_j y_i' - y_i y_j')' dx + (\lambda_i - \lambda_j) \int_a^b w(x)y_i y_j dx = 0,$$

where the first term on the left vanishes by virtue of the boundary condition, resulting in $\int_a^b w(x)y_i y_j dx = 0$, the orthogonality of y_i and y_j for $\lambda_i \neq \lambda_j$.

C.4.1 Orthogonal Polynomial Sequences

Of special interest is the orthogonal polynomial sequence that has unique feature.

Theorem C.4.1 *Suppose that $\{\varphi_j(x), j \geq 0\}$ is an orthogonal polynomial sequence in $L^2([a, b], w(x))$ where $\varphi_j(x)$ is a jth monic polynomial, that is, the coefficient of x^j is 1. Then it admits a three-term recurrence relation:*

$$\varphi_{n+1}(x) = (x - a_n)\varphi_n(x) - b_n\varphi_{n-1}(x), \tag{C.4.1}$$

for $n \geq 1$, where

$$a_n = \frac{\langle x\varphi_n(x), \varphi_n(x)\rangle}{\langle \varphi_n(x), \varphi_n(x)\rangle}, \quad b_n = \frac{\langle x\varphi_n(x), \varphi_{n-1}(x)\rangle}{\langle \varphi_{n-1}(x), \varphi_{n-1}(x)\rangle}.$$

Proof Because $\varphi_{n+1}(x) - x\varphi_n(x)$ is a polynomial of order n, we may write

$$\varphi_{n+1}(x) - x\varphi_n(x) = \sum_{j=0}^{n} c_j\varphi_j(x),$$

where

$$\begin{aligned} c_j &= \langle \varphi_{n+1}(x) - x\varphi_n(x), \varphi_j(x)\rangle \\ &= \langle \varphi_{n+1}(x), \varphi_j(x)\rangle - \langle x\varphi_n(x), \varphi_j(x)\rangle \\ &= \langle \varphi_{n+1}(x), \varphi_j(x)\rangle - \langle \varphi_n(x), x\varphi_j(x)\rangle. \end{aligned}$$

By virtue of the orthogonality, $c_j = 0$ for all $j < n - 1$. We then have

$$\varphi_{n+1}(x) - x\varphi_n(x) = c_n\varphi_n(x) + c_{n-1}\varphi_{n-1}(x).$$

This verifies (C.4.1). Taking inner product on the both sides with $\varphi_n(x)$ yields

$$-\langle \varphi_n(x), x\varphi_n(x)\rangle = c_n\langle \varphi_n(x), \varphi_n(x)\rangle,$$

which gives a_n. Similarly, we have b_n. □

Remark (1) Note that for each polynomial $P_n(x)$ with order n, one may write $P_n(x) = \sum_{j=0}^{n} c_j\varphi_j(x)$ where $c_j = \langle P_n(x), \varphi_j(x)\rangle / \langle \varphi_j(x), \varphi_j(x)\rangle$. (2) If $P_n(x)$ is monic, one has $P_n(x) = \varphi_n(x) + \sum_{j=0}^{n-1} c_j\varphi_j(x)$. Hence,

$$\|P_n(x)\|^2 = \|\varphi_n(x)\|^2 + \sum_{j=0}^{n-1} c_j^2\|\varphi_j(x)\|^2 > \|\varphi_n(x)\|^2,$$

unless $P_n(x) = \varphi_n(x)$. It implies that among all monic polynomials of order n, $\varphi_n(x)$ has the least norm. (3) It follows that $\langle x\varphi_n(x), \varphi_{n-1}(x)\rangle = \langle \varphi_n(x), x\varphi_{n-1}(x)\rangle = \langle \varphi_n(x), \varphi_n(x)\rangle$. Thus, in the theorem

$$b_n = \frac{\langle x\varphi_n(x), \varphi_{n-1}(x)\rangle}{\langle \varphi_{n-1}(x), \varphi_{n-1}(x)\rangle} = \frac{\langle \varphi_n(x), \varphi_n(x)\rangle}{\langle \varphi_{n-1}(x), \varphi_{n-1}(x)\rangle} > 0.$$

Now, suppose $\{\varphi_j(x), j \geq 0\}$ in $L^2([a, b], w(x))$ is an orthonormal polynomial sequence where $\varphi_j(x)$ is the jth polynomial. Let us write $\varphi_j(x) = q_j x^j + \cdots, q_j > 0$, and define Christoffel-Darboux kernel

$$K_n(x, y) = \sum_{j=0}^{n} \varphi_j(x)\varphi_j(y), \quad x, y \in [a, b]. \tag{C.4.2}$$

We then have the following Christoffel-Darboux formula.

Theorem C.4.2 *The Kernel $K_n(x, y)$ can be written as*

$$\sum_{j=0}^{n} \varphi_j(x)\varphi_j(y) = \frac{q_n}{q_{n+1}} \frac{\varphi_{n+1}(x)\varphi_n(y) - \varphi_{n+1}(y)\varphi_n(x)}{x - y}$$

for $x \neq y$. □

Proof Let $\tilde{\varphi}_j(x) = \varphi_j(x)/q_j$ that is monic. By the three-term recurrence relation

$$\tilde{\varphi}_{n+1}(x) = (x - a_n)\tilde{\varphi}_n(x) - b_n\tilde{\varphi}_{n-1}(x),$$
$$\tilde{\varphi}_{n+1}(y) = (y - a_n)\tilde{\varphi}_n(y) - b_n\tilde{\varphi}_{n-1}(y).$$

Multiplying the first equation by $\tilde{\varphi}_n(y)$ and the second by $\tilde{\varphi}_n(x)$, and subtracting yield:

$$\begin{aligned}&\tilde{\varphi}_{n+1}(x)\tilde{\varphi}_n(y) - \tilde{\varphi}_{n+1}(y)\tilde{\varphi}_n(x)\\&= (x - y)\tilde{\varphi}_n(x)\tilde{\varphi}_n(y) + b_n[\tilde{\varphi}_n(x)\tilde{\varphi}_{n-1}(y) - \tilde{\varphi}_n(y)\tilde{\varphi}_{n-1}(x)].\end{aligned} \tag{C.4.3}$$

Notice that

$$b_n = \frac{\langle \tilde{\varphi}_n(x), \tilde{\varphi}_n(x)\rangle}{\langle \tilde{\varphi}_{n-1}(x), \tilde{\varphi}_{n-1}(x)\rangle} = \frac{q_{n-1}^2\langle \varphi_n(x), \varphi_n(x)\rangle}{q_n^2\langle \varphi_{n-1}(x), \varphi_{n-1}(x)\rangle} = \frac{q_{n-1}^2}{q_n^2}.$$

Multiplying both sides of (C.4.3) by q_n^2 yields

$$\begin{aligned}&q_n^2[\tilde{\varphi}_{n+1}(x)\tilde{\varphi}_n(y) - \tilde{\varphi}_{n+1}(y)\tilde{\varphi}_n(x)]\\&= (x - y)\varphi_n(x)\varphi_n(y) + q_{n-1}^2[\tilde{\varphi}_n(x)\tilde{\varphi}_{n-1}(y) - \tilde{\varphi}_n(y)\tilde{\varphi}_{n-1}(x)].\end{aligned} \tag{C.4.4}$$

Repeat (C.4.4) to have

$$
\begin{aligned}
&q_n^2[\tilde{\varphi}_{n+1}(x)\tilde{\varphi}_n(y) - \tilde{\varphi}_{n+1}(y)\tilde{\varphi}_n(x)] \\
&= (x-y)\sum_{j=1}^{n} \varphi_n(x)\varphi_n(y) + q_0^2[\tilde{\varphi}_1(x)\tilde{\varphi}_0(y) - \tilde{\varphi}_1(y)\tilde{\varphi}_0(x)] \\
&= (x-y)\sum_{j=0}^{n} \varphi_n(x)\varphi_n(y),
\end{aligned} \tag{C.4.5}
$$

since $q_0 = 1$, $\tilde{\varphi}_0(x) \equiv 1$ and $\tilde{\varphi}_1(x) - \tilde{\varphi}_1(y) = x - y$. The formula then follows immediately by noting that $\tilde{\varphi}_j(x) = \varphi_j(x)/q_j$. □

It follows immediately from Theorem C.4.2 that

$$
K_n(x,x) = \sum_{j=0}^{n} \varphi_j^2(x) = \frac{q_n}{q_{n+1}}[\varphi_{n+1}'(x)\varphi_n(x) - \varphi_{n+1}(x)\varphi_n'(x)],
$$

due to L'Hôpital's Rule.

C.4.2 Construction of Orthogonal Polynomials (Functions)

As far as we are aware, there are three approaches to construct orthogonal polynomials (functions), that is, Gram-Schmidt procedure, eigenfunctions of differential operators/equations, and integrable operators/equations.

Gram-Schmidt procedure. If $\psi_i(x) \in L^2([a,b], w(x))$, $1 \le i \le s$, define the Gram determinant of $\{\psi_i(x), 1 \le i \le s\}$,

$$
\Delta_s = \Delta_s(\psi_1, \ldots, \psi_s) = \begin{vmatrix} \langle\psi_1, \psi_1\rangle & \cdots & \langle\psi_1, \psi_s\rangle \\ \langle\psi_2, \psi_1\rangle & \cdots & \langle\psi_2, \psi_s\rangle \\ \cdots & \cdots & \cdots \\ \langle\psi_s, \psi_1\rangle & \cdots & \langle\psi_s, \psi_s\rangle \end{vmatrix}.
$$

Then, $\{\psi_i(x), 1 \le i \le s\}$ is dependent if and only if $\Delta_s(\psi_1, \ldots, \psi_s) = 0$.

In fact, if $\{\psi_i(x), 1 \le i \le s\}$ is dependent, then there exist a_i, $1 \le i \le s$, not all zero, such that $\sum_{i=1}^{s} a_i\psi_i(x) \equiv 0$ on $[a,b]$. This implies that the system of linear equations

$$
\sum_{i=1}^{s} a_i\langle\psi_i, \psi_j\rangle = 0, \quad j = 1, \ldots, s, \tag{C.4.6}
$$

has nonzero solution, implying $\Delta_s(\psi_1, \ldots, \psi_s) = 0$.

Conversely, $\Delta_s(\psi_1, \ldots, \psi_s) = 0$ implies the system (C.4.6) has nonzero solution. Rewrite (C.4.6) as

$$\int_a^b w(x)\psi_j(x)\sum_{i=1}^{s} a_i\psi_i(x)dx = 0, \quad j = 1, \ldots, s. \tag{C.4.7}$$

Multiplying each equation by a_j and taking summation over j give

$$\int_a^b w(x)\left(\sum_{i=1}^{s} a_i\psi_i(x)\right)^2 dx = 0. \tag{C.4.8}$$

This yields $\sum_{i=1}^{s} a_i\psi_i(x) = 0$ a.e. by the property of weight $w(x)$. The assertion holds.

Moreover, if $\{\psi_i(x), 1 \le i \le s\}$ is independent, then $\Delta_s > 0$. In effect, define the following determinant

$$\Psi_s(x) = \begin{vmatrix} \langle\psi_1, \psi_1\rangle & \cdots & \langle\psi_1, \psi_{s-1}\rangle & \psi_1(x) \\ \langle\psi_2, \psi_1\rangle & \cdots & \langle\psi_2, \psi_{s-1}\rangle & \psi_2(x) \\ \cdots & \cdots & \cdots & \cdots \\ \langle\psi_s, \psi_1\rangle & \cdots & \langle\psi_{s-1}, \psi_{s-1}\rangle & \psi_s(x) \end{vmatrix}.$$

Multiplying both sides by $w(x)\psi_j(x)$ and taking integration over $[a, b]$, we have $\langle\Psi_s(x), \psi_j(x)\rangle = 0$ for $j = 1, \ldots, s-1$ since the last column will be the same as the jth one, while $\langle\Psi_s(x), \psi_s(x)\rangle = \Delta_s$.

On the other hand, we expand the determinant $\Psi_s(x)$:

$$\Psi_s(x) = a_1\psi_1(x) + \cdots + a_{s-1}\psi_{s-1}(x) + \Delta_{s-1}\psi_s(x) \tag{C.4.9}$$

where $\Delta_{s-1} \neq 0$ due to the independence of $\{\psi_i(x), 1 \le i \le s-1\}$. Multiplying both sides of (C.4.9) by $\Psi_s(x)w(x)$ and taking integration give

$$\|\Psi_s(x)\|^2 = \Delta_{s-1}\langle\Psi_s(x), \psi_s(x)\rangle = \Delta_{s-1}\Delta_s > 0, \tag{C.4.10}$$

so Δ_{s-1} and Δ_s have the same sign. Consequently, all Δ_j have the same sign, while $\Delta_1 = \langle\psi_1(x), \psi_1(x)\rangle > 0$.

Theorem C.4.3 *Suppose that $\psi_i(x) \in L^2([a, b], w(x)), i \ge 1$, (finite or infinite) are independent, $\Psi_s(x)$ is defined as before. Define $\varphi_1(x) = \psi_1(x)/\sqrt{\Delta_1}$, $\varphi_j(x) = \Psi_j(x)/\sqrt{\Delta_{j-1}\Delta_j}$, $j \ge 2$. Then, $\{\varphi_j(x), j \ge 1\}$ is orthonormal.* □

Proof Denoting $\Delta_0 = 1$, $\varphi_j(x) = \Psi_j(x)/\sqrt{\Delta_{j-1}\Delta_j}$, $j \ge 1$. For $s \le j$,

$$\begin{aligned}\langle\varphi_s(x),\varphi_j(x)\rangle &= \frac{\langle\Psi_s(x),\Psi_j(x)\rangle}{\sqrt{\Delta_{j-1}\Delta_j}\sqrt{\Delta_{s-1}\Delta_s}}\\ &= \frac{\langle\sum_{i=1}^{s-1}a_i\psi_i(x)+\Delta_{s-1}\psi_s(x),\Psi_j(x)\rangle}{\sqrt{\Delta_{j-1}\Delta_j}\sqrt{\Delta_{s-1}\Delta_s}}\\ &= \frac{\Delta_{s-1}\langle\psi_s(x),\Psi_j(x)\rangle}{\sqrt{\Delta_{j-1}\Delta_j}\sqrt{\Delta_{s-1}\Delta_s}} = \begin{cases}1, & j=s\\ 0, & s<j\end{cases}.\end{aligned}$$

Remark (1) It is clear that $\varphi_j(x)$ is a combination of $\psi_1(x),\ldots,\psi_j(x)$; and vice versa. More importantly, it follows that the space spanned by $\{\varphi_j(x)\}$ is the same as that spanned by $\{\psi_j(x)\}$.

(2) Since $\{1, x, x^2, \ldots,\}$ is independent on any $[a, b]$, given any density $w(x)$ on $[a, b]$, the sequence can be orthogonalized, and the resultant orthonormal sequence $\{\varphi_j(x)\}$ is unique up to a constant ± 1. See Todd (1963). On the other hand, two orthogonal polynomial sequences $\{\varphi_j(x)\}$ and $\{\psi_j(x)\}$ in $L^2([a, b], w(x))$ have relation $\varphi_j(x) = \alpha_j\psi_j(x)$ with $\alpha_j \neq 0$ for all j. Thus, the orthogonal polynomial sequence is unique up to a constant.

(3) It follows that, a function $f(x) \perp \psi_j(x), \forall j, \Leftrightarrow f(x) \perp \varphi_j(x), \forall j$. As a result, $\{\psi_j(x)\}$ is complete if and only if $\{\varphi_j(x)\}$ is complete. Therefore, the orthonormal sequence generated from $\{1, x, x^2, \ldots,\}$ by the Gram-Schmidt procedure is complete. See Theorem C.4.4 below.

Theorem C.4.4 *Power sequence* $\{1, x, x^2, \ldots,\}$ *is dense in* $L^2([a, b], w(x))$. *Moreover, the orthonormal polynomial sequence* $\{\varphi_j(x), j \geq 0\}$ *generated by Gram-Schmidt procedure from* $\{1, x, x^2, \ldots,\}$ *is complete and* $\varphi_j(x)$ *is a* j*th polynomial; and hence* $\{\varphi_j(x), j \geq 0\}$ *is an orthonormal basis in* $L^2([a, b], w(x))$. □

Proof The first assertion holds because the set of continuous functions is dense in $L^2([a, b], w(x))$, while $\{1, x, x^2, \ldots,\}$ is dense in $C[a, b]$ shown by Theorem B.1.1 (Weierstrass theorem). The second assertion holds because any function that is orthogonal with every element of $\{\varphi_j(x), j \geq 0\}$, and hence of $\{x^j, j = 0, 1, 2, \ldots\}$ is a zero function. □

Example C.4.4 As pointed out above, given an interval $[a, b]$ and on which a density $w(x)$, one always can generate an orthogonal polynomial sequence from $\{1, x, x^2, \ldots\}$. See Table C.1:

Example C.4.5 Here is an another example of orthogonal polynomial sequence generated by Gram-Schmidt schedule. This sequence is similar to the Hermite polynomial sequence in that the orthogonality is defined in the entire real line $\mathbb{R}$, but its density has fatter tails than e^{-x^2}. Thus, it has a broad application area, in particular in finance. This sequence is Logistic orthogonal polynomials.

Standardized logistic density takes the form of

$$f(x) = \frac{\pi}{\sqrt{3}}\frac{1}{\exp(\pi x/\sqrt{3}) + 2 + \exp(-\pi x/\sqrt{3})},$$

Table C.1 Orthogonal sequences generated by powers $\{1, x, x^2, \ldots\}$

Types	$[a, b]$	$w(x)$
Legendre polynomials	$[-1, 1]$	1
Chebyshev polynomials of type I	$[-1, 1]$	$1/\sqrt{1-x^2}$
Chebyshev polynomials of type II	$[-1, 1]$	$\sqrt{1-x^2}$
Jacobi polynomials	$[-1, 1]$	$(1-x)^{\alpha}(1+x)^{\beta}, \alpha, \beta > -1$
Laguerre polynomials	$(0, \infty)$	e^{-x}
Generalized Laguerre polynomials	$(0, \infty)$	$x^{\alpha}e^{-x}, \alpha > 0$
Hermite polynomials	$(-\infty, \infty)$	e^{-x^2}

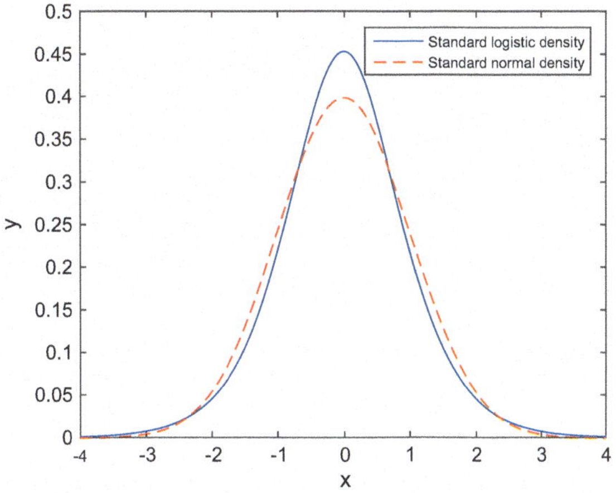

Fig. C.1 Logistic and normal density functions

whose name stems from the sigmoid or "logistic" form of the distribution function

$$F(x) = \int_{-\infty}^{x} f(z)dz = \frac{1}{1 + \exp(-\pi x/\sqrt{3})}.$$

The tail of the logistic density is fatter than that of normal density. See Fig. C.1.

The ith moment of logistic density is

$$\mathbb{E}[X^i] = (2^i - 2)3^{i/2}|B_i|,$$

where B_i is the ith Bernoulli number (i.e., $B_0 = 1$, $B_1 = -1/2$, $B_2 = 1/6$, $B_4 = -1/30, \ldots$).

Define the logistic polynomials $Lo_i(x)$ that are orthogonal w.r.t. logistic density

Table C.2 Comparison of moments between normal and logistic distributions

i	Gaussian $\mathbb{E}(X^i)$	Logistic $\mathbb{E}(X^i)$	Ratio
2	1	1	1
4	3	4.2	1.4
6	15	39.9	2.7
8	105	686	6.5
10	945	18814	19.9

$$\langle Lo_i, Lo_j \rangle = \int Lo_i(x)Lo_j(x)f(x)dx = 0, \quad i \neq j.$$

Here, $Lo_i(x)$ can be generated by Gram-Schmidt procedure

$$Lo_i(x) = x^i - \sum_{j=0}^{i-1} \frac{\langle Lo_j, x^i \rangle}{\langle Lo_j, Lo_j \rangle} Lo_j(x),$$

with $Lo_0(x) = 1$ and the polynomials satisfy the three-term recurrence relation,

$$Lo_{i+1}(x) = x\, Lo_i(x) - \frac{3i^4}{(2i+1)(2i-1)} Lo_{i-1}(x).$$

Moreover,

$$\langle Lo_i, Lo_i \rangle = \frac{3^i (i!)^4}{(2i-1)!!(2i+1)!!}.$$

As shown in Heston and Rossi (2017) (also Theorem C.4.4), $\{Lo_i(x)\}$ is a complete orthogonal polynomial sequence in $L^2(\mathbb{R}, f(x))$ where $f(x)$ is the logistic density.

Differential operators/equations. Let us now consider differential equations of hypergeometric type

$$s(x)y''(x) + v(x)y'(x) + \lambda y(x) = 0, \qquad \text{(C.4.11)}$$

where $s(x)$ and $v(x)$ are polynomials of degree at most 2 and 1 respectively, while λ is a constant independent of x. We shall refer to the solutions of (C.4.11) as *functions of hypergeometric type*. The following lemmas are cited from Nikiforov and Uvarov (1988).

Lemma C.4.1 *All derivatives of the solutions of* (C.4.11) *are still of hypergeometric type; meanwhile, any function of hypergeometric type is a derivative of some function of hypergeometric type with* $\lambda \neq 0$ *in the differential equation.*

Proof Differentiating (C.4.11) and denoting $z_1(x) = y'(x)$ entail that

$$s(x)z_1''(x) + v_1(x)z_1'(x) + \eta_1 z_1(x) = 0 \tag{C.4.12}$$

where $v_1(x) = v(x) + s'(x)$ and $\eta_1 = \lambda + v'(x)$.

Since $v_1(x)$ is a polynomial in x of degree at most 1 and η_1 is independent of x, Eq. (C.4.12) is of hypergeometric type.

Now let $z_1(x)$ be a solution of (C.4.12) and suppose $\lambda = \eta_1 - v_1'(x) + s''(x) \neq 0$. Construct a function $y(x) = -\frac{1}{\lambda}(s(x)z_1'(x) + v(x)z_1(x))$. Then

$$\begin{aligned}\lambda y'(x) &= -(s(x)z_1'(x) + v(x)z_1(x))' \\ &= -s(x)z_1''(x) - s'(x)z_1'(x) - v(x)z_1'(x) - v'(x)z_1(x) \\ &= \lambda z_1(x),\end{aligned}$$

by virtue of (C.4.12). Hence, $y'(x) = z_1(x)$. Therefore, the construction of $y(x)$ (i.e., $s(x)z_1'(x) + v(x)z_1(x) + \lambda y(x) = 0$) implies that $y(x)$ is a solution of Eq. (C.4.11).

It follows from induction that $z_i(x) = y^{(i)}(x)$ is a solution of

$$s(x)z_i''(x) + v_i(x)z_i'(x) + \eta_i z_i(x) = 0 \tag{C.4.13}$$

where $v_i(x) = v(x) + is'(x)$ and $\eta_i = \lambda + iv'(x) + \frac{i(i-1)}{2}s''(x)$.

Moreover, every solution of (C.4.13) for $\eta_k \neq 0$ ($k = 0, 1, \ldots, i-1$) can be represented as $z_i(x) = y^{(i)}(x)$, where $y(x)$ is a solution of (C.4.11). □

Observe that Lemma C.4.1 provides us with a possibility to find out a family of particular solutions of (C.4.11) according to a given λ. Indeed, if $\eta_i(t) = \lambda + iv'(x) + \frac{i(i-1)}{2}s''(x) = 0$, it is evident that Eq. (C.4.13) has a solution $z_i(x) = z_i$ independent of x. Since $z_i = y^{(i)}(x)$, we assert that when $\lambda \equiv \lambda_i = -iv'(x) - \frac{i(i-1)}{2}s''(x)$, $y(x) = y_i(x)$, as a solution of (C.4.11), is a polynomial in x of degree exactly i.

In order to find out the explicit expression of $y_i(x)$, where i is any fixed positive integer, noting that (C.4.13) is valid for $k = 0, 1, \ldots, i$ (that is, i can be substituted by any k), we multiply Eqs. (C.4.11) and (C.4.13) by appropriate functions $w(x)$ and $w_k(x)$ such that they can be written in self-adjoint form

$$(s(x)w(x)y'(x))' + \lambda w(x)y(x) = 0 \tag{C.4.14a}$$

$$(s(x)w_k(x)z_k'(x))' + \eta_k w_k(x)z_k(x) = 0 \tag{C.4.14b}$$

where $w(x)$ and $w_k(x)$ satisfy that

$$(s(x)w(x))' = v(x)w(x) \tag{C.4.15a}$$

$$(s(x)w_k(x))' = v_k(x)w_k(x) \tag{C.4.15b}$$

It follows from (C.4.15) that

$$\frac{(s(x)w_k(x))'}{w_k(x)} = v_k(x) = v(x) + ks'(x) = \frac{(s(x)w(x))'}{w(x)} + ks'(x)$$

which entails that

$$\frac{w_k'(x)}{w_k(x)} = \frac{w'(x)}{w(x)} + k\frac{s'(x)}{s(x)}.$$

Whence we have

$$w_k(x) = s^k(x)w(x), \quad k = 0, 1, \ldots \tag{C.4.16}$$

where $w_0(x) = w(x)$ by definition.

Observing that $s(x)w_k(x) = w_{k+1}(x)$ and $z_k'(x) = z_{k+1}(x)$, it follows from (C.4.14b) that

$$w_k(x)z_k(x) = -\frac{1}{\eta_k}(s(x)w_k(x)z_k'(x))' = -\frac{1}{\eta_k}(w_{k+1}(x)z_{k+1}(x))'. \tag{C.4.17}$$

Hence, when $k < i$ we obtain successively

$$\begin{aligned}
w_k(x)z_k(x) &= -\frac{1}{\eta_k}(w_{k+1}(x)z_{k+1}(x))' \\
&= \frac{(-1)^2}{\eta_k\eta_{k+1}}(w_{k+2}(x)z_{k+2}(x))'' \\
&= \cdots = (-1)^{i-k}\frac{1}{\eta_k\cdots\eta_{i-1}}(w_i(x)z_i(x))^{(i-k)} \\
&= \frac{A_k}{A_i}(w_i(x)z_i(x))^{(i-k)}
\end{aligned}$$

where we denote

$$A_i = (-1)^i\prod_{j=0}^{i-1}\eta_j, \qquad A_0 = 1. \tag{C.4.18}$$

By virtue of that $y_i(x)$ is a polynomial of degree i and $z_k = y^{(k)}, z_i = y^{(i)} = \text{const.}$, we finally have

$$y_i^{(k)}(x) = \frac{A_{ki}B_i}{w_k(x)}[w_i(x)]^{(i-k)} \tag{C.4.19}$$

where $A_{ki} := A_k(\lambda)|_{\lambda=\lambda_i}$ and $B_i = \frac{1}{A_{ii}}y_i^{(i)}(x)$.

Hence, in particular, when $k = 0$, we have an explicit representation of $y_i(x)$ of hypergeometric type

$$y_i(x) = \frac{B_i}{w(x)}\frac{d^i}{dx^i}[s^i(x)w(x)]. \tag{C.4.20}$$

We call (C.4.20) the *Rodrigues formula*, since it was established in 1814 by B. O. Rodrigues for special polynomials of hypergeometric type, namely the Legendre polynomials, for which $s(x) = 1 - x^2$, $w(x) = 1$.

Table C.3 Components of hypergeometric differential equations for classical orthogonal polynomials

$P_i(x)$	$P_i^{(\alpha,\beta)}(x)$	$L_i^{\alpha}(x)$	$H_i(x)$
$[a, b]$	$[-1, 1]$	$(0, \infty)$	$(-\infty, \infty)$
$w(x)$	$(1-x)^{\alpha}(1+x)^{\beta}$, $\alpha, \beta > -1$	$x^{\alpha}e^{-x}, \alpha > 0$	e^{-x^2}
$s(x)$	$1 - x^2$	x	1
$v(x)$	$\beta - \alpha - (\alpha + \beta + 1)x$	$-x + \alpha + 1$	$-2x$
λ_i	$i(i + \alpha + \beta + 1)$	i	$2i$

Lemma C.4.2 *Suppose that polynomials $y_i(x)$ are the solutions of equation of hypergeometric type*

$$s(x)y''(x) + v(x)y'(x) + \lambda_i y(x) = 0 \tag{C.4.21}$$

where $\lambda_i = -iv'(x) - \frac{i(i-1)}{2}s''(x)$. In addition, suppose a density function $w(x)$ satisfies that $(s(x)w(x))' = v(x)w(x)$ and the so-called boundary condition

$$s(x)w(x)x^k|_{x=a,b} = 0, \qquad k = 0, 1, \ldots \tag{C.4.22}$$

where a and b are the boundary points of the support of $w(x)$. Then the $y_i(x)$ are orthogonal on (a, b) with respect to $w(x)$.

The orthogonal polynomial system $\{y_i(x)\}$ with $w(x)$ satisfying conditions in Lemma C.4.2 is called *a classic orthogonal polynomial system* of continuous variables. It is usually considered the auxiliary conditions $w(x) > 0$ and $s(x) > 0$ on (a, b).

Conversely, suppose that $w(x)$ satisfies a first-order differential equation

$$\frac{d}{dx}(s(x)w(x)) = v(x)w(x), \tag{C.4.23}$$

where $s(x)$ and $v(x)$ are polynomials with degree no higher than the second and first, respectively, and satisfy the boundary conditions

$$\lim_{x \to a+} s(x)w(x)x^k = 0, \quad \lim_{x \to b-} s(x)w(x)x^k = 0, \ \forall\, k \geq 0. \tag{C.4.24}$$

It is well known that, depending on $s(x)$ and $v(x)$ up to linear transformations of independent variable, the solution $w(x)$ of (C.4.23) and (C.4.24) is a density function on (a, b) for determining (up to a multiplicative constant) classical orthogonal polynomials, namely, Laguerre, Hermite and Jacobi polynomials (Table C.3).

Here, Jacobi polynomials with parameters α and β can be specified as Legendre ($\alpha = \beta = 0$) and Chebyshev polynomials ($\alpha = \beta = 1/2$ the first type or $\alpha = \beta = -1/2$ the second type) as special cases.

Proof (*Lemma* C.4.2) Observe that $y_m(x)$ and $y_i(x)$ satisfy the following differential equations in self-adjoint form respectively

$$(s(x)w(x)y_i'(x))' + \lambda_i w(x)y_i(x) = 0, \tag{C.4.25a}$$
$$(s(x)w(x)y_m'(x))' + \lambda_m w(x)y_m(x) = 0. \tag{C.4.25b}$$

Operation (C.4.25b)$\times y_i-$(C.4.25a)$\times y_m$ yields

$$\begin{aligned}&(\lambda_m - \lambda_i)w(x)y_m(x)y_i(x)\\ &= (s(x)w(x)y_i'(x))'y_m(x) - (s(x)w(x)y_m'(x))'y_i(x).\end{aligned}$$

Integration by parts gives

$$\begin{aligned}&(\lambda_m - \lambda_i)\int_a^b w(x)y_m(x)y_i(x)dx\\ &= s(x)w(x)y_i'(x)y_m(x)|_a^b - s(x)w(x)y_m'(x)y_i(x)|_a^b = 0\end{aligned}$$

due to the boundary condition (C.4.22).

Hence, if $\lambda_m \neq \lambda_i$, $\int_a^b w(x)y_m(x)y_i(x)dx = 0$, so $\{y_i(x)\}$ is orthogonal with weight $w(x)$. □

Note that $\lambda_i \neq \lambda_m \Leftrightarrow m \neq i$. In fact, $\lambda_i - \lambda_m = (m-i)[v'(x) + \frac{1}{2}(m+i-1)s''(x)]$, but $v'(x) + \frac{1}{2}(m+i-1)s''(x) = 0$ implies both $v'(x) = 0$ and $s''(x) = 0$. Nonetheless, the vanishes of the two simultaneously will not result in a density $w(x)$ that satisfies boundary conditions.

Lemma C.4.3 *For the classical orthogonal polynomial $y_i(x)$ of hypergeometric type with weight $w(x)$ satisfying*

$$s(x)y''(x) + v(x)y'(x) + \lambda_i y(x) = 0, \tag{C.4.26}$$

where $\lambda_i = -iv'(x) - \frac{1}{2}i(i-1)s''(x)$, the derivatives $y_i^{(k)}(x)$, $k \geq 0$, are orthogonal with respect to $w_k(x) = s^k(x)w(x)$ on (a, b).

Proof According to Lemma C.4.1, because $y_i(x)$ satisfies Eq. (C.4.26), $y_i^{(k)}(x)$ is a solution of the following differential equation

$$s(x)[y_i^{(k)}(x)]'' + v_k(x)[y_i^{(k)}(x)]' + \eta_{ki}y_i^{(k)}(x) = 0, \tag{C.4.27}$$

where $v_k(x) = v(x) + ks'(x)$ and $\eta_{ki} = \lambda_i + kv'(x) + \frac{1}{2}k(k-1)s''(x)$.

It is easy to verify that given $(s'(x)w(x))' = v(x)w(x)$, $w_k(x)$ satisfies

$$(s(x)w_k(x))' = v_k(x)w_k(x). \tag{C.4.28}$$

We therefore have a self-adjoint form of Eq. (C.4.27),

$$\{s(x)w_k(x)[y_i^{(k)}(x)]'\}' + \eta_{ki}\, w_k(x)y_i^{(k)}(x) = 0. \tag{C.4.29}$$

On the other hand, suppose that $y_m^{(k)}(x)$ is the kth derivative of $y_m(x)$ of hypergeometric type corresponding to λ_m, then we also have a similar equation to (C.4.29). Aligning them together gives

$$\{s(x)w_k(x)[y_i^{(k)}(x)]'\}' + \eta_{ki}\, w_k(x)y_i^{(k)}(x) = 0, \tag{C.4.30a}$$
$$\{s(x)w_k(x)[y_m^{(k)}(x)]'\}' + \eta_{km}\, w_k(x)y_m^{(k)}(x) = 0. \tag{C.4.30b}$$

A similar derivation as in Lemma C.4.2 yields

$$\begin{aligned}
&(\eta_{km} - \eta_{ki}) \int_a^b w_k(x)y_m^{(k)}(x)y_i^{(k)}(x)dx \\
&= \int_a^b \{s(x)w_k(x)[y_i^{(k)}(x)]'\}'y_m^{(k)}(x)dx - \int_a^b \{s(x)w_k(x)[y_m^{(k)}(x)]'\}'y_i^{(k)}(x)dx \\
&= s(x)w_k(x)[y_i^{(k)}(x)]'y_m^{(k)}(x)|_a^b - s(x)w_k(x)[y_m^{(k)}(x)]'y_i^{(k)}(x)|_a^b \\
&= 0
\end{aligned}$$

by virtue of the boundary condition of $w(x)$.

Therefore, when $\eta_{km} \neq \eta_{ki}$, viz., $m \neq i$, we have $\int_a^b w_k(x)y_m^{(k)}(x)y_i^{(k)}(x)dx = 0$. In other words,

$$\int_a^b w_k(x)y_m^{(k)}(x)y_i^{(k)}(x)dx = \delta_{mi}d_{ki}^2$$

where $d_{ki}^2 := \int_a^b w_k(x)[y_i^{(k)}(x)]^2dx$. □

This lemma shows us that the hypergeometric differential equation with particular λ_i has polynomial solutions $y_i(x)$ of degree i, while whose derivatives $\{y_i^{(k)}(x)\}$, $k \geq 0$, are orthogonal sequence w.r.t. $w_k(x)$. If we define differential operator $D : y \mapsto s(x)y'' + v(x)y'$, then λ_i is such that $-D(y) = \lambda_i y$, and thus λ_i are called *eigenvalues of operator* $-D$, and $y_i(x)$ are corresponding eigenfunctions.

Let us find out the relationship between the squared norm d_{ki}^2 of $y_i^{(k)}(x)$ and the squared norm $d_i^2 := d_{0i}^2$ of $y_i(x)$. Toward this end, rewrite Eq. (C.4.30a) as

$$[w_{k+1}(x)y_i^{(k+1)}(x)]' + \eta_{ki}\, w_k(x)y_i^{(k)}(x) = 0. \tag{C.4.31}$$

Multiplying (C.4.31) by $y_i^{(k)}(x)$ and integrating by parts over (a, b) give

$$\eta_{ki} d_{ki}^2 = \eta_{ki} \int_a^b w_k(x)[y_i^{(k)}(x)]^2 dx \tag{C.4.32}$$

$$= -\int_a^b [w_{k+1}(x) y_i^{(k+1)}(x)]' y_i^{(k)}(x) dx$$

$$= -w_{k+1}(x) y_i^{(k+1)}(x) y_i^{(k)}(x)|_a^b + \int_a^b w_{k+1}(x)[y_i^{(k+1)}(x)]^2 dx$$

$$= d_{k+1,i}^2. \tag{C.4.33}$$

Whence, by induction, we obtain

$$d_{mi}^2 = d_i^2 \prod_{k=0}^{m-1} \eta_{ki}. \tag{C.4.34}$$

where $\eta_{0i} = \lambda_i$.

Integral operators. The third approach of generating orthogonal function sequence is the eigenfunctions of integral operators. Suppose $X(t)$ is a second-order stochastic process that has zero mean and is *continuous in quadratic mean* on the interval $[a, b]$, that is, $\lim_{s \to t} \mathbb{E}[X(s) - X(t)]^2 = 0$ for all $t \in [a, b]$. Let $\gamma(t, s) = \mathbb{E}[X(t)X(s)]$ be its covariance function, $t, s \in [a, b]$. Clearly, $\gamma(t, s)$ is symmetric, $\gamma(t, s) = \gamma(s, t)$ for any $t, s \in [a, b]$.

We claim that $\gamma(t, s)$ is a *positive definite function*, that is, for any $n \geq 1$, and any $t_1, \ldots, t_n \in [a, b]$, square matrix Γ with elements $\gamma(t_i, t_j)$, $1 \leq i, j \leq n$, at its ith row and jth column is nonnegative definite. Indeed, for any vector $a = (a_1, \ldots, a_n)^\top \in \mathbb{R}^n$,

$$\begin{aligned} a^\top \Gamma a &= \sum_{i=1}^n \sum_{j=1}^n a_i a_j \gamma(t_i, t_j) = \sum_{i=1}^n \sum_{j=1}^n a_i a_j \mathbb{E}[X(t_i)X(t_j)] \\ &= \mathbb{E}\left[\sum_{i=1}^n \sum_{j=1}^n a_i a_j X(t_i)X(t_j)\right] = \mathbb{E}\left[\sum_{i=1}^n a_i X(t_i)\right]^2 \\ &\geq 0. \end{aligned}$$

Define integral operator $\mathcal{H}$ on $L^2[a, b]$,

$$(\mathcal{H}g)(r) = \int_a^b \gamma(r, s) g(s) ds. \tag{C.4.35}$$

We say that $\mathcal{H}$ is symmetric, because $\langle \mathcal{H}g, f \rangle = \langle g, \mathcal{H}f \rangle$ for any $f, g \in L^2[a, b]$; also operator $\mathcal{H}$ is positive since $\langle \mathcal{H}f, f \rangle \geq 0$ for any $f \in L^2[a, b]$. In fact,

$$\begin{aligned}\langle \mathcal{H}f, f\rangle &= \int_a^b f(t)\int_a^b \gamma(t,s)f(s)dsdt \\ &= \mathbb{E}\left[\int_a^b\int_a^b f(t)X(t)X(s)f(s)dsdt\right] \\ &= \mathbb{E}\left[\int_a^b f(t)X(t)dt\right]^2 \geq 0.\end{aligned}$$

The following is the Mercer's representation theorem.

Theorem C.4.5 *If $\gamma(t,s)$ is continuous positive definite function, then there exists a sequence of functions $\varphi_i(r)$ called eigenfunctions of $\mathcal{H}$ defined by* (C.4.35) *and a corresponding sequence of nonnegative numbers λ_i called eigenvalues of $\mathcal{H}$ such that $(\mathcal{H}\varphi_i)(r) = \lambda_i\varphi_i(r)$ and*

$$\int_a^b \varphi_i(r)\varphi_j(r)dr = \delta_{ij}.$$

Moreover we have

$$\gamma(t,s) = \sum_{i=1}^{\infty} \lambda_i\varphi_i(t)\varphi_i(s) \tag{C.4.36}$$

where the series converges uniformly and absolutely on $[a, b]$. □

For the proof, see Cucker and Zhou (2007), Berlinet and Thomas-Agnan (2004) and Riesz and SZ.-Nagy (1956). Note that if $\gamma(t,s)$ is not continuous, one may still have expansion (C.4.36) but the series might not be convergent uniformly and absolutely, whereas the convergence holds in L^2 sense. See Riesz and SZ.-Nagy (1956).

It can be seen that the symmetric positive definite operator on $L^2[a,b]$ may produce an orthonormal basis for the space. The following two examples in Phillips (1998) use the orthonormal sequences generated by the covariance function of Brownian motion and Brownian bridge to expand stochastic processes for better understanding spurious regressions.

Example C.4.6 For standard Brownian motion $W(t), t \in [0, 1], \gamma(t, s) = \min(t, s)$ and the integral operator $\mathcal{H}$ generated by this $\gamma(t, s)$ has eigenvalues and eigenfunctions

$$\lambda_k = \frac{4}{(2k-1)^2\pi^2}, \quad \varphi_k(r) = \sqrt{2}\sin[(k-1/2)r].$$

Accordingly, the $\{\varphi_k(r)\}$ becomes an orthonormal basis in $L^2[0, 1]$.

Example C.4.7 Let $V(t) = W(t) - tW(1)$ be the Brownian bridge generated by Brownian motion $W(t)$, $t \in [0, 1]$. The covariance function of $V(t)$ is $\gamma(t, s) = \min(r, s) - rs$. The integral operator $\mathcal{H}$ generated by this $\gamma(t, s)$ has eigenvalues and eigenfunctions

$$\lambda_k = \frac{1}{k^2\pi^2}, \quad \varphi_k(r) = \sqrt{2}\sin(k\pi r).$$

Again, this $\{\varphi_k(r)\}$ becomes an orthonormal basis in $L^2[0, 1]$.

C.4.3 Properties of Particular Orthogonal Polynomials

In this subsection, we shall show the properties of some orthogonal polynomial sequences that are frequently used in the literature.

Legendre polynomial sequence $\{P_n(x)\}$ is an orthogonal basis in Hilbert space $L^2[-1, 1]$. Particularly, $P_0(x) = 1$, $P_1(x) = x$, $P_2(x) = (3x^2 - 1)/2, \ldots$. It has Rodrigues formula

$$P_n(x) = \frac{1}{2^n n!}\frac{d^n}{dx^n}[(x^2-1)^n]. \tag{C.4.37}$$

It is quite clear that the coefficient of x^n in $P_n(x)$ is

$$\frac{1}{2^n n!}(2n)(2n-1)\cdots(n+1) = \frac{(2n)!}{2^n(n!)^2}.$$

The three-term recurrence formula for $\{P_n(x)\}$ is

$$(n+1)P_{n+1}(x) - (2n+1)xP_n(x) + nP_{n-1}(x) = 0.$$

The orthogonality reads

$$\int_{-1}^{1} P_n(x)P_m(x)dx = \frac{2}{2n+1}\delta_{mn}. \tag{C.4.38}$$

To see this, denote $\varphi(x) = (x^2 - 1)^n$, and notice that $\varphi^{(k)}(\pm 1) = 0$ for $0 \le k \le n-1$. Let $Q(x)$ be any polynomial with degree no larger than n. Then, due to integration by parts,

$$\begin{aligned}\int_{-1}^{1} P_n(x)Q(x)dx &= \frac{1}{2^n n!}\int_{-1}^{1} \varphi^{(n)}(x)Q(x)dx \\ &= \frac{-1}{2^n n!}\int_{-1}^{1} \varphi^{(n-1)}(x)Q'(x)dx \\ &= \cdots \\ &= \frac{(-1)^n}{2^n n!}\int_{-1}^{1} \varphi(x)Q^{(n)}(x)dx \\ &= 0.\end{aligned}$$

Thus, if the degree of $Q(x)$ is less than n, then $P_n(x)$ is orthogonal with $Q(x)$, and accordingly $P_n(x)$ is orthogonal with $P_{n-1}(x), \ldots, P_1(x)$ and $P_0(x)$. This means that $\{P_n(x)\}$ is an orthogonal sequence on $[-1, 1]$.

Moreover, letting $Q(x) = P_n(x)$,

$$\begin{aligned}\int_{-1}^{1} P_n^2(x)dx &= \frac{(-1)^n}{2^n n!}\int_{-1}^{1} \varphi(x)P_n^{(n)}(x)dx \\ &= \frac{(2n)!}{(2^n n!)^2}\int_{-1}^{1} (1-x^2)^n dx \\ &= \frac{(2n)!}{(2^n n!)^2}\int_{-\pi/2}^{\pi/2} \cos^{2n+1}\theta d\theta \\ &= \frac{(2n)!}{(2^n n!)^2}\frac{2^{2n+1}(n!)^2}{(2n+1)!} = \frac{2}{2n+1}.\end{aligned}$$

Legendre polynomials $P_n(x)$ satisfy the hypergeometric differential equation,

$$(1-x^2)y'' - 2xy' + n(n+1)y = 0,$$

and boundary condition $P_n(1) = 1$, and their derivatives have the relation

$$\begin{aligned}(x^2-1)P_n'(x) &= nxP_n(x) - nP_{n-1}(x) \\ &= (n+1)P_{n+1}(x) - (n+1)xP_n(x).\end{aligned}$$

Now let us show that Legendre polynomials have generating function

$$\frac{1}{\sqrt{1-2tx+t^2}} = \sum_{n=0}^{\infty} P_n(x)t^n, \quad |t| < 1. \tag{C.4.39}$$

Denote the left side as $G(x, t)$,

$$G(x,t) = \frac{1}{\sqrt{1+(t^2-2tx)}} = \sum_{n=0}^{\infty} A_n(x)t^n.$$

We are about to show $A_n(x) = P_n(x)$.

First, it is readily seen that $A_n(x)$ is a polynomial of degree n, since $A_n(x) = G^{(n)}(x, t)|_{t=0}$ where the derivative is w.r.t. t. Second, letting $x = 1$,

$$G(1, t) = \frac{1}{1-t} = \sum_{n=0}^{\infty} t^n = \sum_{n=0}^{\infty} A_n(1) t^n.$$

This implies $A_n(1) = 1$. Thus, it suffices to show that $A_n(x)$ satisfy the Legendre differential equation. To do so, differentiating $G(x, t)$ w.r.t. t, we have

$$(1 - 2tx + t^2)\frac{\partial G}{\partial t} = (x - t)G.$$

Again, differentiating both sides w.r.t. x gives

$$t\frac{\partial G}{\partial t} = (x - t)\frac{\partial G}{\partial x}.$$

Now, substitute $G = \sum A_n t^n$ into the above equation, and compare coefficients t^{n-1} and t^n. We have

$$nA_n - (2n-1)xA_{n-1} + (n-1)A_{n-2} = 0, \tag{C.4.40}$$

$$x\frac{dA_n}{dx} - \frac{dA_{n-1}}{dx} = nA_n. \tag{C.4.41}$$

Differentiating (C.4.40) and using (C.4.41) (n is replaced by $n - 1$), we obtain

$$\frac{dA_n}{dx} - x\frac{dA_{n-1}}{dx} = nA_{n-1}.$$

Multiplying (C.4.41) by $-x$, adding with the above equation give

$$(1 - x^2)\frac{dA_n}{dx} = n(A_{n-1} - xA_n),$$

for which we differentiate both sides to have

$$(1 - x^2)\frac{d^2A_n}{dx^2} - 2x\frac{dA_n}{dx} + n(n+1)A_n = 0,$$

that is the hypergeometric differential equation for which Legendre polynomials satisfy. Hence, $A_n(x) = P_n(x)$, that is, Legendre polynomials admit the generating function $G(x, t)$.

If we directly expand the generating function into binomial series

$$
\begin{aligned}
G(x,t) &= [1+(t^2-2tx)]^{-1/2} = \sum_{n=0}^{\infty} \binom{-1/2}{n} (-1)^n t^n (2x-t)^n \\
&= \sum_{n=0}^{\infty} \binom{-1/2}{n} (-1)^n t^n \sum_{k=0}^{n} \binom{n}{k} (-1)^k (2x)^{n-k} t^k \\
&= \sum_{n=0}^{\infty} \left[\sum_{k=0}^{[n/2]} \binom{-1/2}{n-k} \binom{n-k}{k} (-1)^n (2x)^{n-2k} \right] t^n,
\end{aligned}
$$

where generally

$$
\binom{\alpha}{n} = \frac{\alpha(\alpha-1)\cdots(\alpha-n+1)}{n!},
$$

we have an explicit formula of Legendre polynomials,

$$
P_n(x) = (-1)^n \sum_{k=0}^{[n/2]} \binom{-1/2}{n-k} \binom{n-k}{k} (2x)^{n-2k}. \tag{C.4.42}
$$

Making an observation, we note that when n is an even number, the polynomial $P_n(x)$ is an even function; and when n is odd, the polynomial is an odd function. Therefore,

$$
P_n(-x) = (-1)^n P_n(x). \tag{C.4.43}
$$

Moreover, from the generating function with $x = 1$, we have $P_n(1) = 1$; and using (C.4.43) yields $P_n(-1) = (-1)^n$. Similarly, $P_{2n+1}(0) = 0$ (this is also a result of odd functions) and

$$
P_{2n}(0) = \binom{-1/2}{n} = (-1)^n \frac{(2n-1)!!}{(2n)!!}.
$$

In addition, the Legendre polynomials have a uniform bound, $|P_n(x)| \le 1$, $x \in [-1, 1]$. In fact, substituting $x = \cos\theta = (e^{i\theta} + e^{-i\theta})/2$ into the generating function, we have

$$
\begin{aligned}
\sum_{n=0}^{\infty} P_n(\cos\theta) t^n &= [1 - t(e^{i\theta} + e^{-i\theta}) + t^2]^{-1/2} \\
&= (1 - te^{i\theta})^{-1/2} (1 - te^{-i\theta})^{-1/2} \\
&= \sum_{k=0}^{\infty} \binom{-1/2}{k} (-te^{i\theta})^k \sum_{s=0}^{\infty} \binom{-1/2}{s} (-te^{-i\theta})^s.
\end{aligned}
$$

When $|t| < 1$, the product of the two infinite sums makes sense. Comparing the coefficients of t^n in both sides gives

$$P_n(\cos\theta) = \frac{(2n-1)!!}{(2n)!!}[e^{in\theta} + e^{-in\theta}] + \sum_{k=1}^{n-1} \frac{(2k-1)!!}{(2k)!!} \frac{(2(n-k)-1)!!}{(2(n-k))!!} e^{i(2k-n)\theta}.$$

Here, all the coefficients are positive, so each term has maximum at $\theta = 0$, so does $P_n(\cos\theta)$, i.e., $|P_n(\cos\theta)| \le |P_n(\cos 0)| = |P_n(1)| = 1$. This completes the claim. Notice also that Szego (1975, p. 164) gives another proof for the uniform bound for $P_n(x)$.

Chebyshev polynomials of the first kind form an orthogonal basis in Hilbert space $L^2([-1,1], 1/\sqrt{1-x^2})$, and they are trigonometric polynomials $T_n(x) = \cos(n \arccos(x))$. The sequence admits a three-term recurrence relation

$$T_{n+1}(x) = 2xT_n(x) - T_{n-1}(x),$$

with $T_0(x) = 1$ and $T_1(x) = x$. It also satisfies $(1-x^2)T_n'(x) = nT_{n-1}(x) - nxT_n(x)$, whose orthogonality reads

$$\int_{-1}^{1} T_n(x)T_m(x)\frac{1}{\sqrt{1-x^2}}dx = \begin{cases} 0, & m \neq n, \\ \pi, & m = n = 0, \\ \frac{1}{2}\pi, & m = n \neq 0. \end{cases}$$

$T_n(x)$ satisfies the hypergeometric differential equation

$$(1-x^2)y'' - xy' + n^2 y = 0,$$

and has generation function

$$\frac{1-tx}{1-2tx+t^2} = \sum_{n=0}^{\infty} T_n(x)t^n.$$

As classical orthogonal polynomials, Chebyshev polynomials have Rodrigues formula

$$T_n(x) = \frac{(-1)^n}{(2n-1)!!}\sqrt{1-x^2}\frac{d^n}{dx^n}[(1-x^2)^{n-1/2}],$$

and clearly the sequence has a uniform bound, $|T_n(x)| \le 1$.

Chebyshev polynomials of the second kind $\{U_n(x)\}$ form an orthogonal basis in Hilbert space $L^2([-1,1], \sqrt{1-x^2})$, the first few of which are $U_0(x) = 1$, $U_1(x) = 2x$, $U_2(x) = 4x^2 - 1$, $U_3(x) = 8x^3 - 4x$, $U_4(x) = 16x^4 - 12x^2 + 1$. The sequence has recursive relationship, $U_{n+1}(x) - 2xU_n(x) + U_{n-1}(x) = 0$, and $(1 - x^2)U_n'(x) = (n+1)U_{n-1}(x) - nxU_n(x)$.

Also, $U_n(x)$ satisfies the hypergeometric differential equation, $(1-x^2)y'' - 3xy' + n(n+2)y = 0$; it admits generating function

$$\frac{1}{1-2xt+t^2} = \sum_{n=0}^{\infty} U_n(x)t^n.$$

The orthogonality of the sequence is

$$\int_{-1}^{1} U_n(x)U_m(x)\sqrt{1-x^2}dx = \begin{cases} 0, & m \neq n, \\ \frac{1}{2}\pi, & m = n. \end{cases}$$

Its Rodrigues formula is

$$U_n(x) = \frac{(-1)^n}{(2n+1)!!}\frac{1}{\sqrt{1-x^2}}\frac{d^n}{dx^n}[(1-x^2)^{n+1/2}];$$

and it has bound, $|U_n(x)| \leq n+1, x \in [-1, 1]$.

Hermite polynomials $\{H_i(x)\}$ are orthogonal in $L^2(\mathbb{R}, \exp(-x^2))$. The space $L^2(\mathbb{R}, \exp(-x^2))$ is large enough for both researchers and practitioners, since it includes all polynomials, all power functions, all bounded functions, and even some exponential functions. More importantly, all functions in the space are defined on the entire real line.

As the basis in $L^2(\mathbb{R}, \exp(-x^2))$, Hermite orthogonal polynomials $\{H_i(x)\}$ are given by Rodrigues formula

$$H_i(x) = (-1)^i \exp(x^2)\frac{d^i}{dx^i}\exp(-x^2), \qquad i \geq 0. \tag{C.4.44}$$

These are the so-called **physicists' Hermite polynomials** in the literature, the first few of which are $H_0(x) = 1$, $H_1(x) = 2x$, $H_2(x) = 4x^2 - 2$, $H_3(x) = 8x^3 - 12x$, and generally

$$H_i(x) = \sum_{k=0}^{[i/2]} \frac{(-1)^k i!}{k!(i-2k)!}(2x)^{i-2k}, \tag{C.4.45}$$

where $[\cdot]$ is the largest integer that does not exceed the argument. These $H_i(x)$ also can be generated from the following expansion

$$u(x,t) = e^{2tx-t^2} = e^{x^2}e^{-(t-x)^2} = \sum_{i=0}^{\infty} \frac{H_i(x)}{i!}t^i. \tag{C.4.46}$$

Due to this, $u(x,t)$ is called the generating function of Hermite polynomials. To verify this, note that

$$\left.\frac{\partial^i u(x,t)}{\partial t^i}\right|_{t=0} = e^{x^2}\frac{\partial^i}{\partial t^i}e^{-(t-x)^2}\Big|_{t=0}$$
$$= (-1)^i e^{x^2}\frac{\partial^i}{\partial w^i}e^{-w^2}\Big|_{w=x} = H_i(x). \tag{C.4.47}$$

Notice also that

$$\frac{\partial u(x,t)}{\partial t} - 2(x-t)u(x,t) = 0, \tag{C.4.48a}$$
$$\frac{\partial u(x,t)}{\partial x} - 2tu(x,t) = 0, \tag{C.4.48b}$$

while $u(x,t)$ is an entire function in both x and t, so that the series in (C.4.46) in any finite interval is uniformly convergent and differentiable term-wisely. It thus follows from (C.4.48a) that

$$\sum_{i=0}^{\infty}\frac{H_{i+1}(x)}{i!}t^i - 2x\sum_{i=0}^{\infty}\frac{H_i(x)}{i!}t^i + 2\sum_{i=0}^{\infty}\frac{H_i(x)}{i!}t^{i+1} = 0.$$

Comparing the coefficients of t^i in each summation yields

$$H_{i+1}(x) - 2xH_i(x) + 2iH_{i-1}(x) = 0, \quad i \geq 1. \tag{C.4.49}$$

In addition, from (C.4.48b) we have

$$\sum_{i=0}^{\infty}\frac{H_i'(x)}{i!}t^i - 2\sum_{i=0}^{\infty}\frac{H_i(x)}{i!}t^{i+1} = 0,$$

which gives

$$H_i'(x) = 2iH_{i-1}(x). \tag{C.4.50}$$

Combining (C.4.49) and (C.4.50), we have

$$H_{i+1}(x) - 2xH_i(x) + H_i'(x) = 0,$$

and taking differentiation on the both sides gives

$$H_i''(x) - 2xH_i'(x) + 2iH_i(x) = 0, \tag{C.4.51}$$

which is the hypergeometric differential equation that Hermite polynomials satisfy.

By letting $x = 0$ it follows immediately from (C.4.46) that

$$H_{2i}(0) = (-1)^i\frac{(2i)!}{i!}, \qquad H_{2i+1}(0) = 0, \quad i \geq 0. \tag{C.4.52}$$

Again, from (C.4.46), we have

$$u(x,t)u(x,v) = e^{2x(t+v)-t^2-v^2} = \sum_{i,j=0}^{\infty} \frac{H_i(x)}{i!} t^i \frac{H_j(x)}{j!} v^j,$$

and further

$$e^{-[x-(t+v)]^2+2tv} = \sum_{i,j=0}^{\infty} \frac{H_i(x)H_j(x)e^{-x^2}}{i!j!} t^i v^j.$$

It follows that

$$\int_{-\infty}^{\infty} e^{-[x-(t+v)]^2+2tv} dx = \sum_{i,j=0}^{\infty} \frac{\int_{-\infty}^{\infty} H_i(x)H_j(x)e^{-x^2} dx}{i!j!} t^i v^j.$$

The left-hand side of the above equation is equal to

$$\sqrt{\pi} e^{2tv} = \sqrt{\pi} \sum_{k=0}^{\infty} \frac{1}{k!} (2tv)^k.$$

Equating them gives the orthogonality of the polynomials,

$$\int_{-\infty}^{\infty} H_i(x)H_j(x)e^{-x^2} dx = 0, \quad i \neq j,$$

$$\int_{-\infty}^{\infty} H_i^2(x)e^{-x^2} dx = \sqrt{\pi} i! 2^i.$$

Next, we show that the sequence $\{H_i(x)\}$ is complete, although we have concluded this statement when we generate orthogonal polynomials from power functions. For an orthogonal system, completeness is equivalent to the fact that the zero function is the only function in the space $L^2(\mathbb{R}, \exp(-x^2))$ orthogonal to all functions in the system. Since the linear span of Hermite polynomials is the space of all polynomials, one has to show that if $f(x)$ satisfies

$$\int_{-\infty}^{\infty} f(x)x^j e^{-x^2} dx = 0,$$

for all $j \geq 0$, then $f(x) = 0$. One possible way to do this is to see the entire function

$$F(z) = \int_{-\infty}^{\infty} f(x)e^{zx-x^2} dx = \sum_{j=0}^{\infty} \frac{z^j}{j!} \int_{-\infty}^{\infty} f(x)x^j e^{-x^2} dx = 0$$

vanishes identically. Notice that when $z = iu$, $F(iu) = 0$ for all real u, and this means by the definition of $F(z)$ that the Fourier transform of $f(x)e^{-x^2}$ is zero. Hence $f(x) = 0$ almost everywhere (a.e.).

The next is Mehler's formula. For $|h| < 1$, we have

$$\sum_{n=0}^{\infty} \frac{h^n}{2^n n!} H_n(x) H_n(y) e^{-(x^2+y^2)/2} = \frac{1}{\sqrt{1-h^2}} \exp\left(\frac{x^2-y^2}{2} - \frac{(x-yh)^2}{1-h^2}\right). \tag{C.4.53}$$

We are now about to prove it. Note that

$$e^{-x^2} = \frac{1}{\sqrt{\pi}} \int_{-\infty}^{\infty} e^{-u^2+2ixu} du,$$

where $i = \sqrt{-1}$ is the unit of imagine number. The left of Mehler's formula is

$$\begin{aligned}
\text{Left} &= e^{(x^2+y^2)/2} \sum_{n=0}^{\infty} \frac{h^n}{2^n n!} H_n(x) H_n(y) e^{-(x^2+y^2)} \\
&= e^{(x^2+y^2)/2} \sum_{n=0}^{\infty} \frac{h^n}{2^n n!} \frac{d^n}{dx^n} e^{-x^2} \frac{d^n}{dy^n} e^{-y^2} \\
&= \frac{e^{(x^2+y^2)/2}}{\pi} \sum_{n=0}^{\infty} \int_{-\infty}^{\infty} \int_{-\infty}^{\infty} \frac{(-2huv)^n}{n!} e^{-u^2-v^2+2ixu+2iyv} dudv \\
&= \frac{e^{(x^2+y^2)/2}}{\pi} \int_{-\infty}^{\infty} \int_{-\infty}^{\infty} e^{-u^2-v^2+2ixu+2iyv-2huv} dudv \\
&= \frac{e^{(x^2-y^2)/2}}{\sqrt{\pi}} \int_{-\infty}^{\infty} e^{-(1-h^2)u^2+2i(x-yh)u} du \\
&= \frac{1}{\sqrt{1-h^2}} \exp\left(\frac{x^2-y^2}{2} - \frac{(x-yh)^2}{1-h^2}\right),
\end{aligned}$$

where the swap between the integral and summation is because

$$\int_{-\infty}^{\infty} \int_{-\infty}^{\infty} \sum_{n=0}^{\infty} \frac{(2\rho uv)^n}{n!} e^{-u^2-v^2+2Au+2Bv} dudv$$

converges when $|\rho| < 1$.

We also can show the Christoffel-Darboux formula about Hermite polynomials by the three-term recurrence relation (C.4.49). Indeed, notice that

$$
\begin{aligned}
&H_{i+1}(x)H_i(y) - H_{i+1}(y)H_i(x) \\
&\quad - 2i[H_i(x)H_{i-1}(y) - H_i(y)H_{i-1}(x)] \\
&= 2(x-y)H_i(x)H_i(y).
\end{aligned}
$$

Divide both sides by $2^i i!$, and take sum for $i = 1, \ldots, n$. We have

$$
2(x-y)\sum_{i=1}^{n} \frac{H_i(x)H_i(y)}{2^i i!} = \frac{H_{n+1}(x)H_n(y) - H_{n+1}(y)H_n(x)}{2^n n!} - 2(x-y)
$$

since $H_1(x) = 2x$ and $H_0(x) = 1$. Then,

$$
2(x-y)\sum_{i=0}^{n} \frac{H_i(x)H_i(y)}{2^i i!} = \frac{H_{n+1}(x)H_n(y) - H_{n+1}(y)H_n(x)}{2^n n!},
$$

that is the formula.

In the literature, there is another kind of Hermite polynomials that is called *probabilists' Hermite polynomials*, because the density used in their orthogonality is the normal density $e^{-x^2/2}$. Specifically, in Hilbert space $L^2(\mathbb{R}, e^{-x^2/2})$, Hermite orthogonal polynomials $H_i(x)$ are given by

$$
H_i(x) = (-1)^i e^{-x^2/2} \frac{d^i}{dx^i} e^{-x^2/2}, \quad i \geq 0. \tag{C.4.54}
$$

The space has $\{H_i(x)\}$ as its basis, the first few of which are $H_0(x) = 1$, $H_1(x) = x$, $H_2(x) = x^2 - 1$, $H_3(x) = x^3 - 3x$. Its orthogonality is

$$
\int H_i(x)H_j(x)\exp(-x^2/2)dx = \sqrt{2\pi}\, i!\delta_{ij};
$$

and it possesses recursion relationship

$$
H_{i+1}(x) = xH_i(x) - H_i'(x), \qquad H_i'(x) = iH_{i-1}(x).
$$

These Hermite polynomials $H_i(x)$ satisfy hypergeometric differential equations $y'' - xy' + iy = 0$. The generating function is

$$
\exp(xt - t^2/2) = \sum_{i=0}^{\infty} H_i(x)\frac{t^i}{i!}.
$$

We do not further pursue the property of probabilistic Hermite polynomials since they are quite similar with the Hermite polynomials orthogonal w.r.t. e^{-x^2}.

Hermite functions in $L^2(\mathbb{R})$ form an orthonormal basis that are constructed from Hermite polynomials, namely,

$$\mathscr{H}_i(x) = (\sqrt{\pi}2^i i!)^{-1/2} H_i(x) e^{-x^2/2}, \quad i \geq 0, \tag{C.4.55}$$

where $H_i(x)$ are orthogonal to e^{-x^2} (physicists's Hermite polynomials).

Straightforwardly from the orthogonality of Hermite polynomials, we have

$$\int_{-\infty}^{\infty} \mathscr{H}_i(x)\mathscr{H}_j(x)dx = \delta_{ij}. \tag{C.4.56}$$

Also, it is easy to see that $\mathscr{H}_i(x)$ satisfies $y'' + (2i+1)y = x^2 y$.

It is clear $L^2(\mathbb{R}) \subset L^2(\mathbb{R}, e^{-x^2/2})$, but most functions in the former are easy to handle because continuous functions in the space are bounded on the real line. In particular, Hermite functions have uniform bound:

$$\sup_x \sup_{j\geq 0} |\mathscr{H}_j(x)| \leq C\pi^{-1/4}. \tag{C.4.57}$$

where C is an absolute constant less than 1.086435. This is the so-called Cramér's inequality.

Denote $h_i(x) = H_i(x)e^{-x^2/2}$ for convenience, and $h_i(x)$ satisfies

$$y'' + (2i+1)y - x^2 y = 0, \tag{C.4.58}$$

with initial values

$$y(0) = H_i(0), \quad y'(0) = H_i'(0).$$

Then, we have

$$\begin{aligned} y(x) &= H_i(0)\cos\sqrt{2i+1}x + H_i'(0)\frac{\sin\sqrt{2i+1}x}{\sqrt{2i+1}} \\ &\quad + \frac{1}{\sqrt{2i+1}}\int_0^x v^2 y(v)\sin[\sqrt{2i+1}(x-v)]dv. \end{aligned} \tag{C.4.59}$$

Note that

$$\begin{aligned} H_{2m}(0) &= (-1)^m \frac{\Gamma(2m+1)}{\Gamma(m+1)}, & H_{2m+1}(0) &= 0, \\ H_{2m+1}'(0) &= 2(-1)^m \frac{\Gamma(2m+2)}{\Gamma(m+1)}, & H_{2m}'(0) &= 0, \end{aligned}$$

where $\Gamma(\cdot)$ is the gamma function, $\Gamma(a) = \int_0^\infty x^{a-1}e^{-x}dx$ for $a > 0$.

Then, we may write

$$y(x) = \alpha_i\left[\cos\left(\sqrt{2i+1}x - \frac{i\pi}{2}\right) + r_i(x)\right], \tag{C.4.60}$$

where

$$\alpha_i = \begin{cases} \frac{\Gamma(i+1)}{\Gamma(\frac{i}{2}+1)}, & i \text{ even}, \\ \frac{2\Gamma(i+1)}{\Gamma(\frac{i+1}{2})\sqrt{2i+1}}, & i \text{ odd}, \end{cases} \tag{C.4.61}$$

and

$$r_i(x) = \frac{1}{\alpha_i\sqrt{2i+1}}\int_0^x v^2 y(v)\sin[\sqrt{2i+1}(x-v)]dv. \tag{C.4.62}$$

Observe that

$$\begin{aligned} |r_i(x)| &\leq \frac{1}{\alpha_i\sqrt{2i+1}}\left(\int_0^{|x|} v^4 dv\right)^{1/2}\left(\int_0^{|x|} y^2(v)dv\right)^{1/2} \\ &\leq \frac{1}{\alpha_i\sqrt{2i+1}}\left(\int_0^{|x|} v^4 dv\right)^{1/2}\left(\int_0^{\infty} y^2(v)dv\right)^{1/2} \\ &= \frac{\sqrt{2^i i!\sqrt{\pi}}}{\alpha_i\sqrt{2i+1}}\frac{|x|^{5/2}}{\sqrt{2}\sqrt{5}} \equiv \beta_i|x|^{5/2}. \end{aligned}$$

Invoking Stirling's formula, when $i \to \infty$,

$$\alpha_i \sim 2^{(i+1)/2} i^{i/2} e^{-i/2}, \quad 2^i i!\sqrt{\pi} \sim 2^{i+1/2} i^{i+1/2} e^{-i}\pi, \tag{C.4.63}$$

which imply $\beta_i \sim i^{-1/4}$. Accordingly, for any $x \in \mathbb{R}$,

$$|r_i(x)| \leq c|x|^{5/2} i^{-1/4}. \tag{C.4.64}$$

It follows that, for any fixed x,

$$y(x) = \alpha_i\left[\cos\left(\sqrt{2i+1}x - \frac{i\pi}{2}\right) + r_i(x)\right], \tag{C.4.65}$$

and also

$$H_i(x) \sim 2^{(i+1)/2} i^{i/2} e^{-i/2} e^{x^2/2}\left[\cos\left(\sqrt{2i+1}x - \frac{i\pi}{2}\right) + O(|x|^{5/2} i^{-1/4})\right]. \tag{C.4.66}$$

The generalized Laguerre polynomials are denoted by $L_i^\alpha(x)$ for $\alpha > -1$, while particular Laguerre polynomials with $\alpha = 0$ are denoted by $L_i(x)$. The polynomials $L_i^\alpha(x)$ are given by

$$L_i^\alpha(x) = \frac{1}{i!}x^{-\alpha}e^x\frac{d^i}{dx^i}[e^{-x}x^{i+\alpha}], \quad \alpha > -1, \ i \geq 0. \tag{C.4.67}$$

The first three polynomials are

$$
\begin{aligned}
L_0^\alpha(x) &= 1,\\
L_1^\alpha(x) &= 1+\alpha-x,\\
L_2^\alpha(x) &= \frac{1}{2}[(1+\alpha)(2+\alpha)-2(2+\alpha)x+x^2],
\end{aligned}
$$

and generally

$$
L_i^\alpha(x) = \sum_{j=0}^{i} \frac{\Gamma(i+\alpha+1)}{\Gamma(j+\alpha+1)} \frac{(-x)^j}{j!(i-j)!}. \tag{C.4.68}
$$

Laguerre polynomials have generating function

$$
u(x,t) = \frac{1}{(1-t)^{1+\alpha}} \exp\left(-\frac{xt}{1-t}\right) = \sum_{i=0}^{\infty} L_i^\alpha(x)t^i, \quad |t|<1. \tag{C.4.69}
$$

In fact, using (C.4.68),

$$
\begin{aligned}
&\sum_{i=0}^{\infty} L_i^\alpha(x)t^i\\
&= \sum_{i=0}^{\infty}\sum_{j=0}^{i}(-1)^j \frac{\Gamma(i+\alpha+1)}{\Gamma(j+\alpha+1)} \frac{1}{j!(i-j)!} x^j t^i\\
&= \sum_{j=0}^{\infty}(-1)^j \frac{x^j}{j!} \sum_{i=j}^{\infty} \frac{\Gamma(i+\alpha+1)}{\Gamma(j+\alpha+1)} \frac{1}{(i-j)!} t^i\\
&= \sum_{j=0}^{\infty} \frac{(-xt)^j}{j!} \sum_{m=0}^{\infty} \frac{\Gamma(m+j+\alpha+1)}{\Gamma(j+\alpha+1)} \frac{1}{m!} t^m\\
&= \sum_{j=0}^{\infty} \frac{(-xt)^j}{j!} \frac{1}{(1-t)^{j+\alpha+1}}\\
&= \frac{1}{(1-t)^{1+\alpha}} \exp\left(-\frac{xt}{1-t}\right) = u(x,t).
\end{aligned}
$$

It can be shown that Laguerre polynomials are orthogonal on $(0,\infty)$ with weight $x^\alpha e^{-x}$,

$$
\int_0^\infty L_i^\alpha(x)L_j^\alpha(x)x^\alpha e^{-x}dx = \frac{\Gamma(1+\alpha+i)}{i!}\delta_{ij}. \tag{C.4.70}
$$

To see this, note that

$$
\begin{aligned}
u(x,t)u(x,v) &= \frac{1}{(1-t)^{1+\alpha}} \exp\left(-\frac{xt}{1-t}\right) \frac{1}{(1-v)^{1+\alpha}} \exp\left(-\frac{xv}{1-v}\right) \\
&= \sum_{i=0}^{\infty} L_i^\alpha(x) t^i \sum_{j=0}^{\infty} L_j^\alpha(x) v^j.
\end{aligned}
$$

Moreover, the integral of the left w.r.t. the weight is

$$
\begin{aligned}
&\int_0^\infty u(x,t)u(x,v) x^\alpha e^{-x} dx \\
&= \frac{1}{[(1-t)(1-v)]^{1+\alpha}} \int_0^\infty \exp\left[-\left(1+\frac{t}{1-t}+\frac{v}{1-v}\right)x\right] x^\alpha dx \\
&= \frac{1}{[(1-t)(1-v)]^{1+\alpha}} \int_0^\infty \exp\left[-\frac{1-tv}{(1-t)(1-v)}x\right] x^\alpha dx \\
&= \frac{1}{(1-tv)^{1+\alpha}} \int_0^\infty e^{-x} x^\alpha dx = \Gamma(1+\alpha)\frac{1}{(1-tv)^{1+\alpha}} \\
&= \Gamma(1+\alpha) \sum_{k=0}^{\infty} \frac{\Gamma(k+\alpha+1)}{\Gamma(\alpha+1)} \frac{1}{k!}(tv)^k = \sum_{k=0}^{\infty} \Gamma(k+\alpha+1)\frac{1}{k!}(tv)^k.
\end{aligned}
$$

Now, integrating the right-hand side w.r.t. the weight and equating with the left give the orthogonality relations.

Furthermore, Laguerre polynomials $y = L_i^\alpha(x)$ satisfy the hypergeometric differential equation

$$
xy'' + (\alpha - x + 1)y' + iy = 0, \tag{C.4.71}
$$

If we denote $z = e^{-x}x^{\alpha/2}L_i^\alpha(x)$, $u = e^{-x/2}x^{(1+\alpha)/2}L_i^\alpha(x)$ and $v = e^{-x/2}x^{\alpha+1/2}L_i^\alpha(x)$, we have

$$
xz'' + (x+1)z' + \left(i + \frac{\alpha}{2} + 1 - \frac{\alpha^2}{4x}\right) z = 0, \tag{C.4.72}
$$

$$
u'' + \left(\frac{i + (1+\alpha)/2}{x} + \frac{1-\alpha^2}{4x^2} - \frac{1}{4}\right) u = 0, \tag{C.4.73}
$$

$$
v'' + \left(4i + 2\alpha + 2 - x^2 - \frac{\alpha^2 - 1/4}{x^2}\right) v = 0. \tag{C.4.74}
$$

The following recurrence formula holds

$$
iL_i^\alpha(x) = (-x + 2i + \alpha - 1)L_{i-1}^\alpha(x) - (i + \alpha - 1)L_{i-2}^\alpha(x). \tag{C.4.75}
$$

Moreover, the Christoffel-Darboux formula reads

$$\sum_{i=0}^{n}\left[\binom{i+\alpha}{i}\right]^{-1} L_i^{\alpha}(x)L_i^{\alpha}(y) = (n+1)\left[\binom{n+\alpha}{n}\right]^{-1} \frac{L_n^{\alpha}(x)L_{n+1}^{\alpha}(y) - L_{n+1}^{\alpha}(x)L_n^{\alpha}(y)}{x-y}. \tag{C.4.76}$$

The special case $y = 0$ gives

$$x\sum_{i=0}^{n} L_i^{\alpha}(x) = (n+\alpha+1)L_n^{\alpha}(x) - (n+1)L_{n+1}^{\alpha}(x). \tag{C.4.77}$$

We also have the following identities

$$\begin{aligned} &\sum_{i=0}^{n} L_i^{\alpha}(x) = L_n^{\alpha+1}(x), \\ &L_n^{\alpha}(x) = L_n^{\alpha+1}(x) - L_{n-1}^{\alpha+1}(x), \\ &\frac{d}{dx}L_n^{\alpha}(x) = -L_{n-1}^{\alpha+1}(x) = x^{-1}[nL_n^{\alpha}(x) - (n+\alpha)L_{n-1}^{\alpha}(x)]. \end{aligned} \tag{C.4.78}$$

The weight estimate

$$e^{-x/2}|L_n^{\alpha}(x)| \le C(\alpha)B_n^{\alpha}(x), \tag{C.4.79}$$

where $C(\alpha)$ is a constant depending on α only, and

$$B_n^{\alpha}(x) = \begin{cases} \theta^{\alpha}, & 0 \le x \le 1/\theta, \\ \theta^{\alpha/2-1/4}x^{-\alpha/2-1/4}, & 1/\theta < x \le \theta/2, \\ [\theta(\theta^{1/3} + |x-\theta|)]^{-1/4}, & \theta/2 < x \le 3\theta/2, \\ e^{-x/4}, & 3\theta/2 < x, \end{cases}$$

with $\theta = \theta_n = 4n + 2\alpha + 2$. See Sharapudinova and Magomed-Kasumova (2018, p. 51).

C.4.4 Convergence in Norm of Orthogonal Series

We have shown that any Hilbert space admits an orthogonal series as its basis. Therefore, once an orthogonal sequence is shown to be a basis in the Hilbert space, any element of which has a convergent orthogonal series expansion in terms of this basis in the norm sense.

The following theorem establishes the convergence in norm sense for orthogonal expansions in terms of Hermite functions without using the message that Hermite functions form a complete orthogonal sequence in $L^2(\mathbb{R})$, otherwise, the result is obvious.

Theorem C.4.6 *If* $g(x) \in L^2(\mathbb{R})$*, define*

$$c_i = \int_{-\infty}^{\infty} g(x)\mathscr{H}_i(x)dx, \quad i \geq 0,$$

where $\mathscr{H}_j(x)$ *are defined by* (C.4.55). *Then we have*

$$\int_{-\infty}^{\infty} \left[g(x) - \sum_{i=0}^{k} c_i \mathscr{H}_i(x) \right]^2 dx \to 0, \quad \text{as } k \to \infty.$$

Proof By the Mehler's formula, if we denote

$$K(x, y, h) = \frac{1}{\sqrt{\pi(1-h^2)}} \exp\left(\frac{x^2 - y^2}{2} - \frac{(x - yh)^2}{1 - h^2} \right), \quad |h| < 1,$$

then

$$\sum_{i=0}^{\infty} h^i \mathscr{H}_i(x)\mathscr{H}_i(y) = K(x, y, h) \geq 0. \tag{C.4.80}$$

Using variable change $y = \frac{2xh}{1+h^2} + u$, we have

$$\begin{aligned}
&\int_{-\infty}^{\infty} K(x, y, h)dy \\
&= \frac{\exp\left(-\frac{1-h^2}{2(1+h^2)}x^2\right)}{\sqrt{\pi(1-h^2)}} \int_{-\infty}^{\infty} \exp\left(-\frac{1+h^2}{2(1-h^2)}u^2\right) du \\
&= \sqrt{\frac{2}{1+h^2}} \exp\left(-\frac{1-h^2}{2(1+h^2)}x^2\right) \to 1,
\end{aligned}$$

as $h \to 1$. In addition, when $|x - y| \geq \delta > 0$,

$$K(x, y, h) \to 0, \quad \text{as } h \to 1,$$

and the convergence for fixed x and bounded y is uniform. Hence, for any $g(x) \in C_0^\infty$ (the class of infinitely differentiable functions vanishing at infinity) and any $\delta > 0$,

$$\begin{aligned}&\int_{-\infty}^{\infty} K(x, y, h)g(y)dy - g(x)\int_{-\infty}^{\infty} K(x, y, h)dy\\ &= \int_{-\infty}^{\infty} K(x, y, h)[g(y) - g(x)]dy\\ &= \int_{|x-y|<\delta} K(x, y, h)[g(y) - g(x)]dy\\ &\quad + \int_{|x-y|\geq\delta} K(x, y, h)[g(y) - g(x)]dy.\end{aligned}$$

Recalling the continuity in C_0^∞ that implies the uniform continuity, for any $\varepsilon > 0$, there exists a $\delta > 0$, when $|x - y| < \delta$ we have $|g(x) - g(y)| < \varepsilon$. Moreover, $|g(y)| < M$ for some $M > 0$ and all y. Thus,

$$\begin{aligned}&\left|\int_{-\infty}^{\infty} K(x, y, h)g(y)dy - g(x)\int_{-\infty}^{\infty} K(x, y, h)dy\right|\\ &\leq \varepsilon\int_{|x-y|<\delta} K(x, y, h)dy + 2M\int_{|x-y|\geq\delta} K(x, y, h)dy,\end{aligned}$$

which gives

$$\int_{-\infty}^{\infty} K(x, y, h)g(y)dy \to g(x), \quad \text{as } h \to 1.$$

Now, multiplying $g(y)$ on both sides of (C.4.80) and taking integral, we have

$$\sum_{i=0}^{\infty} c_i h^i \mathscr{H}_i(x) = \int_{-\infty}^{\infty} K(x, y, h)g(y)dy \to g(x), \quad \text{as } h \to 1,$$

where $c_i = \int_{-\infty}^{\infty} \mathscr{H}_i(y)g(y)dy$. Again, multiplying $g(x)$ on both sides and taking integral imply

$$\sum_{i=0}^{\infty} c_i^2 h^i \to \int_{-\infty}^{\infty} g^2(x)dx, \quad \text{as } h \to 1,$$

and we then have

$$\sum_{i=0}^{\infty} c_i^2 = \int_{-\infty}^{\infty} g^2(x)dx.$$

Back to the general case $g(x) \in L^2(\mathbb{R})$, there is a function $g_v(x) \in C_0^\infty$ such that

$$\int_{-\infty}^{\infty} [g(x) - g_v(x)]^2 dx < \varepsilon,$$

for any given $\varepsilon > 0$.

Let

$$c_{i,v} = \int_{-\infty}^{\infty} g_v(x)\mathscr{H}_i(x)dx, \quad i \geq 0.$$

Then

$$\begin{aligned}
&\int_{-\infty}^{\infty} \left[g(x) - \sum_{i=0}^{k} c_{i,v}\mathscr{H}_i(x) \right]^2 dx \\
&= \int_{-\infty}^{\infty} g^2(x)dx + \sum_{i=0}^{k} c_{i,v}^2 - 2\sum_{i=0}^{k} c_{i,v}c_i \\
&\geq \int_{-\infty}^{\infty} g^2(x)dx - \sum_{i=0}^{k} c_i^2 \\
&= \int_{-\infty}^{\infty} \left[g(x) - \sum_{i=0}^{k} c_i\mathscr{H}_i(x) \right]^2 dx;
\end{aligned}$$

and also

$$\begin{aligned}
&\int_{-\infty}^{\infty} \left[g(x) - \sum_{i=0}^{k} c_{i,v}\mathscr{H}_i(x) \right]^2 dx \\
&= \int_{-\infty}^{\infty} \left[g(x) - g_v(x) + g_v(x) - \sum_{i=0}^{k} c_{i,v}\mathscr{H}_i(x) \right]^2 dx \\
&\leq 2\int_{-\infty}^{\infty} [g(x) - g_v(x)]^2 dx + 2\int_{-\infty}^{\infty} \left[g_v(x) - \sum_{i=0}^{k} c_{i,v}\mathscr{H}_i(x) \right]^2 dx \\
&\leq 3\varepsilon
\end{aligned}$$

when N is sufficiently large. This finishes the proof. □

This theorem is an alternative way to demonstrate the completeness of Hermite functions in $L^2(\mathbb{R})$, although this assertion is an implication of the completeness of Hermite polynomials in $L^2(\mathbb{R}, e^{-x^2})$.

To proceed further, let us first recall some facts. Let $L^2((a, b), w(x))$ admit a complete orthogonal polynomial sequence $\{P_i(x)\}$, each polynomial of which satisfies hypergeometric differential equation

$$s(x)y'' + v(x)y' + \lambda_i y = 0, \quad i \geq 1 \tag{C.4.81}$$

where $s(x)$ and $v(x)$ are polynomials with degree no higher than the second and first, respectively, $\lambda_i = -iv' - i(i-1)s''/2$. Moreover, suppose that $w(x)$ satisfies a first-order differential equation

$$\frac{d}{dx}(s(x)w(x)) = v(x)w(x), \tag{C.4.82}$$

and the boundary conditions

$$\lim_{x\to a+} s(x)w(x)x^k = 0, \quad \lim_{x\to b-} s(x)w(x)x^k = 0, \ \forall\, k \geq 0. \tag{C.4.83}$$

Define a differential operator

$$D = s(x)\frac{d^2}{dx^2} + v(x)\frac{d}{dx}. \tag{C.4.84}$$

Equation (C.4.81) can be written as $-D(y) = \lambda_i y$, so that often λ_i is called an eigenvalue of the operator $-D$.

Let $g \in L^2((a, b), w(x))$ and g is differentiable up to some order that validates what follows. Define the power of the operator D,

$$D^0(g) = g, \quad D^r(g) = D(D^{r-1}(g)), \quad r \geq 1.$$

Denote by $L^2_r(D)$ a subset of all $g \in L^2((a, b), w(x))$ where g have derivatives up to $2r$ order, these derivatives belong to $L^2((a, b), w(x))$ and $D^r(g) \in L^2((a, b), w(x))$.

Moreover, denote $b_i = \|P_i\|$ the norm of $P_i(x)$ in $L^2((a, b), w(x))$. Then, $\{P_i(x)/b_i\}$ is an orthonormal basis in $L^2((a, b), w(x))$. Because Eq. (C.4.81) is invariant under scalar multiplication, without loss of generality we suppose that $\{P_i(x)\}$ is an orthonormal basis in $L^2((a, b), w(x))$.

By Hilbert space theory we have

$$g(x) = \sum_{i=0}^{\infty} c_i P_i(x), \quad c_i \equiv c_i(g) = \langle g, P_i \rangle,$$

and the partial sum

$$g_k(x) = \sum_{i=0}^{k-1} c_i P_i(x)$$

converges to $g(x)$ in norm sense.

The following theorem establishes the convergence rate in norm sense for orthogonal expansion in terms of orthonormal basis $\{P_i(x)\}$ in $L^2((a, b), w(x))$ that satisfies (C.4.81), (C.4.82) and (C.4.83). This includes Legendre, Chebyshev, Hermite, and Laguerre polynomials.

Theorem C.4.7 *Assume that $g \in L^2_r(D)$, associated with $L^2((a, b), w(x))$, that* (C.4.82) *and* (C.4.83) *are satisfied. Also, there is an orthonormal polynomial sequence $\{P_i(x)\}$ that satisfies* (C.4.81). *Then,*

$$c_i(g) = (-1)^r \frac{1}{\lambda_i^r} c_i(D^r(g)), \tag{C.4.85}$$

where $c_i(D^r(g))$ is the coefficient in the orthogonal expansion of $D^r(g)$ in terms of $\{P_i(x)\}$.

Consequently, $\|g - g_k\| = o(\lambda_k^{-r})$ *when* $k \to \infty$. □

Proof By virtue of (C.4.82), multiplying both sides of the differential equation $s(x)P_i''(x) + v(x)P_i'(x) + \lambda_i P_i(x) = 0$ by $w(x)$ yields

$$(s(x)w(x)P_i'(x))' + \lambda_i P_i(x)w(x) = 0.$$

Thus, using integration by parts,

$$\begin{aligned}
c_i = \langle g, P_i\rangle &= \int_a^b g(x)P_i(x)w(x)dx \\
&= \frac{-1}{\lambda_i}\int_a^b g(x)(s(x)w(x)P_i'(x))'dx \\
&= \frac{-1}{\lambda_i} g(x)s(x)w(x)P_i'(x)\Big|_a^b + \frac{1}{\lambda_i}\int_a^b g'(x)s(x)w(x)P_i'(x)dx \\
&= \frac{1}{\lambda_i} g'(x)s(x)w(x)P_i(x)\Big|_a^b - \frac{1}{\lambda_i}\int_a^b (g'(x)s(x)w(x))'P_i(x)dx \\
&= -\frac{1}{\lambda_i}\int_a^b D(g)P_i(x)w(x)dx \\
&= -\frac{1}{\lambda_i}\langle D(g), P_i\rangle = -\frac{1}{\lambda_i}c_i(D(g)),
\end{aligned}$$

where the boundary conditions for w and s, smoothness, and inclusion in the space for g and g' ensure the vanish of the terms in the integral by parts. It then is clear that the relation (C.4.85) holds.

It follows that

$$\begin{aligned}
\|g - g_k\|^2 &= \left\|\sum_{i=k}^{\infty} c_i P_i(x)\right\|^2 = \sum_{i=k}^{\infty} c_i^2 \\
&= \sum_{i=k}^{\infty} \frac{1}{\lambda_i^{2r}} c_i^2(D^r(g)) \le \frac{1}{\lambda_k^{2r}} \sum_{i=k}^{\infty} c_i^2(D^r(g)) \\
&= o(\lambda_k^{-2r}),
\end{aligned}$$

when $k \to \infty$, since $\sum_{i=k}^{\infty} c_i^2(D^r(g)) = o(1)$. □

This theorem gives a decay rate for the coefficients in orthogonal expansion, given a certain smoothness of g, which determines the convergence rate of the series. If

$P_i(x)$ are Jacobi polynomials with parameters α and β, we know that they satisfy the differential equation (C.4.81) with $s(x) = 1 - x^2$, $v(x) = \beta - \alpha - (\alpha + \beta + 1)x$, and density $w(x) = (1 - x)^\alpha (1 + x)^\beta$ on $[-1, 1]$. Thus, (C.4.82) and (C.4.83) are satisfied, and consequently, $\|g - g_k\| = o(k^{-2r})$ because $\lambda_i = i(i + \alpha + \beta + 1)$. In particular, this rate holds for Legendre ($\alpha = \beta = 0$) and Chebyshev ($\alpha = \beta = -1/2$ for type I and $\alpha = \beta = 1/2$ for type II) polynomials. If $P_i(x)$ are either Laguerre ($s(x) = x$, $v(x) = \alpha - x + 1$ and $w(x) = x^\alpha e^{-x}$) or Hermite ($s(x) = 1$, $v(x) = -2x$ and $w(x) = e^{-x^2}$) polynomials, the conditions in the theorem are satisfied and then $\|g - g_k\| = o(k^{-r})$ since $\lambda_i = i$ and $\lambda_i = 2i$, respectively, for Laguerrer and Hermite polynomials.

Remember that $g \in L_r^2(D)$ requires that g is smooth up to $2r$ order and the result of Theorem C.4.7 is $\|g - g_k\| = o(\lambda_k^{-r})$. This is crucial when compared with other theorems that require g to be smooth up to r order so that the results in Theorem C.4.7 seem stronger.

In the supplementary material of Dong et al. (2016), the authors derive the decay rate of the coefficients in the space $L^2(\mathbb{R})$ in a straightforward fashion. Note that Hermite functions form a basis in $L^2(\mathbb{R})$, but Hermite functions $\{\mathscr{H}_i(x)\}$ no longer satisfy hypergeometric differential equation used in the proof of the preceding lemma, while instead they obey differential equation $y'' + (2i + 1 - x^2)y = 0$. The convergence rate in Lemma C.1 of the supplementary material of Dong et al. (2016) is slower than that in the following theorem, although its requirement on the function therein is a bit weaker.

Theorem C.4.8 *Let $g(x) \in L^2(\mathbb{R})$. Then,*

$$g(x) = \sum_{i=0}^{\infty} c_i \mathscr{H}_i(x), \quad c_i = \int g(x) \mathscr{H}_i(x) dx,$$

where $\{\mathscr{H}_i(x)\}$ is the Hermite function sequence. Let $g_k(x) = \sum_{i=0}^{k-1} c_i \mathscr{H}_i(x)$ be its partial sum and $\gamma_k(x) = g(x) - g_k(x) = \sum_{i=k}^{\infty} c_i \mathscr{H}_i(x)$ be the truncation residues. Define $G(x) = g(x)e^{x^2/2}$, and suppose that $D^r(G(x)) \in L^2(\mathbb{R}, e^{-x^2})$, $r \geq 1$, where differential operator D is defined by (C.4.84) with $s(x) = 1$ and $v(x) = 2x$ being coefficient functions in the hypergeometric differential equation that Hermite polynomials satisfy. Then, (i) $\int \gamma_k^2(x)dx = o(k^{-2r})$; (ii) $\int \gamma_k^2(x)x^2dx = o(k^{-(2r-1)})$; (iii) $\int \dot{\gamma}_k^2(x)x^2dx = o(k^{-(2r-2)})$; (iv) $\int \ddot{\gamma}_k^2(x)x^4dx = o(k^{-(2r-4)})$ where $\dot{\gamma}_k(x)$ and $\ddot{\gamma}_k(x)$ are the first-order and second-order derivatives of $\gamma_k(x)$, respectively. □

Clearly, $G(x) \in L^2(\mathbb{R}, e^{-x^2})$ is equivalent to $g(x) \in L^2(\mathbb{R})$, and note that the condition $D^r(G) \in L^2(\mathbb{R}, e^{-x^2})$, $r \geq 1$, is not restrictive. To see this, let $r = 1$, and observe that $D^r(G(x)) = [g''(x) + 2xg(x) + g(x) + xg'(x) + x^2 g(x)]e^{x^2/2}$. Thus, the condition is fulfilled if $g''(x) + 2xg(x) + g(x) + xg'(x) + x^2 g(x) \in L^2(\mathbb{R})$. In particular, when $g(x), g''(x), xg(x), xg'(x), x^2 g(x) \in L^2(\mathbb{R})$ the condition holds.

Proof Recall that $\mathscr{H}_i(x) = \frac{1}{b_i} H_i(x) e^{-x^2/2}$ where $b_i^2 = \sqrt{\pi} 2^i i!$ is the squared norm of $H_i(x)$ in $L^2(\mathbb{R}, e^{-x^2})$. Thus, $\{\frac{1}{b_i} H_i(x)\}$ is an orthonormal sequence in $L^2(\mathbb{R}, e^{-x^2})$.

Note that

$$\begin{aligned} c_i(g) &= \int g(x)\mathcal{H}_i(x)dx \\ &= \int g(x)\frac{1}{b_i}H_i(x)e^{-x^2/2}dx \\ &= \int G(x)\frac{1}{b_i}H_i(x)e^{-x^2}dx. \end{aligned}$$

Accordingly, c_i can be viewed as coefficients in the orthogonal series expansion of $G(x)$ in terms of $\{\frac{1}{b_i}H_i(x)\}$. It follows from (C.4.85) that

$$c_i(g) = \frac{1}{(2i)^r}C_i(D^r(G)), \tag{C.4.86}$$

where $C_i(D^r(G))$ are coefficients in the expansion of $D^r(G(x))$.

(i) By orthogonality,

$$\begin{aligned} \int \gamma_k^2(x)dx &= \sum_{i=k}^{\infty} c_i^2(g) = \sum_{i=k}^{\infty} \frac{1}{(2i)^{2r}}C_i^2(D^r(G)) \\ &\le O(1)k^{-2r}\sum_{i=k}^{\infty} C_i^2(D^r(G)) = o(k^{-2r}). \end{aligned}$$

(ii) From the recursion relation

$$x\mathcal{H}_0(x) = \frac{1}{\sqrt{2}}\mathcal{H}_1(x), \qquad x\mathcal{H}_i(x) = \frac{1}{\sqrt{2}}(\sqrt{i}\mathcal{H}_{i-1}(x) + \sqrt{i+1}\mathcal{H}_{i+1}(x)),$$

and the orthogonality, we have $\int x^2\mathcal{H}_i^2(x)dx = i + 1/2$ and for $i \ne j$,

$$\begin{aligned} &\int x^2\mathcal{H}_i(x)\mathcal{H}_j(x)dx \\ &= \frac{1}{2}\int (\sqrt{i}\mathcal{H}_{i-1}(x) + \sqrt{i+1}\mathcal{H}_{i+1}(x))(\sqrt{j}\mathcal{H}_{j-1}(x) + \sqrt{j+1}\mathcal{H}_{j+1}(x))dx \\ &= \frac{1}{2}\int \sqrt{i(j+1)}\mathcal{H}_{i-1}(x)\mathcal{H}_{j+1}(x)dx + \frac{1}{2}\int \sqrt{j(i+1)}\mathcal{H}_{i+1}(x)\mathcal{H}_{j-1}(x)dx \end{aligned}$$

which assumes $\frac{1}{2}\sqrt{i(i-1)}$ when $j = i-2$, $\frac{1}{2}\sqrt{(i+1)(i+2)}$ when $j = i+2$, and 0 otherwise. Thus,

$$\int \gamma_k^2(x)x^2dx = \sum_{i=k}^{\infty}\sum_{j=k}^{\infty} c_i c_j \int x^2 \mathscr{H}_i(x)\mathscr{H}_j(x)dx$$

$$= \sum_{i=k}^{\infty} c_i^2 \int x^2 \mathscr{H}_i^2(x)dx + \sum_{i=k}^{\infty}\sum_{j=k,\neq i}^{\infty} c_i c_j \int x^2 \mathscr{H}_i(x)\mathscr{H}_j(x)dx$$

$$= \sum_{i=k}^{\infty} c_i^2(i+1/2) + \frac{1}{2}\sum_{i=k}^{\infty} c_i c_{i-2}\sqrt{i(i-1)} + \frac{1}{2}\sum_{i=k}^{\infty} c_i c_{i+2}\sqrt{(i+1)(i+2)}$$

$$= O(1)\sum_{i=k}^{\infty} c_i^2 i = O(1)\sum_{i=k}^{\infty} i i^{-2r} C_i^2(D^r(G)) = o(1)k^{-(2r-1)},$$

using the coefficient relation (C.4.86).

(iii) Note that

$$\dot{\mathscr{H}}_0(x) = -\frac{1}{\sqrt{2}}\mathscr{H}_1(x), \quad \dot{\mathscr{H}}_i(x) = \frac{1}{\sqrt{2}}(\sqrt{i}\mathscr{H}_{i-1}(x) - \sqrt{i+1}\mathscr{H}_{i+1}(x)).$$

It follows from (ii) that

$$\int \dot{\gamma}^2(x)x^2dx = \int\left(\sum_{i=k}^{\infty} c_i \dot{\mathscr{H}}_i(x)\right)^2 x^2dx$$

$$= \frac{1}{2}\int\left(\sum_{i=k}^{\infty} c_i(\sqrt{i}\mathscr{H}_{i-1}(x) - \sqrt{i+1}\mathscr{H}_{i+1}(x))\right)^2 x^2dx$$

$$\leq \int\left(\sum_{i=k}^{\infty}\sqrt{i}c_i\mathscr{H}_{i-1}(x)\right)^2 x^2dx + \int\left(\sum_{i=k}^{\infty}\sqrt{i+1}c_i\mathscr{H}_{i+1}(x)\right)^2 x^2dx$$

$$= o(k^{-(2r-2)}).$$

It is quite clear that assertion (iv) follows in a similar fashion to (iii). □

Next, we consider the convergence rate in $L^2(\mathbb{R}^+, e^{-x})$ where $\mathbb{R}^+ = [0, \infty)$ in norm sense. The derivation in the following theorems is in a straightforward way similar to Lemma C.1 in Dong et al. (2016), and different from the proof of Theorem C.4.7. It is known that generalized Laguerre polynomials $\{L_j^\alpha(u)\}$ are orthogonal basis sequences in $L^2(\mathbb{R}^+, u^\alpha e^{-u})$, $\alpha > -1$. The Rodrigues formula of $L_j^\alpha(u)$ is

$$L_j^\alpha(x) = e^x\frac{x^{-\alpha}}{j!}\frac{d^j}{dx^j}e^{-x}x^{j+\alpha}, \quad \alpha > -1, \ j \geq 0.$$

The orthogonality of Laguerre polynomials reads

$$\int_0^\infty L_i^\alpha(x)L_j^\alpha(x)x^\alpha e^{-x}dx = b_{\alpha,j}^2\delta_{ij}, \quad b_{\alpha,j}^2 = \frac{\Gamma(1+\alpha+j)}{j!}.$$

When $\alpha = 0$, we use $\{L_j(u)\}$ without specifying α; in this case $b_j = b_{0,j} = 1$. Note further that when α is a positive integer, $b_{\alpha,j}^2 = (j+\alpha)\cdots(j+1)$. Define

$$l_j^\alpha(u) = \frac{1}{b_{\alpha,j}}L_j^\alpha(u), \tag{C.4.87}$$

so that $\{l_j^\alpha(u)\}$ forms an orthonomal basis in $L^2([0,\infty), u^\alpha e^{-u})$. Again, when $\alpha = 0$, we use $\{l_j(u)\}$ without specifying α.

Theorem C.4.9 *Suppose that $g(x) \in L^2(\mathbb{R}^+, e^{-x})$, g is differentiable on $\mathbb{R}^+$ up to the rth order, and $g^{(i)}(u)$ belongs to $L^2(\mathbb{R}^+, u^i e^{-u})$, $i = 0, 1, \ldots, r$. Let*

$$g^{(i)}(u) = \sum_{j=0}^\infty c_{i,j}l_j^i(u), \quad c_{i,j} = \int_0^\infty g^{(i)}(u)l_j^i(u)u^i e^{-u}du. \tag{C.4.88}$$

In particular, for $i = 0$, the series in (C.4.88) *is simplified to*

$$g(u) = \sum_{j=0}^\infty c_j l_j(u), \quad c_j = \int_0^\infty g(u)l_j(u)e^{-u}du. \tag{C.4.89}$$

Moreover, for positive integer k, denote the partial sum and residual of (C.4.89) *as*

$$g_k(u) = \sum_{j=0}^{k-1} c_j l_j(u), \quad \gamma_k(u) = \sum_{j=k}^\infty c_j l_j(u). \tag{C.4.90}$$

Then, for $j > r$,

$$c_j = \frac{(-1)^r}{\sqrt{j(j-1)\cdots(j-r+1)}}c_{r,j-r}(g^{(r)}),$$

where $c_{r,j-r}(g^{(r)})$ is the coefficient in the expansion of $g^{(r)}(u)$ in terms of $\{l_j^r(u)\}$, and consequently,

$$\|g(u) - g_k(u)\|_{L^2(\mathbb{R}^+, e^{-u})} = o(k^{-r/2}). \tag{C.4.91}$$

Proof The convergence of the expansion (C.4.89) is shown by Theorems 9.1.5 and 9.1.7 in Szego (1975, p. 246). Here, we are mainly concerned by the convergence rate.

Invoking the Rodrigues formula of Laguerre polynomials, integration by parts gives

$$
\begin{aligned}
c_j &= \int_0^\infty g(u) l_j(u) e^{-u} du = \frac{1}{j!}\int_0^\infty g(u) \frac{d^j}{du^j} e^{-u} u^j du \\
&= \frac{1}{j!}\int_0^\infty g(u) d \frac{d^{j-1}}{du^{j-1}} e^{-u} u^j \\
&= \frac{1}{j!} g(u) \frac{d^{j-1}}{du^{j-1}} e^{-u} u^j \Big|_0^\infty - \frac{1}{j!}\int_0^\infty g'(u) \frac{d^{j-1}}{du^{j-1}} e^{-u} u^j du \\
&= \frac{1}{j!} g(u) e^{-u} \sum_{\ell=0}^{j-1} \binom{j-1}{\ell} (-1)^{k-1-\ell} [u^j]^{(\ell)} \Big|_0^\infty \\
&\quad - \frac{1}{j!}\int_0^\infty g'(u) \frac{d^{j-1}}{du^{j-1}} e^{-u} u^j du \\
&= -\frac{1}{j!}\int_0^\infty g'(u) \frac{d^{j-1}}{du^{j-1}} e^{-u} u^j du \\
&= \cdots \\
&= (-1)^r \frac{1}{j!}\int_0^\infty g^{(r)}(u) \frac{d^{j-r}}{du^{j-r}} e^{-u} u^j du \\
&= (-1)^r \frac{(j-r)!}{j!}\int_0^\infty g^{(r)}(u) L_{j-r}^r(u) u^r e^{-r} du \\
&= (-1)^r \frac{(j-r)! b_{r,j-r}}{j!}\int_0^\infty g^{(r)}(u) l_{j-r}^r(u) u^r e^{-r} du \\
&= \frac{(-1)^r}{\sqrt{j(j-1)\cdots(j-r+1)}} c_{r,j-r}(g^{(r)}).
\end{aligned}
$$

Accordingly, due to the orthogonality of the basis,

$$
\begin{aligned}
&\|g(u) - g_k(u)\|^2_{L^2(\mathbb{R}^+, e^{-x})} \\
&= \int_0^\infty \gamma_k(u)^2 e^{-u} du = \sum_{j=k}^\infty c_j^2 \\
&= \sum_{j=k}^\infty \frac{1}{j(j-1)\cdots(j-r+1)} c_{r,j-r}^2(g^{(r)}) \\
&= O(k^{-r}) \sum_{j=k}^\infty c_{r,j-r}^2(g^{(r)}) = o(k^{-r}).
\end{aligned}
$$

In some situation, we need to consider the convergence rate of the orthogonal expansion in Hilbert space $L^2(\mathbb{R}^+)$. Since $\{l_j^\alpha(u)\}$ defined by (C.4.87) is an orthonomal basis sequence in $L^2(\mathbb{R}^+, u^\alpha e^{-u})$, $\{l_j^\alpha(u) u^{\alpha/2} e^{-u/2}\}$ forms an orthonomal basis sequence in $L^2(\mathbb{R}^+)$, for all $\alpha > -1$. Define

$$\mathscr{L}_j^\alpha(u) = l_j^\alpha(u)u^{\alpha/2}e^{-u/2} \tag{C.4.92}$$

and when $\alpha = 0$ we use $\mathscr{L}_j(u)$ without specifying α for convenience.

Theorem C.4.10 *Suppose that $g(u)$ defined on $\mathbb{R}^+$ belongs to $L^2(\mathbb{R}^+)$, and is differentiable up to the rth order. Suppose further that $[g(u)e^{u/2}]^{(r)}u^{r/2}e^{-u/2} \in L^2(\mathbb{R}^+)$. Let $g(u) = \sum_{j=0}^{\infty} c_j\mathscr{L}_j(u)$, $c_j = \int_0^\infty g(u)\mathscr{L}_j(u)du$, be the orthogonal expansion of $g(u)$ and define $g_k(u) = \sum_{j=0}^{k-1} c_j\mathscr{L}_j(u)$ for positive integer k the partial sum sequence. Then, $\|g(u) - g_k(u)\|_{L^2(\mathbb{R}^+)} = o(k^{-r/2})$.* □

Notice that

$$\begin{aligned}\tilde{g}(u) &\equiv [g(u)e^{u/2}]^{(r)}u^{r/2}e^{-u/2}\\ &= \sum_{\ell=0}^{r} \frac{1}{2^\ell}\binom{r}{\ell} g^{(r-\ell)}(u)e^{u/2}u^{r/2}e^{-u/2}\\ &= u^{r/2}\sum_{\ell=0}^{r} \frac{1}{2^\ell}\binom{r}{\ell} g^{(r-\ell)}(u).\end{aligned}$$

The condition on $[g(u)e^{u/2}]^{(r)}u^{r/2}e^{-u/2}$ is not tough.

Proof The convergence of $g_k(u) \to g(u)$ follows again from Theorems 9.1.5 and 9.1.7 in Szego (1975, p. 246). Here we focus on the convergence rate.

For $j > r$, integration by parts gives

$$\begin{aligned}c_j &= \int_0^\infty g(u)\mathscr{L}_j(u)du = \int_0^\infty g(u)l_j(u)e^{-u/2}du\\ &= \frac{1}{j!}\int_0^\infty g(u)e^{u/2}\frac{d^j}{du^j}e^{-u}u^j du = \frac{1}{j!}\int_0^\infty g(u)e^{u/2}d\frac{d^{j-1}}{du^{j-1}}e^{-u}u^j\\ &= \frac{1}{j!}g(u)e^{u/2}\frac{d^{j-1}}{du^{j-1}}e^{-u}u^j\Big|_0^\infty - \frac{1}{j!}\int_0^\infty [g(u)e^{u/2}]'\frac{d^{j-1}}{du^{j-1}}e^{-u}u^j du\\ &= \frac{1}{j!}g(u)e^{-u/2}\sum_{\ell=0}^{j-1}\binom{j-1}{\ell}(-1)^{k-1-\ell}[u^j]^{(\ell)}\Big|_0^\infty\\ &\quad - \frac{1}{j!}\int_0^\infty [g(u)e^{u/2}]'\frac{d^{j-1}}{du^{j-1}}e^{-u}u^j du\\ &= -\frac{1}{j!}\int_0^\infty [g(u)e^{u/2}]'\frac{d^{j-1}}{du^{j-1}}e^{-u}u^j du\\ &= \cdots\\ &= (-1)^r\frac{1}{j!}\int_0^\infty [g(u)e^{u/2}]^{(r)}\frac{d^{j-r}}{du^{j-r}}e^{-u}u^j du\end{aligned}$$

$$
\begin{aligned}
&= (-1)^r \frac{(j-r)!}{j!} \int_0^\infty [g(u)e^{u/2}]^{(r)} L^r_{j-r}(u) u^r e^{-u} du \\
&= (-1)^r \frac{(j-r)! b_{r,j-r}}{j!} \int_0^\infty [g(u)e^{u/2}]^{(r)} l^r_{j-r}(u) u^r e^{-u} du \\
&= (-1)^r \frac{(j-r)! b_{r,j-r}}{j!} \int_0^\infty [g(u)e^{u/2}]^{(r)} u^{r/2} e^{-u/2} \mathscr{L}^r_{j-r}(u) du \\
&= \frac{(-1)^r}{\sqrt{j(j-1)\cdots(j-r+1)}} c_{r,j-r}(\tilde{g}),
\end{aligned}
$$

where $c_{r,j-r}(\tilde{g})$ is the coefficient in the expansion of $\tilde{g}(u)$ in terms of $\{\mathscr{L}^r_j(u)\}$.

It follows from the orthogonality that

$$
\begin{aligned}
\|g(u) - g_k(u)\|^2_{L^2(\mathbb{R}^+)} &= \sum_{j=k}^\infty c_j^2 = \sum_{j=k}^\infty \frac{1}{j(j-1)\cdots(j-r+1)} c^2_{r,j-r}(\tilde{g}) \\
&= O(k^{-r}) \sum_{j=k}^\infty c^2_{r,j-r}(\tilde{g}) = o(k^{-r}).
\end{aligned}
$$

C.4.5 Convergence in Pointwise Sense of Orthogonal Series

Another important issue about orthogonal series expansion is convergence in pointwise sense. Often, this is encountered in nonparametric estimation in econometric studies by means of series methods. There are several approaches to achieving this goal.

Pointwise convergence in Fourier series expansion. For every $g(x) \in C_{2\pi}$ (the class of periodic continuous functions with period 2π), let $S_k(g; x)$ be the partial sum of its Fourier expansion,

$$
S_k(g; x) = A + \sum_{j=1}^k (a_j \cos(jx) + b_j \sin(jx)),
$$

where

$$
\begin{aligned}
A &= \frac{1}{2\pi} \int_{-\pi}^{\pi} g(x) dx, \\
a_j &= \frac{1}{\pi} \int_{-\pi}^{\pi} g(x) \cos(jx) dx, \\
b_j &= \frac{1}{\pi} \int_{-\pi}^{\pi} g(x) \sin(jx) dx.
\end{aligned}
$$

This partial sum S_k can be viewed as a linear mapping from $C_{2\pi}$ to trigonometric polynomials of order k. We are now about to show that $S_k(g, x)$ can be written as a Dirichlet integral

$$S_k(g, x) = \frac{1}{\pi} \int_0^{\pi/2} [g(x + 2t) + g(x - 2t)] \frac{\sin(2k + 1)t}{\sin t} dt.$$

In fact, observe that

$$\begin{aligned} S_k(g, x) &= A + \sum_{j=1}^{k} (a_j \cos(jx) + b_j \sin(jx)) \\ &= \frac{1}{\pi} \int_{-\pi}^{\pi} g(t) \left[\frac{1}{2} + \sum_{j=1}^{k} (\cos(jt)\cos(jx) + \sin(jt)\sin(jx)) \right] dt \\ &= \frac{1}{\pi} \int_{-\pi}^{\pi} g(t) \left[\frac{1}{2} + \sum_{j=1}^{k} \cos j(x - t) \right] dt. \end{aligned}$$

In the literature,

$$K_N(x) = \frac{1}{\pi} \left[\frac{1}{2} + \sum_{j=1}^{N} \cos jx \right]$$

is called Dirichlet's kernel. Recalling the identity $\cos(\theta) = (e^{i\theta} + e^{-i\theta})/2$ where i is the unit of imaginary number ($i^2 = -1$), we have

$$\begin{aligned} K_N(x) &= \frac{1}{2\pi} \left[1 + 2\sum_{j=1}^{N} \cos jx \right] = \frac{1}{2\pi} \sum_{j=-N}^{N} e^{ijx} \\ &= \frac{1}{2\pi} \frac{e^{i(N+1)x} - e^{-iNx}}{e^{ix} - 1}, \quad x \neq 0, \end{aligned}$$

while clearly $K_N(0) = (2N + 1)/2\pi$.

Further, for $x \neq 0$, multiplying both of the denominator and numerator by $e^{-ix/2}$ we have

$$K_N(x) = \frac{1}{2\pi} \frac{e^{i(N+1/2)x} - e^{-i(N+1/2)x}}{e^{ix/2} - e^{-ix/2}} = \frac{1}{2\pi} \frac{\sin((N + 1/2)x)}{\sin(x/2)}.$$

It follows that

$$\begin{aligned}
S_k(g,x) &= \frac{1}{2\pi}\int_{-\pi}^{\pi} g(t)\frac{\sin((k+1/2)(x-t))}{\sin((x-t)/2)}dt \\
&= \frac{1}{2\pi}\int_{x-\pi}^{x+\pi} g(x-t)\frac{\sin((k+1/2)t)}{\sin(t/2)}dt \\
&= \frac{1}{2\pi}\int_{-\pi}^{\pi} g(x-t)\frac{\sin((k+1/2)t)}{\sin(t/2)}dt \\
&= \frac{1}{2\pi}\int_{0}^{\pi} [g(x+t)+g(x-t)]\frac{\sin((k+1/2)t)}{\sin(t/2)}dt \\
&= \frac{1}{\pi}\int_{0}^{\pi/2} [g(x+2t)+g(x-2t)]\frac{\sin((2k+1)t)}{\sin t}dt.
\end{aligned}$$

Lemma C.4.4 *For any $k \geq 2$, we have*

$$\frac{1}{\pi}\int_0^{\pi/2}\left|\frac{\sin(2k+1)t}{\sin t}\right| dt \leq \frac{1}{2}(2+\ln(k)).$$

Proof By induction, $|\sin nt| \leq n|\sin t|$ for any t. Indeed, for $n=1$, it holds obviously.

Suppose it holds when $n=m$, then $|\sin(m+1)t| \leq |\sin mt \cos t| + |\cos mt \sin t| \leq (m+1)|\sin t|$.

Since $\sin t/t$ is decreasing on $[0, \pi/2]$, $\sin t \geq \frac{2}{\pi}t$ on the interval. Then,

$$\begin{aligned}
&\frac{1}{\pi}\int_0^{\pi/2}\left|\frac{\sin(2k+1)t}{\sin t}\right| dt \\
&= \frac{1}{\pi}\int_0^{\pi/(4k+2)}\left|\frac{\sin(2k+1)t}{\sin t}\right| dt + \frac{1}{\pi}\int_{\pi/(4k+2)}^{\pi/2}\left|\frac{\sin(2k+1)t}{\sin t}\right| dt \\
&\leq \frac{1}{\pi}\int_0^{\pi/(4k+2)} (2k+1)dt + \frac{1}{2}\int_{\pi/(4k+2)}^{\pi/2}\frac{1}{t}dt \\
&\leq \frac{1}{2} + \frac{1}{2}\ln(2k+1) \leq \frac{1}{2} + \frac{1}{2}\ln(ek) \\
&= 1 + \frac{1}{2}\ln(k).
\end{aligned}$$

Theorem C.4.11 *Let $g(x) \in C_{2\pi}$. (1) $\sup_{x\in[-\pi,\pi]}|g(x) - S_k(g;x)| \leq (3+\ln(k))$ $E_k^*(g)$. (2) If $\lim_{\delta\to 0}\omega(\delta; g)\ln(\delta) = 0$, then the Fourier series expansion of $g(x)$ is uniformly convergent. (3) If further $g''(x) \in C_{2\pi}$, then the Fourier series of $g(x)$ converges to $g(x)$ absolutely and uniformly.* □

The first result is due to Lebesgue (1909) where $E_k^*(g)$ is the best approximation error of g by trigonometric polynomials with order no higher than k. See Appendix B. The second one can be found in Theorem 4.2 of Schultz (1969), whereas the condition therein is known as the Dini-Schwartz condition, which is fulfilled by any Lipschtz continuous function. The third assertion shows an alternative sufficient condition that guarantees the convergence of the Fourier series.

Proof (1) Denote $\|f\| = \max_{x\in[-\pi,\pi]} |f(x)|$ the super norm. By Dirichlet integral, $|S_k(f;x)| \le \|f\|(2+\ln(k))$ for any $f \in C_{2\pi}$. Let $T_k(x)$ be the best trigonometric polynomial of $g(x)$. Then,

$$\begin{aligned}|S_k(g;x) - g(x)| &\le |S_k(g;x) - T_k(x)| + |T_k(x) - g(x)| \\ &= |S_k(g - T_k;x)| + E_k^* \\ &\le \|g - T_k\|(2+\ln(k)) + E_k^* \\ &= (3+\ln(k))E_k^*,\end{aligned}$$

where we use the linearity of S_k and $S_k(T_k, x) = T_k(x)$.

(2) can be derived directly by definition.

(3) Integration by parts gives

$$\begin{aligned}\pi a_k &= \int_{-\pi}^{\pi} g(x)\cos(kx)dx = \frac{1}{k}\int_{-\pi}^{\pi} g(x)d\sin(kx) \\ &= -\frac{1}{k}\int_{-\pi}^{\pi} g'(x)\sin(kx)dx = \frac{1}{k^2}\int_{-\pi}^{\pi} g'(x)d\cos(kx) \\ &= -\frac{1}{k^2}\int_{-\pi}^{\pi} g''(x)\cos(kx)dx,\end{aligned}$$

and thus $|a_k| \le 2\frac{1}{k^2}\|g''\|$ where $\|\cdot\|$ is the super norm. Similarly, $|b_k| \le 2\frac{1}{k^2}\|g''\|$.

Hence,

$$\left| A + \sum_{j=1}^{\infty}(a_j\cos(jx) + b_j\sin(jx)) \right| \le |A| + 4\|g''\| \sum_{j=1}^{\infty} \frac{1}{k^2} < \infty,$$

which implies the uniform and absolute convergence of the Fourier series. To show the sum is $g(x)$, suppose

$$f(x) = A + \sum_{j=1}^{\infty}(a_j\cos(jx) + b_j\sin(jx)).$$

Then, $f(x)$ and $g(x)$ have the same Fourier coefficients, and consequently $f(x) = g(x)$ due to the completeness of the Fourier basis. □

Although the theorem is derived under the periodicity of $g(x)$, such requirement can be removed by the argument of the induced function in Appendix B if the induced function satisfies the proviso condition in related theorems; hence the Fourier series expansion possesses the same convergence rate. In addition, in a nonparametric regression context Eubank and Speckman (1991) use trigonometric polynomials plus power functions to conquer the problem that the regression may not be periodic. See the paper for details.

Pointwise convergence of orthogonal series on bounded interval. We now consider the pointwise convergence of the orthogonal series expansion in $L^2([a, b], w(x))$ where $[a, b]$ is bounded, and without loss of generality, $\int_a^b w(x)dx = 1$. Let $\{\varphi_j(x), j \geq 0\}$ be an orthonormal polynomial sequence in $L^2([a, b], w(x))$. Then, for any $g(x) \in L^2([a, b], w(x))$, $g(x) = \sum_{j=0}^{\infty} c_j\varphi_j(x)$ with $c_j = \int_a^b g(u)\varphi_j(u)w(u)du$.

Let $S_k(g; x) = \sum_{j=0}^{k} c_j\varphi_j(x)$ be the partial sum of the orthogonal series expansion, which can be viewed as a project operator from any function of $L^2([a, b], w(x))$ to a k-degree polynomial belonging to the subspace spanned by $\{\varphi_j(x), j = 0, 1, \ldots, k\}$.

For better exposition, denote $\Phi_k(x) = (\varphi_0(x), \ldots, \varphi_k(x))^\top$, $c = (c_0, \ldots, c_k)^\top$ and $\gamma_k(g; x) = \sum_{j=k+1}^{\infty} c_j\varphi_j(x)$. Thence, $g(x) = S_k(g; x) + \gamma_k(g; x)$ and $S_k(g; x) = \Phi_k(x)^\top c$.

Theorem C.4.12 *Suppose that $g(x) \in L^2([a, b], w(x))$ is continuous on $[a, b]$. Let $E_k(g)$ be the error of $g(x)$ approximated by the best polynomial of degree k. If $\|\Phi_k(x)\|E_k(g) \to 0$ as $k \to \infty$, $S_k(g; x) \to g(x)$. Moreover, if $\zeta_k E_k(g) \to 0$ where $\zeta_k = \sup_{x\in[a,b]} \|\Phi_k(x)\|$, then $\sup_{x\in[a,b]} |S_k(g; x) - g(x)| \to 0$ (uniform convergence).* □

Note that the continuity of g is not stringent since as can be seen later we normally require it to be differentiable with certain order in practice.

Proof Let P_k^* be the best polynomial approximation to $g(x) \in C[a, b]$ of degree k. We have

$$
\begin{aligned}
&|g(x) - S_k(g; x)|\\
&= |g(x) - P_k^*(x) + P_k^*(x) - S_k(g; x)|\\
&\leq |g(x) - P_k^*(x)| + |S_k(g - P_k^*; x)|\\
&= E_k(g) + \left|\sum_{j=0}^{k}\int_a^b [g(u) - P_k^*(u)]\varphi_j(u)w(u)du\,\varphi_j(x)\right|\\
&= E_k(g) + \left|\int_a^b [g(u) - P_k^*(u)]w(u)\sum_{j=0}^{k}\varphi_j(u)\varphi_j(x)du\right|\\
&\leq E_k(g) + E_k(g)\int_a^b w(u)\left|\sum_{j=0}^{k}\varphi_j(u)\varphi_j(x)\right|du\\
&\leq E_k(g) + E_k(g)\left(\int_a^b w(u)\left|\sum_{j=0}^{k}\varphi_j(u)\varphi_j(x)\right|^2 du\right)^{1/2}\\
&= (1 + \|\Phi_k(x)\|)E_k(g)
\end{aligned}
$$

by the orthogonality of the basis. Hence, if $\|\Phi_k(x)\| E_k(g) \to 0$ as $k \to \infty$, $S_k(g; x) \to g(x)$.

In particular, $\sup_{x\in[a,b]} |S_k(g; x) - g(x)| \to 0$ (uniform convergence) if $\zeta_k E_k(g) \to 0$ where $\zeta_k = \sup_{x\in[a,b]} \|\Phi_k(x)\|$. □

The relation $|g(x) - S_k(g; x)| \le (1 + \|\Phi_k(x)\|)E_k(g)$ is useful in practice, because we may have the decay order of $E_k(g)$ under certain condition of $g(x)$. Along with $\|\Phi_k(x)\| = O(\sqrt{k})$ shown in Corollary 1.3 of Lubinsky (2009), viz.,

$$\lim_{k\to\infty} \frac{1}{k}\|\Phi_k(x)\|^2 = \frac{1}{\pi w(x)\sqrt{1-x^2}}, \tag{C.4.93}$$

provided that the interval is $[-1, 1]$, the decay order of $E_k(g)$ gives an order of the convergence of $|g(x) - S_k(g; x)|$. However, to obtain a fast rate of $E_k(g)$ certain smoothness of $g(\cdot)$ may be in order.

Theorem C.4.13 *1. For $g(x) \in C[a, b]$, we have (a) $\|\gamma_k(g, x)\| \le E_k(g)$; (b) For any $x \in [a, b]$, $|\gamma_k(g; x)| \le (1 + \|\Phi_k(x)\|)E_k(g)$; (c) In particular, for the first kind of Chebyshev polynomial sequence on* $[-1, 1]$, $\max_{x\in[-1,1]} |\gamma_k(g; x)| \le (1 + \sqrt{k})E_k(g)$.

2. If $h(r) \in L^2[0, 1]$ and the orthogonal sequence, $\varphi_0(r) \equiv 1$ and $\varphi_j(r) = \sqrt{2}\cos(\pi jr)$, $j \ge 1$, is used to expand the function. Define $\gamma_k(h; r)$ similarly. If h is continuously differentiable on $[0, 1]$ *up to the sth order, then* $\max_{r\in[0,1]} |\gamma_k(h; r)| \le Ck^{-s}\log(k)$. □

Proof We only provide the proof of 1(a). Note that $S_k(g, x)$ is a polynomial of order k, and by Theorems C.2.1 and C.2.5 it is such that

$$\|g(x) - S_k(g, x)\| = \min_{p_k(x)} \|g(x) - p_k(x)\|.$$

Let $p_k^*(x)$ be the best approximation polynomial with order no larger than k. Thus,

$$\begin{aligned}\|\gamma_k(g, x)\| \le \|g(x) - p_k^*(x)\| &= \left(\int_a^b [g(x) - p_k^*(x)]^2 w(x)dx\right)^{1/2}\\ &\le \|g(x) - p_k^*(x)\|_\infty = E_k(g).\end{aligned}$$

All other assertions can be found in Lemma A.5 in Dong et al. (2021). □

Note that the assertion 1(c) actually holds for general orthonormal polynomial sequences, since the limit of (C.4.93) may be extended to any orthogonal series on bounded interval. In addition, if g is continuously differentiable on $[a, b]$ up to the sth order, then $E_k(g) \le Ck^{-s}\omega^{(s)}(k^{-1})$ for $k > s$, where $\omega^{(s)}(\cdot)$ is the modulus of continuity for $g^{(s)}$. This along with the assertion 1(b) gives $|\gamma_k(g; x)| \le Ck^{-s+1/2}\omega^{(s)}(k^{-1})$.

The next theorem will give a pointwise convergence for Legendre polynomial expansion of functions that may be discontinuous.

Theorem C.4.14 *If f function is piecewise smooth on $[-1, 1]$, then the Legendre series*

$$f(x) = \sum_{n=0}^{\infty} c_n P_n(x) \tag{C.4.94}$$

where

$$c_n = (n + 1/2) \int_{-1}^{1} f(x) P_n(x) dx, \quad n = 0, 1, 2, \ldots$$

converges pointwise to $f(x)$ at every continuous point of the function f on $[-1, 1]$. At points of discontinuity of f on $[-1, 1]$, the series converges to the average value $[f(x+0) + f(x-0)]/2$. Finally, at $x = -1$ the series converges to $f(-1+0)$, and at $x = 1$ it converges to $f(1-0)$. □

Proof Let us assume that x is a point of continuity of the function f, and consider the partial sum $(-1 < x < 1)$,

$$\begin{aligned} S_n(x) &= \sum_{k=0}^{n} c_k P_k(x) \\ &= \frac{1}{2} \int_{-1}^{1} f(t) \sum_{k=0}^{n} (2k+1) P_k(t) P_k(x) dt \\ &= \frac{1}{2}(n+1) \int_{-1}^{1} f(t) \frac{P_{n+1}(t) P_n(x) - P_n(t) P_{n+1}(x)}{t - x} dt, \end{aligned}$$

where we have used the Christoffel-Darboux formula for Legendre polynomials,

$$\sum_{k=0}^{n} (2k+1) P_k(t) P_k(x) = (n+1) \frac{P_{n+1}(t) P_n(x) - P_n(t) P_{n+1}(x)}{t - x}. \tag{C.4.95}$$

If integrating both sides of (C.4.95) w.r.t. t, we have

$$(n+1) \int_{-1}^{1} \frac{P_{n+1}(t) P_n(x) - P_n(t) P_{n+1}(x)}{t - x} dt = 2,$$

by virtue of the orthogonality,

$$\int_{-1}^{1} P_k(t) dt = \begin{cases} 0, & k \neq 0, \\ 2, & k = 0. \end{cases}$$

It follows that

$$S_n(x) - f(x) = \frac{1}{2}(n+1) \int_{-1}^{1} \frac{f(t) - f(x)}{t - x} [P_{n+1}(t) P_n(x) - P_n(t) P_{n+1}(x)] dt.$$

Set

$$g(t) = \frac{f(t) - f(x)}{t - x}$$

for convenience, and write

$$S_n(x) - f(x) = \frac{n+1}{2} P_n(x) \int_{-1}^{1} g(t) P_{n+1}(t) dt - \frac{n+1}{2} P_{n+1}(x) \int_{-1}^{1} g(t) P_n(t) dt.$$

Because f is piecewise smooth, it follows that g is also piecewise smooth at all $t \neq x$. To investigate the behavior of g at $t = x$, we consider the limit

$$g(x) = \lim_{t \to x} \frac{f(t) - f(x)}{t - x} = f'(x),$$

since x is a continuous point of f. As f' is piecewise continuous, so is g. Thus, both integrals

$$b_{n+1} \equiv \sqrt{n + 3/2} \int_{-1}^{1} g(t) P_{n+1}(t) dt \;\; \text{and} \;\; b_n \equiv \sqrt{n + 1/2} \int_{-1}^{1} g(t) P_n(t) dt$$

converge to zero as $n \to \infty$ because they are expansion coefficients of g in terms of Legendre polynomials. We finally write

$$S_n(x) - f(x) = \frac{(n+1) P_n(x)}{2\sqrt{n + 3/2}} b_{n+1} - \frac{(n+1) P_{n+1}(x)}{2\sqrt{n + 1/2}} b_n,$$

which, together with

$$|P_n(x)| \leq \sqrt{\frac{\pi}{2n(1 - x^2)}}, \quad |x| < 1, \; n \geq 1,$$

given in Andrews (1998, p. 159), leads to the assertion for continuous points.

The assertion for discontinuity of f requires only a slight modification of the above proof. Similar comments can be made about the points $x = \pm 1$. □

Pointwise convergence of orthogonal series on unbounded intervals. When considering the convergence of orthogonal series, mathematicians have different goals other than econometricians. The former would like to find as weak a condition as possible under which the series converges, whereas the latter, bearing in mind the requirement in their econometric research, strive to have the weakest sufficient condition that fulfills their requirement. The following theorems illustrate these two aspects.

First, we consider the pointwise convergence of orthogonal series expansion in $L^2(\mathbb{R})$ where Hermite functions form a basis. Suppose that $g(x) \in L^2(\mathbb{R})$. We already know that

$$g(x) = \sum_{i=0}^{\infty} c_i \mathscr{H}_i(x), \quad c_i = \int g(x)\mathscr{H}_i(x)dx, \tag{C.4.96}$$

converges in norm sense. Note that $\mathscr{H}_i(x) = b_i^{-1} H_i(x)e^{-x^2/2}$ where $b_i^2 = \sqrt{\pi}2^i i!$. Hence, we rewrite (C.4.96) as

$$g(x)e^{x^2/2} = \sum_{i=0}^{\infty} c_i b_i^{-1} H_i(x), \tag{C.4.97}$$

and further denoting $G(x) = g(x)e^{x^2/2}$ and $a_i = c_i/b_i$, we have

$$G(x) = \sum_{i=0}^{\infty} a_i H_i(x), \tag{C.4.98}$$

and

$$\begin{aligned} a_i &= \frac{1}{b_i}\int g(x)\mathscr{H}_i(x)dx = \frac{1}{b_i^2}\int g(x)H_i(x)e^{-x^2/2}dx \\ &= \frac{1}{b_i^2}\int G(x)H_i(x)e^{-x^2}dx, \end{aligned}$$

which are the coefficients of the expansion of $G(x)$ in $L^2(\mathbb{R}, e^{-x^2})$ in terms of $\{H_i(x)\}$.

Theorem C.4.15 *Suppose that $G(x)$ is an arbitrary function defined on $\mathbb{R}$ satisfying the following conditions*

(1) On any finite open set $(-a, a)$, $G(x)$ is a piecewise smooth function.
(2) Integral $\int |x|G^2(x)e^{-x^2}dx < \infty$.

Then, as long as $G(x)$ is continuous at point x, the infinite orthogonal series (C.4.98) *converges to $G(x)$ in point sense.* □

Proof Note firstly that the conditions (1) and (2) ensure the existence of integral $\int G(x)H_i(x)e^{-x^2}dx$, so that a_i in (C.4.98) do exist. In fact, let $a > 1$ be any number and we write

$$\begin{aligned} &\int G(x)H_i(x)e^{-x^2}dx \\ &= \int_{-\infty}^{-a} G(x)H_i(x)e^{-x^2}dx + \int_{-a}^{a} G(x)H_i(x)e^{-x^2}dx + \int_{a}^{\infty} G(x)H_i(x)e^{-x^2}dx \\ &\equiv I_1 + I_2 + I_3, \quad \text{say.} \end{aligned}$$

Because I_2 is always finite regardlessly of what a is, we consider I_3 in what follows while I_1 can be dealt with similarly. It is readily seen that

$$
\begin{aligned}
|I_3| &\leq \int_a^{\infty} |G(x)H_i(x)|e^{-x^2} dx \\
&\leq \frac{1}{2}\left(\int_a^{\infty} |G(x)|^2 e^{-x^2} dx + \int_a^{\infty} |H_i(x)|^2 e^{-x^2} dx\right) \\
&\leq \frac{1}{2}\left(\int_a^{\infty} x|G(x)|^2 e^{-x^2} dx + \int_a^{\infty} |H_i(x)|^2 e^{-x^2} dx\right) \\
&< \infty.
\end{aligned}
$$

Let $S_m(x)$ be the partial sum of the series (C.4.98). We have

$$
\begin{aligned}
S_m(x) &= \sum_{i=0}^{m} a_i H_i(x) \\
&= \sum_{i=0}^{m} H_i(x) \frac{1}{b_i^2} \int G(y) H_i(y) e^{-y^2} dy \\
&= \int G(y) e^{-y^2} \frac{1}{\sqrt{\pi}} \sum_{i=0}^{m} \frac{H_i(x)H_i(y)}{2^i i!} dy \\
&\equiv \int G(y) e^{-y^2} K_m(x, y) dy,
\end{aligned}
$$

where we define

$$
K_m(x, y) = \frac{1}{\sqrt{\pi}} \sum_{i=0}^{m} \frac{H_i(x)H_i(y)}{2^i i!}.
$$

By the Christoffel-Darboux formula,

$$
\sum_{i=0}^{m} \frac{H_i(x)H_i(y)}{2^i i!} = \frac{H_{m+1}(x)H_m(y) - H_{m+1}(y)H_m(x)}{2^{m+1} m!(x-y)}.
$$

Moreover, due to the orthogonality of $\{H_i(x)\}$, we have $\int K_m(x, y) e^{-y^2} dy = 1$. Hence,

$$
\begin{aligned}
S_m(x) - G(x) &= \int [G(y) - G(x)] e^{-y^2} K_m(x, y) dy \\
&= \frac{H_m(x)}{2^{m+1} m!} \frac{1}{\sqrt{\pi}} \int H_{m+1}(y) e^{-y^2} \varphi(x, y) dy \\
&\quad - \frac{H_{m+1}(x)}{2^{m+1} m!} \frac{1}{\sqrt{\pi}} \int H_m(y) e^{-y^2} \varphi(x, y) dy,
\end{aligned}
$$

where we define

$$
\varphi(x, y) = \frac{G(y) - G(x)}{y - x}.
$$

To finish the proof of $S_m(x) - G(x) \to 0$, we need to invoke Lemma C.4.5 below. Regarding a function of y, by the first condition $\varphi(x, y)$ is piecewise smooth on any finite $(-a, a)$, while by the second condition $|y|^3\varphi^2(x, y)e^{-y^2}$ is integrable on $\mathbb{R}$ because for $b > x$,

$$\begin{aligned}\int_b^\infty |y|^3\varphi^2(x, y)e^{-y^2}dy &= \int_b^\infty |y|^2|y|\frac{(G(x) - G(y))^2}{(x - y)^2}e^{-y^2}dy \\ &\le \left(\frac{b}{b - x}\right)^2 \int_b^\infty |y|(G(x) - G(y))^2 e^{-y^2}dy \\ &\le 2\left(\frac{b}{b - x}\right)^2 \int_b^\infty |y|(G^2(x) + G^2(y))e^{-y^2}dy \\ &< \infty.\end{aligned}$$

Thus, by Lemma C.4.5,

$$\lim_{m\to\infty} \frac{(m + 1)^{1/4}}{b_{m+1}} \int e^{-y^2} H_{m+1}(y)\varphi(x, y)dy = 0,$$

$$\lim_{m\to\infty} \frac{(m + 1)^{1/4}}{b_m} \int e^{-y^2} H_m(y)\varphi(x, y)dy = 0,$$

where $b_m^2 = 2^m m!\sqrt{\pi}$, and by virtue of (C.4.66) and Stirling formula, both of

$$\frac{b_{m+1}}{(m + 1)^{1/4}} \frac{H_m(x)}{2^{m+1}m!\sqrt{\pi}} \quad \text{and} \quad \frac{b_m}{(m + 1)^{1/4}} \frac{H_{m+1}(x)}{2^{m+1}m!\sqrt{\pi}}$$

are bounded as $m \to \infty$. Therefore,

$$\lim_{m\to\infty} [S_m(x) - G(x)] = 0,$$

which completes the proof. □

Lemma C.4.5 *Suppose that $\psi(x)$ satisfies*

(a) $\psi(x)$ is piecewise continuous on any finite open set $(-a, a)$;
(b) $\int |x|^3\psi^2(x)e^{-x^2}dx < \infty$.

Then

$$\lim_{i\to\infty} \frac{i^{1/4}}{b_i} \int e^{-x^2} H_i(x)\psi(x)dx = 0,$$

where $b_i^2 = 2^i i!\sqrt{\pi}$.

Proof Note that for any $a > 0$,

$$\begin{aligned} J &\equiv \frac{i^{1/4}}{b_i} \int e^{-x^2} H_i(x)\psi(x)dx \\ &= \frac{i^{1/4}}{b_i} \left[\int_{-\infty}^{-a} + \int_{-a}^{a} + \int_{a}^{\infty} \right] e^{-x^2} H_i(x)\psi(x)dx \\ &\equiv J_1 + J_2 + J_3. \end{aligned}$$

By virtue of the Cauchy-Schwarz inequality,

$$\begin{aligned} |J_1| &\leq \frac{i^{1/4}}{b_i} \int_{-\infty}^{-a} e^{-x^2} |H_i(x)\psi(x)|dx \\ &\leq \frac{i^{1/4}}{b_i} \left(\int_{-\infty}^{-a} e^{-x^2} |x|^{-3} H_i^2(x)dx \right)^{1/2} \left(\int_{-\infty}^{-a} e^{-x^2} |x|^3 \psi^2(x)dx \right)^{1/2} \\ &= \left(\frac{i^{1/2}}{b_i^2} \int_{-\infty}^{-a} e^{-x^2} |x|^{-3} H_i^2(x)dx \right)^{1/2} \left(\int_{-\infty}^{-a} e^{-x^2} |x|^3 \psi^2(x)dx \right)^{1/2}. \end{aligned}$$

Similarly,

$$\begin{aligned} |J_3| &\leq \left(\frac{i^{1/2}}{b_i^2} \int_{a}^{\infty} e^{-x^2} |x|^{-3} H_i^2(x)dx \right)^{1/2} \left(\int_{a}^{\infty} e^{-x^2} |x|^3 \psi^2(x)dx \right)^{1/2} \\ &\equiv (I_1 \times I_2)^{1/2}. \end{aligned}$$

Write

$$\begin{aligned} I_1 &= \frac{i^{1/2}}{b_i^2} \int_{a}^{\infty} e^{-x^2} |x|^{-3} H_i^2(x)dx \\ &= \frac{i^{1/2}}{b_i^2} \left[\int_{a}^{i^\delta} + \int_{i^\delta}^{\infty} \right] e^{-x^2} |x|^{-3} H_i^2(x)dx \\ &\equiv I_{11} + I_{12}. \end{aligned}$$

Let $\delta = 1/6$. We have

$$\begin{aligned} I_{12} &= \frac{i^{1/2}}{b_i^2} \int_{i^\delta}^{\infty} e^{-x^2} |x|^{-3} H_i^2(x)dx \\ &\leq \frac{i^{1/2-3\delta}}{b_i^2} \int e^{-x^2} H_i^2(x)dx = i^{1/2-3\delta} = 1. \end{aligned}$$

On the other hand, invoking (C.4.66) about the asymptotic of $H_i(x)$,

$$
\begin{aligned}
I_{11} &= \frac{i^{1/2}}{b_i^2} \int_a^{i^\delta} e^{-x^2} |x|^{-3} H_i^2(x) dx \\
&\le \frac{\alpha_i^2 i^{1/2}}{b_i^2} \int_a^{i^\delta} \left(1 + c x^{5/2} i^{-1/4}\right)^2 |x|^{-3} dx \\
&\le \frac{\alpha_i^2 i^{1/2}}{b_i^2} \int_a^{i^\delta} \left(2x^{-3} + 2c^2 x^2 i^{-1/2}\right) dx \\
&= \frac{\alpha_i^2 i^{1/2}}{b_i^2} \left(-x^{-2}\Big|_a^{i^\delta} + \frac{2}{3} c^2 x^3 \Big|_a^{i^\delta} i^{-1/2}\right) \le M
\end{aligned}
$$

for some $M > 0$, since $\frac{\alpha_i^2 i^{1/2}}{b_i^2}$ is bounded by (C.4.63) as $i \to \infty$. Thus, I_1 is bounded, while due to the second condition of integrability we may choose a sufficiently large a such that $|J_1|, |J_3| < \varepsilon$ for any given $\varepsilon > 0$.

Fix a. By (C.4.60),

$$
\begin{aligned}
J_2 = \frac{\alpha_i i^{1/4}}{b_i} \Bigg[& \int_{-a}^{a} e^{-x^2/2} \psi(x) \cos\left(\sqrt{2i+1} x + \frac{i\pi}{2}\right) dx \\
& + \int_{-a}^{a} e^{-x^2/2} \psi(x) r_i(x) dx \Bigg].
\end{aligned}
$$

Because $e^{-x^2/2}\psi(x)$ is piecewise continuous, the first integral tends to zero when $i \to \infty$; the second integral also converges to zero since $e^{-x^2/2}\psi(x) r_i(x) = O(i^{-1/4})$ uniformly on $(-a, a)$. Moreover, due to the boundedness of $\alpha_i i^{1/4}/b_i$, we have

$$
\lim_{i \to \infty} J_2 = 0,
$$

which along with $|J_1|, |J_3| < \varepsilon$ implies that $J \to 0$ when $i \to \infty$. □

Under some sufficient conditions, a certain rate of uniform convergence for orthogonal series expansion in terms of Hermite function sequence can be achieved.

Theorem C.4.16 *Let* $g(x) \in L^2(\mathbb{R})$. *Define* $G(x) = g(x) e^{x^2/2}$, *and suppose that* $D^r(G) \in L^2(\mathbb{R}, e^{-x^2})$, $r \ge 1$, *where the differential operator* D *and its powers are given by* (C.4.84). *For the orthogonal expansion*

$$
g(x) = \sum_{i=0}^{\infty} c_i \mathscr{H}_i(x), \quad c_i = \int g(x) \mathscr{H}_i(x) dx, \tag{C.4.99}
$$

its partial sum $S_k(x)$ *converges to* $g(x)$ *uniformly and*

$$
\sup_x |g(x) - S_k(x)| = o(k^{-r+5/12}),
$$

when $k \to \infty$. □

Proof Recall that $\mathscr{H}_i(x) = \frac{1}{b_i} H_i(x) e^{-x^2/2}$ where $b_i^2 = \sqrt{\pi} 2^i i!$ is the squared norm of $H_i(x)$ in $L^2(\mathbb{R}, e^{-x^2})$. Thus, $\{\frac{1}{b_i} H_i(x)\}$ is an orthonormal sequence in $L^2(\mathbb{R}, e^{-x^2})$. It follows from (C.4.86) that

$$c_i(g) = \frac{1}{(2i)^r} C_i(D^r(G)),$$

where $C_i(D^r(G))$ are coefficients in the expansion of $D^r(G(x))$.

Thus, the convergence of (C.4.99) holds because even if $r = 1$,

$$\begin{aligned} |g(x) - S_k(x)| &= \left| \sum_{i=k}^{\infty} c_i \mathscr{H}_i(x) \right| \\ &= \left| \sum_{i=k}^{\infty} \frac{1}{2i} C_i(D^r(G)) \mathscr{H}_i(x) \right| \\ &\le \left| \sum_{i=k}^{\infty} \frac{1}{4i^2} \mathscr{H}_i^2(x) \right|^{1/2} \left| \sum_{i=k}^{\infty} C_i^2(D^r(G)) \right|^{1/2} \\ &= o(1), \end{aligned}$$

as $k \to \infty$, where the uniform boundedness of $\mathscr{H}_i(x)$ is used.

Moreover, for any $r \ge 1$,

$$\begin{aligned} \sup_x |g(x) - S_k(x)| &\le \sup_x \left| \sum_{i=k}^{\infty} \frac{1}{(2i)^{2r}} \mathscr{H}_i^2(x) \right|^{1/2} \left| \sum_{i=k}^{\infty} C_i^2(D^r(G)) \right|^{1/2} \\ &= o(1) \left| \sum_{i=k}^{\infty} \frac{1}{(2i)^{2r}} \sup_x \mathscr{H}_i^2(x) \right|^{1/2} \\ &= o(1) \left| \sum_{i=k}^{\infty} i^{-2r-1/6} \right|^{1/2} \\ &= o(k^{-r+5/12}) \end{aligned}$$

where we have used $\sup_{x\in\mathbb{R}} |\mathscr{H}_i^2(x)| = O(1) i^{-1/6}$ for $i \ge 1$. See Szego (1975, p. 242). □

There is another convergence theorem in Sansone (1959, p. 367) that we restate below for self-content.

Theorem C.4.17 *Let $f(x)$ be defined for all finite values of x and integrable on any finite interval. Also, let*

$$F(x) = F(0) + \int_0^x f(t)dt, \qquad -\infty < x < \infty,$$

and $G(x) = -2xF(x) + f(x)$.

Then, if

$$F(x) = O(e^{kx^2}), \qquad k < 1,$$

and if the integral

$$\int e^{-x^2} G^2(x)dx$$

is convergent, it follows that the series

$$\sum_{i=0}^{\infty} c_i H_i(x)e^{-x^2}, \quad c_i = \frac{1}{b_i^2} \int F(x)H_i(x)e^{-x^2} dx,$$

converges uniformly to $e^{-x^2} F(x)$ *in* $\mathbb{R}$ *where* $b_i^2 = 2^i i! \sqrt{\pi}$, *and the series*

$$\sum_{i=0}^{\infty} c_i H_i(x)$$

converges uniformly to $F(x)$ *on any finite interval.* □

Denote partial sum $S_m(x) = \sum_{i=0}^{m-1} c_i H_i(x)$. The first assertion is

$$\sup_{x \in \mathbb{R}} |[F(x) - S_m(x)]e^{-x^2}| \to 0,$$

when $m \to \infty$, where e^{-x^2} is regarded as a weight on $\mathbb{R}$ that helps measure the uniform convergence of $S_m(x)$; whereas the second assertion does not need this weight, that is,

$$\sup_{a \le x \le b} |F(x) - S_m(x)| \to 0, \quad \forall\, a, b \in \mathbb{R},$$

because the interval is compact. In the literature, these two kinds of convergence are called *type A and H*, respectively.

Proof Integrating by parts and $H'_{i+1}(x) = 2(i+1)H_i(x)$, we have

$$\begin{aligned} c_i &= \frac{1}{b_i^2} \int F(x)H_i(x)e^{-x^2} dx \\ &= \frac{1}{2(i+1)b_i^2} \int F(x)H'_{i+1}(x)e^{-x^2} dx \\ &= -\frac{1}{b_{i+1}^2} \int G(x)H_{i+1}(x)e^{-x^2} dx = -C_{i+1}, \end{aligned}$$

where C_{i+1} are the coefficients of orthogonal expansion of $G(x)$ in terms of $\{H_i(x)\}$.

By (C.4.66), for any x we have

$$|H_i(x)| \leq Ke^{x^2/2}2^{i/2}\sqrt{i!}i^{-1/4}(1+|x|^{5/2}),$$

for some constant $K > 0$. Thus,

$$\begin{aligned} |c_i H_i(x)e^{-x^2}| &\leq Ke^{-x^2/2}2^{i/2}\sqrt{i!}i^{-1/4}(1+|x|^{5/2})|C_{i+1}| \\ &\leq Ke^{-\lambda(x^2/2)}2^{(i+1)/2}\sqrt{(i+1)!}(i+1)^{-3/4}|C_{i+1}| \\ &\leq Ke^{-\lambda(x^2/2)}(2^{i+1}(i+1)!|C_{i+1}|^2+(i+1)^{-3/2}) \\ &\equiv Ke^{-\lambda(x^2/2)}T_i, \end{aligned}$$

for some $0 < \lambda < 1$, where K may be changed in lines but independent of i and x, and

$$T_i = 2^{i+1}(i+1)!|C_{i+1}|^2 + (i+1)^{-3/2}.$$

Because $\|G\|^2 = \int e^{-x^2}G^2(x)dx < \infty$, by Parserval equality

$$\sum_{i=0}^{\infty} 2^i i!|C_i|^2 = \|G\|^2.$$

Accordingly, $\sum_{i=0}^{\infty} T_i < \infty$. This implies that the series

$$\sum_{i=0}^{\infty} c_i H_i(x)e^{-x^2}$$

converges uniformly in $\mathbb{R}$. Let

$$F^*(x) = \sum_{i=0}^{\infty} c_i H_i(x)e^{-x^2},$$

where $F^*(x)$ is continuous and $F^*(x) = O(e^{-\lambda(x^2/2)})$.

By virtue of the convergence $\sum_{i=0}^{\infty} T_i < \infty$, we have, for $N > m$,

$$\left|\frac{1}{b_m^2}\int F^*(x)H_m(x)dx - c_m\right|$$
$$= \left|\frac{1}{b_m^2}\int\left(F^*(x) - \sum_{i=0}^{N} c_i H_i(x)e^{-x^2}\right)H_m(x)dx\right|$$
$$= \left|\int H_m(x)\sum_{i=N+1}^{\infty} c_i H_i(x)e^{-x^2}dx\right|$$
$$\le \int H_m(x)e^{-\lambda(x^2/2)}dx \sum_{i=N+1}^{\infty} T_i = o(1).$$

Therefore,

$$c_m = \frac{1}{b_m^2}\int F^*(x)H_m(x)dx.$$

In view of the definition of c_i in the theorem, we have

$$\int [F^*(x)e^{x^2} - F(x)]e^{-x^2}H_m(x)dx = 0,$$

for all $m \ge 0$. It follows immediately that $F^*(x)e^{x^2} - F(x) = 0$ due to the completeness of the sequence $\{H_i(x)\}$ in $L^2(\mathbb{R}, e^{-x^2})$. Hence, $F^*(x) = F(x)e^{-x^2}$, and therefore

$$F(x)e^{-x^2} = \sum_{i=0}^{\infty} c_i H_i(x)e^{-x^2},$$

uniformly on $\mathbb{R}$, and finally

$$F(x) = \sum_{i=0}^{\infty} c_i H_i(x),$$

uniformly on any bounded interval (a, b). □

As mentioned before, in deriving econometric theory, one may need a certain rate at which the orthogonal series converges. In what follows we give some sufficient conditions that ensure the rate of series convergence.

Theorem C.4.18 *Suppose that* $g(x)$ *is differentiable on* $\mathbb{R}$ *and* $g^{(m-\ell)}(x)x^\ell \in L^2(\mathbb{R})$ *for* $\ell = 0, 1, \ldots, m$ *and* $m \ge 1$. *Consider orthogonal expansion* $g(x) = \sum_{i=0}^{\infty} c_i \mathscr{H}_i(x)$ *with* $c_i = \int g(x)\mathscr{H}_i(x)dx$, *and define* $\gamma_k(x) = \sum_{i=k}^{\infty} c_i \mathscr{H}_i(x)$. *Then,*

(1) When $m = 1$, $g(x) = \sum_{i=0}^{\infty} c_i \mathscr{H}_i(x)$ *converges uniformly and absolutely on* $\mathbb{R}$; *moreover, when* $m \ge 4$, *we have* $g^{(p)}(x) = \sum_{i=0}^{\infty} c_i \mathscr{H}_i^{(p)}(x)$ *where* $p = 1, 2, 3$.
(2) For large m, $\gamma_k(x) = g(x) - g_k(x) = \sum_{i=k}^{\infty} c_i \mathscr{H}_i(x) = o(1)k^{-(m-1)/2-1/12}$ *uniformly on* $\mathbb{R}$; *moreover,* $|\dot{\gamma}_k(x)| = o(1)k^{-(m-2)/2-1/12}$ *and* $|\ddot{\gamma}_k(x)| = o(1)$

$k^{-(m-3)/2-1/12}$ uniformly on $\mathbb{R}$ where $\dot{\gamma}_k(x)$ and $\ddot{\gamma}_k(x)$ are the first and second derivatives of $\gamma_k(x)$, respectively. □

All these assertions are included in Lemma C.1 in Dong et al. (2016), so we omit the proof of the theorem. Next, we consider the point convergence rate in $L^2(\mathbb{R}^+, e^{-x})$ where $\mathbb{R}^+ = [0, \infty)$. Recall that the generalized Laguerre polynomials $\{L_j^\alpha(u)\}$ are orthogonal basis sequence in $L^2(\mathbb{R}^+, u^\alpha e^{-u})$, $\alpha > -1$.

As defined in (C.4.87),

$$l_j^\alpha(u) = \frac{1}{b_{\alpha,j}} L_j^\alpha(u),$$

so that $\{l_j^\alpha(u)\}$ forms an orthonomal basis in $L^2(\mathbb{R}^+, u^\alpha e^{-u})$. Again, when $\alpha = 0$, we use $\{l_j(u)\}$ without specifying α.

Theorem C.4.19 *Under the same setting as in Theorem C.4.9, that is, $g(x) \in L^2(\mathbb{R}^+, e^{-x})$, g is differentiable on $\mathbb{R}^+$ up to the rth order, and $g^{(i)}(u)$ belongs to $L^2(\mathbb{R}^+, u^i e^{-u})$, $i = 0, 1, \ldots, r$. Let*

$$g^{(i)}(u) = \sum_{j=0}^{\infty} c_{i,j} l_j^i(u), \quad c_{i,j} = \int_0^\infty g^{(i)}(u) l_j^i(u) u^i e^{-u} du.$$

In particular, for $i = 0$, the series above is simplified to

$$g(u) = \sum_{j=0}^{\infty} c_j l_j(u), \quad c_j = \int_0^\infty g(u) l_j(u) e^{-u} du.$$

Moreover, for positive integer k, denote the partial sum and residual of the series as

$$g_k(u) = \sum_{j=0}^{k-1} c_j l_j(u), \quad \gamma_k(u) = \sum_{j=k}^{\infty} c_j l_j(u).$$

Then, for $u > 0$ the weighted residue $[g(u) - g_k(u)]e^{-u/2} = o(k^{-r/2+1/4})$ as $k \to \infty$. □

Proof As derived in Theorem C.4.9,

$$c_j = \frac{(-1)^r}{\sqrt{j(j-1)\cdots(j-r+1)}} c_{r,j-r}(g^{(r)}),$$

where $c_{r,j-r}(g^{(r)})$ is the coefficient in the expansion of $g^{(r)}(u)$ in terms of $\{l_j^r(u)\}$.

Accordingly, for $u > 0$ the weighted residue

$$
\begin{aligned}
|[g(u)-g_k(u)]e^{-u/2}| &= \left|\sum_{j=k}^{\infty} c_j l_j(u) e^{-u/2}\right| \\
&\leq \sum_{j=k}^{\infty} \frac{1}{\sqrt{j(j-1)\cdots(j-r+1)}} |c_{r,j-r}||L_j(u)|e^{-u/2} \\
&\leq \pi^{-1/2} u^{-1/4} \sum_{j=k}^{\infty} \frac{1}{\sqrt{j(j-1)\cdots(j-r+1)}} |c_{r,j-r}| j^{-1/4} \\
&\leq \pi^{-1/2} u^{-1/4} \left(\sum_{j=k}^{\infty} \frac{1}{j(j-1)\cdots(j-r+1)} j^{-1/2}\right)^{1/2} \left(\sum_{j=k}^{\infty} |c_{r,j-r}|^2\right)^{1/2} \\
&= o(k^{-r/2+1/4}),
\end{aligned}
$$

where we use an inequality $|L_j(u)|e^{-u/2} \leq \pi^{-1/2} u^{-1/4} j^{-1/4}$ for large j given by Eq. (8.8.3) in Szego (1975, p. 237). □

In some situations, we need to consider the convergence rate of orthogonal expansion in Hilbert space $L^2(\mathbb{R}^+)$. Since $\{l_j^\alpha(u)\}$ is an orthonomal basis sequence in $L^2(\mathbb{R}^+, u^\alpha e^{-u})$, $\{l_j^\alpha(u) u^{\alpha/2} e^{-u/2}\}$ forms an orthonomal basis sequence in $L^2(\mathbb{R}^+)$, for all $\alpha > -1$. As defined in (C.4.92), let

$$
\mathscr{L}_j^\alpha(u) = l_j^\alpha(u) u^{\alpha/2} e^{-u/2}
$$

and when $\alpha = 0$ we use $\mathscr{L}_j(u)$ without specifying α for convenience.

Theorem C.4.20 *Under the same setting as in Theorem C.4.10, that is, $g(u)$ defined on $\mathbb{R}^+$ belongs to $L^2(\mathbb{R}^+)$, and is differentiable up to the rth order. Suppose further that $[g(u)e^{u/2}]^{(r)} u^{r/2} e^{-u/2} \in L^2(\mathbb{R}^+)$. Let $g(u) = \sum_{j=0}^{\infty} c_j \mathscr{L}_j(u)$, $c_j = \int_0^\infty g(u) \mathscr{L}_j(u) du$, be the orthogonal expansion of $g(u)$ and define $g_k(u) = \sum_{j=0}^{k-1} c_j \mathscr{L}_j(u)$ for positive integer k the partial sum sequence. Then, for $u > 0$, $|g(u) - g_k(u)| = o(k^{-r/2+1/4})$ as $k \to \infty$.* □

Proof As derived in Theorem C.4.10, for $j > r$,

$$
c_j = \frac{(-1)^r}{\sqrt{j(j-1)\cdots(j-r+1)}} c_{r,j-r}(\tilde{g}),
$$

where $c_{r,j-r}(\tilde{g})$ is the coefficient in the expansion of $\tilde{g}(u) = [f(u)e^{u/2}]^{(r)} u^{r/2} e^{-u/2}$ in terms of $\{\mathscr{L}_j^r(u)\}$.

It follows that for $u > 0$,

$$
\begin{aligned}
|g(u) - g_k(u)| &= \left|\sum_{j=k}^{\infty} c_j \mathscr{L}_j(u)\right| \\
&\le \sum_{j=k}^{\infty} \frac{1}{\sqrt{j(j-1)\cdots(j-r+1)}} |c_{r,j-r}(\tilde{g}) \mathscr{L}_j(u)| \\
&\le \pi^{-1/2} u^{-1/4} \sum_{j=k}^{\infty} \frac{1}{\sqrt{j(j-1)\cdots(j-r+1)}} |c_{r,j-r}(\tilde{g})| j^{-1/4} \\
&\le \pi^{-1/2} u^{-1/4} \left(\sum_{j=k}^{\infty} \frac{1}{j(j-1)\cdots(j-r+1)} j^{-1/2}\right)^{1/2} \left(\sum_{j=k}^{\infty} |c_{r,j-r}(\tilde{g})|^2\right)^{1/2} \\
&= \pi^{-1/2} u^{-1/4} k^{-r/2+1/4} o(1) = o(k^{-r/2+1/4}).
\end{aligned}
$$

C.4.6 Orthogonal Expansion for Stochastic Processes

Let $X(t), t \in [a, b]$, be a stochastic process with mean zero and finite second moment, continuous in quadratic mean. As its trajectory may be regarded as a function of t, it is possible to expand $X(t)$ into an orthogonal series in terms of a basis in $L^2[a, b]$.

In particular, if one knows the covariance function $\gamma(t, s) = \mathbb{E}[X(t)X(s)]$, as discussed before, one may construct an integral operator $\mathcal{H}$ from $L^2[a, b]$ to $L^2[a, b]$,

$$
(\mathcal{H}g)(t) = \int_a^b \gamma(t, s) g(s) ds.
$$

Hence, $\mathcal{H}$ possesses eigenvalues λ_i and corresponding eigenfunctions $\varphi_i(t)$ that form an orthonormal basis in $L^2[a, b]$. Clearly, $\lambda_i \ge 0$ due to the positive definiteness of $\gamma(t, s)$. In fact,

$$
\begin{aligned}
\lambda_i &= \lambda_i \langle \varphi_i(t), \varphi_i(t) \rangle = \langle \mathcal{H}\varphi_i(t), \varphi_i(t) \rangle \\
&= \int_a^b \int_a^b \varphi_i(t) \gamma(t, s) \varphi_i(s) dt ds \\
&= \mathbb{E}\left[\int_a^b \varphi_i(t) X(t) dt\right]^2 \ge 0.
\end{aligned}
$$

Moreover, by Mercer's theorem, one has

$$
\gamma(t, s) = \sum_{i=1}^{\infty} \lambda_i \varphi_i(t) \varphi_i(s).
$$

Theorem C.4.21 *A random function $X(t)$ that is continuous in quadratic mean on the interval $[a, b]$ has the orthogonal expansion*

$$X(t) = \sum_{i=1}^{\infty} \sqrt{\lambda_i}\xi_i\varphi_i(t), \quad t \in [a, b], \tag{C.4.100}$$

where

$$\xi_i = \frac{1}{\sqrt{\lambda_i}} \int_a^b \varphi_i(t)X(t)dt,$$

that entails $\mathbb{E}[\xi_i\xi_j] = \delta_{ij}$. The convergence of (C.4.100) *is in the quadratic mean sense.* □

This is given by Loéve (1963, p. 478).

Proof In terms of $t \in [a, b]$, $X(t) \in L^2[a, b]$. Thus,

$$X(t) = \sum_{i=1}^{\infty} c_i\varphi_i(t), \qquad c_i = \int_a^b \varphi_i(t)X(t)dt,$$

in the norm sense. Moreover, $c_i = \sqrt{\lambda_i}\xi_i$ and

$$\begin{aligned}
\mathbb{E}[\xi_i\xi_j] &= \frac{1}{\sqrt{\lambda_i}}\frac{1}{\sqrt{\lambda_j}}\mathbb{E}\int_a^b \varphi_i(t)X(t)dt \int_a^b \varphi_j(t)X(t)dt \\
&= \frac{1}{\sqrt{\lambda_i}}\frac{1}{\sqrt{\lambda_j}}\int_a^b\int_a^b \varphi_j(t)\mathbb{E}[X(t)X(s)]\varphi_i(s)dtds \\
&= \frac{1}{\sqrt{\lambda_i}}\frac{1}{\sqrt{\lambda_j}}\int_a^b\int_a^b \varphi_j(t)\gamma(t,s)\varphi_i(s)dtds \\
&= \frac{\sqrt{\lambda_i}}{\sqrt{\lambda_j}}\int_a^b \varphi_j(t)\varphi_i(t)dt \\
&= \delta_{ij}.
\end{aligned}$$

For any positive integer k,

$$\mathbb{E}\left\| X(t) - \sum_{i=1}^{k} \sqrt{\lambda_i}\xi_i\varphi_i(t)\right\|^2 = \mathbb{E}\left\| \sum_{i=k+1}^{\infty} \sqrt{\lambda_i}\xi_i\varphi_i(t)\right\|^2 = \sum_{i=k+1}^{\infty} \lambda_i \to 0,$$

as $k \to \infty$, since $\sum_{i=1}^{\infty} \lambda_i = \mathbb{E}[X(t)^2] < \infty$. □

It is well known that for Brownian motion $W(r)$, $\gamma(t, s) = \min(t, s), t, s \in [0, 1]$. As pointed before, the associated eigenvalues and corresponding eigenfunctions are

$$\lambda_i = \frac{4}{(2i-1)^2\pi^2}, \qquad \varphi_i(r) = \sqrt{2}\sin[(i-1/2)\pi r].$$

It follows from (C.4.100) that

$$W(r) = \sqrt{2}\sum_{i=1}^{\infty} \frac{\sin[(i-1/2)\pi r]}{(i-1/2)\pi}\xi_i, \tag{C.4.101}$$

where ξ_i are i.i.d. $N(0, 1)$. It is easily seen by applying the Martingale Convergence Theorem (for square integrable martingales) that the series is convergent almost surely and uniformly on $r \in [0, 1]$, so this series does converge pointwise.

Another example is Brownian bridge $V(r) = W(r) - rW(1)$, where $\gamma(t, s) = \min(t, s) - ts$, and the associated eigenvalues and corresponding eigenfunctions are

$$\lambda_i = \frac{1}{(i\pi)^2}, \qquad \varphi_i(r) = \sqrt{2}\sin(i\pi r).$$

Accordingly,

$$W(r) = r\xi_0 + \sqrt{2}\sum_{i=1}^{\infty} \frac{\sin(i\pi r)}{i\pi}\xi_i, \tag{C.4.102}$$

where $\xi_0 = W(1)$, and

$$\xi_i = \frac{\sqrt{2}}{i\pi}\int_0^1 \sin(i\pi r)[W(r) - rW(1)]dr, \; i \geq 1.$$

Here, ξ_i are again i.i.d. $N(0, 1)$ sequence. As shown in Hida (1980, p. 73) and Brieman (1992, p. 261), the series (C.4.102) is known to converge almost surely and uniformly for $r \in [0, 1]$.

Some interesting applications of (C.4.101) and (C.4.102) can be found in Phillips (1998).

C.5 Several Crucial Quantities

Regarding of the orthogonal function sequence, $\{f_j(x)\}$ say, used in series methods in econometrics, a crucial quantity is

$$\zeta_k(x) \equiv \left[\sum_{j=0}^{k-1} f_j^2(x)\right]^{1/2}. \tag{C.5.1}$$

That is the Euclidean norm of $\psi_k(x) \equiv (f_0(x), \ldots, f_{k-1}(x))^\top$. One would have to know the divergent order of $\zeta_k(x)$, even $\sup_{x\in\mathcal{X}} \zeta_k(x)$, when $k \to \infty$, where $\mathcal{X}$ is the interval on which the orthogonal sequence is defined. This is because the quantity $\zeta_k(x)$, along with the sample size, governs the convergence rate of a series estimator in nonparametric estimation, as can be seen in the previous chapters and the literature such as Newey (1997).

1. When using cosine orthogonal sequence, $\varphi_0(x) = 1$, $\varphi_j(x) = \sqrt{2}\cos(\pi j x)$, $j \geq 1$, that are orthonormal on (0, 1),

$$\zeta_k^2(x) = 1 + 2\sum_{j=1}^{k-1} \cos^2(\pi j x).$$

Lemma A.4 in Dong and Linton (2018) establishes $\sup_{x\in[0,1]} \zeta_k^2(x) = k + O(1)$ as $k \to \infty$. This is quite straightforward by virtue of the trigonometric identity.

A similar result can be found in Phillips (2005) when orthogonal basis $\varphi_j(x) = \sqrt{2}\sin(\pi(j - 1/2)x)$, $j \geq 1$, in $L^2(0, 1)$ is used.

2. Suppose that $\{p_j(x), j \geq 0\}$ in $L^2((a, b), w(x))$ is an orthonormal polynomial basis. Under this circumstance, the reciprocal of $\zeta_k^2(x)$ is called the *Christoffel's function* in the mathematical literature, denoted by $\lambda_k(x, w(x))$ or $\lambda_k(x)$ in short, which is originally defined by minimization:

$$\lambda_k(x) = \min_{\deg P<k, P(x)\neq 0} \frac{1}{P^2(x)} \int_a^b P^2(u)w(u)du,$$

where deg means the degree of a polynomial. See, for example, (3.3) of Nevai (1986, p. 6), (33) and (38) in Máté et al. (1991, p4.45), and Levin and Lubinsky (1992, p. 18). Note that, for any polynomial $P(u)$ with deg $P(u) \leq k - 1$, we may write $P(u) = \sum_{j=0}^{k-1} c_j p_j(u)$ and $\int_a^b P^2(u)w(u)du = \sum_{j=0}^{k-1} c_j^2$ by the orthonormality of $\{p_j(u)\}$. Thus,

$$\frac{1}{P^2(x)} \int_a^b P^2(u)w(u)du = \frac{1}{[\sum_{j=0}^{n-1} c_j p_j(x)]^2} \sum_{j=0}^{n-1} c_j^2 \geq \frac{1}{\zeta_k^2(x)},$$

by the Cauchy-Schwarz inequality, and the equality holds if we take $c_j = p_j(x)$, $j = 0, 1, \ldots, k - 1$. The assertion follows.

Corollary 1.3 of Lubinsky (2009) shows that in $L^2((-1, 1), w(x))$,

$$\frac{1}{k}\zeta_k^2(x) = \frac{1}{k}\sum_{j=0}^{k-1} p_j^2(x) \to \frac{1}{\pi\, w(x)\sqrt{1-x^2}}, \tag{C.5.2}$$

for every $x \in (-1, 1)$, when $k \to \infty$. This limit might be true for any interval (a, b) as it is only a linear transformation from $(-1, 1)$ to (a, b).

3. For the orthonormal Hermite function sequence $\{\mathscr{H}_j(x), j \geq 0\}$ in $L^2(\mathbb{R})$, and $x \neq y$, by the Christoffel-Darboux formula for $\{H_j(x)/b_j\}$ with $b_j = \sqrt{\sqrt{\pi}2^j j!}$,

$$\begin{aligned}\sum_{j=0}^{k-1} \mathscr{H}_j(x)\mathscr{H}_j(y) &= e^{-(x^2+y^2)/2} \sum_{j=0}^{k-1} \frac{H_j(x)}{b_j} \frac{H_j(y)}{b_j} \\ &= e^{-(x^2+y^2)/2} \frac{2^{k-1}/b_{k-1}}{2^k/b_k} \frac{H_k(x)H_{k-1}(y) - H_k(y)H_{k-1}(x)}{b_k b_{k-1}(x-y)} \\ &= \sqrt{\frac{k}{2}} \frac{\mathscr{H}_k(x)\mathscr{H}_{k-1}(y) - \mathscr{H}_k(y)\mathscr{H}_{k-1}(x)}{x-y}.\end{aligned}$$

Letting $y \to x$ and using L'Hôpital's rule, we have

$$\zeta_k^2(x) = \sum_{j=0}^{k-1} \mathscr{H}_j^2(x) = \sqrt{\frac{k}{2}}[\mathscr{H}_k'(x)\mathscr{H}_{k-1}(x) - \mathscr{H}_k(x)\mathscr{H}_{k-1}'(x)].$$

Recall from (C.4.58) that $\mathscr{H}_k(x)$ satisfies the differential equation

$$y'' + (2k + 1 - x^2)y = 0.$$

Thus,

$$\begin{aligned}\mathscr{H}_k''(x) &= -(2k + 1 - x^2)\mathscr{H}_k(x), \\ \mathscr{H}_{k-1}''(x) &= -(2k - 1 - x^2)\mathscr{H}_{k-1}(x),\end{aligned}$$

from which one has $\mathscr{H}_k''(x)\mathscr{H}_{k-1}(x) - \mathscr{H}_{k-1}''(x)\mathscr{H}_k(x) = -2\mathscr{H}_k(x)\mathscr{H}_{k-1}(x)$. That is, $(\mathscr{H}_k'(x)\mathscr{H}_{k-1}(x) - \mathscr{H}_k(x)\mathscr{H}_{k-1}'(x))' = -2\mathscr{H}_k(x)\mathscr{H}_{k-1}(x)$, and consequently,

$$\begin{aligned}&|\mathscr{H}_k'(x)\mathscr{H}_{k-1}(x) - \mathscr{H}_k(x)\mathscr{H}_{k-1}'(x)| \\ &= 2\left|\int_{-\infty}^{x} \mathscr{H}_k(x)\mathscr{H}_{k-1}(x)dx\right| \\ &\leq 2\left[\int_{-\infty}^{x} \mathscr{H}_k^2(x)dx \int_{-\infty}^{x} \mathscr{H}_{k-1}^2(x)dx\right]^{1/2} \\ &\leq 2\left[\int_{-\infty}^{\infty} \mathscr{H}_k^2(x)dx \int_{-\infty}^{\infty} \mathscr{H}_{k-1}^2(x)dx\right]^{1/2} \\ &= 2.\end{aligned}$$

It follows that

$$\zeta_k^2(x) = \sum_{j=0}^{k-1} \mathscr{H}_j^2(x) \leq \sqrt{2k}. \tag{C.5.3}$$

Interestingly, Theorem 1.1 in Levin and Lubinsky (1992) shows that

$$\sqrt{\frac{2}{k}}\zeta_k^2(x) = \sqrt{\frac{2}{k}}\sum_{j=0}^{k-1}\mathscr{H}_j^2(x) \asymp \left[\max\left(k^{-2/3}, 1 - \frac{|x|}{\sqrt{2k}}\right)\right]^{1/2},$$

uniformly for $k \geq 1$, $|x| \leq \sqrt{2k}(1 + Lk^{-2/3})$, and some constant $L > 0$, where $a \asymp b$ means that there exist constants $c_2 > c_1 > 0$ such that $c_1 \leq a/b \leq c_2$; and for all $x \in \mathbb{R}$ and $k \geq 1$, the theorem gives

$$\sqrt{\frac{2}{k}}\zeta_k^2(x) = \sqrt{\frac{2}{k}}\sum_{j=0}^{k-1}\mathscr{H}_j^2(x) \leq C\left[\max\left(k^{-2/3}, 1 - \frac{|x|}{\sqrt{2k}}\right)\right]^{1/2},$$

for some $C > 0$.

Anyway, both results show that $\zeta_k^2(x) = O(\sqrt{k})$, while (C.5.3) shows $\sup_x \zeta_k^2(x) \leq \sqrt{2k}$.

Appendix D
Comparison Between Series and Kernel Methods

As is well known, series and kernel methods are two popular nonparametric approaches. In this chapter we explore what are their similarities and differences. These are done from a generalized function point of view; and such a comparison may help the reader understand the rationale and decide which one to use in practice.

D.1 Kernel Methods

This section gives the details of how the kernel method was developed in statistics and econometrics. Given a sample $\{X_i, i = 1, \ldots, n\}$ that has distribution function $F(x)$ and density function $f(x)$, to derive an estimator of $f(x)$, consider the empirical distribution function of the sample,

$$F_n(x) = \frac{\text{number of observations} \leq x}{n} = \frac{1}{n}\sum_{i=1}^{n} I(X_i \leq x), \tag{D.1.1}$$

for any $x \in \mathbb{R}$. Though mathematically $F'(x) = f(x)$, one could not obtain the estimator of $f(x)$ by taking a derivative from $F_n(x)$ since $F_n(x)$ is a step function. Intuitively, the difference quotient can approximate a derivative well as the step length is small since the derivative is the limit of the difference quotient as the step length goes to zero. Moreover, in terms of approximating a derivative by a difference quotient, from a geometric point of view, central difference preforms better than both forward and backward differences because, considering $F'(x)$, say, the secant line through a point $(x - h, F(x - h))$ and $(x + h, F(x + h))$ is nearly parallel with the tangent line through $(x, F(x))$ when h is small.

Thus, one defines

C. Dong and J. Gao, *Modern Series Methods in Econometrics and Statistics*, Advanced Studies in Theoretical and Applied Econometrics 45,
https://doi.org/10.1007/978-981-96-2822-3

$$f_n(x) = \frac{1}{2h_n}[F_n(x + h_n) - F_n(x - h_n)], \tag{D.1.2}$$

as an estimator of $f(x)$, where h_n depends on the sample size n approaching zero as $n \to \infty$. Here $f_n(x)$ denotes the proportion of observations falling on the interval $(x - h_n, x + h_n]$ divided by the length of the interval, so-called the *naive estimator* of $f(x)$.

Let

$$K(x) = \begin{cases} \frac{1}{2} & \text{if } x \in (-1, 1], \\ 0 & \text{otherwise.} \end{cases}$$

The naive estimator can be written as

$$\begin{aligned} f_n(x) &= \frac{1}{2h_n}[F_n(x + h_n) - F_n(x - h_n)] \\ &= \frac{1}{2nh_n}\sum_{i=1}^{n}[I(X_i \le x + h_n) - I(X_i \le x - h_n)] \\ &= \frac{1}{2nh_n}\sum_{i=1}^{n} I(x - h_n < X_i \le x + h) \\ &= \frac{1}{2nh_n}\sum_{i=1}^{n} I(-1 < \frac{X_i - x}{h_n} \le 1) \\ &= \frac{1}{nh_n}\sum_{i=1}^{n} K\left(\frac{X_i - x}{h_n}\right). \end{aligned} \tag{D.1.3}$$

Using statistic jargon, function $K(x)$ is called a *kernel* and h_n a *bandwidth* in the estimation.

Let us consider the statistical performance of the naive estimator $f_n(x)$. Observe that $\mathbb{E}[I(X_i \le x)] = \mathbb{P}(X_i \le x) = F(x)$. Thus, for any $x, y \in \mathbb{R}$,

$$\mathbb{E}[F_n(x)] = \frac{1}{n}\sum_{i=1}^{n}\mathbb{E}[I(X_i \le x)] = F(x),$$

and

$$\begin{aligned} \mathbb{E}[F_n(x)F_n(y)] &= \frac{1}{n^2}\mathbb{E}\sum_{i=1}^{n} I(X_i \le x)\sum_{j=1}^{n} I(X_j \le y) \\ &= \frac{1}{n^2}\sum_{i=1}^{n}\mathbb{E}[I(X_i \le x)I(X_i \le y)] \end{aligned}$$

$$
\begin{aligned}
&+\frac{1}{n^2}\sum_{i=1}^{n}\sum_{j=1,\neq i}^{n}\mathbb{E}[I(X_i \le x)I(X_j \le y)]\\
&=\frac{1}{n}F(x\wedge y)+\frac{n-1}{n}F(x)F(y),
\end{aligned}
$$

where $x \wedge y = \min(x, y)$. It follows that

$$
\begin{aligned}
\operatorname{Cov}(F_n(x), F_n(y)) &= \mathbb{E}[F_n(x)F_n(y)] - \mathbb{E}[F_n(x)]\mathbb{E}[F_n(y)]\\
&= \frac{1}{n}[F(x\wedge y) - F(x)F(y)].
\end{aligned}
$$

Moreover,

$$
\begin{aligned}
\mathbb{E}[f_n(x)] &= \frac{1}{2h_n}[\mathbb{E}F_n(x+h_n) - \mathbb{E}F_n(x-h_n)]\\
&= \frac{1}{2h_n}[F(x+h_n) - F(x-h_n)],
\end{aligned}
$$

and

$$
\begin{aligned}
\operatorname{Var}[f_n(x)] &= \frac{1}{4h_n^2}\Big\{\operatorname{Var}[F_n(x+h_n)] + \operatorname{Var}[F_n(x-h_n)]\\
&\quad - 2\operatorname{Cov}(F_n(x+h_n), F_n(x-h_n))\Big\}\\
&= \frac{1}{4h_n^2}\frac{1}{n}\Big\{F(x+h_n) - F(x+h_n)^2 + F(x-h_n) - F(x-h_n)^2\\
&\quad - 2F(x-h_n) + 2F(x-h_n)F(x+h_n)\Big\}\\
&= \frac{1}{4nh_n^2}\Big\{F(x+h_n) - F(x-h_n) - [F(x+h_n) - F(x-h_n)]^2\Big\}.
\end{aligned}
$$

The MSE of $f_n(x)$ is

$$
\begin{aligned}
\mathbb{E}[f_n(x) - f(x)]^2 &= \operatorname{Var}[f_n(x)] + [\mathbb{E}f_n(x) - f(x)]^2\\
&= \frac{1}{4nh_n^2}\Big\{F(x+h_n) - F(x-h_n) + [F(x+h_n) - F(x-h_n)]^2\Big\}\\
&\quad + \left\{\frac{1}{2h_n}[F(x+h_n) - F(x-h_n)] - f(x)\right\}^2.
\end{aligned}
$$

Assume that the first three derivatives of f exist at x and $f''(x) \neq 0$. Then

$$F(x+h_n) = F(x) + f(x)h_n + \frac{1}{2!}f'(x)h_n^2 + \frac{1}{3!}f''(x)h_n^3 + O(h_n^4),$$
$$F(x-h_n) = F(x) - f(x)h_n + \frac{1}{2!}f'(x)h_n^2 - \frac{1}{3!}f''(x)h_n^3 + O(h_n^4).$$

We then have

$$F(x+h_n) - F(x-h_n) = 2h_n f(x) + \frac{1}{3}f''(x)h_n^3 + O(h_n^4).$$

Accordingly,

$$\mathrm{Var}[f_n(x)] = \frac{1}{2nh_n} f(x)(1 + O(n^{-1}))$$

and

$$[\mathbb{E}f_n(x) - f(x)]^2 = \frac{1}{36}(h_n^2 f''(x))^2(1 + O(h_n)),$$

which implies that $f_n(x)$ is an asymptotic unbiased estimator of $f(x)$.

Furthermore, the MSE $\mathbb{E}[f_n(x) - f(x)]^2 \to 0$ as $n \to \infty$ given that $nh_n \to \infty$ and $h_n \to 0$. This by Chebyshev's inequality implies that $f_n(x) \to_P f(x)$ under the same conditions for n and h_n as well as $F(x)$.

To obtain an optimal bandwidth h_n^*, equating the variance and the squared bias

$$\frac{1}{2nh_n} f(x) = \frac{1}{36}(h_n^2 f''(x))^2,$$

gives

$$h_n^* = \left(\frac{18}{n}\frac{f(x)}{(f''(x))^2}\right)^{1/5} = C_x n^{-1/5}.$$

In view of the form of the naive estimator given by (D.1.3), for any suitable density function $K(\cdot)$, one suggests a class of estimators of the form

$$f_n(x) = \frac{1}{nh_n}\sum_{i=1}^{n} K\left(\frac{X_i - x}{h_n}\right), \tag{D.1.4}$$

for the density of the sample $\{X_i, i = 1, \ldots, n\}$ where $h_n \to 0$ as $n \to \infty$. This is called *kernel-type estimator* of density.

One may also consider multivariate density estimate by kernel method using a similar formula as (D.1.4), i.e.,

$$f_n(x) = \frac{1}{nh_n^m}\sum_{i=1}^{n} K\left(\frac{X_i - x}{h_n}\right), \tag{D.1.5}$$

for any $x \in \mathbb{R}^m$, where, given a sample $\{X_i, i = 1, \ldots, n\}$ of m-dimensional multivariate variables, a m dimensional multivariate density $K(\cdot)$ is used, that is,

$$K\left(\frac{X - x}{h_n}\right) = \prod_{j=1}^{d} k\left(\frac{X_j - x_j}{h_n}\right)$$

with some univariate kernel $k(\cdot)$.

Theorem D.1.1 *Let* $(\mathbb{R}^m, \mathcal{B}_m)$ *be the m-dimensional Euclidean space with corresponding Borel* σ*-field, and let* $(\mathbb{R}, \mathcal{B})$ *be the real line and* $\mathcal{B} = \mathcal{B}_1$. *Let* $K : (\mathbb{R}^m, \mathcal{B}_m) \mapsto (\mathbb{R}, \mathcal{B})$ *be measurable such that*

$$|K(z)| \leq M, \quad \forall\, z \in \mathbb{R}^m, \quad \int |K(z)| dz < \infty,$$

and

$$\|z\|^m |K(z)| \to 0, \quad as\ \|z\| \to \infty.$$

Furthermore, let $g : (\mathbb{R}^m, \mathcal{B}_m) \mapsto (\mathbb{R}, \mathcal{B})$ *be measurable such that* $\int |g(z)| dz < \infty$. *Define*

$$g_n(x) = \frac{1}{h_n^m} \int K\left(\frac{z}{h_n}\right) g(x - z) dz, \tag{D.1.6}$$

where $0 < h_n \to 0$ *when* $n \to \infty$. *Then, if g is continuous,*

$$\lim_{n \to \infty} g_n(x) = g(x) \int K(z) dz.$$

And if g is uniformly continuous, the convergence is uniform. □

This theorem shows the rationale behind the kernel estimation. Indeed, if $f(x)$ is a density to estimate, then as $n \to \infty$

$$f_n(x) = \frac{1}{h_n^m} \int K\left(\frac{z}{h_n}\right) f(x - z) dz \to f(x)$$

gives an infeasible estimate, where $K(\cdot)$ is symmetric and integrates to one; notice further that $f_n(x) = \frac{1}{h_n^m} \mathbb{E} K\left(\frac{X - x}{h_n}\right)$ which is the same as (D.1.5) but in the form of population expectation. Once the expectation is substituted by a sample average, $f_n(x)$ becomes feasible and is exactly the kernel estimator of density $f(x)$.

Proof Note that

$$
\begin{aligned}
g_n(x) \quad & g(x)\int K(z)dz \\
&= \frac{1}{h_n^m}\int K\left(\frac{z}{h_n}\right) g(x-z)dz - g(x)\int K(z)dz \\
&= \int K(z)\, g(x-h_n z)dz - g(x)\int K(z)dz \\
&= \int K(z)[g(x-h_n z)-g(x)]dz \\
&= \int_{h_n\|z\|<\delta} K(z)[g(x-h_n z)-g(x)]dz \\
&\quad + \int_{h_n\|z\|\geq\delta} K(z)[g(x-h_n z)-g(x)]dz
\end{aligned}
$$

where $\delta > 0$ is chosen in this way: for any given $\epsilon > 0$, there exists a $\delta > 0$ such that $|g(x-y)-g(x)| < \epsilon$ whenever $\|y\| < \delta$ (by the continuity of g at x). Thus,

$$
\begin{aligned}
&\left|g_n(x) - g(x)\int K(z)dz\right| \\
&\leq \int_{h_n\|z\|<\delta} |K(z)||g(x-h_n z)-g(x)|dz \\
&\quad + \int_{h_n\|z\|\geq\delta} |K(z)||g(x-h_n z)|dz + |g(x)|\int_{h_n\|z\|\geq\delta} |K(z)|dz \\
&\equiv I + I_2 + I_3, \quad \text{say.}
\end{aligned}
$$

Evidently, $I_1 \leq \epsilon\int |K(z)|dz$. For the second term I_2, noting that $h_n^m\|z\|^m\delta^{-m} \geq 1$, we have

$$
\begin{aligned}
I_2 &\leq h_n^m\delta^{-m}\int_{h_n\|z\|\geq\delta} \|z\|^m|K(z)||g(x-h_n z)|dz \\
&\leq \delta^{-m}\sup_{h_n\|z\|\geq\delta}\|z\|^m|K(z)|\, h_n^m\int_{h_n\|z\|\geq\delta}|g(x-h_n z)|dz \\
&= \delta^{-m}\sup_{h_n\|z\|\geq\delta}\|z\|^m|K(z)|\int_{\|z\|\geq\delta}|g(z)|dz \\
&\leq \delta^{-m}\sup_{\|z\|\geq\delta/h_n}\|z\|^m|K(z)|\int |g(z)|dz
\end{aligned}
$$

which will approach zero as $h_n \to 0$. For I_3, notice that

$$\int_{h_n\|z\|\geq\delta} |K(z)|dz = \int_{\|z\|\geq\delta/h_n} |K(z)|dz \to 0,$$

as $h_n \to 0$ since $K(z)$ is integrable over $\mathbb{R}^m$.

When $g(x)$ is uniformly continuous, the choice of δ is independent of x, and by the integrability, $g(x)$ is bounded. Thus, the uniform convergence holds. □

By virtue of Theorem D.1.1, for the estimator $f_n(x)$ in (D.1.5),

$$\mathbb{E}[f_n(x)] = \int \frac{1}{h_n} K\left(\frac{z-x}{h_n}\right) f(z)dz \to f(x) \int K(z)dz = f(x)$$

as $h_n \to 0$ when K integrates one, so it is asymptotically unbiased; and

$$\begin{aligned}
\mathrm{Var}[f_n(x)] &= \frac{1}{n}\mathrm{Var}\left[\frac{1}{h_n}K\left(\frac{X_1-x}{h_n}\right)\right] \\
&\leq \frac{1}{n}\mathbb{E}\left[\frac{1}{h_n}K\left(\frac{X_1-x}{h_n}\right)\right]^2 \\
&= \frac{1}{nh_n}\int \frac{1}{h_n}K^2\left(\frac{z-x}{h_n}\right) f(z)dz \\
&= O((nh_n)^{-1}).
\end{aligned}$$

Next, we shall consider the kernel estimator for the mean regression function $g(x) = \mathbb{E}[Y|X=x]$. As is known,

$$g(x) = \int y f_{Y|X}(y|x)dy = \frac{1}{f_X(x)} \int y f_{Y,X}(x,y)dy,$$

the estimate of $g(x)$ rests on the estimates of the marginal density $f_X(x)$ and the joint density $f_{Y,X}(x,y)$.

Let $K(x,y)$ be a bivariate density function and $J(x) = \int K(x,y)dy$ is the marginal density. Given $\{(X_i, Y_i), i = 1, \ldots, n\}$,

$$f_n(x,y) = \frac{1}{nh_n^2}\sum_{i=1}^{n} K\left(\frac{x-X_i}{h_n}, \frac{y-Y_i}{h_n}\right),$$

and

$$f_{X,n}(x) = \frac{1}{nh_n}\sum_{i=1}^{n} J\left(\frac{x-X_i}{h_n}\right),$$

are estimators of the joint density and marginal density, respectively. We then have

$$
\begin{aligned}
g_n(x) &= \frac{1}{f_{X,n}(x)} \int y f_n(x, y) dy \\
&= \frac{1}{f_{X,n}(x)} \int y \frac{1}{nh_n^2} \sum_{i=1}^{n} K\left(\frac{x - X_i}{h_n}, \frac{y - Y_i}{h_n}\right) dy \\
&= h_n \left[\sum_{i=1}^{n} J\left(\frac{x - X_i}{h_n}\right)\right]^{-1} \sum_{i=1}^{n} m\left(\frac{x - X_i}{h_n}\right) \\
&+ \left[\sum_{i=1}^{n} J\left(\frac{x - X_i}{h_n}\right)\right]^{-1} \sum_{=i1}^{n} Y_i J\left(\frac{x - X_i}{h_n}\right),
\end{aligned}
$$

where normally $m(x) = \int y K(x, y) dy = 0$ if $K(x, y)$ is even in y. Thus, the estimator of the regression function is

$$
g_n(x) = \frac{\sum_{i=1}^{n} Y_i J\left(\frac{x - X_i}{h_n}\right)}{\sum_{i=1}^{n} J\left(\frac{x - X_i}{h_n}\right)}.
$$

The asymptotic properties of $g_n(x)$ can be found in Li and Racine (2007), for example.

D.2 Generalized Functions

Since we found that the impetus of both kernel and series methods is closely related to the rationale of generalized functions, in this section we present some basic conceptions and principles in the field. As is known, generalized functions started with their use in physics, and the most famous one is the Dirac delta function that is actually not a function in the ordinary sense. Mathematicians make the concept of generalized functions rigorous by defining them as functionals acting on tempered test function space S (another test space is D but $D \subset S$). In mathematical context generalized functions also are called distributions or tempered distributions distinguished by the spaces of test functions D and S.

Definition D.2.1 (*Space D*) The space is the set of all functions $\phi(x)$ defined on the real line satisfying

(1) $\phi(x)$ is an infinitely differentiable function defined at every point on $\mathbb{R}$. That is, $\phi^{(k)}(x)$ exists for any positive integer k;
(2) There is a constant $A > 0$ such that $\phi(x) \equiv 0$ for $|x| > A$, or equivalently it has a compact support. □

A function $\phi(x) \in D$ is of C^∞, also known as a test function. There exist many different kinds of functions in D, and it is noteworthy that for any continuous function

$f(x)$ with compact support, there is a function $\phi(x) \in D$ such that $|f(x) - \phi(x)| < \varepsilon$ for all x and any given $\varepsilon > 0$. This implies the denseness of D in any $C[a, b]$. See Gel'fand and Shilov (1964, p. 3).

Definition D.2.2 (*Convergence in D*) A sequence $\{\phi_m\}$ in D is said to converge to a function ϕ_0 if the following conditions are satisfied:

(1) All ϕ_m as well as ϕ_0 vanish outside a common region;
(2) $\phi_m^{(k)} \to \phi_0^{(k)}$ uniformly over $\mathbb{R}$ as $m \to \infty$ for all $k \geq 0$. □

It can be shown that $\phi_0 \in D$, and therefore D is closed under this definition.

Definition D.2.3 (*Generalized function*) A continuous linear functional on the space D is called a generalized function (also a distribution). The space of all generalized functions on D is denoted by D'. □

For the definitions of continuity and linearity of a functional, please see Kanwal (1983, p. 25). The space D' is called the *dual space* of D, and is a linear space itself. The set of generalized functions that are mostly useful are those generated by locally integrable functions. Indeed, if $f(x)$ is *locally integrable* on $\mathbb{R}$, i.e., integrable on any compact set on $\mathbb{R}$, it generates a generalized function $f : \phi \mapsto \mathbb{R}$ through

$$\langle f, \phi \rangle = \int f(x)\phi(x)dx, \quad \forall \phi \in D.$$

Such defined generalized function is called a *regular generalized function*. Remarkably, it is proved in Kanwal (1983, p. 27) that two continuous functions that generate the same regular generalized functions are identical. Moreover, if two locally integrable functions produce the same regular generalized function, they are identical almost everywhere. These enable one to identify functions from the distributions they generate.

Thus, one can identify $f(x)$ by $\langle f, \phi \rangle$ almost everywhere, i.e., if $\langle f, \phi \rangle = \langle g, \phi \rangle$ for any $\phi \in D$, then $f(x) = g(x)$ possibly except a set that has measure zero. To show this, it suffices to prove that if $\langle f, \phi \rangle = 0$ for any $\phi \in D$, then $f(x) = 0$ possibly except a set that has measure zero. In doing so, we reinforce the condition for f for simplicity, that is, f is continuous. Suppose that $f(x_0) > 0$, then there exists a $\eta > 0$ such that $f(x) > 0$ for $x \in (x_0 - \eta, x_0 + \eta)$. Define $\phi_\eta(x) = \exp(-1/(\eta^2 - (x - x_0)^2))$ for $x \in (x_0 - \eta, x_0 + \eta)$ and zero otherwise. Then a contradiction yields by $\langle f, \phi_\eta \rangle > 0$.

All generalized functions other than regular ones are called *singular*. Thus, D' is larger than D, because all $\phi \in D$ are generalized functions so that $D \subset D'$, and there do exist singular generalized functions as illustrated as follows.

Consider a functional $\phi \mapsto \phi(x_0)$, $\forall \phi \in D$, with a particular $x_0 \in \mathbb{R}$. It is linear and continuous, and thus a member in D'. This functional is the well-known Dirac delta distribution (symbolically) given by

$$\langle \delta(x - x_0), \phi(x) \rangle = \int \delta(x - x_0)\phi(x)dx = \phi(x_0).$$

In addition, Dirac delta $\delta(\cdot)$ is a singular distribution as shown in Gel'fand and Shilov (1964, p. 4). Here, we give another approach. Suppose $g(x) = \delta(x)$ is regular and belongs to $L^2[-1, 1]$. Let $\phi_\epsilon(x) = \exp(-1/(1 - (x/\epsilon)^2))$ for $|x| < \epsilon$ and zero otherwise. Then $\phi_\epsilon(x) \in D$ and $\phi_\epsilon(0) = e^{-1}$. By the Cauchy-Schwarz inequality,

$$e^{-1} = \left| \int_{-1}^{1} g(x)\phi_\epsilon(x)dx \right| \le \|g(x)\| \|\phi_\epsilon(x)\|,$$

but $\|\phi_\epsilon(x)\| = \epsilon C \to 0$ when $\epsilon \to 0$, where C is a constant independent of ϵ. Contradiction!

By definition, generalized functions cannot be assigned values at isolated points, while statements about a generalized function on a neighborhood of points can be given a well-defined meaning. This means that generalized functions are determined by their local property. Detailed discussions can be found in Gel'fand and Shilov (1964, p. 5). As is well known, not all ordinary functions are differentiable. In contradistinction, generalized functions always have derivatives that are generalized functions too, and consequently have derivatives of any order.

Definition D.2.4 (*Derivative of generalized function*) Let $f \in D'$. A functional g defined on D given by

$$\langle g, \phi \rangle = -\langle f, \phi' \rangle, \quad \forall \phi \in D$$

is called the derivative of f, denoted as f' or df/dx. □

The definition is motivated by the integration by parts. To be an eligible member of D', note that such defined f' is linear and continuous. Accordingly, all generalized functions have derivatives of all orders. Moreover, the generalized derivative of a regular distribution agrees with the conventional one whenever the latter exists.

Example D.2.1 (Heaviside function) The function given by

$$H(x) = \begin{cases} 1, & x > 0, \\ 0, & x < 0, \end{cases}$$

is called *Heaviside function*. Its value at zero usually is defined as $1/2$, while sometimes it is taken as c for $0 < c < 1$, written as $H_c(x)$. Clearly, it is local integrable. Now, consider the derivative of $H(x)$. By the definition of the derivative of distributions, for any $\phi \in D$,

$$
\begin{aligned}
\langle H'(x), \phi\rangle &= -\langle H(x), \phi'\rangle = -\int_0^{\infty} \phi'(x)dx \\
&= \phi(0) = \int \delta(x)\phi(x)dx,
\end{aligned}
$$

which gives $H'(x) = \delta(x)$.

Example D.2.2 (Absolute function) Let $\rho(u) = |u|$. By the definition, for any $\phi \in D$,

$$
\begin{aligned}
\langle \rho'(u), \varphi(u)\rangle &= -\langle \rho(u), \varphi'(u)\rangle = -\int |u|\varphi'(u)du \\
&= \int_{-\infty}^{0} u\varphi'(u)du - \int_0^{\infty} u\varphi'(u)du \\
&= -\int_{-\infty}^{0} \varphi(u)du + \int_0^{\infty} \varphi(u)du \\
&= \int [-H(-u) + H(u)]\varphi(u)du.
\end{aligned}
$$

Then $\rho'(u) = -H(-u) + H(u)$, and thus $\rho''(u) = \delta(-x) + \delta(x) = 2\delta(x)$, where we use $\delta(-u) = \delta(u)$ given in Kanwal (1983, p. 54).

Definition D.2.5 (*Convergence in D'*) A sequence of generalized functions $f_m \in D'$, $m = 1, 2, \ldots$, is said to converge to a generalized function $f \in D'$ if

$$
\lim_{m\to\infty} \langle f_m, \phi\rangle = \langle f, \phi\rangle, \quad \forall\phi \in D.
$$

A set of generalized functions $\{f_\epsilon\}$ indexed by real ϵ is said converging to f when $\epsilon \to \epsilon_0$, if for $\forall\phi \in D$, $\lim_{\epsilon\to\epsilon_0}\langle f_\epsilon, \phi\rangle = \langle f, \phi\rangle$.

A series of generalized functions $\sum_{m=1}^{\infty} f_m$ converges to a generalized function $f \in D$ if the sequence of partial sum $s_M = \sum_{m=1}^{M} f_m$ converges to f as $M \to \infty$. □

These definitions contain the convergence of ordinary functions as a special case. Indeed, suppose that all members of distribution sequence $\{f_m\}$ are regular, and $f_m(x)$ converge to $f(x)$ uniformly on any compact interval, then

$$
\begin{aligned}
\lim_{m\to\infty} \langle f_m, \phi\rangle &= \lim_{m\to\infty} \int f_m(x)\phi(x)dx \\
&= \int f(x)\phi(x)dx = \langle f, \phi\rangle, \quad \forall\phi \in D,
\end{aligned}
$$

by the Uniform Convergence Theorem.

A consequence of the definition is that if $f_m \to f$ then $f_m^{(k)} \to f^{(k)}$ for any $k > 0$; if $\sum_{m=1}^{\infty} f_m$ converges to f, then the series can be differentiated term by term as many times as required. The most important sequence of distributions is a sequence of regular distributions $\{f_m\}$, so-called *delta-convergent sequence*, that converges to δ distribution. This could be regarded as a bridge between regular and singular distributions.

Theorem D.2.1 *Let $f(x)$ be a nonnegative function defined on $\mathbb{R}$ such that $\int f(x) dx = 1$. Put $f_\epsilon(x) = \epsilon^{-1} f(x/\epsilon)$, $\epsilon > 0$. Then $\lim_{\epsilon\to 0} f_\epsilon(x) = \delta(x)$.* □

The theorem can be proven by the Control Convergence Theorem. Observe that ϵ can be replaced by $1/m$ to have sequence $f_m(x)$ that convergence to $\delta(x)$ as $m \to \infty$.

Example D.2.3 (Delta-convergent sequence)

(1) $f(x) = I(|x| \leq 1/2)$, $f_m(x) = mI(|mx| \leq 1/2)$. Then $\lim_{m\to\infty} f_m(x) = \delta(x)$.

(2) $f(x) = \frac{1}{\pi}\frac{1}{x^2+1}$, and $f_\epsilon(x) = \frac{1}{\pi}\frac{\epsilon}{x^2+\epsilon^2}$. Then $\lim_{\epsilon\to 0} f_\epsilon(x) = \delta(x)$.

(3) Let $f(x) = \frac{1}{\sqrt{2\pi}} \exp(-x^2/2)$ be the density of standard normal variables. Define $f_\epsilon(x) = \frac{1}{\sqrt{2\pi}\epsilon} \exp(-x^2/2\epsilon^2)$. Then $\lim_{\epsilon\to 0} f_\epsilon(x) = \delta(x)$.

(4) Let $f(x) = \frac{1}{\sqrt{\pi}} \exp(-x^2)$, and we define $f_m(x) = \sqrt{m/\pi}\exp(-mx^2)$ considering $\epsilon = 1/\sqrt{m}$. Then $\lim_{m\to\infty} f_m(x) = \delta(x)$.

(5) Consider

$$f(x) = \begin{cases} C\exp\left(-\frac{1}{1-x^2}\right), & |x| < 1, \\ 0, & |x| \geq 1, \end{cases}$$

where C is such that $\int f(x)dx = 1$. Then, we define

$$f_\epsilon(x) = \begin{cases} C\epsilon^{-1}\exp\left(-\frac{\epsilon^2}{\epsilon^2-x^2}\right), & |x| < \epsilon, \\ 0, & |x| \geq \epsilon, \end{cases}$$

and we have $\lim_{\epsilon\to 0} f_\epsilon(x) = \delta(x)$.

In some cases we should consider a space that is larger than D as test function space, in order to extend the compact support of test functions in D to the entire real line.

Definition D.2.6 (*Space S*) The space S of test functions of rapid decay contains all functions ϕ defined on $\mathbb{R}$ that satisfy

(1) $\phi(x)$ is infinitely differentiable, i.e., $\phi(x) \in C^\infty$;
(2) $\phi(x)$, as well as its derivatives of all orders, vanishes at infinity faster than any power of $1/|x|$, i.e., for any $p, k \geq 0$, $|x^p\phi^{(k)}(x)| \leq C_{pk}$ where the constant C_{pk} only depends on p, k and ϕ. □

The space S is linear and clearly $D \subset S$. Accordingly, $S' \subset D'$ because a continuous linear functional on S is also a continuous linear functional on D. Similar to D and D', we may define the convergence of sequence and the derivative of distributions of S and S'.

D.3 The Rationales of Kernel and Series Methods

From the kernel estimate of density function given by (D.1.4), one may observe that the estimate $\widehat{f}_n^{\text{kernel}}(x)$ (in this section the superscript is added to the estimator in order to distinct from its counterpart by series method) is an average of

$$\frac{1}{h_n} K\left(\frac{X_i - x}{h_n}\right)$$

over $i = 1, \ldots, n$. Governed by the bandwidth h_n, the observations X_i close to x have a large contribution to the average while other observations relatively far from x have tiny or no contribution. One may be curious about how this boils down to the density.

To explain the principle behind the kernel estimation clearly, we temporarily and heuristically consider a sequential limit, viz., $n \to \infty$ first and then $h \to 0$. Simply by the SLLN, we have

$$\widehat{f}_n^{\text{kernel}}(x) \overset{n\to\infty}{\longrightarrow} \frac{1}{h}\mathbb{E}K\left(\frac{X_i - x}{h}\right) = \int \frac{1}{h} K\left(\frac{z - x}{h}\right) f(z)dz, \quad a.s. \tag{D.3.1}$$

Notice further that by Theorem D.2.1, $K(y/h)/h$ is a delta-convergent sequence that converges to $\delta(y)$ as $h \to 0$, that is,

$$\int \frac{1}{h} K\left(\frac{z - x}{h}\right) f(z)dz \overset{h\to 0}{\longrightarrow} \int \delta(z - x) f(z)dz = f(x), \tag{D.3.2}$$

whenever $f(\cdot)$ is continuous at x, and the assertion (D.3.2) is proven rigorously in Theorem D.1.1. It follows immediately from (D.3.1) and (D.3.2) that $\widehat{f}_n^{\text{kernel}}(x)$ converges to $f(x)$ a.s. by the SLLN.

Apparently, this is also true in the nonparametric regression function estimate by the kernel method, as illustrated below by sequential limits again,

$$
\begin{aligned}
\frac{1}{nh}\sum_{i=1}^{n} K\left(\frac{X_i - x}{h}\right) y_i &\overset{n\to\infty}{\longrightarrow} \frac{1}{h}\mathbb{E}K\left(\frac{X_i - x}{h}\right) y_i \\
&= \iint \frac{1}{h} K\left(\frac{z - x}{h}\right) y f(z, y) dz dy \\
&\overset{h\to 0}{\longrightarrow} \iint \delta(z - x) y f(z, y) dz dy \\
&= \int y f(x, y) dy,
\end{aligned}
$$

that is the numerator of $\mathbb{E}[Y|X = x]$, where $f(x, y)$ is the joint density of (X_i, y_i).

Thus, the core momentum of the kernel method in density estimation is the delta-convergence sequence in the field of generalized functions.

Now, let us consider the density estimation by series method. As shown in Chap. 4, given a sample $\{X_i, i = 1, \ldots, n\}$ that has common density $f(x)$, its estimator is constructed as

$$
\widehat{f}_n^{\text{series}}(x) = \sum_{j=0}^{m} \widehat{c}_j \mathscr{H}_j(x), \quad \widehat{c}_j = \frac{1}{n}\sum_{i=1}^{n} \mathscr{H}_j(X_i). \tag{D.3.3}
$$

where $\{\mathscr{H}_j(x), j \geq 0\}$ is the sequence of Hermite functions, m is a truncation parameter. Substituting the expression of $\widehat{c}_j$ into $\widehat{f}_n^{\text{series}}(x)$ yields

$$
\widehat{f}_n^{\text{series}}(x) = \frac{1}{n}\sum_{i=1}^{n}\sum_{j=0}^{m} \mathscr{H}_j(X_i)\mathscr{H}_j(x). \tag{D.3.4}
$$

Define

$$
K_m(y, x) = \sum_{j=0}^{m} \mathscr{H}_j(y)\mathscr{H}_j(x). \tag{D.3.5}
$$

It is readily seen that $K_m(y, x)$ is a delta-convergent sequence. Indeed, for any $\phi(x) \in D$ (or S), we have

$$
\begin{aligned}
\int K_m(y, x)\phi(y) dy &= \sum_{j=0}^{m} \int \mathscr{H}_j(y)\phi(y) dy \, \mathscr{H}_j(x) \\
&= \sum_{j=0}^{m} c_j \mathscr{H}_j(x) \overset{m\to\infty}{\longrightarrow} \sum_{j=0}^{\infty} c_j \mathscr{H}_j(x) = \phi(x)
\end{aligned}
$$

since $\phi(x) \in L^2(\mathbb{R})$, and it is sufficiently smooth so that its expansion is convergent uniformly. This means $K_m(y, x) \to \delta(y - x)$ in generalized function sense as $m \to \infty$. Write (D.3.4) as

$$\widehat{f}_n^{\text{series}}(x) = \frac{1}{n}\sum_{i=1}^{n} K_m(X_i, x). \tag{D.3.6}$$

This has the same form as the kernel density estimate (D.1.4) but $K_m(X_i, x)$ replaces $K((X_i - x)/h_n)/h_n$.

In practice, $m = m_n$ depends on the sample size, while, due to the same reason as in the analysis of kernel estimate, we consider a sequential limit for $\widehat{f}_n^{\text{series}}(x)$, that is, $n \to \infty$ first and then $m \to \infty$. Again, by the SLLN and delta-convergent sequence of $K_m(y, x)$, $\widehat{f}_n^{\text{series}}(x)$ converges to

$$\begin{aligned}\widehat{f}_n^{\text{series}}(x) &\overset{n\to\infty}{\longrightarrow} \mathbb{E}K_m(X_i, x) = \int K_m(y, x) f(y) dy \\ &\overset{m\to\infty}{\longrightarrow} \int \delta(y - x) f(y) dy = f(x)\end{aligned} \tag{D.3.7}$$

almost surely as long as $f(\cdot)$ is continuous at x. This means that the series estimator of density is also driven by the delta-convergence sequence.

To see the case in regression, suppose $y = g(x) + \varepsilon$, and $g(x) = \sum_{i=0}^{\infty} c_j p_j(x)$ where $\{p_j(x), j \geq 0\}$ is an orthogonal sequence. Let k be a truncation parameter, and define $\beta = (c_0, \ldots, c_{k-1})^\top$, $\phi_k(x) = (p_0(x), \ldots, p_{k-1}(x))^\top$. Given a sample $\{(x_i, y_i), i = 1, \ldots, n\}$, we have $\widehat{\beta} = (Z^\top Z)^{-1} Z^\top Y$ and define $\widehat{g}(x) = \phi_k(x)^\top \widehat{\beta}$, where $Z = (\phi_k(x_1), \ldots, \phi_k(x_n))^\top$, $Y = (y_1, \ldots, y_n)^\top$. Then,

$$\widehat{g}(x) = \phi_k(x)^\top \widehat{\beta} = \phi_k(x)^\top \beta + \phi_k(x)^\top (Z^\top Z)^{-1} Z^\top (\gamma + e).$$

Thus, $\widehat{g}(x) \to g(x)$ in probability because $\phi_k(x)^\top \beta \to g(x)$ due to the mathematical expressions of c_j and the kernel constructed from the orthogonal sequence $\{p_j(x)\}$, and the second term in the above converges to zero in probability as $n \to \infty$.

Therefore, from the core driving force point of view, the rationales of kernel estimate and series estimate of density are the same, and both of them are driven by some delta-convergent sequence from the generalized function field. Actually, there are some studies in the literature that directly utilize delta-convergence sequence to estimate density; see Walter and Blum (1979) and Susarla and Walter (1981).

The difference between the two methods can be seen from the limit process of the delta-sequence used. In the kernel estimation, $K(y/h)/h \to \delta(y)$ in generalized function sense when $h \to 0$; during this process, the sample points close to x (precisely $|X_i - x| \leq Ch$) are taken into account of the density estimation. This implies that the kernel estimator is in a local sense. On the other hand, since the expectation of $K_m(X_i, x)$ results in a k-term partial sum of the orthogonal expansion of $f_X(x)$, the series estimate of the density converges to $f_X(x)$ when $m \to \infty$. One might conclude that the series estimate is in a global sense.

In terms of nonparametric regression estimation, the momentum that drives kernel methods is still the delta-convergent sequence. The series methods in this case, however, perform quite similarly to the estimate of parametric linear models, because the series expansion of regression function $g(x) = \sum_{i=0}^{\infty} c_j p_j(x)$ parameterizes the nonparametric unknown function. Thus, the series estimation boils down to the estimates of the truncated coefficients c_j though the number of c_j diverges with the sample size; this reveals the difference between parametric and series estimations.

References

Andrews, L. C. (1998). *Special functions of mathematics for engineers*. Oxford: Copublished by SPIE PRESS and Oxford University Press.

Berlinet, A., & Thomas-Agnan, C. (2004). *Reproducing Kernel Hilbert space in probability and statistics*. Boston, MA: Springer.

Brieman, L. (1992). *Probability*. Philadelphia: SIAM.

Cucker, F., & Zhou, D.-X. (2007). *Learning theory: An approximation theory viewpoint. Cambridge monograph on applied and computational mathematics*. Cambridge: Cambridge University Press.

Dong, C., Gao, J., & Tjøstheim, D. (2016). Estimation for single-index and partially linear single-index integrated models. *Annals of Statistics, 44*, 425–453.

Dong, C., & Linton, O. (2018). Additive nonparametric models with time variable and both stationary and nonstationary regressors. *Journal of Econometrics, 207*, 212–236.

Dong, C., Linton, O., & Peng, B. (2021). A weighted sieve estimator for nonparametric time series models with nonstationary variables. *Journal of Econometrics, 222*, 909–932.

Doob, J.L. (1994). *Measure theory*. Graduate texts in mathematics 143. New York: Springer.

Dudley, R.M. (2003). *Real analysis and probability*. Cambridge studies in advanced mathematics 74. Cambridge, U.K: Cambridge University Press.

Eubank, R. L., & Speckman, P. (1991). Convergence rates for trigonometric and polynomial-trigonometric regression estimators. *Statistics & Probability Letters, 11*, 119–124.

Gel'fand, I. M., & Shilov, G. E. (1964). *Generalized functions*. New York: Academic.

Ghosal, R., Ghost, S., Urbanek, J., Schrack, J. A., & Zipunnikov, V. (2023). Shape-constrained estimation in functional regression with Bernstein polynomials. *Comput. Stat. Data Anal., 178*, 107614.

Heston, S. L., & Rossi, A. G. (2017). A spanning series approach to options. *Review of Asset Pricing Studies, 7*, 2–42.

Hida, T. (1980). *Brownian motion*. New York: Springer.

Kanwal, R. P. (1983). *Generalized fuctions: Theory and technique*. New York: Academic.

Levin, A. L., & Lubinsky, D. S. (1992). Christoffel functions, orthogonal polynomails, and Nevai's conjecture for Freud weights. *Constructive Approximation, 8*, 463–535.

Li, Q., & Racine, J. (2007). *Nonparametric econometrics: Theory and practice*. Princeton: Princeton University Press.

Loéve, M. (1963). *Probability theory*. New York: Van Nostrand.

Lubinsky, D. S. (2009). A new approach to universality limits involving orthogonal polynomials. *Journal of Mathematics, 170*, 915–939.

Máté, A., Nevai, P., & Totic, V. (1991). Szegö's extremum problem on the unit circle. *Journal of Mathematics, 134*, 433–453.

Milne, R. D. (1980). *Applied functional analysis*. London: Pitman Publishing INC.

Nevai, P. (1986). Geza Frued, orthogonal polynomials and Christoffel functions. A case study. *Journal of Approximation Theory, 48*, 3–167.

Newey, W. K. (1997). Convergence rates and asymptotic normality for series estimators. *Journal of Econometrics, 79*, 147–168.

Nikiforov, A. F., & Uvarov, V. B. (1988). *Special functions of mathematical physics*. Boston: Birkhauser.

Phillips, P. C. B. (1998). New tools for understanding spurious regressions. *Econometrica, 66*, 1299–1325.
Phillips, P. C. B. (2005). HAC estimation by automated regression. *Econometric Theory, 21*, 116–142.
Riesz, F., & SZ.-Nagy, B. (1956). *Functional analysis*. London and Glasgow: Blackie and Son Limited.
Rudin, W. (1976). *Principles of mathematical analysis. International series in pure and applied mathematics*. New York: McGraw-Hill Inc.
Sansone, G. (1959). *Orthogonal functions. Pure and applied mathematics*. New York: Interscience Publishers Inc.
Schultz, M. H. (1969). L^{∞}-multivariate approximation theory. *Journal on Numerical Analysis, 6*, 161–183.
Sharapudinova, I. I., & Magomed-Kasumova, M. G. (2018). On representation of a solution to the Cauchy problem by a Fourier series in Sobolev-orthogonal polynomials generated by Laguerre polynomials. *Differential Equations, 54*, 49–66.
Susarla, V., & Walter, G. (1981). Estimation of a multivariate density function using delta sequences. *Annals of Statistics, 9*, 347–355.
Szego, G. (1975). *Orthogonal polynomials*. Providence, Rhode Island: American Mathematical Association, Colloquium Publications XXIII.
Todd, J. (1963). *Introduction to the constructive theory of functions*. New York: Academic.
Walter, G., & Blum, J. (1979). Probability density estimation using delta sequences. *Annals of Statistics, 7*, 328–340.

Subject Index

C. Dong and J. Gao, *Modern Series Methods in Econometrics and Statistics*, Advanced Studies in Theoretical and Applied Econometrics 45,
https://doi.org/10.1007/978-981-96-2822-3

T

V

W

Author Index

C. Dong and J. Gao, *Modern Series Methods in Econometrics and Statistics*, Advanced Studies in Theoretical and Applied Econometrics 45,
https://doi.org/10.1007/978-981-96-2822-3

The manufacturer's authorised representative in the EU is Springer
Nature Customer Service Centre GmbH, Europaplatz 3, 69115 Heidelberg,
Germany. If you have any concerns regarding our products, please
contact ProductSafety@springernature.com

Printed and bound by CPI Group (UK) Ltd, Croydon, CR0 4YY

01/10/2026

02225913-0016